COLONIAL SELF-GOVERNMENT

Colonial Self-Government
The British Experience
1759–1856

JOHN MANNING WARD

Challis Professor of History
University of Sydney

University of Toronto Press
Toronto and Buffalo

Published in the United Kingdom 1976 by
THE MACMILLAN PRESS LTD

First published in Canada and the United States 1976 by
UNIVERSITY OF TORONTO PRESS
Totonto and Buffalo

ISBN 0-8020-2203-0

Printed in Great Britain

Contents

Preface

Richard Pares once pointed out, in a context quite different from that of this book, that the most important part of the history of an empire is the history of its mother country. My attempt to discover why it was that between 1759 and 1856 rights of self-government were granted to some British colonies and not to others, and why so many forms of self-government existed in the empire, is an unintended exercise on the theme that Pares stated as an economic historian.

Constitutional change in Britain and, above all, the prevailing views in Britain of good government, political rights and political justice were always at the roots of the development of colonial self-government after American independence. Even when, as in the Canadas in the 1830s, indigenous factors shaped colonial demands that challenged the assumptions of British statesmanship, no solutions were adopted until great changes had taken place in the British constitution and in the associated ideas about large colonies of British settlement. British governments granted colonial self-government in various forms, partly in response to pressure from the colonies, but more in accordance with their own notions of what just British polity permitted and required. In some senses, the British knew better what to do than they knew what they were doing, for policy was rarely explicit or constant.

What I had expected, when I began this book more than ten years ago, to be of great importance, the influence of one colony on another, proved to be always relevant but only occasionally decisive. British interests, economic or strategic, were rarely potent in constitutional matters, partly because stability within the empire was always valued more highly than any 'interest', partly because those responsible for the various 'interests' rarely doubted that imperial ascendancy would be preserved.

I have to thank the Australian Research Grants Committee and the University of Sydney for financial support over a long period on this and a connected project. I thank also the Warden and Fellows of All Souls College, Oxford, who made me a Visiting Fellow in the early months of 1968. The University of Cambridge again placed me in its debt when the Managers of the Smuts Memorial Fund elected me to a Smuts Visiting Fellowship in 1972. The Master and Fellows of St John's College, where I was Dominion Fellow in 1951, welcomed me again and allowed me to live and work in the College. For this, as for much good company, I am most grateful. Sir Stephen Roberts, Challis Professor of History in the University of Sydney from 1929 to 1947 and later Vice-Chancellor, was an invigorating teacher, and till 1971, when his death brought to an end our long association, an unfailing inspiration to write history. I am grateful to the historians who have read parts of the book, or have discussed its arguments with me, and hope that they will recognise that the slightness of this acknowledgement is no measure of my great thanks for patience and scholarship generously bestowed. I am indebted also to the librarians, keepers, archivists and custodians, in England, Australia, Canada and the United States, who indulged my quest for sources and permitted me to quote from the collections in their care.

Every historian of the British Empire has to face the problems of the immense diversity of the imperial experience and the weight of other writers' scholarly researches. I have concentrated, with the aid of my predecessors, on the developments that seemed most significant to well informed contemporaries in Britain and the colonies. To the statesmen, administrators and political economists so placed in the foreground, I have attributed not a great, commanding role, but a sense of history and an ability to perceive from time to time the nature of problems and the course of change.

This book begins in 1759, but contains little about the Thirteen Colonies and the American Revolution. I did write a chapter on the American colonies from 1756 to 1783, but omitted it for two reasons. One was space. The other was the nature of my interpretation of colonial self-government in the British experience. The formal beginning of the post-American trends with which this book is mainly concerned is the Canada Constitutional Act of 1791, to which earlier Canadian experience of British government is an indispensable prelude.

No one could write on the many subjects mentioned in this book without incurring more debts to other historians than he knew of and committing more errors of omission and commission than he dreaded. Almost every reader of the book will be able to suggest questions, of interest to historians, political scientists, or sociologists, to which I have given answers only implicitly, if at all. I shall be content if what I have written is accepted as a contribution towards understanding the nature and growth of colonial self-government within the British Empire.

University of Sydney   JOHN M. WARD
18 March 1974

Abbreviations

AHR	*American Historical Review*
AJPH	*Australian Journal of Politics and History*
CHBE	*Cambridge History of the British Empire*
CHJ	*Cambridge Historical Journal*
CHR	*Canadian Historical Review*
EHJ	*Economic History Journal*
EHR	*English Historical Review*
FJ	*Freeman's Journal*, Sydney
HJ	*Historical Journal*, Cambridge University
HRA	*Historical Records of Australia*
HS	*Historical Studies*, University of Melbourne
HSANZ	*Historical Studies Australia and New Zealand*
IHR	Institute of Historical Research, London
JBS	*Journal of British Studies*, Hartford, Conn.
JMH	*Journal of Modern History*
JPE	*Journal of Political Economy*
JRAHS	*Journal and Proceedings of the Royal Australian Historical Society*, Sydney
ML	Mitchell Library, Sydney
MM	*Maitland Mercury*
NLA	National Library of Australia, Canberra
NeC	Newcastle Papers, University of Nottingham Archives
PA	*People's Advocate and NSW Vindicator*
PAC	Public Archives of Canada, Ottawa
1, 2, 3 PD	Hansard's *Parliamentary Debates*, 1st, 2nd or 3rd series
PH	Cobbett's *Parliamentary History*
PP	British *Parliamentary Papers*
PRO	Public Record Office, London
RHS	Royal Historical Society, London
SMH	*Sydney Morning Herald*
V & P (LC, NSW)	Votes and Proceedings, Legislative Council of New South Wales

1 Introduction

According to John Stuart Mill in 1861, Britain had 'always felt under a certain degree of obligation to bestow on such of her outlying populations as were of her own blood and language, and on some who were not, representative institutions formed in imitation of her own'.[1] What was obvious to Mill then had not been obvious to William Pitt seventy years before. Introducing the Canada Constitutional Bill[2] into the Commons on 5 March 1791, Pitt had declared that, as a great innovation of principle, the Bill would introduce a system of government formed 'in imitation of the constitution of the mother country'.[3] Like his cousin, William Grenville, who had drafted the Bill,[4] Pitt recognised that it broke new ground in British policy towards colonial government.

Mill, looking back over the whole course of British imperial history, from the beginnings of colonisation in the seventeenth century to the granting of responsible government to Canada, New Zealand and Australia in the middle of the nineteenth, was overimpressed by the new liberal concept of self-governing colonies of settlement, a concept that had emerged less than two decades before he wrote. Taking a long view of British policy towards colonial government, he found in it a consistency that neither Pitt nor Grenville had seen in 1791. Essentially, Mill was offering a 'Whig interpretation', based on satisfaction with the most recent developments and on a strong disposition to treat their evolution as a wise unfolding of considered principles.

Pitt and Grenville, as reformers, had been sure of the merits of the aristocratic, parliamentary monarchy under which they themselves lived and, remembering the disasters of American independence, had taken an altogether different view of colonial history from Mill's. They knew that the representative institutions of the West Indian and American colonies before the Revolution had not been bestowed 'in imitation' of those of Britain, but had evolved through expediency from a variety of constitutional precedents that had been followed for reasons other than those that he suggested. They knew that in practice the colonial legislatures had developed in ways that conflicted with official British views of the imperial constitution and had proved irreconcilable not only with changing British constitutional ideas, but also with the basic assumptions of British polity.

In form the political institutions of the colonies had come somewhat to resemble those of Britain, but in function and political character they had been greatly different. Grenville was sure that the old colonial constitutions had developed into mere caricatures of their British counterparts, and had shown themselves incapable of emulating its splendid equipoise of monarchy, aristocracy and people.[5] The old representative system that had emerged slowly and unsystematically in the West Atlantic, Caribbean and North American colonies before the Revolution had possessed clear and misleading resemblances to some parts of the British constitution. Obviously, a governor might be compared with the King, a nominated council with the House of Lords and the Privy Council, and an elected assembly with the House of Commons. Many colonists liked to make the comparison and to say that their institutions were analogous to the British.

Mill, like many of his contemporaries and like many of Pitt's predecessors, may have referred to nothing more than these specious, almost casual, resemblances when he wrote of bestowing 'representative institutions formed in imitation' of those of the mother country. The facts that historically there had been no deliberate imitation, that the resemblances were confined to form and had not generally extended to function or character, and that, during a century and a half, the British and colonial constitutions, like ideas of representative government, had changed in different directions, did not affect a judgement that rested mainly on the common possession of representative legislatures and common subjection to the monarchy. Nor did Mill note that the self-government exercised by the American colonies had been officially condemned in Britain as unconstitutional and politically unsound, or that the colonies had evolved a relationship of governor, council and assembly that was always different from the relationships of King, Lords and Commons at home, which themselves changed greatly and without reference to the colonists. Likewise, he passed over the many instances, in the history of conquered and even of settled colonies, of a grant of representative institutions being deliberately refused. Crown colony government and the many special constitutional arrangements made for anomalous societies such as those of Newfoundland and the penal colonies of Australia had no place in his analysis, unless he intended exceptions to outnumber the supposed general rule.

Pitt and Grenville designed their Bill to correct what they regarded as the highly un-British development of the old representative system in North America. The central principle of the British constitution of the late eighteenth century, the 'mixed government' of sovereign, peers and people, had never existed in North America, and had never been intended to exist there. Conditions on the other side of the Atlantic were so different from those in Britain that attempts to introduce the principle into America were unlikely to succeed. But Pitt and Grenville intended to try. They planned to give Canada not only the benefits of the British constitution, adapted to colonial use and hedged about to preserve colonial subordination, but also the necessary social foundations of their vaunted political system.

Mill, with his interest in reconciling the representative principle of his own times with efficient government, qualified his general comment with a reservation that Pitt and Grenville would have accepted. He contrasted the growth of representative institutions in the colonies with the persistent demand of the mother country 'to be the supreme arbiter even of their purely internal concerns, according to her own, not their, ideas of how their concerns could best be regulated'.[6] According to Mill, the empire had originally been based on commercial monopoly and privilege. The mercantilist policies then followed had supposed the colonies to be subordinate to Britain. The ending of the old commercial system, Mill thought, had been followed by a progressive abandonment of imperial meddling in the affairs of the self-governing colonies that could manage (and pay) for themselves. In the fashion of his time and, until recently, of our own, he believed that the Durham Report had inspired British statesmen to adopt the more liberal attitudes towards colonial self-government that reform of commercial policy between the 1820s and 1840s had made possible.

Mill's chronology was better than his understanding of either the course of British policy towards the colonies, or the reasons why Britain eventually allowed some of her colonies to have institutions formed in imitation of her own, possessing functions and a political character resembling those of similar institutions in Britain and exercising a large measure of autonomy in all domestic affairs. Constitutional and political changes in Britain, the development there of new attitudes to colonisation and colonies (partly as a consequence of enlarged emigration and investment within the empire) and the enormous growth of the colonies themselves, were more important in producing the great shift of policy at the middle of the nineteenth century than was the fall of the old commercial system. The Durham Report, to which Mill gave more importance than its due even before it was written, and which he attributed to Charles Buller and Edward Gibbon Wakefield as much as to Lord Durham,[7] was a mere auxiliary of change, more remarkable to historians as a landmark, and, in our own century, as a guide to colonies seeking what was formerly called dominion status, than it was to contemporaries as an influence on policy making in Britain.

2 The British Constitution for British Colonies: Canada, 1759-1831

I considered the [Canada] Act as the Magna Charta of the colony and that it was my duty to render the province as nearly as may be a 'perfect image and transcript of the British Government and constitution'.

> Lieutenant-Governor Simcoe to Secretary of State, 30 October 1795[1]

While the Thirteen Colonies moved towards independence, Britain began to govern the vast territories acquired from France in North America in 1763. To begin with, the old representative system that had been customary in the Thirteen Colonies and the West Indies was chosen for Quebec (as the new possessions were called), but this was abandoned — first in favour of two illiberal forms of government (one unconstitutional), and then, in 1791, in favour of the earliest attempt to grant to British colonies institutions deliberately fashioned on those of the mother country. But the liberal innovation of 1791 was founded on what turned out to be mistaken assumptions about society and politics, and about the possibility of anglicisation, in British North America. As a result the policy was never fully implemented, although enough of it survived to make its long-term fruits decisive in the political history of Canada.

ABANDONMENT OF THE OLD REPRESENTATIVE SYSTEM

The acquisition of Quebec posed formidable problems of government and defence. In coping with them, British ministers had to consider whether to adapt the old representative system, with its troubled record in America and the West Indies, to the needs of a plural society. Most Europeans in Quebec were French Canadians and nearly all were Roman Catholics; Britain wished to anglicise Quebec by encouraging an immigration of English-speaking Protestants. The Indians, who had maintained a flourishing fur trade and friendly relations with the French, were an additional liability. Fur was important to the new colony and trouble with the Indians was feared, because the rancorous Americans might break the peace with the tribes and the French might seek to recover their lost dominion. South and west of the former French Empire, Spain, neither crushed nor appeased in 1763, remained an American as well as a European power.

Britain had acquired larger possessions than she could, for the time being, either control or exploit commercially.[2] Satiated with territory, jealous of rivals (European or colonial) and dreading attack, she had to find policies for Quebec that would satisfy her complicated set of interests, first among which was peace at home and abroad while the new gains were being assimilated.

A royal proclamation of 7 October 1763[3] declared that Quebec would have a new government on the model of the old representative system. The proclamation made similar promises to Grenada and to East and West Florida. Grenada had been a French colony with a considerable French population; the two Floridas, acquired from Spain, had only meagre European settlement.

In Quebec the proclamation served many purposes. Britain planned to establish a stable colony there, with an English-speaking majority, to offset American trouble-making. The expansive Americans were to be contained within effective British control by new limits on their movement westwards, which had been encouraged while France claimed sovereignty there. Temporarily the limits were set at the watershed of the Appalachian Mountains. All western lands between the Appalachians, the Floridas, the Mississippi and Quebec were reserved for the Indians. No arrangements were made for the civil government of this vast area and the Indian trade was placed exclusively under imperial control. Eastern parts of Quebec, not settled by the French, were added to Nova Scotia and Newfoundland. In this way Quebec lost its most valuable fisheries, and fur became its staple.

The proclamation assumed that the French would be anglicised; it assumed also that English law was already in force and promised its continuance. But, according to English law, established in precedents from the Channel Islands and the Isle of Man, French law continued in Quebec until the conqueror decided otherwise.[4] The Crown took no step to repeal or amend French law, or to introduce English law; French law therefore remained in force. Roman Catholics in the colony were entitled to the free exercise of their religion because of the capitulations and the treaty, and because English laws to the contrary were not in force. A comparable duality of religion had previously existed in Nova Scotia.[5]

The preponderance of the French, then numbering over 60,000, over the few hundred English, Scots, Irish and Americans was a severe impediment to the desired assimilation. It was in order to encourage settlers that the proclamation promised an elected assembly 'so soon as . . . circumstances . . . will admit'. English settlers had entered Nova Scotia in large numbers after the expulsion of the French in 1755 and the establishment of representative government in 1758. Why should not the same happen in Quebec? Perhaps the French would remove themselves to colonies not under British rule.

There was no influx of English-speaking immigrants into Quebec. The Americans regarded it as an economically precarious, isolated settlement of Roman Catholics in a rigorous climate, and were much more attracted to the forbidden country across the Appalachians and to trade with the West Indies. A significant addition of English-speaking colonists to Quebec was always a vain hope so long as the Thirteen Colonies, Nova Scotia and Prince Edward Island could absorb the Scots and Ulster Scots, who were Britain's principal emigrants at that time. Nor was there any exodus of the French. Too numerous to be expelled like the Acadians, they soon became docile subjects, a welcome counterpoise to their American neighbours.

From 1763 to 1815 war cast shadows over British policies in Canada and made French loyalty indispensable. The governors found that the stability, submissiveness and numbers of the conquered race gave it strong claims to preferential treatment. The English in Canada, principally merchants and traders, failed to commend themselves to Government House. The first governor, General Sir James Murray, thought them 'Licentious Fanaticks'[6] and his successors were for long scarcely less Francophile.

The old representative system was never established in Quebec. Most of the French would have been excluded by religion from sitting in the proposed assembly and council, and debarred from appointments as judges, magistrates or civil servants.[7] The *seigneurs*, who might be described as the feudal gentry of Quebec, had no wish for an elected assembly to diminish their own declining authority. The governors had nothing to gain by calling a representative legislature, which the English would have dominated to the irritation and possible detriment of the French.

For a decade Quebec was ruled by governors with the aid of a nominated advisory council. Then not without precedent, the arrangement was later followed in some other colonies. Murray had been given discretion to delay calling an assembly and his instructions allowed him to legislate with a council until an assembly ('impracticable for the present') was summoned. He also had authority to establish courts of justice.[8] The promise to introduce the old representative system was neither forgotten nor kept. The governors continued to rule Quebec under powers intended for a transition period. The British authorities acquiesced, despite complaints from the English-speaking colonists, who protested that their political rights and English law were denied to them, and from the French, who saw that they were under disabilities on religious grounds.

Government in the colony may often have been illegal. The Proclamation of 1763 had exhausted the prerogative power of the Crown to settle the government of Quebec. Murray's commission and instructions did not empower him to establish an alternative form of government.[9] The law was clear from recent experience in Nova Scotia, when the Crown Law Officers had condemned legislation by the council after an assembly had been authorised.[10] What had been unconstitutional in Nova Scotia could not have been constitutional in Quebec.

Quebec also had problems of law. To have adhered to French law (strictly speaking the only course open to the colony) seemed impracticable. As a result Quebec had no certainty, whether under English law, French Canadian law or some mixture of the two. Property, inheritance, commerce and civil liberties were all at stake.[11] The colony developed its own conflict of laws, from which the unscrupulous extracted advantage, while the community at large reaped inconvenience and injustice.

In 1767 the liberal Lord Shelburne,[12] as Secretary of State for the Southern Department, informed Murray's successor, Sir Guy Carleton,[13] that the ministry wished to improve the constitution of Quebec.[14] Only Parliament could extricate law and government from the confusion engendered after the Proclamation of 1763. For the sake of clear law, development and good faith, Quebec would be given a council and assembly, but, in order to avoid minority government, special arrangements for admitting some Roman Catholics into both bodies would be made.

Carleton was ill qualified to follow Shelburne's policies. A successful soldier, well acquainted with North America, he was wary of representative institutions and of Englishmen settled overseas. As an Irishman, he may have been specially sensitive to the problems of French Roman Catholics under British rule. Preoccupied with problems of military security, he shared the preference of his class for the landed gentry rather than the traders or small settlers whom the British government seemed to want to encourage. The *seigneurs* were gentlemen, who might command the loyal obedience of the *habitants*; the English, on the other hand, were a troublesome minority, avid for more political power than their numbers or attitudes to Britain made it wise to grant them. The French were turning away from commerce to concentrate on their lands and their religion; given fair treatment, they would be contented. Security required that the French be reconciled to British rule. A French Canadian army might be raised to overawe or contain the Americans; it might also be used, if the French Canadians were reconciled to British rule, to help repulse any attempts by France at recovering her lost empire.[15]

Carleton believed that the old representative system, as demanded by

some of the English in Quebec, was potentially mischievous in the colony.
In Britain, he thought, men misunderstood the system, thinking it
resembled the excellent constitution under which they themselves lived.
Colonial society, politics and government differed greatly from those at
home. Representative institutions might lead to republicanism if unchecked by monarchy and autocracy.[16] Governor, council and assembly
could never reproduce the splendid equipoise of King, Lords and
Commons in Britain. 'It is impossible for the Dignity of the Throne, or
Peerage, to be represented in the American Forests.' Englishmen would
never resort in sufficient numbers to a country with so ferocious a winter,
and, even if willing to suffer by ice and snow, would they emigrate to a
colony dominated by French Roman Catholics? Only in the event of a
'catastrophe shocking to think of' — that is, the loss of the American
colonies — would Quebec attract many English settlers. Carleton's first
answer to the problems of a plural society in Quebec was to treat the
English as an unwelcome minority contaminated by American subversion,
and to impose arbitrary British rule on the acquiescent French. Shrewdly
and ably, he did so.

THE QUEBEC ACT, 1774

As the probability of military action against the Thirteen Colonies
increased, Carleton's arguments gained weight. London preferred the
certain benefits of reconciling the French and placating the Indians to the
problematical advantages of satisfying the English and promoting development by honouring the promises of 1763. The Bill for the government of
Quebec, introduced into the Lords by Dartmouth on 2 May 1774, was
neither a panic measure nor a part of the coercive programme against the
Americans.[17] Its predominant purpose was to provide lawful, strong and
stable government for Quebec, and its principal author was Carleton.

The new Act gave Quebec a nominated council, called, perhaps for the
first time in British history, a 'legislative' council.[18] It was to have from
seventeen to twenty-three members, all residents of the colony. The
Secretary of State appointed as members the governor, the chief justice
and the provincial secretary, nine French-speaking residents and eight
English-speaking residents.[19] A special oath was instituted so that Roman
Catholics might sit on the council. When engaged on legislative business
the council had to sit in Quebec and, to avoid domination by either race,
ordinances were not to be enacted unless a majority of all members was
present.

By denying Quebec an elected assembly, the Act removed the province
from the orbit of the old representative system, to which it had been
assigned in 1763, and submitted it in essentials to what later became
known as Crown colony government. The King's ministers retained almost
complete and direct authority over Quebec. The small degree of

independence allowed to the new legislature was more strictly controlled than the larger powers of self-government permitted to colonies under the old representative system had ever been. The council could not levy direct taxes or pass ordinances on religion. No ordinance imposing a punishment greater than a fine or three months' imprisonment could be enforced until royal approval had been signified.

The new council had no power for levying taxation, but the Quebec Revenue Act of 1774 imposed customs duties on spirits and molasses, prescribed a fee for the licensing of public houses and continued the French territorial and casual revenues.[20] The moneys collected under the Act were available for the costs of the civil government of Quebec, so that the governor was financially independent of the legislative council and could not be starved into submission as so many governors in America and the West Indies had been.

Long before it came into force in May 1775, the Act was regarded with disfavour in the West Indies and had become anathema to Americans, who thought it conclusive evidence of a British conspiracy against their liberties. They condemned it for favouring the French, condoning popery, denying self-government and blocking American expansion westwards into the Ohio–Mississippi region, where Quebec despotism was to flourish. The First Continental Congress in Philadelphia demanded that the Act be repealed, along with other Acts equally obnoxious to the Americans, and tried in vain to induce the Canadians to rebel against British tyranny. The Declaration of Independence condemned Britain for having abolished 'the free System of English Laws in a neighbouring Province, establishing therein an Arbitrary government and enlarging its Boundaries so as to render it at once an example and fit instrument for introducing the same absolute rule into these Colonies'.

The Act legalised the 'free exercise of the religion of the Church of Rome, subject to the King's supremacy', and, with a sweeping simplicity, ignoring all complications, established French Canadian law in most civil matters, English law in criminal cases, and denied *habeas corpus*. These arrangements satisfied neither English nor French, for both were in some respects subjected to an alien system and both systems of law needed reform.

The illiberality of the Act gratified Carleton. His main care was military defence and he wrongly believed that the new measure had secured the loyalty of the French. He was angry, however, that the Act had not been passed before American trouble made it seem one more item in a calculated programme of repression aimed at the Thirteen Colonies.[21]

THE ATTACK ON THE BILL

Although the government had had the numbers to pass the Quebec Bill, many amendments had been accepted in Parliament and great hostility had raged outside. North's refusal to supply essential information, together with the strongly illiberal tendency of the Bill and the favours granted to the Roman Catholic Church, all roused angry opposition. In the Commons there had been eight divisions; newspapers had protested against despotism and against tenderness to Roman Catholics; Methodists had complained of popery; the City of London had petitioned George III to withhold his assent from a measure that put French law in place of English law, limited the jury system, established the Roman Catholic Church and no other, and instituted a new form of arbitrary government.[22]

Most of the heat came not from any public interest in Quebec, but from anxieties concerning the Thirteen Colonies and from strong public suspicions that ministers had repressive intentions at home as well as in Canada and America, and were unsound on the Catholic question. The Opposition, taking the Bill to be yet another instalment of coercion, rushed to judgement.[23] North and his colleagues had, however, avoided some of the errors of British policy in Ireland.

There was only slight criticism of the novel decision to have Parliament enact a constitution for a colony.[24] No other means existed of circumventing the proclamation of 1763 and the recusancy laws. Parliament had become accustomed to passing strong measures for the colonies, and ministers had forgotten their earlier reluctance to put colonial business before the Commons.

Many speakers attacked the Bill in Parliament. Fox rebuked ministers for attempting to establish a despotism that might be spread to other colonies.[25] When he challenged North to explain why Quebec could not have a representative legislature, the Prime Minister asked whether it would be safe to 'put the principal power in the hands of an assembly of Roman Catholic new subjects'. 'There is something in that religion', he said, 'which makes it not prudent in a Protestant government.'[26] Because only a small number of English Protestant settlers would legally be entitled to vote for an assembly, it would be 'cruel' to empower the minority to legislate for the Roman Catholic majority. Burke, then agent for New York, complained that the Bill violated the promises of 1763 and transgressed the principle, for which he contended, that British colonists were entitled to the laws of England. 'I would have English liberty carried into the French Colonies', he said, 'but I would not have French slavery brought into the British Colonies.'[27] Chatham blamed ministers for planning a despotic rule over Englishmen[28] that might prelude despotism at home. He exhorted the bishops to condemn the policy towards the Roman Catholic Church in Quebec before it damaged the whole empire, by alienating the Protestants in Ireland, outraging the people of England and driving the Americans into rebellion. Parliament had no more right to interfere with the Elizabethan Act of Supremacy for the sake of the French in Quebec than it had to tamper with the Great Charter or the Bill of Rights. All alike were fundamental laws essential to the peace of the King's dominions, and Parliament should never touch them.

The ministry accepted many compromises in the Bill but never conceded that British subjects in a conquered colony had any indefeasible right to English laws or the British constitution as nearly as imperial supremacy would allow. North admitted only cautiously that government in Quebec might eventually conform somewhat to the British constitution after the predominance of the French Roman Catholics had greatly diminished.[29]

CAMPBELL V. HALL, 1774.

A few months after the Quebec Act was passed, the Court of King's Bench decided the case of *Campbell v. Hall*.[30] The decision, of lasting importance in British imperial history, undermined the Opposition's claim that the failure to establish a representative assembly in Quebec had contravened past constitutional practice. Judgement was delivered in November by the Chief Justice, Lord Mansfield, who had been partly responsible for drafting the Quebec Bill earlier in the year, and was one of the government's most powerful spokesmen in the Lords on colonial affairs. Mansfield referred to medieval precedents from Ireland, Wales, the Isle of Man, Guienne, Gascony and Calais in reaching a decision that was as tolerant of conquered peoples as it was insistent on the discretionary powers of the Crown as conqueror to settle law and forms of government.

Alexander Campbell, a British subject in Grenada, sued to recover moneys collected as export duties on sugar, levied under the authority of British Letters Patent of 20 July 1764. The judgement in his favour stated the powers of the Crown in relation to the law and government of conquered colonies. Mansfield declared that the existing laws and forms of government of a conquered or ceded colony continued in force until the Crown exercised its prerogative power to change them. In legislating or constitution making, the Crown had to respect the capitulations, refrain from discriminating between the original inhabitants and the King's other subjects, and heed the authority of Parliament and the policy of English law. When the prerogative power had been used to settle a new form of government, as had happened in Grenada, it was exhausted and could not be used again either to change the constitution or to legislate for the colony.[31]

The Letters Patent of 20 July 1764, purporting to impose the duties of which Campbell complained, had been null and void in Grenada, for they had depended on a power that the Crown had exhausted by instructing the governor to call an assembly. Only the new legislature of the colony, when it met, or Parliament could have enacted the duties validly.

The court did not suggest that the Crown or Parliament was obliged to set up any particular form of legislature, or, indeed, any legislature at all, in a conquered colony.[32] The Crown had promised Grenada (and Quebec) elected assemblies, not because it was legally obliged to do so, but as a deliberate act of conclusive political choice. Once the decision had been formally acted upon, the Crown could no longer legislate for the colony and only Parliament could disturb what the Crown had done. Mansfield imposed no time limit to the Crown's authority; so long as no constitutional change was made to exhaust the legislative power of the Crown, a conquered colony could remain indefinitely under Crown control and legislation, as later happened with some Crown colonies.

FAILURE OF THE QUEBEC ACT

The Quebec Act satisfied only a few of the French Canadians (mostly upper class), while it disturbed the English and disappointed the expectations of its principal author, Carleton. The French, though gratified by the continued protection given their church, were not wholly pleased by the restoration of French civil law, including feudal dues to the *seigneurs*. The *habitants* disliked the Act for having socially and legally put the clock back, and, when Carleton, on orders from London,[33] endeavoured to raise military forces against American attacks, their sullen refusal to co-operate appalled him. In contrast, the clergy were satisfied with the Act, and the *seigneurs*, a diminishing class of sunken prestige, hoped that it might bolster their standing and authority.[34]

The instructions issued from London under the Act showed the 'intention of the Government that under a system of rigid state control, but without harsh persecution, the Roman Catholic Church in Quebec would gradually wither away'.[35] French property, customs and religious practices were to be protected, at least temporarily, for the sake of stability and contentment; but the French Canadians were not to retain their distinctive institutions and privileges for long. Had the instructions sent to Carleton been revealed, French resentment would have overflowed. He was to prepare for the introduction of English civil law, to reintroduce *habeas corpus* by ordinance, to keep the bishops and priests under control, and to reduce and eventually dissolve the religious orders.

The English in Quebec condemned the Act as a statutory embodiment of the Francophile prejudices of the governors and refused to believe that the French could be assimilated. Like North, the English were sure that Catholics were unfit for public office and that Parliament had been unwise as well as unjust to refuse an elected assembly to the King's subjects in Quebec. They protested at the renunciation of *habeas corpus* and the abolition of juries in civil cases. To their irritation, Carleton and his successor Haldimand perverted their instructions by making the executive board, which was nominated from the legislative council, into a Franco-phile junta, perpetually in the service of the governor and generally hostile to the English.

COLONIAL CONSTITUTIONS ON THE BRITISH MODEL

The growing numbers of loyalists from America after 1775 added powerfully to the English case, the more so as it was embarrassing and inconsistent to treat loyalists in Quebec less liberally than loyalists in the maritime provinces. In 1783 there were 40,000 or more loyalists in the maritime provinces of Nova Scotia and New Brunswick and 10,000 in Western Quebec (or Upper Canada). Nova Scotia, as we have seen, had had a representative assembly since 1758; New Brunswick had been separated from Nova Scotia in 1784 and, because it was peopled substantially by loyalists, whom the separation had been partly intended to gratify, had been granted self-government according to the old representative system. So had Cape Breton, which also had been separated from Nova Scotia in 1784, but its population was so small that no assembly was summoned there.

Upper Canada, though its population was still small compared with Lower (or French) Canada, had claims in morality and established British practice to a form of government as liberal as that enjoyed by Nova Scotia and New Brunswick, and by the Thirteen Colonies before the Revolution. Carleton had reported optimistically on the prospects for economic growth in Canada (and Nova Scotia) provided the loyalists settled there. In addition, he had hoped for the growth of a West Indian trade in which Canada would replace the United States, so soon as the loyalists had shown how to 'overturn the lethargic methods of a century and convert a country of wilderness and trading posts into a bursting land of harvest fields and flour mills'.[36] North wrote to Governor Haldimand in May 1783 that the changed condition of Quebec would 'naturally call for some alteration in the Measures of Civil Government'. Four months later the 'ancient' English Canadians petitioned for an elective assembly, and they were joined by the loyalists in a similar petition at the end of 1784.[37]

Haldimand, conservative in opinion and autocratic in temper, opposed all plans to repeal or amend the Quebec Act. If the constitutional bulwarks were overthrown, what could stay a headlong rush to republicanism and, perhaps, annexation to the United States? On the other hand, if the local legislature altered those parts of the old French civil law that notoriously impeded commerce, and adapted English criminal law to local conditions, the French would be contented enough to withstand American influences, and the English merchants would be satisfied that their complaints against French civil law had been remedied. The loyalists had suffered too much 'by Committees and Houses of Assembly' in America to find the Quebec

Act irksome so long as the colony was quiet and prosperous.[38] He was wrong. The loyalists continued to ask for English (instead of French) land tenures, for law reform and for representative government on the models of Nova Scotia and New Brunswick.

At first, Pitt and his colleagues refused to believe that the Quebec Act would have to go. Lord Sydney, the Home and Colonial Secretary, a man of intermittent energy and no originality, tried to believe Haldimand's confident assertions that no change in the Act was needed. Pitt, however, was uncertain, the more so because of the storm in Anglo-Irish relations that followed his attempt to readjust Ireland's position in the empire after the grant of legislative independence in 1782. He told the London committee of Canadian merchants, when they petitioned for an enlarged legislative council (nominated for life) and an elected assembly, that he would consult the Cabinet on amendments to the Quebec Act.[39]

The ministry was more willing for reform than either Pitt's caution or the appointment (in April 1785) of Lord Dorchester as governor-general might have suggested. Dorchester was the former Carleton, but his friend William Smith,[40] the new liberal chief justice of Quebec, was to help him report on the 'real state' of public opinion on constitutional change. He was also to consider the case for partition, which would allow Upper Canada (mainly English) to have a constitution modelled on the old representative system, while leaving Lower Canada (predominantly French) under the less liberal form of government that seemed appropriate to its condition. The government warned Dorchester, however, that if the English part of Canada were freed of French constraints it might be infected by American republicanism.[41]

Dorchester respected the just claims of the King's newly arrived subjects, but could not see how to satisfy them without alarming the French, whose numbers had nearly doubled since 1760 and who claimed that their religion, culture and social structure had been guaranteed by the capitulations, the treaty and the Act. An increasing proportion of their own educated classes and some Scots sympathisers might have welcomed an elected assembly in undivided Quebec, provided that representation gave the French a majority in the legislature according to their numbers. But this was the judgement of an élite, and Dorchester still thought that any assembly would breed discord and challenge his own authority.

Dorchester's doubts were neither unintelligent nor unintelligible, but they were useless to the troubled ministers in London, whose thinking on Quebec was soon interrupted by George III's first fit of insanity and the following Regency crisis. No new constitution was drafted until the King had recovered and W. W. Grenville, whose father had carried the Stamp Act of evil memory, had replaced Sydney as Home and Colonial Secretary in June 1789. By then the inevitability of reform in Quebec was notorious in London and only its direction was undecided.

The failure of the Quebec Revenue Act, which had provided only a fraction of the costs of civil government, had also been recognised. Britain was said to be spending £100,000 a year on Canada, in addition to the costs of defence, and ministers resented a burden the principal benefits of which were questionable prestige and obscure potentialities.[42] No easy remedy was possible. Only Parliament could confer on a colony whose constitution Parliament had enacted a power to levy tax, and without new taxation Quebec would lack revenue for development. Parliament, however, was unlikely to confer such a power on an unrepresentative legislative council.[43]

Grenville believed that the loyalists were fit for, and would be satisfied with nothing less than, the old representative system, of governor, nominated council and elected assembly. But neither he nor any other leading politician retained much faith in the prospects of the old form of colonial government. Conventional wisdom in Britain attributed the loss of the American colonies to too much, rather than too little, liberty, both within each colony and in the colonial relationship with Britain. Whatever form of government was introduced into Quebec needed, like the British constitution itself, to have a strong executive and a powerful upper house, capable of balancing the elected representatives of the people.

Grenville doubted whether any form of government would keep Quebec in the empire for long. A generous grant of self-government might bind the colony more closely to Britain, or might generate a demand for independence. He decided to risk everything by establishing British institutions rather than the old representative system, which lacked the most essential virtues of British forms of government.[44] Grenville had considerable faith in the British constitution. France had collapsed in revolution and the political unsoundness of most of Europe was painfully evident, but British institutions remained stable and secure. Eminent European savants had praised them. Not even the catastrophe of the American War, which had revealed so many imperfections of government in Britain, had shaken the faith of British statesmen in their mixed constitution. Pitt had considered limited parliamentary reforms in 1785, but when revolution began in France he condemned change as inexpedient and encouraged satisfaction with things as they were. In addition, Grenville shared with most of his contemporaries a faith in the ability of institutions to mould men. Given a long period of peace and prosperity, the French in Canada would be partly anglicised through learning to manage their political affairs under a British constitution. Thus the plural society across the Atlantic might benefit from British institutions as if it had been wholly heir to their traditions and enjoyed the social system in which they had evolved.

Having reached this judgement, Grenville soon decided on that separation of English Canada from French Canada that Sydney had meditated, Dorchester had condemned and the Cabinet had favoured. Quebec, already divided 'in fact, thou' not by law' was to become two Canadas.[45] The conspicuous failure of the Anglo-French Assembly in Grenada provided yet another reason for not establishing any similar body in Quebec.[46]

In deciding on partition Grenville disapproved a proposal from Chief Justice Smith for a general federal legislature of all the North American colonies, including the maritimes.[47] Smith had known the Thirteen Colonies well and believed that 'wisdom and moderation' were never to be expected from 'petty Parliaments'.[48] A general legislature might absorb colonial animosities before they could reach Britain, and be more imperially minded than provincial legislatures had ever been, especially if the Crown established a general executive council for all British North America. Smith knew enough of the Dutch in New York to doubt whether the French would be easily assimilated, and he wanted to give political predominance to the English party immediately. Grenville disliked Smith's proposals, which he thought mere clever devices. He did approve, however, the reference to a general executive.[49] Federation seemed American and was no part of the British constitution. Vast distances would make it unworkable in North America, and the French would oppose a legislature that the English would dominate. Perhaps, remembering the Continental Congress, he also feared that a general legislature would challenge the sovereignty of Parliament.

In reaching his decision Grenville also ignored the fateful advice of the merchants of Montreal and Quebec, conveyed to him by Adam Lymburner, their agent in London. The Great Lakes and the St Lawrence river, Lymburner declared, were an economic and geographic unity that only folly would rend asunder. Grenville was too interested in assimilating the French and laying the social and political foundations needed for the British constitution to heed economic geography or commercial pleading.[50]

ADAPTING THE BRITISH CONSTITUTION

In adapting the British constitution to meet the case of Quebec, Grenville remembered the faults of the old representative system. Chief among these in America had been the absence of a hereditary aristocracy.[51] He wished the Canadas to have, as nearly as possible, the balance wheel of the English political structure — that is, the House of Lords. Titles and other hereditary honours, conferred without regard for creed, would give the new legislative council high social rank and political standing. The same principle also was thought of for Ireland, where Pitt was willing to give power to the propertied class, Roman Catholic as well as Protestant, in order to curb republicanism and to assimilate leading Catholics into the totality of Irish public life.[52] In the Canadas Grenville hoped to appoint to the councils substantial landholders and successful merchants. The Bill authorised the nomination of life members, upon whom the King might confer hereditary titles to which might be annexed a descendible right to be summoned to the legislative council (Sections 3, 5). Through use of these powers the legislative councils might gradually become hereditary.[53] Fox ridiculed the proposal, but it became law — unavailingly, however, for no hereditary honours were ever conferred.

Fox, in this respect like Burke, did not dispute the basis of the government's policy, but differed from Pitt and Grenville on how to make the legislative councils analogues of the House of Lords. He would have made them neither nominated nor hereditary, but 'totally free and independently chosen, in a manner as independent of the Governor' as possible, elected on a property franchise 'infinitely higher' than that for the assemblies. He argued that property, not title, was the true basis of aristocracy, that aristocracy was essential to 'mixed' government, and that a 'mixed' government was the essence of a free constitution.[54]

Parliament preferred the traditional wisdom of the British constitution to Fox's abstract reasoning, which was thought to smack of the republican practices of the United States. According to Pitt, an elected upper house, however safely founded on property, 'would render the poise nearer to the people than it was to the Crown in the British constitution' and so upset the equilibrium of 'mixed government'.[55] So it was settled in 1791, although the problem of deciding whether colonial legislative councils should be nominated (the apparent equivalent to the Lords in communities where hereditary honours were inappropriate) or elected on a special franchise (so as to gain standing and authority comparable with that of the Lords) long troubled policy makers whose norm for colonial institutions was the constitution of Great Britain.

The Constitutional Act[56] barely mentioned the executive councils and defined neither their functions nor their relationships to governors and legislators. The separation of the legislative and executive functions of the councils was unprecedented and so was the name 'executive council'.[57] In the old representative system the councils had been governors' (or 'privy') councils, as well as upper houses of the legislatures and (with the governors) colonial courts of appeal. The Howe Peace Commission of 1776 had offered to 'constitute colonial councils as separate and independent branches' of the American legislatures.[58] In 1791 Grenville carried out this reform in order to make the legislative council more like the House of Lords.

Few duties were specified anywhere for the new executive councils.[59] Their main responsibility was to advise and assist the governor and they had no formal relationship to the legislature. Grenville presumably intended them to be analogous to the Privy Council rather than the

Cabinet, which was not a body known to the law. Partly because appointments to the legislative councils were to be especially prestigious and to be held (in general) for life, while those to the executive councils were to be held only during pleasure, the legislative and executive councils were formally separated from one another although allowed to have members in common. Assemblymen also could sit on the executive council.

The executive councils were intended also to strengthen the governors, who under the old representative system had sometimes been unable to carry out imperial policy because of obstruction by the assemblies. Grenville had been gratified by Pitt's decision in 1785 to appoint a governor-general of all British North America, because so high an officer might be able to control a strong executive and carry out orders from London.[60] Governors with strong executive councils and carefully nominated legislative councils[61] might in addition be able to restrain the democratic tendencies of elected assemblies, just as the monarch and the Lords offset the Commons at home.

The government planned to extend the Church of England in the colonies to help assimilate the Canadian constitution to that of Britain. Many British politicians still blamed the American Revolution partly on the lack in the Thirteen Colonies of an essential part of the British constitution, the Established Church. No one wanted to push anglicisation against Roman Catholics and Presbyterians; equally, no one at the British end foresaw the imminent rise in Upper Canada of vigorous non-conformity, firmly anti-episcopal and aggressively Protestant, or expected the strength of Roman Catholicism to endure in Lower Canada. Pitt had persuaded himself that the French would be assimilated through experience of the constitution and by contact with Upper Canada and the maritime provinces. Looking to the future, the Act allowed the provincial legislatures to introduce English civil law at their discretion, permitted freehold land tenure in Lower Canada (while safeguarding existing tenures) and required freehold tenures for the future in Upper Canada.

Section 2 of the new Act declared that the Crown would divide Canada into two provinces.[62] Section 3 gave the legislative council of Upper Canada a minimum of fifteen members and that of Lower Canada seven. The property franchise for electors of the assemblies was more liberal than for electors of the British Commons. Almost no part of the Canadas lacked representation and practically all men except artisans and the small class of landless farm workers could vote. The *habitants* were included as copyholders. Assemblies were to be elected for four years. The new constitution came into force on 26 December 1791. Conditions in North America, which Grenville never understood, and the outbreak of war with France, which he had not foreseen, undermined his attempt to introduce British forms of government into the Canadas and frustrated his desire to assimilate the French. But in the long term the Act was not a failure. It set both the Canadas on the way to British parliamentary government. Decades of difficulties and turmoil were followed in the 1840s by the establishment in united Canada of a constitution resembling that of Britain in substance as well as form.

LIMITATIONS OF THE POLICY OF 1791

Parliament had not made, and could not have made, the new institutions in the Canadas more than pale shadows of their English archetypes. The Canadas were colonies. Their governors were not kings, but servants of the King, bound to obey the instructions of his ministers. The colonial legislatures were subordinate to the sovereign imperial Parliament, which could make laws for the whole empire and repeal colonial enactments. The Constitutional Act specified no limits on provincial or imperial legislation, beyond reserving entirely to Parliament the power to control trade, commerce and navigation between the Canadas, or between either of them and any part of the world. At law, the power of Parliament to legislate for the colonies was limited only by the Declaratory Act of 1778, which it could repeal. The Crown might disallow Acts of the colonial legislatures within two years and control the business that governors put before them. The executive councils were only slightly comparable with either the Privy Council or Cabinet. They were nominated advisers of the governors, who might however disregard them, and who as imperial officers were themselves under orders from London.

Pitt and Grenville had trusted the theory of 'mixed government' sufficiently to believe that a representative of the sovereign, a legislative council standing for aristocracy and an assembly elected by men of property, would evolve harmonious conventions appropriate to a colony under imperial control, the more so as the new executive council was intended to have high standing. They had not, however, sufficiently appreciated the gulf that separated the aristocratic, hierarchical tradition of society and government, in which they had been bred, from the increasingly different traditions of society and politics, English as well as French, in North America.

In Britain most ministers were aristocrats, or had aristocratic connections, and all ministries owed part of their political strength to the power of the Lords in relation to the Commons, the King and the people. It was their own power (largely a landed aristocrats' power), as well as the influence of the Crown, that ministers used to prevent the government from being defeated at any of the elections between 1742 and 1830. Pitt and Grenville recognised that the Canadas lacked an aristocracy like the British one, which provided an important part of government as well as balancing the representatives of the people. Grenville's plan to appoint successful merchants and large landholders to the legislative councils and to confer titles on some of them would formally have been the nearest possible approach to the aristocracy that he so greatly wished to establish, but it failed. Early in the nineteenth century the assemblies in both Canadas complained that the councils, whether legislative or executive, were dominated by officials, placemen and cliques with no valid claims to special privilege and no dedication to the service of a colony as a whole.

Within a decade the Constitutional Act was full of troubles in Britain as well. Official disenchantment with the Act began early and was increased by evidence that British North America would never succeed the Thirteen Colonies as a main trading partner of the West Indies.[63] The Act itself, as we have seen, obstructed the commercial growth of the St Lawrence River trade by dividing its control between Upper and Lower Canada, at a time when rising American competition demanded vigorous and uniform control. Commercial frustration followed in Montreal, Quebec and later Toronto.[64]

In addition, the French Revolution had as baleful an effect on liberal trends in colonial policy as on liberal movements at home. The policy of the Act was soon an anachronism. Within twenty years of its passing most Tories and many Whigs, on the rare occasions when they thought about Canada, condemned the Act for separating the provinces, for excessive liberality, and for allowing French Lower Canada the same form of government as English Upper Canada. Grenville's immediate successor at the Home Department, Henry Dundas, used the Canadas as a rich field of patronage (for loyalists and Scots) and ignored the objectives of 1791. He fatally compromised Grenville's policy of a strong governor-generalship when he allowed Simcoe, the lieutenant-governor of Upper Canada, to correspond directly with the Secretary of State, instead of through the governor-general. In 1810 Liverpool, as Secretary of State for War and the Colonies, regretted that he could not have the Act repealed.[65] In 1822, his successor, the third Earl Bathurst,[66] unsuccessfully attempted to reunite the Canadas and modify drastically the grant of British institutions.

CONFLICTS IN UPPER CANADA, 1791–1820

The legislative councillors of Upper Canada, whom Grenville had intended to have greater prestige than members of the assembly, were commonly magistrates and men of substance, notably officials or wealthy merchants. Englishmen, Scots or American loyalists, they were accustomed to deference and possessed strong class solidarity. Similarly, the members of the executive council (many of whom sat also on the legislative council) regarded themselves as superior to members of the assembly in rank and judgement. The assembly, whose members were mostly less well established than the gentlemen of the councils, contained growing numbers of

Americans and Irishmen, as well as Englishmen and Scots; many were farmers, or agricultural frontiersmen suspicious of urban power, both commercial and official.

The social differences dividing the assembly from the councils came to coincide with major conflicts over the development of the colony; the ensuing struggle for power eventually produced complaints that the Constitutional Act had been subverted by an oligarchy of powerful families aided by the Colonial Office, which favoured the men of property, education and stability who made up the privileged classes. As time went on, successful merchants aligned themselves with the councils; but farmers, especially small farmers, and professional men tended to predominate in the assembly.

By the 1820s leading members of the councils, confident of their political and personal superiority to the assembly, had evolved a sort of 'Family Compact'.[67] The antagonism of the assembly to this high-minded group (with whom governors were usually allied) gave constitutional questions in Upper Canada some distinctive features. In the eyes of the assembly, the legislative council was remote and unresponsive to the people at large, while the executive council was not only remote, but also, in a constitutional sense, irresponsible, because it owed a duty only to the governor and his superiors in London and not to the legislature or the people of the province. As the assembly, fearing administrative corrosion, discouraged its own members from accepting nomination to the executive council and, for similar reasons, would not allow the government to send representatives to its meetings to explain official policy, the distance between the councils and the elected representatives of the people became wider than the Act itself required.

The liberal electoral franchise aggravated the problem. The assembly was much more representative than the House of Commons, even after 1832. A provincial Act of 1820 allocated one member to areas and towns with populations of over 1000 and two members to areas with over 4000 people. The number of members rose from twenty-six in 1826 to sixty-nine in 1836. Because they represented small numbers of constituents, although some electorates were very large, members felt closely in touch with their electors and preferred their own claims to political power over those of the nominated councils, whose privileged members represented nobody but themselves. The people whom the assembly represented included politically inexperienced agricultural frontiersmen — English, Scots, Irish or American. The councils often thought of them as selfish, factious and ill-informed.

In 1824 the Upper Canadian elections for the first time returned an assembly with a majority against the entrenched conservatives. Lieutenant-Governor Maitland appealed urgently to the Colonial Office for help on the longstanding aliens question, which arose principally from American immigration and had become more difficult after the War of 1812. Bathurst recognised that the naturalisation laws would have to be changed,[68] but the changes were not made until after the assembly, the legislative council, the lieutenant-governor and two Secretaries of State (Bathurst and Goderich) had displayed the worst features of the colonial status and the sectional government of the province. With the aid of American settlers, victory went to the assembly and the cause of rapid economic development, not to the lieutenant-governor and the councils, with their conservative preferences and stiff attitudes towards republicans from across the border.

Maitland believed that British policy had betrayed the natural allies of the mother country, as a result of fears that, if the American settlers were not wholly assimilated, United States influence might grow in Upper Canada, or some colonists might seek incorporation within the American republic.[69] Imprudent concessions, he was sure, would generate reckless demands. Iron-clad in duty, he did not perceive that his own administration had been a prolific source of discontent among those who thought it illiberal, extravagant, class-based and detrimental to the province as a whole. His support of Anglican monopolies in clergy reserves, university education and the celebration of marriages was much condemned. The Bank of Upper Canada, chartered in 1824, had a virtual monopoly of banking in the province and was widely regarded as a creature of the ruling clique. Expenditure on St Lawrence river canals was thought to help only the merchants. The colonial government was charged with neglect of all education, except of the rich and well-connected. There was anger at the land policy, with complaints that prices were too high, that large land grants to the disadvantage of settlers were made to men with influence at Government House, and that the reservation of vast areas for the Crown and for clergy reserves was disastrous.

No politician or official in Upper Canada was charismatic enough to earn for himself the distinction of bridging the gap between the lieutenant-governor and the councils on the one hand and the assembly on the other. Maitland was too rigid and socially prejudiced to be a conciliator. There were, however, outspoken radicals, notably William Lyon Mackenzie,[70] a Scot, that captured public notice even from men who thought their ideas exaggerated and their motives suspect. Mackenzie had arrived in Upper Canada in 1820 and had launched himself as editor of the *Colonial Advocate* in 1824. At first no republican, he persistently attacked the government of Upper Canada, comparing its lack of achievement with the relative triumphs in the richer lands across the American border, and he castigated the Colonial Office for not allowing Upper Canada to develop freely, untrammelled by either British interference or the selfishness of entrenched rulers. His articles continued to be read, even by those who knew that he doted on excess and fed on fighting.

In 1827—8 the Willis affair, much exploited by Mackenzie, plunged Upper Canada into a political crisis. John Walpole Willis, a puisne judge of the provincial King's Bench, outraged the government and was suspended by Maitland. An inquiry by a Privy Council committee led to his removal from office. R. W. Hay, the Permanent Under-Secretary at the Colonial Office, thought Willis 'a silly fellow . . . the tool of . . . malcontents in Up. Canada',[71] but Hay was a Tory in England. In the province the reformers saw the suspension as conclusive proof that Maitland was an insufferable tyrant and in 1828 the electors inflicted a severe defeat on the governor and the conservatives.

In the new assembly the leading reformers were John Rolph, an English-born lawyer and physician, who had strongly opposed Maitland over the aliens question; Marshall Spring Bidwell, an American lawyer of moderate reforming views, whose behaviour had hardened Maitland against naturalising aliens; Dr William Baldwin, Irish-born and, like Rolph, both physician and lawyer; and, from 1829, Baldwin's fastidious son Robert, another lawyer, who became the most persistent, respectable and thoughtful of the colonial advocates of responsible government. Rolph called the meetings of these men a 'cabinet';[72] certainly they thought of themselves as leaders of a reform party. In the summer of 1828 they drafted a petition to Parliament for the remedy of their grievances.[73]

The petition revealed as much knowledge of British constitutional practice as colonial lawyers could be expected to have had: they knew history and practice from reading Blackstone, De Lolme, the histories, the quarterlies and the newspapers; but, significantly, they did not know how to introduce into the colony the responsible government that they sought. They thought that a local Act might effect their purpose and, when they spoke of an imperial Act on the subject, failed to see that a Bill designed to introduce so subtle, complicated and evolving a convention as responsible government was most unlikely ever to be drawn up in Britain. The Canadian reformers trod their own road to responsible government, deriving their ideas from Canadian problems and observing that constitutional practice in Britain, so far as they knew it, would meet their needs well.

The petition, signed by 3000 Upper Canadians, repeated the reformers' complaints, protested against the dismissal of Willis and condemned the 'total ineptitude of military men for civil rule in this province'. The legislative council was charged with lack of independence, and the executive council with 'practical irresponsibility', because only the governor and Secretary of State could call it to account. Both councils were criticised for overlapping membership and hostility to the assembly. The petition asked for a provincial Act to permit the removal of members of the executive council when they lost the confidence of the assembly, and in addition it sought a right to impeach officials. When the reformers learned that Wellington had become Prime Minister in January 1828,

William Baldwin sent him a special plea for responsible government as it existed in Britain, declaring that it was a necessary part of the constitution granted in 1791.[74]

Baldwin clearly wished the sovereign's representative to have under the prerogative a discretionary power to appoint, retain or remove 'ministers' and, especially, to remove them if they lost the confidence of the assembly. The power was to be discretionary, so that the governor would not be compelled to part with advisers who were defeated in the assembly.[75] Baldwin's understanding of British constitutional practice in 1828 was broadly correct. In leaving the governor so much discretion, he was not considering the wish of the Colonial Office to keep the executive under imperial control, but the problems of Upper Canada and the constitutional position then existing in Britain. The events in Britain during the next decade showed that the sovereign could still remove ministers who had the confidence of the Commons and retain ministers who lacked it. Baldwin was not seeking the modern principle of responsible government through the rule of a majority party, which emerged in Britain in the 1840s (although not always not followed there) and was soon afterwards extended to North America. He was asking that relations between the governor and his advisers in Upper Canada should be as nearly as possible the same as those that he observed between the sovereign and his ministers in London. Similarly, when he asked that a minister should be responsible for every act of the Crown and that no judge should serve on the executive council, he intended nothing more than that existing British practice be adopted.

Pitt and Grenville had not intended, when giving the colonists a constitution modelled partly on that of Britain, to provide them with a claim to the most advanced conventions controlling the relations of King, ministers and Parliament at home. The instructions issued to the governors had continued to be based on those used in colonies under the old representative system. They had allowed a governor complete power under the King to choose his advisers regardless of the wishes of the legislature. Indeed, the governor in his colony had more power than the King himself had in Britain, because the King's ministers, unlike a governor's advisers, sat in Parliament, took responsibility there for his public actions and were liable to censure. In effect, though not yet in law or convention, the King's ministers had to be acceptable to Parliament. A governor and his advisers were not accountable to the colonial legislature and were effectively responsible to no one save the Secretary of State.

CONFLICTS IN LOWER CANADA, 1791–1818

In 1791 Pitt and Grenville had not wished to force the anglicisation or assimilation of the French Canadians. They had expected Lower Canada to be transformed by living under a British constitution, and through influences from other parts of British North America. Before long, however, it became clear that the Constitutional Act, instead of helping assimilation, had increased the French sense of racial difference. The Napoleonic Wars, moreover, destroyed all Grenville's hopes of a long peace in which quiet anglicisation might succeed.

The majority of assembly members were French Roman Catholics, whose interests were predominantly agrarian and whose leaders came principally from their own professional classes. The French found two great merits in the 1791 constitution: the privilege of practising their religion freely, and the possibility (recognised by about 1805) of using their superior numbers in the assembly to combat measures promoting the special interests in business, land, law and fiscal policy of English merchants in Montreal and Quebec; these the French regarded as injurious to their society and agriculture. However, they did not learn how to control the assembly until after the councils had become predominantly English and begun to grasp more power than Pitt and Grenville had intended.[76] A few French leaders studied the British constitution to discover how the assembly could prevail over the councils, and eventually the French were more eager to uphold the Act strictly than the English were. Some governors then supported the English party in arguing that the French did not deserve the great powers they were coming to hold in the assembly.[77]

British policy had originally favoured keeping the *seigneurs* on the legislative council, where, under the Quebec Act, and because of the fact that as a class they were the nearest colonial equivalent to the British landed aristocracy, they had held an important position. But, for a variety of reasons, French influence on the legislative council declined after 1791 and the council became a preserve of the dominant group of English merchants and officials, known as the Château Clique. Both councils shared the tacit unwillingness of the Colonial Office to permit liberal development of parliamentary government in Lower Canada and justified their position by denigrating the French. The Colonial Office, controlling an extensive patronage, gave most of the important posts to men who were not Canadian by birth. Many office holders were loyalists or their sons; all assumed that British ascendancy should be maintained. The loyalists were notable beneficiaries of large land grants made through the executive council, and held many grants in favoured areas simply for speculation. The assembly complained that land needed for *habitants* and immigrants had been squandered on the favourites of the Crown.[78]

Under French domination, the assembly complained that the councils were too close to each other, and that both were dominated by the English party, who ignored the people's representatives and ran the province as a profitable monopoly. In retaliation the assembly held itself aloof and objected to the nomination of its members to the executive council, lest they be corrupted by oligarchy.

In 1807 Sir James Craig became lieutenant-governor. He was a soldier and distrusted the French, the more so as war with the United States seemed likely. Making the quarrel of the English his own, he dismissed French leaders from their government offices, including posts in the militia, and hoped to suppress their party for ever. He warned the Secretary of State, Castlereagh, that the French wanted him to change the membership of the executive council whenever the assembly so wished.[79] He exaggerated. The French claim that he found most alarming was probably only that the assembly should have the right, as the Commons had, to attack and impeach the advisers of the Crown,[80] not that the assembly should be able to force the governor to dismiss all his advisers collectively, a power that the Commons did not then possess in England.[81] Yet even the more limited claim would have involved extensive change. The governor would have remained under the orders of the Secretary of State, but members of his executive council would have been liable, collectively or individually, to attack and impeachment for his actions, whether taken on their advice, on his own initiative, or on orders from Downing Street. The power would have given a strong assembly considerable control over most governors. Craig angrily concluded that the French party was ill suited to its legislative duties.[82] When the elections of 1809 showed that the people did not agree with him he soon dissolved the new assembly, only to find his position worse than before, because his action was not approved in Britain.

The imperial government agreed with Craig 'that it had been a mistake to grant Lower Canada representative government'. Castlereagh wrote temporisingly about the difficulties of controlling so turbulent a body as the assembly of Lower Canada; he regretted particularly that Craig did not have at his disposal the influence of the Crown and extensive patronage, which were what helped ministers to keep control over the Commons.[83] But he would do no more. Only urgent necessity would have induced him to lay the constitutional problems of the Canadas before Parliament in wartime, so soon after the Act of 1791, and while the Opposition was rancorous.

Liverpool, who succeeded Castlereagh in October 1809, also dreaded a storm in Parliament over the Canadas.[84] Grenville was believed to treasure his brainchild of 1791 and to control many votes in the Commons. Radicals in Britain might support the French in Lower Canada and British prestige would then be undermined throughout North America. Toleration of Roman Catholics in Canada was still a sensitive subject in Britain, where emancipation was twenty years away (Liverpool opposed it) and religious tensions were stimulated by attacks on the Act of Union. Moreover, amendment of the constitution of Lower Canada might alarm the Upper Canadians with fears of being yoked again to the more numerous, Roman Catholic, racially proud French.

Privately Liverpool told Craig, 'We are all fully convinced of the evils which have arisen from the Act . . . and of the absurdity of attempting to give what is falsely called the British constitution to a people whose education, habits and prejudices render them incapable of receiving it.'[85] Publicly he asked whether the assembly might meet less frequently or for only short periods.[86] The governor had a large revenue, and armed forces to ensure his independence. Also in public, Liverpool advised Craig to conciliate the French as far as he could while maintaining a 'firm, temperate but persevering resistance to all the Encroachments and Usurpations of the Assembly'; if necessary Craig could punish the assembly by dissolving or proroguing it.

Liverpool would not agree to make the executive council responsible to the assembly, and said that 'It would . . . have been wholly inconsistent with the nature of a Colony, and its necessary connection with the Mother Country, that the Executive Government should have been placed in the same state of dependence upon a local Legislature, as most usefully subsists reciprocally between the Crown and the Parliament of the United Kingdom.'[87] In Britain ministers were appointed and removed by the King, governed in his name, followed policies that he approved, and answered in Parliament, where he possessed great power, for every act of state. In a colony the executive council was appointed by the King on the nomination of the governor, who controlled no votes in the assembly and lacked the special authority of the sovereign. Members of the executive council were responsible to the governor and through him to the King; like the governor they were subordinate to the King's ministers and could not reasonably be subject to the control of the colonial legislature as well, especially so angry and vehement a body as the assembly of Lower Canada. If they were made responsible to the assembly, imperial control over the governor and the colonial executive and legislature would be at an end. For over thirty years Liverpool's declaration continued to represent British policy towards any form of responsible government in colonies.

The election of a determined radical, Louis Joseph Papineau,[88] as speaker of the assembly in 1815 brought to the foreground a new champion of French Canada, agrarian, nationalist and egalitarian, who detested the way in which a minority of English-speaking colonists had gained privileges and wealth to dominate the whole province. Although later a strong republican, he was in 1815 still a loyal monarchist, protesting that the Colonial Office and the two councils were wrongly denying the assembly its legitimate powers. A few liberally-minded non-French members of the assembly supported him, most notably John

Neilson, a Scot, who had married a Frenchwoman and learned constitutional law from Bédard, one of the coolest and best informed of the
French leaders.

THE REUNION BILL OF 1822

For both Canadas the St Lawrence river was the vital link with the outside
world. Upper Canada, lacking a seaport of its own, shared with Lower
Canada the revenue from customs duties collected at Quebec. Beginning in
1819, the Assembly of Lower Canada declined to extend the two-year
agreement over customs receipts that had been made with Upper Canada
in 1817. Troubled by loss of revenue, the legislature of Upper Canada
empowered the lieutenant-governor to borrow against the security of
duties to be received later and in 1822 sent the attorney-general, John
Beverley Robinson, to lay the problem before the imperial authorities in
London. Robinson, at thirty, was already eminent in the Family Compact
and ranked among the ablest conservatives in the colonies. A descendant of
Bishop John Robinson, who had served as ambassador and Lord Privy Seal
under Queen Anne, he belonged to the privileged classes of Britain.[89]

In London Robinson found the Colonial Office at work on Lower
Canadian projects to reunite the Canadas.[90] The partition of 1791 had
never been acceptable to the English and Scots merchants in Montreal and
Quebec, because it had cut them off from the progressive inland province
of Upper Canada and tied them to the anti-commercial French. In the
early 1820s they tried hard to undo partition. The merchants were
supported by some 30,000 English-speaking colonists, who had settled in
the Eastern Townships of Lower Canada.[91] Mostly Americans, they
resented lack of representation in the assembly. Electoral divisions had
been established before the Townships were much populated and redress
of the immigrants' wrongs was slow. Reunion of the Canadas would join
the Eastern Townships with the English of Upper Canada in a bloc
opposed to the French.

Liverpool's government, which did not approve the principles followed
by Pitt and Grenville in 1791, and was presiding elsewhere over the growth
of Crown colony government, willingly considered reunion. 'Bear' Ellice
(Edward Ellice the elder), son of a Montreal merchant, uncle of John
Richardson (the leader of the English in Lower Canada), brother-in-law of
the second Earl Grey, and absentee *seigneur* of Beauharnois, won support
for reunion from the Under-Secretary for Colonies, R. J. Wilmot-Horton.[92]

Robinson did not agree with the persuasive Ellice.[93] Like other Tories
in Upper Canada, he shared British disenchantment with the policy of
1791, and feared that a new, united legislature would be as tumultuous,

democratic and persistently at loggerheads with the executive government as the assembly of Lower Canada was. The only united legislature he desired was one meeting at long intervals to pass laws on trade and customs revenue.

No one in London knew for certain, while the Reunion Bill was being drafted, that Robinson's misgivings about opinion in Upper Canada were well founded. The colonial tories, like others who objected to incorporation with the too numerous French (still three-fifths of the population of the Canadas), or who dreaded rule from Montreal or Quebec, should the capital be established there instead of Toronto, strongly opposed reunion. But they knew nothing of the new proposals until after a Bill to reunite the Canadas had been presented.[94]

The Bill embodied the aspirations of the English party in Lower Canada, whose zeal for strong government and commercial development were thoroughly congenial to Tory notions on the utility of colonies.[95] Anglicisation and some of the formal structure of the proposed new government were all that was to be saved from the policy of 1791. Not self-government on the British model, but an anomalous form of constitution with a strengthened executive favourable to English interests had become official policy.

The Bill gave each province equal representation in the new legislature of united Canada and made English the official language (although assembly debates might be in either language for the first fifteen years). The new legislative council, to be composed from the two existing councils, with additional members nominated by the governor-general, would have been predominantly English. Roman Catholics were guaranteed freedom of worship, but priests were not to receive their tithes until collated to their benefices by the governor. The Eastern Townships were to be enfranchised and their elected members counted as part of the representation of Quebec in the new assembly. Because the Townships could be counted upon to return English-speaking members, and the total number of members from each Canada was to be the same, the assembly was certain to have an English majority. To these guarantees of English supremacy was added a barrier against democracy in the shape of higher property qualifications for members of the legislature. A slight attempt to bridge the gap between the assembly and the executive was made by giving the governor-general power to summon two executive councillors from each province to attend the assembly and speak, but not vote.[96]

The government planned to rush the Bill through Parliament before opposition could muster in Britain and North America; not even the governor-general was informed. A heavy responsibility rested on the over-confident Wilmot-Horton,[97] to whom a masterful role in policy making was ever congenial. Although he knew that the Bill would be unpopular in Lower Canada, he expected a good reception in Upper Canada, provided that Parliament passed it by a large majority. He was doubly wrong: Upper Canada was opposed to reunion even if English supremacy were guaranteed, and Parliament was unwilling to legislate for colonies, whose affairs were understood in Britain only obscurely, but whose capacity to make trouble was obvious.

In the Commons Sir James Mackintosh, the reformer and historian, attacked the ministry for haste and proposed a delay of six months.[98] Wilmot-Horton smoothly replied, with good law and bad sense, that a constitution that Parliament had granted, Parliament could take away. Mackintosh, who was not opposed to reunion (should the colonists want it), admitted that Parliament could lawfully do all that was proposed, but condemned reckless indifference to colonial opinion. As an old Whig, he valued representative legislatures as safeguards of political stability and detested provocation of the people.

Ministers, who had wrongly expected an easy passage for their Bill, were alarmed by the support given to Mackintosh and gladly took advantage of the end of the session to postpone Wilmot-Horton's precipitate measure. In announcing the decision, Castlereagh rejected the argument that Britain should not legislate for colonies without consulting them. Such a restriction, he said, could never be tolerated by an imperial Parliament.[99]

In Lower Canada the French party interpreted the Bill as a punitive measure aimed at the assembly.[100] The French, whose nationalism had been greatly stirred, aroused fears in Upper Canada that the province's independence would be forfeited to British imperial interests and its identity merged with that of Lower Canada.[101] Early in 1823 Neilson and Papineau visited England to protest against the ministry's procedings. They wanted the peaceful development of French Canada within the empire, but free from British, American and Upper Canadian interference. So far as reunion was concerned, their journey was not necessary. The government had learned such a lesson from the swift massing of opposition in Britain and North America that ministers did not dare take such a policy to Parliament again. Bathurst admitted to Wilmot-Horton that fear of driving the Canadians into the arms of the United States 'makes me a Coward & influences me strongly in all my proceedings with the North American Colonial assemblies'; better inaction than wrong action.[102]

Bathurst did, however, assist the English in the Canadas with a variety of measures on tariffs, trade and land tenure. The concessions made to the English on land tenure were resented by the French as compulsory anglicisation. No such measures would ever have been passed by the assembly and their enactment by Parliament was condemned as ignorant, high-handed and injurious. However, the commutation rate set by the executive council was so high that the new facilities were little used.[103]

THE SELECT COMMITTEE OF 1828

In Lower Canada in the 1820s, clashes between the executive council and the assembly, or between the English and French parties, often took the form of disputes over financial control.[104] The colonial government, as we have seen, had exclusive control without reference to the legislature over moneys received under the Quebec Revenue Act, the casual and territorial revenues of the Crown, the proceeds of certain provincial Acts and the profits of justice; of these, the first was most important. In the 1820s the financial independence of the executive was, however, being eroded by rising expenditure, which the assembly was called upon to finance from general revenue.[105]

Years of increasing difficulty brought Governor-General Dalhousie and the assembly to a deadlock over supply in 1826–7. Dalhousie appropriated provincial funds to meet a deficit; his action was illegal, although it had precedent, and was the more objectionable because the assembly had voted nothing. To punish the assembly, Dalhousie dissolved it. To his chagrin, the elections returned the radicals in increased strength. When the assembly re-elected Papineau as speaker, Dalhousie with doubtful right demanded that another choice be made. The assembly refused and he prorogued it at once. 'Here I sincerely hope will be an end of Parliament in this Province', he wrote.[106] He was too optimistic. The new Secretary of State, Huskisson, could not ignore the clamour that he had roused and recalled him. Dalhousie went to command the troops in India, while his superiors reaped the whirlwind.[107]

Dalhousie's behaviour had produced such a storm that even London newspapers reported it. However, they continued to ignore the no less extraordinary ambitions of the French party, which Governor-General Kempt summed up as aiming 'to get . . . the whole of government into . . . [its] hands'.[108] Papineau no longer admired the British constitution and was beginning to overcome his misgivings about the United States.[109] The French radicals added to their demands for legislative control of all expenditure a further demand, that the legislative council be made elective, so that the majority of members would be of their own race. A French majority in both houses could bring the executive council under control. Supreme power in the colony under Britain – not independence – was Papineau's objective in 1827.

Early in 1828 a delegation from Lower Canada asked Huskisson to consider the state of the province and its government. The memorable debate of 2 May,[110] when the House considered his motion for a select committee, revealed what informed men had long known, that Lower Canada had not been governed according to the Act of 1791 because British governments had distrusted the French and tried to rule through the English minority. It also revealed that a few liberals had a strong belief that Britain should lean towards effective grants of self-government to all colonies where political rights would be exercised equitably and efficiently, despite the risks that self-government might lead to independence. The first signs of the new concept of self-governing colonies of settlement, which was so important in policy from the 1840s onward, were already appearing.[111]

Huskisson, a reforming Tory, combined robust faith in empire with an active businessman's desire to develop the colonies and enrich British commerce. He blamed the French for delaying the growth of Canada. Lethargic in commerce, troublesome in politics, they should have been anglicised long before. Freedom of religion they could have, but Lower Canada had to be an English colony, absorbing British capital and emigrants and swelling British shipping and trade.

He knew that some reform of the Canadian constitutions was inevitable, but would not allow the colonists to undertake the task for themselves, and did not think of independence as anything more than a guide (never a goal) for long-term policy. The assembly's claims to appropriate the Crown revenues he condemned as 'neither founded in law nor practice', although he allowed that the revenues might be exchanged for a civil list, paying the salaries of the highest officials and judges.

Huskisson's strong assertions were rejected by the Radicals, by Mackintosh, and by the moderate young Whig, Henry Labouchere, who was of French descent and had travelled in Canada in 1823. Labouchere, later Secretary of State for the Colonies, praised the Act of 1791 as the 'charter' of French Canadian liberties. If it were honestly applied, the colonists could be left to solve their own problems.

Mackintosh demanded a new policy towards self-governing colonies so as to reduce their subordination to Britain. The Canadians should manage their own affairs, 'except in cases of the most urgent and manifest necessity', and not be ruled by an unpopular, pro-British minority. Rather than have the Commons set up a committee, he would have preferred the Canadians to decide constitutional changes for themselves. He recommended five 'maxims' of colonial policy:

A full and efficient protection from all foreign influences; full permission to conduct the whole of their internal affairs; compelling them to pay all the reasonable expenses of their own government, and giving them . . . a perfect control over the expenditure of the money; and imposing no restrictions of any kind upon the industry or traffic of the people . . . . These . . . are the only means by which the hitherto almost incurable evil of all distant governments can be either mitigated or removed.

Mackintosh scorned the argument, to which Huskisson has leaned, that the English party in Lower Canada should continue to be treated as a privileged minority, although the French outnumbered them by five to one. Did not the French own most of the landed property? Had they ever used their majority in the assembly against the English? In Ireland, England had dealt out 'six hundred years of misery' by establishing a 'ruling caste'. That mistake should never be repeated in Lower Canada, whatever the government's sympathy with English interests and Protestant ascendancy. In Upper Canada Britain had already pandered shamelessly to the special interests of the Church of England and the conservative minority who were its leading members.

Mackintosh would have had colonial policy aim not at subordination or assimilation, but at virtual autonomy under the Crown. To rule through privileged, unpopular minorities in the colonies was dismal folly, certain to produce resentment and strife. If just grievances were remedied and the colonists left to govern themselves, Britain would share their prosperity and goodwill.

The House appointed a liberally composed committee of twenty-one members, whose report[112] strongly criticised past policy as illiberal and vacillating. The committee vindicated most of the constitutional complaints of the assembly of Lower Canada and rejected Huskisson's charge that French laws and customs had worsened the colony's problems. The Canadas were thought to have suffered less from defects in the 1791 constitution than from maladministration and the monopolising of government by privileged groups serving their own selfish ends.

By gratifying the French, the report irritated the English in Lower Canada. In Upper Canada English opinion was divided. Some reformers saw the report as a triumph. The radical *Colonial Advocate* praised it as 'prudent, just and conciliatory'.[113] Land titles, the clergy reserves, the electoral system, the jury system and, above all, the councils had all been found to need reform. Most conservatives, however, found it obnoxious.

There was a world of difference between Bathurst's policy in Canada — that of supporting the friends of the British government, such as the officials and conservatives on the councils — and the favour shown by the select committee to self-government and the people at large. Bathurst, a moderately conservative aristocrat, was quite out of touch with views that emphasised not privilege, responsibility, authority and the need to protect the English minority in Lower Canada, but the politics of representative government. Typically, he had expected the committee, whose appointment he had regretted, to be swayed by its ministerial members and to smother disturbing thoughts. The implied attack on his own administration apparently did not move him, for he was either indifferent to such things or wished to seem so. He was alarmed by the damage that the report might do to the empire: was it not in effect an invitation to the colonists to oppose their established rulers? He blamed Huskisson for having had the committee appointed, and other ministers for not having kept the report within reasonable bounds.[114]

To help the colonists remedy their own grievances, the committee recommended that the numbers of officials on the legislative councils be reduced, in favour of independent members of good standing. The report did not mention responsible government. Reunion, although advocated before the committee by Ellice and Stephen, was dismissed as impracticable.[115] Decentralisation, as sought by Papineau, was ignored.[116] The only proposal to amend the constitution was in respect of the Quebec Revenue Act. The committee wished the whole of the public revenue to be placed under the control of the assembly in each province, provided that the salaries of the governors, high officials and judges were established by statute as a fixed civil list, and not left to annual votes of the legislatures.

The committee's report was available before Parliament considered the petition drafted by the Baldwins and their colleagues.[117] The debate on the petition added little to British thinking on the Canadian problem.[118] Wellington and Goderich defended British policy; Wellington was particularly firm in the faith that Britain knew what was best for her colonies, and believed that no colony with a foreign power on its borders could be allowed the reforms that the Baldwins sought. Stanley rejected the Baldwins' pleas with confident vigour. He had visited the Canadas in 1824 and thought them listless and backward;[119] he had served energetically on the 1828 committee. In 1829 he told the Commons that Upper Canada was quite unfit for cabinet government, even if the innovation could be reconciled with colonial status.

However, in 1829 even the Tories conceded that some reforms had become necessary in the Canadas. Without reform, the officials and merchants, who were close to Government House, could not preserve the tranquillity of the provinces, sustain the commerce that made them useful to Britain, and restrain disloyal attempts to promote annexation to the United States. But reform was not a grateful word to most Tories[120] and reform in the Canadas to make the 1791 Act work as intended might transfer power to men – such as Frenchmen, Americans and new settlers with doubtful antecedents – on whose judgement and fidelity Britain ought not to rely. Moreover, reform in the colonies might rouse expectations of new reforms at home.

BEGINNINGS OF LIBERAL REFORM IN BRITAIN

When the Whigs took office in November 1830 under the second Earl Grey, the Colonial Secretary was Goderich and the Parliamentary Under-Secretary at the Colonial Office was the Prime Minister's eldest son, Viscount Howick.[121] Because Goderich was in the Lords and lacked decisiveness and vigour, the ambitious Howick had, like Wilmot-Horton, a larger share in policy making than would otherwise have been allowed him.

Reformers in the colonies were glad when the Whigs took office, for change seemed possible at last. The Whigs had not enunciated any clear colonial policy;[122] but it was well known that they hoped for economies in the administration of the empire, which could not be achieved without reforms, and also that many Whigs regarded moderate reform as the bulwark of their political strength in Britain. Fresh in office, they condemned friction between Britain and the Canadas as a discreditable product of Tory intransigence.

Of the many papers on Canada that were to be found in the Colonial Office when the Whigs took power, none pointed to immediate action so strongly as James Stephen's memorandum of September 1828.[123] Stephen, a lawyer, had declared that the assemblies had never exploited the full powers granted them in 1791. In Lower Canada larger claims of authority would have been made had it not been for the 'docility and habit of obedience' of the French. On the other hand, the executive governments in both provinces had exercised greater powers than the constitution allowed them. Attacks on their overprivileged authority were certain to increase. Prolonged conflict between Britain and the assemblies would reveal how weak the position of the governors under the Act of 1791 really was. In theory the Act had established monarchical institutions in the Canadas, but in practice it had almost created 'two new Republics upon the continent of North America'. At law the Crown was weak against assemblies that chose to use their full powers, especially their financial powers.

Howick was well acquainted with Stephen's ideas on Canada and ready to act on some of them. He drafted at once,[124] on behalf of Goderich, a Bill to release to the colonial legislatures the whole of the moneys collected under the Quebec Revenue Act. The Bill made no stipulations about a civil list, for Howick wished merely to suggest to the provincial legislatures the provision that they should make for the salaries of governors, judges and officials. Privately he thought of the Bill as a measure of repeal, to strike down an irksome and impolitic barrier to colonial self-government. Publicly he deplored the ways in which the Colonial Office and the governors had perverted the legislative independence granted in 1791 in order to sustain executives amenable to imperial control.[125] He persuaded himself that the complaining colonists were moderate men, whose just wrath had been correctly apprehended by the committee of 1828. His view was generous, impulsive and too simple, a young man's reaction to Tory failure to get on with basic reforms.

Howick always spoke publicly as if the Bill were designed to carry out the recommendations of the 1828 committee. He reminded the Commons that the Tories themselves had begun to remedy some evils of which the committee had complained and had brought down (but abandoned) a Bill similar to his own. The number of officials on the legislative councils was already being reduced; fourteen new, independent members had been appointed; judges other than the chief justice had been asked to stay away from council meetings and keep out of politics. In a burst of radical generosity he declared, 'I rejoice ... that the Canadas have had the intelligence to know their constitutional rights, and the spirit and determination to assert them .... What use or advantage can it be to this country, that the government should have the power of control over the internal affairs of the colonies which seems to be so much valued by some people here?'[126] The second part of this statement, which he qualified later with reservations too subtle for most colonists to comprehend, always remained fundamental in his colonial policies. It contained principles on which autonomy of colonies could be founded. Repression, Howick told the Commons in 1831, could not fail to be discreditable; conciliation and concession, neither of which should ever have become necessary, were the only just and prudent policy. The Bill, which Hume praised warmly,[127] attracted little notice and became law as 1 and 2 William IV, c. 23.[128]

In Upper Canada, where conservatives had regained control of the assembly, the magnanimity of Howick (and Goderich) was justified. The legislature at once granted a civil list lasting for the life of the King, though providing less than Goderich suggested. Radical reformers, led by Mackenzie, perceived the conservative side of Howick's liberalism and denounced the 'Everlasting Salary Bill', which had deprived the elected representatives of the people of the readiest means of bringing pressure on the governor and the executive council.[129]

In Lower Canada, where conditions were greatly disturbed, the demands of the French leaders had become insatiable. The assembly had asked for the establishment in the colony of a tribunal empowered to impeach public officials, and for extensive reforms of land policy, the judiciary and public finance.[130] Howick's investment in colonial goodwill came too late. Papineau sought an entire capitulation that would surrender all the casual and territorial revenues of the Crown to legislative appropriation. When the assembly refused to vote salaries for the officials except on an annual basis,[131] the legislative council rejected the Supply Bill for 1832 on the ground that a civil list lasting for the life of the King ought to be enacted. The dispute continued for years, while salaries, which eventually were made up from 'army extraordinaries',[132] went into arrears. Another indication of the failure of concession was Papineau's refusal to accept the seat that Goderich allowed him on the executive council in the hope of narrowing the distance between the council and the assembly.[133]

The unhappy results of Howick's Act in Lower Canada prejudiced Cabinet and Parliament against attempts to escape from the *damnosa heriditas* of the decades in which Britain had relied on privileged colonial oligarchies instead of working the 1791 Act as Pitt and Grenville had intended. Before long, talk of effective self-government and even possible independence for the Canadas was not, as it had been with Mackintosh, a matter of respectable speculation in the House of Commons, nor, as it had been in Howick's generous speech, one of reasonable inferences; instead it was a frenzied affair of immediate aspiration by Papineau and his followers, and of alarming predictions, from Hume and his allies, of strife and bloodshed. Extremism in the colonies silenced almost all the friends of reform in Britain except the most liberal Whigs and the Radicals.

3 The Canadas Troubles, 1831-41

> The Whigs ... did have firmly held principles. They really believed in giving the colonists control over their own internal affairs, and had the colonial assemblies been able to agree as to the form of self-government they wanted, they would probably have got it between 1835 and 1837.
>
> H. T. Manning[1]

The Howick Act of 1831 soon became the short test of British politicians' views on the Canadas. Ought it be repealed, suspended, or followed by further concessions? Was it a late return to the policy followed by Pitt and Grenville in 1791, or a mere palliative to reduce colonial dissatisfaction?

Running through the discussions was a conflict of old and new ideas about the objects of reform, the conventions of the constitution in Britain, the future of commercial policy and the permanence or impermanence of empire. In the Canadas themselves reform was no less contentious. Constitutional conflicts were part of a struggle for power in which the British authorities were usually regarded as natural allies of conservatives already entrenched in power. Extreme groups in the colonies pleaded for constitutional autochthony, hoping to design their own forms of government on North American principles, which would be different from those underlying the government of Britain.

THE CONCEPT OF REFORM IN BRITAIN

There were many ways in which the nature of British and of colonial politics differed, raising barriers to understanding on both sides of the Atlantic. British wariness of colonial self-government generally was roused by dislike of the French Canadian reformers and inflamed by suspicious jealousy of the United States of America. Political and social differences between the mother country and the Canadas suggested that the colonies were not really suited to British political institutions: 'The frame of society in the colonies is essentially and necessarily democratic; in the mother country it is still essentially aristocratic. Whenever, therefore, the colonists . . . insist upon their just claims to a government conformable to their genius and character, a collision is inevitable.'²

The Reform Act had made aristocratic power in Britain safe for decades to come. In the Canadas, where the claims of aristocracy to govern had been formally recognised in the Act of 1791, both provinces lacked an aristocracy. The Family Compact in Upper Canada and the Château Clique in Lower Canada had often attempted to play aristocratic roles, but, although the British government recognised their loyalty to the Crown and their claims to authority, they were opposed in the colonies. Until the late 1830s, the gulf dividing them from the bulk of the colonists was apprehended only obscurely by British observers. Men of affairs in Britain often regretted the growth of colonial democracy, believing that it rose from social and political instability, complicated by American influence; perhaps it might also be a grim indicator of future trends in Britain. The inability of the Château Clique to command a degree of respect remotely comparable with that enjoyed by the aristocracy in Britain was mystifying in London, except on the assumption that racial hostility induced animosity, while attacks on the Family Compact seemed the more ominous because they lacked the specious comprehensibility that racial differences gave to the troubles of Lower Canada.

Another difficulty for British politicians studying Canadian problems came from their own concepts of reform. The Act of 1832 had been passed for a variety of reasons, among them the desire to safeguard the existing pattern of rulers by making political power and economic power more nearly coincident with one another. Whig reforms were essentially conservative, designed to save and not to transform the existing order. ' "Reform on a truly conservative principle", as Grey called it, could be applied to every established institution and became a virtual Whig maxim.'³ But it provided no key to Canadian problems. The Whigs, though ready to adapt institutions for the sake of stability, could not see what reforms acceptable to themselves were likely to succeed in the colonies. Did not the Canadas already have liberal electoral franchises, representative institutions resembling those of the mother country, and governments conspicuous for loyalty to the throne, respectable attitudes to property and trade, and views on society acceptable to Whig aristocrats? The Whigs were pulled both ways at once. Elected assemblies, securely based on property, ought to have authority and trustworthy judgement, but their complaints about lack of authority were so intemperate as to undermine faith in their judgement. Nominated upper houses, on the other hand, even if not aristocratic, had important conservative functions and sometimes seemed necessary for stability and for maintaining British power over the colonies.

The Whigs could find no reform of colonial constitutions to prevent a dangerous disintegration of colonial politics in Lower Canada and sharp conflicts in Upper Canada. Independence, if achieved peaceably and not followed by annexation to the United States, was occasionally palatable to the Whigs when out of patience with colonists apparently bent on separation from Britain, but independence was too drastic a measure to be a regular basis of policy making, and no ministry would survive in Britain if it lost colonies in America. Extensive changes, like those sought by Papineau or Mackenzie, or the less radical reforms proposed by the Baldwins, were far beyond the range of safe Whig reforms, which were to be compounded of economy, benevolence and firm maintenance of aristocratic supremacy. 'A reform which is not radical', Jeremy Bentham wrote in 1828, 'is a moderate reform; and a reform which is moderate is a Whig reform.'[4] No moderate reform of consequence was in sight for the Canadas after the Howick Act, and another attempt at repression in North America was unthinkable. The Whigs hesitated and were lost.

Tories were in a simpler position than Whigs in facing Canadian demands for reform. Out of office for most of the 1830s, they could make political capital out of Whig difficulties with colonies. Having opposed reform in 1832, on the grounds that a successful legislature ought not to be disturbed and that the authority of the Lords and the King should be maintained, they had few inhibitions in rejecting or modifying demands for reform in the colonies. Only receding memories of 1776 and 1822, and painful recollections of the committee of 1828 restrained them.

In constitutional principle, neither Whigs nor Tories found the demands of Lower Canadian radicals easy to comprehend or safe to satisfy. In Britain in 1832, 'overnight, as it were, the constitution had ceased to be based on the principle of prescription and had come to be based on the principle of representation'.[5] But men were slow to recognise how great a change had been made and continued to think of government as if its foundations were still wholly prescriptive. In the Canadas, according to the law, the constitutions were established by authority of the King in Parliament; but in Lower Canada the majority leaders of the assembly were claiming powers, and recommending a form of constitution making, that could be justified only if the representative principle were given the amplest, and an altogether unprecedented, scope. To the Tories in Britain, who feared that the Reform Act might have weakened the Crown and endangered Church and State, the claims of the Lower Canadian assembly, when noticed at all, seemed evil reminders of unknown perils yet to emerge from the Act of 1832. To most Whigs, when Canada caught their notice, the prospect seemed little better, for the implications of the demands from Lower Canada obviously threatened the established bases of British colonial rule.

Again, everyone in Britain knew that the conventions requiring Lords and Commons to support the King's government, so long as independent men of conscience could, might be weakening but were undoubtedly still alive. Obviously those colonists who emphasised the principle of popular representation, instead of the power and the duty of the King in Parliament to rule, knew no such convention. The turmoil of politics in Lower Canada bewildered British politicians because it seemed so irresponsible: why was authority not respected, and why did reasonable concessions so rarely produce reasonable responses?

In Britain every fear that colonial politics were unsound was increased by the success of the colonial radicals in enlisting the aid of the Radicals on whom the Whigs had to depend in the Commons. Papineau and Mackenzie were supported publicly and privately in Britain by Brougham, Hume, Roebuck and Molesworth. Moderate Whigs and the Tories feared that concessions to the reformers in the colonies would produce as many evils there as unbridled radicalism would produce at home. Canadians already had too much obvious temptation to try out republican and democratic forms of government; some of them wished to be absorbed into the American Republic, or to abandon British monarchy and parliamentary government in favour of American models.

When Mackenzie visited England in 1832 and 1833, he was assisted by Hume, received by Stanley and Howick, and had a cordial interview with Goderich.[6] He also met R. S. Rintoul[7] of *Spectator*, which was dedicated equally to colonial reform and destruction of the Colonial Office, and John Black[8] of *The Morning Chronicle*, the most uncompromising of the opposition newspapers. Neither Stanley nor Howick liked Mackenzie's notions of reform, but they heard him patiently. Stanley declined to agree either that members of the two councils and the governors 'should always be such as possess the confidence of the country', or that legislative councils should be elected, and he merely noted Mackenzie's wholesale condemnation of British policy on trade, defence, lands, navigation of the St Lawrence, postal services, and boundaries with the United States.[9] Howick, reacting against 'the old Tory system' of exploiting colonies for patronage while subordinating them to Britain economically, was alarmed by charges that the law officers of Upper Canada always opposed reform, and encouraged Mackenzie to inform Goderich that not all classes were fairly represented in the ... Assembly' of Upper Canada.[10] Goderich thought Mackenzie unexpectedly civil for so strong a radical, but too embittered to be credible as the representative of more than a minority of Upper Canadians. Mackenzie found Goderich 'naturally a kind, liberal and benevolent man' but appallingly ignorant of the colonies he had to administer.[11]

Goderich's ignorance was profound, for he rarely received political information from Upper Canada, where Lieutenant-Governor Colborne did not think it important to report what the politicians were doing. Ignorance was closely related to the confusion of which Stephen complained in 1832:

> The British Government has never followed a course, consistent in principle, for two years regarding Canada. After a system of opposing all claims of the Assembly, they went on to a plan of measured concession, then to the suspension of all measures pending a Parliamentary inquiry, then again to a more rigid assertion of the rights of the Crown, from which they again reverted to the plan of liberal concessions. At last they are forced to admit that the popular party is not conciliated except by the virtual abdication of all the rights of the Crown, and probably not even then.[12]

Stephen was right, but this is not to say that no one in office was willing to work hard to solve problems that may have been in the short term insoluble, or that British policy was unchanged between 1831 and the reunion of the Canadas in 1841. Among the Tories, Peel and Aberdeen had firm objectives, although their policies were fortunate not to have been put to the test. If ever clear proposals of moderate reform had been received from the Canadas, the Whigs would gratefully have tried to adopt them. Some Whigs, most notably Howick, were willing to consider reforms that were far from moderate, that contradicted political principles generally held in England, and that were inconsistent with established colonial policy.

Howick was the outstanding Whig willing for large reforms; he went far beyond his father's cautious concept of reform as something to preserve stability. His Act of 1831 had been a deliberately taken risk and half of it had misfired. He had worked hard for the Reform Act. In the Colonial Office he had dedicated himself to emancipating the slaves, and had been the moving force behind the Ripon Regulations for land policy in Australia. Already a free trader, he associated with leading economists and was not a reforming Whig only by inheritance. Already a great man in his party and destined for high office, he was liberal by intellectual conviction but not by temperament. A determined enemy to waste and inefficiency, which he found everywhere in colonial administration, he was irritated by the frustrations of colonial self-government, which perpetually prejudiced efficiency and economic advance, and was willing for radical constitutional reform. A natural authoritarian, he chafed at opposition, resenting the failure of men less committed and less knowledgeable than himself to approve changes that he regarded as indispensable to colonial contentment and imperial efficiency.

Howick was allowed to keep in close touch with colonial affairs long after his formal connections with the Colonial Office ended in 1833. His associations with Stephen, with Henry Taylor of the West India section, and with his kinsman Sir George Grey, Parliamentary Under-Secretary to

Glenelg and Spring-Rice, kept him in touch with official sources about the empire. He had a family interest in Canada through 'Bear' Ellice, his uncle by marriage. Partly through Stephen's guidance, he learned early that subordination of dependencies was not a wise principle to apply to the Canadas. The seeming generosity of 1791, when the colonists were granted constitutions modelled on the British, threatened to end in a chaos of disorder and recrimination. Should not the colonists be allowed to settle their constitution for themselves? So long as they maintained the monarchy and imperial supremacy, and preserved imperial interests, which included justice among the King's subjects as well as trade, investment and immigration, why should not colonists capable of administering their own affairs decide their own forms of internal government?

On the whole, Howick's attempts to influence events and policy in the 1830s were unsuccessful. He had many blind monents in dealing with the Canadas. Inability to convince the Cabinet reduced his usefulness to reform. Twice he erred greatly in his judgement of men. His sincerity was unquestioned, but ambition and seeming arrogance made his zeal for master strokes suspect. Although a notable speaker in the Commons, he could win support only by argument and integrity, for he was neither conciliatory nor persuasive.[13] His voice was harsh, his style of speaking awkward and his manner in conversation cold, haughty and abrupt, making him the epitome of a nervous illiberal liberal. Unflagging devotion and considerable intellectual power earned him respect, but his judgement was too easily driven to extremes by opposition and he could be impetuous and incautious in both speech and writing. In the 1830s he was a lonely and usually ineffective advocate of colonial reform.[14] But a reformer of the imperial system he clearly was, both through his advocacy of free trade and through his insistence on the need to revise fundamentally the political and constitutional relationships between Britain and the self-governing colonies. It is easy to recognise in Howick the third Earl Grey, who in the 1840s ordered the introduction of responsible government into Nova Scotia and Canada.

REFORM MOVEMENTS IN UPPER CANADA

In Upper Canada in the early 1830s the most powerful force in the colonial government was still the 'quasi-aristocracy of bureaucrats and professional men (principally lawyers)', the Family Compact.[15] Critics complained that members of the Compact used their powers to turn the colony's land, patronage, banking and canal building to their own advantage. In truth, however, the Compact was neither a conspiracy to monopolise government for gain, nor an entrenched group of selfish reactionaries. It was a small group of officials, lawyers and others, united in the main by loyalty to Britain, belief in the Established Church, social conservatism and faith in a balanced (or 'mixed') constitution that could not tolerate an increase of democracy. Inevitably the Compact was anti-American, but intelligently so, and its standards of political acumen were high, although events sometimes made its role appear reactionary.

The popular discontents of Upper Canada were expressed constitutionally in demands that government be brought closer to the people and away from the Colonial Office, the governor and the established rulers of the province.[16] The link between executive and legislative authority, on which the power of the Compact partly rested, was notorious. Of the twenty-two men who sat on the executive council between 1820 and 1827, fifteen were also members of the legislative council. 'Every one of the small charmed circle of eight men [at the head of the Family Compact] sat, or had sat, in the Councils.'[17] An elected legislative council, in order to break the unpopular nexus with the executive, was the constitutional reform most often sought in Upper Canada; other demands included reductions of official privileges and salaries, election by ballot, and the accountability of the executive council to the assembly, the elected representatives of the people. An executive government controlled by ministers responsible to the assembly was sought only by small groups, such as the Baldwins and their associates, who wanted the colonists to have what they believed to be the British cabinet system. Responsible government commanded little attention outside the restricted, mainly upper middle class circle of the Baldwins. Men unfamiliar with British politics did not know how a parliamentary executive would work in a colony accustomed to a nominated executive council, and were unaware of the benefits that responsible government might bring.

Up to the early 1830s the popular reformers appealed with some success to new immigrants from the British Isles, telling them that Upper Canada was ruled by an Anglican clique, whose oligarchical interests in land policy, clergy reserves and commercial development conflicted directly with those of the mass of the population engaged in agriculture. As the population soared from 177,000 in 1828 to 320,000 in 1832, reformers like Mackenzie, Marshall Spring Bidwell and the Methodist clergyman Egerton Ryerson all found many sympathisers but few firm supporters. Noisy attacks on government in Britain and in the colony, perpetual clamour for change, and a disposition to find in the Age of Jackson an American millenium that Upper Canada ought to emulate sometimes drove electors into supporting the existing government for the sake of stability under British protection. The Family Compact saw how the reformers over-reached themselves, and shrewdly played on settlers' fears of political disintegration and the breaking of imperial ties. Successful immigrants, some of whom had arrived almost without capital, enjoyed as landowners an independence that most of them had never known before, and drifted into conservatism. The increasing proportion of

British immigrants and the decline of immigration from the United States also hindered the radical reformers.

Most electors in Upper Canada, irrespective of politics, thought of the constitution as a government granted prescriptively by the King in Parliament, and not to be modified except in Britain. They found the representative principle, which some radicals favoured and which would have allowed the people to make or amend their own constitution, unduly American and disturbing.[18] Mackenzie's open admiration for American forms of government[19] marked him as a radical and, among colonial tories, as a reckless demagogue. He had come to see the American model of two elected houses and an elected executive as preferable to the British system of hereditary monarchy and Lords, elected Commons, and a Cabinet chosen from both houses of the legislature. Without aristocracy, which the 1791 Act had tried in vain to introduce, he could see no case for a nominee upper house. The established power of aristocracy in Britain, he suspected, made Parliament and the Colonial Office hostile to the democratic ideas of North America. This opinion, which many Radicals in Britain shared, was partly correct.

Mackenzie may have owed some of his ideas on elected upper houses to the Radicals in Britain, or even to liberal Whigs, among whom plans for the reform of the House of Lords were much discussed after 1832.[20] However, it is more probable that he worked for an elected council because the nominee upper house blocked the will of the elected assembly, and seemed to represent British or Compact interests, not the people's. He cited the constitution of the United States, where social conditions were more like those of the Canadas than conditions in Britain had ever been, mainly in order to buttress convictions already formed by local conflicts. He asked also for elected governors, in the hope that chief executives directly accountable to the people would be more responsive to the popular will than the representatives of the Crown had been in Upper Canada.[21]

Colonial conservatives opposed any increase of the power of the people's representatives, whether by making the legislative council elective or the executive council responsible. Either change, they thought, would be contary to British constitutional principles, injurious to their own predominance, and damaging to provincial stability. Reform and reformers alike seemed too republican and too capable of producing in Upper Canada the vulgarity and venality that conservatives often found in the United States.

Sometimes the conservatives failed to distinguish between the loyal respectability of the Baldwins' proposals, which were carefully reasoned with little appeal to political or social passions, and the tempestuous demands of colonial radicals, who sought to establish a North American constitution in North America and overthrow rule by an élite of officials, placemen and merchants. The Baldwins tried to hold aloof — socially and intellectually as well as politically — from 'common radicals' and would undertake no action that was not strictly constitutional.[22]

The winds of opinion in Upper Canada varied greatly. Much depended, especially at elections, on the role of governors, the state of the economy, and influences from Lower Canada and the United States. A conservative assembly in Upper Canada was better able than a reforming assembly to work harmoniously within the framework of the 1791 constitution as it then existed.

In the 1830s the electors leaned towards the established ruling class whenever political storms or economic distress became alarming. Conservatives with a moderate policy of development and progress under Britain held power in the assembly from 1830 to 1834 and from 1836 to the rebellion.

CONSTITUTIONAL AUTOCHTHONY DEMANDED IN LOWER CANADA

In Lower Canada the French remained a permanent, mainly agrarian majority in the assembly, opposing the oligarchy of officials, wealthy merchants and placemen on the executive and legislative councils. The English party, which dominated the councils and on whom the imperial authorities relied, tried in vain to increase its representation in the assembly. A great change from the situation in the 1820s was that only the older French leaders, such as Neilson, still wished for due performance of the Constitutional Act of 1791. Papineau and the radicals, partly moved by the 1830 revolution in France, increasingly preferred to break the system. Lower Canada, they thought, should have its own form of government, giving the French majority power to rule and reducing the British connection to a minimum until independence as a republic was attained. Another great change from the 1820s was economic. Wheat production had declined and the province suffered through the international financial crisis of 1837. The *habitants*, pressed by rising population, by the *seigneurs'* wish to hold land for timber, and by prodigal land grants to favoured immigrants and privileged persons, complained of land shortage and rising rentals. French political leaders attributed the ills of the *habitants* to the ceaseless flow of immigrants from Britain and Ireland and to the selfishness of the oligarchy on the councils.

Politically, 1832 was a dividing line in Lower Canada. Papineau then broke with the moderate Neilson and, as his belief in separation of Church and State came to be expressed more stridently, clashed with the Roman Catholic Church. A violent election in Montreal involved the use of British troops.[23] Immigration from the British Isles, which had reached 50,000 a year in 1831, alarmed the French[24] but was welcomed by English merchants, who hoped to offset the numerical superiority of their rivals and to enlarge the commercial empire of the St Lawrence. Many immigrants were desperately poor; having crossed the Atlantic in timber ships returning to Canada in ballast, they stayed near Quebec or Montreal simply because they lacked the means, health or enterprise to go on to Upper Canada, with its superior attractions. After the terrible cholera outbreak of 1832 'immigration became, to certain wild French-Canadian eyes, an English conspiracy to wipe them off the face of the earth'.[25]

Also in 1832 the British American Land Company was formed in London.[26] It eventually acquired for British migrants over half a million acres in the Eastern Townships, on condition that it built roads and made annual payments to the Treasury in London. The French party resented almost equally the arrival of more British and the disposal of the colony's land by the metropolitan power. But, to the English in Lower Canada, the work of the company 'became ... a symbol of the whole energizing revolution which they were anxious to effect. It meant immigration and progress; it threatened feudalism and stagnation.'[27] The legislative council supported the company; the assembly opposed it. Likewise, the council favoured the development of banks, while the assembly distrusted them as insidious agents of the twin evils of modern commerce and British money power. Commercially the *patriotes* in the assembly were reactionary, while the Château Clique and the English merchants were all for progress.

In 1833 the assembly and the council both complained to the King. 'Mr. Papineau and his party', commented Governor-General Aylmer, 'have ... [as] their avowed object ... to alter the whole ... constitution, and Government of the Colony.'[28] The assembly wanted the legislative council to be elective (but on a higher property franchise than that applying to the assembly, and with special property qualifications for membership) and indissoluble, so as to be beyond the power of the governor.[29] It demanded a popular convention established by British statute to plan constitutional reform. Papineau was sure that any British constitution would be inappropriate to Lower Canada.[30] He said that the will of the people, not the mandate of the sovereign or of Parliament, gave authority to a constitution, and Lower Canada had never been allowed to decide its own form of government. Democracy and nationalism together led Papineau into extreme political positions. Men who did not agree that representation was the true source of constitutional authority resented his challenge to the bases of colonial polity[31] and the council complained that his proposals would 'drench the country with blood, ... the inhabitants' of Upper Canada will never quietly permit the interposition of a French republic between them and the ocean'.[32]

In February 1834 Papineau persuaded the assembly to adopt the Ninety-Two Resolutions,[33] which complained that conditions had deteriorated since the select committee's report of 1828 and that rebellion now threatened. The American constitution was praised as better for Lower

Canada than any British constitution could ever be. Only a constitution that the people had drawn up for themselves would distribute power equitably and promote the true interests of the province. If reform were withheld, declared the eighty-sixth resolution, the province might separate from Britain, as the Thirteen Colonies had done, and 'seek elsewhere a remedy for . . . [its] afflictions'. Papineau hoped that the assembly, where he was so powerful, would become the supreme organ of provincial government, at the expense of the councils where the hated English party predominated. To begin with he sought social democracy, and then in order to obtain it, was driven to demand political democracy and the autonomy, or even the independence, of Lower Canada.

Aylmer called the Resolutions a 'Declaration of Independence'.[34] Read literally, they were; but they were principally a platform for the provincial elections in autumn 1834 and were less influential than Papineau had hoped. His growing anti-clericalism was already turning the Church and the faithful against him. His incessant talk of an American constitution and his intemperate attacks on judges and officials alienated those who had no wish to disturb existing forms of government and society, provided that power was not monopolised by oligarchies enjoying special relationships with the mother country. When the moderates grouped themselves at the centre of provincial politics, between the English party and Papineau's followers, he became more extreme and rejected all British attempts at reform of the existing constitution.

BRITISH LIBERAL CONFUSION ABOUT LOWER CANADA

The Ninety-Two Resolutions attracted little notice in Britain, where the break-up of Grey's ministry overshadowed threats of rebellion in Lower Canada. Hume's Radical protégé J. A. Roebuck, who had spent part of his youth in French Canada and was the paid agent of the provincial assembly, had, however, already given notice of motion for a new select committee on Canadian affairs.[35] He excitedly told the Commons that Lower Canada was 'in a state of revolution' and that armed rebellion was probable unless the legislative council were abolished or made elective. If rebellion occurred, the United States might step in to make 'the Canadas . . . part of the great Federal Republic'.

The House appointed a select committee, as Stanley, the Secretary of State, wished.[36] When the committee approved most of what Goderich (together with Howick) and Stanley had done,[37] Roebuck alleged that its decisions were mere jobbery. The committee, 'by and large aristocratic and, therefore, anti-democracy', had been blind to the problems of colonists in a remote country. 'Unless some immediate steps be taken to redress . . . their grievances' Roebuck again warned the House, '. . . they will rebel.' Peel justly rebuked the remark as 'irresponsible', but Hume supported it, comparing the state of Lower Canada with the condition of England in 1831–2.[38]

The Whigs were in a state of liberal confusion over Lower Canada. Grey himself, while still Prime Minister, had had to prevent an open breach between his son and Stanley over the Howick Act.[39] Parliament had not touched the Act when Stanley left the ministry in June. His successor, Spring-Rice, floundered in search of a policy. Attempting to solve the salaries problem, he was accused by the French and by the Radicals in Britain of illegal resort to dishonest shams instead of genuine reform.[40] The Whigs received no help from the obtuse, obscure dispatches of Governor-General Aylmer[41] and were dismayed at the advice given to the Cabinet by the Colonial Office.[42] Stephen explained to his superiors that Papineau wanted a republic, which Britain could never allow, and that the French radicals had a political philosophy and theory of the constitution entirely opposed to British ideas. How the French party should be checked or appeased had not been decided when William IV abruptly dismissed the Whigs and called on the Tories.

The new Prime Minister, Peel, gave the Colonial Office to Aberdeen, a man of strong religious principle and high sense of duty, fully prepared to combat Canadian demands for reform and threats of independence. Aberdeen resolved to maintain the constitution and the law and to call on the Whigs to support his policy. 'Aberdeen', wrote Peel, 'has laid the foundation for a complete settlement of the Canada question, or a complete conviction of the Canadian Party of the intention to rebel and separate.'[43] The Tories proposed to send a royal commissioner to Quebec to negotiate with the assembly of Lower Canada on the basis that, although the Ninety-Two Resolutions were rejected, the Howick Act would be interpreted generously. (At one stage Howick himself was thought of as a possible commissioner.)[44] If the assembly granted a civil list for the lifetime of the King, as Upper Canada had done, Crown revenues would generally be submitted to legislative appropriation. Established injustices, including those over land tenures, would be examined, but, Peel assured the Commons, 'We do not mean to declare any new principle of government in the colonies.' If the assembly rejected the implied ultimatum, Parliament would have to punish Lower Canada, presumably by repealing the Howick Act.[45]

Peel and Aberdeen seemed prepared for their policy to produce demands for independence. They were so confident that Lower Canada should remain in the empire only on conditions decided in Britain that they preferred the risk of separation to further discreditable drift. Their policy lacked neither optimism nor determination; while they were rejecting major reforms, Papineau was demanding American institutions and calling the Radicals of England to his aid, and Aylmer was gloomily predicting that even the English party might be driven to adopt the politics of force.[46]

Before the Tories could send a commissioner, the Whigs had returned to power, Glenelg taking the Colonial Office, and Howick maintaining a lively, if ineffectual, watch over the empire from his place as Secretary at War. The new ministry, depending mainly on reform for its reputation and on Radicals and Irish members for its majority, boggled at the risks the Tories had been prepared to run in the Canadas and laid down no clear policy at all.

Howick, predictably, was less hostile to the firm decisiveness of Aberdeen than to the liberal confusions of his own colleagues. In late 1835 he still believed that large concessions might calm the French radicals and wanted the government to send out a strong commissioner to settle constitutional questions on the spot. He was prepared to make the executive council of Lower Canada into 'something very much resembling the cabinet in this country, choosing its members from the leaders of the legislature, and rendering it practically the Governing body, subject of course to that sort of control from the Govr and the Secretary of State which is in this country exercised by the King'.[47] The executive council was to be chosen from both houses of the legislature. Although Howick's colleagues in the Cabinet knew that he was not proposing so great a change as one to responsible government, they preferred their own hesitant courses to his proposals,[48] which remained abortive.

The Whigs decided to send their own commissioner to Lower Canada, not to negotiate a settlement or present an ultimatum, but to silence the Radicals who criticised Whig ineffectiveness.[49] Glenelg was slow to issue instructions; when they were demanded of him, he withdrew to his home and refused to see anyone.[50] Neither he nor the Cabinet knew what to do. The Canadians were not thought fit for any larger degree of self-government than they already had, and there was indeed little that could be allowed them consistent with the views that then prevailed in Parliament regarding the British constitution and the imperial relationship.

The instructions eventually issued were meagre: to conciliate, to gain information and to put the finances of Lower Canada on to a satisfactory basis.[51] The commissioners, led by the second Earl of Gosford, who was also governor-general, were to report on all matters raised in the Ninety-Two Resolutions, except the demand for a constitutional convention, which Glenelg rejected as unconstitutional. The complaints of the English party were specially mentioned, for Cabinet feared to alienate the men on whom Britain depended so greatly for loyal administration.[52] The only promise at the commission's disposal was the longstanding offer to grant the legislature full control of the revenues of the Crown if a fixed civil list were established for ten years.

There was never much to hope for from the Gosford commission, except accurate reporting,[53] and the irregular behaviour of the new

lieutenant-governor of Upper Canada, Sir Francis Bond Head,[54] soon
gravely embarrassed the commissioners. Head let the assembly in Toronto
know his instructions, which were understood to be identical with
Gosford's as governor-general. Everyone learned that both men had orders
to conciliate and to discourage every demand for reform. Gosford, whose
amiability with the French had enraged the English, was assailed from
both sides when the French party learned how little he could do for them,
for the English, esteeming themselves privileged defenders of the British
connection, were already outraged by his favours to their opponents.

The commission's six reports, so far as they were unanimous,
recommended no constitutional change beyond suspension or amendment
of Howick's Act. For reasons already familiar in Britain and the colony,
the commissioners rejected all demands for reform. An executive council
responsible to the elected assembly would be inconsistent with colonial
status. An elected upper house would be anti-monarchical, American,
difficult to organise electorally (unless it merely duplicated the assembly)
and unacceptable to the English party because it would deprive them of
their only point of strength in the legislature. Control of Crown revenues
could not be surrendered, because a fixed civil list was indispensable to
stable administration. Public lands were an imperial trust and could not be
entrusted to colonists with selfish interests to promote.

The reports did however confirm many French complaints, notably
that membership of executive and legislative councils overlapped excessively and that the French were too much excluded from public office.[55]
The commissioners also agreed with the French in opposing the immediate
reunion of the Canadas, although they favoured it as a long-term policy.
The possible suspension of the assembly of Lower Canada was mentioned
only to be rejected. So drastic a step would outrage all the colonies in
North America, and Lower Canada should not be made a second
Massachusetts.

Howick believed that the most important feature of the reports was
that the commissioners had altogether failed to agree on a diagnosis of the
colony's ills and the treatment to cure them.[56] He noted that the reports
clearly implied the inadequacy of the Cabinet's conciliation policy. Unless
British ideas on Canadian politics, the imperial constitution and colonial
self-government changed extensively, radical French leaders would go on
demanding an American constitution and, perhaps, independence under
American protection. The Cabinet had neither the vision nor the principles
to escape from such difficulties.

THE RESPONSIBLE GOVERNMENT QUESTION IN UPPER CANADA

The choice of Head, as a reputed liberal of wide experience, to govern
Upper Canada was the mistaken response of the Colonial Office to the
grievances of the province. Mackenzie's visit to London in 1832—3, the

elections of 1834 and the assembly's Grievances Report in 1835 had persuaded Whig ministers that radical reformers in Upper Canada had to be placated if tranquillity were to be preserved. Colborne's dispatches had been too inept to correct such a false impression. The Family Compact knew the truth, for its members recognised that the new immigrants, who were the ones most affected by the radicals, would not follow extreme leaders far, and that discontented farmers, professional people and town workers were, despite their complaints, unlikely to menace constitutional government. In Britain, however, the noisy propaganda of the Radicals, the Whigs' own liberal confusions over reform, anxieties over the crisis in Lower Canada and a lively dread of American influences all obscured the quiet consolidation of strength effected by the conservatives in Upper Canada after the elections of 1834. Being unable to understand the colony's problems well enough to devise an adequate, constructive policy, and distrusting the capacity of Upper Canada to govern itself, the Cabinet decided on conciliation and a minimum of change, just as in the neighbouring province.

Francis Bond Head had seemed the man of the hour. Even Howick, who believed so strongly that fundamentally new policies were needed in colonial government, supported Head, overcame Glenelg's doubts and obtained the 'grumbling consent' of Melbourne himself.[57] Head's instructions,[58] like those of the Gosford commission, assumed that efficient, tactful administration, and judicious insistence that the governor and members of the executive council were responsible to no one but the imperial authorities would solve all constitutional problems. 'New and hazardous schemes' were condemned. Head was instructed to consult the wishes of the assembly whenever he reasonably could, but was forbidden to introduce responsible government. Heads of departments who opposed the governor ought, wrote Glenelg, to resign. Head was to preserve the old order by making the most he could out of minimum concessions.

In the province Head's reputation as a liberal survived the publication of his instructions. Hume had written to Mackenzie that Head was a 'tried reformer',[59] and the governor retained credibility and goodwill. Ostensibly for the sake of conciliation and in conformity with his instructions, he proposed to add some moderate reformers to the executive council. Robert Baldwin, after twice refusing the governor's invitation (because responsible government was not to be introduced), agreed in February 1836 to join the executive council, in the hope that Head might adopt new principles. At last, remarked *The Correspondent and Advocate*, Upper Canada might have 'what it had never had before, an executive that will inspire general confidence'.[60]

Head's intentions were soon revealed to be not as conciliatory as Glenelg had intended. If the reformers resisted Head's view of the constitution, he planned to drive them into 'radical' courses that he could stigmatise as disloyal. This he did, alleging that his authority was subverted and delivering a tremendous public blast against suggestions that his advisers were responsible to the assembly. All executive councillors then resigned and Head claimed that his own position under the Act of 1791 had been made impossible.[61] He was sure that all the reformers were republicans, and that most republicans learned their vile creed from the United States.

The assembly, whose liberal majority was shocked by Head's actions, passed resolutions on the dispute between him and the council[62] without, however, displaying much knowledge of Baldwin's principles. It also passed a motion of no confidence in Head's new, conservative council, which he dissolved soon afterwards as he prepared to stage an electoral struggle between British monarchy and American democracy. He 'hoped through his own personal influence to extinguish all party feeling in the ... assembly' and have there none but supporters of the King's government.[63] Then Glenelg would have to feel satisfied and grant him a peerage.

At the elections in June the reformers were routed. Head appealed to the people to make a clear choice between, on the one hand, monarchy, the British constitution and orderly development of the province, and on the other, party, republicanism, American political principles and consequent chaos. The basis of authority was at stake. Would the province retain the constitution granted by the King and Parliament, or risk the unknown by opting for constitution making in the name of the people? The electors, perhaps mainly because they believed Head, voted the reformers out. Robert Baldwin had already temporarily retired from politics. Mackenzie lost his seat and with it the last vestiges of restraint. The only reformer of standing left in the assembly was John Rolph, who had shared some of Baldwin's experiences on Head's executive council.

The election of 1836 cannot be explained wholly in constitutional terms.[64] Most electors were probably not interested in the principles of government disputed between Head and the reformers. Electors were colonists, intent on economic growth and its necessary condition, political stability. On such matters the Family Compact, for all its oligarchic tendencies, was nearer to the mass of the people than were the reformers, who seemed less interested in attracting immigrants and capital than in gaining control over colonial patronage and revenue and attacking British policy.

The immigrants themselves largely supported authority in 1836. As landowners they had become instinctive conservatives. Half-pay officers, some with land for the first time, were a doubly conservative force, habituated to authority and elevated, as they thought, to the role of local gentry. Ryerson kept the growing population of Wesleyan Methodists respectably loyal to the governor. Orangemen, their numbers continually augmented with Protestant Irish, co-operated so strongly with Roman Catholics in supporting Head that Mackenzie complained of 'Orange Papists'. The Orangemen were more worried by allegations of republicanism and separatism among the reformers than by the activities of the comparatively few Roman Catholics in the Province. The Anglican clergy, the magistrates and the officials also made themselves spearheads of conservatism in the electoral contest.[65] Head's sensational jingoism won the day because men feared domestic violence and believed that economic progress, stable government, the British connection and internal tranquillity all depended on an official victory.

Before the elections were held, Robert Baldwin had gone to London to attack Head's policies,[66] but Glenelg, warned by Head and fearing the tories in Upper Canada, refused to see him. 'To what purposes', wrote William Baldwin to his son, 'are applications to Ministers? Lord Glenelg's conduct in refusing you an audience is quite disgusting – it manifests a timidity of honest men – he fears an Intercourse with truth.'[67] However, Glenelg enabled him to see Lord John Russell, the most powerful member of the Cabinet where colonial business was concerned. Russell rejected responsible government as irreconcilable with colonial status, but recognised Baldwin's loyalty to Britain.[68]

On 13 July Baldwin wrote to Glenelg presenting the case for responsible government.[69] He sought a parliamentary executive whose members would 'generally, if not uniformly, be in one or other of the Houses of Parliament'. The governor would be in the same position with respect to the colonial legislature and ministry as, according to Baldwin, the King was with respect to Parliament and Cabinet in Britain. Britain could lose nothing. The prerogative would not be touched and monarchy would be unaffected. Only the domestic affairs of the colony would be within the control of ministers responsible to the assembly. Imperial matters would continue to be controlled by the Secretary of State or the governor.

Baldwin made three recommendations. Members of the executive council were, as far as possible, to be appointed, retained or removed as if they were members of the British Cabinet. The new policy should be introduced by inserting a 'Specific Clause in the general Royal Instructions for the Government of the Province'. Head was to be recalled, and a 'Successor appointed who shall have been practically acquainted with the working of the Machinery of a free Representative Government': no soldiers or officials, but someone who understood the British political system.

After the election results became known in Britain, where they caused jubilation, the Colonial Office brushed away Baldwin's enquiries[70] and he, concluding that all lawful roads to reform were closed,[71] returned to private life in the colony. A moderate man, who believed in the empire and was a devoted Anglican and sound constitutionalist, he was frustrated both in the colony and in Britain.

Head was too rash to enjoy for long the fruits of his strange victory. While Mackenzie declared that 'The conduct of the executive towards the people of Upper Canada and Lower Canada, has been such as ... to absolve them from ... allegiance' and thought it vain to appeal to London,[72] the governor set out to destroy his defeated opponents by dismissing from office those believed to have opposed him in the elections. Swollen with vanity, he rebuked the Colonial Office itself for weakness in the face of 'low-bred antagonist democracy'.[73] Howick and other original supporters of his appointment were first dismayed, then outraged.[74] Before the year was out, even patient Glenelg had decided that Head must be recalled. His successor was to be Sir George Arthur, a soldier, who had done well as a strong lieutenant-governor in the penal colony of Van Diemen's Land.

THE END OF THE ROAD

When the Cabinet considered the first and second reports of the Gosford commission in April and May 1836,[75] the majority wanted to suspend the Howick Act. But Palmerston and Howick steered the discussions to larger projects of reform. According to Howick, Palmerston broached in the Cabinet the great question that the Tories had answered in 1835, that of whether Britain '... had any interest in governing the N. American colonies in a manner distasteful to themselves, and expressed the opinion, which ... was ... generally acquiesced in, that our great object ought to be to prevent a contest wh. wd bring disgrace and defeat upon us, and not to dream of keeping up the connection for ever'.[76] The Cabinet agreed to a committee on the reform of the legislative council of Lower Canada, and Stephen prepared a minute, which Glenelg presented on 30 April 1836.[77]

Stephen suggested that the existing objects of British policy in North America were 'few and simple', including the maintenance of the British connection, the use of the colonies for poor emigrants from Britain and the fostering of trade. But other objectives would eventually become necessary. British North America already had 1,200,000 inhabitants, and was rapidly

> ... assuming a distinct National character; ... the day cannot be very remote when an Independence, first real, and then avowed, will take the place of the present subjection of these Provinces to the British Crown, provision should be deliberately made for the peaceful and honourable abdication of a power, which ere long it will be impossible to retain and for raising up on the North American Continent a counterpoise to the United States.[78]

Deaf to the challenge to their statesmanship and unwilling for separation, the Whigs continued to mull over the details of short-term reforms. Stephen advised them against repealing or suspending the Howick Act, which he thought a necessary concession to colonists on their way to nationhood, and favoured in the Canadas reforms suggested to him by the recent course of reform in Britain. The legislative councils could be improved by converting what were in practice life appointments to appointments held only during pleasure, and by being made to preserve harmony between the houses. The legislative councils would have been invested with some of the flexibility that had been so important in persuading the Lords to pass the Reform Bill. The assembly of Lower Canada might also be reformed, again in the spirit of recent changes in Britain, in order to improve representation of the areas settled after 1791 and in which, as it happened, English and American settlers predominated. Stephen could find no solution to the problem of the executive councils. Responsible government was unthinkable for the time being, because the Canadas were colonies.[79] Palliatives, such as employing British techniques of patronage and allowing executive councillors to be impeached for misconduct, were, however, permissible means of strengthening the executive in dealing with the legislature.[80]

The Cabinet found the Canadian problem too difficult. On 14 May Glenelg came out at last against tampering with the Howick Act. William IV swung the ministry against proposals to reform (or abolish) the legislative council. Any change in the upper house of the colony appeared to the King to menace the House of Lords, which he had a constitutional duty to defend. Howick, who favoured reform of the Lords, fought to the last for reform of the legislative council of Lower Canada.[81] He threatened to resign from the Cabinet and warned Melbourne that public indignation would rage against ministers if they lost Canada: their 'total want of vigour and foresight will be justly regarded as the cause of the calamity'. Melbourne, unimpressed by so much vigour from one who had proposed so many plans of little foresight, continued to ignore colonial policy, except in so far as it might embarrass the ministry with the King or with the Irish and Radicals in Parliament.[82]

To Howick's disgust, Glenelg virtually told Gosford that the Cabinet had no constructive policy to offer.[83] The bland generalities with which the Secretary of State futilely sought to soothe the assembly of Lower Canada included the extraordinary statement that Britain would allow a 'responsible and popular government'. Glenelg wrote that this reform would require no more than the ample exchange of information between the executive and the legislature, together with unfailing inquiry into complaints against colonial officials, and instructions to governors to heed their assemblies when they could. Howick's exasperation at his colleague's failure to understand the discontents of Lower Canada was just, but he himself committed as great an error when he credited Papineau with entire sincerity in demanding from Britain reform of the legislative council. Papineau knew that the reforms he sought were impracticable in London and sedulously nurtured the irremediable grievance in order to confuse the imperial government and rally his followers.[84]

By the second half of 1836 British policy towards the Canadas was nearing the end of the road. Melbourne's government lacked the resolution to be liberal in reform, since it seemed that concessions made in the Canadas might imperil its own majority in the Commons. 'If 1837 should be as fruitless of any decision ... as 1836 has been', wrote Stephen to Howick in August, 'I suppose the result will be some convulsion in Lower Canada which will cut the knot that we are unable to untie.'[85]

Three months later, despairing of any other solution to the Canadian problems, and partly drawing on a suggestion from Sir Charles Grey, who had served on the Gosford commission, Stephen proposed the Federation of British North America.[86] Federation was not a new principle for the British Empire, for Stephen and Howick had considered it a few years before as a key to some problems of government in the West Indies.[87] Tocqueville's great work had recently described its operation in America. Stephen's suggestion in 1836 was that Lower Canada be partitioned and allowed to enter a federation of all British North America, in which the French would be in a minority. After further thought, he looked to less drastic action, hoping that a 'new Congress on the North American Continent' might grow from joint control of common interests such as customs duties and communications. Through it British rule might draw peaceably to its close, with 'the Euthanasia of the present Constitution'.[88] The plan had some attractions for the government, because it would have allowed ministers to seem in control of a situation that was really beyond their statesmanship.[89] However, the fatal flaws in the plan were soon obvious: the assembly of Lower Canada would never co-operate in any such British-proposed measure,[90] and the other colonies, even if they were willing to enter into a federal union with the French, would object to amendments to their constitutions.

When none of these alternatives remained, the Cabinet, despite Howick's continued opposition, authorised Russell's Ten Resolutions,[91] which rejected the demands of the French radicals and allowed the governor of Lower Canada to appropriate the colonial revenue without authority of the legislature. At the same time, however, ministers recognised the paramount necessity of bringing the various parts of the colonial government into harmony with one another. Russell admitted that the legislative council had not worked as Pitt and Grenville had intended, but would not make it elective.[92] (He had already thought of encouraging legislative councillors to resign their life appointments so that the vacant places might be filled alternately by English and French new members.)[93] In the Commons, a Radical amendment to make the council elective was badly beaten by 318 votes to fifty-six, at which Howick was greatly astonished.[94] Russell's rejection of responsible government became memorable: 'That part of the constitution which requires that the ministers of the Crown shall be responsible to Parliament, and shall be removable[95] if they do not obtain the confidence of Parliament is a condition which can only exist in one place, namely, the seat of empire. Otherwise we should have separate independent powers[96] existing . . . in every separate colony.' The separation of the executive council from the legislature he condemned as a mistake proposing that in future the council should contain two or three officials, together with members drawn from both legislative houses; these members the governor would appoint and remove at his discretion.[97] This would not have been responsible government, only a remote approximation to it judged suitable to a troubled colony. Nor would it have been a new arrangement: the Reunion Bill of 1822 had contained a comparable device, to ensure that the legislature was informed of executive policy; Spring-Rice and Glenelg had been willing for assembly representatives to be added to the executive council in New Brunswick, and Howick and Glenelg had thought of a similar arrangement for Nova Scotia.[98]

Another important aspect of the Resolutions was implicit. Britain resisted any claim from Lower Canada to make its own constitutional reforms. The clearest reason adduced for this stand was that offered by George Grey, who said that nothing should be done to weaken the power of the English minority, who sustained the British connection in the province. This argument, as conservative as any ever used by Bathurst and equally aggravating to the French, was accepted by the Commons. Members were not impressed when O'Connell and the Radicals tried to find analogies between Lower Canada and Ireland, or when Hume, Roebuck and Molesworth predicted bloodshed. The Resolutions cost the government some Radical support but suited the general tenor of members' attitudes to colonies.

In July Glenelg wrote to Gosford to implement the policy of harmonising colonial institutions that Russell had outlined to the House. Gosford was empowered to set up a new executive council in Lower Canada, and was himself to choose (subject to royal approval) the nine members he appointed. He was to reduce the overlapping of the executive and legislative councils and to let it be understood that he could at any time change his advisers, either individually or collectively, without imputing fault to them. 'The Executive Council should be so composed as to secure as much as possible of the confidence of the people',[99] but it was not to be changed merely at the will of the assembly. This was the limit of reform. The new policy, limited though it was, could have been of great importance in the hands of a stronger governor than Gosford, or one with a keener perception than he had of the nuances of assembly politics. But it could do nothing to satisfy French radicals, who wanted republicanism and the right to make their own constitution. Roebuck was nearer their ideas when he pleaded for the abolition of the legislative council, arguing that, since Britain would not make it elective and the colony could not endure it nominated, the only course was to bring the executive and assembly directly into touch with one another, as in the old representative system.[100] Howick was tempted by the idea, but no British government with any respect for the House of Lords would have dared to abolish the legislative council of Lower Canada.

REBELLION

In Lower Canada the French radical leaders, already looking on annexation to the United States as almost inevitable, resorted to the tactics that the Americans had adopted against the British sixty and seventy years before. They boycotted British trade and prepared for military action. The English party, which also contained some advocates of violence, disliked the Ten Resolutions, for they offered no prospect of peace. In August the assembly condemned the Resolutions and again refused to pay the salary arrears. Gosford prorogued it. A few weeks later he warned London that he might have to suspend the constitution, because Papineau was openly working for a republic and separation from Britain. In alarm Melbourne asked Howick whether Gosford should be recalled for talks, 'as it appears . . . most inexpedient to be too readily putting upon paper expectations of the ultimate separation and the recommendation of measures which may ultimately lead to its taking place quietly and amicably'.[101]

Short of planning separation, which would outrage British opinion, the ministry had exhausted its statesmanship. North America was passing into acute financial difficulties, with much commercial distress, just when the Ten Resolutions were becoming notorious. Stephen feared violence or civil disobedience; Howick was impatient with Glenelg, disgusted with Head and inclined to think that Lord Durham ought to be sent out to Canada as a strong man to restore order; Ellice thought of Durham for the Colonial Office.[102] But nothing was done except to decide to recall Gosford as well as Head, and to consider again the possibility of confederating all the provinces of British North America, so as to transfer some of the problems of Lower Canada to a wider arena, in which French influence would be diluted.[103]

Late in December London heard that in Lower Canada there had been a rash attempt to arrest Papineau, and that this had been followed by uprisings in both provinces. Although there was only a minor rebellion in Lower Canada and little more than an isolated revolt in the neighbouring colony, the government in London scarcely knew what to expect and, in the short term, was nearly powerless in North America. The rebellions might be serious; the United States, to which Papineau fled, might intervene. In fact, however, the radicals had, during the last few months before the rebellions, become so extreme that their support was fast diminishing. In Lower Canada the Roman Catholics, and in Upper Canada the Methodists — that is, the two most powerful churches — had both rallied men against violence. In London the truth was not known and the Cabinet felt certain of nothing but trouble. Its sympathies were naturally with law and order — with the business leaders who wanted to develop the St Lawrence river trade, rather than with either the radical *patriotes* preaching French Canadian nationalism and agrarian democracy, or the small number of radicals in Upper Canada.

A meeting of ministers resolved at once that Parliament should resume on 16 January instead of 1 February.[104] Before the end of the session (just before Christmas), Hume, Leader and Morpeth all made speeches that Howick described as 'beyond measure both violent and stupid'.[105] Molesworth outranted them:

> ... if unhappily a war does ensue, may some early victory crown the efforts of the Canadians, and may the curses and execrations of the indignant people of this empire alight upon the heads of those Ministers, who, by their misgovernment, ignorance and imprudence, involve us in the calamities of civil discord and expend our ... resources in an unhappy struggle against liberty.

The first effect the rebellion had on the ministry was to close the ranks against separation. The common ground between the majority, led by Melbourne, Lansdowne and Duncannon, who favoured coercion to restore law and order, and the minority, consisting of Howick and some others, that wanted coercion joined with reconstruction, was the necessity of defeating the pessimists who would let the empire disintegrate in rebellion and its aftermath. The independence of Lower Canada, which George Grey had condemned in March as unfair to the English, was rejected more robustly in December because the government would fall if it happened. Melbourne asked Russell for a policy to avert the double catastrophe. Howick recorded that even Roebuck wished the North American colonies to remain within the empire rather than join the United States.[106]

Stephen, excelling himself in clarity of analysis and futility of planning, reminded his superiors that

> We are acting on the assumption that between colonial dependence, and national independence there is no resting place or middle point. . . . British North America has become a considerable nation. The time rapidly approaches when it must assume a character very remote from that which it has hitherto borne. To maintain the honor of the Crown, and the integrity of the Empire, are the only rational objects of British

policy towards these provinces. The silent substitution of a federative union, for dominion on the one side, and subjection on the other, would accomplish both these ends in the most effectual manner which is now possible.[107]

These principles, he added, could have averted the American Revolution.

Stephen thought that the characteristic weakness of British policy — that it concentrated on day-to-day decisions and lacked direction — had produced the failure in Canada. The English, who had always known the right thing to do, had only rarely known what they were doing:

> ... the error of acting upon a policy which is merely occasional and transitory, has been the source of our greatest national misfortunes. It lost us the United States. It has rendered Ireland what we now see it to be. It overspread the land with pauperism. It created slavery in the West Indies, and has converted Australia into a den of thieves. To the same cause our Canadian trouble may very fairly be ascribed, and if they are now met by expedients which look no farther than the passing day, those troubles will infallibly issue in national disaster and disgrace.

Stephen proposed a convention of all the North American colonies, in the hope that reforms could be made on its advice without appearing to give way to the rebels. The United States, which could not restrain its citizens from border raids, would be impressed by a conspicuous act of unity, while those French Canadians who had not rebelled would be grateful. His policy unchanged, Stephen hoped for a joint commission of the colonies, to co-ordinate matters of common interest. If its labours gave it the status of a federal union, or if the proposed convention recommended federation, he would be glad, for the British government could then relax its control and substitute influence for domination. He wished to 'place the Brit. North American Provinces, rather in a Federal, than in a Colonial relation to Gt Britain'.[108]

Melbourne promptly rejected 'the beautiful creature of Mr Stephen's fancy', seeing it as a short road to the independence of all British North America.[109] Howick disagreed. Stephen's plan resembled one of his own projects and he approved it 'entirely'.[110] Melbourne saw the difficulty of calling on Parliament to allow the colonies virtually to decide their own constitutional future. Why give the rebels a platform to declare independence? Why infect the maritime provinces with the disloyalty of Lower Canada? Why leave so much political power to the unreliable French? Hitherto the colonies had never produced good plans of reform; would rebellion have improved their ability to do so? Howick himself proposed to suspend *habeas corpus* and the assembly of Lower Canada for a year, entrusting powers of legislation to the governor and executive council.[111]

Early in January the Cabinet, on Russell's advice, rejected every plan for a constitutional convention in Canada and decided to ask Parliament to suspend the legislature of Lower Canada for a year, giving its powers to the governor and a special council of seventeen members (on the model of the Quebec Act.[112] Under pressure from Howick and George Grey, Cabinet then agreed to empower the governor-general to call an advisory convention for the two Canadas, limited to delegates not involved in the rebellion. Howick and Grey hoped that this body might be given (as 'Bear' Ellice had proposed in December) a power to amend the Act of 1791, subject to approval by the Queen in council; but Cabinet again declined to allow the colonists to determine their own constitutions.[113]

THE DURHAM MISSION AND THE DURHAM REPORT

Cabinet did not expect these meagre plans to disarm its critics, who would be eager for blood when Parliament reassembled on 16 January. A master stroke was necessary. For over a year, various members of Cabinet, mainly of the Grey family, had thought of Durham as a strong man for Canada.[114] Melbourne himself, in the summer of 1837, had invited Durham to be governor-general.[115] The Whigs had other, less creditable reasons for wanting to employ Durham in Canada. After his return from the ambassadorship in St Petersburg, he had resumed his role as a leading and troublesomely ambitious Radical. If he went to Canada he would either help restore the government's reputation or imperil his own, and the Radicals, on whose votes the ministry depended, might agree to suspend the legislature of Lower Canada and abate their criticisms of past policy.[116]

There were other approaches to the employment of Durham. Russell, whose principal wish was to send out a strong man of established political ability, was willing to employ either Durham or Sir James Kempt, the able governor-general of 1828–30.[117] Like Melbourne, Russell wanted political skill and firmness, not new ideas on colonial policy. Howick, independent as ever, still hoped for liberal reforms. Durham, whose views appeared to coincide with his own,[118] might do great good. Howick was so convinced that Durham would succeed (if only out of vanity) that he decided to remain in office if Durham were appointed. Otherwise he would resign, rather than share responsibility for so many blunders.[119]

Durham accepted appointment as governor-general and high commissioner on 15 January 1838, the day before Parliament resumed.[120] Russell asked the Commons to suspend the legislature of Lower Canada until November 1840 and to provide for legislation in the province to be carried out in the interim by the governor-general and a special council.[121] He also announced that Durham would go to Canada. The news reduced but did not silence Radical attacks on the ministry. The government gained from confusion among the Radicals, most of whom were not at all prepared to let the Canadas go, although they continued to warn of impending separation and the possible incorporation of British

North America in the United States.[122] Charles Buller, the most popular Radical, who had worked with Durham on the Reform Bill and was about to go with him to Canada, told the House that 'the colonies do not want to separate' and warned the government against reading lust for independence into every project of reform.

The government was in no mood for reform and, with the rebellions fresh in mind, was under no political pressure to speak as if it were. In the Commons it yielded much to Peel, who refused to play politics with the Canada question, insisted that Tories let the Bill through,[123] and exacted a high price: the reference in the Bill's preamble to a convention to advise the governor-general had to be dropped. So disappeared for the time the last remnants of the convention policy on which Howick and Stephen had set such store.[124]

The government had few instructions for Durham,[125] but did suggest federation as a possible answer to the problems of the Canadas.[126] Howick had pressed this idea on the Cabinet and included it in the draft dispatch to Durham, which he helped Stephen and George Grey prepare and showed to Durham before sending it to Glenelg.[127] Again, federation was partly intended to contain the French, by transferring to a common body the economic matters over which English and French differed most. A federal body interposed between the provinces and the Colonial Office might also absorb local frictions without transmitting them to London, much as Chief Justice Smith had suggested when the Act of 1791 was planned.[128]

Federation was suggested to Durham from many quarters. Roebuck, a supporter of Brougham and not well disposed to Durham, claimed to have pressed it on him. Roebuck, to whom the American model of government was attractive, wanted to impose federation on the Canadas and let the other provinces join when they wished.[129] Peel and Ellice also supported federation in one form or another. Before leaving England, Durham drew up a plan for Canada in which federation played a part.[130]

Durham was not sent to Canada to write a report, nor to put down an insurrection; Cabinet had had enough reports on Canada and hoped for peace in the provinces before he arrived.[131] His instructions were clear: 'The most important part of Your Lordship's Mission is . . . the settlement of the affairs of Her Majesty's dominion in North America . . . under a form of Government corresponding in its general principles with that of this Kingdom, so far as such correspondence is compatible with the essential differences . . . between the Metropolitan State and its Provincial Dependencies.'[132] Glenelg ruled out every possible major reform, such as making the legislative councils elective or introducing responsible government.

Ministers were disillusioned with Durham before he left England. He delayed his departure inordinately; he made inconvenient demands of rank and privilege; and he appointed a 'shady entourage' (Howick's phrase),[133] which included the most notorious of the 'colonial reformers', Edward Gibbon Wakefield (whose ideas are discussed later), and a radical lawyer of blemished reputation, Thomas Turton. Wakefield had been imprisoned for abducting an heiress; Turton had 'offended against the moral law' with his wife's sister. Their appointment involved the government and Durham himself in considerable public difficulty. In Canada Durham behaved with ill considered ostentation and, by imprudently spending by far the greater part of his time in Lower Canada, irritated the loyal tories of Upper Canada and confirmed his own worst misjudgements, attributing Canadian troubles to racial conflicts and driving himself to the conclusion that the French had to be assimilated. After much inquiry he was led to reject every proposal of federation for British North America, largely on the grounds that any form of federation would depend excessively on the goodwill of the unreliable French and might leave a dangerous amount of power in their disloyal hands. He precipitated an extraordinarily angry political conflict in Britain by banishing some of the rebels to Bermuda (where he had no jurisdiction) on pain of death if they returned to Canada. This was an illegal sentence. Melbourne mismanaged the crisis that the Tories contrived out of Durham's blunders. Durham himself, complaining that Melbourne had betrayed him, resigned and issued a proclamation to vindicate himself to the people of Canada. Howick thought the proclamation a calamitous error of judgement and condemned Durham's decision to return home with his mission incomplete.[134] A second rebellion was imminent when Durham left Canada, after having been recalled as well as having resigned.

A failure as governor-general and high commissioner, Durham returned to England boasting of triumph. When he wrote the *Report on the Affairs of British North America* he had no official status to give standing to his opinions or to compel ministers to read them. But the Whigs, not daring to ignore him, asked what information he could give, although Melbourne doubted whether anything useful could come from such a source.[135]

Durham's position in writing the Report was difficult. He could expect little sympathy from the Whigs. Few radicals still supported him and among them only Molesworth, more eloquent than important, was enthusiastic. The Tories would condemn whatever he proposed. Ministers wanted no recommendations in favour of responsible government or major reforms of the legislative councils, although they would have welcomed a proposal to federate the colonies, preferably with a strong form of local government in each province. For a man who wanted to recommend responsible government, legislative union of the Canadas (instead of federation) and a considered programme of municipal reform, the outlook was bleak. Boldness was the only course and boldness Durham never lacked.

The eloquence of the Durham Report[136] and the long-term coincidence between its recommendations and the subsequent course of imperial history formerly persuaded historians that successive ministers had gratefully acted upon his enlightened counsel.[137] The beginnings of responsible government in British North America were attributed to him. He was even hailed as its true originator in Australia, New Zealand and South Africa. Established notions, bearing so splendid an aura of aristocratic leadership, proconsular grandeur and spirited disputation with a shuffling government at home, have died only slowly. How much less difficult it has been to attribute the coming of responsible government to Durham, or, like J. S. Mill, to Durham and his associates jointly with the triumph of free trade, than to look into the tortuous course that history actually took.

It has been the easier to credit Durham with originality and great influence because he did advocate a form of responsible government for Canada and did believe that its adoption would save British North America for the empire. Like Pitt and Grenville, and in harmony with the letter, if not the spirit, of his instructions, he wished Canada to have, so far as a colony could, the benefits of the British constitution. He agreed with the moderate Canadian reformers, notably the Baldwins, that British political institutions granted to the Canadas would never work smoothly unless the colonies were allowed some degree of responsible government, of the kind he believed to exist in Britain, and granted appropriate legislatures. In 1839 no minister agreed with him.

Less than a decade later, when the third Earl Grey decided that a limited form of responsible government might be allowed in British North America, the great decision rested not on the recommendations of the Durham Report, but on changes in Britain and the colonies, including changes in the British constitution and British ideas concerning colonies of settlement. However, none of the matters that then influenced Grey had the spectacular, publicly reasoned quality of the Durham Report. Durham caught the tide of history, with a broad, bold outline of policies long agitated by other men.

Durham advocated responsible government (with important limitations) for the united provinces of Upper and Lower Canada. His object was to still internal strife, to suppress the French and to keep united Canada for the empire. He had had no intention of supporting responsible government when he went to Canada,[138] and learned it there from the Baldwins and other moderate reformers. When, very briefly, he visited Toronto, he interviewed both William and Robert Baldwin and asked them to put into writing the views that he had not the time to discuss. William recommended four reforms, of which responsible government was the first.[139] Robert, who had been impressed by Durham's hopes that the connection between Britain and the North American colonies might be preserved, pleaded against proposals to federate the Canadas, which might separate them from the mother country. All that was needed to keep the Canadas loyal to Britain was to allow the colonists the same control over their own government in domestic affairs as their fellow subjects (according to Baldwin) exercised in the mother country – that is, they should be allowed responsible government. He enclosed a copy of the letter he had written to Glenelg in July 1836.[140] Durham also received several copies of *The Examiner*, a moderate reform newspaper founded not long before in Toronto; its editor, Francis Hincks, a young Irish friend of the Baldwins, advocated responsible government.

Except in drawing a clearer line between imperial and colonial affairs than the Baldwins had proposed, Durham accepted their reasoning on responsible government.[141] As a Radical, he had been well disposed towards liberalising Canadian institutions. By supporting responsible government (even in a limited form), he threw the weight of his authority against the idea, widespread in England, that the colonial demand for it was the 'watchword of every rebel'[142] or a hypocritical prelude to attempts at separation from the mother country. He helped to make responsible government for colonies a subject that Gladstone himself could condemn in Parliament merely as impracticable and not as wholly regrettable.[143]

Durham's analysis of the constitutional problems of the Canadas rested on two premises, one relating to the past, the other to the future. He repeated the usual criticisms of the separation of the executive councils from the legislatures and regretted the departure from normal British practice, both domestic and colonial. In Lower Canada the executive council, the law officers and the heads of departments had been 'placed in power, without any regard to the wishes of the people or their representatives'. The governors had been in the hands of advisers, who were normally pro-British and often opposed to the assembly. In Upper Canada the executive council seemed to have been more important than either house of the legislature and there had been a 'monopoly of office and influence'. The Family Compact, though loyal, had exploited the separation of the executive from the legislature in order to force its own selfish policies onto the province. He especially criticised partial administration of the clergy reserves and hostility towards moderate reformers, who had properly asked for administration by 'men possessing the confidence of the Assembly'. 'It is difficult to understand', he concluded, 'how any English statesmen could ever have imagined that representative and irresponsible government could be successfully combined.'[144]

Durham's second premise was that British, not Canadian or American, institutions were needed to restore tranquillity and ensure progress. He was sorry that even in Upper Canada some men looked 'with envy at the material prosperity of . . . the United States, under a perfectly free and eminently responsible government'.[145] The attractions of the American political system to Papineau and his deluded followers were notorious. Durham believed that the problems of representative government in British North America could be solved by adopting 'those principles which have been found perfectly efficacious in Great Britain'.[146] In answer to the colonial radicals' assertion that North Americans needed a North American constitution he confidently insisted on the superior merits of the British constitution, which combined monarchy, aristocracy and the people. The British constitution was the standard of excellence in government and Durham believed that the English-speaking colonists were capable of operating it and of bringing the French within its scope.[147]

The Canadas already had representative legislatures designed on the British model. The Crown, therefore, should carry on government in the colony as at home, 'by means of those in whom that representative body has confidence'.[148] Responsible government by ministers serving the Crown, and answerable to the elected house in all matters of purely domestic concern, would solve the constitutional problems of Canada. In Britain a ministry was doomed (as Durham wrongly thought) if it ceased to 'command a majority in Parliament on great questions of policy'. Similarly, in the Canadas, 'Every purpose of popular control might be combined with every advantage of vesting the immediate choice of advisers in the Crown, were the Colonial Governor to be instructed to secure the co-operation of the Assembly in his policy, by entrusting its administration to such men as could command a majority.'[149] The governor should act in all purely colonial affairs on the advice of ministers possessing the confidence of the assembly, and should call on British support only where the colony's relations with the mother country were involved.[150] Such a change could be introduced without the aid of Parliament, by relying on the royal prerogative to settle the form of the executive.[151]

Durham was placing great trust in the political knowledge and abilities of the English in the Canadas when he advised the home government to let them conduct their own business in their own way. If the colonists mismanaged their domestic affairs, whether by electing a bad assembly or by allowing bad ministers to hold office, the principal sufferers would be themselves and, as voters, they would possess appropriate remedies. Neither the governor nor the Secretary of State in London should attempt to interpose his own wisdom either between the colonists and the assembly, or between the assembly and the ministry.[152] If a governor wished to keep his advisers after they had lost the confidence of the assembly, or if they offered advice that he could not accept, the Colonial Office ought not to intervene. In the former case the governor could, if necessary, dissolve the assembly and appeal to the electors; in the latter, he could seek new advisers and, if he chose, hold an election. If the governor persisted in keeping his advisers in office, despite defeat at the polls, which was improbable, the Colonial Office still ought not to intervene, for the assembly could end the impasse by refusing supplies.

Durham nowhere showed greater faith in the English Canadians than when he rejected fears that, if left to themselves, they would, as Russell had supposed, embarrass the mother country with follies, illegalities, or actions injurious to the honour of the Crown and the faith of the sovereign.[153] In his opinion the only substantial 'question at issue' in deciding whether or not to grant responsible government to Canada was whether Britain had an interest or a duty 'to confer colonial appointments on one rather than another set of persons in the Colonies'.[154] Britain could not sensibly hope to control the internal affairs of Canada and had no good reason for attempting to do so. If the grievances of the colonists against Britain were redressed and the worst errors of 1791 corrected, the bonds of kinship and common institutions, of investment and commerce, would join the mother country and united Canada in lasting amity.

Responsible government for Canada, as Durham advocated it, required a workable distinction between colonial matters, in respect of which the colony would be nearly independent, and imperial matters, control of which would be reserved to London. Durham's list of matters that he regarded as necessarily imperial severely restricted the degree of autonomy that a colony could enjoy under responsible government and included 'the constitution of the form of government – the regulation of foreign relations, and of trade with the Mother Country, the other British colonies, and foreign nations – and the disposal of the public lands'. On these the governor would continue to receive his instructions from Britain and legislation would be by the imperial parliament. The constitution itself, moreover, would establish a fixed civil list to pay the governor, other principal officials and the judges.[155]

The restrictions were important. Colonial radicals, especially among the French in Lower Canada, had long demanded that they should draw up their own constitution. Howick and others had asked that the colonists be allowed to do so, subject to imperial approval. Durham, however, wished the constitution to be drawn, approved and amended in England. The regulation of foreign relations was obviously less a matter of exclusive imperial concern in Canada than it was in any other part of the empire. The proximity of the United States affected almost every aspect of commerce and trade as well as domestic security and territorial integrity. That Britain should be responsible for external relations (and defence, which Durham did not mention) was probably inevitable in 1839; that the responsibility should continue to be exclusively hers in the future was, however, difficult to accept as necessary or prudent. Were the Canadians not to control their own militia? Similarly, the general power claimed over all commerce outside the boundaries of United Canada was traditionally imperial, but the case for the claim was weakening; already the commercial interests of the colonies were not always compatible with those of Britain. The power reserved for Britain over imperial lands had also been claimed and acted upon (as a trust) by Britain in the past, but its imperial character was becoming difficult to sustain as the population and economy of the colony grew and the colonists demanded full control of their own resources. Durham glibly made nothing of these difficulties; the matters he was reserving to imperial control were already all in imperial hands; given restraint and wisdom in Britain and responsible government of domestic matters in the colonies, there should be no difficulty.[156]

Because responsible government was a British institution, requiring constant reference to British political experience, Durham was not prepared to trust it to the French alone. He recommended the union of Upper and Lower Canada in order that the English might dominate the French, whom he stigmatised as a backward and rebellious race.[157] With the prejudice of his class, and the strong contempt of an improver for a conservative, agricultural people, he ignorantly condemned the French as unskilled in government, indifferent to commerce and blindly obstinate in clinging to a religion and a social system that he abhorred. 'The British people of the North American colonies', on the other hand, were 'a people on whom we may safely rely, and to whom we must not grudge power.'[158] The remedy for what he wrongly thought of as the problem of two nations warring in the bosom of a single state was to unite the Canadas in a single province, in which English-speaking colonists would predominate, and to entrust it with the largest powers of self-government consonant with the British constitution and the imperial connection.[159] Union, intended also to foster feelings of Canadian identity, was confidently regarded as a sound basis for permanent attachment to Britain and permanent protection against the absorptive power of the United States. There was to be an end to 'the vain endeavour to preserve a French Canadian nationality in the midst of Anglo-American colonies and states'.[160]

Durham hoped that, even among the French, there would be a general increase of political skill and contentment in Canada when elective local government was introduced throughout the united province. Municipal self-government was to spread political interest and experience and liberate the provincial legislature from parish problems. He probably did not think of local government, as some English policy-makers had thought of partition and district councils, as a means of cutting down the powers of the new legislature. The local government bodies were, however, to be 'subordinate to the general legislature'.

The proposals he made had, like responsible government, been steadily supported for a long time. Durham's distinctiveness with regard to local government is that he would have introduced it by imperial Act, to prevent the province from encroaching on the municipalities, and that he looked to it to improve the quality of the men serving at the provincial level.[161]

Durham did not match his eloquence in recommending responsible government for Canada with precision in defining it, either as it existed in Britain or as it might exist in the colony. If his views on responsible government, judged solely on a literal reading of the Report, were collected together, they would appear incomplete. Little is gained by exploring the Report for obscurities in the details of responsible government when its main outlines are so clear. Neither Durham nor anyone else at the time could have drawn up a blueprint for introducing the new system into the colonies. Twenty years later, after responsible government had been operating in British North America for a decade, Labouchere, as Secretary of State for the Colonies, was not certain of important practical details.[162] What Durham wrote was as clear and specific as barring a truly superhuman foresight, anything at the time could be: 'The Governor, as the representative of the Crown, should be instructed that he must carry on his government by heads of departments, in whom the United Legislature shall repose confidence; and that he must look for no support from home in any contest with the Legislature, except on points involving strictly Imperial interests.'[163] The governor and his secretary were, however, to be responsible to the authorities in Britain, not to the colonial legislature. Every prerogative of the Crown was to remain intact.

Durham intended united Canada to have the British cabinet system of 1839.[164] The responsibility of ministers 'should be secured by every means known to the British Constitution.'[165] Members of the executive council were to be a ministry, all of them belonging to one or other of the legislative houses and serving as heads of departments in the colonial government. Their responsibility to the legislature was to be collective, not individual, so that all would resign if they lost the confidence of the assembly. So long as it retained the confidence of the assembly, the ministry would normally be entitled to expect the governor, with whom it was to consult regularly on every matter of policy, to act on its advice in all matters (other than patronage) that were colonial rather than imperial. In addition the governor was to exercise the same prerogative powers as the sovereign then still enjoyed in Britain; to choose ministers, or to keep them in office, despite defeats in the assembly, until they were forced out by a vote of no confidence or a defeat at elections. He was also to be able to remove advisers, individually or collectively, whom he no longer trusted or whose relations with the assembly were unsatisfactory — subject in the last resort to the ability of his new ministers to obtain from the assembly the measures and money needed for their policies. Durham clearly left a governor the option of being virtually his own prime minister if, for example, the colony had no party or faction capable of forming a ministry that would command a majority in the assembly. A governor so placed would have had to keep his advisers, his policies, a majority of the assembly and the Secretary of State in harmony with one another.

On imperial matters the governor was to continue to act on instructions from London and his advisers were not to be entitled to have their advice taken, although he might consult them. If his advisers positively declined to assist in carrying out an imperial policy on imperial matters, the governor would presumably have had to seek other advisers and endeavour to obtain for them a majority in the assembly. Durham did not consider this point. Nor did he speculate about what should happen if a governor or the Secretary of State differed with colonial ministers, or with one another, on whether a matter were imperial or colonial. He was silent also on matters that had both imperial and colonial aspects, such as immigration and investment.

Much else concerning responsible government was obscure in the Report, either because British practice was not yet settled, or because its application to colonial politics was still in the future. The point of greatest obscurity was the role of the governor[166] in appointing, retaining and removing advisers, and in the making of the policies that he and they were jointly to follow.

RUSSELL, HOWICK AND GLADSTONE ON THE DURHAM REPORT

From first to last, Howick and Russell were the important members of the Melbourne government in deciding policy towards responsible government for colonies.[167] Howick, as we have seen, was the only able statesman of the period who was truly a specialist in colonial matters. He was also the first minister to escape from the traditional limits of thinking on colonial self-government. He did not measure a colony's fitness for self-government principally in terms of its ability to operate political and administrative institutions analogous to those of Britain while preserving proper subordination to imperial supremacy. His tests were simple: was the colony capable of governing itself in ways consistent with monarchy, the imperial system and the need to maintain justice and equity among the Queen's subjects? Did Britain have any interests in the colony that could be preserved only by withholding self-government? Provided that monarchy and imperial supremacy were preserved, he was willing that a colony that was fit for self-government should design its own constitution, to be approved and enacted by Parliament.

Despite the liberality of his views on colonial self-government, it was not until the middle 1840s that Howick supported responsible government of colonies. Between 1837 and 1841 he made incessant criticisms of the way in which Russell was settling British policy towards Canada, without once questioning Russell's principle, that responsible government of colonies was irreconcilable with imperial supremacy. His views did not alter until after the conventions of the British constitution had changed, a new concept of colonies of settlement had emerged in Britain, and the practical difficulties of Russell's policy had been revealed by experience in Canada.[168]

In 1839 Howick was not on close or cordial terms with Durham. The near friendship that had existed between them some years before — based on political affinities, Durham's early helpfulness to the younger man, and the marriage of Durham to Howick's sister Mary — had lost warmth as animosity grew between Durham and the second Earl Grey. Howick's respect for Durham's abilities, which had led him to think of him for Canada in 1837 and 1838, had been undermined by the record of the famous mission and its abandonment. The fatal qualities of Durham's defects had been revealed and Howick's wife Maria reminded him constantly that Durham wished him no good. She also repeatedly complained, reviving old family and political differences, that the Durhams had snubbed her on their return from Canada.[169]

Howick was nevertheless wedded to principles rather than personalities, wanted reform in the Canadas, and was wary of quarrelling politically with Durham. He met his brother-in-law on his return[170] and read the Report immediately it was available, praising it highly before he had grasped its recommendations correctly.[171] Perhaps he was swayed by Russell's private, inaccurate remark that Durham's recommendations resembled plans that Howick had proposed three or four years before.[172] Durham acknowledged Howick's letter most cordially, for he needed a strong spokesman in the Cabinet, but Wakefield warned him not to discuss the Report with Howick until it was known who would replace Glenelg as Secretary of State.[173]

Howick applauded the guiding assumption of the Report, that the Canadas should be encouraged to remain within the empire; but he objected to the plan of reunion and preferred the scheme that had been commended to Durham before his departure, for federation of all the provinces in British North America. Durham had eventually rejected federation because he thought it would leave too much power in the hands of the French, whom he wished to deprive of political identity, and because he wished to reserve to imperial control most of the matters normally belonging to a federal government.[174] Howick, who knew that reunion was an old idea that had always aroused implacable opposition in the Canadas, thought that a convention should be called in Montreal, where the colonists themselves could consider reforms of the constitution of 1791. Durham had seemed to favour this idea when he discussed it with Howick in January 1838,[175] but experience in North America had shown him that conditions there were unfavourable to constitution making by colonists.

Although he rejected reunion, Howick sympathised with Durham's wish to increase Canadian self-government. Were it not for the views that he stated to Parliament a year later,[176] his early, unguarded comments on the Report would suggest that he already supported responsible government: 'I entirely concur with your leading notions of allowing to the Colonists the most complete self-government upon Matters of mere internal regulation and local interest.' Unless Howick is to be credited with a double change of mind, not otherwise attested on this occasion, this sentence must not be interpreted as support for responsible government. He wished merely that the colonists should manage their own affairs without intervention from Britain, not that their executive governments should be controlled by men responsible to the elected assemblies.

Howick soon received from Canada another, plainer version of the case for responsible government. His brother, Colonel Charles Grey,[177] who was in the colony with his regiment and had worked with Durham, wrote to their father that the case for responsible government was overwhelming, while that for federation was weak.[178] The Greys were a close-knit family and Howick almost certainly saw his brother's letters. On 24 June 1839 Colonel Grey answered the familiar objection, proposed by his father,[179] that in a colony the executive government could not be responsible to the assembly without abrogating the supremacy of the mother country:

I cannot say I exactly know what . . . has been demanded. But if it is merely that the Executive Officers, nominated by the Governor, shall be so far responsible to the House of Assembly that they shall be changed like the Government at home when proved not to have the confidence of the People as expressed through their Representatives, I must say that it seems to me the inevitable consequence of giving Representative Government at all, and that I do not think it will be long *possible* to withhold so much. More, of course, could not be granted, nor, do I believe, more would be required.

This was a fair statement of Durham's and Robert Baldwin's views, but coincided only partly with Grey's and Howick's understanding of the British constitution in 1839. Neither Grey nor Howick believed that responsible government, in the sense intended by Baldwin and Durham, was then fully part of the constitution in Britain. In a letter to his son in Canada, Grey commented significantly on events at home: he commended Melbourne for having resigned over the Jamaica question when his majority had been dangerously diminished, because good government was impossible when ministers could not count on having a majority to pass their measures; but he added that Melbourne had been right to resume office after the Bedchamber Crisis, although the ministry was 'inefficient' and its majority still as insecure as when Melbourne had resigned. The Queen had wanted Melbourne back in office and had not wanted Peel to be her minister; Grey, therefore, did not blame Melbourne for returning to office, nor for having failed to consult the country immediately in order to increase his support in the Commons.[180] He regarded the principle that a ministry ought to command a majority in the Commons as a flexible guide to political behaviour, not a firm rule of the constitution. The principle was less important than the question of fact, of whether a ministry could carry the necessary measures through the Commons. To Grey in 1839, ministers were the Queen's servants, owing her a duty that was no mere formality. Melbourne's responsibility was to serve the Queen; to do this, he had to get himself a majority in the Commons, and not resign (against her wishes) merely because he lacked a stable following in the Commons. If the Queen wished him to remain in office, he had to stay until the Commons or the electorate forced him out, or until he clearly could not carry measures that he judged essential to the welfare of the nation. Howick concurred in his father's judgements on Melbourne's behaviour. Privately he thought the return to office precipitate, but not otherwise constitutionally mistaken. Publicly he acquiesced in the decision of his colleagues and later defended them in Parliament.[181]

The other key figure in determining Whig attitudes to the Durham Report was Lord John Russell, leader of the government in the Commons and its most powerful member on most colonial questions. Harassed by the weakness of the ministry and fearful that Durham might yet detach some of the Radicals from the Whigs, he approached the Report cautiously. Reunion he eventually approved, but he rejected altogether Durham's case for responsible government, finding it merely another instalment of the Baldwins' persistent advocacy.

When the Cabinet looked at Canadian affairs in March 1839 the Secretary of State was Normanby, but Russell dominated the deliberations, from which Durham was totally excluded.[182] Most ministers were reluctant to restore the constitution of Lower Canada, where a second rebellion had occurred only months before. They leaned uncertainly towards legislative union, which Durham had recommended, in the hope that it would contain the rebellious French, favour the loyal English and preserve the imperial connection. Howick continued to prefer federation to legislative union and vigorously opposed every plan for legislating for the Canadas without consulting the colonists, at least in Upper Canada.[183]

The Cabinet was confused. At one stage it almost decided to reject both union and federation in favour of a plan of divide and rule, which had first been proposed in December 1838 by 'Bear' Ellice. Ellice would have given the Canadas a strong central government for specified matters of common interest, such as trade and navigation on the St Lawrence, and have supplemented this by extensive local government. In this anomalous form of government the central legislature would necessarily have had an English majority, and the French would have had little power except over their own local affairs. On the other hand, only the merchants of Montreal and Quebec were likely to approve the plan, which would have offended Upper Canada by reducing provincial powers of government, and Lower Canada by its obviously anti-French intentions. The Cabinet rejected it late in March.[184]

Before the month was over, the Cabinet turned to Russell's proposals for legislative union. Howick at once objected that the colonists ought to be empowered to decide for themselves between legislative union and federation. The Cabinet overruled him, but did consider whether to ask Parliament to enact a legislative union, or to authorise the colonial legislatures to prepare their own plan of union. Voting was evenly divided when Howick left the meeting to go to his new home at Datchet (near Windsor); Russell then won the majority over to the traditional view, that all constitution making had to be undertaken in Britain. The Cabinet proceeded to deal with Russell's detailed plan of legislative union, with devolution of some matters from the colonial to the municipal level, somewhat as Durham had intended.[185]

The willingness of ministers to impose a legislative union on the Canadas was powerfully reinforced by events outside North America. The troubles of Jamaica (referred to in the next chapter), the extreme precariousness of the government's situation during the political clash over Jamaica and during the following Bedchamber Crisis (discussed in Chapter 6), and disasters in Afghanistan all helped to produce a general exasperation with colonies and the troubles they caused in Parliament. Ministers wanted either strong, decisive action or no action at all. Even Russell's scheme had critics and difficulties. In May, Normanby was willing to put off the whole of the Canada business for a year, on the ground that it presented too many problems.[186] In June, dispatches from Upper Canada, loaded with the hostility of colonial tories to any change in the councils where they held sway, gave the government cause to halt. The Durham Report was much detested by the conservatives of Upper Canada and many, perhaps most of them, opposed reunion.[187]

The Cabinet decided to ask Parliament to continue the emergency government of Lower Canada until 1842 and to take no further action in Upper Canada until its legislature had agreed to reunion. Ministers had not been convinced by Howick's arguments in favour of consultation. They remained nervous about Upper Canada. The slight uprising of 1837 had shaken their notions of its loyalty, and the colonists' bitter judgements on the Durham Report suggested to them that there was much they did not understand about the province. They were still more apprehensive about their own weak position in Parliament, where the Upper Canadians who had for so long loyally supported Britain had many friends.

On 3 June Russell put before the Commons the latest policy proposals. These took the form of two resolutions: one to reunite the Canadas, the other to continue till 1842 the arrangements made in 1837 for the government of Lower Canada.[188] Russell praised the Durham Report, especially the proposals made for local government and the control of colonial revenues by the assembly, but rejected responsible government on the grounds that he had stated in the Ten Resolutions on Lower Canada in 1837.[189] He did concede, however, in answer to a question from Buller, that, subject always to imperial supremacy, 'the executive should be carried on in such a way that their measures should be agreeable and acceptable to the representatives of the people'. Parliament agreed to both of Russell's resolutions, although Peel and Buller criticised the government for delay, Hume objected to everything proposed, and Buller puffed Durham. That sick and weary man was, however, temperate.[190]

The Cabinet, having decided not to legislate for the Canadas without consulting the colonists, sent a leading Whig, Poulett Thomson (soon to be Lord Sydenham), to be governor-general. By February 1840 he had persuaded the legislature of Upper Canada and the special council of Lower Canada to accept the official plan of union. The next step was Russell's. He had succeeded Normanby at the Colonial Office in September, and in March he introduced the Reunion Bill. Ellice and Peel criticised its local government provisions and Russell withdrew them in order to have the Bill passed.[191] Parliament then reunited the Canadas,[192] but not on the basis agreed with them through Sydenham and not as Durham had recommended. The affairs of the Canadas were settled arbitrarily in Britain to suit the convenience of ministers searching for majorities, and the wishes of the colonists, though officially ascertained, were disregarded.

In 1839 the only concession that Russell made on the question of responsible government was, as we have seen, to tell the Commons that he disliked carrying on the government of North American colonies through executive councils not in sympathy with the assemblies. Otherwise he adhered to a particularly rigid form of Liverpool's principle of 1810,[193] and informed Poulett Thomson that, in colonies, responsible government would necessarily conflict with imperial authority:

> It may happen . . . that the Governor receives at one and the same time instructions from the Queen and advice from his Executive Council, totally at variance with each other. If he is to obey his instructions from England, the parallel [with Britain] of constitutional responsibility entirely fails; if, on the other hand, he is to follow the advice of his Council, he is no longer a subordinate officer, but an independent sovereign.[194]

Russell had two anxieties. He feared that a colonial governor might be steered by his advisers into conflict with the Secretary of State. A second fear is indicated by the words 'an independent sovereign'. In Britain in 1839 responsible government had not evolved to the point at which the sovereign was bound to accept the advice of ministers commanding the confidence of the Commons, whether approving of it or not. The Queen still had power to appoint and remove ministers at will and, although she could not control majorities in the Commons as her predecessors had done, she could, had she so chosen, have influenced the policies that her ministers placed before the House. The record of Francis Bond Head in Upper Canada showed that Russell had solid reason to fear that some equally egocentric representative of the sovereign might disdain the prospect of his own recall (a slow business in 1839) and appoint advisers unacceptable to the Secretary of State, who might then on behalf of the Crown, have to give the appointments an approval that was merely forced and nominal. Such a governor could follow policies, suggested by the advisers of his choice, that would be no less objectionable in London than those dictated by a democratic majority in an elected assembly.

In some respects Russell's famous statement was as much a criticism of any form of colonial self-government as it was of responsible government. He still wished Britain to retain final power of decision on all colonial matters, and assumed that Britain would provide better government, based on a more informed consideration of imperial and colonial interests, than a colony ever could. Specifically, he judged the Canadians unfit for a further grant of self-government.

On all these points there was much in the recent history of British colonies to support his gloomy judgement,[195] while the hostile comments on the Durham Report that were pouring in from Upper Canada confirmed him against conceding responsible government to any of the colonies in North America.[196] Buller wrote to Durham on 4 June that, its proposals for reunion apart, the Report had been thrust aside.[197] Durham, already seriously ill, did not protest as his disciple hoped.

The famous 'tenure of offices' dispatch,[198] which Russell sent out as a circular on 16 October 1839, made no concessions to responsible government beyond the principles involved in Glenelg's instruction on the executive council of Lower Canada in July 1837.[199] The immediate origins of the dispatch were in a minor South Australian problem that had drawn attention to the desirability of reforming the tenure on which officials held their offices.[200] In practice, appointments made nominally during pleasure were commonly held for life, subject to good behaviour. This was no longer to be the case. A dispatch to this effect, drafted by Stephen, was sent to North America soon after Poulett Thomson had been informed that the Cabinet was unalterably opposed to responsible government.[201] The dispatch stated that:

... hereafter the tenure of colonial offices held during Her Majesty's pleasure, will not be regarded as equivalent to a tenure during good behaviour; ... not only will such officers be called upon to retire from the public service as often as any sufficient motives of public policy may suggest . . . , but a change in the person of the governor will be considered as a sufficient reason . . . subject to the future confirmation of the sovereign.

Judges were excepted. The dispatch referred particularly to the colonial secretary, treasurer, attorney-general, solicitor-general and 'members of the council, especially in those colonies in which the Legislative and Executive Councils are distinct bodies'. Pensions and indemnities were mentioned briefly.

As Russell explained to Lieutenant-Governor Sir Colin Campbell of Nova Scotia, the dispatch empowered, but did not compel, a governor to remove councillors who were out of harmony with his administration or 'the deliberate opinions of the people at large and their representatives'.[202] Presumably, however, a councillor would not have been removed for supporting an imperial policy, whether acceptable to the legislature and the people or not; and, because every change of advisers would have had to be effectively, and not merely nominally, approved in Britain, the prospects that a governor might make himself 'an independent sovereign' or that the legislature might compel him to appoint advisers unacceptable to the Secretary of State appeared insubstantial. Although the purpose of the dispatch was to strengthen the governor in relation to his advisers and the assembly, the effect, as Buller predicted, was to open the way to allowing the assembly to insist that the governor treat his advisers as responsible to the elected representatives of the people.[203]

Russell's rejection of responsible government immediately provoked two powerful responses. Joseph Howe, the ebullient reformer in Nova Scotia, published four open *Letters to Lord John Russell*,[204] in which Russell's objections to responsible government were ridiculed with robust use of arguments *ad absurdum*. Crude and vigorous, the *Letters* may have been influential in Nova Scotia, where there was solid, respectable opposition to the reform that Howe advocated so powerfully; but, when first published, they did not have the desired influence on Russell or on any other political leader in Britain. They are memorable principally for Howe's certainty that the real tie between Britain and her settled colonies was kinship and national affection, not commercial policy or defence.[205]

In the long run the more persuasive answer to Russell in 1840 was Buller's, published as a series of articles in *The Colonial Gazette*.[206] 'Power without representation', Buller wrote, 'is not so great an evil as representation without executive responsibility. It is better to be without a fire than to have a fire without a chimney.'[207] In Canada the assemblies had been 'deprived of control over the ultimate results of government' and, in consequence, had assailed the executive violently. The governor's advisers should be men commanding a majority in the assembly, for otherwise the governor and his council would be continually involved in strife, and this could weaken the imperial connection. Buller saw no insuperable difficulty in demarcating imperial and colonial powers and claimed that conflict between Britain and every colony into which responsible government was introduced would be diminished. Buller emphasised party, recognising that a governor's choice of advisers might sometimes be no more than the choice of the party with the largest following in the assembly. Just as in Britain, however, considerable discretion was to be left to the Crown:

> Sometimes the Executive must take the first hint on the part of the representative body, and dismiss its advisers on the first indication of the hostility of a majority. Sometimes, again, it may with perfect safety make a long resistance to the majority, wait for repeated declarations of their will, and not submit even then, unless it finds on trial that they are backed by the people.[208]

This was considerably different from the sort of responsible government that, within a few years, became a convention of the constitution in Britain. Buller's version left the governor a large, independent discretion, such as the sovereign still possessed in Britain, in appointing and removing his advisers. In 1839 Durham and Robert Baldwin were also advocating responsible government in this sense. As we have seen, the role allowed to the governor was potentially so powerful as to threaten to reduce to a mere formality the Secretary of State's power to confirm or disallow appointments. The prospect that the representatives of the sovereign might select their advisers in order to suit either their own policies (instead of those of the Secretary of State) or majority opinion in their legislatures was only slightly less prejudicial to imperial authority than the prospect, which emerged a few years later, of governors bound to accept on behalf of the Secretary of State whichever advisers could control the elected houses of the legislatures.

The Durham Report, Buller's lucid articles and Howe's vigorous pleading all failed to change British policy in 1839–40. The Report, so famous later, was already almost forgotten, except when some Durhamite occasionally brought it to notice.[209] In spring 1840, when Parliament debated the Bill to reunite the Canadas,[210] Durham went almost unnoticed; both Houses opposed any increase of colonial self-government and few members referred to the principle that British colonies should have the British constitution. Hume, almost alone in asking for responsible government, spoiled his case by the extravagant claim that the colonists had accepted union in the belief that responsible government would be granted when the provinces had been reunited. The Tory Pakington, Secretary of State in 1852, praised Russell for having refused un-British reforms – including responsible government, an elected legislative council and control of colonial finances through the assembly — sought by 'democratic and republican' agitators; and Gladstone accepted Russell's case against responsible government for colonies and declared that its advocates in Canada could only be French Canadians, republicans, or persons otherwise hostile to the imperial connection.

Gladstone was one of two members to ask the basic question of whether British colonies should have British institutions. His answer was clever, comprehensive and well in accord with established British attitudes. So long as Britain maintained colonies 'as receptacles for our surplus population', he told the Commons, the mother country must preserve at least a semblance of British institutions there. But the similarity of British and colonial institutions was not to be measured by mere comparison of their forms of government, for the differences between British and colonial societies was already great in attitudes to property, aristocracy and the establishment of religion.

Gladstone was attracted by the idea that British colonies should have British forms of government as a possible means of preserving the integrity of the empire, but he excused himself, on the grounds of great differences between British and colonial society and the probable impermanence of the colonial connection, from any attempt to follow so large a proposition through to fulfilment. He had already recognised that mere assertions of imperial authority in the Canadas would be profitless and that British policies founded on sympathy with the English party in Lower Canada or the tories in Upper Canada could no longer succeed.[211]

Buller, regarding himself as the voice of Durham (then near death), commented that Gladstone was too beguiled with words to be a safe guide on such questions. He stated the case for responsible government again, reminding members of Durham's great principle, that it was this system 'on thich the government of every country having representative institutions must be conducted'. The reunion of the Canadas would soon necessitate responsible government, because a colony of 1,100,000 people could not be administered peaceably except according to the wishes of its inhabitants, and most of them already desired, or soon would desire, government by executive councils responsible to the assembly. Buller praised the 'tenure of offices' dispatch, believing that it would be the means of introducing responsible government in the limited sense that he then thought appropriate to a colony.

Howick doubted the case for union, but voted for it, shrewdly declaring that, if the colonists wanted independence, reforms of their constitutions would not deter them from seeking it. He added what he had often told the Cabinet, that he was willing for the constitution of Canada to be different from that of Britain. The form of the constitution, he thought, was a local matter, provided only that the colonists, so long as they wished to preserve the British connection, safeguarded the monarchy, respected imperial supremacy, and guaranteed justice and equity among the Queen's subjects. At heart he would still have preferred the Canadians to hold a convention and make a constitution, preferably a federal one, for themselves.

Howick and Russell, especially Howick, were open to change of view on responsible government as soon as they could be liberated from their conviction that responsible government was inconsistent with the status of a colony. Gladstone, however, firmly believed that so great a concession would necessarily destroy the imperial connection and cause events to run down the slope leading colonial society and politics to mere democracy. To Gladstone, and to Russell, it seemed inevitable that the colonists would eventually want to frame constitutions to suit their own special conditions; when this happened, they believed, the British connection would necessarily be dissolved, preferably in peace and with goodwill. Howick, taught by Stephen, was less fearful of colonial excesses and did not believe that a constitution drawn up in a colony would necessarily be unacceptable to Britain as a part of imperial government. Long before 1839 he had asked whether Britain had any real interest in maintaining a control of last resort over every colonial question. Between 1839 and 1846 he came to see that larger settled colonies did not have to be subordinate to the mother country, save in respect of a few imperial matters. Subordination so attenuated might make independence lose its attraction.

4 The Crown Colony System

Until the accession of his present majesty, with the exception of a few inconsiderable factories on the coast of Africa, and a few not less inconsiderable in India, no body of Englishmen had ever been established as a colony on foreign soil, without partaking the enjoyment of the British constitution. The smallest rock in the West Indies exhibited a sort of miniature of the British constitution.

> Sir James Mackintosh in the House of Commons, 1819[1]

The experience of Ireland and of the W. Indies proves . . . that of all bad Govts by far the worst is that carried on under popular forms by a minority constantly dreading a successful resistance of the great majority of the population.

> Howick to Melbourne, 3 January 1839[2]

The stormy history of self-government in the Canadas was contemporary with the development, elsewhere in the empire, of the illiberal system of Crown colony government. Unknown by that name before 1828,[3] it existed in many different forms in the conquered colonies of the West Indies, Ceylon, Mauritius and the Cape and in the settled colonies of New South Wales and Tasmania. Although its beginnings were in wartime arrangements for conquered colonies, it had precedents of a kind in British imperial experience. The Quebec Act of 1774 had established a form of government that embraced every essential feature of Crown colony government.[4] Similarly, other colonies had been left without representative institutions and sometimes without any local means of making laws. Georgia, Nova Scotia, Cape Breton and Grenada were all, at various times in the eighteenth century, under the rule of the Crown, legislatively as well as administratively.

IMPULSES TO AUTHORITARIAN GOVERNMENT

The conflict with the American colonies in the eighteenth century had convinced British ministers that in colonies with representative institutions the executive power needed to be strong, as it was in Britain. Colonial assemblies encroached on the powers of the governors and councils, through whom Britain partly exerted her authority within the colonies. In Crown colony government, as it emerged in the 1790s, there were at first no representative institutions and sometimes no local power of legislation. The denial of self-government, though possibly congenial to the Tories in a period of reaction, was not originally planned as a new system of colonial rule and was long defended as something temporary and exceptional. Bathurst was planning to liberalise the system when he left office in 1827. In the 1830s the Whigs were confident that Crown colony government was, for the most part, a halfway house to the old representative system. The illiberal rule of the Crown was justified only when a colonial society was so backward, or so divided by race, nationality, religion, wealth or servitude, that no group capable of working the old representative system was likely to provide good government in the interests of the population as a whole.

The principle of trusteeship embodied in this attitude was common to both Whigs and Tories. It rested partly on dread of instability in colonies misruled by powerful minorities, and partly on distrust of any kind of self-government in colonies to which British institutions were inappropriate. It owed something also to the special difficulties of incorporating Frenchmen, Dutchmen, Spaniards and other foreigners into the empire, and was reinforced by the growth of British humanitarianism in the early nineteenth century. Humanitarianism was often inseparable from the evangelical revival; evangelicalism itself, 'the rock upon which the character of the nineteenth century Englishman was formed', owed much to the impetus of the Indian connexion'. Similarly, the anti-slavery movement helped to transform the morals and opinions of great numbers of people, inculcating responsibility for the welfare of others, at home and abroad.[5]

In settling the forms of colonial government, the important examples of authoritarian rule came from India. From Chatham onwards, men had wondered 'whether the possession of a despotically ruled empire might not prove fatal to the cause of liberty in England'.[6] On the eve of the American Revolution Lord North's Regulating Act had given responsibility for the government of British possessions in India to the East India Company. Scandals and financial ineptitude soon showed how unequal the Company was to the task. Two Parliamentary committees persuaded the Commons that the independence of the Company's rule in India had to end. Pitt's India Act of 1784[7] established a new department of government, the Board of Control, to which all the Company's dispatches, except those on commercial matters, had to be submitted. In emergencies the Board could transmit its own orders to India and recall, though it did not appoint, the Company's servants.

The success of the Act largely depended on the appointment of a strong man as governor-general of Bengal. When Lord Cornwallis was persuaded to accept the post in 1782, he stipulated that as governor-general he should be authorised to override the nominated council, which was established, under the Act, to share the governor-general's responsibilities. Remembering the fate of Warren Hastings when confronted by a hostile council in 1775, Cornwallis required statutory recognition of his own supremacy. Pitt conceded the point to get the man and answered objections by pleading that vast responsibilities needed vast powers.[8] Parliament gave Cornwallis the authority that he sought and similar powers were conferred on the governors of Madras and Bombay.

The governor-general was empowered to overrule his council, positively or negatively, and to require its members to sign his orders even if they disagreed with them. Their protection was that the Act placed responsibility on the governor-general alone and that they could record their views in secret consultations transmitted to London. The governor-general could not use his supreme powers in judicial matters, nor for the making of general regulations in matters of civil government. Before long, British ministers used the prerogative powers of the Crown to endow some governors of conquered colonies with powers that, in law, were no less than those bestowed on Cornwallis.

At first, autocracy of this kind was established in the conquered colonies, where the power of the Crown to settle the laws and decide the form of government was undoubted.[9] New colonisation by settlement had temporarily ceased after the founding of Georgia in 1732, apart from the special cases of Sierra Leone in 1787 and New South Wales (then most of the eastern half of Australia) in 1788. Wars and the fact that, geographically speaking, the most obvious territories for new settlement were too distant to be easily colonised[10] were important reasons why Britain did not, at this time, found any new colonies of settlement, although she did acquire valuable new territories in the West Indies, Africa and the East. Some of the additions to the empire were unsuited to white settlement. In some others, white settlement already existed and there were immediate claims to representative government.

All such claims were denied. Crown colony government emerged in the so-called 'King's colonies', which were the conquered dependencies in the West Indies, Mauritius, Ceylon and the Cape. Eventually a similar form of government was adopted for New South Wales. Parliament did not challenge the new system until 1819, when Joseph Hume, obsessed with the costs of empire, complained that wealthy and important colonies, requiring tremendous sums to defend, were wholly removed from legislative scrutiny and subject to the Secretary of State alone.[11] Parliament was not interested, even though taunted that, while it debated the spending of a few hundred pounds, Bathurst, without reference to the Commons or anyone else, spent hundreds of thousands of pounds in the

King's colonies. Henry Goulburn, the Under-Secretary for Colonies, limited his answer to Hume to the question of financial controls and asserted that government in the conquered colonies was in the form settled by the treaties acquiring them, and had not been decided upon by ministers. Only Sir James Mackintosh was restless at Goulburn's evasion[12] and the House dropped the matter. Some months later Hume returned to the question of colonial revenue and challenged the refusal of legislative powers to the King's colonies. The House agreed to ask for financial returns from some of the colonies ruled by orders-in-council, but did not protest against their system of government.[13]

Three years later Hume instigated another debate on colonial finances and condemned what he thought abuses in the King's colonies: 'In some of these colonies, a large revenue was collected by the local government under an authority directly contrary to the spirit of the British constitution, which said that no subject should be taxed but by an act of the legislature. They ought to have a share in their own law making, or the amount of the revenue ought to be sanctioned by the House.' Apparently Hume thought it better to repeal the Act of 1778, which pledged Britain not to tax some colonies, than to continue to levy taxes on the authority of the Crown. This would allow a revenue to be raised on the authority of Parliament. The new Under-Secretary, Wilmot-Horton, did not comment on Hume's constitutional ideas, nor explain to the Commons why the Crown had power to raise a revenue in the colonies, though Parliament had not. He promised that the Crown colonies would be fully discussed on some other occasion. Henry Bright, the only other significant speaker, warned against the assumption, common among Radicals and the more liberal Whigs, that every colony would sooner or later be suited to some form of the British constitution. Hume then withdrew his motion on finances and Wilmot-Horton's proposed consideration of Crown colony government never took place.[14] Members would already have known that, in endeavouring to ameliorate the conditions of slavery, Parliament and the Colonial Office had had more success with Crown colonies than with colonies able to interpose their legislatures between themselves and British reforms. Moreover, Goulburn and Wilmot-Horton both hinted at military reasons for not allowing representative government to the conquered colonies. In the new, conquered colonies, where English settlers were small minorities, surrounded by non-European and servile inhabitants, the case against disturbing the course taken by the Crown seemed too obvious for discussion.

THE CONQUERED WEST INDIAN COLONIES

In the course of the long Napoleonic Wars Britain conquered, lost and reconquered many Caribbean colonies. At the peace in 1815 she kept Trinidad, Tobago and St. Lucia, together with Demerara, Essequibo and

Berbice (later united as British Guiana), all of which already had European populations ruled by European laws. Experience in Quebec and Grenada suggested that the old representative system, which the West India colonies had done so much to discredit,[15] was not suited to conquered colonies, whose free populations consisted principally of foreigners lacking experience of self-government.

While war lasted, speculation on the government of colonies that might be returned to the enemy at the next peace seemed useless. In 1794, when civil government had to be introduced into the conquered colonies of San Domingo and Martinique, the governors' commissions were abridged forms of those regularly used in self-governing colonies, with references to councils, assemblies and local powers of legislation struck out. The governors' instructions, however, were specially drawn for the new colonies. Each was to be ruled according to its 'ancient Laws and Institutions', subject to directions from England and to the vesting in the governor of all executive power, both civil and military. No legislative authority was established in either island. Both had to depend for new laws on British orders-in-council and executive proclamations by governors. A small council selected from the élite of the landholders was to advise each governor, but not to entangle or restrain him. When he disregarded its advice, members in opposition were, on the model of the Indian councils, to record their reasons and submit them for consideration by the Secretary of State.[16] Roman Catholics were allowed to sit on the councils, taking the form of oath prescribed in the Quebec Act, and to practise their religion. The existing fiscal system, laws and courts system were all retained, and appeal could be made to the Privy Council in cases involving more than £500. In effect the conquered colonies were allowed to retain their laws and institutions, subject to a minimum of change. They had, of course, already become well accustomed to control from the centre of an empire.[17]

These precedents were generally followed in most other conquered colonies, except Tobago, which had been ruled twice before by Britain and to which the old representative system, granted in 1768, was restored. Neither Martinique nor San Domingo, which was ruined in the famous race war, remained in the British Empire. At the Peace of Amiens in 1802 Britain kept only Trinidad and Ceylon of the colonies that she had gained for the first time in the war.

Trinidad, conquered from Spain in 1796, was always important in the early shaping of the Crown colony system. The Spaniards had administered it as part of Venezuela and left the fertile island largely undeveloped. From the 1780s on, Roman Catholic settlers of every nationality had been encouraged to settle there, and a considerable immigration of French colonists had followed the return of the Ceded Islands to Britain and the spread of the Revolution to the Caribbean in

1791. Shortly after the conquest the largest group of free inhabitants were the coloured peoples (mostly French-speaking), who numbered nearly 3000. In addition there were 1000 Frenchmen, 500 Spaniards and about 660 Englishmen, together with 10,000 slaves and 1000 or more aborigines.[18]

In settling the original form of government for Trinidad no one tried to look beyond the war. The new Secretary of State, Lord Hobart, was 'anxious . . . to give a British Constitution to Trinidad . . . as soon as it can prudentially be effected',[19] but the instructions issued to Governor Thomas Picton in 1801 were on the same lines as those issued to the governor of San Domingo.[20] The prerogative powers of the Crown were used to vest all executive powers in the governor, assisted by a nominated council of advice. Legislative powers, apart from governor's proclamations, were retained in London, to be exercised through orders-in-council.

Spanish forms of government were difficult even for Picton, who knew the language and was liked by the Spanish inhabitants, to ascertain and apply. A growing number of British merchants, openly engaged in illicit trade with the Spanish empire in South America, demanded English law, especially commercial law, and English courts, together with the old representative system. Their cool assumption[21] that only English, French and Spanish men of property would be admitted to the franchise, although the free coloureds outnumbered all the Europeans, worried Picton:

> Popular Elective Assemblies have been productive of much ruinous Consequence in some of the neighbouring Islands where the Elements of Society are too different to admit of a similar Composition with that of the Mother Country. An Elective Assembly will unavoidably introduce a question which cannot fail to generate the seeds of lasting Fermentation in a Country composed of such Combustible Materials.[22]

If an assembly were granted without the numerous free coloured people being enfranchised, they would be justly resentful. If they were enfranchised, their numbers and talents would give them control of the assembly, and the Europeans would object. If no assembly were granted, possibly only the English settlers, a minority, would complain.

The plans of the settlers for the development of Trinidad caused fears in Britain that they might lead to a revival of the detested slave trade.[23] In May 1802 Canning warned the Commons that if Trinidad were developed as a sugar-producing colony in the normal West India style a million slaves might perish. As the price of sugar would fall when such a bountiful supply reached the market, great cruelty would not even reap great profits. He moved that land grants be stopped until regulations had been made to prevent plantation slavery in Trinidad. Canning hoped for development by small resident proprietors, who would provide political stability and serve as militia to defend the island against envious foreigners. Although the motion was not carried, the Prime Minister, Addington, promised further measures against the slave trade and declared that no more land grants would be made without reference to Parliament. Addington and Hobart were willing to look at the prospects of encouraging an emigration of small settlers, including Scots Presbyterians.[24]

With so many plans under discussion, Hobart decided on an inquiry into the laws and government of Trinidad. He informed Picton that the island would not be granted 'the form of Legislature existing in the old West Indian colonies' until there was no doubt that the reform would benefit all the inhabitants and Britain. English law could not be introduced without a legislature to adapt it to local conditions.[25]

The commission of inquiry that Hobart appointed was a notorious failure. Picton himself was virtually superseded by a triumvirate in which he was a junior member. Clashes of personality and the fundamental conflicts between the British desire to protect free coloureds and slaves and the desire of the planters and merchants to exploit the island destroyed its work and went near to paralysing local administration.[26]

Hobart recalled the commissioners and in 1804 ordered the new lieutenant-governor, General Sir Thomas Hislop, to report on the laws and government of the island.[27] Hislop was to consider three forms of colonial government already existing in the empire, the first of which would not be allowed to Trinidad:

1st — That which obtains in all the Old Colonies; namely a Legislature, consisting of *The Governor* as His Majesty's Representative with a *Council* and an *Assembly*.

2dly — That which consists of a *Governor* and *Council* without an Assembly; as was formerly the Government of the Province Quebec and is at present of the Island of Cape Breton.

3dly — That which prevails in a conquered Territory governed, during His Majesty's Pleasure, by its ancient laws under the Sovereign Authority of the King delegated to His Representative *The Governor* as is at present the case in the Island under your Charge and in St Lucia.

Hobart preferred the second alternative, to introduce into Trinidad the form of government established by the Quebec Act in 1774. He added, however, that the government certainly wished Trinidad to advance slowly to 'the further benefits of the constitutions of the other British colonies' in the Caribbean.

No reforms followed Hislop's inquiries, although he and the attorney-general, Archibald Gloster, proposed that for an interim period of from three to five years legislative powers should be vested in the governor and a nominated council, like that of Quebec from 1774 to 1791 but with power to tax. Because most Europeans in the island were foreign Roman Catholics, Hislop and Gloster thought a 'free and liberal form of government' obviously unsuitable, but wanted some English law, essential to merchants and traders, introduced at once, leaving the governor and new council to adapt it to local conditions and prepare for British forms of government.[28]

Changed circumstances made these recommendations, however close to Hobart's first wishes, unwelcome in London. The risks of war with Spain were powerful arguments against interfering with the Spanish (and French) in Trinidad, who outnumbered the English settlers and whose loyalty to Britain was slight. The free coloureds, most of them French-speaking, were thought to be republicans.[29] Fears for the security of the island outweighed concern for the complaints of English merchants, who claimed that trading was obstructed by Spanish civil law and cumbersome court proceedings in the Spanish language, and of the settlers, who had discovered the disadvantages of the Spanish law of property and were demanding English law and the old representative system.

Apart from the war, the most conclusive argument against liberalising the government of Trinidad was the humanitarian. The passionate liberator of slaves, James Stephen the elder, who had practised law in St Kitts and had many powerful friends in Britain, had since 1802 been conducting a campaign against the European exploitation of Trinidad. He roused fears of extensions of the slave trade and proposed that part of the island be reserved for cultivation by free negroes. Above all he wanted Trinidad to be controlled from Britain, so that power would never get into the hands of planters willing to use slaves and of merchants caring only for profit. He declared significantly that there were not enough men of property and character in Trinidad to make representative government there creditable to the British name.[30] Stephen agitated in high places and in 1808 Spencer Perceval found him a place in the House of Commons.

War and fear of the slave trade had given the government an overwhelming case for doing nothing about Trinidad, and nothing was done. When hostilities with Spain ceased in 1808 the island's problems of government were pressing. Castlereagh, the Third Secretary of State, sent out the eccentric George Smith, who had been chief justice of Grenada (and later complicated the judicial affairs of Mauritius), to act as chief judge and report on the reform of law and government. Smith was a friend of Stephen and sympathised with Castlereagh's ambitious plans to spread Christianity among the slaves and mulattos, to protect the negroes and free coloureds and to establish the Church of England. In Trinidad he quarrelled with Hislop and most of the English population, whom he despised as 'the offal of the Community', unfit for British self-government:

If you mean to ruin the colony you will give us the British Constitution, a form of government whose foundation ... on the general liberty becomes an absolute caricature in a community where

four-fifths of the population are slaves; and in which ... the rights of
humanity can only be guarded by an executive government holding
over the masters an authority bearing some proportion to that which he
claims over his slaves.[31]

In Britain his view was not easy to accept. Hobart had been willing to
introduce government on the model of the Quebec Act; Hislop and the
Advisory Council had asked for it, meaning it to be followed at an
appropriate time by the old representative system. The English merchants
asked why conquered West Indian islands should be treated differently
from the old West India islands: was not slavery common to them all?
How could a common institution be a reason for refusing to the merchants
and planters of Trinidad what they would have been entitled to anywhere
else?

In 1810, with the Trinidad government nearly bankrupt and severe
problems in administering Spanish law, the planters and merchants
interested in the island's trade agitated again for the 'British Constitution'
and English law. Liverpool, the Secretary of State, knew that the ministry
was too weak in Parliament to risk a challenge to its West Indies policies.
He decided to play for time by asking Hislop and the council to advise him
again whether to give Trinidad 'the British Laws and constitution upon an
equal footing of advantage with the other Islands'.[32]

Embarrassing advice came from the governor and council. English
law should be introduced, together with the old representative system.
But Chief Justice Smith still preferred the existing system of
government, and, as had long been expected, the free coloured population,
still by far the largest group of free men in the island, petitioned not to be
excluded from any form of representative government granted to
Trinidad.[33]

Liverpool, faced with a triple choice of rule from London, rule by the
Europeans and rule by all free people, and hounded by the humanitarians
to concede nothing to Hislop, rejected everything except the curt advice
from Smith. How could he introduce a representative assembly into a
colony that lacked a loyal, respectable, responsibly minded population?
Was he to hand over the island to the free coloureds and make the English
there a minority among a minority? Or should he attempt, on some
principle unknown to English law and contrary to the capitulations, to
exclude free men of colour and property from the franchise? He was no
more willing for reform in Trinidad than he had been in favour of it in
Lower Canada.

Liverpool gave his decision in November 1810. The existing form of
government was to continue. Neither the old representative system nor the
model of the Quebec Act could work smoothly in a colony where so few
of the free population were accustomed to British institutions and in

which the special problems of the free coloureds had to be added to those presented by the many Spanish and French settlers. Because Britain had committed herself in 1807 to abolishing the slave trade, she needed the fullest possible control of the colony's development.

Liverpool deferred the request for English law, but declared that the Crown might delegate some of its prerogative power of legislation to the governor. Ordinances issued by the governor would, of course, be subject to amendment, disallowance or repeal in London.[34]

Under what Harlow called 'Colonial Office government', the least liberal form of Crown colony government, Britain reserved to herself the entire control of the affairs of Trinidad. By doing so she aroused strong opposition in the island and among the merchants in England; but an attempt to have Parliament reverse Liverpool's decision failed.[35] Colonial Office government in Trinidad avoided the difficulties of producing a consensus of the island's diverse free populations, left the way open for humanitarian action from Britain in the interests of the slaves and free coloureds, and prevented a challenge to Parliamentary sovereignty. Taxes were imposed, revenue collected and spent, and administration controlled on the authority of the Secretary of State. The governor's delegated power to legislate by proclamation grew progressively and was not often checked from London. Important legislation, however, was provided by orders-in-council, drawn in the island by the governor or chief justice and presented by the Secretary of State to the Privy Council with little alteration.[36]

Similar arrangements were made for similar reasons in the other conquered West Indian colonies. Liverpool disliked the reactionary compromise forced on him in Trinidad and thought that the more liberal form of government established in Ceylon was 'the best administration of all the King's Colonies [i.e. Crown colonies] in any quarter of the globe'.[37] So far as he could he adopted the Ceylon form of government for Mauritius, after that island's capture in 1810. Trinidad, with its mixed population and special interest to the humanitarians, he had to leave as it was.[38]

THE AMELIORATION CONTROVERSY: LEGISLATIVE COLONIES AND CROWN COLONIES

Problems of the slave trade and slavery powerfully affected British attitudes towards the West Indian colonies from the late eighteenth century to halfway through the nineteenth. Ministers had to steer a middle course between demands from Quakers, evangelicals, humanitarians, and 'Saints' generally, for strong efforts to mitigate or abolish slavery, and the conviction of many people in Britain that, in the eyes of God and reasonable men, slavery was not wrong and that obstructing planters' rights of property in their slaves would not promote amelioration.

The constitutional problems raised by the slavery question seemed simple at first. All those in Britain who wished to ameliorate the conditions of slavery and ultimately abolish it declared that Parliament could and should compel every colony, whether a legislative or a Crown colony, to undertake reforms. The old legislative colonies, however, denied that Parliament had power to do anything of the sort and contested every attempt to interfere with their internal affairs. The Crown colonies also resisted British attempts to reform slavery and used legal arguments to supplement their subterfuges, evasions and defiance.

From 1812 the Saints pressed, with varying degrees of public support, for a Slave Registration Act, to help enforce the severe laws against the slave trade. The matter became urgent when, after the war, the Franch colonies were returned without stipulations against the evil trade and rumours arose that British colonies were recruiting slaves through Demerara from the Spanish and Portuguese colonies. In 1815, when Wilberforce gave notice in the Commons of a Bill to require slave registration in every British colony, he precipitated an angry reappraisal of the rights of self-government as well as of the state of slavery in the old British colonies.

Wilberforce's proposed Bill resembled closely orders-in-council passed for Trinidad in 1812 and St Lucia in 1814 to establish slave registers. It provided also for a central slave registry in England, where duplicates of the island registers would be kept, and for fees and fines to make the system work.[39] In Parliament the West Indians were quick to claim immunity to imperial control, condemning the Bill as unprecedented tyranny and the proposed fees and fines as taxation contrary to the Declaratory Act.[40]

Though clear half a century earlier, the basic constitutional question of whether Parliament had power to legislate for the internal affairs of colonies to which representative assemblies had been granted[41] had been complicated since by misapprehensions of law and special circumstances. The Declaratory Act of 1766[42] had asserted the supremacy of Parliament throughout the empire. But supremacy had produced disastrous consequences in North America, and Parliament, having no great interest in colonial government, had after the American Revolution been reluctant to exercise its powers or assume responsibilities in the colonies. The Act of 1778, renouncing the power to tax colonies, save for the regulation of external commerce, acquired a standing in men's minds far beyond its limited intention: some thought a statutory embodiment of a new convention restraining Parliament from legislating for colonies on matters on which they could legislate for themselves. In 1796, when Sir Philip Francis sought leave to introduce a Bill to make the West Indian governments instruments for preparing the slaves for freedom, he invoked 'the transcendent power of Parliament to make laws for every part of the

British empire'. The power, he said, still existed, although reserved for 'great emergencies', especially cases in which no colonial legislature had authority to act. His motion was lost. Members supported Henry Dundas, who thought it useless to legislate for colonies unless 'we had the concurrence of the colonies themselves'. There was no means of compelling them to accept British legislation and the right to legislate ought not to be agitated, 'except in cases of necessity'. Five years later Hobart accepted the advice of the Law Officers, that Parliament had made it a principle not to interfere with the internal legislation of the colonies, although still claiming a right to do so.[43]

These assertions of principle carefully hedged about with arguments for inaction, posed an obscure legal question in place of a plain one. The new question was, did Parliament abstain — merely on grounds of political expediency, or because a new convention of the constitution limited its powers and duties with respect to the legislative colonies — from using the authority that it had possessed in 1766 and 1778?

Amelioration of slavery was not the only problem to raise such constitutional questions with the West Indian colonies. Contributions to the costs of imperial defence were again being sought, and in the slave colonies troops were needed to hold the servile population in obedience. After 1815 Britain maintained colonial garrisons at much above pre-war levels, and the slave uprisings of 1795–6 in Grenada and St Vincent and of 1816 in Barbados did much to justify her policy. On 31 July 1816 Bathurst told the West Indian governors[44] that Britain needed a larger colonial contribution to the costs of the garrisons, in the way in which Jamaica was already contributing (and which Britain wished to increase). Nothing was gained by his rather tentative inquiries, though reinforced with hints that garrisons might be reduced or withdrawn.[45] Amelioration continued to dominate British policy towards self-government in the West Indies.

The Saints knew that Wilberforce's Bill raised severe problems for the government. Colonial resistance was certain and would be partly on constitutional grounds. Planters might visit their resentment on the slaves, to mock efforts at amelioration.[46] On the eve of Wilberforce's motion James Stephen the elder wrote to Bathurst, 'relying ... on the candour and indulgence I have always experienced from your Lordship' to suggest that, if the Bill failed to pass, Bathurst should introduce a government measure at once. No other course would be tolerable. The government had aggravated the slave problem by acquiring Demerara, Essequibo and Berbice, which needed slaves and could be used to pass slaves through to other British territories. The old colonies needed a registry Act as efficient as the orders-in-council passed for Trinidad and St Lucia.[47]

The government, fearing its own weakness in the Commons, was perplexed. Castlereagh admitted that slave registers were needed, but asked the House not to proceed with the Bill until the assemblies had had a chance to legislate for themselves.[48] Wilberforce then let his measure lapse. Intense agitation followed. The Saints and West Indian opponents of the Bill assailed the Colonial Office and members of Parliament with contradictory arguments, mainly constitutional, sometimes circumstantial. Angry colonists denied that any significant slave trade existed in the West Indies and charged that registration was a dishonest prelude to emancipation. Supporters of the Bill attempted to refute West Indian ideas of the constitution and pointed out that the arguments used before 1807 to prove the futility of abolishing the slave trade, on the ground that slaves could easily be smuggled in the Caribbean, showed how essential registration was. In Jamaica the assembly denied that Parliament, in which no colony was represented, could legislate for its internal affairs. Jamaica and Great Britain were linked with one another only by having the same King. One part of the King's dominions could not lawfully have power over any other part that possessed rights of self-government.[49]

The first months of troubled peace after Waterloo were a bad time to press against arguments like these and Wilberforce recognised that political opinion was against him. Bathurst was an old friend and the prudent course was to let him persuade the colonial legislatures to introduce their own registration acts. Bathurst explained to the Lords that '. . . it was the intention of the government to recommend to the colonial legislatures the adoption of some measure . . . calculated to answer the purposes of the slave registry bill. He did not deny the right of the British Parliament to bind the colonies by such a law, but it would be very indiscreet to act upon that right, unless . . . the object could not be accomplished by another method'.[50] If the legislative colonies failed to enact their own measures, Wilberforce could revive his Bill.

'For the first time, at any rate since 1783', commented Helen Taft Manning, 'the colonial minister deliberately and with great force used the threat of parliamentary action as a club to bring the colonial legislatures into line'.[51] But Bathurst had most studiously refrained from inviting Parliamentary action and there is little evidence that either Lords or Commons would have passed a Bill to establish registers in the legislative colonies. Stephen the elder resigned his seat in disgust.

Bathurst again reminded the governors that Parliament was sovereign throughout the empire and instructed them to have their legislatures at once enact registry Acts along the lines of Wilberforce's Bill.[52] Recalcitrant assemblies, he wrote, would forfeit respect for their privileges. The assemblies, for all their fire and fury, were not yet so despairing as to ignore an appeal to reason, backed, as it was, by their own representatives in London. By 1819 all the colonies except Bermuda had passed Acts approximating to Bathurst's directions.[53] An imperial Act was then passed to require duplicates to be lodged in London.[54] It provided that no sale or mortgage of a slave would be valid in the United Kingdom unless his name and description were on the central registry. As planters depended heavily on London credit, this was a severe provision.

Bathurst's tactics had succeeded. Whether they had indicated weakness or produced weakness in Britain's constitutional powers over the colonies has been debated. Schuyler, impressed by the Colonial Office's failure over the next ten years, to force legislation on the old West India colonies, thought that Wilberforce's withdrawal of his Bill had been a triumph for the Caribbean malcontents who disputed British authority.[55] But Bathurst was as opposed to using the powers of Parliament as the Jamaicans were; he believed that the powers existed and was sure that it would be folly to invoke them. He left the powers intact and used them in 1823, when he effectually began the destruction of the legislative powers of the old colonies.[56]

The Saints disliked the rate of progress under Bathurst's cautious statesmanship. In January 1823 they formed the Anti-Slavery Society (the Society for the Mitigation and Gradual Abolition of Slavery throughout the British Dominions) to press for a single, enlightened policy towards slavery throughout all the colonies. In May the Commons adopted the famous resolutions with which Canning parried Thomas Fowell Buxton's motion for the gradual abolition of slavery. These had been drafted after discussions between Liverpool, Bathurst and prominent West Indians belonging to a special committee that had been formed by Caribbean interests in London to check any far-reaching resolution from Buxton; the West Indians feared that news of the debates in Parliament might provoke the slaves to insurrection. Canning declared that the government itself would introduce an orderly programme of reform leading to emancipation. However, reforms could be imposed on the Crown colonies only; in the legislative colonies the government would have to rely on exhortation. If the colonies were contumacious the government would come to the House for counsel.[57]

The Cabinet agreed on the programme of reforms that the colonial governments would be ordered, or recommended, to effect. On 28 May 1823 Bathurst sent Canning's speech and the Commons resolutions to Governor John Murray in Demerara, with a request that he lay them before the court of policy.[58] The reforms proposed included two that even Wilberforce thought ambitious: prohibitions of the flogging of women (generally more difficult to control than men) and of the use of the driving whip in the fields. Because Demerara was a conquered colony, Bathurst could have proceeded by order-in-council, but its representative institutions (inherited from the Dutch and not well understood in Britain) had sometimes been treated as though they were assemblies. Bathurst left Demerara to act through its legislature, if it would; but if nothing were done he proposed to act by order-in-council. The governors of the Crown colonies of Trinidad and St Lucia were ordered to prepare the planters for an order-in-council instituting the proposed reforms, or, preferably, to anticipate British reforms by taking their own actions to reform slavery.[59] Also on 28 May, Bathurst sent a public circular dispatch to the governors of the old West India colonies[60] commanding them to lay Canning's resolutions before the assemblies and ask for appropriate legislation. Confidential dispatches of the same day told the governors that Parliament would intervene if the required laws were not passed.[61]

From London the Society of Planters and Merchants urged the colonies to adopt the reforms and even go beyond what had been requested. Only strong, positive leadership from the islands, the Society pointed out, could save them from rebellious slaves looking to Britain for emancipation, and from violation of their internal self-government by intervention of Parliament.[62] To the West Indian assemblies this seemed an aggravating counsel of despair, offered by men so close to the Saints and politicians of Britain that they had lost touch with the painful realities of slavery in a declining plantation economy.

Bathurst's proposals had disastrous consequences in Demerara. Persuading themselves that the King had set them free and that their masters were selfishly concealing the fact, the slaves rebelled to demand liberty. Governor Murray, whom Goulburn described as 'well-meaning with no very great capacity'[63] behaved with courage but small judgement. There were bloody and savage reprisals, and amelioration found a notable martyr: the Rev. John Smith of the London Missionary Society, a friend of slaves, died of illness while imprisoned under sentence of death illegally imposed by court-martial. Thereafter, men who thought the government weak or wrong in not compelling all the West Indian colonies to ameliorate slavery had a name on their lips with which to reject every suggestion that anything good was to be hoped for from the old colonies. Smith's case, the Demerara uprising and the violent treatment of missionaries in Barbados all made slavery for a time the great public question in England. Religion, humanitarianism and law itself had been outraged and indignation blazed that such crimes in British colonies could be neither prevented nor punished from London.[64] It was possible to condemn murder and cruelty without rejecting slavery.

The first news of the Demerara uprising reached England in October. Liverpool and Bathurst, worried already by West Indian claims that British action to ameliorate slavery would precipitate rebellion, at once assumed that a slave war had begun and decided on substantial military and naval reinforcements in the West Indies. Wellington feared another Maroon War. Ministers with lively memories of the race war in San Domingo experienced a short period of gloom before they learned that peace had been restored in Demerara. The uprising, unfortunate in origin and disastrously suppressed, had exacerbated the fear and anger of the West Indian assemblies, and in London had made the slavery problem seem ever more difficult and dangerous.[65] Opponents of slavery were quick to see the importance of writing off the Demerara incident as exaggerated: Brougham ridiculed the government's alarm at the 'slight commotion . . . among the negroes' and charged that the incident had been deliberately inflated in order to excuse lack of progress with Canning's resolutions.[66]

Reassurance from Demerara was the more welcome to Bathurst because on 9 July he had sent out to governors of West Indian colonies another circular dispatch, with further proposals for amelioration.[67] These included religious instruction, which the planters thought unsettling, and inconvenient reforms such as a prohibition on separating man and wife in slave sales, abolition of restrictions on manumission, recognition of negroes as witnesses in certain cases, and an obligation to keep a sworn register of punishments. Bathurst warned the governors of the old colonies that their legislatures must not lag behind the Crown colonies, in which Britain would proceed by order-in-council. Assemblies that resisted would forfeit friends and reputation in Britain and deserve intervention by Parliament.

In Demerara there was the special difficulty that the court of policy regarded itself as an assembly.[68] Bathurst cut through the difficulty, which lacked substance in law, by telling Governor Murray that the British Government could issue an order-in-council to enforce what ought to have been adopted by the court of policy.[69] When the court asserted that it had an exclusive right of internal legislation in Demerara, Bathurst settled the matter with two orders-in-council, declaring the right of the Crown to legislate for Demerara (and Berbice).[70]

Early in 1824 only Trinidad had complied with Bathurst's directions; its response had been so prompt that an order-in-council for Trinidad was passed on 10 March, laying down the slave code that the government then invited the legislative colonies to adopt.[71] Otherwise there was little but failure and tumult to report.[72] Bathurst's intention to go to Parliament to force amelioration on the colonies, expressed in the secret and confidential dispatches of 28 May and 9 July 1823, had become known in the colonies to the great prejudice of the government and its policy. There were immediate protests from the legislatures of Barbados, Dominica (where there was active slave unrest), St Vincent and, above all, Jamaica. Fear of further uprisings persuaded the Cabinet to abandon coercion for the time, even in Crown colonies.[73] Because compulsion by an imperial Act was 'much too delicate to be mooted',[74] the government continued to promote amelioration by other means. Among its less effective measures was the appointment of two bishops and other clergy, for the sake of religion and morals and in pursuance of the policy of 9 July 1823. Canning, a member of the Merchant Seamen's Auxiliary Bible Society, declared that the Church of England in the West Indies was 'no more calculated for the negro than for the brute animal that shares his tools'.[75]

Liverpool could never think of the old West India colonies without remembering the American Revolution. In America, he wrote to Canning, Britain had committed herself to positions that foresight would have shown to be untenable. Could past errors be avoided in present troubles, which involved the same principles? Canning thought the problem of 'most awful importance' and warned the mild Bathurst against forcing the Trinidad order-in-council onto unwilling colonies. In the same letter, however, he asked how far the colonies had complied with official policy and looked to see what further action might be possible.[76]

The famous quarterlies contradicted one another on colonial rights of self-government. The Tory *Quarterly Review* thought that policy, rather than law, made the ministry cautious. Neither the slaves not the West Indian colonies ought to be at risk. How easy it would be to push slave owners into repression and tyranny! The West Indian colonies might leave the empire in disgust. In a strong rebuke to political economists who denounce colonies as burdens to the mother country, the *Quarterly* argued that loss of the West Indies would cost Britain £218 million of investments, a twelfth of her annual exports and a quarter of her imports.[77] Ministers, however, were more impressed by the risks of a servile rebellion or a discreditable assertion of independence than by the threat that the West Indian colonies might take their privileged trade elsewhere, to face competition in foreign markets.

The Radical *Westminster Review* found the government's scruples pusillanimous. Distrusting colonies and detesting slavery, it scoffed at colonial claims to legislative independence. Authoritarian, like all Benthamites with a cause to promote, it credited Britain with 'an unlimited right to interfere in the West Indies'; colonies had legislatures only because local laws might best be made by men with local knowledge. Subordinate assemblies could not block imperial legislation and an imperial Act obviously prevailed over any colonial law repugnant to it. Negroes were not mere chattels, as some slave owners thought: they were the King's subjects and slavery was merely a right, sanctioned by ancient usage and by Act of Parliament, to enforce their services.[78] From every point of view, amelioration and abolition were imperial problems, which Parliament clearly had ample powers to solve.

The *Edinburgh Review*, determined to support both amelioration and emancipation, offered the most striking estimate of the government's constitutional difficulties. An article probably written by Brougham[79] summed up the law boldly. Parliament had justly asserted its sovereignty in 1766 by the Declaratory Act; the Act of 1778, referring only to taxation, had not touched its supremacy in any relevant way: 'The general right of legislation ... stands exactly as it did before the American War'. Doubters who feared to invade supposed conventions limiting the sovereignty of Parliament ought to remember that no legislature in a colony whose inhabitants were mostly uncivilised slaves and depressed free coloureds could be compared with the Parliament of free men in Britain.[80]

Fears of constitutional impropriety, Brougham thought, ought not to delay reform. If amelioration were not effective, the 'feebleness of the Government at home' would be justly blamed for every negro rebellion that followed. White resistance was less to be feared than large-scale black rebellion.[81]

True to its tradition of irritable resistance to imperial authority, the Assembly of Jamaica charged the House of Commons and Bathurst himself with arrogant assaults on its liberties and directed that its protest be circulated among British and American newspapers.[82] The Jamaica agent in London, wealthy George Hibbert, pressed difficulties on Bathurst and corresponded with the assembly. In 1825 he told Bathurst that Jamaica ought not to be asked to adopt the Trinidad code before time had shown how it worked. He also reported to Jamaica on Bathurst's dread of the 'lengthened debates in parliament' that would follow if the government introduced legislation for the old West India colonies. The Parliamentary discussions would be as embarrassing in the Caribbean as in Britain, because the slaves would suspect their masters of denying them liberties that Parliament had already granted. Bathurst, according to Hibbert, would be content with almost any action in the spirit of the Trinidad code; exact compliance was not required.[83]

In April 1826 Hibbert told Bathurst of the constitutional ingenuities with which the assembly hoped to fend off an imperial Act. An imperial statute to ameliorate slavery, or to 'extinguish' it gradually, would conflict with many Jamaican enactments, including some relating to property. In the Jamaican view, no imperial Act could repeal a colonial law approved by the King in council. The governor's instructions, unchanged for more than a century and a half, limited disallowance to colonial laws 'not before confirmed' by the Crown. Thus any law that the Crown had confirmed could not be disallowed. Would Jamaican courts have to decide whether to obey Parliament or obey the lawful assembly of the island?[84] The argument was unacceptable to anyone who could distinguish between the Royal disallowance of a colonial Act and the repeal by Parliament of a statute, British or colonial; but it raised problems of expediency. James Stephen the younger, then Counsel to the Colonial Office, was troubled by the lack of precedents for Parliamentary repeal of colonial statutes and not disposed to argue that, because Parliament was sovereign, any colonial law inconsistent with its enactments was necessarily void to the extent of repugnancy.[85]

Bathurst continued reluctant to provoke the West Indian legislatures too far.[86] The colonists could discredit the colonial system by defying the mother country and make amelioration practically impossible by becoming heedless to reason.[87]

In all the doubts that afflicted the ministers responsible for amelioration, no one doubted that the imperial Parliament could regulate the relations of colonies with one another. In July 1824 Parliament forbade the removal of slaves other than personal servants from one colony to another, except in instances where the transfer would benefit the slave.[88] Stephen Lushington, the eminent lawyer and abolitionist, warned Bathurst that the new provision would be contested, which it was, though not on constitutional grounds. Objections were made to interference with rights of property rather than to unconstitutional action. Similarly, when Bathurst forbade the restoration to their masters of slaves escaped from foreign colonies, the principal West Indian complaint was that he had destroyed the basis for restoration of British slaves escaped to foreign soil.[89]

While constitutional questions were agitated in Britain and the West Indies, amelioration progressed slowly in Demerara, Berbice and St Lucia. On 6 October 1824 Bathurst wrote to Governor D'Urban in Demerara[90] that the court of policy should adopt the Trinidad order 'in spirit and in substance'. D'Urban, a soldier, who had governed Antigua successfully, sympathised with the planters.[91] Successive draft orders were sent from Demerara to the Colonial Office, but none satisfied Bathurst's conditions. When D'Urban recommended constitutional reforms, Bathurst decided to restore the system of government that had existed at the beginning of the century. Amelioration lagged until he accepted one of the Demerara drafts, regretfully admitting that the scheme of manumission that the Colonial Office had pressed on the court was unsuitable to Demerara.[92]

Bathurst had also overcome trouble in Berbice, another former Dutch colony with inherited institutions, fortunately less complicated than those of Demerara. When the council of advice would not comply with his wishes, he dissolved it by order-in-council and introduced a more pliant council in its place. The desired results were obtained in 1826, and in the same year the Crown colony of St Lucia also adopted the Trinidad code.[93]

Bathurst continued to hope that the old colonies, under private and official pressure from Britain, would enact slave codes resembling the Trinidad order-in-council. On 17 March 1826, with an election pending and the Saints more restless because of it, he persuaded the House of Lords to adopt unanimously the Canning resolutions of 1823.[94] The slight earnest of the government's intentions was needed. Two months later Brougham asked the House to express regret at the failure of the West Indian legislatures to comply with the government's proposals and threatened to introduce for the next session 'such measures as may appear necessary for giving effect to the said resolutions'. His motion was defeated by 100 votes to thirty-eight.[95]

While Parliament considered the unimpressive record of attempted amelioration, Bathurst announced that he would send out to all the colonies the Trinidad code in the form of eight draft Bills. When he did so the law officers of each colony were instructed to prepare suitable measures on the basis of the drafts. Nevis complied sufficiently well for its slave laws of 1828 to be praised by Stephen.[96] Elsewhere there were idle promises or open defiance.

Until he left the Colonial Office in April 1827, Bathurst continued to fear that Parliamentary discussion of slavery would 'irritate the Negro Population'.[97] He remained also uncertain about whether Britain could solve the problems of slavery without weakening the empire or ruining the colonies. Dread of an open clash with the assemblies led him in 1826 to approach Huskisson, President of the Board of Trade, with a request for speedier consideration of colonial Bills awaiting the King's pleasure, because the government could not afford a single source of possibly legitimate reproach from the West Indies.[98]

Under Bathurst's immediate successors, Goderich, Huskisson and Murray, the tail-ends of his policies were gradually caught up. Dominica in 1826, Tobago in 1829, St Vincent in 1830 and Jamaica in 1831 were all equipped with tolerably satisfactory slave codes. In February 1830 an order-in-council applying to all the Crown colonies was issued, to enforce the government's policies. Bathurst had decided on this step, but the changes of ministry and the doubts of Wellington and Peel concerning such a means of introducing important changes of law blocked action for some time.[99] The order-in-council of 1830 was more extensive than the famous Trinidad order and contained an important provision admitting slaves, without restriction, as witnesses in law cases.[100] Although the order may have been too late to help the slaves it showed the power of the imperial government. The Demerara enactment that Bathurst had disliked was overridden and the claims of the court of policy to be an assembly were rejected.[101]

At the end of Murray's brief term, the government decided to teach the legislative colonies that Parliament was both able and willing to legislate on slavery. A proposal that Bathurst had made in 1827, to have Parliament enact that slave evidence was admissible in courts throughout the whole empire, in legislative colonies as well as in Crown colonies, was revived. The importance of the measure, remarked Stephen, was 'less in the change of law which it would have effected' than in asserting 'the right and determination of Parliament to legislate for the internal affairs of the Colonies on the subject of slavery'.[102] Such a Bill would probably have become law and been notice to the legislative colonies that Parliament would intervene if they did not follow the government's wishes. The resignation of Wellington's ministry in November 1830 prevented the experiment from being put to the test.

A year later, under Goderich and Howick, a revised order-in-council of 2 November 1831 was applied to all the Crown colonies with slaves.[103] It was sufficiently liberal on food, clothing, corporal punishment and hours of labour to provoke bitter predictions of utter ruin. Whether the Whigs would proceed to have Parliament pass laws for the legislative colonies remained to be seen. As a party they had no binding commitment to abolition. Goderich certainly abhorred slavery, sharing Howick's view that it was economically wasteful as well as morally indefensible. Both men respected the advice of the evangelical Stephen, who had chosen to work in the Colonial Office, rather than at the Bar, so that he might see the slaves emancipated. They respected also the advice of Henry Taylor, the senior clerk on the West India side of the Office, who was strongly for amelioration and disposed towards authoritarian solutions.

The decline of economic conditions in the Caribbean soon gave the Whigs means other than admonition for bringing the legislative colonies into line. In 1830–1 sugar and coffee prices slumped, mainly because of increased production in the new colonies. A Commons committee drew attention to planter indebtedness to mortgagees in England, the financial dependence of planters on British merchants, the frequent changes of plantation ownership and the growth of absentee proprietorship. The decline of the planter class,[104] which so impressed the select committee, gave the Colonial Office a lever to influence the West Indian colonies. The committee itself had suggested that attention be given to possible reductions in British duties on colonial sugar and various administrative and financial changes.[105] The Whigs decided to make economic relief conditional on progress with amelioration. 'Admonition, temperate and authoritative' having failed, the other course outlined by Canning in 1824 was to be tried: fiscal pressure. Only colonies that adopted slave codes identical with the revised order-in-council would receive the benefits of the proposed reduction of sugar duties, which, of course, the Crown colonies, already subject to the order-in-council of 2 November, would receive automatically.[106]

The new policy had a bad start. Rumours of emancipation led to a serious slave rising in Jamaica at Christmas 1831, with the usual sequel of court-martials, hangings, floggings and great destruction of property. Goderich warned the Jamaicans to introduce quick reforms in order to save themselves.[107] Resistance in Jamaica was, however, running wild, with futile attempts being made to blame the slave troubles on Goderich, on evangelicals and humanitarians at home, or on missionaries on the island. The Jamaica Insurrection Act was passed to indemnify free persons for all acts committed during the disturbances; Stephen thought it intended to save those who had attacked the missionaries.[108] Extremists in the assembly denied that Jamacia belonged to Britain and longed for the protection of the slave-owning United States. Lunacies of this kind ran their course and then subsided when the moderate majority asserted itself in disgust and found powerful aid in the new governor, Earl Mulgrave.

The uprising in Jamaica strengthened belief in England that there were more dangers in withholding emancipation than in granting it. Taylor was among those who feared that the evangelicals were making the pace too fast. He warned Howick, who was preparing an elaborate and wholly impracticable scheme of emancipation, that the Reform Act might lead to a strong Parliamentary move to abolish slavery at once, producing chaos in the colonies. Rather than risk destroying the fabric of West Indian society and politics by precipitate emancipation, he would have been better satisfied if all the West Indian colonies had adopted the policy of November 1831 and the slavery question been left to rest, for fifteen years if necessary. His own plan was for gradual emancipation.[109]

The sudden upsurge of plans of emancipation was not the government's only embarrassment after the Jamaica troubles. In April 1832 Goderich agreed too readily to a request in the Lords for a select committee to consider the state of the West Indies after the outbreak of violence in some colonies and hurricane damage in Barbados, St Vincent and St Lucia. According to Stephen, fourteen of the committee of twenty-five were large slaveholders, six were peers pledged to oppose the government and two were prelates, who would be inactive. Howick, Stephen and Taylor almost despaired. How could a legislative colony be induced to adopt the policy of the revised order-in-council while a Lords committee was investigating conditions in the West Indies? The assemblies might even try to hold the government to its promise of fiscal relief, while pleading respect for the Lords as excuse for not adopting the order-in-council.[110]

Goderich, although pressed by Howick to go on forcing the order-in-council onto the legislative colonies, and by Stephen to preserve the discriminating qualities of the promised concessions, weakly decided to withdraw for the time being his formal request for adoption of the policy of the order-in-council. The 'boon' of differential sugar duties, he told Howick, was inadequate for its intended purpose, and he criticised the anti-slavery party for constantly hounding the government to declare its intentions before Parliament could be consulted.[111]

These anxious meditations were already obsolescent. The Reform Act had given Britain a House of Commons in which opinion against slavery was impatient and strong, and the West Indian interest had lost its power of obstruction. The Caribbean assemblies, besides reducing Goderich to despair, had thoroughly discredited themselves with informed opinion in England. Young Whigs like Howick and Althorp were as eager for abolition as for the Reform Act. Slavery, Francis Baring wrote to Wilmot-Horton, would now be dealt with for certain because 'the question had become too much agitated to stop'. The constitutional barriers against imperial legislation for colonies with their own representative institutions looked thin in the face of aroused British opinion.[112] Even Lord Grey, the Prime Minister, was impressed. Howick told him that it was time to challenge the assemblies' claim to exclusive competence to make laws for the internal affairs of the colonies, and to insist, as public opinion demanded, on using Parliamentary sovereignty to stamp out slavery.[113]

The Whigs rallied to popular reform. The Act 3 and 4 William IV, c. 73, emancipated the slaves from 1 August 1834, with compensation to their former owners. The assemblies were left to enact detailed legislation for a period of apprenticeship smoothing the transition from servitude to freedom. For the Crown colonies a comprehensive order-in-council was passed in 1834.[114]

Only after the assemblies had betrayed their own cause by obduracy and violence — that is, when it became clear that they had morally isolated themselves in Britain and that the slave colonies were becoming economic liabilities rather than assets — was even a Whig government, committed to reform and with a large majority in the Commons, willing to invoke the sovereignty of Parliament to emancipate the slaves. The legislative colonies' existing rights of self-government were respected so long as there was any prospect that a ministry that asked Parliament to intervene for the sake of the slaves might be turned out of office for its pains.

Looking back fifteen years later on the struggle with the colonies over slavery, T. F. Elliot, one of the clear-headed administrators of the period, was almost appalled by the systematic ruthlessness with which the Colonial Office, even under Bathurst, had set about forcing the West Indian assemblies to pass laws that they regarded as unjust and injurious to property. Still greater rigour had been practised on the Crown colonies. By its own 'distinguished vigor, perseverance and ability' concluded Elliot, the Office had earned the 'undying hatred of the white Inhabitants of the West India Colonies and of all connected with them in this country' and gone far towards obliterating the differences between legislative colonies and Crown colonies.[115]

CONSTITUTIONAL REFORM

The long struggle with the legislative and Crown colonies on the matter of amelioration often prompted Downing Street to consider constitutional change. In 1825, a year after the order-in-council for the new model slave code in Trinidad had been passed, Bathurst thought of gratifying the old, strong demands from colonists in Trinidad, St Lucia, the Cape and Mauritius for constitutional reform by introducing a form of government resembling that recently granted to New South Wales.[116] He would have given the colonies small, nominated legislative councils, to act under, rather than with, the governors. Supreme power, both in legislation and administration, would have remained in Britain, but the colonists would have helped make some of their own laws and the governors would have been in a stronger position politically than when served by mere advisory councils without responsibility. With an advisory council, the governor was the sole legislature. With a legislative council, ordinances were issued by the governor with the advice and consent of the council.[117] The Crown would have retained its general power to legislate for the colonies by order-in-council.

Bathurst stayed his laggard hand when the reports of legal commissioners inquiring into the judicial systems of the West Indian colonies began to arrive and showed a need for larger measures than he had contemplated. Although constitutional questions had not formally been within their terms of reference, the commissioners had not been able to disregard them.[118]

Wilmot-Horton, on seeing the first report, declared that change was needed urgently[119] and advised Bathurst how to introduce reforms into legislative colonies that habitually resented imperial interference.[120] The first and simplest method would be for Parliament to legislate; this he rejected on the familiar ground that in the eyes of colonists an Act of Parliament might not prevail over a colonial enactment repugnant to it. The second was for Parliament to pass an Act that the colonies would be empowered to adopt, on the model of Robinson's Trade Act of 1822. The third was to invite the colonies to legislate for themselves.

Wilmot-Horton was troubled by his own rejection of the first alternative and wanted Parliament to be asked to declare that it reserved an ultimate power, 'to be resorted to in the case of irremediable necessity', to legislate for any colony, when faced with 'contumacious resistance' or actions 'strictly incompatible with the interests of the Empire taken as a whole'. His strange mixture of law and expediency was consistent with Dundas's doctrine approved by the Commons in 1796,[121] but Bathurst declined to support a resolution so provocative and ambiguous and implying that the sovereignty of Parliament was limited.[122] James Stephen the younger also found great difficulties. If an imperial Act were passed, the colonists would deny that it repealed any of their own enactments that conflicted with it.[123]

Stephen's advice, accepted by Bathurst, was to follow the second of Wilmot-Horton's alternatives, to have Parliament pass an imperial Act and invite the colonies to copy it.[124] But Bathurst, as we have seen, proposed to insert a clause allowing slave evidence to be received in courts of law. Possibly no colony would have adopted the whole of his intended Act, but in April 1827, before the Bill could be drawn, the Liverpool ministry broke up.

During this period, however, one important reform was accomplished without reference to Parliament. The slavery question and improving standards of public administration at home led the Colonial Office to look closely at the internal administration of colonies, both legislative and Crown. Stephen and Taylor began to insist that the Crown had the right not only to advise and instruct governors, but also to control the administrations over which they presided. The new procedures involved no legal changes to colonial status. The colonies did, however, lose part of an important *de facto* liberty, the freedom to administer their own governments.

Otherwise Bathurst left the future of self-government in the Caribbean colonies in doubt. His reluctance to legislate for the old colonies had, as we have seen, been virtually overcome. He hoped to liberalise the constitutions of some Crown colonies, albeit only in cautious stages, so as to keep the executives strong enough to protect slaves, former slaves and other persons of colour. Generally, he was wary of general plans of constitutional reform, knowing that what was good in one country might be bad in another, and that British institutions might be actively dangerous in some of the colonies.[125] 'A sceptic with little faith in the possibility of improvement ... in men themselves or in the conditions in which they lived',[126] he was willing to press the colonies for reform when great pressures were exerted on Parliament or on ministers, but had no wish to see the Colonial Office actively control the whole empire. Changes that he did not approve and forces that he could not resist produced the rapid growth of the Colonial Office and its functions during the latter part of his long reign there.[127]

At the end of the Parliamentary session of 1830, Horace Twiss, Murray's under-secretary, set to work on the West India political reports. 'The fleshiest incubus' of the Parliamentary under-secretaries who 'laid the weight of their authority upon ... the Colonial Office',[128] as Taylor called him, convinced himself that the conquered colonies all needed new constitutions as well as improved judicial systems. Twiss was fascinated by the problems of Demerara, whose complicated institutions attracted his powers of legal analysis. Demerara had inherited from the Dutch a court of policy, which advised the governor on political and financial matters, made ordinances (subject to his prior sanction) and had general responsibility for law and order, but no power to tax. It consisted of the governor, three other official members and four elected members, elected every eight years by the College of Kiezers, who were chosen for life by the larger landowners. As the governor had a double vote, officials usually dominated the court of policy. There was also a combined court (or financial assembly), which decided how to raise revenue and examined accounts, but did not sanction expenditures and could not legislate, except to tax. It consisted of the court of policy and six colonists elected for two years as financial representatives by the freeholders of the colony. The elected majority in the combined court was less important than its numbers suggested, because official salaries and military charges were generally beyond the control of the court.[129]

In 1812 Major-General Carmichael, an acting governor sick with fever, decided to establish the supremacy of the English population in Demerara and assimilate the constitution to the British one, which he greatly admired. Unfortunately, he could recall British institutions only imperfectly, would not wait to be informed, and was acting contrary to orders. By proclamation he changed the electoral franchise to increase the power of the merchants, shopkeepers, and professional men in George Town, who were mostly English, at the expense of the planters, who were predominantly Dutch. His second change was to dissolve the College of Kiezers and replace it with a College of Kiezers and Financial Representatives, chosen by the new electorate and holding office for two years. The seven members of the new college were to replace the former financial representatives on the combined court. Carmichael formally allowed the combined court full recognition of the financial powers, including the appropriation of supplies, apparently because he wished it to be an analogue of the House of Commons. Bathurst neither approved nor disallowed these changes.[130]

The financial representatives embarrassed Carmichael's successor, Major-General John Murray, by claiming power to reduce government offices and receive petitions. The combined court assumed that its control over finance must be as absolute as that of the House of Commons. 'The Court of Policy . . . acted in practice on the view that, being an executive Council of Advice, it could advise upon all branches of government.'[131]

Complaints from Murray, who was governor for eleven years, and from his forthright successor, D'Urban, who became governor in 1824, led Bathurst, as we have seen, to decide to restore the original constitution. For the sake of amelioration he wanted a strong executive, to ensure that the court of policy and the combined court carried out British policy. He wanted to expunge everything that Carmichael had done.[132] Constitutions however, do not stand still. The colony had accustomed itself to the Carmichael reforms and D'Urban had allowed the court of policy to exceed its powers. Bathurst's simple solution was impossible. He left office with only two points clear, that Demerara needed constitutional reform and that the Crown had power to make reforms without reference to Parliament.[133]

In 1830 Twiss produced his own scheme for the government of Demerara, intended to be a model for the government of other colonies without elected assemblies. He proposed uniform constitutions for British Guiana (to be formed by uniting Demerara, Essequibo and Berbice), and Trinidad, St Lucia, Mauritius, the Cape Colony and Ceylon. Each colony was to have a legislative council, half its members nominated and half elected by a college of electors. The council was to consider measures recommended by the Crown, and to be prevented by a hedge of restrictions from becoming yet another irresponsible colonial legislature. The executive council was to consist of the governor and some officials.

Twiss's proposals are known only through the severe criticisms that Stephen made of them.[134] In law they were a good sketch for a model of Crown colony government, but Twiss had little knowledge of colonial societies or of government from a distance. He wrote a lawyer's exercise, not an essay in statesmanship. Stephen regarded the proposals as disturbing, incompatible with capitulations made at the conquests (a tendentious point, which on occasion he conveniently forgot) and impracticably ambitious. In rejecting Twiss's plan, he made suggestions of his own, adding, however, that uniform constitutions would never be possible in the British Empire:

> I would have in each a Legislative Body, in which a certain number of Officers dependant on the Crown should meet an equal number of Proprietors, who are exempt from any such Dependance. I would define in each Colony the limits of the Legislative Authority in the same terms, and in each I would prescribe certain forms of proceedings for the enactment of Laws. The rules should be the same throughout the whole range respecting the transmission of their Laws to England, and respecting the exercise of the Royal prerogative, and respecting the time and manner in which Colonial Enactments should take effect.

Stephen would have allowed 'blended' legislatures,[135] composed both of Crown nominees and elected members, to Trinidad, Demerara and Berbice, in all of which the colonists had sufficient experience of elected bodies to work them satisfactorily. But, after the experiences of Lower Canada, he was not prepared to try blended legislature in the former French colonies of St Lucia and Mauritius, 'where French minds would misunderstand and French fervour would pervert' the new privileges. The Cape Colony and Ceylon he also thought unready for such legislatures, unless their governors proposed reforms. Much, indeed, would have to be left to the governors, 'not perhaps men of very large capacity; their proximity to the scene is an advantage which in this case would more than compensate for every other incompetency'.

Stephen was not drawing up model constitutions: 'Had I the understanding of Jeremy Bentham himself, I should distrust my own judgment as to what is really practicable in such remote and anomalous societies.' He wanted constitutions that would foster the growth of liberal self-government and the social bases needed for it, while avoiding friction between legislatures and executives and leaving the Colonial Office full power to decide such questions as amelioration and abolition. Tranquillity and efficiency might proceed more surely from institutions to which men were accustomed than from lawyers' models of colonial government. Twiss's proposals for Demerara were eventually altered (how is not clear) to satisfy Stephen's view that they should conform where possible to the colony's traditional institutions and to the 'fundamentals of the capitulation'.[136]

While Murray was still Secretary of State, important decisions were taken regarding the constitutions of Trinidad and St Lucia (and Mauritius) as well. All were to have executive councils consisting of the governor and three officials. Only the governor could propose matters for discussion at a meeting; other members had to submit their proposals in writing. If the governor did not allow a matter to be discussed, the letter of request could be preserved in the minutes transmitted to the Secretary of State. The governor could disregard the advice of his executive council, in effect for as long as he pleased, by referring any matter to Britain for directions. Each colony was also to have a nominated legislative council, half of its members to be officials and half non-officials. All nominations were to be made by the Secretary of State, so relieving the governor of a hazardous occupation and strengthening the possible hold of the Colonial Office over the governor, whenever the Secretary of State had knowledge and will to select his own nominees. In the legislative councils only the governor could propose measures; and, except in emergency, no ordinance was to take effect until approved by the King in council. It would be difficult to think of a system that more reluctantly allowed the King's subjects so minor a share in making laws for their own government, or one in which so many precautions were taken to preserve the governor from his councils. Murray left office with the dispatches to Trinidad and St Lucia written, and the legal instruments for proceeding by order-in-council completed, but with nothing sent to the colonies.[137]

When Goderich and Howick entered the Colonial office, they found that the principal reason for delay had been Stephen's sensible insistence that orders-in-council ought not to be used to alter colonial constitutions. He wanted to follow established procedures and issue new commissions and instructions to the governors, so that the colonies would continue to derive their constitutions from the Crown, through him, on the authority of the Secretary of State. The Law Officers supported Stephen.[138]

Neither Goderich nor Howick had fixed opinions on colonial government (although Howick soon developed them). Both had the general Whig willingness for reforms, especially reforms relating to economy or enlarged participation in government. Both believed in representative institutions and in free public discussion of public policy. So long as slavery existed, however, the Whigs were as anxious as the Tories to retain a tight control over the Crown colonies. They had little difficulty in taking over the Tory programme for constitutional reform and accepted Stephen's advice on procedure. Their principal change in the plans was to increase the size of the councils in Trinidad and Mauritius, in order to broaden public involvement in colonial affairs and introduce the safeguards of good government that public discussion might provide.

The concessions that Murray and Goderich made to the Crown colonies were intended not only to gratify the demands of the colonists, so far as prudence allowed, but also to answer criticisms in England that government in the King's colonies violated the rights of Englishmen. Hume, who had said as much in the Commons in 1819 and 1823, returned to the problem on 16 August 1831. During the debates on the Reform Bill he proposed that all the colonies, including India, should be represented in the Commons by nineteen members.[139] The proposal was not taken seriously, although it had distinguished precedents, and arose from views of representation expressed in the debate.

In Demerara the Whigs followed Bathurst's policy of 1826, as revised by Stephen, to return as nearly as possible to the original constitution.[140] Some changes showed the scars of the amelioration controversy. A 'protector of the slaves' and one unofficial member were added to the court of policy, and all legislative ordinances had to be transmitted to London for confirmation by the Secretary of State. When Demerara, Essequibo and Berbice were united as British Guiana, the Demerara constitution became the constitution of the new colony, with appropriate enlargement of the court of policy. The court received some of the increased legislative powers that it had demanded, but, as before, only the governor could propose legislation and the right of the Crown to legislate by order-in-council was expressly reserved. The judicial system was reorganised by order-in-council of 23 April 1831, much as the commissioners had recommended.[141]

Qualified return to the old constitution brought no respite to problems of government in Demerara. The elected members of the court strove for independence of British control. They raked up old disputes of 1810 to 1812 to justify claims to examine estimates as well as to consider ways and means. In April and September 1832 they prevented the combined court from voting supply.[142] Goderich and Howick firmly resisted encroachments on imperial authority and zealously safeguarded the independence of the executive from every control except that of the Secretary of State. In 1832 Goderich reaffirmed the prerogative power of the Crown to rely on orders-in-council to legislate for the Crown colonies and to establish their forms of government. One dispatch threatened that Parliament would legislate to settle the affairs of British Guiana if the colonists failed to act as required of them.[143]

In March 1831 the new commission and instructions were sent to the governor of Trinidad.[144] The nominated legislative council (or 'council of government'),[145] half official and half unofficial, was to have twelve members instead of ten, as originally proposed. Its functions were those belonging 'to the business of passing Legislative Ordinances'. The executive council, composed of the governor, colonial secretary, attorney-general and colonial treasurer, was purely advisory. The arrangements made for Trinidad were intended as models for all Crown colonies. The same instruments were issued to the governor of St Lucia in 1832 and the system was extended to Mauritius the same year, to Ceylon in 1833, Malta in 1835, the Gambias and the Falkland Islands in 1843 and the Gold Coast in 1850.[146]

In every case the Secretary of State retained full power over both policy and administration. The legislative councils (their unofficial members all nominated by the Secretary of State) were not intended to be properly representative, but merely to ventilate colonial law-making with a light current of local interest and local knowledge. To Goderich and Howick the new system seemed a cautious prelude to a later grant of representative institutions; the councils could at least give the colonists political experience. Howick distrusted arbitrary government and thought it justifiable in Mauritius (or the Caribbean) only because of slavery.[147] Goderich, on 25 May 1831, wrote to the governor of Trinidad to explain why an elected assembly had not been granted to the island. He conceded as obvious that representative institutions were to be preferred to nominee institutions, wherever they could be granted with safety to the colony and Britain, but he could not find a case for giving Trinidad an elected legislature because 'a very large majority of the people are in a state of domestic slavery, and ... those persons who are of free condition are separated from each other by the indelible distinction of European or African birth or parentage'.[148] When a group of planters and merchants complained that Trinidad had taxation without representation and that revenue raised by local taxes was expended without popular control, he commented that 'Society in Trinidad is divided into castes as strongly marked as those of Hindustan, nor can any man who has but an ordinary knowledge of the history and general character of mankind, doubt what must be the effect of such distinctions when in addition to their other privileges, the superior race are entrusted with legislative authority over the inferior.'[149] To gain representative institutions, Trinidad would have to do away with slavery and show that distinction of race or colour were not perpetual political and social barriers that would prevent the successful operation of British forms of government. Other colonies receiving the Trinidad constitution were given the same advice.

THE PERILS OF REPRESENTATIVE GOVERNMENT

In the Colonial Office one strong voice objected from the first that representative institutions could not safely be allowed to Mauritius and the

Crown colonies in the Caribbean. Henry Taylor was sure that the white inhabitants should never have exclusive powers to make laws or control administration in colonies where slaves, former slaves or other free persons of colour were liable to be oppressed. 'Measures entirely favourable to the negroes in a Slave Colony can be successfully carried into effect only by means of a despotic government', he wrote, referring to Mauritius, but with a larger context in mind.[150] He strongly criticised the reforms already made in the Crown colonies when they produced great trouble in Mauritius. 'The real use of the New Council in the Crown colonies', he thought, 'consists in the check which it places upon the Governor's statements to the Secretary of State.'[151] Taylor was a man who united great talent with over-confident faith in his own judgement.[152] Howick told Goderich of Taylor's view that 'we have gone too far in attempting to combine a liberal policy as regards the Whites with a liberal policy as regards the Blacks, and . . . it is impossible in a slave colony to carry any effective measures for the improvement of the condition of the slaves otherwise than by arbitrary power . . . . I entirely agree in the last of these positions.' But, Howick added, if the government forced its policies on the colonists, Hume and others would charge ministers with oppression.[153]

Howick developed a totally unconvincing argument that Crown colony government could be liberalised with perfect safety to Britain and all classes of the colonists. He emphasised the dependence of the governor and colonial officials on the authorities at home. In every slave colony, he strangely added, a great majority of the population had 'interests diametrically opposed to those who are engaged in a struggle with the Government' and the masters could not 'proceed to extremities in their resistance to lawful authority, without teaching the slaves to do the same'.

If ever a would-be statesman stood self-convicted of ignorance, Howick did after writing these words on the slave colonies. When he went on to support enlarged public debate of public issues in such colonies he showed decent Whig faith in liberal institutions rather than shrewd appreciation of the difficulties of forcing amelioration and emancipation on reluctant planters. The strongest parts of his case for continuing to lead the Crown colonies to representative government were his insistence that the colonists had to gain political experience somehow, and his condemnation of a strange proposal from Taylor — that the colonists be disarmed in the slave colony of Mauritius.

Three months later Goderich assured Howick that policy was unchanged; the Crown colonies might be told that 'upon the extinction of Slavery . . . they should receive the boon of a more direct share in their internal Government, particularly as regards taxation and expenditure'.[154] Crown colonies were to be kept in line by being promised reforms rather than by being subjected to Taylor's iron measures.

In the early 1830s Goderich and Howick, while adopting a liberal policy towards the Crown colonies, tightened again the imperial powers of control in the legislative colonies. Howick in particular attempted, with Stephen's help, to increase direct control from Britain in the executive governments of the smaller colonies. In part they hoped to increase the independence of governors and high officers by giving them means and courage to oppose their assemblies.[155] The reforms were made by the Crown without reference to Parliament, except on salaries.[156]

Goderich and Howick saw nothing inconsistent about increasing the local independence of the colonial executives and, at the same time, calling on the colonial legislatures to follow British leadership. The executives were to be instructed, and the legislatures persuaded, to follow identical courses. That the new policies might be resented as attempts to reduce the powers that the legislatures had by convention acquired over the executives counted for little against the strong desire to abolish slavery and produce economy of administration; Howick, especially, had nothing but contempt for men who opposed either purpose.[157]

Taylor, although willing that the powers of the Secretary of State be increased in the legislative colonies, would have preferred more direct action against the assemblies: 'To effect by force from without the greatest of all social changes and yet to leave the political framework of this totally different society the same as it was, would seem, even in a more theoretical view, to be in the nature of a political solecism.'[158] He lacked the faith of Goderich, Howick and Stephen that the former slaves and other persons of colour would, through their numbers, eventually be on equal political terms with the dominant white minority. The liberal views of his superiors, strengthened in some cases by religious conviction, led them to think of every man as the best judge and protector of his own interests, and they were reluctant to admit that the structure of society might be a fatal obstacle to their liberal intentions. Taylor was too conscious of human depravity to expect anything but terrible dangers in the West Indies when slavery ended.

When Stanley succeeded Goderich in March 1833 and himself gave way to Spring-Rice in June 1834 there was no change in the comfortable Whig view that, after emancipation had been completed, all the West Indian colonies, Crown or legislative, could soon be left to govern themselves. Britain would not need to exercise great powers in the colonies, because colonial societies would have changed sufficiently for British institutions to be entrusted to them all and proper self-government introduced. A dead end to such thinking was reached relatively soon, and it was sharply interrupted during Peel's ministry, while Aberdeen was at the Colonial Office (December 1834 to April 1835). While it lasted there were straws in the wind to show how strongly the Whigs held their opinion. Stanley and Spring-Rice both took at face value complaints from Trinidad, that Goderich had 'pledged' representative institutions to the island.[159]

Stanley was willing for immediate minor reforms and considered whether some unofficial members of the legislative council might be elected instead of nominated; but in the end he decided to make no change until apprenticeship was over.[160] Spring-Rice was willing to inquire into the possibility of representative government when 'the relations between the different classes of society shall have acquired under the new social system maturity and strength'.[161] Stanley did his best to concede to the combined court in British Guiana, in return for a civil list, the powers of appropriation that it claimed. In so doing he admitted that Goderich's decision to the contrary had been correct in law, but suggested that the colony would have a better prospect of frugal, vigilant adminstration when more authority over financial matters had been transferred to a body with local knowledge.[162]

THE JAMAICA PROBLEM: RETROGRESSION OF COLONIAL SELF-GOVERNMENT

The imperial Emancipation Act interposed the authority of Parliament in the colonies in a spectacular way, but, as we have seen, it left the West Indian legislatures to provide for apprenticeship on the model of the order-in-council by which emancipation was effected in ·the Crown colonies.[163] In passing their own Acts, the colonial legislatures carefully refrained from appearing to rely on the Emancipation Act. Stephen, although severely critical of the colonial Acts, did not object to the way they had been made:

> The right of Parliament to make laws binding on British colonists (with the exception of Laws by which internal Taxes are imposed, or the produce of Duties, whether internal or external, appropriated) is distinctly established. But it is no less settled that every such interference with the internal Economy of the Colonies is a departure from a General Rule — an infringement of a settled habit of the Constitution — which rule or habit rests upon grounds of the utmost solidity and importance. Whatever may have been the practice, at a more remote period, it is clear that since the American contest, this
> . right of Parliamentary legislation for the Colonies, had been numbered amongst the latent resources of government, to which the Imperial Legislature would resort, only under the pressure of some extreme and indisputable exigency.[164]

The lay terms 'rule or habit' suggested that the limits to Parliamentary authority were expediency, not a new convention of the constitution.

In practice, Whig secretaries of state, for some years after emancipation, refrained on policy grounds from playing a dominant role in the affairs of the West Indies. Goderich, Howick, Stanley and Spring-Rice had all hoped to grant representative institutions to the Crown colonies in the West Indies after emancipation had removed the paramount reason for British intervention in their affairs.[165]

The Tory Aberdeen held the contrary opinion, just as he had over Lower Canada, and was supported by Taylor's pleas for Crown rule in the former slave colonies. Foreseeing great obstacles to allowing the negroes to enjoy political rights, Aberdeen believed that it would 'only be after a protracted series of years' that they would be able to participate in politics to their own advantage. In some colonies the choice would effectively be between 'an independent irresponsible Oligarchy ... and ... the Crown'.[166] He was already thinking of establishing Crown colony government in colonies that had legislatures, and not merely of delaying the grant of representative institutions to the Crown colonies.

The Whigs, from liberal views of what was owing to a representative assembly, unwillingness to go against the reforming spirit of their party, and an economic desire not to stir up trouble, preferred inaction to a firm choice between alternatives proposed by Aberdeen. Their only strong intervention in this period was to disallow, on Stephen's recommendation, two Jamaican Acts of 1834 and 1836, which had been designed to exclude the liberated negroes from the electoral franchise without declaring racial grounds for doing so.[167]

In 1836, after Stephen had become Permanent Under-Secretary and when the Colonial Office was being reconstructed, Glenelg and George Grey, the Parliamentary Under-Secretary, assumed that legislative colonies, whether in the West Indies or North America, would normally be allowed to manage the whole of their own domestic affairs. The Office would not settle their policies for them, although it would ensure justice and equity among the King's subjects, and deference to Parliament, the law, and the Secretary of State in matters that were imperial.[168]

The arrangements made in the Office were the more remarkable because Glenelg, George Grey and Stephen all knew that substantial Parliamentary intervention in the West Indian colonies was already contemplated. Stephen had always known, despite his hopes of liberal policies, that there were serious risks in trusting the legislative colonies with apprenticeship: he foresaw terrible dangers if the plantation economy ran down through lack of a disciplined labour force. Jamaica, he wrote to Howick in 1835, needed an 'army of Schoolmasters and Missionaries' with power to compel attention to their teaching, or 'the year 1840 will . . . find Jamaica a disorganised Horde of uncivilised Men, acquainted with just so much of the Arts and Manners of Europe as will be necessary to render their Vices and internal Contests more Destructive than they would otherwise have been.[169]

But Stephen could not bring himself to recommend strong measures. When Lord Sligo, the governor of Jamaica, reported that the assembly would 'assuredly never know how to establish or maintain a dominion in which the Whip is not the Direct Instrument', Stephen remarked that he was unable to make any recommendation consistent with the respect that he owed to a British legislature.[170] His superiors were less restrained. Glenelg informed Sligo that, if the assembly continued to 'render itself obnoxious both to the mass of the population and to the most respectable inhabitants', 'I am compelled to anticipate the early arrival of the period at which His Majesty must seek the support of Parliament against the Pretensions which the House of Assembly of Jamaica seems disposed to advance'.[171]

In 1836 the Commons took the unusual step of passing a Bill to prolong to 1840 (unless the Jamaica assembly had already done so) an Act that Jamaica had passed at the request of the Secretary of State, to amend the colony's own Abolition Act. Sligo was instructed to call the assembly together and invite it to pass a colonial Act to anticipate the imperial Act. The assembly immediately renewed its own enactment and condemned the British intervention as irregular, wanton and tyrannical: 'All laws for internal regulation should be propounded and framed in this House.'[172]

Meanwhile in Britain the government defended apprenticeship against strong attacks by the abolitionists. On 2 April 1838 Glenelg sent dispatches to all the West Indian governors pointing out that apprenticeship would have to end earlier than had originally been planned.[173] In the same month Parliament passed an Act to remove abuses in apprenticeship; the Act also repealed certain provisions relating to slaves in the Jamaica Police Act of 1837.[174] Political passions over colonies were then running high, partly because of apprenticeship, partly because of Molesworth's motion of censure charging Glenelg with having reduced the empire to frustration and rebellion.[175] In May the ministry was defeated (by ninety-six to ninety-three) on a snap vote in a thin House, when John Eardley Wilmot, a notable liberal with strong connections at Exeter Hall, moved for the entire abolition of apprenticeship on 1 August 1838.[176] The vote apparently asked for the impracticable and six days later George Grey with Peel's aid carried a resolution (250 votes to 178) that it was inexpedient to implement Wilmot's resolution at once.[177] Apprenticeship was however, abolished everywhere, by 1 August 1838, the West Indian legislatures having acted with extreme promptness on Glenelg's hint.

On 16 June 1838, when the new governor of Jamaica, Sir Lionel Smith, signed the colonial Act to end apprenticeship, the assembly resolved that:

Jamaica is dependent on the Crown of England, and she admits the rights of the English Parliament to regulate the commerce of the empire, but she rejects, with indignation, its claim to make other laws to govern her . . . this island has of right, confirmed by time, usage, and law, an independent legislature; ... by its authority alone can taxes or other burdens be imposed on the people of Jamaica, repealed, or altered, or new laws be enacted.[178]

According to the assembly, British colonial policy already lay in ruins; Parliament was inefficient, overworked, possibly corrupt and certainly so ignorant of the empire as to be at the mercy of any Secretary of State willing to mislead it. How long would colonies remain within an empire so grievously misruled? 'We dread a system of government which has, notwithstanding so many efforts, failed to pacify Ireland, has just caused a rebellion in the Canadas by its capricious policy, and scarcely escaped a war with the United States.' Natural law aside, the protests of the Jamaica assembly in 1838 were very much like those of Massachusetts or Virginia on the eve of the American Revolution. They were also well designed to embarrass the Whigs and, if necessary, hamstring them by detaching their Radical allies.[179]

The assembly had expected that, with the ending of apprenticeship, British interference in Jamaican affairs would cease. Disillusion came in October. Three months before, Parliament had hurriedly enacted a measure to control prisons in the West Indies, for prison conditions and treatment of the negroes were closely related.[180] The new Act empowered the Privy Council or the governor in council to regulate prisons and workhouses in a colony without reference to its legislature. Governor Smith was appalled by the assembly's 'violent resentment' of the new measure. The hopes of Howick and others, that the assemblies might become more reasonable as free coloured men gained political rights, were dashed when Smith pointed to the powers of bribery and influence: 'All the coloured members of the House, with the exception of two, have gone over to the enemy.'[181]

The assembly had protested that the Prisons Act violated its 'inherent rights', and declined to transact any business. Smith prorogued, then dissolved, it for contumacy. The elections returned most of the old members. On 4 December Smith prorogued the new assembly till 5 February 1839 and tried to stir the unwilling Whigs to intervene in Jamaica for the sake of law, order, good government and the welfare of the negroes.[182] He suggested that Jamaica should be governed by orders-in-council, because, 'If the Assembly is left alone as it hopes, the bulk of the people will be again placed in slavery.' To Glenelg and his advisers the problems of Jamaica were merely the most critical of the many difficulties in West Indian colonies in the aftermath of slavery.[183] On 19 January 1839 Taylor drew up a minute, in which he challenged sharply both British and West Indian ideas on the government of the Caribbean part of the empire, for Glenelg to present to the Cabinet.[184] Could any West

Indian assembly be trusted to legislate fairly in respect of the emancipated slaves, or, indeed, to legislate responsibly at all? Alternatively, there was the danger that the ascendancy of the planters might be replaced by an even worse ascendancy of newly liberated, politically inexperienced and socially disaffected blacks.[185]

Taylor proposed that all the West Indian assemblies be abolished. Following abolition, either a legislative commission should visit the West Indian colonies to make whatever laws might be needed or, preferably, Parliament should turn the legislative colonies into Crown colonies. Taylor wanted to strip every West Indian colony of its claims to autonomy and to transfer every significant power of initiative and control to London.[186]

Glenelg, advised by Stephen, who favoured suspension of the Jamaican constitution, and by George Grey, who combined optimism with caution, feared another debacle like those that had just occurred in the Canadas, and balked at the Draconian measures advocated by his masterful subordinate.[187] Glenelg presented Taylor's memorandum to the Cabinet most ineffectively.[188] Too intelligent to deny that there was a case for decisive action, Glenelg continued too irresolute to argue for it decisively. He suggested a compromise: to suspend the constitution of Jamaica only. Under his embarrassed guidance, the Cabinet, already split over Canada, had the greatest difficulty in coming to grips with the problem: 'Glenelg', thought Howick, 'made a most wretched statement and proposed a most paltry measure.'[189] Howick himself, on good terms with Taylor and always attracted by resolution and strength, wrote a powerful paper for the Cabinet and told Melbourne and Russell that he would resign if some strong policy were not adopted. The Cabinet, however, rejected his complicated, triple proposal: to suspend all the West Indian assemblies for two years, to provide emergency means of legislation, and to establish municipal institutions as 'the best means of training the ignorant negroes so as to fit them by degrees for taking an active share in the government'. Glenelg's less extensive measure was adopted and Howick again threatened to resign.[190]

The Cabinet was so far from satisfied with Glenelg that Melbourne, who may himself have leaned towards Taylor's policy on Jamaica, at last decided to compel Glenelg to go.[191] In the West Indies Glenelg had merely shelved the problems of providing stable, effective government in colonies where emancipation and the falling price of sugar had transformed the social basis of politics.[192] His successor, the Marquis of Normanby, had, as Earl Mulgrave, governed Jamaica from 1832 to 1834. Taylor arrogantly wrote him off as 'a man of some little talent with a weak mind', for ever doing what was wrong and popular, rather than what was unpopular and right;[193] but Normanby had had notable successes as Lord-Lieutenant in Ireland, was close to Russell and was believed to be conciliatory.

In April and May the government tried to persuade the Commons to suspend the constitution of Jamaica for five years.[194] Members had to consider whether the recent Prisons Act had been necessary and whether it transgressed any limits imposed by convention to the exercise of Parliamentary sovereignty throughout the empire. They had also to consider whether Parliament had power to suspend the constitution of Jamaica, and whether to do so would be an act of wisdom, essential to justice among the King's subjects, or merely, as some Tories thought, a precipitate blow struck at colonial liberties by a weak and exasperated ministry.

The prolonged debates over Jamaica were full of the factious spirit of those impatient Tories (not including Peel),[195] whose real object was to thrust the Whigs from office. The irresponsibility with which the Tories had harassed Durham, and the irresolution of the Whigs in failing to support him were close to the Jamaica debates, in spirit and in time. Both parties insisted that Parliament was supreme throughout the empire, and agreed that strong measures were needed in Jamaica; but neither understood how greatly the old order had already changed in the colony, nor wished to force the self-governing colonies into the straitjacket of the Crown colony system. The Whigs, declaring their sense of responsibility to the former slaves, wanted immediate action against the assembly; the Tories and the Radicals deplored their impatience and wanted the assembly to have a second chance before Parliament intervened.[196]

Peel steered a course between defending the right of Parliament to intervene in Jamaica as in any other colony, and condemning ministers for having proposed 'a complete despotism'. The power to legislate for a self-governing colony was 'an arcanum of empire, which . . . exists, but . . . should be veiled. It should not be produced on trifling occasions, or in cases of petty refractoriness, or temporary misconduct. It should be brought forward only in the utmost extremity of the state; where other remedies have failed, to stay the raging of some moral or political pestilence.' Peel did not compare the representative system, established in Jamaica (and recently suspended in Lower Canada), with Crown colony government as it existed in some other West Indian colonies and might come to exist in Jamaica. But he did warn that the government's measure flouted the principle of no taxation without representation, and added that the effects of punitive action against Jamaica would not 'be stifled by the limits of the island'.

The Tories rallied firmly, although inconsistently with their views on Lower Canada, to defend colonial autonomy in Jamaica. The way was prepared for them by William Burge QC, former attorney-general of Jamaica, who had been a member of Parliament and became the colony's agent in London. Appearing at the bar of the House to speak against the Bill, he called on history and law to declare Jamaica's rights of self-government within the empire.[197] His case was essentially that of the Americans, who had contested the sovereignty of Parliament on grounds other than natural law. It had already been used by Jamaica in 1815 to argue that the Slave Registration Bill proposed by Wilberforce was unconstitutional interference with 'mere municipal regulation and internal peace'.[198]

Was there not, asked Burge, an important 'line . . . drawn between the supreme superintending power of the Imperial Government and the right of internal legislation which is left in the possession of the colony'? British subjects in a British colony were entitled to representative government, because they had no representation at Westminister. A Parliament in which they were not represented could not make laws for them, still less suspend the constitution that Charles II had confirmed in 1661. His contention was bad law: what Charles II had granted Parliament could certainly take away; and it was strange history to argue, as Burge did, that Charles II's proclamation, on which Jamaican self-government was formally founded, was no more than a guarantee of rights and privileges already existing at that time, and not in any sense an 'original grant to the people of Jamaica'.

Burge imputed haste and tyranny to the Colonial Office and folly or worse to Governor Smith. He compared the political problems of Lower Canada with those of Jamaica. The Constitutional Act of 1791 had given slighter powers of self-government to Lower Canada than Jamaica had enjoyed since 1661, but Lower Canada — which had refused supply, demanded 'an organic change' of its constitution and rebelled — had been punished no more severely than Jamaica would be if its constitution were suspended. This was a skilful appeal to opinion outside the House, which was rallying to the assembly rather than the slaves and eventually settled in favour of colonial liberties rather than humanitarianism.

The great question answered by Burge, independently of the contested facts in the case, was whether Parliament had power to interfere in the domestic affairs of Jamaica and revoke its constitution. Burge denied that the power existed, but, for greater security, argued also that there were many precedents against invoking the power (if it did exist) in any but the most grave and urgent cause. The Tories, in their desire to attack the government, relied on much of Burge's case, however ill it matched their general positions on the rights of Crown and Parliament in the colonies. An earlier Tory view had been to deprecate discussing such matters at all.

Government speakers asked how, without suspending the constitution of Jamaica, Britain could preserve her supremacy in face of the defiance offered by the assembly. Supremacy that was not asserted would certainly be lost. Without British intervention the humanitarian policies that had produced emancipation would be frustrated. Reform, in this case illiberal reform, was needed to preserve the great achievement of 1833. Political opinion was, on balance, willing to deny self-government to colonies where a white minority might oppress a coloured majority, but not willing that an actively oppressive white minority should be deprived of rights of self-government that had long been possessed and that the Reform Act somehow made appear indefeasible.

Charles Buller, who had been in Canada with Durham, unexpectedly favoured suspension, although complaining that ministers had not disclosed proper grounds for suspending the constitution. His first principle was sound doctrine in all parties, that colonial self-government should normally be treated as sacrosanct. But Britain had a paramount obligation to the former slaves. The oppressive oligarchy that ruled in Jamaica had to be replaced for the sake of the negroes, who were not yet ready to exercise their new political rights. Neither the white minority nor the black majority could be trusted to rule Jamaica; therefore, the constitution had to be suspended to ensure equity among the subjects of the Queen.

Expecting a division on party lines, Russell remained unreasonably confident to the end; according to Greville[199] the government expected a majority of twenty in favour of the Bill. But at about two o'clock on the morning of 7 May, on the motion that the Speaker leave the chair, the government's majority was only five; ten of its supporters crossed the floor, five Tories voted with the government, ten Radicals stayed away, and another ten went over to the Tories. Possibly the Radicals were more interested in constitutional liberty for Jamaican whites than in the emancipation of the slaves; this is not certain.[200] The majority was too small for a government that was steeling itself to introduce controversial measures on the Canadas as well as on Jamaica, and Melbourne resigned.[201]

The Whigs returned to power after the Bedchamber Crisis[202] and introduced a modified measure on Jamaica. Labouchere, the Parliamentary Under-Secretary, then complained that the political tactics of the Tories were so notorious that the colonists resented being made the sport of party politics in Britain. Nothing other than party politics, he said, had forced the ministry to abandon the proposed suspension of the Jamaican constitution. Although that policy was still best, the government now proposed that the Jamaican assembly be called together and invited to reconsider the decision not to transact any business. If the assembly remained contumacious, the governor in council would be empowered to make laws for the well-being of the former slaves, on the model of the orders that had been sent from London to the Crown colonies. Labouchere stated, fairly enough, that the new policy restricted to a minimum the intervention of Parliament in the domestic affairs of Jamaica.[203]

In proceeding with 'the inferior Jamaica measure'[204] the government hoped to disarm the Opposition, for its proposals resembled those that Peel himself had advocated a few weeks earlier. Had Labouchere not taunted the Opposition with playing politics at the expense of the empire, and had the Tories not been enraged by the Whigs' return to power, the second Jamaica measure might have passed the Commons easily. Instead, time was spent acrimoniously in going over again the merits of the original Prisons Bill and the limits of Parliamentary intervention in self-governing colonies. No one considered whether all the legislative colonies in the West Indies ought to be under Crown colony government.

The case for modifying the original measure was not nearly so much a matter of political animosities as Labouchere implied. At any time after the American Revolution the suspension of a colonial constitution was an unusual and drastic step. Even in Australia Whig policy on Jamaica seemed illiberal.[205] Lower Canada had virtually suspended its own constitution. Would the cautious Whigs have proceeded so drastically against Jamaica, as trustees of the former slaves and in order to protect imperial supremacy, if they had not so recently punished Lower Canada? The step finally taken by the Melbourne government, of allowing the assembly a chance to repent, was closer to normal Whig benevolence than was the sharp discipline that Taylor had recommended, Howick (and perhaps Melbourne) had partly supported and the Cabinet had agreed to administer in a weakened form. Conciliation of a troubled self-governing colony was nearer to Whig maxims of conservative reform than coercion for the sake of oppressed negroes could ever be. Trusteeship was important, but so were established rights of self-government.

Suspension of the constitution had not been proposed without some attempt to placate Jamaica. Although Normanby had supported suspensions, he had always attributed part of the colony's problems to the officious zeal and tactlessness of Governor Smith. The dispatch that informed Smith of the proposal to suspend the constitution also warned him that he would soon be recalled, because his vigour had identified him so firmly with one party in the colony.[206] 'He was a warm friend of the negro, and heartily sympathised with the missionaries', wrote one observer, 'but he had not sufficient generosity to foregive the planters for the hard things they had said about him.'[207] His successor was intended to be Sir Richard Bourke, who had been a wise and temperate governor of New South Wales.[208] When Bourke declined, the post was given to Sir Charles Metcalfe, an adroit administrator with extensive experience in India. Metcalfe restored a measure of official harmony in Jamaica and warned the Secretary of State against any further drastic measures.[209] Matters were left to drag on in Jamaica with institutions unsuited to the new conditions and without decisive action to forfend the constitutional crises that quickly succeeded one another in the late forties, fifties and sixties, until the old representative system was abandoned in 1866.[210]

Political and official opinion in 1839—40 had favoured the continuance of colonial self-government unless gross and immediate evils, clearly apprehended by public opinion in Britain, could be removed by no other authority. In 1839, as George Grey recalled a decade later, the people rallied to the popular assembly, not to the British government and the slaves.[211]

5 Anomalous Societies: Newfoundland and New South Wales

Everyone will admit the broad doctrine that colonies should, as far as possible, be self-governed.

James Stephen[1]

The composition of society in New South Wales is such as to be constantly replete with the danger of insubordination and tumultuous resistance to the law.

Colonial Office Memorandum of 1836[2]

Crown colony government developed in the conquered colonies because British ministers would not establish representative institutions that would work only tumultuously or fall into the hands of oppressive minorities. An elected assembly in Trinidad, for example, would not have functioned peacefully if it had represented all men of property and would have been an unpopular and possibly tyrannical body if it had represented only English or European settlers.

In some of the colonies where political groups had claims, based on property, education and loyalty to the throne, to representative institutions, and these could not be granted to them, a new sort of legislature evolved. This was the 'blended' or 'mixed' council, a single legislative chamber containing both the nominees of the Crown and the elected representatives of the people. In blended councils the dangers of representative government by an unpopular minority, or by men of doubtful goodwill, could be checked by bringing elected members, in any desired proportion, into direct contact with Crown officials and nominees. Further, there was no need with these councils to labour futilely to establish upper houses where the materials to fill them did not exist. The blended council would contain its own monarchical, or aristocratic, element, more likely to be an effective counterpart of the Lords than any specially devised upper house would ever be. Later, when some colonies with blended councils became ready for the change, the transition to normal bicameral institutions proved to be particularly easy, because nominated and elected elements already existed.

In addition, the blended council promised a simple remedy to conflicts between elected assemblies and nominated councils, which had plagued the old representative system and poisoned the politics of the Canadas. In a blended council the principal members of the executive met for legislative purposes in the same chamber as the elected representatives of the people, and met separately (with other officials) only as an executive council. At the least, some of the perils stemming from the legislature's ignorance of the executive's intentions, and *vice versa*, might be avoided; at the best, the special knowledge of executive members might be harmonised with the political feelings of the electorate. Government would not be 'responsible', but it would be informed and, perhaps, responsive.

The original advocate of the blended council in the nineteenth century was James Stephen,[3] who intended it first for Newfoundland, but saw it applied there and in New South Wales only after he had concluded that the principle was specious and unsuited to British colonies. Stephen did not invent blended councils. They had existed in Demerara and other colonies inherited from the Dutch. They had existed also, at least in practice, in the American colonies of the seventeenth century. In Virginia there were joint sessions of governor, council and representatives until 1666, in Maryland to 1650 (with a brief revival in 1660), in Rhode Island to 1696 and in Connecticut to 1698.[4] Stephen (and Twiss), as we have seen, had planned to apply the principle to some colonies fit to advance beyond the most illiberal forms of Crown colony government but not to be trusted with either the old representative system or the Canadian model of 1791.

NEWFOUNDLAND

The constitutional history of Newfoundland, where Stephen wished to establish a blended council, had been full of obscurity of principle and tyranny of execution. Originally Britain had encouraged fisheries in the island but discouraged settlement, so that the fisheries might produce as many seamen as possible. Primitive arrangements for law and order were enforced by the fishing 'admirals' — that is, for every harbour, the first captains to arrive each year.[5] Official discouragement failed to prevent settlement, and in 1729 judicial and administrative institutions that were slightly less crude, but still fragmentary, were provided. A naval officer was to serve as governor, aided by resident justices of the peace, one of whom would deputise for the governor while the latter was at sea. No powers of legislation were granted and conflicts of jurisdiction between the fishing 'admirals' and the justices of the peace were not resolved. Settlement though much dispersed, continued to grow, and by the middle of the eighteenth century 'a true colony had grown up'.[6] A court of superior civil jurisdiction was established in 1791, but the island was still not granted legislative power. The first resident governor, appointed in 1817, issued proclamations as his predecessors had done. When a good, but somewhat rigid lawyer, Francis Forbes, became chief justice (later succeeding to the equivalent post in New South Wales), the sham legislative edifice of the island crumbled. In *Jennings and Long v. Beard* (1821) Forbes decided that governors had never possessed any legislative power and that all proclamations were therefore invalid. Bathurst then conceded that the colony needed a constitution.[7]

Forbes advised Bathurst that the island was unfit for representative government. The permanent population was small; communications among the scattered settlements were bad; and there were fierce internal dissensions between Protestants and Roman Catholics, and between merchants and fishermen. Bathurst accepted Forbes's advice rather than transfer power to a possibly oppressive minority, who would abuse British forms of government to promote their own interests.

When, in the Commons on 25 March 1823, Wilmot-Horton sought leave to introduce a Newfoundland Law Bill, to deal with fisheries, judicature and local legislative powers, a few liberally minded members had a field day. Lushington charged that no colony had ever been so neglected as Newfoundland. Hume, refusing to legislate 'in the dark', asked for a committee to report on the island's needs.[8] Leave was given, however, to bring in the Bill. Two months later Hume again asked for a committee on Newfoundland and strongly supported the small number of educated colonists, mostly wealthy Protestant merchants, who wanted a representative legislature.[9] But the government again got its way and he was defeated (by forty-two votes to twenty-seven) in a thin House.

Three Acts of 1824 made Newfoundland a colony rather than an outpost, but left it without self-government.[10] Two years later a young naval officer, Sir Thomas Cochrane, was made governor, with a commission establishing an illiberal form of Crown colony government. Newfoundland was given a nominated advisory council, composed of the governor and principal officials, meeting when convened by him to consider business that he set before it, and with power to assist him in making ordinances on certain local matters.

Cochrane, energetic and provocative, exasperated both the colonists and his superiors and failed to understand island politics. Opinions in Newfoundland on constitutional reform were as savagely discordant as on most other subjects. Cochrane erred badly when he underestimated the strength of the educated, Protestant group's desire for the old representative system as it existed in Nova Scotia and New Brunswick.

James Stephen had never wished Newfoundland to have the illiberal form of Crown colony government bestowed on it in 1826. Knowing how much the island had suffered from arbitrary rule, he had proposed a blended legislative council.[11] His superiors had declined such an experiment in a colony where legislative institutions of any kind would be a novelty and the population was so divided as to make the peaceable transfer of power to men of property and education impossible.

Considering the problem again in 1831, Stephen reviewed the working of representative institutions in British colonies generally.[12] Where populations were homogenous, as in Upper Canada, New Brunswick and Nova Scotia, elected assemblies were of 'inestimable benefit', but where the population was 'divided into castes as in the West Indies, or composed of different nations as in the Cape of Good Hope and Lower Canada' a representative assembly was not likely to work well. In either sort of colony, a nominated legislative council would probably embarrass Britain. Nominated upper houses had nothing good in common with the Lords, could not protect governors from clashes with the people's elected representatives and were often discreditably preoccupied with assertions of privilege and rank.

Stephen wanted Newfoundland to have an elected assembly, which would immediately convert itself into a blended legislature. The governor was to be empowered to convene an assembly and then propose, on a plan that the Crown would bind itself to approve, that it pass a Bill to allow a certain number of government officers to sit with it. The council would be dissolved for ever as soon as it had agreed to the assembly's Bill incorporating some council members into the elected house. Stephen did not propose that Parliament establish the blended council, because attacks on the innovation might precipitate awkward discussions of colonial policy. He also feared, remembering the disappointment of 1826, that the plan for a blended assembly would somehow be reduced to one for a council composed only of official members and other nominees. He intended a fairly liberal constitution, not some new form of legislation by a governor with the advice of an enlarged council. An essential part of his plan was to require the assembly to vote a civil list for the salaries of the governor and the judges, in return for which the Crown would surrender its revenues to appropriation by the assembly.

Goderich hesitated. Demerara had so many problems of government that he did not favour a scheme partly suggested by its constitution. Moreover, as he wrote to Howick, 'there may be some difficulty in the way of *two* houses; but I had rather stick to precedent unless it were really impracticable'.[13] By July 1832 experience of the legislative colonies of the West Indies and the Canadas had undermined Goderich's faith in bicameral legislatures and he agreed to a blended council for Newfoundland, although still fearing its implications for more important dependencies and for Britain itself. Howick privately informed the governor that the Colonial Office had had too much trouble with conflicts between councils and assemblies to wish to try the old representative system again.[14] The Newfoundland Act of 1832 (2 and 3 William IV, c. 78) assumed the establishment of a representative legislature under the prerogative and conferred certain constituent powers. To relieve any fear that the new blended assembly might be dominated by official members with knowledge and abilities superior to those of elected members, Goderich ordered that only three officials and no nominees be incorporated in it. This was not part of Stephen's plan; he had thought that the nominees in blended councils should include non-official as well as official members.[15]

Cochrane lacked the political skill to reconcile the colonists to their new constitution. The assembly indignantly rejected the proposal that it should absorb part of the council as not 'in accordance with the principles of the British Constitution'.[16] His explanations left the conservatives firmly convinced that they would suffer under an elected, democratic assembly without the safeguard of an upper house. Their opponents, on the other hand, concluded that the blended house was a clever device to prevent liberal reform.[17] All parties suspected the Colonial Office of trying to maintain autocracy in the island and few trusted Cochrane.

Goderich wanted no contest with Newfoundland over its form of government and soon abandoned Stephen's plan. Orders were sent to the governor to summon a new council of six (later nine) members, to have legislative powers as an upper house concurrent with those of the assembly of fifteen members. The council was to be on the model of the old representative system, with both legislative and executive powers.

From 1832 to 1841 Newfoundland had an increasingly unsatisfactory assembly and an almost equally unsatisfactory council. The political life of the colony was shaken by tremendous antagonisms — especially that between the assembly (predominantly Roman Catholic and including poor people like domestic servants, small farmers and fishermen) and the council (predominantly Protestant, mercantile and composed of men of education, property and standing). In April 1839 Aberdeen presented in the Lords a petition from Newfoundland conservatives, praying for 'the abolition of the colonial legislature'. Normanby, as Secretary of State, Durham, Ripon (formerly Goderich) and Brougham convinced themselves of little except that the truth was obscure. Durham asked for a parliamentary inquiry. Troubles continued. While Normanby was Secretary of State, the Protestants feared that he would be 'pro-Catholic', as he had been in Ireland. Elections were disgraced by bloodshed and arson and in 1840 by riots so violent that Stephen wished the right to vote to be withdrawn from the 'herds of wild people' in Newfoundland. In March 1841 the Tories persuaded the Commons to appoint a committee of inquiry.[18] The constitution was virtually suspended for nearly two years, during which no assembly was elected.

Sir John Harvey, governor from 1841, advised that the council be divided (as in the Canadas) into separate legislative and executive councils; that the executive council contain three officials and three members from each legislative house, to be nominated by the governor; and that the franchise and electoral laws be reformed. Stanley decided the fate of Newfoundland with little regard for Harvey's advice. There had to be an end, he wrote, to the 'fancied analogy to the Imperial Parliament', which had inspired bicameralism in colonies quite unsuited to so elaborate an institution. Newfoundland should have the blended constitution that Stephen had thought of in 1826 and recommended in vain in 1831, and which Stanley was about to introduce into New South Wales. Harvey agreed doubtingly. Some time elapsed before he recognised that Newfoundland could not provide sufficient men of quality for a bicameral legislature. He stipulated that the executive council should be distinct from the blended council, as Stephen's proposal required, and that three members of the blended legislature — to be chosen by himself and to include, perhaps, the speaker — should sit on the executive council. This was not part of Stephen's plan.[19]

Parliament, professedly as a temporary measure and against the opposition of Charles Buller, the Irish and the Radicals,[20] passed an Act (5 and 6 Vict., c. 120) to raise the minimum property qualifications of voters in Newfoundland, to give the Crown power to establish there an executive council distinct from the legislative council, and to amalgamate the legislative council with the assembly. In the single blended assembly so formed, the nominees of the Crown were not to exceed two-fifths of the total membership. Parliament also reserved to the governor the exclusive right to initiate money votes. In this way Stephen's cure for clashes between irreconcilable councils and umbrageous assemblies in anomalous societies unsuited to normal institutions of representative government became part of British policy in North America. O'Connell compared the Newfoundland Bill with the suspension of the constitution of Jamaica in 1839. Certainly, in Newfoundland the reform was retrogressive, although in New South Wales, where a blended legislative council was created by another Act of Parliament in the same session, it was accepted as a step towards representative self-government.

Ironically, Stephen in 1842 no longer believed in blended legislatures and was displeased by the adoption of the policy that he had formerly advocated. He disclaimed any responsibility for Goderich's earlier attempt to set up a blended legislature in Newfoundland and strongly defended the old representative system as preferable to it:

... a single Chamber, composed partly of elected and partly of nominated members, must turn out to be nothing more nor less than a pure Democracy. The nominated members will either form a distinct party and consolidate the opposite party, and be overpowered by them — or they will shrink from so invidious a position, and rescue their independence from suspicion by an exaggerated and extravagant exhibition of it. In either case, the Governor will be left to contend with the Assembly single-handed.

He distinguished the case of Guiana (Demerara), on which he had founded his proposal in 1831, pointing out that the court of policy was not an assembly, that the governor belonged to it and that it was checked by the College of Keizers and Financial Representatives. Further, the Crown retained power to legislate in Guiana by order-in-council, which was not to be the case in Newfoundland or New South Wales.[21]

Stanley lacked patience with such subtleties. Newfoundland was an anomalous society, too divided and too backward to be able to work the old representative system. It was no better fitted for the normal institutions of colonial self-government than was the equally anomalous society of New South Wales. A blended legislature, however, might keep colonial disputes away from the Colonial Office, strengthen the governor, and give some representation without risk of either unrestrained democracy or offensive minority rule. The system lasted only six years.

THE PENAL COLONY OF NEW SOUTH WALES

In New South Wales a blended legislative council was established by Parliament only after part of the anomalous social structure that made it seem necessary had begun to disappear, and long after a local, spontaneous movement for it had emerged. In Sydney, as in London, men of political experience thought that the special constitutional problems of a penal colony moving towards representative government could best be solved by permitting the elected members of the legislature to sit in the same chamber as Crown nominees and officials. The great variety of schemes considered for New South Wales in the 1830s showed a continuing preference for some form of blended legislature, and revealed some notable consistency in British thinking on the problems of transfer of power to rival colonial factions, neither of them likely to rule in the interests of the colony as a whole.

Like Newfoundland, New South Wales had unsatisfactory constitutional beginnings.[22] When, in 1786, Britain decided to plant a penal colony on the east coast of Australia, it entered on an unprecedented imperial enterprise. An ordinary colony of settlement could, like Georgia half a century before, have been founded by the Crown. But New South Wales was not to be such a settled colony, at least in the first instance. The founders were to be prisoners of the Crown, plus military forces and officials, all of them subordinate to a governor with almost absolute powers; and the colony was to be within the monopoly area of the East

India Company. The old legal fiction that a colony planted among the 'infidel' was necessarily a colony of conquest and therefore subject to the absolute powers of the Crown would have been useful in founding New South Wales, but was too long dead to be revived.

New South Wales was to be a penal settlement, founded in a territory of over a million square miles, its governor having jurisdiction also over the 'adjacent' islands of the South Pacific. The acquisition of so vast a territory reflected lively awareness of the nexus of strategy, possessions and trade, rather than specific objectives (other than the founding of a penal colony). That trade would come to the new colony was obvious, both for geographical reasons and because economic development was needed to make it self-supporting. Convicts whose sentences had expired were likely to stay in the colony until they died, for most would lack the means of returning home. Officers and soldiers might also settle there; free immigrants might be needed or might choose to go to New South Wales. In one way and another a free population would grow, and complicate the discipline of the penal settlement.[23]

The convict part of the new project was given impeccable legal foundations with two Acts of Parliament, one authorising the Crown to designate, by order-in-council, places overseas to which convicted criminals might be transported, the other empowering the governor to set up a criminal court without trial by jury.[24] A court of civil justice was established by the Crown without statutory authority. Many doubts of its legitimacy were expressed, although Stephen, as counsel to the Colonial Office, confidently advised that the Crown had prerogative power to establish colonial courts administering English law, so far as applicable to the colony, provided that the courts were modelled, as nearly as conditions permitted, on those at Westminster.[25]

The first governor, Captain Arthur Phillip RN, received two commissions.[26] The earlier, dated 12 October 1786, was a commission to a military governor of a fortress or garrison. The second, issued on 2 April 1787, was in the traditional form, giving Phillip powers appropriate to a settled colony, except that no advisory or legislative institutions were established. The bizarre settlement planted in New South Wales on 26 January 1788 endured thirty-five years of autocratic rule by governors with little knowledge of law and generally without competent legal advice. Growing numbers of free immigrants and of emancipated convicts protested at their lack of the most prized political rights of Englishmen. A supreme court was established in 1815, as was a governor's court with power to try minor cases, but civil juries were not permitted and the court of criminal judicature was not changed.[27]

More fundamental, though less angry, difficulties appeared when the governor's powers as sole legislative authority for the colony were challenged. All the early governors had had to issue orders and proclamations and compel obedience. Jeremy Bentham, in *A Plea for the Constitution* (1803), objected, and was soon followed by irate free settlers, the Solicitor-General in England, and men who had had judicial office in the colony.[28] The House of Commons Select Committee on Transportation, appointed in 1810, recommended that the colony be given an advisory council on the Indian model (as already suggested by the Solicitor-General, Sir Thomas Plumer).[29] Bathurst rejected the proposals, assuring Governor Macquarie in 1812 that he would never sanction changes that might disturb the discipline of the penal colony.[30] His answer in 1815 to Ellis Bent, a New South Wales judge, who doubted the legality of the governor's orders, was memorable: 'The power of the Governor to issue Government and General Orders, in the absence of all other Authority and the Necessity of obeying them, rests now on the same foundation on which it has ever stood since the first foundation of the Colony'.[31]

Nothing could have been clearer, but in 1819, when public attention was turning to the 'illegal despotism' in New South Wales, Bathurst consulted the Law Officers on the validity of the colony's 'legislation'. Their answer was disturbing. The Crown did not have — or, at least, no longer had — any power to raise taxes or customs duties in a settled colony except through a representative assembly, or Parliament. Bathurst thereupon procured an Act of Indemnity, which was renewed in 1820 and 1821 and made perpetual in 1823. Later, Stephen reported on two proclamations issued by Macquarie and Brisbane, declaring both to be illegal and adding, extremely, 'they have no law at all which can properly be called such'.[32]

The Parliamentary debates of February 1819[33] on complaints of unlawful government, unconstitutional law making, public extravagance and religious intolerance[34] in New South Wales embarrassed the Tories, who were already resisting Whig and Radical charges of despotism at home. Manifestly, there was tyranny in New South Wales. Sir James Mackintosh, an advocate of penal reform as well as of representative self-government, declared, indignantly and wrongly, 'Until the accession of his present majesty, with the exception of a few inconsiderable factories on the coast of Africa, and a few not less inconsiderable in India, no body of Englishmen had ever been established as a colony on foreign soil, without partaking the enjoyment of the British constitution.' Challenged by Canning to remember Trinidad and be mindful that New South Wales was a penal colony, Mackintosh denied that he wished 'the terrors of the law' to be diminished: he sought a middle way between despotism and full representative government. The government pointed out that every matter the critics raised was already under inquiry. The House of Commons was setting up a committee to look into prisons. The basic question, whether New South Wales was a penal station or a settled colony with a supply of convict labour, had already been referred by Bathurst to a special commissioner of inquiry.[35]

These assurances did not stop complaints, and the question whether New South Wales were a unique colony to which British subjects resorted at their peril was raised repeatedly in Parliament. Henry Grey Bennet, radical Whig member for Westminster, who in 1817 presented a petition from the free immigrants against Macquarie's autocratic methods, and in 1819 attacked the colony's administrative system, published a letter in 1820 arguing that New South Wales had either to be a gaol, in which case the free settlers should return home, or a normal colony with a 'rational, limited, legal government'. He asked not for a representative assembly, but for the rule of law.[36]

Bennet drew part of his case from the *Statistical, Historical and Political Description of ... New South Wales*, which William Charles Wentworth, the colony's first popular leader, had published in London in 1819.[37] The son of a convict mother and a medical superintendent (later principal surgeon) who had been tried four times, without conviction, for highway robbery, Wentworth had recently encountered the social rebuffs of the colonial exclusives, the people without a convict taint. He had also resented the conscious superiority of the official class and the arbitrary power of the governor, and had been humiliated in London when his father's record in the criminal courts was exposed by Grey Bennet and Jeffery Hart Bent, a former judge of the colony. His book combined hope for the future and venomous hatred of the wealthy exclusives, whose large land grants had made them the aristocracy of the colony. Wentworth completed the book just after the collapse of his hopes to marry the daughter of John Macarthur, who ranked first among the founders of the wool industry and whose family had formerly befriended him.[38] Although he had been away from the colony for three years, studying in England for the bar, he boldly declared that the colonists expected all the ordinary political privileges of Englishmen and might appeal to the United States if tyranny continued. He also warned London that government in New South Wales must not be allowed to fall into the hands of the 'aristocratic junta', who would always try to refuse political and civil rights to former convicts. Wentworth would have given political rights to anyone, free or freed, who had sufficient property, unless transported for life or convicted of a new crime in the colony.[39]

Wentworth advocated a bicameral legislature, with an assembly elected on a low property franchise, and an upper house as nearly as possible a colonial House of Lords. He had no objection to a colonial aristocracy; a relative of the fourth Earl Fitzwilliam, he believed in the social and political uses of aristocracy and wanted to belong to it. Possibly he intended the upper house to have executive and advisory, as well as legislative, funtions, on the model of the old representative system. If so, his general point, that New South Wales should have the institutions granted to the Canadas in 1791, was not well sustained. He asked also for law reform, trial by jury, an end to taxation without representation, and the appointment of a colonial secretary to systematise civil administration. Wentworth's dreams contrasted strangely with the sober views of Alexander Riley, a magistrate of the colony, who had gone there as an official and remained as a woolgrower and merchant. In evidence to the 1819 committee on prisons he proposed an advisory council to limit the governor's autocracy; it was to consist of persons 'independent of any other situation in the colony', by which he presumably meant gentlemen other than officials. Riley thought that many emancipists had become 'useful inhabitants, acquiring property and bringing up families', and were likely to do well if kept from old, evil associations in Britain. However, he did not ask for representative institutions.[40]

Wentworth's proud attempt to equate New South Wales with Upper Canada,[41] even only incipiently, destroyed his case. The Act of 1791 had been passed primarily for the sake of reputable loyalists, to whom Britain owed a debt, and the French, who were to be assimilated. The special privileges granted to them were not to be allowed to some thousands of allegedly reformed criminals and the much smaller number of settlers and officials, who together made up the free population of the penal colony. New South Wales in 1821 had 7556 emancipists (with 5859 children) and only 1558 settlers (with 878 children).[42] Even those never convicted were divided among themselves, between the principal officials and wealthier settlers and their families, and, below them, the mass of free immigrants and the majority of persons born in the colony. As Howick declared ten years later, New South Wales was more like a West Indian colony, with convicts instead of slaves, emancipists instead of free coloureds, and free settlers instead of planters, than it was like any part of North America. Similarly, the *Edinburgh Review* thought the 'land of convicts and kangaroos' incapable of finding suitable legislators; and the *Quarterly*, which five years before had thought of handing the colony and its convicts over to the Americans, dismissed Wentworth as a 'stripling Australian', foolishly adopting a 'dictatorial and menacing tone'.[43]

The supreme exclusive, John Macarthur Senior, read Wentworth's book with disgust. Economically, its best ideas had been taken from him without licence; politically, it was mischievous: 'Anything in the shape of a Legislative Assembly in the present state of our society . . . would seal the destruction of every respectable person here.' A colony in which so many men of property were former convicts was obviously not qualified for representative government. He exhorted his eldest son John, then the family's representative in London, to use every connection he had to combat the pernicious influence of Wentworth's book.[44]

Another emancipist case for reform was stated by Edward Eagar, an

Irish attorney transported for uttering a forged bill of exchange and conditionally pardoned in 1813. Eagar had rehabilitated himself except among the few who doubted evidences of reformation consisting largely of wealth and sedulous support of the Wesleyan church. In October 1819 he wrote to Bathurst's special commissioner in New South Wales to propose reforms. More prudent than Wentworth, he looked not to Canada, but to the Caribbean colonies, to help his case. If the old West India colonies, overlaid with slaves and persons of colour, and whose white populations were not wholly English, could have representative institutions, why refuse New South Wales normal political privileges? Jamaica had fewer Europeans than New South Wales, Barbados had only half as many, Dominica only one-sixtieth. Convicts were less dangerous than slaves and were wholly excluded from participation in public life.[45]

Unlike Wentworth, Eagar knew that emancipists were more concerned with problems of legal and economic status than with political privileges.[46] He hoped to blot out the distinction between exclusives and emancipists and in 1823 tried to persuade Bathurst that the conflict between the classes had been unimportant until judicial decisions threw doubts on governors' pardons and emancipist rights to own property and go to law. Judge Barron Field had injured Eagar by abuse of the legal process; Macarthur Senior had become the leader of a 'party determinedly hostile to the Emancipists and their hitherto undoubted, undisputed rights and privilidges'.[47]

Bathurst's commissioner of inquiry was John Thomas Bigge, formerly chief justice of Trinidad, an able man long acquainted with complex colonial societies and well connected with both Whigs and Tories.[48] He was to inquire how New South Wales might be kept a place of dread to criminals, yet be developed later as a settled colony, after transportation had eventually ended. He was especially to report on the relations between emancipists and free settlers and on the 'propriety of admitting into Society Persons who originally came to the settlement as Convicts'. Bigge was not forbidden to recommend constitutional reform, but had to keep within the narrow ambit of penal policy that Bathurst wished to maintain.

Guided by his instructions and advice received from the Macarthurs in London and the colony, Bigge proposed almost no changes of government.[49] He had found no demand for either a legislative or an executive council. The petitions sent to the Colonial Office in 1819 from all classes of the colonists and in 1821 from the emancipists had not asked for legislative institutions. Only the committee of 1812, together with Wentworth and Eagar, had asked for a law-making authority other than Parliament and the governor. Presumably these people represented nobody but themselves; they certainly were not agreed on what they proposed. Bigge was sure that in New South Wales there were social barriers as formidable as those that separated white planters from free coloureds, however wealthy, in the West Indies; representative institutions, therefore, could not work well and would impose improper burdens on a governor responsible for penal colony discipline. He defended the political position of the governor as sole legislative authority and recommended only that his ordinances be given a secure legal foundation. An Act of Parliament might authorise the governor to make regulations on specified subjects (principally police and convicts) after consulting a majority of the magistrates and subject to the approval of the Crown. 'All my father's measures are advocated', wrote Edward Macarthur to his brother John.[50]

THE FIRST LEGISLATIVE COUNCIL IN NEW SOUTH WALES

While the Colonial Office considered Bigge's reports, it was also examining the complaints made against Barron Field by Governor Sir Thomas Brisbane, who had succeeded Macquarie on 1 December 1821. Bathurst decided to recall Barron Field and replace him with Forbes of Newfoundland, who would be appointed chief justice of a new supreme court. Dr William Redfern, a leading emancipist transported for a youthful part in the Nore mutiny, thought Forbes 'clever, and sensible' with 'a very proper notion of the distinction between law and justice', but John Macarthur Junior noted with concern that Forbes, though 'of great talent and of very estimable character', had 'theoretical views concerning liberty'.[51]

Between his return from Newfoundland and his departure for New South Wales, Forbes worked with Stephen in drafting the Bill of 1823, which was to give the colony its first legislative council and its present supreme court. In Forbes's first draft the only legislative powers conferred on the governor were those proposed by Bigge — that is, to make local regulations upon defined subjects with the consent of an unspecified number of magistrates. After Stephen had read the draft it was amended, probably by him, to give the governor a general power, with the approval of any six magistrates, to make laws or impose taxes, provided that nothing repugnant to the laws of England was enacted, and subject to disallowance by the King in council. Forbes did not want to confer on the governor and magistrates so large and undefined a legislative power, which would be as great as that of the governor, council and assembly in Jamaica and be 'without precedent in other colonies, properly British'.[52]

In Newfoundland, where there was a free population of over 50,000 people without political experience, greatly divided among themselves and dispersed among isolated settlements, Forbes had not recommended either a normal legislature or a general legislative power. Instead he had proposed that power be given to a committee of residents to enact, under the governor, any local regulations indispensable to law and order. He was impressed by Bigge's case for establishing only a limited legislative power in New South Wales, the more so because Newfoundland was discussed in Parliament by Wilmot-Horton, Hume and others on 14 May 1823, the day before Forbes wrote his memorandum on giving legislative powers to the governor and magistrates.[53]

When, at Wilmot-Horton's request, Stephen and Forbes conferred, it was Stephen's view, based on long experience, that prevailed. As a result, substantial legislative powers to be exercised by the governor and magistrates were written into the Bill. Forbes's continuing doubts on how these powers might be exercised led to a late decision, for which Stephen probably hoped, to establish a legislative council.[54] Forbes thought the decision wrong, for it would 'engender the idea of popular representation' and disturb the penal colony.

John Macarthur Junior, whom Wilmot-Horton consulted more than once about the Bill, reminded the Under-Secretary in October 1823 that 'both Mr Forbes and myself objected to the clause proposed by Mr Stephen, which established a regular Council, contending that all difficulties would be obviated by simply authorising the Governor to pass any local regulations, after consulting the Magistrates, as advised by the Commissioner'.[55] Forbes had wanted no more than this. The legislative council in the 1823 Act was essentially the upshot of disagreement between the legal experts drafting the Bill, and reflected Stephen's dislike of giving power to a select group like the magistrates, whose rule would be resented by other men of property and education. Administrative convenience was also involved; Forbes himself admitted that the original draft Bill had had to catch up many outstanding legal problems that needed the intervention of Parliament but were too remote and too 'complex . . . for discussion in Parliament'. It was easiest to give New South Wales clear legislative authority to solve them in the colony.[56]

Similarly, in the Cape Colony a little later, an advisory council of officials was established by order-in-council to mitigate the autocracy founded in 1796. English settlers arriving after 1815 had demanded representative institutions, but the original Dutch settlers, whose knowledge of English language and law and of British institutions was meagre, had opposed the English colonists on reform of government. They wanted to rule themselves through local institutions and be remote from English interference. With such a division of races and political ideas, the British government would not establish a legislative council and took the safe course, taken in other Crown colonies of mixed population, of establishing an advisory council composed of officials discussing and voting on measures either proposed by the governor or accepted by him after proposal in writing by another member of council. The governor had power to act without his council, but had to report to the Secretary of State when he disregarded its advice.[57] The New South Wales council, although Wilmot-Horton referred to it at least once as advisory, was in fact legislative, and had to be established by Parliament not by order-in-council, because New South Wales was a settled colony.[58]

In introducing the New South Wales Jurisdiction Bill on 7 July, Wilmot-Horton did not refer to the legislative council, but stated that in the new measure New South Wales was for the first time treated 'in the light of a British colony' and not as the 'destination of . . . individuals . . . sentenced . . . to be transported'. Henry Bright denounced the legislative council as too slight a concession to be safe. Although few members spoke, criticism of the Bill led the government to stress that conditions in the colony were changing rapidly, and Canning, who privately thought that the Bill had 'come up with too little notice', proposed that its operation be limited to five years. Wilmot-Horton agreed at once and the Bill, amended in both Houses, became law as 4 Geo. IV, c. 96.[59]

The new legislative council was a limited body whose history was vexed by failure to revise the whole Bill thoroughly when the late decision to establish the council was abruptly taken.[60] The Crown was to appoint a legislative council of from five to seven 'persons resident in the said Colony'. No business was to be considered unless laid before the council by the governor. If the council rejected a measure, those voting against it were to record their reasons, for transmission to the Secretary of State. The governor might override the council if he thought a rejected Bill essential to the safety of the colony, provided that at least one member agreed with him. In addition, in the event of rebellion, either actual or apprehended, the governor might legislate without the council (Section 25). These principles were adapted from those relating to Indian councils.

The governor's financial powers were strong. Section 27 gave the council power to tax and Section 28 conferred a similar power on the governor without the council, although this was perhaps only an unintended survival from earlier drafts of the Bill. The governor had a further power, independently of the council, to dispose of revenues arising from any Act of Parliament and from the duties that Parliament had validated retrospectively in 1819–22. As John Macarthur Junior wrote to Wilmot-Horton, the outstanding feature of the Bill was that the powers of the governor remained great and were placed beyond legal challenge.[61]

To the loyal son of a father who boasted that he had broken more than one governor and was confident of great influence in Downing Street the changes were not wholly welcome. An astute governor who knew his own powers was in a stronger position than before and might use the council to protect himself from the Secretary of State. John Macarthur Junior, a lawyer who associated with leading Tory lawyers, suggested that the governor's advisers should not all be officials, subordinate to his authority and dependent on his goodwill, but should include four or five of the colony's principal landholders and merchants, according to the precedents of the American and West Indian colonies. He wanted appointments to be made by the Secretary of State on his own inquiries (which would probably include a reference to Macarthur) and not be left to the governor, who might surround himself with sycophants. Bathurst's first appointments included Forbes, James Bowman (a Macarthur relative), who was colonial surgeon, and Major Frederick Goulburn (brother of Henry Goulburn, the former Under-Secretary), who was to be the first colonial secretary.[62]

Apart from the unfitness of Brisbane, a gallant officer and impecunious gentleman, to govern such a colony, there were constitutional reasons why the governor was less powerful under the new system than Macarthur had feared. The governor did not sit on the council: the Act had been inexcusably vague on his membership of it, and Brisbane weakly accepted Forbes's advice not to sit. He opened the meetings of the council and was responsible for most of the business before it, but otherwise had no part in its deliberations. Forbes, prevailed upon by the other members, presided. This was an unfortuate decision, because the Act laid upon him, as chief justice, the responsibility of certifying that every proposed law was consistent with the law of England, and he began to compare his position with the Lord Chancellor's.[63]

The origins of Section 29, which required the chief justice's certificate to proposed laws, were largely accidental,[64] and its history mainly troublesome. It repeatedly brought the governor and chief justice into conflict, especially after General Sir Ralph Darling succeeded Brisbane in December 1825. Darling was the exact type of 'military Governor, assisted by a very small body of official counsellors', for whom Stephen had designed Section 29. Forbes's liberal views clashed with Darling's hopes of strong government, and their differences coincided disastrously well with bitter political conflicts in the colony. Stephen always argued that Section 29 was neither intrinsically bad nor necessarily unworkable. Might not any judge have to decide in court whether a colonial law were invalid because of repugnancy to the law of England? Why should he not give his opinion before the law was made? The man who asked the question was counsel to the Colonial Office, not chief justice of a turbulent colony.[65]

POLITICS OF REFORM IN NEW SOUTH WALES, 1823–8

As Forbes had predicted, the establishment of the new council stimulated a strong demand for larger reforms. At first there was no liberal 'party' to combat the exclusives, whom Bathurst had entrenched in power.[66] When Wentworth returned to the colony in July, he set out to create one. The third edition of his book had condemned the new 'wretched mongrel substitute for a Legislative Assembly' and complained of the lack of judicial reforms. Fortunately, he wrote, the Act would expire in five years

and it had given the colony a lawful, if regrettable, legislature. The
ministry had been misled by Bathurst's 'booby commissioner', himself
'either the unconscious dupe or the corrupt coadjutor of as turbulent and
tyrannical a faction as ever any community was yet cursed with'. In the
Quarterly Barron Field contemptuously rejected these allegations against
the ministry and condemned colonial assemblies generally for 'obstruc-
tions, factions, feuding and the sacrifice of the public good to the private
interest'.[67] In New South Wales, however, Wentworth found an audience
among emancipists and the free settlers, who detested domination by
exclusives and officials.

On learning the temper of the colony, Wentworth concentrated for a
while on the emancipists' favoured causes – trial by jury, abolition of a
court of appeal consisting of the governor alone, and the fullest possible
individual and commercial liberties. In co-operation with a Cambridge
friend, Robert Wardell, Wentworth began to publish *The Australian*, the
first independent newspaper in the colony. Brisbane tolerated it and mildly
sympathised with plans to mould the emancipists and new free immigrants
into a cohesive, anti-exclusive party.

On 21 October, at a meeting that adopted an address to Brisbane on his
retirement, Wentworth persuaded those present to urge the governer to
advocate trial by jury and a representative legislature of at least 100
members.[68] Brisbane declined to support the absurd demand for so large
an assembly, but did 'consider the colony to have arrived at that state in
which the popular institutions of the parent country may be further
introduced with mutual advantage'.

The exclusives resented the clamour at Brisbane's departure. Through
John Macarthur Junior they assured Bathurst in July 1826 that men of
respectability still resisted the dangerous ideas of low-class agitators and
emancipists. The meeting of 21 October, they said, had been a mere rabble
of former convicts, failed businessmen, drunkards and undesirables, whose
shallow resentments had been exploited by demagogues and a 'licentious
press'. The exclusives asked for reform to diminish the power of the
autocrats in Government House, some of whom had foolishly favoured the
emancipists. The colony needed also 'an Executive Council (composed of
the officers of government) with all the powers of an upper house'. The
legislative council should be enlarged to at least fifteen members, selected
by the King from the respectable landholders and merchants of the
colony.[69]

The exclusives' case was subtle. Under Darling's instructions an executive
council had already been sworn in on 19 December 1825.[70] Bathurst
intended it to check the governor's autocracy and help regulate his work
with the colonial secretary, colonial treasurer and attorney-general. The
governor presided over the council and had to consult it on every matter
save those too unimportant or too exeptional to require or permit him to

do so. Only he could bring a matter before the council; other members might propose, in writing, subjects for his consideration, and these, with his replies, were to be entered in the minute books. The council was a normal body in British colonies and had been favourably received in New South Wales.[71] The exclusives' proposal to make it into a legislative upper house, while continuing its executive functions, would have revived one of the most troublesome features of the old representative system. In effect they proposed two nominated councils, both chosen by the Secretary of State, whom the Macarthurs could influence. Such a legislature would have been unprecedented for a colony of the wealth and population of New South Wales. Possibly they intended only to suggest that their plan was the most liberal form of government prudently conceivable and that anything more liberal would be dangerous. Bathurst read their petition with interest and heeded it as far as he could. He entirely agreed that representative institutions would disturb the tranquillity of New South Wales. Hay wrote privately to Darling, assuring him that his political difficulties were understood and that he need not fear private representations from any source. The colonists were 'totally' unfit for the changes they sought.[72]

Hay's reassuring letter crossed with a dispatch from Darling to Bathurst, complaining that Macarthur Senior, 'factious and turbulent', was the head of the only 'party' (used pejoratively) in New South Wales, and that, although unpopular in the colony at large, he had great influence with the unofficial members of the council.[73] Macarthur's 'party' would have been difficult to define. It was exclusive, in the sense that it wished to withhold social recognition and political and jury service privileges from emancipists. It was constructive, for the Macarthurs, at least, had clear ideas on how to develop the colony through gentlemen pastoralists employing convict labour. It condemned the emancipist leaders and their sympathisers for loose living, corruption and indifference to religion and authority. Like the Family Compact in Upper Canada, the exclusives were men of principle as well as of privilege, property and power.

In London, the reasonable conclusion to draw from the squabbles at Brisbane's departure was that New South Wales had two sets of reformers. One, in the main wealthy, usefully involved in the valuable pastoral industry (which absorbed many convicts at safe distance from Sydney), and agreeably conservative in its ideas of reform, was well known in England and was supported by high officials in the colony. In Britain it was generally represented by young Mr Macarthur, who associated with respectable Tory lawyers such as Lord Lyndhurst, met under-secretaries in their clubs, and had favourably impressed Bigge. Except when his irascible father denounced the opposition too furiously, the conservatives seemed calm, lucid, well informed and able to offer advice discreetly. Their ideas on law, religion, family and society were consonant with what English gentlemen could publicly support. Even if not all the exclusives possessed the adroitness and moral purpose of the Macarthurs, they at least allowed the Macarthurs to speak for them.

How different were their opponents! Wentworth and Eagar, one the son of a convict, the other a former convict, were loud, clamorous and notorious in private immoralities. They spoke for an extraordinary assortment of free and freed, some poor, some wealthy, some ne'er-do-wells, some getting rich faster than honesty permitted. Wentworth and Wardell controlled a vitriolic newspaper, which persistently denigrated authority and had broken with Governor Darling. Like E. S. Hall's *Monitor*, founded in May 1826,[74] it repeated or hinted at stories so scandalous that, if true, they were better suppressed, and, if false, they ought to be convincingly denied, which they hardly ever seemed to be. Reform demanded from such sources, in extravagant language and backed by rowdy meetings, was condemned by the character of its advocates. Ministers and officials in Britain, struggling with irate West Indian assemblies in the long conflict over emancipation and amelioration, thought that wisdom, judgement and 'respectability' were all on the side of the exclusives, who might come to represent in New South Wales the class that the West Indies had lost when the great planters became absentees.

Wentworth, Wardell and their sympathisers had not yet learned that to demand justice with discordant howls of vituperation against authority and the exclusives was to guarantee that Downing Street, which dreaded convict excesses, would not heed them. Why transfer power to a loud-mouthed, partly criminal rabble? Little wonder that a gentleman like Brisbane, distinguished in war (he had had Edward Macarthur as his brigade major), zealous in astronomy, and a friend of Sir Walter Scott, should have lost his way in such a society. Even Frederick Goulburn had been embittered by the turmoil of New South Wales. The radicals in the colony were condemned by their own behaviour, while their opponents seemed upright, harassed men in a shameful land.

The information that Darling, who after all had first-hand knowledge of the colony, sent home, confirmed these notions. He had been sensibly non-committal when an address on his arrival referred to 'the danger of deferring a popular elected legislature' and to the prevailing 'state of vassalage, so opposed to the rights and immunities enjoyed by our fellow subjects in the Canadas and in the West Indies'. As acting governor of Mauritius for over a year and a soldier in the West Indies, he had learned the language of colonial faction. He tried to conciliate Wentworth and was on fair terms with Wardell until the notorious Sudds and Thompson affair of late 1826 disrupted the political life of the colony and forced him over to the exclusives' side.[75]

Sudds and Thompson, two soldiers wishing to leave the army, committed theft. They expected to be convicted, discharged from the service, imprisoned and, on release, to settle in the colony. Darling, troubled by similar events, decided on exemplary action. His proceedings, though not brutal by the standards of the time, were partly illegal, and within a few days Sudds, who had been ill, died. At once *The Australian* and *The Monitor* used the affair 'to induce the People to unite in petitioning Parliament to extend their privileges by granting them Trial by Jury, a Legislative Assembly, and such other institutions as are recognised by the British Constitution'.[76] First Wardell and then Wentworth tried to make a martyr out of Sudds and prove that New South Wales was writhing under a military despot who controlled even the soldiery by illegal acts of mortal tyranny.

Neither Darling nor Forbes was deceived about Wentworth's intentions or unaware of the gap that divided natural public concern at Sudds's death from the boundless ambitions of Wentworth. That 'vulgar, ill-bred fellow, utterly unconscious of the Common Civilities, due from one Gentleman to another', Darling confided to Wilmot-Horton, wanted to lead the emancipists and 'appears to have taken his stand in opposition to the Government'. Was he seeking independence for the colony and dictatorship for himself? Forbes, less rigorous than the martinet at Government House as regards the civilities due between gentlemen, and, as a lawyer, somewhat critical of Darling's actions, agreed that 'the case of Sudds . . . is a political juggle'.[77]

Wentworth cared little what Darling reported; at last he had a case to interest Parliament. Possibly because of private affairs and personal reverses in New South Wales politics, he made little in England of the death of Sudds until 1829–30.[78] No Secretary of State ever regarded the accidental killing of a soldier convicted of crime as evidence that New South Wales ought to have a representative legislature, civil juries or any other liberal reform. The petition adopted at Wentworth's instigation by a public meeting held on 26 January 1827 had little impact in Britain, although supported by many free immigrants, including the Blaxlands and Sir John Jamison. It attacked 'certain private Families' of the colony — that is, those most respected in Downing Street — and repeated the demand for an assembly of 100 members. Without such a safeguard against the exclusives, the petitioners declared, representation would be a mockery and the council better unreformed. Darling reported that 100 suitable legislators were not to be found; possibly only three men of merit in the colony would have time and inclination for such work. He thought the demand for an assembly a mere political manoeuvre; the one reform strongly desired was civil juries.[79]

Darling's own advice on a Bill to replace the 1823 Act varied considerably. In December 1826, before Wentworth's petition, he was sure that the thinking part of the community did not want a legislative assembly. Discussions with Forbes, Alexander McLeay (the colonial secretary) and Macarthur had persuaded him that the existing council might be enlarged to twelve members (Macarthur would have gone to fifteen) and (Forbes dissenting) that the official majority might be safely given up. After the public meeting of January 1827, however, he had more elaborate views. Confident that the official majority did more harm than good, he was willing for a sliding scale, reducing the proportion of officials according to the size of the council. The chief justice, he declared, should be kept off both the councils. Surprisingly, because he feared trouble in Parliament when Wentworth's petition was presented, Darling suggested a blended council. From eight to twelve unofficial members might be elected to a council that had from fifteen to twenty members. Local problems had shown him that there was possible advantage in having elected members sitting with official members and Crown nominees, since this would allow the advantages of yielding to the demand for representation to be combined with those of retaining a nominated bloc. His arguments for a blended council resembled Stephen's. To Hay he explained, 'I throw out these observations *only* in the event of the Question being taken up earnestly in the House of Commons.' He may also have intended that a new legislative council be united with the executive council against Forbes.[80]

In December 1827 Macarthur Senior called on Darling to discuss the new constitution, Forbes, and Macarthur's pastoral interests.[81] They agreed that the jury question should be decided dispassionately in London, where Macarthur Junior would contradict wild notions sent home by radicals like Forbes. They agreed also that it would be dangerous to establish a representative assembly, although the legislative council might be enlarged to twelve. Darling abandoned his proposal for a blended council, because its elected element would be too liberal. Macarthur persuaded Darling to report to London that Forbes had failed to inform him when proposing extensive amendments of the constitution a year before.[82] Darling added to his report that Forbes had been 'anxious [in his draft Bill] to perpetuate and extend his own power, and to curtail that of the Governor'. Darling's anxieties and Macarthur's shrewdness aside, Forbes certainly approved much of the 1827 petition and admired republican institutions, although he disclaimed 'concurrence' with the political opinions of Wentworth and Wardell. Such distinctions were too fine for an exasperated governor and a suspicious exclusive.

In London Forbes was known to have used his powers under Section 29 with little regard for the governor, and to have failed to keep his judicial office out of politics.[83] Charges that he was a radical, an enemy to Darling and prejudiced against exclusives would have influenced every official who read his letter of November 1827 to Hay. Written about the time when Wentworth, Wardell and Hall were heaping insults on the absent governor in the public privacy of the Turf Club, Forbes's letters contained liberal proposals offered in good faith. He asked to be relieved of the duty of certifying each proposed law. He recommended trial by jury, subject to a high property qualification for emancipists as evidence of their rehabilitation. Believing proposals for an elected assembly to be premature, he suggested that the Colonial Office establish, as it thought best, a legislature that would have contacts with the people. (This could have been a blended council.) In order to restrict arbitrary rule from Government House, he wished the executive council to be treated somewhat as a cabinet responsible to the governor, so that each high official would have independence under the governor's supervision.[84]

Already the Secretary of State had had one Bill (substantially Forbes's second draft of 1826) introduced into the Commons. This had been presented in 1827, and strong opposition had led to its withdrawal. Its severest critic outside the House, John Macarthur Junior, persuaded Wilmot-Horton and Stephen that the provision of limited trial by jury and a future grant of a legislative assembly were dangerous. Agitators would argue incessantly that the time had come to convene an assembly, which could be filled only be electing the former prisoners of the Crown. Macarthur asked for delay. His pleas, coinciding with the change of view in Sydney, were heard with respect. By 1828, Stephen was arguing, in almost the same terms as Macarthur had used the year before, against a power in the Crown to establish an assembly.[85] After the 1827 Bill had been withdrawn, Parliament extended the Act of 1823 for another year.

When Stephen again reviewed policy towards the New South Wales constitution, he had before him the views and amended views of Darling, Forbes and Macarthur, and the Wentworth petition of January 1827. There was nothing else from Wentworth except a promise of evidence to impeach Darling for crimes against humanity.[86] Eagar was still in London, and his pamphlet *Remarks and Objections on the part of the Colonists of New South Wales*, attacking the 1827 Bill and proposing a blended council for New South Wales, was known to Stephen. Colonel Dumaresq, Darling's secretary and brother-in-law, also then in London, reminded the Colonial Office that Eagar was a person of 'very equivocal virtue', falsely asserting that New South Wales wanted an elected assembly. (Since 1823 Eagar had been living in London with Ellen Gorman, who bore him a large family; his own wife was Wentworth's mistress in Sydney.) Eagar was heard, not heeded.[87]

If Downing Street ever hesitated about ignoring the emancipists, and probably it never did, some conservative was always at hand to relieve anxieties. Discreet reminders about the licentious press, the immoral behaviour of leading emancipists and the depravity of the colony were always available. Virtue and wisdom apparently belonged to the governor and the exclusives, folly and crime to the emancipists and their supporters.[88]

THE NEW SOUTH WALES ACT OF 1828

Stephen's memorandum on a possible Bill[89] was concise and well reasoned. His superiors were harassed by the political changes in which the Colonial Office passed from Bathurst to Goderich (April 1827), to Huskisson (September 1827) and to Murray (May 1828). The Bill that Huskisson presented to Parliament in 1828 was Stephen's work and was as agreeable to Tories in Britain as to exclusives in New South Wales.[90] Much of it had originally been drafted by Forbes, but Stephen settled its final form and decided the most controversial provisions. In 1823 he had had a lawyer's reasons for wanting the colony to have a legislative council; in 1828 he had other reasons for believing that any form of political representation would be dangerous. A dedicated evangelical, more interested in man's relations to God than in human rights, abhorring drunkenness and loose living or any other evil that might blind men to their Saviour, he doubted the reformation in New South Wales of 'the scourings of our gaols'. Like most of the 'Saints', he preferred the rule of the intelligent, righteous few to the boisterous democracy of the many. He found the leading emancipists regrettable and Forbes a troublemaker who, inflated with Benthamite ideas of man and society, strained Acts of Parliament to suit his own notions of colonial government.[91]

Stephen's outline of policy was fatal to the hopes of Forbes, the radicals and the emancipists. He followed all parties in the colony in being willing to enlarge the legislative council, recommending that it have between ten and fifteen members, all nominated, without statutory distinction between official and unofficial seats. The governor was to preside, with both an original and a casting vote. But, as Darling had wished, the governor was to lose his sole right to initiate laws, his emergency power to legislate without the council, and his power to legislate against the opinion of the majority. The council was, so far as law making was concerned, to be placed above the governor, who would lose his unenviable role as court of appeal. The jury system was not to be reformed.[92]

Like Forbes, Stephen wished the new legislative council, rather than Parliament, to undertake as much as possible of the colony's law making. The greater the council's responsibilities, the more likely it was to rise above sectional interests. The Act empowered the governor and legislative council to make laws and ordinances for the peace, welfare and good government of the colony, provided that their measures were consistent with English law. The royal power of disallowance was extended to four years, instead of three. The chief justice was relieved of the duty to certify that Bills were consistent with the laws of England. Instead, each Act had to be enrolled in the supreme court, so that the judges might declare within fourteen days any misgivings on the score of repugnancy.[93] Some limits were placed on the repugnancy rule. Only those laws and statutes in force in England at the time of the passing of the new Act, and not inconsistent with it, were to be in force in New South Wales and Tasmania from the time of its commencement. This gave the colony the benefit of many law reforms effected since 1788, including Peel's reforms of criminal law. In doubtful cases the governor and legislative council might pass declaratory ordinances, defining the extent to which English laws were applicable in the colony.

The justification given in Parliament for refusing representative assemblies to New South Wales and Tasmania was probably Huskisson's, not Stephen's. Huskisson was then presiding over the select committee on Canada and he stated policy in Canadian terms. New South Wales and Tasmania, he said, might be ready for constitutions on the 1774 model, but not on that of 1791, although they might aspire to it.[94] The reference to the Quebec Act was partly inaccurate. The legislative councils of New South Wales and Tasmania, unlike that of Quebec, were to have power to appropriate all revenues except those arising from the properties of the Crown, most notably land; further, the special powers of taxation that had been continued in the 1823 Act (Sections 27, 28) were continued again (Clauses 36 and 37). Clause 25 limited the taxing power by requiring that no tax or duty be imposed except for local needs, and that the purposes to which revenue would be appropriated had to be stated in every taxing Act.

On 18 April, when the Bill was before the House, Mackintosh presented the petition of January 1827 asking for representative government and trial by jury.[95] No other colony of the wealth and population of New South Wales, he said, had ever been denied the rights of all the King's subjects. Huskisson answered that over half the inhabitants were convicts, and that concessions would therefore be disadvantageous. Of the 36,680 inhabitants of New South Wales, 15,660 were convicts and 7520 had been convicts.

In the Commons again on 20 June, Mackintosh, prompted by Eagar,[96] tried to amend the Bill so as to establish a blended council (one-third elected) until such time as an assembly were called, and to provide for trial by civil jury in both civil and criminal cases. Electors for the blended council were to be men who had been free inhabitants for three years and had a clear annual income of £100. Mackintosh spoke ably, but did not touch the matters that swayed the ministry. He said nothing of the West Indian problems that made the Colonial Office so wary of prejudiced juries and irascible assemblies. He was irritatingly over-confident that the 'foul stains' of convictism might be removed by access to British institutions. Huskisson accepted his general principles and mildly explained that New South Wales was too special a case to be allowed the liberal institutions normal in British colonies. The Bill became law as 9 Geo. IV, c. 83, in force in New South Wales from 1 March 1829. John Macarthur wrote to his father with joy at the exclusives' great victory: 'It will be a death-blow to the radical party and has . . . excited the bitterest feelings in the minds of the delegates and their friends in England. Mr Eagar imputes the failure of their hopes to Mr [Gregory] Blaxland, and the latter retorts upon him that the infamous behaviour of their leaders in New South Wales has prejudiced every one against their cause.'[97] Eagar was wrong and Gregory Blaxland was right. In so far as anyone could be blamed for having failed to extract from a Tory government, sorely harassed with problems in Canada and the West Indies, a liberal measure contrary to every precedent in the history of colonial self-government, it was the emancipist and radical leaders in New South Wales. Violence of language, extravagance of behaviour and contempt for authority had discredited a cause that had always been hopeless.

The new legislative council, nominated by the Crown, had seven official and seven non-official members.[98] The latter included John Macarthur Senior; a majority of the group were his natural allies, and the supplementary list of eight names to be used in filling casual vacancies was scarcely less favourable to his cause. *The Australian* condemned the Act for denying liberty, failing to restrain the 'pride, intolerance and tyranny of Governors', and for creating a council composed of old exclusives.[99]

THE PARALLEL WITH THE WEST INDIES

In September 1828 E. S. Hall was prosecuted for criminal libel in *The Monitor* of 5 July, where he had ridiculed Archdeacon Scott as a greater enemy to public liberties than John Macarthur. Hall, sent to gaol, wrote to the Secretary of State, attacking Darling for abuse of patronage, nepotism and making such excessive land grants to the exclusives and officers that nothing was available to the native-born and the emancipists. According to Hall, the families of Macarthur, McLeay, Berry, Throsby and others were hand in glove with high authority; they dominated the legislative council and could sway Downing Street itself.[100] His complaints resembled those of Upper Canadian radicals under Governor Maitland.

Two days before Hall's letter was sent to London, 115 members of the respectable classes, whom he hated, had assured Darling that they deplored malign attacks on his administration and feared dangerous repercussions among the convicts and lower orders. They referred not only to Hall's attack, but also to Wentworth's savage indictment of the governor as a sadistic and corrupt tyrant; this together with his own defence, Darling had just sent off to London.[101]

Darling told his sympathisers that Wentworth's calumnies bore their own antidote, for no one in authority would believe them. Wentworth and Forbes, both 'Americans at Heart', had supplied most of Hall's thunder. If the wicked triumvirate could be driven out of the colony, New South

Wales would again be a place of order and contentment.[102] He deceived himself. Wentworth and Hall were intemperate journalists, but their ideas of reform commended them to many free immigrants, emancipists and, generally, all those who opposed transportation of convicts. In the Commons, Hume and Daniel O'Connell demanded that Hall's case be reviewed. Edward Macarthur, then in London, warned his father and his brother James to keep out of brawls and petitions in the colony and rely on prudent and private representations in Downing Street.[103]

In Sydney the reformers were already trying to state a reasoned, temperate case. A public meeting of 9 February 1830 appointed a committee to draft a Constitution Bill and adopted a respectful petition to the Commons, to show that 'the efforts of Parliament have not kept pace with the advancement of society'. The petition was presented to the Commons in June 1832 by Henry Lytton Bulwer, later agent of the Australian Patriotic Association. He rashly denied that New South Wales was any longer a place of 'thieves and pickpockets' and asked the House to think of it as place to take 'the stream of our stifled and dammed up . . . civilization'. The onus of proof rested on those who opposed, not those who sought, normal privileges of British subjects. How could representative government be refused to a colony yielding a higher revenue than the Thirteen Colonies before the Revolution? Tyranny had become unconscionable.[104]

Fortunately for the colonial radicals, the government's spokesman was Howick, who announced that Goderich had already authorised the new governor, Sir Richard Bourke, to introduce trial by jury in criminal cases. Although he was ready to extend self-government in the Canadas, Howick would not agree to a representative assembly for New South Wales. To give the emancipists 'a paramount influence in the legislation of the colony', such as their numbers would entitle them to, would be totally inadmissible. To transfer power to the exclusives, who were a minority, would be equally objectionable. Having heard Howick, Bulwer withdrew his motion on juries and the House divided against him, by sixty-six to twenty-six, to support the ministry on the assembly.

In February 1834 Howick sent his private thoughts on New South Wales to the Prime Minister. He compared New South Wales and its emancipists and convicts with the West Indian colonies under slavery. Convictism had demoralised New South Wales, just as slavery had demoralised the West Indies. Howick was appalled by the 'close correspondence between the state of society in the W. In. & in the penal colonies'. In both the landowning class had been corrupted by cheap labour, and in New South Wales by cheap land as well. Transportation had lost its terrors in Britain, but not to its power to depress the society in which the exported criminals of the mother country became in effect the slave labour of greedy and imprudent capitalists.[105]

In deciding whether New South Wales were fit for representative institutions, informed British observers concentrated on the future of transportation, the corrosive effects of convictism and the true state of the great fissure in colonial society. There could be no representative institutions unless the colony had a social structure such as would let them operate efficiently and fairly. From the late 1820s there were occasional signs that educated opinion was swinging mildly towards the emancipist view, that New South Wales would inevitably develop into an ordinary colony of settlement.[106]

BLENDED COUNCIL OR INDIRECT ELECTION?

When the liberally minded Bourke, who believed in generous political representation, became governor on 3 December 1831, his views on the emancipist question were so well known that Edward Macarthur warned his father to discuss no public business with him until he had been acclimatised. In the colony Bourke immediately ran into trouble on the jury question, and with great difficulty produced a liberal compromise.[107] After two years he wrote to the Secretary of State[108] that the colony was divided into two parties, 'usually designated emigrants and emancipists, although the respective bodies are not confined to that exact description of persons, for, . . . with the latter, are to be found a great number of free emigrants, and, generally, those who advocate liberal principles'. The legislative council was not representative of the public opinion, but opposed to it. Non-official members were mostly from the exclusive party (the 'emigrants'), whose prejudices and aspirations were shared by the official members, with whom they mixed socially. Government by a single party already existed in New South Wales, although fear of such a situation had been the principal reason given by Howick on 28 June 1832 for not allowing a representative assembly to the colony. Howick had dreaded a party of former convicts or a minority party of the exclusives. Bourke disliked the party of the respectable exclusives and high officials. Howick concluded that, until conditions in New South Wales improved, the council should be liberalised only gradually, while the community gained political experience. Bourke's solution was also gradual. He sought a blended council as a prelude to a more liberal form of government. The existing council might be enlarged to twenty-four members, two-thirds elected by the most populous districts in proportion to their inhabitants, one-third (including a president) nominated by the Crown. Emancipists should be enfranchised, but not allowed to sit on the council.

Forbes agreed with Bourke's plan for a gradual transition to representative government by way of a blended legislature, as nothing more liberal was likely to be granted. When no reply to Bourke's proposal was received from the Colonial Office, he prepared a Bill for a legislative assembly of thirty-six members, twelve nominated by the Crown, twelve elected by the counties and twelve by the towns; the blended assembly so formed might have power to add up to another twelve elected members. Forbes thought that twelve nominees would be a 'sufficient counterpoise to the popular election'. Emancipists were to be eligible as electors, but not as members of the assembly. The Bourke—Forbes Bill was dispatched to the Colonial Office on 26 December 1835, Bourke hoping that the political rights of the emancipists would be decided by Parliament away from 'the heat and discord of Party' in the colony.[109] The ship carrying the dispatch was wrecked and the duplicates did not reach London until July 1836.

Bourke meanwhile wrote to Hay on 1 February to plead urgency,[110] because the Australian Patriotic Association, representing the emancipist or 'liberal' party, was preparing to battle with the exclusives in London. Bourke's sympathies were with the Association, which had been established at a public meeting on 29 May 1835, and had Henry Lytton Bulwer as its Parliamentary agent. Wentworth was a vice-president; E. S. Hall was secretary, soon succeeded, however, by the emancipist surgeon William Bland, a friend of Forbes. The president, Sir John Jamison, was a liberal member of the colonial gentry and highly respected by Bourke. The Association sent Bulwer two Bills drafted by Wentworth, together with a letter of instructions supplying details omitted from the Bills.[111] Both Bills provided for trial by jury and the repeal of the enactments establishing the existing legislative council. Bill 'A' — for a bicameral legislature, with a nominated council of fifteen members and an elected assembly of forty members — was rather on the model of the Canada Constitutional Act, although the nominees in the upper house were to hold their seats for fixed terms, not for life. Bill 'B' was for a single blended chamber, clumsily named the 'House of Legislative Council and Assembly'. It was to have at least fifty members, ten nominated and forty elected. Emancipists were not to be disfranchised. The copies of the Association's Bills that Bourke sent officially to London travelled on the same ship as his own draft Bill and also suffered shipwreck.

The exclusives opposed nearly all the reforms that Bourke, Forbes and the Association supported. Led by James Macarthur, they sent a petition to the King through the governor. Macarthur had insisted that the petition should not criticise Bourke personally, but allowed it to comment scathingly on the legislative council for its failure to command public confidence. Its failings were attributed to small size, the official majority, closed meetings and the presence of the governor and chief justice. The exclusives asked for no sudden change. The council might be increased in size, but an inquiry ought meanwhile to be held into the convict system, the laws on land and marriage, the prospects of free immigration, the condition of former convicts and the expediency of reforming the council as a step towards representative government. Delay was not the whole object of the exclusives: they expected any competent inquiry to confirm their judgements of the unfitness of the colony for representative institutions. Some new commissioner might do as much for them as Bigge had done, in justice and honesty. Looking to the distant future, they asked that property should never be made the sole test of an elective franchise in New South Wales, because in the colony property guaranteed neither respectability nor public service.[112]

The Patriotic Association watched these proceedings anxiously. Bourke sympathised with the emancipists, who warmly supported him as a liberal, but in London only Radicals were likely to side with the Association. If James and Edward Macarthur worked together, the exclusives' view would be presented superbly to the Colonial Office and members of Parliament. Wentworth warned the emancipists that it would be better to go back 'to the old despotic form of government', in which the governor was both legislature and executive, than to suffer under the existing legislative council or any substitute that the exclusives might contrive.[113]

There was, however, some common ground between exclusives and emancipists. Apart from their shared interest in reform of the land and marriage laws, both groups objected to British policy on colonial finances, claiming that the whole of the land revenue of the colony should be spent on immigration and that all colonial revenue should be appropriated by the governor and legislative council. Similarly, both groups resisted British attempts to transfer part of the costs of maintaining police and gaols to the colonial budget. None of these grievances was sectional and all 'gave to emancipists and exclusives a common field of action'. On the other hand, neither exclusives nor emancipists wanted control of finances to be transferred to the colony if political power were monopolised by their antagonists.[114]

Before the Bourke and Forbes draft Bill of December 1835 reached London, the Colonial Office itself drew up a Bill, based partly on Bourke's dispatch of Christmas Day 1833.[115] The Bill was printed and circulated to the Cabinet, but was never presented to Parliament. Probably the work of Stephen, it encountered the fatal hostility of Howick and set him to work on a variety of special constitutions based on elected municipal organisations from which a colonial legislature would be established indirectly.

Stephen's draft Bill provided for the establishment, for nine years, of a blended legislative council of unspecified size, two-thirds elected and one-third nominated. Emancipists might be electors, but not members. The council was to 'make laws and ordinances for the peace, welfare and good government' of the colony, provided that these were not repugnant to the laws of England, and to appropriate the whole of the revenue, but not to vote money except on the governor's recommendation. Education and religious instruction were to absorb not less than one-tenth of the colony's revenues.

The liberality of the draft Bill provoked Howick, who was doing his best to win concessions for the Canadas, to declare to Stephen his strong hostility to representative government for New South Wales:

Knowing as we do how very depraved a society exists there, I cannot think such a step could be taken with safety . . . when the rulers are more enlightened than the Governed and have no interest opposed to theirs I very much doubt the Policy of giving to the People themselves sole power of making general Laws, and I cannot help thinking that in Australia this power would be more wisely exercised by the Govnrs assisted by the Councils than by popular Assemblies.[116]

Howick's policy towards Canada, the West Indies and the emancipation of the slaves ('he had slaved his life out for the last two years on the question of the Niggers', said his father)[117] acquitted him of calculated illiberality in colonial affairs. He thought New South Wales a den of iniquity, where convicts were unreformed, and where most settlers, divided irreconcilably into free and freed, were so corrupted by cheap labour and cheap land that they lacked the qualities that made men of property a satisfactory electorate in Britain.[118]

Howick looked to land reform and free emigration to improve colonial society, to remedy some of the ills of transportation and perhaps to expedite its abolition. Transportation neither deterred criminals in Britain nor reformed convicts in New South Wales. It rotted colonial society by debasing free immigrants, degrading standards of behaviour and producing the worst effects of gross disproportion of the sexes.[119] Bourke, a liberal himself, recognised that Howick was an intelligent, although autocratic and prejudiced, reformer and was sorry when he left the Colonial Office in March 1833.[120]

Howick recognised that the colony needed a form of government to satisfy 'the natural desire of the Inhabitants' to manage their own affairs, and have scope for public discussion and 'the Contests of Political Ambition'. He proposed tutelage. Calling on his knowledge of government in Prussia and of the English Municipal Reform Act (1835), and possibly influenced (though he did not say so) by Tocqueville's account of local government in America,[121] he made his first proposals for a 'system of Local or municipal organisation' that would provide district administration and also be the means of electing indirectly the members of a colonial legislature.

A central legislature, Howick thought, would contribute nothing to the political advantage of districts remote from Sydney and, as Canadian experience showed, would either take good men away from the rural districts, where they could ill be spared, or fall into the hands of 'Adventurers or Attorneys and Lawyers of the Capital'. Indirect election he defended by citing Tocqueville's opinion that the Senate was superior to the House of Representatives in the United States partly because it was not directly elected by the people.

Stephen, though he depended on Howick for his own advancement in the Colonial Office[122] and for co-operation in making Canadian policy, rejected his proposals for New South Wales in alarm. Municipal institutions, he conceded, might be good training grounds for politics, and indirect election might have great advantages, but Bourke had recommended very different reforms and Parliament would consider his dispatches. How could the government refuse to act on Bourke's advice when every member would know that his proposals were nearer to ordinary policy than Howick's? 'A miniature British Constitn in a little slave Colony tho' the grossest of absurdities will command twenty fold more votes than the most perfect scheme of Colonl polity wh. Locke or Bentham could have devised. I should fear that your Lordship's plan would be summarily put down by the House of Commons as ... un-English, unprecedented & so on.' A blended council was composed of recognisably British elements; Howick's scheme was not. 'Moral abasement' could not delay representative institutions for long, because 'generations must elapse before the hereditary taint will be purged away'.[123] The colony was gaining wealth and population so rapidly that the best course was to adopt Bourke's advice at once, treating a blended council as the limit of prudent concession.[124]

Howick was unconvinced. A new Bill was drawn, setting his views into statutory form; he rejected it at once and immediately thought of another, similar scheme. Bourke's dispatch of December 1835 with Forbes's draft Bill then introduced new material and drew attention to the Patriotic Association. Bulwer received Wentworth's two draft Bills and the emancipist petition at about the same time, and their contents became known to ministers before Bourke's official duplicates reached the Colonial Office, replacing the originals lost at sea. With so much conflict of opinion and, as a result of Canadian and West Indian troubles, so many fundamental doubts about self-government, no course seemed right.[125]

With only five weeks of the parliamentary session remaining, Glenelg decided not to enact a new constitution in 1836, but to extend the 1828 Act for another year. He was sure that Howick's proposal, to govern the 'vast sheep-walk' of New South Wales as though it were a set of English corporations, was mistaken. The presence of the emancipists required no such elaborate means to offset it; why not adopt the English legal principle distinguishing between crimes that were, and those that were not, wholly expiated by punishment? Howick was furious at the delay, but not sure enough of himself to offer to resign, as he frequently did over Canada when his liberal proposals were blocked. Bulwer asked a hostile question in the Commons, but was put off by George Grey's claims that new information had been received from the colony and that the government most earnestly wished to promote emigration.[126]

No constitution was enacted for New South Wales until 1842, although in the late 1830s Howick and James Macarthur contrived many variations on the themes of blended councils and municipal organisation of colonial politics. Howick's contribution to delay was enormous, especially after he and Macarthur had reinforced one another's convictions that the colony was unfit for representative government. Forbes also worked with Macarthur and to a certain extent passed under his influence.

On arriving in England in August 1836, Forbes at once rejected as impracticable and unacceptable to the colony Howick's plan to make local government the foundation of a new legislative system. Although he was bold in his opposition to Howick's plan, his hopes that the Cabinet would accept the plan that he and Bourke had made were receding. Before Macarthur reached England, Forbes decided to modify the official New South Wales proposal a little, by reducing the proportion of elected members from two-thirds to one-half. He told Bourke that he despaired of liberal reform from ministers who would run no political risks to liberalise the government of a colony.[127]

Shortly after Forbes offered his first advice, James Macarthur arrived in London and at once spoke with Sir George Grey, a friend of his military brother Edward, about the exclusives' petition. He shrewdly emphasised the matters on which the Colonial Office and the exclusives were most agreed, such as encouraging good working men to emigrate – the more important as transportation might soon end. A little later Macarthur met Stephen and enjoyed the shy Under-Secretary's jests about sending the convicts and radicals of New South Wales to join 'Mr Radical Papineau in Quebec'. Macarthur can have had little doubt of what Stephen thought of Wentworth. When Glenelg received the exclusives the next day, Macarthur explained the case for limiting reform during the next seven to ten years to enlarging the legislative council so as to include 'men of all parties'. Stephen saw at once that this might entrench the exclusives in power again, but does not seem to have objected strongly. Macarthur conceded that, if some elected element were desirable, a blended council might be possible. Emancipists could then be allowed to vote, subject to high property qualifications, but only magistrates and certain officials should sit on the council. Glenelg agreed to present the exclusives' petition in the Lords while Grey presented it in the Commons, but he declined to give judgement on Macarthur's proposals.[128]

Macarthur, when he published *New South Wales; its Present State and Future Prospects* (London, 1837) to support the exclusives' petition, proposed a blended council.

A portion of the colonists are of opinion that a council of thirty members ... should be appointed by the Crown, ... practically to represent the different interests of the community. Other parties, holding ... extreme opinions, and comprising but a small portion of the property and intelligence of the colony, desire a House of Assembly. The petitioners conceive that the latter would be at present a most dangerous experiment, and earnestly solicit . . . a middle course; . . . the reconstruction of the Legislative Council upon an enlarged basis, and that the nomination of one-third, or one-half of the members should be in the Crown, the remainder being elected by the colonists.[129].

Although Macarthur assumed that emancipists would be kept off the council, however much of it was elected, Forbes, after 'unrestrained conversations' with him, wrote to Stephen supporting principles closely resembling those laid down by Macarthur. The difference between them at this stage was diminished, although still significant. Macarthur would have excluded from the council all former convicts and everyone not qualified in property and respectability to be a magistrate. He was sure that most emancipists had such low ethical standards, and such indifference to the public welfare, that they ought never to sit on the council. Forbes was willing to exclude the emancipists from the council (as in other British colonies), but did not otherwise wish to impose tests as severe as those Macarthur sought.[130] Appropriately, the *Herald* in distant Sydney chose to publish in its issue of 23 February 1837 an article declaring that the cleavage between free and freed would be permanent.

Sir George Gipps, when consulted in mid-1837, before he left to succeed Bourke in New South Wales, had the prestige of work in Lower Canada to support his recommendations. Although often an advocate of local government, he decided that Howick's municipal proposals were unsuited to the colony and agreed, with reservations, to a blended council. Like Stephen he recognised that, whether the council were merely enlarged as a nominated body or made partly or wholly elective, the 'conservatives' would dominate it. He preferred conservatives restrained by electors to conservatives restrained merely by respect for the Crown, whose policies they had so often contested. The risk that a blended council would split into government and non-government factions did not alarm him, and he regarded the council as a stage of tutelage on the way to conventional representative institutions.[131]

Although Glenelg, Stephen, Gipps, Forbes and Macarthur had all objected to Howick's proposals that municipal government should serve as the basic institution of legislative politics in New South Wales, the idea remained obstinately alive, and Macarthur himself soon swung towards it, appreciating its conservative qualities. Late in 1837 Howick was working on a particularly illiberal form of the municipal policy. His elaborate plan of December 1837 provided for a strong executive-cum-legislature consisting of the governor and a small council. This council, to have no more than five members (including the colonial secretary, treasurer and attorney-general), would be given exclusive powers to initiate laws and the annual budget, but would be required to publish its proposed measures and submit them for criticism to five elected local councils. The governor in council could override objections from the local councils, but had to inform the Secretary of State whenever this happened. Howick treated the relationship of the governor in council to the municipal councils as an analogue of the relationship of governor to members in councils on the Indian model. His plan included special provisions for consulting the local councils on finance. At the beginning of each financial year a meeting attended by two representatives from each council was to be held, to consider the budget proposed by the governor in council. Any objection to a new tax or expenditure would have to be referred to the Secretary of State. Local councils were to be elected by householders of three years' residence. Emancipists whose political rights had been expressly restored and not forfeited by subsequent conviction were to be allowed to vote.[132]

Macarthur at first liked the broad outlines of this scheme.[133] Later, on 4 December, he told George Grey that Howick's plan could not gratify the ambitions of the colonists for reform of the legislative council. He added, however, that he still adhered to Howick's fundamental principle, developed in earlier plans, of enlarging the legislative council by adding members elected by municipal bodies from among their own numbers. He did not expect any conflict between nominated and elected members in a council so composed. Would it not be a wholly conservative body? When he gave these views to George Grey, Macarthur was remembering Howick's active role in the Cabinet and also, perhaps, the social advantages that he himself enjoyed with the Grey of Howick family, whose naval son Frederick had been entertained by the Macarthurs on their Camden estate.[134]

Early in 1834 Charles Buller, the famous 'colonial reformer', and, possibly, Macarthur and Eagar as well were all invited by the Colonial Office to consider the various plans proposed in the past two years. Buller, who had succeeded Bulwer as agent of the Association, and was to be a key figure in the introduction of responsible government into Nova Scotia in 1847, sent to Sydney a report of a new official plan that closely resembled Howick's latest design. He neither wholly approved nor wholly rejected it, for he was caught between admiration for Macarthur's ideals and unexcelled knowledge of the colony, and fidelity to his own liberal principles and to the Association. Before long he developed his own plan for combining municipal elements with a blended council.[135]

'Ideally', wrote Buller as a good Radical, 'the best mode of securing peace and content is to leave these remote colonies to govern themselves.' So long, however, as transportation continued and political activity was necessarily concentrated in Sydney, because of dispersion of settlement, the ideal was unattainable. Buller proposed to extend the existing Act to

1839 and divide the colony into six municipal districts, subdivided into wards. Municipal councillors would be elected triennially from the wards by voters with moderate qualifications in occupation or ownership of property. Annually, through district courts, the councillors would elect twenty-four members to an assembly that would also contain the governor and twelve nominated members.[136] Indirect election, he agreed, was the answer to the problem of enfranchising emancipists. The legislature so formed would make laws on all internal matters other than public lands and land revenue.

Buller did not much like his own plan, which he intended as a compromise acceptable to Macarthur, who had partly inspired it. His own preference was still for a bicameral legislature with a nominated upper house. He felt so strongly about the defects of unicameral legislatures that he wished the governor to have power to propose amendments before he assented to a Bill. If a blended legislature were the best that the colony could have, Buller would have preferred most nominated members to be non-officials.[137]

On 9 April Buller, in duty bound, presented the emancipist petition to the Commons and was met with George Grey's familiar talk of convicts and the possible ending of transportation.[138] On the same day Macarthur adroitly used Buller's plan, which had been drafted as a Bill and presented to Glenelg, to sound a cautionary note. Buller's plan was best, he told Glenelg, only if the government felt obliged to introduce representative institutions at once; but, was it safe to do so? Would Glenelg give power to 'mere adventurers in politics', unworthy of 'important trusts'? Did he believe that the emancipists were right to claim that the colony belonged, not to free immigrants, but to convicts, former convicts and their offspring? Why not just enlarge the existing council for a few years, adding six to ten members (not fifteen as sometimes proposed), and await the effects of the expected change in transportation policy?[139] In order to gratify Howick and Buller and to extract conservative advantage from their proposals, Macarthur proposed that the legislative council be empowered to establish municipal bodies as a platform on which representative institutions could be based when the time was ripe.

Having presented the conservative point of view with subtle skill, Macarthur temporarily retired from politics. The occasion was his engagement to Amelia (Emily) Stone, daughter of a Lombard Street banker, and kinswoman of George Grey, the Barings, the Normans, the Cavendish-Bentincks, the Bonham-Carters, Spring-Rice and Labouchere.[140] The marriage took place in June and cemented the links between the Macarthurs and British families eminent in finance and politics.

Buller learned of Macarthur's true opinions just as he was about to leave for Canada with Durham, and he decided to support Macarthur in advocating, as a short-term measure for only three years, the enlargement of the legislative council and the opening of its proceedings to the public. He supported also an instruction to the council to discuss a municipal system.[141] His own basic views had not changed; he acted from expediency. After discussions with Russell, he wrote to him that New South Wales really was ready for representative government and that doubts were stronger in Britain than in the colony. In a cordial letter to Howick, he told him of the change of plan, made because 'you and other enemies of representative government' would allow nothing better.[142]

Howick and Macarthur had successfully barred the way to significant reform. Neither was reactionary; both believed that New South Wales was too anomalous to be trusted with normal representative institutions. As the end of transportation was in sight, they had a strong argument for wait-and-see. Buller, so ill informed that he had to get his facts about the colony from Macarthur, was no match for them.[143] Glenelg (and Melbourne) thought the New South Wales problem difficult, with few political advantages to be won from it in Britain. Howick was the only member of Cabinet much interested in the colony, and he thought it depraved.

Eventually Glenelg did less than Macarthur and Buller had recommended, although Eagar supported Macarthur and Buller in asking that further nominees be added to the council. On 24 August Glenelg wrote to Governor Gipps with a copy of the Act renewing the 1828 constitution for another year. Nothing would be done to change the constitution, he explained, until the new Select Committee on Transportation had reported. He did not mention enlargement of the council or municipal government.[144]

THE ENDING OF ANOMALY

From about 1838 the great anomaly produced by the antagonism of exclusives and emancipists began to disappear. The economic growth of the colony through the wool industry and general trade gave wealthy emancipists and wealthy exclusives important common causes and enhanced standing in Britain. Both classes suffered from shortage of labour and wondered whether transportation should be abolished in the hope of encouraging free immigration. Increasingly, both classes complained against British land policy, especially the abolition of free grants in 1831 and the attempts to block the great squatting movement of the late 1820s and the 1830s. Both classes were opposed by many of the free immigrants who had no capital, and by wage earners and small businessmen and farmers, some of them poor emancipists, who complained that the government favoured men of large property.

The transportation question was fundamental in every matter affecting either the colony's progress towards representative government, or the increasing desire of its leaders to have control of land policy and public finance transferred from Britain to New South Wales.[145] In 1838 transportation was obviously near its end. In Britain it was attacked for lacking 'salutary terror', and for being too expensive, degrading to the colonies, uncertain in its treatment of individuals and incapable of reforming criminals. It was reviled also because it damaged the prospects of the new colony of South Australia (which had no convict labour to attract settlers) and caused 'unspeakable' immorality among the prisoners of the Crown. In March 1837 Russell told the Commons that New South Wales could no longer absorb 4000 to 5000 convicts a year without becoming the most depraved community the world had ever seen.[146] The argument was shrewdly matched to the mood of Whigs, wary of colonial scandals and only too willing to retrieve their own (then rather tarnished) reputation as reformers. His comment appealed also to the systematic colonisers, mostly disciples or associates of Edward Gibbon Wakefield, whose hopes of a middle-class empire of settlement in Australia were vain so long as transportation discouraged free emigration.

On 7 April the government agreed to a motion by the Radical Molesworth for a select committee to report on transportation and its effects on the moral state of the colonies. The committee included Wakefield supporters (among them Buller), as well as Russell, Howick, Peel and George Grey; Bulwer was added later. Its conclusions, were never in doubt. Glenelg wrote to Bourke on 26 April 1837 that, because of the evils of the assignment system (by which convicts worked for individual settlers), the government hoped to end transportation and stimulate free emigration. Bourke was ordered to prepare the colonists for the change.[147]

Under the chairmanship of Molesworth, the committee set out to prove that convictism had made New South Wales a moral dunghill. Bourke, who knew the truth, was disgusted.[148] Molesworth, whose own moral character displeased the censorious Howick,[149] encouraged witnesses to besmirch the colony. Macarthur, however, proudly remembered that he was an Australian, and Forbes was embarrassed. Unusually, the committee published part of its scabrous evidence at the end of the 1837 session, although its report was not tabled until April 1838.[150]

Spreading its net in constitutional waters, the committee questioned Macarthur about government in New South Wales. Buller wanted to know why the colony could not have the British constitution, Molesworth whether the principles of the Canada Act would be appropriate. Macarthur stated firmly that no customary form of representative government would be safe in a colony peopled so heavily by former convicts. The Rev. John Dunmore Lang, a Presbyterian anxious to build up a free Protestant society in New South Wales, also appeared before the committee. His constitutional views had recently been stated in the second edition of *An Historical and Statistical Account of New South Wales*. Lang condemned the legislative council as an 'irresponsible oligarchy' and the Patriotic Association as a 'Colonial Rag-Fair attended by all the blustering attorneys in the colony'. He sought, as an interim measure, an illiberal blended council of thirty members, ten nominated by the Crown, twenty chosen by the magistrates of the colony. In *Transportation and Colonization*, also published in 1837, Lang attacked the legislative council for its dependence on the government. 'Flogging' Mudie of Castle Forbes, whose angry *Felonry of New South Wales* (1837) described the colony as a 'huge penitentiary', attacked the Patriotic Association and asked for an increase in the number of unofficial nominees on the legislative council.[151]

The evidence given to the committee supported Macarthur's final position on constitutional reform and justified the committee's principal recommendation, that transportation to New South Wales and the settled districts of Tasmania be discontinued as soon as possible. When, on 6 March 1838, Molesworth moved a motion of no confidence in Glenelg, he emphasised the unfitness of New South Wales for representative government. The 'convict and once convict inhabitants of New South Wales', he told the Commons, like 'the ignorant and superstitious millions of India', 'the motley and not half or even quarter civilized population' of South Africa, and 'the labouring rustics for whom Parliament has provided the means of settlement in South Australia' were unfit for self-government.[152] Nevertheless, the Transportation Committee planned to make New South Wales something better than an anomalous society unfit for normal institutions of colonial government, and proposed an increase of free emigration, to compensate for loss of labour and improve morality. It also proposed that the price of land be raised from five shillings an acre (the minimum upset price established in 1831) to a fixed uniform price, somewhat on Wakefield's principles.

Soon after the Transportation Committee reported, the government introduced a Bill to continue the 1828 constitution for another year. At the third reading Buller complained that the colonists paid high taxes without representation and that transportation had continued too long. Ineptly, he gave away his own case: 'Five years of well-conducted emigration would place these colonies in the condition of being fully capable of taking care of themselves, and of enjoying those free institutions without which Englishmen ... would never be content.'[153] Only a 'very indifferent advocate', as Edward Macarthur thought Buller, would have admitted that the colony was still five years away from being fit for normal representative government. Buller failed to state that the gap between exclusives and emancipists was narrowing fast.[154] Unmoved by his advocacy, the government merely promised that, as transportation was about to end, a more liberal constitution would be proposed in the next session.

When Russell became Secretary of State for the Colonies in September 1839, he wrote to Howick that, in order to give free institutions to New South Wales, he had to 'rid that colony of its penal character as soon as possible'. Convict transportation to New South Wales was to cease, not only because it was offensive to the colony, but because of its rising costs, the abhorrence with which it was regarded in Britain, its failure either to deter or reform criminals and the policy complications in constitution making that arose from the anomalous state of society in the antipodes.[155] An order-in-council of May 1840 withdrew New South Wales from the list of places to which convicts might be transported.

In New South Wales the committee's report helped exclusives and emancipists to see that, although they might not readily enter one another's drawing rooms or sit in the same jury box, they did have common interests. No one, apart from lunatic extremists, approved the vilification of New South Wales. Neither the leading emancipists nor the exclusives, however, wanted transportation suddenly abolished, at the expense of the labour supply, unless free immigration replaced it at once. In June 1838 the council resolved that transportation was a cheap, effective punishment, and that convict labour was essential to colonial prosperity.[156] So the leaders of the emancipist party came into closer sympathy with Macarthur and the exclusives. The common interest in maintaining transportation was the more important because of the hostility to convictism among the rest of the community, which believed that transportation depressed wages, discouraged free emigration from Britain, made society and government illiberal and created social problems of which affluent emancipists and exclusives were unaware.[157]

The Patriotic Association, when its Committee of Correspondence wrote to Buller concerning his actions in April 1838, attacked the basis of British official thinking on the colony's constitution. It denied that there was 'any thing peculiar in the ... social state of these Colonies' to justify withholding representative institutions. Crime was no more rife in the colony than in Britain, whence the convicts came. Buller's plan for government through municipal institutions was strongly condemned as likely to produce an 'oligarchy of the worst description ... a *plutocracy*', lacking the virtues, such as they were, of English aristocracy. The committee rightly concluded that Buller had been over-persuaded by Macarthur and desired him to press for Wentworth's two draft Bills. Buller himself preferred Bill 'B', which proposed a blended legislature, as politically the more practicable, but saw little chance of having any such measure passed: Parliament was in turmoil over Canada and convinced of the wickedness of New South Wales; the Tories considered nothing on its merits and the Whigs exhausted themselves in clinging to office. The

Macarthurs, with quiet satisfaction, thought much the same, and the Patriotic Association in New South Wales carried on its work to have transportation continued.[158]

THE BLENDED COUNCIL ACHIEVED IN 1842

Constitution making from 1839 to 1842 was greatly different from in 1836–8. Forbes, a sick man, had returned to New South Wales, and died there in 1841. Howick's extraordinary influence at the Colonial Office ended when he resigned from the ministry in August. One of his last acts of interference was to urge George Grey to borrow on the security of the colonial lands in order to keep up free emigration to New South Wales. Bourke, though in retirement, was still consulted by the Office. His successor, Gipps, was again proving himself active, intelligent and too unbending. James Macarthur and his bride had gone to New South Wales, where he entered the legislative council in May 1840 and played an unexpectedly liberal role in colonial politics. The family's affairs in London were in the care of his brother Edward, less astute than James and lacking his political gifts, but assiduous and well connected.[159]

The return of James Macarthur to the colony marked the beginning of the end of his family's special power in the Colonial Office. Its final flowering between 1836 and 1838 was due partly to ignorance and confusion, in Downing Street, partly to the fact that Glenelg, Howick, George Grey and Stephen all sympathised with Macarthur's ideals of public duty and hierarchical society. They had respected his desire to combine the general good with the advancement of his own family, because that was the common aspiration of the classes to which they themselves belonged. The Macarthur influence in Downing Street declined because Canadian and West Indian problems and the rise of systematic colonisation dragged imperial problems into the full glare of politics; because of the growing size of the Colonial Office itself; and because changing conditions in New South Wales produced conflict between British policy and Macarthur's objectives.

Changing political circumstances in the colony, as leading exclusives came together with leading emancipists, and the numbers of free immigrants, remote from convictism, increased spectacularly, shifted Macarthur's position. The ending of transportation and the growth of free immigration turned Macarthur from an enemy of liberal constitutional reform into its most respectable advocate.

Free Immigration into New South Wales[160].

1831	407	1837	3477
1833	2685	1839	10549
1835	1428	1841	22483

By 1840 Macarthur wanted men of wealth and standing to decide in New South Wales, not in Britain, the great questions of land policy, land revenue and immigration on which colonial development depended. In order to bring about the necessary transfer of power from London to Sydney, he had to persuade British ministers of the opposite of what he had argued hitherto, and convince them that self-government was safe and overdue.

While colonial politics were in transition, Durham's famous *Report on the Affairs of British North America* was noted, but misunderstood, in New South Wales, and it had little influence there.[161] In the 1830s it had been fashionable for *The Sydney Herald*,[162] for example, to publish Canadian news, to show that the Colonial Office was incompetent everywhere. The *Herald* was politically independent, favoured respectable landholders and business and professional men, and was as vigorously hostile to Wakefield and the theorists of imperial land policy as to Molesworth the calumniator. The rebellions of 1837 and Durham's mission were reported as evidence that other British colonies also suffered under Whig misrule. The *Herald* thought Durham an ignorant, arrogant aristocrat whose behaviour in Canada was not above criticism. The Report itself, despite the boasts of Wakefield and Buller, fell flat in Australia. *The Sydney Gazette* published the text; long extracts appeared in the *Herald*, *The Australian* and *The Monitor*; but no newspaper understood it. *The Australian* complained of Durham's lack of 'originality or greatness of thought' and said he had overlooked the importance of the French in Lower Canada. The *Herald* was bewildered by Durham's account of responsible government and concluded that the main reason for reading the Report was to learn that Canada had been no better governed than New South Wales, the Cape or Jamaica. Crown lands particularly were mismanaged throughout the empire and no colony had sufficient self-government. Generally, the Report had no influence on the course of New South Wales politics. Five years later, when Wentworth referred to it in his demand for responsible government, he was relying more on mistaken notions of constitutional practice in Canada than on what Durham had written.[163]

The Colonial Office lagged behind the changing ideas of Macarthur and the leading exclusives. In 1839 it was studying Wentworth's Bill 'B' of 1835, and proposals received from Gipps, who, after experience, had decided to support most of Bourke's ideas.[164] Gipps rejected all plans to base colonial politics on municipal government and wanted a blended council of from twenty-four to thirty-six members, at least half and not more than two-thirds elected triennially. Emancipists were to be excluded from membership, but to be allowed to vote. After nine years, he thought, the colony would be ready for normal representative government. Gipps would have allowed the governor power to propose amendments to Bills submitted for his assent, to initiate Bills by message (as he was not to sit in the council) and to have the sole right to initiate money Bills. His ideas of the relationship of the executive with the legislature were informed by Canadian experience.

Had not land problems complicated proceedings, New South Wales would have received a modified version of the Gipps constitution in 1840. In the Commons, only Radicals would have opposed it. But the Colonial Land and Emigration Commissioners, appointed by Russell in 1840 to apply a common policy to the empire as a whole, pressed for land reforms and intruded theoretical notions of imperial development into what had been the relatively simple matter of deciding, on generally accepted criteria, whether New South Wales were fit to have a blended legislature. The commissioners wanted a uniform fixed price for land throughout Australia, except in the Nineteen Counties (proclaimed in New South Wales in 1829) and certain towns. They wanted the proceeds of the land sales to be spent on emigration and an emigration loan to be raised on the security of the land fund. Gipps scoffed at parts of their proposals, and the pastoralists condemned them fiercely, but Russell favoured them in a modified form and decided to partition New South Wales into three separate districts, each with its own land price and eventually its own government.[165] In this way the new enthusiasm for colonies of settlement delayed constitutional reform in Australia.

A Bill combining Gipps's proposed form of government and Russell's partition policy was introduced into the Commons on 30 June 1840. The blended council was to be established for ten years, after which New South Wales (but not any new colonies erected out of it) would be given the North American form of representative government. Subject to a civil list, the proposed new blended council was to appropriate all the colonial 'taxes, duties, rates and imposts', provided that the land revenues remained under imperial control. The Crown was empowered to subdivide the colony, and each new colony so established was to have a legislative council of at least seven members, including the lieutenant-governor. The Bill aroused strong opposition, because it did not discriminate against emancipists, did not transfer the land revenue to the control of the colony and inflicted partition on a colony known to value its own integrity. Russell withdrew the Bill on 14 July, believing that the ministry was too weak to fight on so uncertain a cause.[166]

In New South Wales reports of the Bill were received with mixed feelings. The Patriotic Association praised its constitutional principles. *The Australian* commended it for not penalising emancipists and for allowing a measure of representation, but condemned it for failing to surrender the land revenue to colonial control and for partitioning the colony, a measure that was seen as an unwarranted assault on the integrity and wealth of the colony. The representation allowed was criticised as tending to create 'a spirit of party and dissension between the advocates of popular rights on the one side and the defenders of the Government on the other'. Pastoralists, whether exclusives or emancipists, rejected the new land policy as a doctrinaire attempt to deprive them of cheap land and as a hazard to free immigration. Towards the end of 1840 New South Wales entered on a long depression, for which British policy was blamed so much that little but total ignorance and arrogance of power were expected from Downing Street.[167]

Later in the year a new Act (3 and 4 Vict., c. 62) continued the 1828 constitution for a further twelve months and empowered the Crown to separate islands within the government of New South Wales and erect them into colonies. (The power was used at once to separate New Zealand, which had for a short time been a dependency of New South Wales.)[168] Originally the Bill would have empowered the Crown to partition New South Wales, but Edward Macarthur prevailed on Peel to object against inserting a permanent provision into a temporary measure that should have been non-controversial.[169]

No one doubted that some form of representative government would soon be granted to the colony. *The Sydney Herald*, having at last learned how the Colonial Office looked at such problems, pointed out that, because transportation had ended, the colony's claims to a grant of representative institutions were as strong as the claims of old West Indian colonies like Jamaica to retain them. The *Herald* also argued that the colonists should be allowed to manage all their own affairs, including, most specifically, land settlement and the land sales fund, on which assisted immigration depended.[170]

At two public meetings in Sydney on 7 January and 4 February 1841 Macarthur called for a new era in colonial politics. Downing Street, he said, had evidently passed under Wakefield's dangerous influence, and its land policy had to be resisted. He did not explain that the Macarthurs, having extended far beyond their original vast freehold possessions in the Nineteen Counties, to join the squatting leaseholders in the south and south-west of New South Wales, had compelling reasons of their own for resisting Wakefield's doctrines. He preferred to explain generally that it was time to close the breach between exclusives and the emancipist party, so that representative institutions and power to control great matters of policy might be gained from Britain without delay.[171] He also failed to point out that Russell had already decided to make no special provisions, either in the new constitution or in the new municipality of Sydney, for emancipists, and that Wentworth also was urging that the old conflict be given up. Both meetings, forgetting that less than a year earlier Macarthur had wanted convict origins recorded in the census, readily supported his demands.[172]

The union, advocated by Macarthur, of leading exclusives and leaders of the emancipist party was always imperfect,[173] but it nevertheless alarmed less affluent colonists, who condemned as selfish the fears of the great pastoralists about rising land prices, partition of the colony and shortage of labour. The alliance of men of large property was almost a necessary condition of constitutional reform, but it was also politically unsettling within the colony and meant that, when Britain did transfer power from London to Sydney, power was given to men who thought that they should control land policy, the land fund and immigration.[174]

The tottering Whig government fell without putting Russell's constitution of 1840 onto the statute book. In March 1841 Edward Macarthur, following the same policy as his brother in Sydney, informed Russell that, provided that the colonists received representative institutions together with control over the lands, the land fund and immigration, they would pay for police and gaols. In April, when George Grote raised the same matter in the Commons, Russell's tired, cliché-ridden speech could have meant that he conceded part of what Edward Macarthur had asked: the colonists could have representative government, provided that they met the whole of the disputed expenditure. But the ministry was falling and could gain no credit by legislating for New South Wales. Russell's intentions were probably indicated when in July he cancelled his instructions on the alienation of Crown lands and ordered the governor to restore sale by auction.[175] In this way the case for partitioning the colony for the sake of land policy disappeared. A new Act (4 and 5 Vict., c. 44) continued the 1828 constitution for yet another year and *The Sydney Herald* called for protest meetings throughout the colony. In Feburary 1842 Macarthur, at a large Sydney meeting, again demanded representative government.[176]

As soon as the Tories took office, Buller pointed out to the new Secretary of State, Stanley, that all parties in the colony wanted a blended council. Stanley asked him for proposals for a Bill. Buller, instead of sending Wentworth's draft Bills of 1835, which he could neither find nor correctly remember, or reviving his own draft of 1838, pressed for Russell's Bill, subject to certain amendments.[177] He was particularly insistent that the Bill should not mention emancipists, because the emancipist party (which, through the Patriotic Association, employed him) was of diminishing importance, while free immigration had already changed the tone of colonial society.[178] Emancipists and their supporters, he declared, were far from radical. They had depended so long on the favours of the Crown and of governors that they were certainly not enemies of the British connection or lawful authority. If, asked Buller, Macarthur himself believed that the great anomaly of New South Wales society was no longer politically significant, why should a constitution Bill mention it? He could have added that Gipps and the Patriotic Association were of the same opinion. Buller was confident and pressing. In Sydney men were glad that the vacillating Whigs had gone and that a rising man like Stanley had taken the Colonial Office.[179]

Stanley hastened where his predecessors had delayed. He consulted Edward Macarthur and the New South Wales attorney-general, who was in London. Macarthur reported to his brothers with satisfaction that partition was abandoned, that the blended council would have twelve nominated and eighteen elected members (without discrimination against emancipists) and that provision was to be made for local government. Both Houses passed Stanley's Bill 'without a single dissentient voice'. Bourke, more liberal than the Tories, would have preferred a larger council, a lower elective franchise and a smaller proportion of nominees.[180]

The Australian Constitutions Act (No. 1), 5 and 6 Vict., c. 76, gave New South Wales the blended council that Darling, Forbes, Wentworth, Eagar and Buller had recommended. Stanley thought such a council appropriate for societies like those of Newfoundland and New South Wales, which were too divided, too lacking in political experience and too embarrassed by large numbers of inhabitants unsuited to political power to be granted conventional forms of representative government. New South Wales, however, did not receive its blended council until the major anomaly of its social structure, the great division between the emancipists and the exclusives, had been sufficiently diminished for most men of property to be willing to work together politically.

The new council was to have thirty-six members, two-thirds elected, one-third nominated by the Queen or the governor (subject to royal approval). Both sorts of member were to hold office for five years. Elected members were required to have a freehold of £2000 value (or £100 annual value), which was a rather high property qualification. No qualifications were prescribed for nominated members, not more than six of whom were to be officials, nominated by office or by name. The council might enlarge itself, subject to royal assent, but not so as to disturb the proportions of nominated and elected members. Electors had to have a freehold of £200 value, or the occupancy of a dwelling house of a clear annual value of £20. This was a fairly low qualification, for most dwelling houses in the towns were worth at least £10 a year; but it was high enough to be a barrier against the 'mob' who had supported Wentworth in his swash-buckling days and been so strongly condemned by John Macarthur Senior. Stanley recognised that some wealthy squatters might be excluded from electoral privileges because they were not freeholders, and asked Gipps to consider whether a leasehold qualification might be accepted in country districts. He also suggested that pastoral areas should be overrepresented, by fixing constituencies in terms of area as well as of population.[181]

The council that met for the first time in 1843 was so constructed that respect for property, profits and privilege was guaranteed, but respect for Downing Street and for governors was less well assured. A fixed civil list (the so-called 'Schedules') guaranteed £33,000 a year for the salaries of the governor, judges and principal officials, £18,600 for civil administration, and £30,000 for public worship. Revenue from fines, penalties and Crown lands was not subject to the council's appropriation. The governor was not to sit in the council (which elected its own speaker), but could require it to consider legislation that he proposed and could propose amendments to Bills that the council had passed. He could assent to, or withhold his assent from, or reserve for the royal pleasure, the Bills that the council passed; and his instructions required him to reserve some sorts of Bill anyway. The Crown retained power to disallow any colonial Act within two years. The governor could dissolve or prorogue the council at discretion and only he could recommend appropriations of the revenue that the council nominally controlled. The governor's responsibilities to the Crown for every act of colonial administration were unchanged. In theory, he had enough power to have some real independence of the council, but on terms that the council was certain to resist. Stanley had not yielded the power over lands and land revenues that Macarthur and other reformers in the colony had desired so strongly.

The governor and his imperial masters were intended to be strengthened by the system of local government established under the Act, but Stanley was hasty and the system was unworkable. Drawing on North American experience rather than on Howick's ideas, the Act provided for district councils with power to establish schools, manage roads and bridges, enact local bylaws, levy rates and tolls, and defray half the costs of the police (the other half being paid by the colony at large). Stanley looked to the district councils to check the authority of the new council and to ensure that the police were properly maintained. The first district councils were to be nominated by the governor; later they were to be elected, with the governor possessing power to fill vacancies caused by default of election. In practice, the local government provisions of the Act were resented in the colony as a cumbersome attempt to limit the power of the new council and had little practical importance.[182]

The governor and legislative council were empowered to make laws for the peace, welfare and good government of the colony, provided that no law was repugnant to the law of England, that the Crown lands and land revenue were reserved to imperial control as trusts for the empire as a whole and that Bills affecting customs duties, the salaries of the principal officers, or the constitution of the council (for instance, those affecting electoral divisions and the size of the council) were reserved for the royal assent. The Crown was empowered to define the borders of New South Wales and to establish new colonies north of latitude 26°S. The Port Phillip District (later Victoria), which resented Sydney domination, was given six of the elected members.

Stanley, increasingly involved in Canadian troubles between the executive and the legislature, doubted whether the governor would really have a working majority in the new council. Like the governor-general in

Canada, the governor in New South Wales had virtually to be his own prime minister, making policy and defending it, and contriving majorities in the legislature, although he did not sit there.[183] On 5 September Stanley suggested privately to Gipps that certain officials should hold elected seats, not so as to be responsible to the legislature, but so that the governor might have in the chamber the largest possible contingent obliged to follow his wishes,[184] and enjoy the political advantage of having his officials approved by the people. The colonial secretary, chief justice, bishop (if he sat on the council) and the officer commanding the troops were not to face election, but the collector of customs, the attorney-general, solicitor-general, treasurer and auditor-general might all contest seats. If they did not win a place, but were needed, Gipps could nominate them to the council. Similarly, he could appoint at his discretion any of the existing non-official members who failed to be elected. Gipps persuaded some officials to stand, but only the attorney-general was elected, and he in circumstances owing more to the large schemes of James Macarthur than to the calculations of Gipps or Stanley.[185]

The new constitution was introduced at the same time as the Australian Land Sales Act of 1842 (5 and 6 Vict., c. 36), whose principles of systematic colonisation were anathema to most landholders in the colony.[186] Taken together, the Constitution Act and the Land Sales Act kept the land fund entirely out of the colony's control and so deprived it of the richest revenue for colonial development. Imperial land policy was attacked in the colony as a fatal impediment to progress.

Colonial leaders wanted London to transfer to Sydney sufficient political power for the colony to have extensive control over its own development. They correctly regarded the systematic colonisers as enemies of colonial self-government, because Wakefield's policies assumed the supremacy of imperial interests over colonial interests, and of British political wisdom over colonial opinion. The clash that developed between British ministers (who claimed that the Crown lands and their revenue were imperial trusts, which could not be handed over to the colony) and colonial politicians (who demanded the right to control what they thought of as their patrimony) immediately weakened the new system of government and engendered clashes between the governor and the council, and the council and Britain.

Stephen opposed both Stanley's Acts of 1842. He condemned the fixed minimum price as wrong in policy and mistaken in detail, and believed that either the colony should have full control of its land revenue, or that the whole of the land revenue should be devoted to emigration.[187] He also opposed the establishment of a blended council, because he had lost faith in the utility of seating the nominees of the Crown in the same chamber as the elected representatives of the people. In 1848 he wrote to

Lord Grey, then Secretary of State, as if he had never supported blended councils:

> Former administrations devised in Newfoundland and New South Wales the scheme of a single Chamber. Having predicted with earnestness the failure of these schemes, I am probably under a bias when I conclude that they have failed. . . . the longer they are tried the more complete the failure will be. All colonial history — all theory — and I believe all recent experience are in favour of two Chambers.[188]

Stephen was then a tired and ill man.[189] When he had changed his mind on blended councils is not clear. As late as 1839, when he prepared the Cabinet papers on the New South Wales constitution, he had given no hint that he opposed blended councils, although allowing his judgement of other matters to be implied. In 1849, when his health and equanimity were somewhat restored, his only criticism of blended legislatures was that they were more liberal than the old representative system. He did not appear to regard this as a great fault.[190]

New South Wales did not receive its blended council, itself an anomalous form of government, until transportation had ceased and Britain had decided to promote settlement by immigration. These changes marked the counterpart in Britain to Macarthur's declaration, in New South Wales,' that the time had come to give up thinking of the social chasm between exclusives and the emancipist party as important in constitution making. Full representative government was thought of by Stanley as impossible for another five or ten years, by which time changes in the social structure of the colony should have made the working of normal institutions of colonial representative government entirely possible.

The blended council came too late to prevent rising political dissatisfaction in New South Wales.[191] The richest and most powerful colonists had enough confidence in their own cohesiveness, and sufficient resentment of British policy on lands, police and gaols, to be anxious that London should transfer to Sydney extensive power over the internal affairs of the colony. The old exclusives, in whom British ministers and officials had formerly placed so much trust, were at one with the leaders of the emancipist party in demanding more effective self-government and in disliking Stanley's doctrine that the governor had to be kept strong and assured a working majority in the new legislature.

6 Responsible Government in Britain

The most important thing in the history of an empire is the history of its mother country.

Richard Pares[1]

Parliamentary Government . . . requires the powers belonging to the Crown to be exercised through Ministers, who are held responsible for the manner in which they are used, who are expected to be members of the two Houses of Parliament, the proceedings of which they must generally be able to guide, and who are considered entitled to hold their offices only while they possess the confidence of Parliament and more especially the House of Commons.

Third Earl Grey[2]

The Upper Canadian reformers who during the 1830s sought responsible government were seeking, as historians have since agreed, to gain the established conventions of the British constitution. Some of the reformers, most notably Robert Baldwin, were certainly asking for what they believed to be the British constitution, promised in 1791 and modified by changing conventions. They sought, in respect of all the internal affairs of the colony, a parliamentary executive, instead of an executive council that was remote from the assembly and rarely changed in membership. They expected the governor to exercise a personal discretion in appointing and removing his advisers, whether individually or collectively, so as to keep them in harmony with the assembly. This system the reformers named 'responsible government', contrasting the responsibility that they wished members of the government to owe to the elected assembly with the lack of such responsibility in existing practice.[3]

In the 1830s Baldwin and his supporters did not seek responsible government in the modern sense. Britain herself did not then have a parliamentary executive composed of ministers depending collectively for their title to office on retaining the confidence of the elected house of the legislature. This form of government did not become a convention of the constitution until the 1840s. Apparent exceptions and special cases were common for another three decades, and one important part of the principle was not clear until 1929. In Britain in the 1830s the sovereign still had a large enough discretion in appointing and removing his advisers to be able to ignore the wishes of Parliament, at least in the short run. The King's ministers depended on his confidence for their title to office and on the confidence of Parliament (especially the Commons) for their ability to legislate and govern. The King appointed or removed ministers at his discretion; Parliament might contest their tenure of office. Substantially, this was the system that Robert Baldwin desired for Upper Canada. He wished the governor to have an independent discretion to change his advisers, so often as the public interest appeared to him to require, instead of letting them hold office for life. Obviously, the governor would have to maintain harmony between the executive and the legislature, but Baldwin did not then claim that the assembly should have constitutional power to compel the governor to change his advisers, or that all the governor's advisers should be members of the legislature.

In the early 1840s, while responsible government in the modern sense emerged as a convention of the constitution in Britain, it was demanded in North America with vigour and determination.[4] There a system of government approximating to that sought by Baldwin in the 1830s had been introduced by Governor-General Sydenham in 1841 and failed to gratify either local aspirations or its original sponsors. For reasons that were principally colonial, rather than the result of influences proceeding from constitutional changes then occurring in Britain, Baldwin and his allies in united Canada sought government by party or parties responsible to the assembly, with the governor-general's discretion in appointing and removing ministers reduced to a minimum of special cases. The reformers were wholly dissatisfied with the Sydenham system, and, beginning with Nova Scotia in 1846, party government was conceded to most of the provinces of British North America.

According to administrators and political men in Britain, a colony could not be allowed to govern itself except according to British polity; its laws had to be made by representatives of the free men of property, and they themselves had to form a class that could reasonably be trusted to legislate and govern on behalf of the colony as a whole. Changes in a colony could bring it nearer to, or farther from, a grant of increased self-government. Similarly, changes in the constitution and government of Britain could affect the requirements that British statesmen imposed when looking at colonial demands for self-government.

So far as the colonies were concerned, the great importance of the coming of responsible government in Britain was that the sovereign lost to the Commons the power to choose ministers and determine policy. If Britain could have party or parliamentary government, as the new system of government through ministers depending for office on the confidence of a majority of the Commons came to be called, why should the system not be permitted in British colonies that already had representative institutions? Party government was not inconsistent with monarchy or the stability of the realm. In colonies that had men of property and political understanding to represent the community as a whole as legislators, what could Britain lose if the governor had to entrust the administration to members commanding a majority in the elected house, instead of to executive councillors chosen and appointed by the Crown? What British interests were served when the governor or the Secretary of State appointed and removed heads of departments in the self-governing colonies? Would not Britain gain political advantages by containing within each colony every political question on which the mother country did not reasonably need to have the final word? These were questions that Howick had asked since 1831, and that Durham too had asked; reformers like Baldwin were sure of the answers.

In seeking responsible government, Baldwin and his colleagues did not ask for power over matters in which Britain clearly had her own or general imperial interests to preserve. They were willing that the responsible government of a colony be limited to its domestic concerns, allowing such imperial matters as foreign policy, the constitution and form of government, or the public lands to be controlled by the British Parliament and by ministers responsible to the House of Commons. The problem of sovereignty was solved without precision, but with faith in the good sense and goodwill of all concerned, by assuming that Britain would retain her supremacy, that she would not exercise it in purely colonial matters, and that there would be no great clashes over the demarcation of imperial and colonial questions.

Before responsible government was granted in British North America, major changes occurred to make the great reform possible. In Britain, as this chapter shows, responsible government became a convention of the constitution. A sea change occurred in attitudes to colonies of settlement, which came to be regarded as part of an imperial destiny to plant British people and institutions overseas. The triumph of free trade in the 1840s helped to make colonies of settlement more attractive than they would otherwise have been. At the critical stage in this decade, when responsible government was granted, colonial policy was controlled by men (notably Grey and Russell) who thought of colonies of settlement as commercial partners and complements of the mother country in a free trade empire (see Chapter 7). Lastly, experience in North America showed that no political system other than responsible government was likely to keep valuable colonies within the empire (see Chapter 8).

The introduction of this form of government into the empire was not the consequence of the triumph of free trade, as used to be thought, but rather, a direct continuation of the long process by which British statesmen thought of colonial self-government in British terms and allowed it only where it would flourish according to British polity. Free trade affected the introduction of responsible government only in so far as the coming of free trade and of the new concept of colonies of settlement were inextricably linked during the 1830s and 1840s.

SOVEREIGN, PARLIAMENT AND MINISTERS

When William IV became King, neither Whigs nor Tories accepted the modern principle of government by ministers responsible to Parliament. Probably the Whigs were moving faster than the Tories away from eighteenth-century ideas of a mixed form of government, in which the checks and balances regulating the relations of sovereign, Lords and Commons had generally favoured the throne. The sovereign had his own sources of influence in both Houses of Parliament, and benefited from the convention that loyal subjects supported the King's ministers as long as they could in conscience do so. The critical tests of the changing conventions of the constitution were the rise, to respectability and place, of His Majesty's Opposition, who opposed the King's ministers and might replace them, and the declining ability of the sovereign to change his ministers and command electoral support for them if the Commons disapproved his choice.

Between 1835 and 1841 both Sir Robert Peel and Lord Melbourne were able — for considerable periods and with the strong support of the sovereign — to hold office as Prime Minister without commanding a majority in the Commons. Neither William IV nor, to begin with, Victoria faced any determined challenge to the royal claim to appoint, remove and retain ministers, whether or not they controlled majorities in the Commons. Indeed, the prerogative power of the sovereign to choose his or her own ministers was not substantially checked until after the changes following the Reform Act had combined with the growth of the constitutional Opposition and the decline of the 'influence of the Crown' (the power of the sovereign to control seats in the Commons) to alter profoundly the relations of ministers with Parliament.[5]

The question of whether a ministry had a duty to resign if it lost the confidence of the Commons had been debated in the early months of 1784, soon after Pitt had taken office as Prime Minister although supported by only a minority of the Commons.[6] Fox, moved by opposition to Pitt and resentment at his own dismissal by George III, declared that ministers not supported by a majority of the Commons ought to resign. The Commons were 'stationed as sentinels by the people' and had a right to compel ministers to resign. He moved that the House send an address to the King, 'that the continuance of an administration, which does not possess the confidence of the representatives of the people, must be injurious to the public service'. Pitt answered that ministers had to resign only in the improbable event of losing a general vote of no confidence, containing specific charges. The disapprobation of the House 'placed ministers in an awkward and unpleasant situation; but that it should force them to retire . . . was an unconstitutional doctrine, hostile to the prerogative of the crown, and to that balance of power, on which the excellence of our government depended'.[7] Fox's motion was carried by 201 votes to 184, but Pitt stayed in office.

After an unprecedented number of addresses from counties and boroughs had supported the King, the government and the constitution, Pitt obtained a dissolution; the King had suggested it in January, but Pitt, despite the inconvenience of defeats in the House, had preferred to wait. At the elections the influence of the Crown and an appeal to support the King's ministers helped him to a victory that virtually confirmed the royal proceedings since the fall of North.

In 1784 Fox challenged not only the King's prerogative powers, but also the important convention that members of Parliament should support the King's government so long as honest men could.[8] Fox argued that the convention could not prevail over the right of the Commons to get rid of ministers. George III and Pitt relied on it triumphantly; in the 1830s it still survived, though more among Tories than among Whigs.[9]

After 1784, dissolution before the end of a Parliament's normal life of seven years became 'a powerful aggressive weapon in the hands of the King' to enable ministers to carry on despite the hostility of the Commons or to give new ministers a favourable House.[10] George III and his successors used dissolution as a means of exercising their power to appoint and remove ministers. The general elections of May 1796, June 1802 and June 1818 followed dissolutions intended to improve the position of the ministry; those of Marcch 1784, October 1806, April 1807 and September 1812 were intended to improve the position of new administrations. The Opposition attacked as abuse of the prerogative the growing use of dissolutions after the King had changed his ministry: ministers unable to command a majority in the Commons ought to resign, and not appeal to the country save in extraordinary circumstances. Ministers, however, strongly defended the King's powers to appoint and remove his advisers and to dissolve. How, they asked, could it ever be wrong to appeal to the sense of the people?

The use of the prerogative to dissolve became risky for the King as the ability of his ministers to win general elections waned. The influence of the Crown had been declining gradually for over half a century before the Reform Act extinguished it almost entirely. Its destruction, wrote Foord, 'was effected, not by any enactment or group of enactments, but by a long train of legislation, administrative reform, and changed attitudes to public life'.[11] Even before 1832 the Crown could no longer determine a majority in the House of Commons. While the influence of the Crown declined, and not merely because of the decline, the strength and power of the Opposition increased. 'By the mid-1820's it was generally accepted that "His Majesty's Opposition"[12] constituted an essential part of the state's political machinery . . . as an alternative Government'. In the Commons two loosely organised parties, or groups of parties, both loyal to the throne and both potentially capable of commanding a majority in the Commons, contended for power. The way was opening for the Commons to choose for itself between the competing sets of ministers. Similarly, opposition in colonial assemblies and (more rarely) councils began to be accepted as neither contumacy nor disloyalty, but as the just, lawful presentation of alternative policies, which the executive was bound to consider. Governors, many of them soldiers, were more reluctant to admit this change than were their political superiors at home.

These changes were less apparent to contemporaries than they have been to historians since. For example, the increasing (and successful) use of the King's name in elections helped to disguise the effects of the decline in the royal power of patronage. Careful assessments of the constitution failed to notice the changes that had already occurred. The peculiar sequence of ministries that followed the death of Liverpool, when in less than a year Canning, Goderich and Wellington succeeded one another to the post of Prime Minister led even shrewd Bathurst to think that party was declining: 'The Events of last year have dissolved all great political attachments, by which a powerful Party is kept together; and there is not at present any great political Question, which would force men to range themselves on one side or the other which might . . . reconstruct the Elements of a Party.'[13]

Before Bathurst died in 1834, Parliament had emancipated the Catholics, reformed the franchise, decided to emancipate the slaves, and run into trouble on the Irish question. In March 1827 Stephen R. Lushington, then Joint Secretary to the Treasury, still attributed to the King an authority, almost unlimited by the constitution, to choose his ministers, although he admitted that political pressures might affect the choice.[14] Some contemporaries foresaw that the Reform Bill, if passed, would radically change the relations of sovereign, ministers and Commons. During the debates on the Bill Peel asked, 'How could the King hereafter change a Ministry? How could he make a partial change in the administration, in times of public excitement, with any prospect that the Ministers of his choice, unpopular perhaps from the strict performance of necessary duties, would be returned to Parliament?'[15] The Act left the King in command of only twenty or thirty seats at a general election and embodied the great change, from prescription to representation, in the principles of the constitution. The Commons took ten years to learn that it had gained the means of controlling the royal choice of ministers.

When Parliament met after the first elections under the Act, Charles Greville, Clerk of the Council, and formerly private secretary to Bathurst, thought that 'The Government has evidently no power over the House of Commons. . . . we are now reduced to . . . Lord Grey's Government or none at all; 'should he be defeated on any great measure, he must either abandon the country to its fate, or consent to carry on the government upon the condition of a virtual transfer of the executive power to the House of Commons.'[16] Greville predicted that the Commons would make itself as powerful as the Long Parliament had been and reduce the authority of the Crown 'to a mere cypher'. By the end of the session he thought his own judgement too severe, although he considered its general tenor not mistaken.[17] The power of the Crown in the Commons was diminishing and the power of the Commons to control the King and his ministers was growing.

In the 1830s these were strong trends, but not yet conventions of the constitution. In 1841 the Commons debated on whether the government could be carried on constitutionally by ministers who did not command a majority in the House. In 1835 more voices were raised, both in and out of Parliament, to defend the prerogative power of appointing and removing ministers, regardless of the will of the Commons, than were raised to condemn it. Looking back to the crisis of 1783–4, men criticised George III for having granted a dissolution to Pitt, rather than for having dismissed Fox and North. The government, they thought, was the King's government; the sovereign would judge more wisely than the politicians because kingly duty and attributes lifted him above party and personality; politicians should bow to his choice. Not until 1841, when the Commons debated Peel's motion of want of confidence in Melbourne's government, was the essential principle of responsible government, that the will of the Commons must prevail in appointing and removing ministers, accepted by the House in a way that politicians came to regard as generally binding.

The principles claimed for Upper Canada in the 1830s, that the executive of the colony should be parliamentary, and responsible to the elected assembly in all colonial matters, were objected to in Britain on three distinct grounds. The reformers were asking that the governor should appoint his advisers from among the members of the legislature and change them (within an undefined area of discretion) when they lost the confidence of the assembly. A majority of the assembly might force him to use his discretion to remove advisers of whom he approved, or whom the sovereign's ministers in Britain preferred to retain. In Britain in the 1830s the constitutional position was quite different from this. The sovereign was altogether more powerful and more august than any governor could ever be, and had his own sources of power in both Houses. The Commons did not insist that the royal prerogative to appoint and remove ministers should be exercised only according to its will. Peel, as we shall see, went to extraordinary lengths to avoid even the appearance of such a limitation to the prerogative. The King's ministers might be forced out of office by prolonged failure to carry their measures through Parliament, or, more doubtfully, by a vote of general censure containing specific accusations; but their title to govern, as distinct from their ability to do so, rested on the confidence of the sovereign, not of the Lords and Commons. Whigs and Tories still had to learn that the power of the Crown to have a House returned in favour of the King's ministers was by 1832 a thing of the past. The colonial demand for responsible government, without the restraints of an old and privileged monarchy, seemed so inconceivably dangerous in Britain, when understood at all, that even the liberal Howick failed to comprehend it correctly.[18]

Again, every commonsense view of the imperial constitution suggested that the introduction of responsible government into colonies could never be reconciled with their proper subordination to Crown and Parliament. A governor might have to accept as his advisers persons advocating policies that Westminster could not approve and be exposed to the dilemma that Russell stated so memorably in 1839. Lastly, it was difficult for men of affairs in Britain to trust the democratic assemblies of the colonies. Britain, Gladstone reminded the Commons, was in its ideas of rank, property, inheritance and culture, an aristocratic country.[19] The bases of polity in Britain and the colonies seemed so different that for long it appeared neither wise nor safe for Britain to allow colonial legislatures to have a strong influence, perhaps even a decisive voice, in the appointment of colonial governments.

THE DISMISSAL OF MELBOURNE AND THE 'PREMATURE CONSCRIPTION'[20] OF PEEL

When George IV was near death in April 1830, the Whig lawyer Lord Campbell remarked that he had been a perfect constitutional monarch, having 'stood by and let the country govern itself'.[21] William IV, however, firmly asserted a right both to appoint and to remove ministers according to his own ideas on policy, regardless of what the Commons might think. When he did so men were astonished, but offered little effective criticism on constitutional grounds; politicians and the country alike felt obliged to acknowledge the King's right to change his ministers at will.

After Lord Grey resigned as Prime Minister in July 1834, the King feared that the country would be given over to reforming Whigs like Lord John Russell. He sent for Melbourne, not to form a Whig ministry, but to promote a coalition ministry of Whigs and Tories that would command a majority in the Commons and follow conservative policies. Melbourne declined to serve on these terms, and Peel agreed with him that what the King desired was impossible.[22] Eventually Melbourne was allowed to form a government according to his own ideas. The little confidence that his ministry enjoyed at the palace was shattered when the moderate Lord Althorp, leader of the government in the Commons, went to the upper house on the death of his father, and Russell succeeded to his office in the Commons. The ministry's policy towards the Irish Church convinced the King that he must rid himself of such dangerous advisers and in November 1834 he dismissed them and called on the Tories to govern in their stead. Parliament was not in session; the Whigs had a majority in the Commons and the Tories did not.[23]

'It is quite clear', wrote Howick in his journal, that the fall of the government 'was far from the thoughts of any of the ministers thus unceremoniously dismissed. . . . Can the King have taken this step without being assured that the Tories would undertake the government?'[24] He had;[25] his action embarassed the Tories and enraged the Whigs. Of the Tory leaders, Peel was in Italy and Wellington would not form a ministry. In order that the King's government might be carried on, however, Wellington made himself a one-man caretaker administration until Peel could return from the Continent.

Two and a half years earlier, in the famous 'Days of May', Peel had declined to join Wellington in forming a government to pass the Reform Bill. He had recognised that the Bill would pass, because the Whigs, if necessary, would take office in order to pass it;[26] the King had then had an alternative government available. In 1834, however, Melbourne had been dismissed after only four months in office and there was no alternative government ready to replace the Whigs. The King had jeopardised the prestige of the Crown, and Peel believed that William IV had left him no choice: 'I could not reconcile it to my feeling, or indeed to my sense of duty, to subject the King and the monarchy to the humiliation, through my refusal of office, of inviting his dismissed servants to resume their appointments. My refusal could only have been on avowed disapprobation of the course taken by the King.'[27] He took responsibility for the King's actions, including the dismissal of Melbourne and the summoning of Wellington, and formed a ministry with the support of less than a quarter of the Commons.[28]

The Whigs greatly resented their fall from power. Some considered the King's actions unconstitutional; a majority was determined to force Peel out of office, whatever his policy might be. Nothing comparable had occurred since George III had rid himself of Grenville's Ministry of All the Talents. Campbell, who had become attorney-general, thought William's action 'preposterous', but neither he nor any other prominent person chose to attack the King publicly. The Whigs had no wish for a trial of strength with the throne. They complained vigorously of Peel's choice of ministers and criticised his decision (contrary to Pitt's precedent of 1784) to dissolve Parliament during the recess, before the government had tried its strength there. They attacked Wellington and defended Melbourne, but they did not object publicly to the constitutional principles on which the King had acted.[29]

The country greatly supported the King's action: William IV was popular and appeared to have acted from honest sense of duty. Cobbett defended 'the undoubted prerogative of the King, which has been given for our security'.[30] The electors, responding to what Melbourne called 'the natural influence . . . of the King's name',[31] swung to the Tories, although not sufficiently to make Peel safe. Greville wrote that,

> Though the Crown is not so powerful as it was, there probably still remains a great deal of attachment and respect to it, so that if the King can show a fair case to the country, there will be found both in Parliament and out of it a vast number of persons who will reflect deeply upon the consequences of coming to a serious collision with the Throne, and consider whether the exigency is such as to justify such extremities.[32]

The Westminster Review, however, which had been founded to reflect Radical and working-class opinion, attacked the King's actions as inconsistent with parliamentary government. This hostile judgement required a clear innovation of principle; neither Lords nor Commons claimed that such a great constitutional change had occurred. Even those who would have agreed with a correspondent in *Spectator*, that the King's actions were 'incompatible with Parliamentary Government', would also have agreed, that the matter was one for grumbling wonder, not great protest.[33]

The elections gave Peel neither a majority in the Commons nor sufficient men of quality to win support there. Even in the Admiralty boroughs and other constituencies where the influence of the Crown still existed the Tories lost, apparently because the voters thought their tenure precarious and treated the Whigs as though they were still the King's government.[34] Peel suffered for his sovereign's old-fashioned notions of the constitution. To those who could read the signs correctly, it was clear that dissolutions could no longer be trusted to produce a majority for the ministers of the King's choice.

The debate on the address at the opening of the new Parliament touched only incidentally on the constitutional aspects of the King's change of government. Lord Sandon, who moved the address, denied the suggestion sometimes made outside Parliament, that the Reform Act had in practice limited the prerogative power of the King to choose his ministers. Sandon had voted for the Reform Bill, but in 1835 he still believed that 'the prerogative . . . was essential to protect the liberties of the people from the domination of the factions'.[35] Lord Morpeth, who moved the Whig amendment to the address, admitted that the sovereign had an 'undoubted prerogative' to dismiss ministers, but insisted that this power existed along with the power of the Commons to accept or reject the King's ministers: 'Whether before or after the passing of the Reform Bill, the power must reside with this House — and through this House, with the people of this country — of deciding who the Ministers of the Crown are to be.'[36] Morpeth, as the actions of the Whigs between 1835 and 1841 showed, meant only that the Commons, though it would normally acquiesce in the sovereign's choice of ministers and would always endeavour to do so, claimed a right to reject his choice. This was still fairly close to the practice of the later eighteenth century, apart from the fundamental difference, not mentioned by Morpeth, that the King's government could no longer be certain to win a general election.[37]

Throughout the debate on the address no one challenged the constitutional right of the minority to govern. When an amendment condemning the dissolution as unnecessary was carried, two well connected observers — Croker, the former Tory secretary to the Admiralty, and Greville — thought that the ministry might have to resign because it was in a perpetual minority and the vote was virtually one of no confidence. However, the Opposition did not press its advantage and Peel remained uncomfortably in power.[38]

William IV was shaken to learn that Peel did not command enough votes to control the election of the Speaker, and the rigidity of the Opposition, together with Peel's inability to command support among moderate Whigs, astounded him.[39] Was it not a duty to support his minister? His own rashness had left him dependent on the constancy of Peel, on the surviving forces of deference to the sovereign and of loyalty to the King's government, and on the probability that the Opposition would not turn the ministry out until some great question gave them public justification.

Russell, the leading member of the Opposition in the Commons, charged Peel with having contravened the principles of representative government, but did not spell out the accusation in detail nor attempt to overthrow the government.[40] In the country the King was too popular and his powers still too unchallenged to encourage the Whigs to attack, as strongly as they could have done, the ministers of the King's choice. *Fraser's Magazine*, whose politics were Tory, remarked that most of the Commons, whatever their party, were pledged to their constituents to offer 'no factious opposition' to the King's government and would not use the money power of the Commons to stop supply and force the government to resign.[41] The Whigs were restrained also by lack of unity. 'They are gone as a party to the Devil', wrote Creevey to Countess Grey.[42] The Whig leaders were landed aristocrats, but their following in the Commons after 1832 owed much to urban and non-English constituencies. Opposition of interests within the party embarrassed its leaders because majorities composed of discordant Whigs and of Irish members and Radicals were always uncertain.[43] Nor was the problem of who should lead the Whigs solved. If the Tories were driven from power, which Whig aristocrat would become Prime Minister? The King would have hoped for Grey; a majority of the party might have preferred Melbourne; Russell had his own ambitions. Stanley, already moving towards the Tories, disliked the government but was 'unwilling to vote for anything which might have the effect of turning them out without seeing by what sort of government they are likely to be succeeded'.[44] No one could hope to dislodge Peel until some great question united the Whigs and their allies and gave them some popular support for ousting the ministers whom the King had so recently appointed.

The Tories, on the other hand, were too weak to take advantage of the divisions among their opponents. Howick, after a poor showing by the government, wrote pityingly, 'I never saw a man look more wretched than Peel did'.[45] 'Bear' Ellice thought that 'Peel's fate depends rather upon the incapacity and unpopularity of his colleagues and supporters, than upon any union ... on the part of his opponents. He fights his battle well; pleads his duty to the King as a justification for submission to the personal mortifications which his position necessarily exposes him to.'[46] Disturbed by threatened motions of no confidence, which were never brought forward, Peel pleaded for a 'fair trial' while he governed according to the wishes of the King. Defeats inflicted on his ministry he described as merely 'accidental', not implying lack of confidence and not requiring resignation.[47] Parliament did not debate this view of the constitution until six years later, when Peel drove Melbourne from office and had to reconcile criticisms of the Whigs with his own behaviour in 1835.

In March Peel wrote to his colleagues to defend staying in power and to prepare for leaving it: 'Nothing can, in my opinion, justify an administration in persevering against a majority, but a rational and well-grounded hope of acquiring additional support, and converting a minority into a majority. I see no ground for entertaining that hope.'[48] He set no time limits to the 'rational and well-grounded hope' of the King's ministers, but he did outline the dangers to good government, ministerial prestige and the prerogatives of the Crown that might result from a prolonged attempt to govern with a minority. Political misjudgement might imperil the constitution, he thought, but Wellington and the King urged him to carry on so long as he possibly could.[49]

Events soon forced Peel's hand. On 20 March the government introduced a Bill for the commutation of Irish tithes. Ten days later Russell moved for a committee of the whole house to consider the temporalities of the Irish Church. Peel sent a circular to Cabinet, pointing out that Russell had moved a virtual vote of no confidence. If Russell won, the government might have to rule Ireland either on principles that

ministers did not accept, or (if the Lords rejected the Whig policy) on
principles not acceptable to the Commons. The question was 'practical,
and fearfully practical'. The Commons passed Russell's resolution and, on
his further motion, resolved that the government's Bill be amended to
allow the surplus revenues of the Irish Church to be appropriated for
education in Ireland.[50]

Peel's position was hopeless: 'The longer we protract the struggle, if
that struggle shall be ultimately unavailing,' he wrote to Wellington on 4
April, 'the more certain will be the blow at the Royal authority.' The
Whigs were already at work 'forming a new Government'/that would have
a majority in the Commons. Grey was aiding them /in the hope that
Howick might be in the ministry, even if he himself stayed out. The danger
to the Crown, thought Peel, was that if the King accepted a Whig ministry
he would appear to have been merely the servant of the Commons: 'When
it is actually installed, it will have to the whole world the appearance of
having been nominated by the House of Commons, having been dictated
to the King, and of continuing in office independently of his will and
control.'[51] This would have been responsible government almost in its
modern form, and Peel was appalled at so great a change in the
constitution.[52] His resignation on 8 April was an attempt to preserve
the prerogatives that the King had overstrained: 'the House of Commons,
having been habituated to the exercise of functions not properly belonging
to them will be unwilling to relinquish it, . . . the Royal prerogative and
. . . authority will inevitably suffer from continued manifestations of
weakness on the part of the Executive Government'.[53] Having lost Peel,
the King would have welcomed Grey's return to office, but the old earl,
uncertain of support among the Whigs, preferred Howick Hall to Downing
Street. Melbourne formed the new government, for only he seemed likely
to command a majority in the party.[54]

Since William IV no sovereign has attempted to dismiss a ministry in
Britain, and in 1835 the House of Commons did eventually make its will
prevail. But, like George III in 1784, the King had been able to keep his
ministers in power for months, despite constant defeats in the Commons.
He had also ignored their rejection by the country, a rebuff that his father
had been spared.

Brougham summed up the position in 1835 in terms that implied some
change in the constitution: 'The Crown has the power of making a
Ministry, but not such a Ministry as the people will not have. . . . Within
certain limits the choice exists; only it is not absolute and universal.' The
'limits' were still wide enough in 1835 to accommodate Peel's view that
the first responsibility of the King's ministers was to him and not to
Parliament. They might hold office while seeking a majority, and had no
duty to resign merely because of defeat at elections or because the
Commons was against them on a particular question, unless their position

as a government trying to implement a course of policy was quite hopeless. They would then give up office on political, not constitutional grounds.

When Melbourne succeeded Peel, the King exchanged a government that could not carry its measures in the Commons for one united principally by opposition to the Tories. The *Edinburgh Review*, which supported the Whigs, claimed that, although King, Lords and Church might oppose them, the people were for them. Brougham thought that he had observed the beginnings of an important constitutional change: 'We are now stating the most precious result of the Reform, namely, the intimate connection between the people and the Ministry, and the fact of the Ministry being now the people's servants rather than the Crown's.'[55]

Croker also recognised that such a change might be occurring, but, as a conservative, regretted the rising power of the Commons and the people. He hoped for a return to constitutional government with ministers properly responsible to the sovereign, instead of allowing government to fall into the hands of 'factions and cabals', who would lead the country into anarchy.[56] *Fraser's Magazine*, then gaining popularity as a conservative journal interested in limited reform, believed that the fall of Peel might have introduced a novel principle – that a ministry, even if not formally censured, had to resign if it lost the support of the Commons. *Fraser's* condemned the alleged new principle strongly. The Commons ought never to gain supreme executive power in addition to its already large share of legislative power, for it would rob 'the true executive' of all authority and become the effective ruler of the country. Ministers were the King's ministers, and should have his confidence; but constitutionally they did not need the confidence of the Commons, either collectively or individually. *Fraser's* disliked the growth of parties, preferring the days when a ministry might have the regular support of only a third of the Commons, and need to win the support of independent gentlemen loyal to the King's government in order to pass its measures.[57]

Fraser's had read the writing on the wall before it was legible to most of the Commons. The sovereign's power to appoint, remove and sustain ministers was never as great after 1835 as before, although some elements of it remained and were used by Victoria. Another great change, for which *Fraser's* could have held William IV partly responsible, was the regeneration of the Tory Party throughout the country. With the revival of Tory strength came a hardening of party lines. 'It was clear now what post-reform politics would be about and where post-reform party lines could be drawn.'[58]

THE BEDCHAMBER CRISIS AND COLONIAL POLICY

Melbourne's new government survived the smouldering hostility of William IV and won eager royal favour when Victoria became Queen in June 1837.

As a result the Whigs campaigned with panache for the elections held in July, on the demise of the Crown; but, although their position was strengthened, they failed to win a reliable majority to carry their measures in the Commons. Radicals and Irish members remained the Whig's necessary, but uncertain, allies. Howick believed that misgovernment continually eroded support for the administration, both in the Commons and in the country. Grey agreed that the ministry had more than a reasonable share of incompetents, and criticised Melbourne for not taking a strong line of policy that might capture popular support, compel the irresponsible Radicals to behave sensibly, and permit the Queen's ministers to govern effectively.[59]

When news of the Canadian rebellions reached England just before Christmas 1837, the Whigs first looked to save themselves from the imminent danger of united attack by Tories and Radicals. Peel advised his party not to make capital out of the rebellion, the effects of which on British prestige were incalculable.[60] His wisdom saved the Whigs from the worst they feared, but could not prevent his followers attacking Durham's mission to North America. Objections to the appointment of Wakefield and Turton to Durham's staff, legal criticisms of Durham's actions (especially the famous Bermuda Ordinance of 29 June), and blasts at the special council through which Durham was to work were used to enlist votes that might harry the Whigs, come what may in North America. Melbourne himself, evasive and equivocal, failed to give Durham proper support. Howick, although never willing to support Durham at every point, was ashamed when Melbourne announced that the Bermuda Ordinance would be disallowed, and chafed at his own inability to insist on a proper course.[61]

In August, with the Tories in full cry, the Durham crisis seemed likely to overthrow the ministry. Howick soon complained that Melbourne's tactics of bowing to any storm rather than surrender office had discredited the government with its natural supporters, liberals throughout the country. He cheerfully awaited its destruction at the hands of the Tories. Russell, weary and petulant, blamed the Lords for the government's misfortunes in Canada and attributed every problem, from the national debt to 'a bad law for Canada', to the errors of Pitt.[62]

The troubled year ended without the overthrow of the government and without any claim in Parliament that it was unconstitutional of the Whigs to cling to office while so weak in the Commons. They remained the Queen's government, graced with her favour. Elections had been held only a year before and the Tories lacked the numbers and, possibly, the will to drive the Whigs into resignation. But constitutional questions were in the air. *Fraser's* wanted to know how Melbourne's privileged position at Court could be reconciled with the duties of a Prime Minister.[63] Greville, at the end of the session in August 1838, reflected on how difficult the position of the Tories had become:

> The great mass of the Tories are always fretting ... at the Whigs' retaining possession of office ... but the wiser ... know that, however weak the Whigs may be as a Government, ... they are fortified in their places by certain barriers which their adversaries are still more powerless to break through; for they have the cordial, undoubted support of the Queen, they are the Ministers of her choice and they have a majority in the House of Commons.[64]

If it had been right for William IV to place Tories in power in 1834, without the support of the Commons, how much more right was it for the Queen to keep the Whigs in power, when they were still supported by a majority, however variably composed, of the Commons?

Throughout 1838 Lord Glenelg had continued weak and ineffective as Secretary of State for War and the Colonies. Sir William Molesworth's motion in March to censure his administration was used by the Tories to discredit the government as a whole. Although the Whigs had a majority of twenty-nine when the motion was put, and thus frustrated some wild Tory hopes of overthrowing Melbourne, the debate lowered the government's reputation and glaringly exhibited Glenelg's inefficiency. Early in 1839 Grey remarked angrily on the 'helpless imbecility' of Glenelg. Other prominent Whigs urged Melbourne to remove a minister who possessed intelligence and application but lacked decision. Howick protested constantly at the ministry's failure to come to grips with the problems of Canada, the West Indies, Ireland, New Zealand and New South Wales.[65]

In 1839 Parliament was prepared to follow the Whigs on the question of Canada, but not on that of the West Indies, regarding which Glenelg was more than usually vacillating.[66] Howick was exasperated to the point of being willing to break up the ministry. After a Cabinet meeting in January, he had a fruitless discussion with Russell and went home to write his resignation. Next morning he received word from Russell that he also would resign if Howick did — and on the same grounds of 'dissatisfaction about colonial policy'.[67] That day Howick and Russell exchanged further letters, and Howick had an unexpectedly pleasant interview with Melbourne. The Prime Minister had decided to give way, and the Queen was agreeable. How distasteful if would be to broach the matter with Glenelg, Melbourne remarked, for Glenelg himself was 'quite unconscious of his inadequacy to the duties of his office'.[68] Howick decided not to resign.

When Glenelg, to his great chagrin, was removed, Melbourne and Russell did not — perhaps could not — prevent some of the blame from attaching to Howick.[69] Moreover, Glenelg's office was not given to Howick, although both he and his father had confidently expected his appointment. Melbourne had to appease the Radicals as well as Russell and the Greys, and wanted a man of achievement, not, like Howick, of constantly changing ideas. Accordingly he gave the Colonial Office to the Marquis of Normanby, who had been closely associated with Durham over the Reform Bill, had governed Jamaica from 1832 to 1834 and been Lord-Lieutenant of Ireland from 1835 to 1839. The disappointed Greys told one another that the new minister was only doubtfully better than Glenelg. Howick rightly regarded Normanby's appointment as another victory for procrastination and as a formal declaration by the Cabinet against his own views on colonial policy. Grey, who had suffered a painful accident when a portrait of his wife fell on him, testily warned his son to trust neither Russell nor Melbourne. Russell especially he regarded (unjustly) as having no interest in forwarding Howick's political career.[70]

The Greys prudently kept their anger to themselves. Grey grumblingly agreed that Howick had to choose between supporting the Whigs or retiring from public life. Howick continued to regret that he had not resigned.[71] Outwardly the Greys in February 1839 supported the Whig ministry, but privately they disliked its policies and doubted whether it could command the majority in the Commons necessary for it to be able to govern and legislate effectively.

On 9 February Howick's self-control snapped and a bitter dispute occurred in the Cabinet between him and Spring-Rice, the Chancellor of the Exchequer, over the relations of the War Office with the Treasury. Melbourne was alarmed and told the Queen that, despite her support, he could not remain Prime Minister much longer if discontents continued in the Cabinet.[72] He feared a vote of no confidence less than a disintegration of his own leadership, such as Grey had suffered in 1834. A month after the incident in the Cabinet, the government was defeated in the Lords over Ireland, and Melbourne then repeated to the Queen the assurance that he had given in 1836: 'I would maintain my post so long as I possessed the confidence of the Crown and of the House of Commons.'[73] He did not speculate on how far the cordiality of his sovereign might outweigh the displeasure of the representatives of the people. Nor did he distinguish, as Russell did in 1841, between the confidence of the sovereign, which gave ministers their title to office, and the confidence of the Commons, which gave them ability to legislate and govern. He assured the Queen that none of the defeats suffered by the ministry (in the Lords or in the Commons) had implied loss of confidence. Even if the confidence of the Lords were lost, he declared, the Cabinet believed that a counteracting vote of confidence by the Commons would set matters right.

Glenelg's resignation had coincided with the publication in *The Times* of Lord Durham's Report. The government feared the angry Radical's ambition and dreaded his revenge. Would he overthrow the ministry, which still needed the support of his (dwindling) allies? What was to be done in Canada? Whig problems with Durham, however, were short-lived, for the perturbator had lost much Radical support and was entering his last illness. He showed more interest in promoting the policy of the Report than in unseating the government.

Whigs and Tories found it easier to agree on Canada than to settle a policy towards Jamaica. Tory opposition to the government's proposals for Jamaica prompted Melbourne to write to the Queen concerning the defeat that the government might soon suffer in the Commons: 'If Sir Robert Peel should persist . . . and a majority of the House of Commons should concur with him, it will be such a mark of want of confidence as it will be impossible for your Majesty's Government to submit to.'[74] He did not make clear whether ministers would resign merely on the political ground that they could no longer implement their policies, or on the constitutional ground that defeat in the Commons would imply a loss of confidence needed by government to justify continuing in office. Melbourne probably thought little of such distinctions, and consulted only his convenience, his duty to the Queen and the wishes of his colleagues.

The government, as we have seen, proposed to suspend the constitution of Jamaica for five years; no similar action was sought in respect of the other West Indian colonies. Peel, Hume and the Radicals criticised the measure strongly. On a motion that the Speaker leave the Chair, the government's majority fell to five (304 to 299), for the Radicals either voted with the Tories or stayed away.[75] Melbourne and Russell decided to resign, not because the Whigs had been defeated (the majority had supported them), but because of the strong probability that Parliament would not accept their Jamaican policy, and also because of earlier defeats and many divisions in the Cabinet.[76] Wellington was said to have thought the action precipitate.[77] but Melbourne was weary of the exertions of office and probably preferred resignation over a colonial question to resignation over a home or Irish problem. *The Times* declared pontifically that he ought to have resigned much earlier, for the government had never enjoyed 'the confidence of the House'.[78] This was a political, not a constitutional, judgement. *The Times* did not suggest that he had erred constitutionally by continuing in office while suffering defeats that implied the loss of confidence of the House.

The Queen had learned most of her politics from Melbourne and wished neither to lose his suave counsels nor to surrender her government to his opponents. He correctly advised her on 7 May to send for Wellington and, as Melbourne had foreseen, the duke persuaded her to invite Peel to form the new administration. The Queen had so long given the Whigs such generous public instances of her favour, while doing little to conciliate the Tories, that Peel was troubled by the presence of vehement Whigs among the ladies of the Court. He asked Victoria to change some whose political interests were notoriously opposed to his own. The Queen was dismayed;

she consulted Melbourne and Russell and, armed with their opinions — irregularly sought and irregularly given — refused the request.[79]

The Whigs did not at first understand that Peel had asked for the removal of only some, not all, of the ladies, and they sympathised with the tearful young woman on whose favour they depended. Peel recognised that in wishing to help the Queen and in hoping to cling to office they had lost sight of strict constitutional propriety. His own position, however, was weak in Parliament and he needed clear signs of royal favour. He resigned his commission and allowed the Whigs to return to office. Melbourne accepted responsibility for the Queen's actions, and the Whigs extracted what credit they could from association with the throne. As Greville caustically observed, they were back in power 'without the removal of any of the difficulties which compelled them to resign, for the purpose of enabling the Queen to exercise her pleasure . . . in the choice of the Ladies of her household. . . . It is a high trial to our institutions, when the wishes of a Princess of nineteen can overthrow a great ministerial combination.'[80]

Howick also was disturbed and, both privately and in the Cabinet, was more than usually critical of Melbourne. He believed that further explanations should have been sought from Peel, because the differences between him and the Queen might turn out to be (as in fact they were) smaller than the Whigs believed. He and Grey would have preferred the Tories to have formed a government and the Whigs to have gone out of office until able to command the confidence of the Commons.[81] Nevertheless, Howick continued in the ministry rather than give up office or ally himself with the Tories or the dissident Radicals. In the Commons in January 1840 he defended his conduct during the Bedchamber Crisis by pleading 'the duty which I thought was owed to her Majesty, to support her . . . against a pretension which . . . was unjust and ungenerous'.[82] The words were loyal to his party colleagues rather than candidly revealing of his own thoughts during the crisis and afterwards, which were that the Whigs had placed themselves and the Queen in a bad constitutional position.

In 1839 Melbourne was himself full of doubts:[83] he knew that in Parliament he would be no stronger than when he had resigned. He knew also that weighty constitutional arguments were being raised against his proceedings, both in advising the Queen to decline Peel's request and in returning to office. Nevertheless, he vigorously defended the Queen's actions (and his own) in a 'capital' speech in the Lords, while in the Commons Russell was nervous, feeble and ineffective.[84] All the principal speakers were generous to the Queen.

That the Queen and the Whigs had stretched the constitution shamelessly was apparent at the time, or soon afterwards, to many of those most involved. In 1841 Melbourne himself admitted (to George Anson, the Prince Consort's Private Secretary) that only 'the forbearance of the Tories' had 'enabled himself and his colleagues to support H.M.' The Queen ought to have acted on Peel's advice, given on a matter of patronage; she ought not to have consulted Melbourne or Russell; and she ought not to have been ready to take back the ministers who had resigned.[85] On the first two points she had acted unconstitutionally; on the third she had merely been impolitic.

Nothing could disguise the government's weakness in Parliament, and Melbourne, kept in office by his commitments to the Queen, again remade his Cabinet in a futile endeavour to win support. This time the principal head to roll was Howick's. When he resigned in August 1839, his decision, taken after prolonged correspondence with his father, was partly precipitated by Melbourne's failure to promote him when Normanby gave up the Colonial Office, as well as by dissatisfaction with the government's colonial policy and its failure to appeal to the moderates in the Commons.[86] Russell himself took the Colonial Office, a change that Howick criticised only on the ground that, as leader of the House, Russell would lack time for the colonies.[87]

Melbourne and Russell may have been secretly glad[88] to lose the most censorious and inflexible of their colleagues, but they paid a price for letting him go. That Grey would support his son had been taken for granted in Downing Street, and the cost of hostility had been calculated before Howick was allowed to go.[89] Howick's own behaviour, on the other hand, was probably not foreseen. In less than a year, despite his protestations of continued support for Melbourne, he inflicted (not quite intentionally) a defeat on the government that contributed notably to its downfall.

The reconstruction of the Cabinet did not strengthen Melbourne's position. In the Commons the ministry suffered many reverses, while in the country its vaunted monopoly of royal favour provoked attack.[90] 'I cannot imagine the possibility of the government's lasting. If it does, woe to the country', wrote Grey to his son-in-law, Charles A. Wood.[91] On 16 January 1840 Sir John Yarde Buller, the respected Tory member for South Devon, unexpectedly gave notice of a motion of want of confidence in the government, to be moved in twelve days' time. Peel had been reluctant to press matters so hard against the ministry, for his own supporters had neither the numbers nor the unity to form a government, and the Court continued hostile to the Tories. He supported Buller's motion, however, because of the 'uncontrollable temper of his followers'.[92]

When the motion came before the House,[93] the restless Tories did not challenge Melbourne's title to govern. Buller raised no constitutional questions except obscurely to allege that the ministry wished to separate Church and State. His attack was on the government's administrative record and its habit of 'exciting the people' outside in order to carry its measures through the Commons. His seconder, Alderman Thompson, almost challenged the right of a government to hold office without a majority in the Commons when he quoted Melbourne's words of 31 May in the Lords: 'Unquestionably, the worst Ministry was that which did not possess sufficient of the confidence of Parliament and the country to carry out those measures that they thought necessary for the well-being of the country.' But he did not draw the conclusion that Melbourne, who was in such a position, ought, on that ground alone, to resign.

When Macaulay, for the Whigs, tried to distinguish between the government's executive and legislative responsibilities, so as to require the confidence of the House for only the former, Peel answered him severely by pointing out what would happen, 'If every Government may say, "We feel pressed by those behind us, we find ourselves unable . . . to command the majority and retain the confidence of our followers; our remedy is an easy one; let us make each question an open question, and thereby destroy every obstacle to every possible combination." ' The consequences would be mediocre or bad government, for honourable and just men would keep out of public life. Peel put his case strongly, but there was nothing in it to harm the ministry. Stanley also was characteristically sharp and critical, but did not challenge the ministry's right to govern.

Howick wondered why Peel had not pressed the obvious question with which he might have overthrown the ministry:

> If he had wished to turn them out . . . he might have left to Lord John the embarrassing alternatives of disgusting either his Whig or his Radical supporters by declaring distinctly whether or not greater encouragement than before was to be given to Radical views and whether any more of the propositions for organic change are to be made open questions . . . I cannot help suspecting that he purposely avoided pressing the advantage and did not really wish to turn out the Government.[94]

In the Commons Howick did not challenge the constitutional correctness of Melbourne's behaviour in clinging to office. Instead, he blamed the Opposition for having moved an untimely vote of censure. Such a motion, he declared, was capable of overturning a ministry and, therefore, belonged only to 'circumstances of great and unusual difficulty and necessity'; no one had alleged that the condition was met. He rebutted the charges that the government was incompetent and weak (which he himself believed) by blaming the Tories for having made 'questions involving the very highest interests of the empire the battle fields of party contention'. The government had resigned in May, he said, because 'it did not possess that amount of confidence and support on the part of this House and the country, which would enable . . . [it] to conduct its affairs with advantage'. When constitutionally obliged to resume office in duty to the

Queen, who had wished her old ministers back in office, it had been in an extremely weak situation. Melbourne had then tried to strengthen his ministry, as was constitutionally proper.

On the whole Grey approved his son's tendentious reasoning, for it left the family free to criticise Melbourne's Cabinet reconstruction without implying that the Whigs ought not to have supported the Queen against Peel.[95] The Greys conceded that the Queen's government had to be carried on as she wished and that Melbourne might for a reasonable time persevere, in order to transact essential business and endeavour to win a stable majority in the House. This was exactly what Peel had done in 1835.[96] But there were limits: the Queen's ministers had to govern and, therefore, had to get their business through Parliament; if they could not do so, they ought to resign for the sake of the sovereign and the welfare of the country. They might imperil the constitution if they did not resign, but the constitution did not positively require their resignation.

The debate on Buller's motion lasted four nights and ended in a victory for the government by twenty-one votes (308 to 287). Howick voted with the ministry. Grey drew several interesting conclusions.[97] He believed that only Peel had profited from the debate, for he had made an admirable, restrained speech and had not tried to snatch power. Peel's great obstacle, Grey thought, was still the hostility of the Queen rather than the balance of the parties in the Commons, where the Whigs themselves relied on dangerously mixed support for their victory. The radical H. G. Ward, for example, who had openly boasted of his recent differences with the ministry, had been welcomed among Melbourne's supporters. A majority so contrived could offer no stability for the future. While the debate was still on, Grey wrote to Howick that a victory of twenty or thirty votes might have to be reckoned morally as a defeat. The Queen's government could not be carried on with such slender support and she should be advised to seek other ministers to provide a stable administration. When Melbourne continued in office with his strangely composed majority of twenty-one, Grey was so disgusted that Howick and Wood had to assure him that neither of them had promised the Prime Minister unconditional support.[98]

Howick knew that Melbourne would cling to office, however precarious his majority, and he knew also that the Prime Minister was meditating a dissolution, although the country was swinging to the Tories. So events continued throughout 1840, while Peel harassed the government with debates and divisions but made no decisive move against it. In September *Fraser's* challenged Melbourne's claim to govern: he had nominally the support of 339 members of the Commons, with only 319 against him, but he could not get his measures through Parliament. By continuing in office he abandoned his own declared principle, that the Whigs would govern only so long as they possessed the confidence of the House of Commons. On

1 January 1841 a leading article in *The Times* stated that the 'public'
condemned the government but would not become excited on the
question until Peel gave a lead. As troubles over the Irish franchise
increased, Grey became increasingly gloomy over the injury that Melbourne's dependence on so uncertain a majority was inflicting on Crown
and country. Great questions were becoming the spoils of faction, and the
throne, while the government comforted itself with the favours of the
young Queen, was being compromised.[99]

In April Howick himself helped to bring matters to a head. Largely
through his intervention the government was defeated on its Irish Voters
Registration Bill, 'the Government Bill of the session'. Disliking the Bill, he
moved an unsuccessful amendment. When his amendment was lost, he and
his friends voted against the Bill and so 'the government was beaten in Full
House on a government measure by ten votes'.[100]

In modern usage the defeat would certainly have implied want of
confidence. Melbourne, however, did not resign, nor was he pressed to do
so. Stanley privately told Howick that the Tories felt 'very indignant that
nothing had happened'. Howick, uncomfortable about his own part in the
affair, was relieved when Russell declared that the government would not
resign.[101] This was brave Whig talk with little to support it, except that, if
challenged, Russell would have denied that defeat on the Irish measure
implied general loss of confidence in the ministry. The majority that had
voted against it was unlikely to unite again on other matters, especially if
the government trimmed its policies to suit the Commons and take
advantage of the divided state of the Tories.

Politicians talked incessantly of dissolution or resignation.[102] On 9
May Anson called on Peel (with the knowledge of Melbourne and possibly
at his prompting) to assure him that if he had to form a ministry he need
fear no problems over the ladies of the household.[103] Less than a
fortnight later every member of Cabinet except Melbourne and Normanby
declared for a dissolution.[104] Melbourne hesitated to face an election in
which the people might reject the Whigs although they were the Queen's
government; such an unusual rebuff, he warned the Queen, would be 'an
affront to which I am very unwilling to expose the Crown'.[105] However,
the more optimistic members of the Cabinet, notably Palmerston, hoped
to appeal to the country with a programme of commercial reform revising
sugar, timber and corn duties.[106] The Queen's government, in their view,
was still likely to win enough seats to put its ability to govern beyond
doubt.

As an ardent free trader, Howick was interested in the government's
change of fiscal policy and would have rejoined the ministry, despite his
father's objections, had he been invited to do so.[107] When no sign came
from Downing Street he cheerfully awaited the downfall of the government. On 18 May he noted that Palmerston, when answering Peel's

criticism of the sugar duties, had not been able to 'say one word . . . as to the conduct of the Government in clinging to office with the House of Commons against them and bringing forward measures of such vast importance without the power of carrying them'.

The government was defeated that day by thirty-six votes on its proposal to reduce drastically the preference on colonial sugar, a matter that united a miscellany of well organised groups in opposition.[108] The Cabinet decided by a majority of one to remain in office and to introduce a Bill to levy a fixed duty on corn instead of the sliding scale of duties that protected growers in Britain and, after them, growers in the colonies, against foreign competition.

A majority of the Cabinet believed that the Corn Law proposal would be defeated in the Commons, and hoped that if the Queen granted a dissolution[109] the electors would vote for the Whigs and fiscal reform. Harvests had been lean since 1838 and grain prices had been high enough to remove effective discrimination against colonial grain and even some of the heavy discrimination against foreign grain. A few ministers hoped for a motion of no confidence against the government, which they could defeat by two or three votes, so justifying, as they believed, their staying in office. Melbourne and Normanby, however, would have preferred to resign at once (although not on constitutional grounds), rather than hold an election on fiscal policy or stay uncomfortably in power.[110]

So soon as Peel understood what the Cabinet intended, he decided that before Parliament could discuss the proposed amendment of the Corn Law, which, as he knew, would split his own followers,[111] he would move a motion of want of confidence. He thought that Melbourne was attempting a shameful manoeuvre, which the Opposition ought to disclose to the electors, and he gave notice of a motion to include the significant charge that the government's 'continuance in office, under such circumstances, is at variance with the spirit of the constitution'. A large muster of Tories acclaimed the notice.[112]

Most ministers were resolved from the first not to resign if Peel's motion were carried, although recognising it as a vote of censure. They proposed to ask the Queen for the dissolution that she herself favoured, and fully intended that, whatever happened, they would stay in office until after the estimates up to October had been carried. Their obstinacy was compounded of unwillingness to be driven out of office, resistance to Peel's constitutional assertions, vain hopes of victory at the election and respect for the wishes of the Queen.[113]

THE DEBATE OF 1841[114]

Parliament was at last to discuss a fundamental principle of responsible government in its modern sense: namely, that on losing the confidence of the elected house of the legislature, whether in an explicit vote of censure or by implication, through defeat on a significant measure of legislation, a ministry must resign (or, in some circumstances, seek a dissolution) and not sustain itself in power by pleading the confidence of the sovereign. C. S. Emden has pointed out that 'The considerable length of the debate and the energy expended in discussing whether the defeats already suffered were vital to the Ministry or not, are to be explained by the incomplete recognition of the dependence of the Ministry on the House of Commons up to that time'.[115]

Peel's speech on 27 May claimed that the principles of responsible government, for which he was contending, had existed 'since the Hanoverian accession'. He cited precedents from Walpole, North, Sidmouth, Liverpool and Wellington to show that loss of confidence, however indicated, ought to lead to resignation. But his history was unconvincing. The first plain example of the resignation of a ministry on the ground that it had been defeated in the Commons was that of Wellington's ministry in 1830, and it was far from conclusive. The ministry had lost a general election and used its defeat by twenty-nine votes on a minor question as an excuse to resign rather than face certain defeat on reform.[116]

Peel admitted that his own proceedings in 1835 might appear an exception to the rule that he was laying down in 1841. That they were so, he denied: had he not resigned so soon as he was 'positively obstructed in legislation'? He did not argue in 1841 that the wishes of William IV had justified him in governing the country without possessing a majority in the Commons. He had remained Prime Minister, he said, enjoying the confidence of the King, until the Commons had clearly withdrawn its confidence in his administration. The defeats that he had suffered before coming to grief over Ireland had been too minor and disconnected to imply loss of confidence. The gravamen of his charge against the Whigs in 1841 was that they had suffered a series of defeats, demonstrating beyond doubt their loss of the confidence of the House, and that they had disregarded a clear constitutional duty, which he explained, to resign.

The strength of Peel's case did not lie in his lengthy historical demonstrations, of which many were mistaken or inconclusive, but in the growing belief among politicians that the will of the Commons as representatives of the people must prevail against both sovereign and ministers. Everyone knew that the Whigs could not pass important Bills through Parliament and that there was a strong probability that the electorate would support Peel, whatever the Queen might say.[117] The sovereign no longer had the means of having a House of Commons returned in her favour, and members felt no compelling obligation to support the Queen's government out of loyalty or deference.

Melbourne could not hope to go to the country victoriously, as Pitt had done in 1784. Peel sardonically told the House that the Whigs, who had changed the franchise in 1832 to suit their own advantage, would not, in 1841, be able to win a majority from the electors whom they themselves had chosen. The continuance of Melbourne's weak administration, he added, would injure the nation and the empire. He warned of dangers to both Crown and Parliament if a trial of strength developed between them:

> That the Crown could support its Ministers without a majority might superficially have seemed to prove the strength of the royal prerogative; but the interests of the Crown and of the House were identical and to injure one was to injure the other. Being maintained in power by the Crown could be no compensation for the insufficiency and lack of authority of the Government.

This was a firmer statement against uncontrolled use of the prerogative than any that had been made in the House in 1835; Peel explained that ministers were 'the proper guardians of both the royal prerogative and Parliamentary privilege' and therefore 'should possess the confidence of the House'. The growing strength of political parties pointed to the same conclusion. 'The influence of the party', he said, 'could not be obstructed in England and obstruction would inevitably follow an attempt to govern by a minority.'

Although he did not specifically state that the government had no business to dissolve the House and appeal to the electors, Peel set limits to calling on the people's will to keep a ministry in office. 'While . . . [ministers] could dissolve the House at any time', he said, 'he still felt it his duty to call on the House to declare whether the Government had its confidence.' He warned the government that it was 'dangerous to set up the supposed opinion of the constituencies against their declared and authorised organ', the Commons. Melbourne's government had lost sixteen of the twenty by-elections held in the life of the Parliament and could not possibly win the country.

Late in the debate he clarified his attitude towards the events of 1835 by declaring that a ministry did not have to resign whenever it was 'defeated on an important legislative measure'. The essential question was whether it had lost the confidence of the House, not whether any particular Bill passed. He conceded, further, that ministers who were obstructed in attempting to form a Cabinet need not resign because of early difficulties, but might try again. Some defeats on financial measures also might be inconclusive on the question of confidence. Having in this fashion justified his own behaviour in 1835, he insisted that the only judge of loss of confidence was the House itself; the opinions of ministers on such a question could not be decisive. Melbourne had suffered many defeats and had already resigned in 1839 on the Jamaica Bill because he could not carry on as he wished and believed that the House did not desire him to do so. After the events of April and May 1841, when the government had gone from one severe reverse to another, 'it was not respectful to the representative principle that the Ministers should remain in office'.

Government speakers attacked Peel's history zealously, controverting his precedents with others — or with different interpretations of the cases that he had cited. Although both sides claimed that their principles were founded on the established practice of the constitution, both relied mainly on the situation confronting Crown, Parliament and people in 1841. Precedents merely set the terms of the debate.

Russell knew that it was useless to argue that the 'royal prerogative or personal favour of the sovereign should protect the Ministers from a vote of no confidence'. He admitted Peel's contention that, 'If the House refused its confidence to the Ministry, it was impossible for them to continue in office.' He contended, however, that this was a matter of practical politics, not of binding, constitutional convention.

The government's case, as put by Russell, depended not only on the claim that ministers enjoyed the confidence of the Queen, and so had a clear title to office, nor just on denying that ministers needed the confidence of the House in order to govern effectively, but also on two contentious statements of fact. Ministers, he said, still had the confidence of the Commons and nothing in their record was a possible ground of loss of confidence. In effect Russell admitted, more clearly than Melbourne had done in 1836 and 1839, that the government in order to function, needed the confidence of the Commons as well as the confidence of the Queen, which was their title to office. Further, he did not deny that loss of the confidence of the House might be indicated by defeats on important legislative measures, as well as by explicit votes of censure. On this view the Queen could dismiss her ministers, or keep them in office, as she chose, but the practical needs of politics would force them into resignation if the Commons persistently withheld confidence. Similarly, in replying to Peel's attack on the proposed dissolution of Parliament, Russell professed not to see that a dissolution might be either desired or needed, and strongly defended what Peel had not attacked — that is, the Queen's prerogative to dissolve. Did Peel intend, asked Russell, 'an unjustifiable interference with the royal prerogative'?

The tactics of admitting some of Peel's principles, while denying the force of his precedents and contradicting him on questions of fact, did not save the ministry from making laborious efforts to explain away its many defeats. The Whigs tried hard to distinguish between defeats that necessarily implied loss of confidence, and defeats that raised no question of confidence at all. Peel himself had declared in 1835 and again in 1841 that such a distinction was necessary, but the Whigs disagreed with his view of how to make it. They would have left a ministry to decide for itself (unless there were a formal motion of want of confidence) whether a defeat signified a need to resign on the ground that the House would reject essential legislative proposals.

Russell referred to another significant change in British politics. Legislation had so greatly increased in volume, he said, that no government could be held as a matter of confidence to the whole of every Bill that it introduced. When the Commons debated a measure, ministers ought to be able to accept amendments, even fundamental amendments and direct negatives, without forfeiting their right to hold office. The duty of Parliament was to discuss, improve and enact measures, not to pass every Bill the government introduced. Russell's attempt to state his case in an extreme form took him near to doing away altogether with the special responsibilities of ministries to introduce and promote legislation.

George Grey also overstated Peel's propositions in order to rebut them more easily: 'The resolution is a sort of declaratory law of the principles of the constitution, which would lead to the inference, that any government which may be unable to carry measures which they believe essential to the prosperity and welfare of the country, are bound at once to yield to the opinion of an existing Parliament, and resign.' Was a government to have no opportunity of winning support for its measures, and the sovereign to have no choice but to surrender to a majority, perhaps an ephemeral majority, of the Commons her prerogative power to appoint and remove ministers? Were ministers to hestitate to bring down a Bill in which they believed, because defeat on some part of it might cause the fall of the government?

At three o'clock in the morning of Saturday, 5 June, the House gave Peel a majority of one (312 to 311) and there were frantic cheers from the Opposition benches. On the following Monday Russell, prompted by Peel, announced that Parliament would be dissolved, that meanwhile only urgent business would be laid before it, and that, after the elections, Parliament would meet again as soon as possible.[118]

These were extraordinary decisions. The House had, explicitly as a matter of principle, condemned ministers for remaining in office despite clear proof that they did not enjoy its confidence. Instead of resigning after defeat on a vote of censure, the government persevered with its plan to go to the country. *The Times* had declared on 28 April that it would be 'base and politically profligate for a retiring ministry to harass the country by dissolution without any hope of gaining a majority'. Grey had told Howick that, with the government so weak in the country, a dissolution would be 'an act of such desperate wickedness' that he could not believe it possible. He had pressed Howick to cut all ties with Melbourne and Russell and so avoid being touched by the scandal of the intended dissolution.[119] In his article 'The Old and New Ministries' Croker condemned the Whig record after 1839 as wholly unconstitutional and dishonest. Melbourne had been right to resign in May 1839 when he could not rely on

Parliament to pass his Jamaica Bill. By resigning he had demonstrated that even Whigs accepted the 'unwritten ... well-understood constitutional axiom' that ministers unable to carry measures on which they had decided ought to leave office or, in certain cases, appeal to the country by an immediate dissolution. Melbourne's return to power, according to Croker, was the first ever attempt at setting that constitutional axiom to 'open and protracted defiance' and it had driven Peel to the extraordinary course of proposing a direct vote for the expulsion of the ministry. Nothing could justify an appeal to the country in 1841.[120] The Queen could no longer guarantee victory for her ministers.

The Queen and the ministry, however, decided to take their case to the people, as they were constitutionally entitled to do. Melbourne knew the chances of victory were slight and dreaded the effects that a dissolution followed by defeat would have on the monarchy and the party. Peel, despite Tory complaints, had everything to gain from an election, as he was certain to win a majority.[121]

Employing in Britain a weak version of the tactics that Sydenham and Metcalfe later used in Canada, or of the tactics of the Pittites who had made the elections of 1807 a 'referendum in support of George III',[122] many Whigs claimed that a vote against them was a vote against the Queen.[123] Lord Lincoln (later fifth Duke of Newcastle) quoted a satirical verse on their attachment to the throne:

> Ministers by Kings appointed
> Are, under them, the Lord's anointed,
> *Ergo* — 'tis now the self-same thing,
> To oppose the Minister or King,
> *Ergo* — by consequence of reason
> To censure statesmen is high treason.[124]

Much of the press represented the Queen as personally involved in the result of the election.

Peel won a majority in the Commons of over ninety. The Whigs still did not resign and strictly were under no additional obligation to do so before the House met. When challenged in the Lords with having lost the confidence of the Commons by defeat at the elections, Melbourne correctly defended himself by citing Burke's theory of representation: 'Members are sent *ad consultandum de rebus arduis regni*. We are not ... to judge what the conduct of Members may be by their declarations on the hustings.'[125] The party system was not then strong enough to make Melbourne's comment absurd, nor were elections yet seen to be held in order to choose a government. Moreover, 1841 was the first modern election in which a majority ministry in the Commons was defeated by an Opposition that had been a minority.[126] Melbourne remained Prime Minister until the Commons had carried an amendment to the address by ninety-one votes.[127]

Disraeli then complained that the government ought to have resigned in June, when defeated by Peel on the vote of confidence, and added that Melbourne had had no case at all for remaining in office after his defeat at the elections.[128] The first criticism was well founded but confused: Melbourne was widely blamed for having advised the Queen to dissolve, when he ought to have resigned and allowed the Tories to form a government. He had condemned the Whigs to defeat and the Queen to humiliation, but his actions after defeat had not been unconstitutional. The second criticism was ill founded; there was no rule in 1841, nor until long afterwards, to require that a ministry that had lost its majority at elections should resign before Parliament met. George V and his advisers thought the matter doubtful in 1923[129] and it was probably not settled until Baldwin resigned after defeat at elections in 1929. When Disraeli made his point in 1841, Stanley and Graham, though on his side of the House, appeared to disagree.[130]

No prime minister in Britain ever again remained in office after the Commons had formally asserted want of confidence in his administration. The distinction between the confidence of the sovereign, which gave ministers their title to govern, and the confidence of the Commons, which enabled them to do so, soon disappeared. It had lacked vitality ever since the sovereign had lost the power to influence elections in the interests of his chosen ministers.

Melbourne, equivocal to the end, advised the Queen to state that she parted from her ministers in deference to Parliament, although her own confidence in them was unimpaired. He referred to his defeat in the new House, not to Peel's motion in June or to the result of the election. The Queen refused to believe that 'the verdict of the electors deprived her of the right to feel confidence in ministers of whom the voters had disapproved'. Five years later she wrote to Russell 'that she [had] made a mistake in allowing the dissolution in 1841; the result had been a majority returned against her of nearly one hundred votes'.[131]

Whatever the Queen might think and whatever Melbourne could bring himself to state, 'a cardinal principle was secured as a result of the debate on Peel's motion in 1841'.[132] Henceforth, a government that lost the confidence of the Commons had to resign, except when the loss of confidence was implicit (through defeat on legislation) and the sovereign, due to there being a great public question at stake, granted a dissolution.[133] The Queen could no longer constitutionally keep in power a ministry that did not have the confidence of the Commons; equally, she could not — except, perhaps, for some grave and altogether exceptional reason — dismiss, as William IV had done in 1834, a ministry that was supported by a majority of the Commons.

Between 1834 and 1841, three or four other principles that were greatly to affect British policy towards self-government of colonies were established. The sovereign would no longer be actively involved in choosing a ministry, except, conceivably, in such special cases as when there were no clear leaders of a majority in the House of Commons.[134] The Queen would have in law to accept the advisers that the Commons gave her, whether or not she approved their policies. Remonstrance, influence, advice and much other political action were still open to her, but the Commons would in law have the first and last say in choosing or removing a ministry, however much they might choose to heed the opinion of the sovereign. Government by ministers commanding a majority in the Commons would normally be government by a party. Peel had made this point expressly and had predicted that the influence of party would grow and could not be obstructed. The Cabinet, supported by a majority of the Commons, had become 'the only link which secured harmony between the Executive and the Legislature'. It mediated between the Crown and the legislature and eventually came to control both. Perhaps, after 1841, yet another principle was established: that the electorate, when it chose the Commons, also chose the King's ministers, or — so soon as party discipline and alignments became binding on members — gained the power to do so.[135]

The significance for colonial policy of the events of 1834 to 1841 passed without notice in Britain and the colonies. Throughout the debates of 1841 no one commented on the resemblances of principle between the case put by Peel and the form of responsible government claimed in British North America. Although Gladstone had ponderously declared in 1840 that members of Parliament were 'familiarised with the name and practice of responsible government',[136] the debates of 1841 contained almost no use of the term. 'Responsible government', to people in Britain who knew the term, was a constitutional device wrongly claimed by colonists, or merely the old rule that ministers were responsible for every public act of the sovereign. The question whether ministers ought to depend on the confidence of the Commons for their title to office was discussed at Westminster without raising problems about the colonies.

Howick, who was to institute responsible government in the British colonies a few years later, had bitter cause to remember the fate of the Whigs in 1841. He had said almost nothing in the debate (keeping silent because his father so strongly disapproved Melbourne's conduct), but he had voted with the government. Personal ambition, hopes of free trade if the Whigs remained in power, loyalty to his associates, hostility to the Tories, and, probably, a measure of agreement with Russell on the constitutional questions involved, all moved him.[137] He recognised that the Queen's government needed a majority in the Commons in order to pass its measures; he knew that Melbourne did not command such a majority; he believed that, as a matter of the public benefit and for the sake of the throne, Melbourne ought to resign; but he was not yet persuaded that Melbourne was under an absolute constitutional obligation to resign or go to the country.

Grey had objected strongly to Howick's attitude towards Melbourne's discredited ministry. At first he refused to help his son win re-election in Northumberland. When he relented, his help was too little and too late: Howick lost by sixty-two votes and temporarily retired from politics. Irked at such a reverse to the family, Grey relented, and a few months later Howick won a violent, troubled by-election in Sunderland. He returned to the Commons as an active worker for free trade.[138]

RESPONSIBLE GOVERNMENT, PARTY AND THE SOVEREIGN, 1845–6

The majority that Peel won in 1841 endured with some setbacks until 1845, when his policies began to break up his own party. In June 1844, when the government was defeated on sugar duties, the Cabinet made the matter one of confidence and the Tories rallied to give Peel a majority of twenty-two votes. He thought this majority too slight to offset the earlier defeat. The practical effects on the ministry's responsibility to the Queen to govern the country on avowed principles troubled him: 'Declarations of general confidence [such as he could command] will not . . . compensate for that loss of authority and efficiency which is sustained by a Government not enabled to carry into effect practical measures of legislation which it feels it to be its duty to submit to Parliament. . . .'[139] Authority was lost in 1845 when his policy of increasing the Maynooth grant seemed to Disraeli and many others to repudiate the principles of the Tory Party. At the third reading of the Bill for the grant, over half the party voted against Peel.[140] The Home Secretary, Graham, wrote that 'The bill will pass but our party is destroyed. The result may probably resemble the consequences which ensued on the carrying of the Relief Act.'[141]

On the Corn Law, as on the Maynooth Bill, Peel again precipitated a crisis of conscience for many of his followers. Although only two members of Cabinet opposed his policy strongly when he announced it to the Cabinet on 2 December, Peel knew that the assent of many others had been reluctant and that a majority of the party would not support him. Rather than carry his new fiscal policy with the mixed support of some Tories and most Whigs, which would conflict with his responsibility to party, or prejudice the reform by failing to carry it at all, which would be contrary to his responsibility to the Queen and the country, he decided to resign.

No Tory was willing to succeed Peel and the Queen called on Russell to form a ministry. The Whig leader had had hopes of the prime ministership for more than ten years, but did not wish to take office in December 1845, when the free trade question might convulse political life and the Whigs were in a minority of between ninety and 100 in the Commons. The headstrong insistence of Grey (the former Howick) on the immediate abolition of protection troubled him[142] and he feared the political consequences of moving towards free trade, unless Peel gave him public support. The Prince Consort warned Peel that Russell might not form a government without a promise from Peel of significant support, but Peel agreed only to private co-operation and the help of his friends in an 'adjustment' of the Corn Laws. Russell then declared that differences between Grey and Palmerston made it impossible for him to form a strong Cabinet.[143]

Peel and Russell both assumed that a new government would have to be based on one of the existing parties; neither favoured the project, discussed among some free traders, of a government of Whigs and Tories, led by Peel, and pledged to repeal the Corn Laws. Peel, indeed, dreaded his possible fate as the prisoner of a coalition and wrote to the Prince Consort that he would not 'relinquish the power of free independent action, which will constitute my chief strength' (in repealing the Corn Law).[144]

When Peel announced his intention of carrying one, Stanley resigned from the ministry and was replaced at the Colonial Office by Gladstone, who returned to the government after having left it over the Maynooth grant. The majority of ministers stayed with Peel rather than entrust 'the reins of government to men so thoroughly reckless as Lord Grey and Mr. Cobden'.[145] At the opening of Parliament on 22 January 1846 Peel justified his attempts to change Tory policy in terms that reconciled his responsibilities to Queen and to party: 'I have thought it consistent with true Conservative policy, to promote so much of happiness and contentment among the people that the voice of disaffection should be no longer heard, and that thoughts of the dissolution of our institutions should be forgotten ....'[146] The problems facing Britain in 1845 and 1846, argued Peel, would be solved best by promoting trade and industry, by subduing class and sectarian conflict, by taking the sting out of Irish discontents, by smothering Chartism with prosperity and by making proper concession to the Anti-Corn League. Those Tories who regarded themselves as the natural representatives of agricultural interests rejected him as a traitor, and dismissed as false in law and mistaken in policy his contention that the Queen's first minister might prefer his own ideas of what was good for the nation to the tenets of the party that sustained him in office.

Peel was not acting, as Croker and some others argued in *The Quarterly Review*, as an enemy of party.[147] He believed in the duty of leadership, both within the party and within the government. The party was a group united by principle to serve the Queen, when called upon to do so; the party would serve her best under a strong leader, who would discharge his duty to the sovereign by guiding and controlling the party that guaranteed his position in the Commons. The leader's first duty, however, was to Queen and country, not to party.

Peel told the House that the Queen's government had to be carried on and that, as her minister in office, he took responsibility for doing so:

> I do not hesitate to say . . . that the noble Lord having failed, and the colleagues with whom I had heretofore acted not thinking it advisable to form an Administration, I did inform Her Majesty . . . that I would return . . . as Her Majesty's Minister . . . . I resolved to meet them [his colleagues] in the capacity of the Minister of the Crown, and to submit to them the measures I proposed to bring before Parliament.[148]

If, disregarding party, he formed an administration that the House would support and carried out the policies in which he believed, his duty to the Queen, and in the long run, therefore, to the party and the country, would have been done. Any other course, Peel (and Wellington) were sure, would have been evasive. To have advised the Queen to call on Stanley or some other Tory would have been a 'useless parade', as none of them would have agreed to form a ministry.[149]

The bewildered Tories found a spokesman in Disraeli, who had his own reasons for attacking Peel. Making a virtue out of party loyalty, he accused his former leader of having forsaken the first principle of honourable public men: 'Let men stand by the principle by which they rise, right or wrong . . . . Above, all, maintain the line of demarcation between parties, for it is only by maintaining the independence of party that you can maintain the integrity of public men and the power . . . of Parliament.'[150]

Steering his own course as head of the government and as Tory leader, Peel continued as Prime Minister in January 1846 rather than leave the Queen without advisers or abandon policies that, as the Queen's first minister, he believed essential to the welfare of the nation. In June, however, when the Queen had an alternative government available, and after Parliament had enacted the major part of his policies, he resigned rather than continue in the embarrassed condition of Prime Minister lacking the support of an organised party in the House of Commons. He could not continue to discharge his duty to the Queen while having to contrive majorities to pass necessary measures through the House. His actions confirmed the principle that government by ministers responsible to the Commons was normally party government, through which alone could stability be regularly established.

In June, the Bill to repeal the Corn Laws passed its third reading in the Commons by 327 to 229 votes, after five months' debate and with more than half the Tories opposing it.[151] At the end of May, Ellenborough, First Lord of the Admiralty and one of the more forceful Tories, had asked Peel whether, in the event of his having to resign, he would undertake to assist the formation of a Tory government.[152] Peel had refused on two grounds, of which the certainty that a Tory ministry would be protectionist was the second. The first and more compelling reason was partly constitutional:

> ... the Queen ought in the event you suppose to have a perfectly unfettered choice in respect to those whom she might be disposed to select for her confidence. It clearly would not be unfettered were those who retired from her service and by retirement left her in great difficulty, to intimate to her that they would support only one particular set of Ministers.[153]

To Peel, the Queen's government was still a ministry of her servants, with a duty to the Crown and the country, and bound to serve so long as they had a satisfactory majority in the Commons. When a government had maintained itself with uncertain support from the Opposition and found it could no longer do so, she should be free of all commitments in looking to Parliament for a more stable ministry.

Knowing that he was courting defeat, Peel chose to go on with the Irish Coercion Bill, which had been introduced into the Lords in February. He believed that the measure was needed, but was certainly not obliged, except in conscience, to endanger the government by bringing it forward. The Tory protectionists would oppose the Irish measure in order to overthrow him; Russell and the Whigs might also oppose the Bill. When Russell decided to join the protectionists in opposing the Bill, Peel accepted defeat as inevitable,[154] declining either to withdraw the Bill, which he thought necessary for good government, or to ask for a dissolution: 'Unsuccessful dissolutions are, generally speaking, injurious to the authority of the Crown. The dissolution of the Whigs in 1841 was, I think, an unjustifiable one. Dissolution now, if the result is likely to be the same, would be at least equally so.'[155] A few days before his defeat he wrote, in a memorandum for the Cabinet, that 'no ministers ought to advise the Sovereign to dissolve Parliament without feeling a moral conviction that Dissolution will enable them to carry on the Government of the country'[156] with the support of a body of men 'honourably and cordially concurring with us in great political principles'. He would not campaign on free trade, because too many of those who had supported him on that agreed with him and one another on little else.

Peel sent his reflections on party and on the nature of parliamentary majorities to Wellington. A government needed the consistent support of an organised party in order to have a majority in Commons and carry out its responsibilities to the Queen. Wellington, detesting the Tories who were driving Peel from office, would have gone to the country 'on the simple question of the Irish Assassination Act'.[157] Peel replied that 'A government ought to have natural support. A Conservative government should be supported by a Conservative party.'

Peel was sure that he ought to go ahead with the Coercion Bill, sure that, when he failed to pass it, he ought to resign, and sure that without the Bill his ministry could not govern Ireland. A combination of Tories, Whigs, Radicals and Irish members defeated him[158] and he resigned the day after the Corn Bill was passed. *The Times* commented, 'It was a resignation of power in the moment of a great success. . . . The Minister resigns, not merely because he is beaten on one particular question, important as it is, but because he has not the general confidence of a majority in Parliament.'[159] Peel resigned because he lacked, in his own phrase, a 'natural' majority to implement the policies that, as the Queen's first minister, he deemed essential for Ireland, and also because he was bound, after 1841, to regard the defeat as a vote of no confidence.

Peel's prestige remained so high that in some senses he resigned from office rather than from power. The Whigs could not command a majority in the Commons even with the support of Radicals and Irish members. Peel, together with his followers in the Tory Party, proposed to support them so long as he approved their policies. He did not think it wrong for Russell to become Prime Minister with the aid of the Peelites, for Russell was supported by an unbroken party and by allies fairly well united with him in broad concurrence of principle; a majority so based would be more 'natural' and better able to serve the Queen than any majority that he himself might contrive to command.

Peel was applying in practice the principle stated by Grey in 1858, that a ministry should normally be able to guide the proceedings of the Houses of Parliament.[160] A government ought not to sustain itself in power by relying on the temporary, tenuous majorities that might occur during the passage of unusual measures. It ought always to have a secure, stable majority to enact the policies that it thought necessary for the well-being of the country. Responsible government, or 'parliamentary government', as Grey called it, was party government, and without the rule of party (or coalition of parties or groups) it would not exist.

Some forms of party government, as Grey elsewhere pointed out, had 'long flourished' in Britain.[161] What was new was the recognition that the sovereign had lost so much power in the Commons and in the country that choice of the party (or coalition) to hold office, like the decision to force a party out of office, was no longer the personal prerogative of the sovereign. The Queen's ministers served her subject to the wishes of the party or parties that gave them their majority in Parliament, and subject also to whatever influence she might exert through rank, experience and public acclaim. The government could lawfully be carried on in her name and require her formal participation even though she objected to its actions or its members. Whether ministers chose to ignore or to heed her objections was a political, not a constitutional, matter. Only the Commons or the electorate could relieve her of ministers she distrusted. For twenty years or more, party remained weak in Britain, but the constitutional position was not really in doubt.

The implications for colonial policy of the changed conventions of the constitution in Britain were obvious when men had cause to see them.[162] If party government, as it had evolved at home, were perfectly consistent with monarchy, why should the Queen's representative in a self-governing colony not be served by parties, just as she was? Why should a colonial government be ruled by a party in Britain, rather than by a party in the colony? In colonies that seemed politically mature enough to be able to work a system of party government, the only remaining constitutional difficulty was the alleged necessity of colonial subordination. The growth of the new concept of the self-governing colonies, then coming to be viewed as extensions of Britain overseas, soon reduced subordination to a list of reserved powers that the mother country needed to retain and encouraged a more generous attitude towards colonies, which were seen to be the heirs of the British political system.

7 The New Idea of Self-Governing Colonies of Settlement

> The new empire was founded largely on land and settlement, but, however economic was its emphasis, there was not the economic bondage of the old one.
>
> J. C. Beaglehole[1]

> It is a sort of instinctive feeling to us all, that the destiny of our name and nation is not here, in the narrow island which we occupy; that the spirit of England is volatile, not fixed.
>
> H. Merivale[2]

'A very different way of thinking' about empire became prevalent as England was being industrialised, wrote Richard Pares in 1937.[3] For a long time, historians were too interested in the rejection of mercantilism in the 1840s to appreciate correctly what Pares called the 'positive theory of empire', the beginnings of which were coeval with the coming of free trade. Belief in active colonisation by settlement was a vital part of the 'positive theory of empire' and involved a sense of imperial destiny through self-governing colonies, which would inherit British culture and enjoy British institutions. Over forty years ago W. P. Morrell suggested that a 'new imperialism' had begun 'with the great migration of the second quarter of the nineteenth century'.[4] In 1970 A. G. L. Shaw reached a similar, rather more extensive conclusion: 'Very broadly, in place of the old conception of empire, based largely on the alleged advantages of controlling imperial trade, ... a new one was arising, based on humanitarianism, migration and investment'.[5]

Morrell and Shaw were both at odds with R. L. Schuyler's thesis, originally stated in two articles in 1917 and 1922, that between the American Revolution and 1870 Britain experienced a rise of 'anti-imperial' sentiment, reaching its climax in the 1860s. Schuyler thought that this popular feeling was related to the collapse of the old commercial system, which had supposedly dominated men's thoughts on colonies before the triumph of free trade and *laissez-faire*. He saw a period of anti-imperialism and relaxation of imperial economic controls as necessary for the triumph of liberal views of colonial government and for the establishment of the new imperial constitution that led to the emergence of the British Commonwealth in the twentieth century. In the very short run, free trade nearly dissolved the empire, by breaking up the old political and economic unity. In the long run it allowed the colonies to escape from subordination and become virtually independent within the empire.[6] Schuyler's work, like much of C. A. Bodelsen's *Studies in Mid-Victorian Imperialism,* ignored or assessed inadequately the territorial expansion of the empire, the new belief in imperial destiny, and the development of colonial self-government, factors that so strongly characterised the second quarter of the nineteenth century. To Schuyler, the granting of responsible government in the 1840s and after was a prudent step to ensure the peaceful disintegration of the empire after the old commercial system had been abandoned. He did not see it as the deliberate and confident sharing between Britain and some of her colonies of a great constitutional change. Bodelsen, overimpressed by the hostility among political economists and Radicals towards the empire, made a *deus ex machina* of the 'colonial reformers' in order to explain the liberal, expansive trend of British imperialism in the middle of the century and so accommodate it to his belief in a period of anti-imperialism. He took the 'reformers' at their own estimation, an error that many historians have repeated.

Part of the celebrated article 'The Imperialism of Free Trade' by Gallagher and Robinson[7] strongly attacked the view that there had been in Britain during the nineteenth century a period of anti-imperialism or indifference to empire. Reforms like responsible government were seen as concessions made from a position of strength by an empire that, formally and informally, was growing constantly in territory, wealth and power. After the coming of free trade had destroyed the old colonial system, economic and other links between Britain and her colonies of settlement remained strong enough to allow considerable progress to be made towards colonial self-government, for the sake of political tranquillity and without prejudicing effective British supremacy over the colonies. Imperial domination by Britain continued, largely through economic power, though this apparatus of political control was partly dismantled when responsible government was granted, and was soon still further reduced. There is much substance in this view, but it overestimates the weight of economic factors, disregards the expressed opinions of the statesmen (most notably the third Earl Grey) who introduced responsible government, ignores the 'new imperialism' to which Morrell referred, and seems indifferent to the long history of self-government in the empire. Changing forms of government in Britain had always greatly influenced accepted political ideas on the nature and form of self-government of colonies.

Shaw cautiously observed that Gallagher and Robinson, Galbraith[8] and other writers had made it 'doubtful if there was any period of anti-imperialism in nineteenth-century England. There were always anti-imperial writers, but at no period did they represent the mood of very powerful groups.'[9] MacDonagh also, who tellingly criticised Gallagher and Robinson for having taken too extreme a position, concluded that in Britain between about 1845 and 1860 imperialism prevailed against its critics, who were reduced to relative impotence though not to silence.[10]

THE NEW EMPIRE

Changes in Britain were the crucible of the new idea of an empire of settlement. Colonial developments helped to bring it about. The granting of responsible government, even to colonies that did not seek the reform, was its confident expression. Some doubters thought reforms of colonial government merely sagacious steps towards a friendly separation from Britain. The men in high office between the 1830s and 1850s who were friendly to reform included some doubters, like Russell, and some men of faith who occasionally doubted, like Grey. All of them believed that, whether or not the self-governing colonies remained in the empire for ever (or for a long time), they would remain Britain transplanted and continue British in outlook, civilisation and attachment.

The new imperial concept of a destiny to be achieved through the self-governing colonies was impregnated with pride in the spread of British civilisation (with which Protestantism was usually equated), English law and British institutions. Emigration had come to be regarded as the desirable movement whereby members of most classes of British society, including the respectable middle classes, helped to plant new Britains overseas. Colonies peopled with British stock and inheriting British traditions were, on the principles implicit in colonial policy after 1791, likely to be granted forms of government based on the British constitution, provided that imperial supremacy were preserved. Political liberties and constitutional privileges familiar to men of property in Britain were not denied to colonies with the population, wealth, social stability and political experience necessary to reproduce essential elements of British polity. If, in the absence of aristocracy, colonial societies and politics were more democratic than those at home, the fact was the less alarming to liberals in Britain because of the example of the United States and because many persons of the highest respectability in Britain had long thought the House of Lords more valuable as a chamber based on property than as a meeting place of hereditary aristocracy.[11]

THE POLITICAL ECONOMISTS

If ever there was a period in British history in which economists were widely quoted, praised and reviled by public men, it was while the first industrial nation adapted its economic policies to changed economic circumstances. The economists may not greatly have influenced the course of imperial policy, but they did set the terms in which free trade, the utility of colonies, the wisdom of investing men and money in the empire, and the case for colonies of settlement (of which they became persistent advocates) were discussed. They and their ideas were familiar in the corridors of power; they were consulted by parliamentary committees and secretaries of state. Through the famous reviews and in their own persons they were known also in the country houses and the city clubs, where much of the nation's political business was transacted.

Many of the politicians responsible for the colonies between the 1820s and the 1850s read political economy. Goderich was described by Ricardo in 1823 as a 'tolerable political economist, and well-inclined to liberal principles of trade'[12]. As F. J. Robinson, he had been a notable reformer of the commercial system. 'A very timid man', wary of agrarians in the Tory backwoods, he belittled in public the economic knowledge that he gained in private.[13] Liverpool, who kept a ministry uncertainly together from 1812 to 1827, and had been Secretary for War and the Colonies from 1809 to 1812, concealed neither his interest in promoting free trade nor his willingness to consult with political economists.[14] Huskisson, the most famous commercial reformer before Peel, was a direct link with Pitt and Adam Smith and was a friend of Ricardo. In 1819 Peel himself supported Ricardo, on the resumption of specie payments, and sympathised with Wilmot-Horton, the famous Under-Secretary for Colonies, when he advocated emigration to relieve pauperism. Wilmot-Horton's own correspondence with Malthus, Senior and McCulloch marked him as a political economist of standing. In the 1830s Peel told the Commons that he had read Smith, David Hume, Ricardo, McCulloch, Torrens, Malthus and the French economists and marvelled at their disagreements.[15] In the 1840s, when he attacked the Corn Laws, he presented a sophisticated economic argument well based on a critical reading of (in particular) Ricardo and McCulloch.[16] Poulett Thomson, scion of a merchant family, president of the Board of Trade, and later governor-general of Canada, participated in trade debates as both a statesman and an economist.[17]

The two outstanding Whigs in the making of imperial policy on colonial government in the 1830s and 1840s, Russell and Howick, both studied political economy. Russell had Senior as his 'economic adviser' and read Smith, Malthus, Ricardo, McCulloch, Greg and J. G. Hubbard to prepare for the free trade debates. His understanding of economics may have been superficial, but he did use terms and arguments derived from economic writers.[18] Howick had, for a Victorian aristocrat of his rank and fortune, a social and intellectual acquaintance with political economists that was mildly surprising. From the 1820s he knew McCulloch (his first tutor in political economy), Senior (whose political judgement he greatly admired), Wilmot-Horton, G. J. P. Scrope (brother of Poulett Thomson) and the Mills. His Journal records his reading in the political economists (some French) and mentions his father's advice to study monetary theory; Howick did so with McCulloch's edition of Smith.[19] After retiring from office he wrote two books — *Colonial Policy of Lord John Russell's Administration* (1853) and *Parliamentary Government* (1858) — that earned respect among intellectuals and administrators.[20] Contemporaries regarded him as a man well versed in political economy, though not an original thinker.[21]

In the Colonial Office James Spedding, famous as the editor of Bacon, wrote on political economy for The *Edinburgh Review*, and Herman Merivale, who succeeded Stephen as Permanent Under-Secretary, had, like Senior, been Drummond Professor at Oxford. Merivale's *Lectures on Colonization* (1841) analysed the economics of empire building and the problems of colonial government.

Many of the political economists were active in politics. Ricardo, Robert Torrens, Wilmot-Horton and Sir Henry Parnell were members of Parliament. Both the Mills held high office in the East India Company and were closely connected with men of influence and authority in public affairs. The Political Economy Club, which Ricardo founded in 1821, brought together Malthus, the Mills, McCulloch, Torrens, Thomas Tooke, Howick, Poulett Thomson, Wilmot-Horton, Spring-Rice, Parnell, Althorp and Buller, as well as bankers and businessmen (like G. W. Norman) with a taste for abstract speculation on policy.

COLONIAL THEORIES OF SOME CRITICS OF MERCANTILISM

Britain never lacked defenders of empire, even after the Thirteen Colonies had successfully rebelled. The idea of empire as strategy and trade lived on; Britain continued to acquire colonies and, in Sierra Leone and New South Wales, to plant new ones for special reasons. Adam Smith and many of his contemporaries found advantages in colonies, as well as calamities in their mismanagement. From early in the nineteenth century, at least beginning with Brougham in 1803, some political economists believed that colonies of settlement were necessary to British growth, prosperity and greatness. Until the 1820s, however, proposals for founding new colonies of settlement were few and of slight consequence. Demobilised soldiers, the unemployed and other disadvantaged persons were settled on various occasions along the imperial frontiers, and from 1818 men of capital were encouraged to go to New South Wales; but these were all sporadic attempts to solve particular problems, not constructive imperialism by settlement. British North America continued until the late 1820s to be regarded as a special case, a congeries of settled colonies valuable in strategy and trade, chancing to have a large English-speaking population because of the loss of the Thirteen Colonies. No one planned to establish new colonies of settlement as an act of imperial policy.

Adam Smith's view of empire was more favourable than his famous attacks on mercantilism and the East India Company might suggest. He certainly though that mercantilism had restricted commerce and diverted capital from investment at home, but, as a historian of commerce, he believed that the settled colonies in North America had enriched part of the nation, enlarged the mercantile marine and helped to strengthen the navy. Colonial trade, like any other trade, might increase productivity and open markets for products that Britain could not sell at home. Until free trade was adopted by Britain and other great commercial powers, rates of profit might fall through competition of capital seeking investment. Colonies could help sustain rates of profit by checking undue accumulation of capital at home.[22]

None of Smith's historical observations or remarks on colonies and capital affected his case against mercantilism and for free trade. Mercantilism, he believed, limited the gains to be had from colonies and was justifiable only for defence or unusual conditions of trade.[23] The rich trade with North America could not justify policies that had been bad in principle. Monopoly, maintained on behalf of a conspiracy of merchants and 'the private interest of the governing part of the nation', had encouraged prodigality and war, without helping the nation as a whole. In principle Smith would have preferred Britain to give up empire. Because no power would part voluntarily with such an apparently prolific source of profit, prestige and power, he hoped for free trade within the empire, which in 1776 still included the Thirteen Colonies. He planned to keep the colonies contentedly within it by allowing them to share with the mother country the law making and administration of the whole empire. Britain and her principal colonies were to be partners in a single imperial sovereignty. The participation of each colony was to depend partly on the size of its English-speaking population.[24]

The Rev. Thomas R. Malthus criticised Smith's emphasis on industry and trade and lacked his vision of a rich empire of settlement; but he did, directly and indirectly, contribute to the belief that colonisation by settlement could help solve the economic and social problems of the mother country. The basic proposition of Malthus's political economy was that Britain owed her wealth not to 'commerce and manufactures', but to her superior agriculture. Was not land 'incontrovertibly the sole cause of all riches'? External trade, whether with colonies or foreign countries, was exploitative and probably ephemeral, and could not guarantee economic pre-eminence. Temporary prosperity arising from industry and trade was dangerous because it discouraged concentration on the land, turned capital away from agriculture and raised the price of food.[25]

Although he adhered to these principles, Malthus was eventually driven by fears of rising capital and population to find merit in trade, commerce, and colonisation by settlement. He believed that population tended to increase in geometrical progression, while the means of subsistence might increase in, at most, arithmetical progression.[26] He therefore opposed the mercantilist position — that prosperity depended on a large, dense population — and was sure that in Britain population would come to press hard on resources, first because of reckless procreation among the poor.[27] Poverty, produced by and arising from the heedless increase of population, would imperil the social fabric by impeding the growth of the middle classes and endangering aristocracy itself.

The occasional use of colonies to accommodate some of Britain's redundant population might, Malthus eventually conceded, be to the national advantage. Only a 'slight palliative' could result, however, because the most 'redundant' parts of the population lacked the foresight to emigrate and because the colonies would not welcome shiploads of unemployed from Britain. Malthus, who wanted the poor laws gradually abolished, was reluctant to spend public money on emigration. He opposed state interference in economic matters, doubted whether a government ought to promote movements of people, and distrusted British colonial administration as economically unsound. The only sure remedy for overpopulation was, not emigration, but misery, which could limit reproduction by forcing men and women to control their instincts. Colonies might sometimes absorb part of the surplus population already existing; they could not justify letting the population grow.

Malthus also saw that colonies might be outlets for capital investment in agriculture. An industrial country with growing trade would suffer a fall in the rate of profit as a result of the continued 'increase of capital in a limited territory'.[28] Britain had in her 'rich colonial possessions' a 'large *arena* for the employment of an increasing capital' without depressing the rate of profit. Colonies might also be used, with tolerable safety, to increase food supplies, since trade with them would not be liable to the precarious interruptions attendant on trade with foreign countries. 'The British empire might .. be able, not only to support from its own agricultural resources its present population, but double, and, in time, perhaps even treble the number.'[29]

Malthus despite himself became almost a progenitor of the new imperialism of emigration and settlement. Wilmot-Horton drew on his ideas in planning emigration of the poor at public expense.[30] Wakefield used his criticisms of industrial society to argue that the surplus of capital and labour with which he believed Britain to be afflicted could be relieved only by systematic colonisation, to make the rich British possessions overseas into large producers of food for Britain and sure markets for her surplus manufactures. When Malthus's agrarian sympathies led him to write for the *Quarterly*, he found himself, ironically, in the company of those who most supported colonisation.[31]

In 1820 Malthus published *Principles of Political Economy*, partly to answer Ricardo's *Elements of Political Economy* (1817). Ricardo was then generally regarded as the principal exponent of the new industrialism of free trade, and, as such, as the theorist of the English manufacturers, who dreamed of the economic conquest of the world. Malthus, oversimplifying, saw Ricardo as an anti-agrarian; Ricardo thought Malthus an unreasonable enemy of industrialisation and change. In the context of colonial theory, however, the differences between the two economists were less important than the resemblances. Ricardo, like Malthus, concluded that there was normally little economic gain in colonisation. Overseas trade, he thought, was limited mainly by capital, which colonies might not increase, and was valuable only to increase the range of products available to a nation or to confer occasional advantages through the comparative costs of goods exchanged. Colonies could be no more valuable in this analysis than were foreign countries, and had the dangerous disadvantage that they might drain capital away from Britain.

On the other hand, in a way reminiscent of Smith, Ricardo thought that in some circumstances colonies might help to arrest a decline of profits. In Ricardo's system, profits fell because of diminishing returns when inferior land was cultivated to feed an increasing population. In Britain the area cultivated for food had long been increasing, but yield per acre had risen only a little. Growth of population forced Britain to be a net importer of food in most years. Failing universal free trade, which would allow the workshop of the world to import food as part of her prosperity and power, settled colonies might be valuable. 'If with every accumulation of capital, we could tack a piece of fertile land to our Island, profits would never fall.'[32]

Ricardo never supported colonisation as a national policy, for food or for markets, or to prevent a fall of profits or check capital accumulation at home. A *laissez-faire* economist with strong utilitarian leanings, he doubted the case for colonisation, although he left his followers considerable leeway to look favourably on empire. As he died in 1823, he did not see the mid-1820s boom in colonial investment, nor the most serious alarm over population increase.

The Philosophic Radicals, Bentham and James Mill, originally opposed empire strongly. Bentham's *Emancipate your Colonies!*, addressed to the French National Convention in 1793 and not published until 1830, is famous. Neither he nor Mill found much economic advantage in colonisation, which diverted capital from investment in Britain. If emigration of capital were needed to sustain rates of profit, foreign investment was better than colonial because it would not call on Britain for more capital than it was in her interest to provide. Trade was 'the child of capital' and efforts to develop new markets in colonies could not increase the total volume of trade, although they might divert trade from old markets to new.[33] Mill also, arguing (like Malthus) from Say's Law, was convinced of the relative unimportance of trade as a stimulus to economic captivity. Any gain from enforced cheapness of colonial products in British markets would be offset by the loss incurred in flouting the principles of free trade.[34]

At first the Philosophic Radicals thought colonisation active evil, as well as error. They condemned colonies and trade as prolific causes of war and linked attacks on the state of Britain to their criticism of colonies. Empire was to the advantage of only 'the ruling Few', who, by abuse of patronage and twists of fiscal policy, entrenched themselves in the colonies at the expense of the 'subject many'. In Britain, government suffered from the perpetual 'complications of interest, the indistinct views, and the consumption of time, occasioned by the load of distant dependencies'.[35] In the colonies, ruling minorities resorted to methods that could only prejudice constitutional government at home. Hume led a Radical demand, with which young Whigs like Howick partly agreed, that colonies should have self-government for the sake of efficiency and economy.[36] Crown colonies were particularly condemned, because their inhabitants had no means for insisting on economical administration, and in them Britain practised an expensive 'jobbery' under the name of patronage.[37] Inconsistently, Mill wanted to retain India as a place where Radical reforms might be usefully attempted.[38]

Radicals were well aware that emigration need not be to British colonies. An article in *The Westminster Review* in 1825 advised emigrants not to stay within the empire from loyalty, but to consider going to the United States (which Bentham then admired). 'All new countries must be good customers to Britain' and the growth of colonies was no better for British trade than was the growth of other new countries. In July 1827 Roebuck wrote, and many Radicals probably believed, that the Canadians hoped to leave the empire and accept American protection.[39] No country, Roebuck thought, was so well governed as the United States, and Anglo-Canadian trade was too small to justify the expense and trouble of keeping the colony. Ireland, likewise, ought to be emancipated, but not India, which was a conquered colony, where a rich field awaited Benthamite wisdom. Separation would deprive Britain of nothing except doubtfully valuable prestige and the opportunity to misuse colonial patronage. Emigration would still be possible and trade would be safe, for it would naturally flow in the same channels after independence as before.[40]

THE EARLY CASE FOR COLONIES OF SETTLEMENT

After the American Revolution Britain still possessed the largest colonial empire in the world and never lacked writers to record the uses of colonies of settlement. None of the arguments used in the 1830s and 1840s to introduce the new concept of self-governing settled colonies was wholly novel. In some form, all had occasionally been used in the period when the consensus among political economists was unfavourable to existing colonial policy and doubtfully permissive of colonisation.

Brougham, the future Lord Chancellor and 'Apostle of Free Trade', wrote on colonies in 1803, celebrating the advantages of colonial trade and imperial monopoly and arguing for emigration to the colonies by working-class and middle-class people, who could not prosper in Britain. Overproduction of goods, overpopulation and the amassing of surplus capital (profits on which might disappear 'in a state of overgrown magnificence') could all be relieved by colonies and the settlement of colonies overseas.[41]

Robert Torrens, officer in the marines and later member of Parliament, was a forward-looking, latter-day mercantilist whose intellectual history epitomised the change in British thinking on empire and colonisation. In 1808 he criticised mercantilist ideas on bullion and the balance of trade, but supported restrictions on colonial trade, to benefit the mother country. Later, responding to changed economic conditions in Britain, he began to elaborate a grand vision of an empire of trade. By 1815 he wanted a gradual transition to free trade in corn, so as to release capital from agriculture and help sell British manufactures abroad. Britain could obtain 'a species of property' in the soil of other countries (including colonies) by exporting manufactures that cost her less to produce than she would have to spend to produce for herself the food that she bought in return for exports. A country with so limited a territory as Britain had to look outside, to foreign trade and to colonies, if she were not to be inferior to France, Austria or Russia. In 1817 Torrens thought that a 'well-regulated system' of colonisation could be a 'safety valve to the political machine', while emigration could relieve the unrest of those who found no opportunity in Britain. In 1821, seeing Britain as the workshop of the world, Torrens explicitly rejected Say's Law, to which he had formerly inclined, and predicted gluts of production, capital and labour. Anticipating Wakefield by a decade, he argued that all three forms of glut could be relieved through colonisation as well as by foreign trade.[42]

The views that Brougham and Torrens reached by economic reasoning strongly resembled the proud Toryism of *The Quarterly Review*, which in 1811 gave the colonies much credit 'for our commerce, our manufactures, our naval wealth, the high state of our agriculture and the progressive cultivation of our waste lands'. In 1812, commenting on the apparent rise of population, it boldly quoted Scripture ('Be fruitful and multiple: replenish the earth and subdue it') and argued, as a corollary to Holy Writ, that the miseries of Ireland, the Scottish Highlands and many parts of England should be relieved by emigration to the colonies. Otherwise, social and political unrest might overturn the established order of the state.[43]

In 1824—5 the *Quarterly* rejected McCulloch's 'shop-keeping' principles of imperial economics as incompatible with common sense, national honour and prestige. It condemned the much publicised Radical alternative — of keeping the colonies to the detriment of Britain and themselves, or of letting them go for the common good — as wholly false and based upon the 'palpable quackery' of political economists. If a colony wanted to separate and could defend itself, then as American experience showed, the sensible course would be to let it go; but most colonies did not wish to leave the empire and certainly could not defend or govern themselves if they did. Colonies were valuable and should be sought, promoted, settled and so governed as to maximise economic progress and political tranquillity.[44] 'The discouragement of colonisation is *not* the feeling of the great majority of Englishmen', Sir John Barrow declared in the *Quarterly* in 1829.[45]

The *Quarterly* believed that part of its differences with the economists arose from the conflict of basic political principles in Britain: 'These visions of the economists may appear ludicrous; but they are coupled in a sinister manner with persevering abuse of all Britain's moral, religious and political institutions.'[46] If the 'lower orders' were, as the *Edinburgh* claimed, 'making good progress' in learning political economy from Ricardo, who was prejudiced against agriculture and hankered after manufactures and free trade, where would the infusion of pernicious doctrine end? The masses would use 'their numerical force to compel a mutual exchange of property' — that is, to expropriate their employers. Colonies, the empire, the proper subordination of class to class, monarchy and Christianity itself, all of them part of the fabric of Great Britain, would be destroyed. To abandon shipping or the colonies would imperil the whole edifice. Not for the last time, the most conservative position was the most favourable to colonies.

Huskisson, for all his concern with trade and commerce, was touched by the larger Tory views expressed in the *Quarterly* (and *Fraser's*)[47] and wanted colonies that would spread Britain throughout the world, not merely increase trade. In a speech on the civil government of Canada in 1828 he declared that 'England cannot afford to be little. She must be what she is or nothing . . . in every quarter of the globe we have planted the seeds of freedom, civilization and Christianity.'[48] Although Huskisson believed that the colonies might eventually become independent, he insisted that Britain had a traditional responsibility for 'young and distant communities dependent upon her protection'. She should keep the colonies as long as they were willing, and make them as British as possible in culture, institutions and economic ties before they acquired political independence. It was a good businessman's policy, with an enlightened eye on values other than profits.

Although the colonies could not provide markets to equal those of Western Europe, the United States, Latin America and the Far East, Huskisson nevertheless wanted empire. As Morrell wrote, 'The real significance of Huskisson in the history of colonial policy lies in the fact that he defended Imperial preference on political rather than on economic grounds.'[49] Huskisson had a strong, imaginative vision of Britain's duty and destiny to settle colonies overseas.

In the Tory years a large territorial growth of the empire in Australia, South Africa, Asia and the Caribbean was accompanied by the beginnings of new forms of systematic settlement. State-aided emigration to Canada and South Africa was intended to solve British problems by helping ex-servicemen and unemployed, and to assist the colonies by increasing settlement along vital frontiers. From 1818 the Colonial Office carefully tried to interest men having £500 of capital in emigrating to New South Wales, offering land in proportion to money taken to the colony. New South Wales clearly had enough poor already, and an addition of English and Scots farmers was thought likely improve the prospects of satisfactorily employing convicts, while relieving the condition of those hard put to keep up their positions at home. The numbers involved in this movement were never large, but the significance of the decision to transfer middle-class people to the antipodes for the benefit of themselves, Britain and the colony was not lost on propagandists of emigration in the 1820s.[50]

The settled colonies participated in the great boom of capital investment in Britain and overseas in 1824—5. The Canada Land Company and the Australian Agricultural Company were 'real estate undertakings ... of moment in the history of the respective colonies'. The Canadian company adopted with official sanction a policy of company colonisation. The Company was to buy waste land, clear it, open up communications and bring out and assist a 'steady industrious agricultural population'.[51] It received nearly 2·5 million acres at low prices. In the same year the Australian Agricultural Company, which was well connected in Downing Street, began the colonisation of the new country between the Hunter and Manning rivers in New South Wales and received nearly half a million acres.[52]

In the financial crisis that followed the boom of the mid-1820s, many weak points in British prosperity became apparent and helped to divert attention to colonisation by settlement.[53] The blunting of expectations of South America as a field for investment turned attention to other expanding economies. The United States was attractive to investors, exporters and emigrants, but was becoming such a rival to Britain that patriotic arguments helped stimulate interest in British North America. It was an easy step to surmise that 'there must be profitable areas of exploitation in other undeveloped parts of the empire'.[54]

The ending of the boom turned men's thoughts to colonisation. The fears of the agrarian economists, that gluts were inevitable in any economy that was industrial and commercial rather than agricultural, appeared to be confirmed when factories shut down and dismissed workers became 'redundant'. Colonies might relieve gluts. Dread of declining rates of profit and of dangerous dependence on foreign food also served to justify and so strengthen the case for colonisation. By the mid-1830s over half of Britain's total area of almost 57 million acres was under cultivation or used as pasture; acreage under wheat was close to its highest point ever. Despite the growth of population and the growing demand for better food, the number of enclosure bills diminished, as if the limits of profitable expansion had been reached.[55]

Disturbing social and political signs of economic strain had long been apparent. While population rose, so did unemployment in many parts of England and Scotland, and many thought this cause and effect. Violence and unrest pursued the new industrialism, and the misery of the unemployed, both agricultural and industrial, was too plain to be denied. In 1816 Parliament voted £50,000 for the emigration of unemployed labourers and in 1819 the same amount to assist settlement at the Cape. Lord Sidmouth had remarked in 1817 that many thousands of people in Britain apparently faced the alternatives of emigration or death,[56] and in the same year the Select Committee on the Poor Law signalised the long connection between unemployment relief and colonisation by recommending that no obstacles be placed in the way of unemployed seeking work outside Britain and that every reasonable facility be afforded to those 'who may wish to resort to some of our colonies'.

In 1819 the Poor Law Committee pointed out with stronger emphasis than before that the unemployed should be helped to find work overseas. The colonies had plenty of unoccupied land on which the 'labour of man, assisted by a genial and healthy climate, would produce an early and abundant return'.[57] The committee hoped that the existing Poor Law, which subsidised idleness, would be removed. In 1824, when Britain had a surplus of labour, laws prohibiting the emigrating of workmen and the export of machines were repealed. 3000 Scots emigrating to Canada, and several thousand Irishmen, most of whom also went to Canada, received assistance from Parliamentary grants in the 1820s. Although doubts of the success of the programmes led Parliament to resolve against further grants after 1825, until the Select Committee on Emigration (under Wilmot-Horton) had reported, the flow of voluntary emigrants continued. Men of education and capital were among the emigrants to the United States, Canada and, in small degree, Australia. Their interest was settlement, not trade, and their movement from England was watched with growing public and official interest. In 1825 there were 14,891 emigrants from the British Isles, 485 of whom went to Australia and over half to British North America. Gradually the proportion going to Australia increased, until in 1829 2016 out of a total of 31,198 emigrants went there, while 13,307 went to British North America and 15,678 to the United States.[58] Reports of drought then reduced the Australian proportion for some years, while that of Canada fluctuated widely as circumstances there changed.

SOME REVISIONS AMONG THE POLITICAL ECONOMISTS

After 1825 'the general feeling [among economists] against colonization' was replaced by a 'movement pressing the economic case for colonies'. From 1830, apart from McCulloch, 'no prominent economist ventured to attack colonization in principle or to object to England's retaining her colonies', whether for settlement or trade.[59]

In his old age Bentham revised his colonial theories because changed social conditions in Britain made an empire of settlement attractive. Fears of overpopulation and the example of the United States as a new country, apparently without hindrances of tradition and law to obstruct rational government,[60] led him to look kindly on planned emigration to the colonies. Mill had already been impressed by the prospects of emigration as a relief to overpopulation. He had advocated education against the imprudence of passion and supported emigration from overcrowded countries 'so long as the earth is not peopled to that state of fulness which is most conducive to human happiness'.[61] Colonial soil should be richer than the soil the emigrants left, and the expenses of their removal should not involve damaging loss of capital to the mother country. When Bentham gave up hope of limiting population growth by contraception,[62] he approved colonisation as a means of relieving the population, 'of preventing its excess, by providing a vent for those who find themselves over-burthened upon their native soil'. Colonisation had to be planned deliberately and in good time, and never be 'performed without appropriate preparation . . . under pressure of distress'. It would produce 'a new people, with whom we shall possess all the connexions of language, of social habits and of national and political ties'.[63]

Philosophic Radicals concluded that colonies in tutelage were as attractive to authoritarian reformers as India was. Bentham's postscript of 1829 to *Emancipate your Colonies!* looked on 'the colonial empire as a vast field for experiments in philanthropy and reform'. In 1831, at the request of Wakefield (through Francis Place), he drew up a scheme for a joint stock colonisation society to conduct emigration on approved principles. The society was formed and among its members were the young Benthamites George Grote, Sir William Molesworth and John Stuart Mill.[64]

According to the Rev. Thomas Chalmers, an underconsumptionist, who influenced Wakefield, colonisation might provide outlets for capital, while emigration sometimes absorbed redundant population. Britain in 1832 was saturated with capital and suffered from 'low interest, a high-wrought agriculture, ... redundant population among the labourers, and ... redundant capital among the mercantile classes'. New countries such as the United States and the British colonies had vast 'unbroken tracts ... open for cultivation', but old countries had little land not already under cultivation and, therefore, could have only 'gleams of prosperity' while they were strangled by increase of population, glut of capital and prolonged underconsumption.[65] The available remedies, other than unrelieved hardship to reduce overpopulation, were emigration, colonisation and free trade; none of them, however, could permanently correct or offset the evils of industrial society. State aid to emigration and colonisation, Chambers had written in 1821, might, like other charitable measures, merely encourage further, dangerous increases of population. At best, state-aided emigration might help relieve temporary crises of redundant population.[66]

Wilmot-Horton, the Tory Under-Secretary for Colonies, became the principal exponent of the opposite view, that the state should promote and assist the emigration of the redundant poor. His arguments were partly derived from Malthus, especially the 1817 *Additions to ... An Essay on Population*, and from Torrens's *Paper on the Means of Reducing the Poor's Rates* (1817). Unlike the classical economists, he believed that a fairly rapid adjustment of excess labour to demand was possible. Surplus labour could be 'abstracted' by colonisation, at home or, preferably, abroad, where soil fertility was high and there would be little danger that assisted workers would return to the labour market.

Wilmot-Horton's plans of emigration were elaborated in great detail and varied considerably, especially over finance. But the basic objectives were constant and did not deserve Buller's gibe that they were merely a 'shovelling out of paupers'. Wilmot-Horton wished to remove part of the 'relatively redundant population' from Britain, as the 'main remedy' for the unhappy condition of the working class. Colonists were to be planted 'in a soil prepared to receive them, aided by a small portion of capital to enable them to take root and flourish' and become proprietors. Normally, skilled workers would not be redundant, so that most assisted emigrants would be unemployed labourers.

Wilmot-Horton supported overseas colonisation by assisted emigrants because he did not see how 'the superfluous population [could be] abstracted . . . more economically and more advantageously at home than abroad'. Like Malthus, he expected redundancy of population to set in again after emigration had removed the original surplus (on the 'vacuum principle'), but he hoped this would not take place until the expenses of the emigration had been covered, and he believed that the costs of emigration would be less than the expense of maintaining paupers in idleness at home.[67]

Wilmot-Horton wished also, but only secondarily, to build up the empire.[68] He found Upper Canada the most suitable colony to receive assisted emigrants. It had a general shortage of labour and plenty of new, unappropriated land. Emigrants who went there rather than to the United States would be over three times as valuable to Britain as customers, and capital invested there would be as safe as, or safer than, capital invested in the United States. He was not sufficiently impressed by Canadian objections to immigrant paupers to propose sending emigrants to distant Australia.

Wilmot-Horton won eminent support. Torrens, who in 1817 had expressed alarm at 'the perpetually accelerating pace' at which the poor rate increased, approved his plans until he himself went over to Wakefield's version of systematic colonisation.[69] Assisted emigration, wrote Torrens with his wide vision, might 'work almost unlimited advantage to Great Britain' beyond simply relieving excess labour, for it would 'spread the British name and British laws, and British influence throughout all climes of the world'.[70] Goderich, Wellington, Peel and Alexander Baring (of the banking family) also sympathised with Wilmot-Horton's objectives, on humanitarian and economic grounds, and Senior, the architect of the Poor Law Amendment Act of 1834, generally favoured his principles. Even if emigration cost more than keeping paupers in England, thought Senior, when questioning one of Wilmot-Horton's more optimistic premises, emigration was still to be preferred, as it would reduce discontent at home. Senior did point out in 1836, however, that emigration could not keep the population down, and after Wilmot-Horton's death he came close to becoming a Wakefieldian.[71] McCulloch and Ricardo both expressed general approval of Wilmot-Horton's plans, although their position on capital loss and wages-fund theory predisposed them against him. McCulloch, indeed, was willing for the government to spend large sums to promote emigration from Ireland and to prevent resettlement of vacated areas. The Benthamite *Westminster Review* also generally approved, although it wanted emigrants to be carried as 'labourers', not as 'colonists', and opposed payments for travel to distant New South Wales.[72]

Strong opposition to Wilmot-Horton came from some classical economists and, most publicly, from Hume. As a Radical, Hume condemned the emigration plans for extravagance and risk of capital loss. Hume thought so ill of British colonisation that the imperial aspects of assisted emigration could not appeal to him. Voluntary emigrants, he thought, should go to the United States, where they were most likely to prosper. As for overpopulation, he agreed with Malthus that the only sure remedy was to limit procreation. Public funds should never be spent on emigration. Malthus himself firmly insisted that emigration would never curb population growth, although it might temporarily relieve crises of redundancy.[73]

In 1831–2 Wilmot-Horton suffered double defeat. Howick, as Parliamentary Under-Secretary, introduced early in 1831 a Bill to promote pauper emigration from the parishes of England and, if possible, Ireland also. He declared that the Bill was based on Wilmot-Horton's ideas, and both the *Edinburgh* and the *Quarterly* gave it a good reception. Wilmot-Horton, however, objected to the Bill as inadequate to carry out his policies. When Parliament was dissolved in April, the Bill lapsed, but the government completed certain administrative arrangements connected with it that had been recommended by Wilmot-Horton's select committee in 1827. An Emigration Commission of five members, including Howick and Hay, was appointed on 22 June and wound up in August 1832, after spreading information to possible emigrants and sending skilled labourers and young women to New South Wales. 'Lord Howick prefers the personal superintendence of Emigration to the continuance of a board, and we have expired having done however some good', wrote one of the commissioners to Wilmot-Horton. Howick had convinced himself that most parishes could neither select suitable emigrants nor protect them from fraudulent shipowners. Boggling at the expense of state control, he dropped the Emigration Bill and effectively abandoned the far from whole-hearted attempt to promote emigration on Wilmot-Horton's model.[74]

Meanwhile Wilmot-Horton had committed the last of his many political misjudgements. Having destroyed his own chances of a great ministerial future, he had hoped to be governor-general of Canada and promote his ideas from there. He accepted the governorship of Ceylon, to which assisted emigration was impossible, and so removed himself from England just when Wakefield had brought his ideas under attack. 'I might be said', he wrote to Howick, 'to have incurred the penalty of exile'. Before his death ten years later, the victory had gone to Wakefield's version of systematic, middle-class colonisation.[75]

WAKEFIELD'S IDEAS ON EMPIRE

In the 1820s Wilmot-Horton was the outstanding advocate of state-aided emigration. Wakefield naturally turned to him when, for reasons private as well as public, he joined the advocates of colonisation in 1829. While in Newgate Prison serving a three-year sentence for abducting an heiress, he read political science, penology and social reform, and then, using ideas from the political economists, planned systematic colonisation. As a propagandist in so national a cause, he hoped to rehabilitate himself while satisfying his powerful urge for achievement, profit and recognition.

'The sensation created by *A Letter from Sydney*', which Wakefield published in 1829, 'was possible only because of the public attention attracted by the tide of emigration [already flowing] to North America and by the pleasing descriptions appearing in books and journals of the possibilities of settlement in New South Wales.'[76] In 1830, before Wakefield was out of prison, his friend Robert Gouger set up the National Colonisation Society to promote 'systematic colonisation' and persuaded Wilmot-Horton, whose inspiration he had already acknowledged,[77] to join. Enough philanthropists, clergymen, politicians and persons of respectability became members to make the association immediately notable. J. S. Mill, H. G. Ward, Sir Francis Burdett, Sir John Hobhouse, Buller, Roebuck, Charles Tennant, Sir William Molesworth and William Hutt were among the early members.

Conflicts soon developed in the association between Wakefield and Wilmot-Horton, originally over Wakefield's insistence on concentration of settlement in specified districts and arrogant insistence that his principles were universally valid. The differences between the two men were fomented by Wakefield and his ally Tennant until in April 1831 Wilmot-Horton withdrew from the Society.[78] For the next two decades Wakefield was the best publicised advocate of systematic colonisation and the most deliberate propagandist of empire by settlement.

Wakefield's ideas were remarkable for neither consistency nor originality. His striking defects of character have obstructed academic discussion of them. Some historians, regretting the praise lavished on him by writers who took him at his own valuation have condemned him as a criminal seducer of young girls in his youth, a scavenging author, a cunning businessman in middle age and an unscrupulous politician in old age. June Philipp, who tried hard to see him warts and all, charitably concluded that 'he always retained something of the unscrupulous intriguer, of the rash and fanciful adventurer'. 'Something' is a mild word. Upright men like Howick and Stephen abhorred him. Howick, who had to deal with him in public, tried to maintain an appearance of cordiality towards the best known advocate of systematic colonisation, who was notorious also as a swift and remorseless enemy.[79] Wakefield habitually vilified opponents, made inflated claims for himself as an original thinker, and exaggerated his importance to every cause he served.

When he demanded systematic colonisation, Wakefield was pushing on an almost open door. When he alleged that British governments opposed careful emigration and the controlled use of land, he deceived himself and his followers. As we have seen, selected free emigration to New South Wales had begun before he wrote a word on such questions. The Colonial

Office had decided to sell Crown lands in Australia, instead of granting them, before his ideas on the subject were known in Downing Street.[80] T. F. Elliot of the Colonial Office told the House of Lords Select Committee on Emigration from Ireland that, 'It is . . . a mere Delusion to suppose that there is something called Colonisation, which is wilfully or negligently set aside', adding that the Wakefieldians condemned as mere emigration what they would have praised as colonisation, had it been promoted under their own auspices.[81]

Personal failings aside, Wakefield did, however, propagate 'a great view of things'.[82] His ideas on empire[83] appeared most clearly in *England and America*. Here, in terms that were familiar to educated readers in 1833, he analysed the economic structure of Britain to show the sources of the distress and poverty afflicting the richest nation in the world: 'In England, those who compose the bulk of the people are too cheap to be happy. If their condition be such that it must be worse before it can be better, the crisis is coming.' England was permeated with distress because of the 'small proportion which the field of production constantly bears to capital and labour'.[84] Capital accumulated without finding employment; population became more redundant. Capital competed with capital and wage earners with wage earners, so forcing rates of profit and wages perpetually downwards. Most wage earners could not save and most capitalists had to diminish their capital; an enormous frustration of normal human desires resulted as careers were blighted, marriages postponed and enjoyments denied. A few capitalists, richer than the rest, accepted low rates of profits on vast investments and steadily improved their position. The poor and the new poor might be driven to opt for a 'revolution of property' that would destroy society.

As a social conservative, Wakefield deplored the march to revolution. In an age that contained Malthus, Chalmers and Marx, predictions of catastrophe were not unusual. Wakefield's were distinguished by a brassy confidence that he could halt the march to destruction.

In democracy he saw yet another threat to stability, but one that colonisation might remove. The traditional 'judgment and moral courage' of Englishmen would mitigate the rigours of 'pure', levelling democracy, but the growing inequalities of society would dispose men towards democracy and its inevitable conflict with 'high civilization'. Until inflammable social conditions had passed away, Parliament and the government should be as sensitive to the public will as if the Commons had been democratically elected. The root danger had to be removed. Democracy would lead to the overthrow of the accepted order of property and society unless wages rose and unemployed resources of men and capital were put to work. 'To raise wages immediately, the field for the employment of English capital and labour must be enlarged.'[85] The first step was to adopt free trade. Its efficacy, however, would be blunted by the opposite policies of other countries. The second step was to found new colonies, for settled colonies would be the safety valve of troubled Britain (as Torrens and Senior had already suggested).[86] Colonies that were moulded to the needs of the mother country and properly governed, without either 'monopoly or dominion', would be linked with her almost perpetually. They would be planned extensions of Great Britain, reproducing the best aspects of its society and politics, absorbing its unemployed capital and population and designed to suit its economic needs. Settled colonies would spread English civilisation, culture, government and law across the world, a subject on which Wakefield was as enthusiastic as any Tory.

In the colonies, political liberty was to be the child of a balanced social order, not its parent. To ensure that the desired social structure existed within each colony, settlement should be concentrated in carefully regulated areas. In this way land prices would be kept up, labourers would have to work for wages for some years, and standards of comfort and civilisation would be high enough among proprietors to attract the middle classes, whose capital, political ideas and social preferences were essential to the enterprise. The social structure so engendered would induce responsible attitudes in all classes, guaranteeing men of property and education their just respect. Wakefield was particularly anxious that the middle classes should emigrate, overcoming their prejudiced belief that every emigrant was a convict or a failure or unwanted in Britain.

In advocating free trade and systematic colonisation together, Wakefield and his supporters had to combat old established notions of commercial monopoly and protection as the true basis of empire, and also much new thinking about free trade. 'The possession of colonies', declared The *Edinburgh Review* in 1842, 'would be useless to the country possessing them, if freedom of trade were universal and perfect'.[87] Some economists, such as G. P. Scrope, advocated colonisation only so long as universal free trade seemed impossible. Some of the Manchester School were glad that, by destroying protection and, therefore, the traditional reason for having colonies, free trade would rid Britain of the cost and danger of administering and defending an empire that spread throughout the world.[88]

The arguments most commonly used by the Wakefieldians to prove that, in addition to free trade, systematic colonisation was necessary to Britain were put to the Commons by Buller in 1843. When Britain adopted free trade, he said, other countries probably would not follow, but colonies would have to do so: 'I must not be understood to propose colonisation as a substitute for free trade. . . . its effects in extending employment must be slower. But . . . it will probably be surer; and will be liable to no such interruptions from the caprice of others, as trade with foreign nations . . . . The commerce of the world is narrowed now not only by our legislation but by that of other powers.'[89] The great colonies of settlement, Buller continued, could produce exactly the food and raw materials (including timber and wool) that Britain needed, and could buy in exchange the manufactures that Britain had to sell. Buller committed the common error of all the colonial reformers, including Durham, and of Russell and Grey, when he assumed that after the introduction of free trade Britain would be able to continue to control the fiscal policies of her colonies. They would be compelled to adopt free trade, and not be allowed to raise 'hostile tariffs' against her.[90]

Wakefield had other economic arguments to reconcile systematic colonisation with free trade. Britain needed more land to prevent decline of profits and stagnation, at least so long as other countries did not go over to free trade. The great colonies of settlement possessed enough fertile land to increase food production almost indefinitely without diminished returns. (He knew little of droughts, floods, soil erosion and prolonged bad seasons.) Their own prosperity and rising populations would make them expanding markets for British capital as well as British exports. Together with immediate repeal of the Corn Laws, vigorous colonisation would work to produce enormous benefits for the British people.

Torrens had his own ideas on free trade and systematic colonisation. He feared that if Britain went over to free trade and came to depend more heavily on imported foodstuffs and raw materials their prices might rise while Britain's own export prices fell. Confident of the future of the 'Anglo-Saxon race' and anxious to integrate the home and colonial economies, he proposed a colonial customs union. Britain was to export capital and labour to the colonies, where food and raw materials could be produced cheaply, make markets of the colonies, and insist on free trade throughout the empire. If strict reciprocity were maintained in dealings with other countries, they might be induced to adopt free trade.[91]

Wakefield by choice involved himself in disputes with the political economists. In particular he attacked what he thought were Ricardo's ideas on capital accumulation and employment, referring back to Adam Smith to find arguments against the master of the new orthodoxy.[92] He knew that some of the political economists, most clearly James Mill, had propounded severe theoretical objections to Wilmot-Horton's humanitarian schemes of emigration, and he was also well aware that notice from the political economists could keep him above the ruck of dubious company promoters and propagandists of Utopia, to which *The Times* had once consigned him.[93] Eventually he was accepted as a political economist in his own right, even if his understanding of the theories that he criticised was imperfect.

John Stuart Mill, the most eminent economist to accept most of Wakefield's analysis, tried to reconcile it with Ricardian orthodoxy and, in doing so, departed from or weakened much of the classical position. Mill agreed with Wakefield in emphasising the economic importance of expanding markets and in teaching that new settlements could end people's frustrations in Britain. He allowed that export of capital might be beneficial and did not expect money spent on emigration to be lost to people remaining in Britain. 'Colonization in the present state of the world', he concluded, 'is the best affair of business in which the capital of an old and wealthy country can engage.'[94] Mill went beyond Wakefield in recognising that state aid was necessary for large emigration.

Whether Mill reconciled Wakefield's ideas with Ricardian orthodoxy (he claimed that Wakefield was merely stating corollaries of Ricardo's principles) mattered less to the shrewd propagandist than the fact that the last classical economist had attempted to do so and had become an advocate of systematic colonisation. Wakefield could easily endure the persistent hostility of, for example, the *Edinburgh*, because every attack drew attention to ideas that Mill, Senior and Torrens commended and that Merivale, the Permanent Under-Secretary at the Colonial Office from 1847, partly accepted.[95]

What Wakefield achieved with systematic thinkers, he also accomplished with politicians and the public. Samuel Sidney, one of his severer critics, outlined the methods of Wakefield's success:

> Energetic, tenacious, indefatigable, unscrupulous, with a wonderful talent for literary agitation, for simultaneously feeding a hundred journalists with the same idea and the same illustrations in varying language, for filling eloquent, but indolent, orators with telling speeches ... at one time he had rallied round him nearly every rising man of political aspirations, and secured the support of nearly every economical writer of any celebrity.[96]

Wakefield's influence was wide. The Ripon Regulations of 1831 on waste lands in Australia, the new form of assisted emigration to New South Wales (dating from the same year), the foundation of South Australia, the Select Committee on the Disposal of Lands in the British Colonies (1836), the Select Committee on Transportation, the Durham Report, the establishment of the Colonial Land and Emigration Commission in 1840, the many endeavours to promote company colonisation in New Zealand and the founding of five colonies there, the Select Committee on South Australia in 1840 and the Australian Land Sales Act of 1842 all owed something, often small, sometimes large, to his incessant agitation. When his influence was opposed, or when his ideas bore no fruit or a scheme failed, he complained of ignorance, jealousy and obduracy in high places. When his influence was large, or a scheme succeeded, he claimed to be the sole source of whatever had merit or significance. Debarred from Parliament by a disreputable past, he gathered 'a band of disciples — the brilliant, witty and popular Buller, the logical, vigorous, outspoken Molesworth, and other lesser men — and through them he set about converting Parliament'.[97] These were the self-styled 'colonial reformers', who shared Wakefield's opinions on the condition-of-Britain question and on colonisation as its remedy. Some shared also his unenviable ability to denigrate opponents, puff themselves, decline to believe that anyone outside their circle of influence understood colonial policy, and persuade historians to take them at their own valuation. Rintoul, the founder of The *Spectator*, was their constant ally, but the good and scholarly Spedding, who served in the Colonial Office for some years, estimated them correctly: '. . . a small, compact vigorous and able body of men have repeatedly and unscrupulously attacked anybody hostile to their views without provoking any reply as the only persons concerned are either Ministers, who cannot take issue with the periodical press, or subordinate officers who can only speak in their own defence if so directed by their chiefs'.[98]

Howick, who as third Earl Grey became the most powerful minister supporting both the spread of empire and free trade, and who introduced responsible government into British North America, was for some years a systematic coloniser. He refused, however, to associate with Wakefield, whose character and reputation, as we have seen, appalled him, and he sympathised with the victims of the so-called reformers' character assassinations. Privately he was even more critical of Wakefield's plans, inconsistencies and tergiversations than some of his less guarded public speeches suggested. The only Wakefieldians with whom he was closely connected were Buller and Merivale, and though often reaching conclusions similar to theirs, he maintained clear intellectual independence of them both.[99]

Howick did not accept Wakefield's diagnosis of the condition-of-Britain question. He attributed unemployment and other evils to the faults of commercial policy and did not believe that colonial emigration would improve conditions at home except in emergencies and by extending British commerce with free trade markets. Britain, he told the Lords in 1848, had never had 'any real or permanent excess of population'. Her vast undeveloped resources could be used profitably 'now that the shackles are removed from industry'. 'Those who look to emigration for relief from the distress to which the industrious classes are occasionally exposed' had not perceived that 'any diminution of the population by artificial means would necessarily . . . be followed by an acceleration in the rate of increase of the population, which would more than meet the vacuum so occasioned'.[100] In retrospect in 1853, he wrote that population itself had never been 'superabundant'. Unemployment had resulted from want of capital, wrong commercial policy, bad seasons and overspeculation in railways and other new industries. Howick was an ardent supporter of empire, for the sake of responsibility to colonies already acquired, and for prestige, mission, imperial destiny, wealth, power and the spreading of free trade. Like Wakefield, he looked to the colonies to strengthen Britain by deploying men and capital to greater advantage than at home. Unlike Wakefield, he stressed imperial responsibility, free trade and self-government, rather than private profit and 'systematic' colonisation on fixed principles.[101]

A few critics tried to deflate the empire-building aspects of systematic colonisation. *The Economist* thought that overseas territories would be no 'less open to the reception of our super-abundant population . . . if each had their own government and was a separate state'.[102] Cornewall Lewis, whose *Essay on the Government of Dependencies* became a text for British statemen, proposed the paradox that systematic colonisation did not require colonies: 'If it were advantageous for a new settlement to employ a portion of its public revenues in procuring immigrants, its government would naturally devote a portion of its revenues to this purpose, whether the settlement were dependent or independent.'[103] Lewis thought colonies expensive and liable to provoke wars and to corrupt government in Britain.

These arguments, so close to the Radical attacks on empire, made little headway against the proud and growing aspiration to spread Great Britain throughout the world; the increasing attractiveness of colonies as sources of prestige, markets and sound investments; and the dread of diminished standing and impaired strategy if colonies were lost. Some writers deplored the gains made by the United States when immigrants went there instead of to the empty lands of Canada and Australia. Generally, the view prevailed that, as emigration of men and capital was inevitable and probably beneficial, risk of loss was diminished and prospects of gain increased if people and investments stayed within the empire.[104]

From the 1840s onward, belief in the future of the empire became popular. Tens of thousands of men and women, drawn from all social classes, left the mother country for Britain overseas. There was a prolific outpouring of books and articles telling people at home what the British settlements overseas could offer them. British North America, for example, had James Buckingham's *Canada, Nova Scotia, New Brunswick and other British Provinces in North America* (London, 1843), which described the colonies and called for an orderly programme of free trade and extensive colonisation to save England from ruin by developing her transatlantic possessions. The *Foreign and Colonial Quarterly*, first appearing in January 1843, gave much space to Australia and Canada in the opening issues and to New Zealand in the seventh. Generally it favoured emigration of British people to British colonies overseas, where they would live under British institutions. The old Tory *Quarterly* continued as strongly imperial as ever. A memorable article in September 1841 looked to emigration to cure the ills of England, strengthen the empire and increase the sum of human happiness.[105] *The Illustrated*

London News, *Blackwood's* and *The Times* were scarcely less favourable. Carlyle's *Past and Present* (1843) was neither novel nor unusual when it argued for the emigration of honest willing workers to the new lands. The interest in Britain overseas remained strong throughout the 1840s, 1850s and early 1860s. It appeared in masses of emigrant manuals, in popular fiction (including Dickens) and in such serious works of observation and reflection as W. Howitt's *Land, Labour and Gold* (2 vols, London, 1855), which described the Australian colonies and pointed out that England was reproducing herself there on a larger scale than would ever be possible at home. Howitt saw Australia as one of the places to which Britain was taking freedom, Christianity and civilisation.

IMPERIAL DESTINY

It would be wrong to claim that the principles of systematic colonisation, which Wakefieldians supported so sedulously, were well understood or generally accepted in Britain by the 1840s. But the idea of an empire of settlement as the destiny of imperial Britain had certainly captured political and popular notice; Australia and New Zealand, as well as British North America, had begun to be attractive to British emigrants; many men in high places, both politicians and civil servants, were firm believers in active colonisation by settlement, if necessary using state funds; and the colonies themselves warmed to the idea of an imperial destiny that they could share.

Emigration, declared *The Westminster Review* in 1840, with some indifference to its own earlier pronouncements, was 'no longer confined to the wretched', for the educated middle classes and 'aristocratic cadets' had come to favour it. Colonies founded with such people, according to true principles of systematic colonisation, would start at the same level of civilisation as the mother country and, free of its trammels, might surpass it. Twelve years earlier, Huskisson had gloried in the triumphs of colonisation, which carried 'the language, the free institutions, the system of laws' of Britain to 'every quarter of the globe' and so contributed to freedom, peace, order and Christianity. 'The extension of English law, language and morality are of great value,' declared the *Quarterly* in 1829, when reviewing a book on the precarious Swan river settlement. In comparison with the splendid achievements open to cultural imperialism, the expense of colonisation was 'trifling'.[106] Christianity itself seemed the special care of Protestant Britain, and missionaries enjoyed esteem and deference as flowers of British civilisation.

After over a decade of propaganda for systematic colonisation and growing public interest in emigration to Canada, Australia and New Zealand, Cobden himself told the Commons that, though he abhorred the old commercial system and the apparatus of privilege, jobbery and autocracy with which formal empire had been invested, he was 'as anxious as anyone that the English race should spread itself over the earth'.[107] Torrens, who had been a systematic coloniser before Wakefield, was sure by 1844 that emigration would serve 'the mission of the Anglo-Saxon race to multiply and replenish the earth'. The manifest destiny of England was to 'become a vast industrial metropolis' and of the colonies to be her complementary 'agricultural provinces of unlimited extent'.[108] Gladstone, to whom glorious destiny was sober duty, agreed that 'we have an obligation to provide ... what semblance we can of British institutions and a home as nearly as might be like that which the emigrants have left, and to which they ... retain a fond attachment'.[109] Merivale was sure of imperial destiny:

> It is a sort of instinctive feeling to us all, that the destiny of our name and nation is not here, in the narrow island which we occupy; that the spirit of England is volatile, not fixed; that it lives in our language, our commerce, our industry, in all those channels of inter-communication by which we embrace and connect the vast multitude of states, both civilized and uncivilized, throughout the world.[110]

The confident liberalism that wanted to take to India English ideas of law, justice and morality[111] was comparable with the belief, often expressed from the 1820s onward with respect to the settled colonies, that Britain had been appointed by Providence to spread her civilisation throughout the world. Archibald Alison, historian, lawyer and protectionist, declared that the 'British race' was peopling the western and southern hemispheres; in time, 200 million people 'on the shores of the Atlantic, and in the isles of the Pacific, will be speaking our language, reading our authors, glorying in our descent'.[112]

Belief in the cultural mission of Britain was common to men of all parties and was held strongly by the Wakefieldians. Grey himself was a believer: 'The authority of the British Crown is at this moment the most powerful instrument, under Providence, of maintaining peace and order in many extensive regions of the earth, and thereby assists in diffusing amongst millions of the human race, the blessings of Christianity and civilization.'[113]

Conviction of racial superiority confirmed the growing sense of imperial destiny. Evidence placed before the Select Committee on Aborigines (Buxton's Committee) in 1835—7 showed that the growth of European population in British North America and Australia had led to the dying out of the indigenous race and scandalised some humanitarians into opposing colonisation or insisting that it be under strict official control. Sometimes, however, the evidence was regarded as proof that 'the extinction of the non-Europeans was part of natural evolution'. White superiority, thus brutally attested, was taken as an additional and natural sanction appertaining to colonisation among other races, who would be subdued, assimilated or allowed to expire. Thomas Arnold thought that the English was the last great creative race, charged with a unique duty to spread itself throughout the world. Robert Knox, the anatomist and ethnologist, who influenced Disraeli and Bulwer Lytton and wrote for both the *Edinburgh* and the *Westminster*, believed that the 'Saxon' was the great race and that 'wars of the races' were a source of human creativity. Although climatic reasons dictated that Europeans could survive only in Europe, so that in Australia, for example, they would need the refreshment of constant immigration, they should go out to the world and fulfil their destiny. Many frontier colonists took the most ruthless view of white superiority and rejected the misgivings of Exeter Hall with angry contempt.[114]

Advocates of cultural imperialism and of spreading British people and institutions throughout the world were well aware of the rich rewards, more material than pride and spiritual satisfaction, that interested political economists and businessmen. Grey observed that when Britain spread her influence, or her religion and law, among 'barbaric' peoples, she made customers out of those whom she raised in the scale of civilisation.[115] When she sent her own people to North America, Australasia and South Africa, she nobly spread her civilisation, culture, government and free trade. She also developed ideal sources of food and raw materials, reliable export markets and safe, dependable outlets for investment. Colonisation, its advocates generally claimed, benefited the whole world by spreading Christianity, free trade, British culture and British forms of government. It also raised the level of profits at home and developed abroad – to the benefit of British power and prestige, and ultimately of mankind – human and capital resources that would otherwise have been wasted.

Grey, who looked on his own political life as an inherited, aristocratic responsibility, thought of the empire as a duty laid on Britain, and of free trade as a moral imperative binding on him as on everybody else.[116] Free trade was a policy of such universal wisdom, so fundamental and immanent in society, so self-adjusting in practice, that, when Britain was converted to its principles, the colonies must have them also. Every colony was another territory in which Britain must make free trade prevail. On this ground alone every argument that colonies should be given up along with the old commercial system had to be rejected. As colonies needed revenue from customs duties, Grey favoured federal unions,[117] especially in British North America and Australia, so as to guarantee the maximum flow of trade, unhampered by customs duties, within the empire. Taxes should be laid on external trade only and never so as to constitute preferences or restrictions.

Grey was sure that free trade would strengthen the empire.[118] If the principles of free trade could reconcile the interests of all nations, how could they produce disharmony between Britain and her colonies? If the empire had formerly been held together by the erroneous belief that the old commercial system benefited the colonies as well as Britain, how much better would it cohere when, after free trade had been imposed from Britain, she and her colonies experienced a new accession of prosperity and wealth? Until the whole would went over to free trade, all parts of the empire would be able to enjoy it together, and Britain had a duty to ensure that this was so.

THE NEW IDEA OF COLONIES OF SETTLEMENT

The new idea of great colonies of settlement was strongly apparent in Britain from the 1840s on, and was materially different from any earlier way of thinking about the empire. Colonies were still regarded as part of an imperial system of commerce, although for many people the system was becoming free trade, not protection, preference and privilege. Colonies were also still regarded as subordinate to Britain and believed to be a vital element of her strength and prestige. The new aspect was confident expectation of a great imperial destiny, in which the colonies of settlement would be extensions of Britain overseas, peopled from the British Isles, reproducing vital parts of British polity and society, developed with British capital, under some British control (economic as well as political), and sharing in British culture, civilisation, law and government. Even if they became independent they would remain British in character and attachment.

If the idea had existed before in British history, it was certainly not in the history of the old American colonies. They had grown up with little planning and no intention of a vast empire of settlement. They had become objects of jealousy in Britain when they acquired wealth, numbers and a distinct civilisation, whose origins were only partly British, with which to challenge the supremacy that Britain tried to assert from the middle of the eighteenth century onward. Nor had the idea existed when Pitt and Grenville planned the Act of 1791, for they had thought only of the Canadas, had been obsessed by the French problem and had lacked any vision of a vast empire of settlement reproducing Britain overseas. From the 1840s onward, British North America, Australia, New Zealand and, increasingly, the Cape Colony, though enormous in extent and scattered, seemed to await development by Britain's excess of capital and people, and to be certain (their French and Dutch elements perhaps excluded) of becoming and remaining societies as like Britain as ever distant colonies could be.

Parliamentary debates on New Zealand and on free trade showed how the new concept of settled colonies was growing. Among the themes that recurred most often during the New Zealand debates of June 1845[119] were the attractiveness of the colonies to British settlers, the rights of British subjects in the colonies to the fullest possible degree of representative self-government, the destiny of Britain to spread her culture, her law and her people, and the overcoming of humanitarian inhibitions concerning British settlement among such indigenous peoples as the Maoris. The inadequacy of commercial explanations of empire was apparent throughout the debates, which arose from the tangled relationships of the New Zealand Company (Wakefield in the background and Buller its Parliamentary spokesman), the systematic colonisers generally, the Colonial Office — anxious to uphold the Treaty of Waitangi and protect the Maoris against the Company — and Stanley, who had to defend inept officials in New Zealand, disliked the Company and had to do his best with the treaty.

Two aspects of the debate were clear from the first. Although the acquisition of New Zealand in 1840 had been against the wishes of Parliament and the Colonial Office, no one in 1845 disputed that British colonisation of New Zealand should continue.[120] Moreover, the existence of new colonies of settlement was understood to require changed principles of colonial government, or, at least, a return to the principles of 1791 in a new and wider context. 'Bear' Ellice told the Commons:

> Our old habits and associations with respect to Colonial Government have been completely lost sight of subsequent to the Quebec Act [the Canada Constitutional Act, 1791]. Since that time we have only learnt to maintain in conquered colonies the French, Spanish and Dutch intitutions we found there, and to establish Penal Colonies, the administration of all of which has been conducted by Orders in Council .... Is it intended ... to persevere in the system with your new Colony of New Zealand?

Buller, who had opened the debate the previous day, had answered Ellice's question when he had emphasised that the Company was spreading British settlement and trade, British culture, power and institutions and the English language. He strongly attacked the Treaty of Waitangi, which had recognised Maori sovereignty and guaranteed the Maoris in the possession of their lands, calling it a mere device to get round the practice, inspired by missionaries, of treating the Maoris as a civilised nation, responsible for law, order and good government throughout the islands.[121] Like most of the colonial reformers, Buller had firm faith in racial superiority. He ignorantly dismissed the Maoris as 'inferior to the Caffres, and to all the Indian tribes who people the West Indies and the American continent from the equator to Labrador'. He blamed the Colonial Office for having 'thwarted' a sound colonising policy by 'feeble views and minor jealousies' — that is, for having protected the Maoris, distrusted colonisation by companies connected with Wakefield, and

delayed in acquiring New Zealand. He saw the ambitions of the Company
as part of the great imperial destiny of Britain, to elevate primitive peoples
and to use God's gifts of land and resources by cultivating the 'wilderness'
and encouraging an extensive and planned emigration from the British
Isles.

The Parliamentary Under-Secretary, G. W. Hope, denied that Stanley
opposed colonisation, for no one opposed it any longer. But colonisation
in New Zealand had to be subject to the Treaty of Waitangi and the moral
obligations of Britain to the indigenous people. His arguments carried little
weight. Howick and Benjamin Hawes, on behalf of the Whigs, supported
colonisation by settlement as a national imperative, recognised that it
involved the most liberal possible grant of self-government to the colonists,
and refused to believe that it would be impossible to reconcile the interests
of British settlers and the Maoris in these 'magnificent islands'. Russell
spoke of New Zealand as 'a branch of this mighty Empire'. General Sir
Howard Douglas, who had governed New Brunswick and knew British
North America from military experience, introduced transatlantic notions
into the debate by declaring that the settled colonies sustained and
strengthened Britain. Although he claimed that these opinions were 'as old
as the days in which the foundations of this great Empire were laid',
Koebner rightly remarked that they were 'anything but traditional'.[122]
Peel, though he thought the Treaty of Waitangi binding on the
government, condemned some of its legal premises and strongly advocated
representative government on a municipal basis for the scattered British
settlements in New Zealand. He wanted them to have the nearest
approximation to British institutions that would be possible for some
12,000–14,000 settlers widely dispersed in large and distant territories.
The debate was so favourable to systematic colonisation that Buller's
motion to go into committee on 'the state of New Zealand and the case of
the New Zealand Company' was lost by only fifty votes (223 to 173).

Substantially, Buller and the systematic colonisers had won. Stanley at
once issued new instructions on land grants, which satisfied some of the
Company's complaints, and provided land for the Free Church of Scotland
to plant a settlement at Otago.[123] Later developments, some of them
mentioned briefly in Chapter 9, confirmed that, although the Company
could not carry out its own intentions, political opinion in Britain
recognised that colonisation of a new kind had begun in New Zealand,
and, moreover, that special arrangements were needed to introduce British
political institutions in forms suitably adjusted to local conditions.

Although the free trade debates of 1846 were preoccupied with the
problems of Britain rather than of the colonies, important indicators of
the new idea of colonies of settlement appeared in them. Some
protectionists and some free traders were sure that Britain had already
acquired to her immense advantage vast colonies of settlement, of almost

unlimited potential, in which, so long as she retained them, she could reproduce her society and civilisation as well as grow rich. Free traders taking this view had, of course, to oppose the vociferous Manchester School and, particularly, Cobden, who thought that when free trade was achieved the empire could be allowed to disintegrate as fast as inescapable responsibilities permitted. Opponents of empire had their eloquence fired by radical hostility to the aristocratic privileges and offices so notoriously associated with colonisation, by general unwillingness to spend British money on the many colonial wars of the period, and, above all, by consciousness of their own failure to retard the growth of empire. As Shaw remarked, the stridency of the enemies of empire was that of the defeated, not of the victors.[124]

Naturally, protectionists, who were Tories, were sufficiently aware of the glory of empire to look beyond merely commercial arguments when they defended it and opposed free trade. When Peel and Stanley were attacked in 1842 for preserving colonial preferences in their reformed tariff, Stanley praised colonial trade and colonial ties with Britain in language 'not heard from a British minister since William Pitt had solicited the Commons to accept his Irish treaty project'.[125] Colonial trade, he said, 'more than any other employed our shipping, consumed the produce of our manufactures, and gave encouragement to native and to colonial industry – and . . . kept entire that strong . . . beneficial tie of nationality . . . of mutual connection between the different parts of this great empire, which constituted its protection from war and its strength and glory in peace'.[126] Although Stanley, like Peel, still thought the commercial tie the most important part of empire, he conceded strength and vitality to 'nationality'. Gladstone dismissed 'political' considerations from the debate, not because he thought them mistaken or overstated, but because he doubted their relevance to the question before the House.

In January 1846, when Peel proposed the immediate removal of duties on grain imported from the colonies (and the immediate reduction of duties on foreign grain, which were to end on 1 February 1849),[127] the protectionists mostly treated the colonial question as secondary and fought to defend British agricultural interests. Members opposed to Peel, who did look at the colonial question, argued as if the destruction of colonial preference would inevitably lead to the fall of the old commercial system and so to the end of empire. Howard Douglas maintained that colonies would no longer have value to Britain and was sure that a merely political connection between the mother country and the colonies would have no influence on trade. Francis Scott, the Parliamentary agent for the legislative council of New South Wales, predicted that Canada would leave the empire first, followed in succession by the other colonies. Stanley argued forcibly that, because protection was the 'basis upon which your colonial system rests', its destruction must weaken the attachment of the colonies. He attacked those free traders who would have welcomed the dissolution of the empire. Whether protection continued or not, he said, Britain ought to keep her colonies, for their sake as well as hers. Commercial independence might be a step to political independence. Could British manufacturers afford the loss of their most secure market overseas? Was Britain to break the promises implicitly given to British North America in the Canada Corn Law of 1843 (6 and 7 Vict., c. 29)?[128]

Peel and Grey gave the critical answers to Stanley and the protectionists, who feared that repeal would weaken or destroy the empire. Peel denied that the colonial system was based entirely, or even principally, on commercial exclusiveness, preference and prohibitions. There were political, military and cultural ties of no less importance than those of trade. He expected the colonies to benefit from the coming of free trade and to be held to Britain by the common advantages of new commercial links that would strengthen other, older ties. Grey enthusiastically went farther than Peel and gave an unusually optimistic view of an empire of settlement founded on free trade and colonial self-government:

> . . . the connexion between the colonies and the Mother Country was a mutual advantage, requiring no such support [as commercial protection] to maintain . . . . He believed that if they pursued a liberal policy in other respects towards the colonies, by extending to them the dearest right of Englishmen, the privilege of self-government, and not needlessly interfering in their domestic concerns . . . they would bind them to us with chains which no power on earth could break; and the connexion between them and the Parent State would continue until they far exceeded ourselves in population.[129].

Since the 1830s Grey had advocated considerable extension of colonial self-government in colonies qualified to enjoy it beneficially. He believed in the active advantages of free trade to every part of the world to which it extended. He believed also in the new empire of settlement, in which commercial advantages to Britain and the colonies would exist, but whose spirit and justification were the spreading throughout the world of British people, culture and civilisation.

A few months later Gladstone summed up the position that most imperial free traders had reached. When the Canadians objected to the loss of their preferences in British markets, he was Secretary of State for the Colonies. His slightly tendentious dispatch to Governor-General Cathcart had one paragraph epitomising the new concept of empire. Significantly, to show that he was writing of a general idea of settled colonies, not merely of Canada, he cited Australian experiences to justify the view that empire did not rest on commercial preferences. If the distant Australian colonies flourished in close ties with Britain without a vestige of preference to their principal products, why should not the Canadians look to the benefits of free trade and the established virtues of empire to reconcile themselves to the new imperial policy?

> It would ... be a source of the greatest pain to Her Majesty's Government if ... the connexion between this country and Canada derived its vitality from no other source than from the exchange of commercial preferences. If it were so, it might appear to be a relation consisting in the exchange not of benefits of burdens; ... it would suggest ... that the connexion itself had reached ... the legitimate term of its existence. But Her Majesty's Government ... augur for it a longer duration, founded upon a larger and firmer basis — upon [military] protection rendered from one side and allegiance freely and loyally returned from the other — upon common traditions of the past and hopes of the future — upon resemblances in origin, in laws, and in manners — in what inwardly binds men ... together, as well as in the close association of ... material interests which ... are destined not to recede but to advance, not to be severed but to be more closely and healthfully combined under the quickening influences of increased commercial freedom.[130]

Gladstone and Grey were both too reserved to use the expansive language of grand destiny; but they did state unambiguously a new view of colonies of settlement. In Britain, and in the colonies, an increasing number of public men no longer looked on the colonies that had been peopled from Britain as merely part of a commercial system, or as special communities such as Upper Canada had been. Empire to them still meant India, the Crown colonies, the trading posts and regions of influence and strategy; it meant also, however, the growth of new British communities overseas, sharing common traditions of law, government, manners and civilisation as well as British trade and commerce, participating in one another's defence and adding to one another's prestige. The empire of British settlement was the transplanting of Britain overseas, as people, capital, culture and institutions. When, in July 1846 and with the sufferance of Peel, Russell became Prime Minister and Grey Secretary of State for War and the Colonies, power passed to the men who believed in the empire of settlement, of free trade and of the largest possible degree of self-government for colonies.[131]

SELF-GOVERNMENT OF 'BRITISH COMMUNITIES' OVERSEAS

The new concept of empire as 'British communities'[132] overseas obviously challenged British statesmen to grant to the large settled colonies political institutions as nearly as possible the same as those existing in Britain. In order to reproduce English society in the colonies, as Wakefield never tired of pointing out, the middle classes had to be induced to emigrate; they would expect political rights comparable with those they had possessed in Britain.

In *A View of the Art of Colonization* Wakefield contrasted two main principles of colonial government, the 'municipal' and the 'central' — that is, local self-government and government from the metropolis.[133] Britain had founded the American colonies, he thought, on the correct municipal principle, but lost them by attempting central control. 'This wound to our national pride seems to have brought the municipal into disfavour, just when it should rather have produced aversion to the central.' Convict colonies and all the conquered colonies, other than Quebec, had been thought unfit for municipal government, so that 'by degrees the central system prevailed over the municipal' and a large part of the empire came to be ruled ignorantly and incompetently by the Colonial Office. Inconsistently, liberal forms of government in Britain existed side by side with tyrannical misrule of colonies, whose affairs rarely came to public notice. 'The only real exceptions from the rule of Colonial-Office supremacy have occurred when gross errors of administration, as in Canada and New Zealand, have drawn public attention in this country to a colonial subject.'[134] There was enough accuracy in his specious attacks on British policy to sway the uninformed, the more so because Grey, Stephen and other principal victims of his slanders lacked a popular following.[135]

Wakefield, according to himself, was prepared to allow responsible government to colonies, and he carefully described some of its essential features in *The Art of Colonization*.[136] But his defence of Sir Charles Metcalfe's administration in Canada,[137] his conduct in New Zealand, when his personal interests conflicted with his supposed principles, and his later blindness to the merits of what Grey (Howick) and Elgin achieved in Canada showed that he himself was no true or thorough supporter of the great constitutional concession. Like Durham, he restricted severely the possible range of responsible government in colonies. He would have retained for Britain full power over the waste lands and their land revenue, the defence forces, coinage and currency, external trade and foreign relations, the constitution and the succession to the throne. As a systematic coloniser, he had strong reasons for wishing imperial supremacy to be maintained.

If either Durham or Wakefield had had half the prescient understanding of colonial societies with which admirers have credited them, they would have perceived the futility of attempting to keep out of the hands of colonists matters of the most vital importance to them, such as lands and trade.[138] Grey, who made the same mistake, has generally had it charged against him as evidence of his inability to comprehend the aspirations of colonists. Wakefield has been strangely excused.

COLONIAL DEMOCRACY AND THE AMERICAN EXAMPLE

American political experience helped to reconcile British statesmen to the democracy that was certain to follow if the institutions of the mother country were bestowed as nearly as possible on the new British communities overseas. Monarchy, aristocracy and hereditary owners of large estates would all be lacking in the colonies. Would British institutions, which had themselves become so much more liberal than before, be safe there? The publication in 1835 of an English translation of Tocqueville's *Democracy in America* roused the strong interest of J. S. Mill, Howick and other thinkers on representative government. Tocqueville was already well known in England, where his friends included Nassau Senior, the Grotes, Roebuck, Cornewall Lewis, John Austin and Reeve, his translator. Howick, as we have seen, read *Democracy in America* and thought it unusually interesting; whether it influenced him is not known. British statesmen who knew Tocqueville's commentary on their own country[139] as well as his conclusions on America were interested in his expectation that democracy in England might be mitigated by the blending of the power of aristocracy and tradition with the power of the people. British colonies of settlement, although monarchical in government, lacked traditional governing classes and seemed impatient of the distinctions that made a conservative social structure proper. What could mitigate 'levelling democracy' in the colonies? Fortunately, Tocqueville had found that, even in the United States, democracy was not unrestrained. The United States, Gladstone remarked in 1852, was 'the great source of experimental instruction, so far as colonial institutions are concerned'.[140]

As interpreted by J. S. Mill,[141] who supported both colonisation and representative government, Tocqueville regarded the United States as a middle-class country, liable to democratic excesses, but dominated effectively by its more responsible citizens. Mill himself found in the United States many normal manifestations of a modern commercial society, such as Britain was becoming, rather than distinctively or alarming American traits. His conclusion was that in every society the institutions of government were in the hands of its 'active powers', that the United States was a bourgeois country with powerful conservative forces, and that the people there learned political wisdom through representative government and gave large powers to an élite. America was not a mere democracy, unchecked except for such institutional safeguards as federalism. The absence of hereditary monarchy, hereditary legislators and powerful privileged classes had not produced instability. Mill was, in fact, less pessimistic about democracy than was Tocqueville.

The Whig economist Senior, whose liberal views on colonial self-government are mentioned in the next chapter, also found much to praise in American political institutions and preferred them to those of any country other than Britain.[142] Universal suffrage, he believed, would be disastrous in Britain, which was industrial and heavily urban, but it might succeed in new, agricultural countries like the United States.[143] Merivale, who noted that the people of Britain regarded the United States as 'the land of requital and redress . . . in which fortune opens her arms to the courageous', followed Tocqueville in accepting the inevitability of democracy and, like Senior, thought it safer in a new, agricultural country than in an old, industrial one.[144] Although British conservatives criticised the 'pervasive electioneering spirit' of American public life and deplored American rough manners, lack of deference and intolerance, Coleridge himself welcomed the 'possible destiny of the United States of America as a nation of a hundred millions of freemen . . . under the law of Alfred, and speaking the language of Shakespeare and Milton'; it would become 'Great Britain in a state of glorious magnification' and sneering attacks on the republic were contemptible.[145] If democracy in America were consistent with such a destiny, how could democracy in the colonies be dangerous, especially when it would be checked by imperial subordination and the governors?

The connection between American forms of government and society and the future of British colonies of settlement was often noticed. Durham emphasised two points already familiar to British politicians: that the United States would object to illiberal forms of government anywhere in North America, and that the Canadians would continue to look to American government for models in adapting their own institutions to local needs. He drew attention also to the strong 'natural tie of sympathy between the English population of the Canadas and the inhabitants of the frontier states of the Union' and insisted that Britain could not afford to allow Canada to be less attractive to British emigrants than the United States was. Like some Canadian critics of colonial government, Durham believed that the superior pace of growth that the United States enjoyed as compared with British North America was partly to be attributed to the superiority of some American institutions of government.[146]

Roebuck highly praised the American political system[147] and his book *The Colonies of England* (1849) drew special attention to the United States as an example of successful colonisation, both by Britain and later by the United States of America.[148] The conditions of successful colonisation, he thought, were self-government and free trade, together not apart: 'Where there were complete self-government, and an entirely unrestricted trade, there success, even with an adverse soil and climate, was most rapid and extensive; where there was no self-government, there was no success; where there was self-government, but so far checked as a restricted trade implied, there was only a partial, and slowly advancing improvement.' Roebuck's book is not always easy to understand,[149] but it is clear that Roebuck thought the colonies considerably mismanaged and that he did not want Britain to lose them. He made a special case of Canada, allowing three alternatives: annexation to the United States (which he opposed), friendly independence as a great 'Northern Confederation of British American Provinces', or some other degree of separation that would preserve the British tie while allowing substantial autonomy in all Canadian affairs. Roebuck's book appeared after he had passed the zenith of his reputation as a colonial specialist. At about the same time, Molesworth suggested (without details or deliberation) that the American federal system might be the model for the imperial constitution: 'The United States is a system of States clustered around a central republic. Our colonial empire ought to be a system of colonies clustered round the hereditary monarchy of England.'[150] More discriminatingly, Sir James Mackintosh thought that the American republic worked successfully, despite excessively liberal institutions, because of special, propitious circumstances. His list of the causes of American success coincided well with the conditions that most British colonies of settlement could be expected to provide. They included the prevalence of isolated rural communities, few large towns, no rancorous proletariat, and relatively large numbers of landholders or other proprietors with vested interests in a middle-class society of established values, and with plenty of land available as a safety valve for discontent.[151] Merivale saw more clearly than most contemporaries that the changing technology that led Britain to free trade was also profoundly affecting politics in ways important for democracy. Steam, he wrote in 1846 in reviewing C. Lyell's *Travels in North America*, was rendering the action of the people on the government in great emergencies both inevitable and irresistible.[152] Improved communications were engendering progress towards democracy as news, opinions and influence, instead of being confined to relatively small areas or limited classes of privilege, were made capable of touching a whole country and bringing its remotest territories into contact with the centres of political power. The example of the United States showed that 'we must accustom ourselves to the contemplation of space and numbers as the greatest future elements' of politics.[153] In a colony, as in Britain, the imperial government would have to reckon with the action of the people as a whole, not merely of select leaders, elites and elected representatives. In the 'civilised' parts of the empire, pre-eminently the colonies of settlement, political power was inevitably passing into the hands of the people as a whole. To attempt to control such communities from Britain, or to deny them all the self-government they asked, would be blind and absurd.

Grey, however, doubted whether British colonial policy had anything to learn from the example of the United States. He disliked American democracy, blaming it for the reckless course of American foreign policy (particularly over the Oregon and Maine boundaries), and distrusted the apparent inability of the American government to control Irish Americans and other anti-British elements when they fished in the troubled waters of Canadian discontent.[154] He was, however, keenly aware of the importance of American political examples to Canada and dreaded the political consequences of allowing Canadian discontent to fester while the United States prospered in the Age of Jackson.

8 Party Government in British North America

> Of whatsoever party your Council may be composed, it will be your duty to act strictly upon the principle . . . of not identifying yourself with any one party, but instead of this, 'Making yourself both a mediator and a moderator between the influential of all parties'. . . . you will carefully avoid any acts which can possibly be supposed to imply the slightest personal objection to their opponents . . . .
>
> Grey to Harvey, 3 November 1846[1]

Henry George, third Earl Grey, Secretary of State for War and the Colonies in Lord John Russell's first administration, wrote to Sir John Harvey, Lieutenant-Governor of Nova Scotia, on 3 November 1846, instructing him to allow responsible government in the colony. Shortly afterwards he authorised Lord Elgin, the new governor-general of Canada to allow responsible government there as well. In 1847 he sanctioned it in New Brunswick and in 1851, after much hesitation, in Prince Edward Island. These well known decisions reflected an important change of mind for Grey. In May 1840, while Lord Howick, he had told the Commons that responsible government was impossible in colonies:

> If by responsible government it were meant that the Executive Government of the colony should be directly responsible to the Colonial Assembly, . . . responsible government so defined would be incompatible with the maintenance of Colonial Government. But . . . if the Government at home, as well as the authorities in the colonies, were to pursue a system of protective government, guided by a conciliatory spirit, and a desire to consult the wishes of the people, then such a form of government would answer the object that those who were loudest in their clamour for a responsible government had in view.[2]

What produced Grey's change of mind between 1840, when he thought responsible government impossible in colonies, and 1846, when he ordered its introduction in the extensive form of party government?

GREY'S CHANGE OF POLICY

There have been two traditional answers to the former question (and none to the latter). Although the answers are consistent with one another, neither is satisfying and both are probably wrong. The older answer, derived from John Stuart Mill, was mentioned at the beginning of this book. Mill believed that Britain had maintained a tight control over the internal affairs of her colonies until, first, the ending of the old commercial system had removed important reasons for doing so, and, second, 'a new era in the colonial policy of nations began with Lord Durham's Report'.[3] In effect, Mill attributed the beginning of responsible government in colonies to the change in British commercial policy and the wisdom of the Report. Most historians have thought the same.

There are difficulties in Mill's account. Neither Grey nor Russell was convinced by Durham's case for responsible government in 1839, or at any later time.[4] When they allowed responsible government in British North America, seven and more years later, they did not refer to Durham. When responsible government was challenged in Parliament in 1849 they did not rely on his authority. Grey simply stated that colonies developed their own forms of government according to their needs, that Canada had sufficient political maturity to enjoy responsible government on the British model, and that Britain could gain nothing good by withholding from 'British communities overseas'[5] the power to manage their own internal affairs. The form of responsible government that he allowed in North America was not what Durham had advocated in 1839, because Canadian demands and the conventions of the British constitution had both changed since then. Britain had gone over to responsible government by party[6] and, as we shall see, the Canadian reformers were demanding the new system at least as early as 1841, when it first appeared in Britain. The struggle in Canada for party government, instead of the limited form of responsible government in which the governor-general was effectively his own prime minister (although his advisers sat in the legislature and had to be in harmony with it), found no place in Mill's brief sketch. The limited form of responsible government that Russell and Lord Sydenham made into a system was, however, wholly consistent with that proposed by Durham,[7] even if it owed little to him. The party government that Grey actually granted was more liberal than that Durham had thought of in 1839.

Mill's emphasis on Durham, even if correct in its main premise, rested on a gross foreshortening of British history and considerable obliviousness to events in Canada. The refusal of Russell, Stanley and Gladstone, when Secretaries of State to British North America, to allow responsible government in the full sense of party government had become so strained by 1846 that Grey (and Russell) were partly bowing to immediate political necessity when they made their great concession. 'Lord Grey', wrote C. P. Stacey, 'went to the Colonial Office determined to end the pitiful tragi-comedy that had been in progress in Canada.'[8] Mill passed over the 'tragi-comedy', enacted for seven years after Durham had reported, as if it had been some insignificant, forgettable overture to a great new policy, and did not ask why so eminent a cast, all of whom had known Durham and had read his Report, should have prolonged it so painfully. Nor did he ask why responsible government was strongly opposed by most colonial conservatives, even after conservatives in Britain had either given up opposing it or actually decided to support it.

The other difficulty in Mill's position concerns free trade. To Grey, the coming of free trade certainly did not imply that Britain should give up her control of the commercial policy of the colonies. A doctrinaire free trader, he was, while Secretary of State, incessantly active in promoting the new commercial policy. He wished duties of customs to be raised for revenue only, opposed tariff preferences favouring one country's products over another's (imperial preference was included in the ban), and objected to subsidies or other public assistance to any form of industry. When free trade triumphed, Grey thought that Britain had an imperial duty to insist upon it throughout the empire. Free trade did not imply freedom of fiscal policy for the colonies:[9] rather, every part of the empire had to adopt free trade policies.

Grey was glad that the coming of free trade reduced the imperial supervision of colonial laws and administration, which had provoked trouble with the Americans and had long been declining in extent and significance.[10] But in his eyes the great revolution of commercial policy did not otherwise affect the limits of British control over colonial affairs. When Grey granted responsible government he assumed that commercial policy was necessarily reserved for imperial control. Colonial societies had to be saved from their natural propensity to protect infant industries and thwarted in their desire for preference in imperial markets.

The coming of free trade certainly helped those Radicals who wanted to reduce the costs of empire and argued, therefore, that colonies not bound to Britain by commercial preferences and restrictions could not be worth defending and administering.[11] The triumph of free trade also raised the question, in Canada as well as in Britain, of whether colonies would any longer accept restrictions on their rights to self-government after Britain had given up the commercial system, the benefits of which allegedly justified subordination of colonies. But the voices of the critics and doubters of empire — strongest during the Canadian troubles of 1849, after responsible government had been granted — were drowned in Britain for most of the 1840s and 1850s by the rise of confidence in the future empire of settlement, in which Grey and also Elgin believed. It is significant that when the 'colonial reformers', Grey's bitterest critics at the end of the 1840s, tried to drive him from office they accused him of not doing enough to preserve the empire and of failing to press ahead with systematic colonisation.[12]

The simple assertion (no one appears ever to have demonstrated the point) that the triumph of free trade cleared the way for the coming of responsible government by helping to relax imperial control of the colonies cannot be accepted. It mistakes the whole history of British colonial government after the American Revolution. It treats Grey and Russell, who introduced responsible government, as too obtuse to understand the greatest imperial changes with which they were identified. It assumes a similar lack of perspicacity in their contemporaries, who rarely discussed responsible government and, when they did, generally failed to find the advent of free trade relevant to the granting of the greatest of all reforms in the history of colonial self-government. Equally it ignores the confident spirit of the new ideas of an empire of settlement and proceeds as if, for the first time since the 1760s, British policy towards the government of colonies had been determined as a matter of economic interest rather than as a matter of giving 'British communities overseas' the fullest possible control of their internal affairs. Doubtless, the economic interests of Britain were served by maintaining contentment in the great colonies and by keeping them in the empire as places to absorb the men, capital, exports and technology that Britain could not profitably employ at home. But this is not to say that it was the coming of free trade and the abandonment of the old commercial system that made possible the introduction of full responsible government, or that responsible government was a device of free trade imperialism.

The acceptance of party government as a convention of the British constitution allowed the Whig leaders to regard it as legitimate and permissible in suitable colonies when demanded there. Grey and Russell both believed that in colonies of British settlement where no ruling group was likely to be sectionally oppressive[13] Britain gained nothing by maintaining any more control than was indispensable for defence, foreign policy, lands policy, commercial policy and constitutional change.

THE POLITICS OF PARTY GOVERNMENT IN CANADA, 1841–6

The history of responsible government or various approximations to it during the administrations of Lord Sydenham, Sir Charles Bagot, Sir Charles (later Lord) Metcalfe and Earl Cathcart has been analysed so thoroughly by Canadian historians that nothing more is needed here than to identify what was important in the general history of colonial self-government.[14] In united Canada, responsible government was sought from the first by Robert Baldwin and his supporters as the one great reform needed to reconcile differences between Britain and the colony and harmonise English—French relations in Canada. Baldwin's view of the scope of responsible government became steadily larger under pressure of Canadian politics, and also, possibly, from the example of party government in Britain. Above all, it was Baldwin's alliance with the French Canadians, which he found necessary in order to make the executive council responsible to the assembly, that impelled him towards the British system of party government. Underlying the responsible government question, wrote J. M. S. Careless, 'running through and beyond it, is the deeper theme of the relations of the French and English-speaking peoples within the United province'.[15] Responsible government, as a political question within the colony, had potency and significance quite outside its importance in imperial relations. It fed on the strains and stresses of reunion of the Canadas, which the French resisted as a threat to their cultural autonomy.

United Canada was inaugurated on 10 February 1841. The French, neither assimilated as Pitt and Grenville had hoped in 1791, nor subjugated as Bathurst and Wilmot-Horton has contemplated in 1822, were incorporated against their will in the same province as the English-speaking Upper Canadians. Lower Canada had long had within its own territories an English-speaking minority in the Eastern Townships, as well as a powerful citadel of English merchants in Montreal and other large towns. These groups were expected to make common cause with old Upper Canada (or Canada West, as it became known), rather than with Lower Canada (or Canada East). The only visible welcome to the union in Canada East was that of the English, especially the merchants of Montreal, where the Moffatts and the McGills looked forward to exploiting the commercial empire of the St Lawrence in unimpeded co-operation with the merchants of Canada West. Most French Canadians feared new threats to their national distinctiveness, which union had been intended to obliterate. Lower Canada had had no proper legislature between 1838 and 1841; consent to the union had been given by the unrepresentative special council that replaced it, and this consent did not represent the sentiments of the French.

The Reunion Act gave Upper Canada, with only 450,000 inhabitants, the same number of representatives in the new assembly as Lower Canada, with 650,000 inhabitants. As Lower Canada contained English-speaking minorities and gerrymandering was taken for granted, the French were rightly apprehensive. Overrepresentation of Canada West had not been recommended by Durham: he had wished the population to be represented as a whole, without internal division. The Act allowed no change in the representative proportions except on two-thirds majority votes in both houses of the new legislature. The French feared repression, or neglect, and dreaded incorporation with the active, commercial English. Canada West, as they saw it, was loaded with debt because of heavy spending on canals to improve transport on the St Lawrence. The debt would be transferred to the united province, so that the French would lose the benefits of their own financial restraint. Perhaps union itself was a device to get Canada East to help pay the debts of Canada West, to end haggling over customs revenue and improve prospects of fund-raising in London. These ideas, which occurred to the French as resentful suspicions, were held with ill conceded gratification in Montreal and Toronto, and in London with real purposiveness. F. T. Baring of Baring Brothers, the firm that underwrote most Upper Canadian securities, had been Melbourne's Chancellor of the Exchequer.[16] As the agriculture of Canada East was still depressed and rural unemployment remained widespread, the future looked bleak in 1840. The supreme insult to the French was that English was made the sole language of the official records of the legislature, although French might be used in debate. However, the rights granted to the Roman Catholic Church by the Quebec Act in 1774 remained intact.

John Neilson, veteran of many agitations to give Lower Canada its rights under the British constitution, and owner of the bilingual *Quebec Gazette*, became the outstanding advocate of repeal of the union He favoured survival by withdrawal, but another French constitutionalist, Louis Hippolyte La Fontaine (formerly a follower of Papineau), in whose firm, cool hands much of the future lay, proposed to extract the maximum advantage for the French from the new system. To this end, he decided that the French must find allies in Canada West.

At first the French knew little and cared less about responsible government: their concern was to find a trustworthy alliance in the new legislature. Baldwin and Hincks looked as though they might supply it and be suitably grateful for French support in working for *le gouvernement responsable*. From 1839 Hincks negotiated with La Fontaine, showing him how responsible government, which might put the majority party in the new assembly into executive power, could be used to the advantage of the French.

Two conspicuous obstacles delayed their alliance. In Upper Canada union was on the whole popular, although many details of the Act were disliked. Toronto resented the choice of Kingston as the new capital and the old high Anglican tories loathed reincorporation with the French, but most of the province looked forward to a new access of commercial strength as a result of the more energetic policies likely to be followed after reunion in the development of Canada East. In the last few months before union, moreover, Thomson had persuaded the legislature of Upper Canada to make a moderate settlement of the old clergy reserves question, and this satisfied nearly everyone except extremists. Stability and growth seemed to be on the side of the new regime, with little to be gained by agitating for responsible government or forming a political alliance with the French.

Sydenham himself was their other obstacle. He had strict orders from Lord John Russell not to tolerate responsible government in Canada, but to select as his advisers 'Men whose principles and feelings were in accordance with the majority' and administer all purely Canadian affairs in agreement with the wishes of the legislature. The executive council was responsible to him, not to the legislature, and he was responsible to nobody save the Queen's ministers in London. Thomson, whose popularity alarmed La Fontaine, made responsible government seem a tedious and unpopular cause, obstructing the good that he could do for the colony, and was gratuitously offensive to the tories of Canada West, who saw him as 'anti-British'. Thomson had the further advantage that Canada West was prosperous again: timber and wheat were doing well in 1841. Their prospects depended largely on British tariff policy, on British assistance with loans for the further development of the St Lawrence and on British action in maintaining as much free trade as possible between Canada and the United States (so that the St Lawrence would get the carrying trade of the northern part of the Middle West).

Few governors have ever been so incessantly active in the politics of a colony with representative government as Thomson was in Canada. A practised and confident political manager, a free trader who had been president of the Board of Trade and worked with Howick on colonial questions, he believed in Russell's policy on responsible government. High in the confidence of the Whigs and little over forty, he foresaw a limitless future for himself, should he do well in Canada. That he would triumph he could not doubt. Brusque, open ways and shrewd understanding of men and affairs put him on excellent terms with most of the colonists. The mass of the people, he wrote optimistically, 'are sound, moderate in their demands and attached to British institutions, but they have been oppressed by a miserable little oligarchy on the one hand and exacerbated by a few factious demagogues on the other. I can make a middle reforming party, I feel sure, which will put down both.'[17]

Sydenham had his own reasons for welcoming the famous tenure of offices dispatch that Russell had written on 16 October 1839.[18] It fitted well with his (and Russell's) plans to reorganise the government departments. He no longer had to provide for the old oligarchy on the executive council and could insist that the head of each department sit on the council and that each councillor hold a seat in the legislature.[19] He intended not responsible government, but 'harmony' between the executive council and the assembly, to be obtained through his own political skill. He would be 'prime minister' (although not sitting in the legislature) as well as governor-general, and manipulate men and measures, changing advisers and policies to keep a steady majority in the assembly for his executive council. His advisers, appointed and removed by him as he thought the public service required, would in practice be responsible to him, not to the assembly. He reserved to himself the entire power of patronage, which was useful to a politician governor.

The new legislature, to which Sydenham and Russell to some degree tied the executive, was conventional in fórm. It comprised a nominated legislative council of at least twenty members, appointed for life on good behaviour, and an elected assembly of eighty-four members, half from Canada East, half from Canada West. The franchise was based on low property qualifications, giving a decidedly democratic electorate, but considerably short of manhood suffrage. The assembly elected its own speaker; the governor-general appointed the president of the council. The governor-general had all ordinary powers to assent to Bills that the legislature had passed, or to withhold assent or reserve them for the royal pleasure. The executive council, as in the Act of 1791, was little mentioned, but its power was potentially large and the contest between the governor-general and the assembly for its control, on which Baldwin, Hincks and La Fontaine had resolved, was one for the commanding heights of government. A fixed civil list was prescribed in the Act; otherwise all Crown revenues, including territorial revenues, were available for appropriation in the colony.

When, before a legislature had convened, Sydenham nominated the first executive council of united Canada, he included two conservatives from Canada West, William Draper and Robert Baldwin Sullivan (his namesake's cousin), and three reformers — Robert Baldwin, who agreed to serve only because he believed that Sydenham would introduce responsible government, Samuel Bealey Harrison and John Henry Dunn. All had been members of the last executive council of Upper Canada. Draper, a man of ability, had alienated some old tories by supporting Sydenham on reunion and clergy reserves. From Canada East the governor-general took three of the old executive councillors, two of them Montreal tories and the third the non-party perennial of executive councils, Dominick Daly.

Robert Baldwin had problems of conscience. His views of responsible government had already advanced beyond Durham's, or his own in 1836. He complained to Sydenham that he had no confidence in the members of the new council apart from Dunn and Harrison, who were reformers, and Daly, who was outside party. He informed the other members of what he had done and gave his reasons.[20] In 1836 he had been willing for some members of the council not to sit in either house, and had required them to have the confidence of the assembly individually, not necessarily collectively.[21] At that time Melbourne's government in Britain had contained very great differences of opinion and. ministers had openly lacked confidence in one another. In 1841 Baldwin took a much more extensive view than in 1836. He asked for government by party, and wanted ministers to depend collectively for office on the confidence of the assembly. He no longer wished the governor-general to retain a real choice of members of the executive council once the new system of government had been fully inaugurated. Sydenham answered Baldwin equivocally, saying that he would consult his council when he chose: 'If they cannot agree, then will be the time for me to decide between their conflicting opinions ... and then ... would be the fitting time for any member of the council to declare his opinions.'[22] Neither man wished to push matters to extremes until the elections had been held and the political preferences of the colony disclosed. Baldwin still hoped that Sydenham would allow responsibble government in practice, for he could not conceive of Russell's policy of 1839, nor of Sydenham's statement of 1840,[23] leading to any other result. He had an early reward for his restraint when La Fontaine declared publicly, *'Je suis en faveur de ce principle anglais du gouvernment responsable.'*

Sydenham managed the elections from behind the scenes with unrelenting vigour. Electorates were gerrymandered; in Canada East polling places were established near the government's supporters and away from its opponents; in some constituencies the governor-general indicated his favoured candidates. Violence and riots were suppressed efficiently only if likely to obstruct the official cause. In Canada East Sydenham won nineteen or twenty of the forty-two seats, an extraordinary result in a region that still sullenly resented reunion. In Canada West, where violence had been less necessary (although some had been fatal), Sydenham won in the name of loyalty to Britain and the Queen, of prosperity and growth. His likely supporters won twenty-eight or twenty-nine of the forty-two seats, and were mostly moderates; ultra-reformers and tories polled less well. In the assembly as a whole Sydenham had a working majority, although the strength of Baldwin and his ultra-reformers made it undependable.

In England Howick was disgusted with the methods that Sydenham used to drum up a government majority. In his home territory he was no stranger to violent elections, or to allegations of corruption: he soon endured both at Sunderland, when he won Thomson's former seat. Violence from one's opponents at the polls was, however, different from violence used by the government for its own ends.[24]

Sydenham soon had to decide whether to do without the ultra-reformers. Baldwin, acting with Hincks and La Fontaine, wrote to him that in the new assembly the 'United Reform Party' of Canada East and West had a clear majority. Therefore the governor-general should change his council to make it conform with the opinions of the new assembly. He should remove all the conservatives from the council, replacing them with reformers from Canada East. Sydenham acted promptly at this double threat, to assimilation and to his scheme of responsible government: he treated Baldwin's letter as a resignation ('of the most crotchety impracticable enthusiast I ever had to deal with'), accepted his departure 'without the least regret', and told him, the day before the legislature met, that his behaviour had been 'in the highest degree unconstitutional, as dictating to the crown who are the particular individuals whom it should include in the ministry'.[25] No other member of the council resigned.

Having wrested the initiative from Baldwin, Sydenham played his most powerful card when the legislature opened. He announced that Britain would guarantee a loan to Canada of £1·5 million, to reduce colonial debts and allow work to proceed again on the canals. He also mentioned likely British assistance to immigration. His speech left no room for the 'United Reform Party' to win. The assembly supported Sydenham, passing the address in reply with a large majority and, a little later, defeating Neilson's motion against the Act of Union. Sydenham, although not out of danger, counted his chickens. 'I have got rid of Baldwin and finished him as a public man forever', he boasted to Russell.[26] He was encouraged again when he produced a rift between Baldwin and Hincks, attracting Hincks towards the official group by his vigorous financial policy and practical achievements. .Hincks told old William Baldwin that the battle for responsible government was no longer worth fighting, for the executive council was acting as a ministry and 'we have *practical* responsibility'.[27] Sydenham had another victory when the District Councils Act, which extended to all Canada the system that he had introduced into Upper Canada, passed the legislature with Hinck's support and against Baldwin's opposition.

Sydenham thought his victory complete. He had reported to Russell,

The great and harassing question of Clergy Reserves and Reserves and Responsible Government settled, the Offices of Govt arranged so as to ensure responsibility in those who are at their head and an efficient discharge of their duties to Governor and Public. The Legislature assembled, acting in harmony with the Executive, and really employed in beneficial measures of Legislation ... nothing ... can now prevent or mar the most complete success, and Canada must henceforward go on well except it be most terribly mismanaged.[28]

Sydenham overestimated his ability to detach his opponents from one another. The French were unreconciled and uncommitted except to themselves. The Common Schools Act of 1841, which had passed through the legislature with little difficulty, enraged them because public education clashed with Roman Catholic schooling and endangered cultural autonomy. Baldwin decided to capitalise on this discontent before failure destroyed all hope of a 'United Reform Party' and before Neilson's alternative policy for the French, withdrawal and separation, gained headway. In August he proposed that La Fontaine should stand for the more safely liberal of the two seats that he himself had won at the elections, and the Frenchman was elected in September. On 3 September

Baldwin moved in the assembly a set of six resolutions on responsible government.[29] They declared that the executive council was a ministry responsible to the legislature and that on colonial matters the governor-general had always to accept the advice of ministers, who were responsible for every government action. Baldwin carefully made it plain that responsible government did not extend to imperial affairs. Sydenham won his last notable victory when he had Harrison propose four amendments, possibly drafted by himself, that were subtly and significantly different from Baldwin's. The key resolutions were:

> 2. That the head of the executive Government of the Province, being within the limits of his Government, the representative of the Sovereign, is responsible to the Imperial authority alone; but that, nevertheless, the management of our local affairs can only be conducted by him, by and with the assistance, counsel and information of subordinate officers in the Province.
> 3. That ... the chief advisers of the representative of the Sovereign, constituting a Provincial administration under him, ought to be men possessed of the confidence of the representatives of the people . . . .

A fourth resolution stated that the colony should be administered 'in the manner most consistent' with the 'well-understood wishes and interests' of its people. Rather than go down to complete defeat, Baldwin supported Harrison's amendments. He lost little, because it was clear that ministers would have to resign on a vote of no confidence.[30] Draper thought that Sydenham had conceded too much, but voted for the resolutions.

The day after the resolutions were passed, Sydenham's horse stumbled and the governor-general was injured. Only a fortnight later he was dead from lockjaw, leaving behind him not an obedient executive council supported by a docile assembly, but an incipient party ministry and an assembly full of troubles. Sir George Arthur, the lieutenant-governor, warned Russell to wait for another election before accepting Sydenham's claims on the state of colonial politics.[31] Howick advised George Grey in June not to ask to succeed Sydenham, 'because I could not anticipate a favourable result from the union of the Provinces' and the next governor-general was certain to be discredited. As Peel recognised two years later, 'Lord Sydenham's death, untimely as it might be in every other respect, was a very timely relief to him from Canadian embarrassments . . . his policy was on the eve of exposure.'[32]

Sydenham's death closely followed the fall of Melbourne's administration and the replacement of Russell at the Colonial Office by Stanley. No change in Canadian policy was to be expected. Sydenham had recommended to Russell that the new governor-general should be 'some one with House of Commons and Ministerial habits — a person who will not shrink from work, and who will govern, as I do, *himself*.[33] Russell passed this letter to Stanley. Charles Buller, who had gone to Canada with Durham and who was to be at Grey's right hand when responsible government was ordered for Nova Scotia, wrote to Peel that Sydenham had done wonders: 'he has had *majorities* for his *measures*, but it remains for his successors to create a steady and reliable majority for *the Government*'.[34] Buller did not quarrel with Sydenham's highly limited doctrine of responsible government; Durham himself had allowed that a governor might be his own prime minister and that his advisers might be responsible individually, rather than collectively, to the assembly. Buller, however, saw that Sydenham had not treated the French Canadians wisely: 'if rightly managed', he wrote, they could be 'the natural instrument by which the Government could keep in check the democratic and American tendencies of Upper Canada'. The new governor-general, who would have to manage the French for this complicated purpose, would also have to be something of an 'Ambassador to the United States' and have the prestige to command personal respect in the colony. Stanley had already declared that the governor-general must be capable of applying the 'soothing system' and have had Parliamentary experience.[35] The government's choice fell on the sixty-year old Sir Charles Bagot, nephew of the Duke of Wellington, and a man of diplomatic but little political experience. Bagot had done well as ambassador to Washington after the War of 1812 and spoke fluent French.

Bagot's instructions[36] charged him to 'know no distinction of National origin or Religious Creed', for assimilation was not to be pushed so strongly as to increase French resistance to the union. He was to discourage abstract discussions of colonial government and concentrate on colonial development, choosing as his advisers men of standing in the legislature, who could help frame policy. He was to conciliate the assembly, maintain harmony between the two houses of the legislature, and never to allow party government. Stanley's policy in 1841 differed little from Russell's.

Like the Whigs, the Tories hoped that, as French clamour against reunion subsided, political parties would disappear and demands for any more responsible government than a narrow reading of the Harrison–Baldwin resolutions allowed would die away. The governor-general had to be his own prime minister; how else could the colonial status of Canada be preserved?

Bagot's faith in his instructions did not last long. Six weeks after reaching Kingston in January 1842, he thought the province tranquil and party less strong than before.[37] No party in Canada, he reassured Stanley, was large or strong enough to provide a government. Sydenham's principal difficulties had been with an 'unnatural . . . alliance' of French Canadians, ultra-reformers, and old tories in Upper Canada, all of whom had abandoned principle in order to defeat the government on individual measures. Canadian parties behaved like factions. Bagot hoped to bring them to a better view of politics and to detach the French Canadians from the ultra-reformers, of whom only Baldwin had great influence. A strong public works programme and sensible policies of development might erode faction and stifle the beginnings of party by occupying men with business, not politics.

Bagot won easy successes before events taught him that French Canada still resented reunion, that all parts of Canada opposed the British settlement of the civil list in the Reunion Act, and that he would have great difficulty in reconstructing the executive council. Bagot had none of Sydenham's tough skill in managing politicians. The principal beneficiary of his manoeuvres to get a satisfactory executive council was Baldwin, who rallied followers by pointing out that Bagot had shown how essential it was to have cohesion among all liberals. Bagot was no longer confident that his advisers would be safe when the legislature met.

Draper wanted him to bring French Canadians into the council, so as to have strong French support in the assembly.[38] Unless this were done, Draper explained, the French would side with Baldwin. Could they not be attached to the government by beneficial consideration? They were not indifferent to patronage and power. Bagot, thinking Sydenham imprudent for not having conciliated the French, had already recognised that to admit them as a party would contradict his instructions.[39] He appealed to Stanley: 'What is to be done? Are we to bide our time and wait till immigration hems in and overwhelms French population and French Power? This must happen some day or other – but . . . meanwhile I may lose my majority in the Legislature, and we may then have to begin all over again.'[40] He soon had to warn Stanley that there was no alternative to admitting the French to the council, virtually as a party and on their own terms, although still hostile to the union and much of Sydenham's legislation. He asked for advice before the legislature met early in September, and admitted that the French would insist on having Baldwin in the ministry and that Baldwin would demand formal recognition of responsible government by party.[41]

Stanley was 'in the North' for the summer and the threat to British policy in Canada did not persuade him to return.[42] When he picked up the reins again, late in August, he told Peel that if the French and ultra-reformers were admitted to the council as a party 'the union is a failure, and the Canadas are gone'.[43] Peel agreed with this Tory view of the imperial relationship, but it was too late for their opinions to reach Bagot before the legislature opened.

As the fateful day of 8 September approached, Bagot became convinced that the executive council would not survive without the admission of the French.[44] Just before the expected storm broke, he told La Fontaine that the French Canadians would be invited to join the executive council, not as individuals, but as a party.[45] La Fontaine then asked for four places on the council, including one for Baldwin. Bagot, reluctant to concede so much, found two pistols pointed at his head. Draper, who was willing to let Baldwin and the French into power and to resign himself, informed him that the whole council would certainly resign if the assembly condemned it with a motion of no confidence; and Baldwin moved such a motion. Bagot concluded that he had either to see his ministers forced out as a body, to be replaced by a council made up of the French and the ultra-reformers, or to yield all the French demands.

The simple course of waiting to see whether the assembly really would force the council out seemed too dangerous and Bagot tried a stratagem from diplomacy, by allowing the assembly to know the details of his offer to La Fontaine.[46] Macnab and the old tories, who still hated the union, were furious at what had been done; the French party, which had been kept largely ignorant, was electrified. By 20 September, when the dust had settled a little, Baldwin had withdrawn his motion of no confidence and Bagot had a new council that the assembly supported by fifty-five votes to twenty-five.

The French and Baldwin made up four members of the council; six former members remained so that the council was not a one-party ministry, but the French were in it as a party and it was more disposed to reform than its predecessor had been. The tories were furious, foreseeing responsible government by party, the end of British rule and other disasters.[47] The *Montreal Transcript* attacked Bagot's 'infatuated imbecility', while the Toronto *Herald* thought that, if traitors had to be bribed to let the union continue, Canada would be parted from Britain within a generation.[48]

Meanwhile Stanley had concluded that Bagot was too pessimistic.[49] He passed on Peel's opinion — 'It is a fine opportunity for playing the game of *Divide et impera*' — and advised against admitting the French 'until all other means have been tried'. Stanley, courageous in another's trouble, wanted Bigot to play the game of *vendus*, detaching individual French Canadians to join the council, at the risk of alienating them from their own people, and so avoid conceding party government. He still thought in terms of loyal English and disloyal French, still hoped for assimilation, and still believed that the governor-general should choose his own advisers and make his own policies, except when under orders from London.

It was easy in England to criticise Bagot's actions. *The Times* blamed him for making the English French, instead of the French English.[50] Wellington was astounded at his nephew's behaviour.[51] Some Whigs thought that Bagot should have waited for the assembly to defeat the council, if it dared to do so, rather than resort to such drastic measures.[52] Only the liberal *Morning Chronicle* among the major organs of opinion hailed the change in the council as a triumph for 'Lord Durham's principle of responsible government'. 'The rational system of representative government', it remarked on 15 October, 'is ... established in Canada in the most marked manner.'

Although Bagot comforted himself that he had not transferred all power and patronage to the reformers, he did not deny that responsible government 'virtually' existed.[53] Peel was too shrewd to make a bad case worse; Bagot, who had not formally conceded any new principle, was coolly informed that the government acquiesced in what he had done.[54] Privately, Stanley told him that the wisdom of his tactics was not established and reminded him that 'you act in concert with your Executive Council, but the ultimate decision rests with yourself, and you are recognised, not only as having an opinion, but as supreme and irresponsible, except to the Home Government, for your acts in your executive capacity'.[55] Bagot was dying and had the last word: 'I leave the world not satisfied that my measures will be successful, but ... I ... had no choice ..., if the Union were to be maintained.'[56]

His successor, Sir Charles Metcalfe, came to Canada at the age of fifty-eight with a useful reputation for liberality won as governor of Jamaica, and experience as a benevolent despot in India. Devoted, resolute, kindly and rigid, he had instructions to refuse responsible government by party, to uphold the resolutions of 1841 and to insist on his own independence. His advisers were to be answerable individually in the assembly, but he was to control their policies and continue to be responsible to the Queen and the imperial government for the welfare of Canada. He himself was to choose 'ministers', taking them from among the moderates, and to consult them and listen to their advice, but not necessarily to act on it.[57] When he proposed to lift the restrictions on the use of French as an official language, he was firmly reminded that the Cabinet still hoped for assimilation.[58]

Metcalfe had been in Canada only two months when he reported that Bagot had surrendered so much that only one constitutional problem remained: 'whether the Governor shall be solely and completely a tool in the hands of the Council, or ... have any exercise of his own judgment in the administration of the government'.[59] He recommended that if there were a test of strength it should be over patronage and not the civil list, which would be best settled by a local Act followed by repeal of the relevant provisions of the Act of Reunion.

Stanley was resolute on patronage. Metcalfe was to keep 'the patronage of the Crown in his own hands and refuse to apply it exclusively to party purposes'. Without it, the governor's power would be diminished and the moderate loyalists, in whom the British authorities still trusted, would be denied official advancement, for reformers would never give them offices or salaries.[60] Metcalfe agreed. He knew that the reformers on the council wanted patronage to entrench themselves in power and he expected their favourites to include rebels of 1837. The growth of parties sustained by the public purse alarmed him: 'In an independent State all parties must generally desire the welfare of the State. In a colony . . . it may happen that the predominant party is hostile . . . to the Mother Country, or has ulterior views inconsistent with her interest.'[61] Metcalfe's sympathies were with the conservatives, but he tried to conciliate all moderates and hoped that concessions to the French would reduce their forced appetite for responsible government.

Metcalfe was sorry that any form of responsible government had ever been allowed in the colony. If the governor co-operated with the council, he seemed a partisan; if he did not do so, no one trusted him and his power for good declined. His own policy, he told Stanley, would be to satisfy all parties and by good government show the people that the imperial connection promoted their welfare. British guarantees of loans for public works and special conditions for the import of wheat and flour from Canada would help him.[62]

A clash over patronage was avoided until the troubled legislative session that began in September 1843. Metcalfe's relations with Baldwin then worsened and politicians in Canada West suspected that the government was, for its own political reasons, excessively preoccupied with the welfare of Canada East. Metcalfe warned Stanley that there would be no end to the 'unavailing' struggle in Canada 'until the object of the Council and the Assembly, namely Democratic and Party Government, is fully admitted'.[63] Already he was little more than a 'tool in the hands of a Party'.

On 24 November, after Metcalfe had made important appointments without consulting the council and contrary to its desires, Baldwin and La Fontaine demanded that in future the colonial patronage be exercised only after advice from the council. Baldwin had foreseen in 1836 that responsible government might lead to a demand for full control of patronage; at first he had thought that no more than a right to advise would be expected. However, in the crude conditions of young colonial politics, just as in Britain, the most high-minded reformers wanted the resources of the state to gratify their followers. Metcalfe refused the demand to surrender the Crown's prerogative of patronage and repeated the refusal when the council addressed him on the question. All but one of the councillors resigned on 26 November, and Metcalfe, fortified by Stanley's letter of 1 November, prepared for battle. 'Whatever may happen', he wrote private to Stanley, 'I do not mean at any time to take back Mr La Fontaine or Mr Baldwin. Both are intolerable.' By forty-six votes to twenty-three the assembly supported the resigning councillors, and Metcalfe prorogued it on 9 December.[64]

A few days later he formed a provisional council that was a coalition between Draper and the old French Canadian nationalist Denis-Benjamin Viger. Draper agreed with Metcalfe on the patronage question. Viger, a man of prestige and a cousin of Papineau, shrewdly saw merit in Metcalfe's position. The hopes of French Canadians for national survival, he thought, might be better served through co-operation with the governor, who depended on them, than by risking everything on the 'unnatural' alliance of English reformers and French nationalists. Unfortunately for Metcalfe, Viger brought him little French support.

Formally, the issue between Metcalfe and his old council was the question of whether the Harrison—Baldwin resolutions of 1841 required the governor to use powers of patronage only on the advice of the council. Metcalfe claimed that an independent power of patronage was an essential prerogative of the Crown and that Canada already had the fullest degree of representative government possible in a colony. Baldwin argued that the power of patronage had been given up when the Crown accepted the 1841 resolutions. Metcalfe complained that he was being asked to surrender the 'patronage of the Crown . . . for the purchase of parliamentary support' by the council and to reduce his own independence.[65] The French, after their long exclusion from office in Lower Canada, were notably interested in patronage.[66] Baldwin's supporters spoke of it, as Metcalfe did, as the means of forging a party on the anvil of 'spoils for the victors'.

Metcalfe was sure that if he gave up patronage he would make himself 'merely an instrument of putting the sign manual to . . . [the] dictation' of whatever ministers chanced to have a majority in the assembly.[67] 'I have avowed my adherence to Responsible Government views to the fullest extent which it can be avowed in a Colony, and it must be either Blindness or Disaffection that can desire to get further', he told Stanley.[68] The French and the reformers no doubt wanted provincial independence within the empire, retaining British protection but ending all subordination to Britain, and working towards democracy on the worst American pattern.

Tormented with cancer of the face, Metcalfe could still win greater victories than he expected. La Fontaine blocked his efforts to use Viger (or Neilson) to win the French over to moderation, but could not prevent the steady accretion of strength to the governor-general in Canada West. Metcalfe's public stand, that the practical limit of responsible government in a colony had been reached, and his charge that the reformers merely lusted after the profits of office won more and more support. Businessmen and the loyalists in Canada West, who remembered the War of 1812 and the rebellion of 1837, came to his side. The organiser of moderation and loyalty in Canada West was Draper. He had strong support in the press from Egerton Ryerson, who attacked the liberalism of George Brown's new paper, the Toronto *Globe*.

In Britain, where Tory ministers were scandalised by the idea of party government in a colony, but wished most whole-heartedly to keep Canada within the empire, Metcalfe was praised almost universally. The Canada

Corn Act of 1843 (6 and 7 Vict., c. 29) had recently allowed special privileges in British markets to Canadian exports of wheat and flour. In the debate on the Bill,[69] Buller and Hume had both assumed that the wishes of the Canadians were good enough reason for passing it. The Whigs, especially Howick and Labouchere, had criticised it as a belated new preference and even the protectionists had been uneasy about granting such a privilege; Disraeli voted against it. But Peel had insisted that Canada needed the protection to make profitable use of the expensive St Lawrence river canals and profit from the British loan of 1841. By Feburary 1844 Peel was in a strong position to tell the Canadian reformers that they were overstepping the limits of self-government within an empire that loaded them with benefits, just as he and Aberdeen had been willing to send an ultimatum to Lower Canada in 1835, and just as he had been certain, when the Maine boundary settlement was negotiated in 1842, that Britain could sacrifice too much to the susceptibilities of restless colonists:[70]

> It is a hard bargain enough to have to give every advantage of connexion with the Mother Country, and to undertake the serious responsibility and charge of providing for internal tranquillity and for defence from external attack. ... To be met at every turn by a captious and quibbling spirit, and above all to be denied the means of well governing the Province, of ensuring the independent and respectable adminis- tration of justice and the employment of honest and efficient Civil servants, will make the connexion too onerous to be borne. We shall have to tell these factious people there is one limit to our concessions – We will not govern you in a manner discreditable to us or injurious to you.[71]

The surrender of Canada to party government with a power of patronage would, Peel was sure, make the governor-general a mere political machine in all the internal affairs of the colony. As the prisoner of the ruling party, he might not be able to implement imperial policy on matters admittedly imperial, such as defence and commercial policy, or have ordinary guarantees of honest, efficient administration. A colony held on such terms was not worth holding.

This was not an extreme or reactionary view. Wakefield supported Metcalfe in contending that patronage should be reserved to the Crown. He was in Canada and had fallen out with the ministry over land and canal development. Having given up the reformers as incompetent, incapable and possibly corrupt, he defended Metcalfe as a man of energy and judgement, who was upholding responsible government in its correct colonial interpretation.[72] The radical *Spectator* in London agreed with Wakefield that the reformers had forced the patronage dispute onto a liberal governor-general, and warned the colonists against 'losing the substance that was quietly growing up in a fidgety attempt to force its maturity'.[73]

The extent of support for Metcalfe became apparent when, in May 1844, Roebuck raised the patronage question in the House of Commons. Although he predicted that Metcalfe would lose the next elections and so be forced into an intolerable situation, he could find only Hume to agree with him strongly.[74] Buller defended Metcalfe on patronage and showed that Durham had been willing for the governor-general to be his own prime minister. Buller did not reject responsible government in the sense of party government, but recommended continued support for Metcalfe in the conditions then existing in Canada. He believed that the final decision would have to be taken by the colonial legislature, or, if necessary, Metcalfe could dissolve the assembly and appeal to the people.

What might happen if Metcalfe were rejected both by the assembly and the electorate was plain enough from Peel's brief speech. He denied that the governor-general's position was analogous to the Queen's and denied further that Canada could be ruled on wholly the same principles as Britain. If the Canadians were out of patience with their status, their relationship with Britain would be 'better broken than maintained by force'. If they wanted full party government, entire control of their own civil list and patronage, and no dominant role in their government for the Queen's representative, they should be independent. No governor could ever rely on influence and rank as the Queen did, for he was only a great imperial official, whose powers and duties should be clearly defined.

Stanley also thought that the Canadians' demands were wholly 'inconsistent with monarchical institutions, and with relations which should exist between mother-country and colony'. Only in an 'independent republic' could the governor-general either accept all the advice offered to him by the ministers who chanced to possess majority support in the assembly, or give up the reality of power in selecting his advisers. Stanley believed that no acceptable division of imperial and colonial affairs could ever be made and, on this ground alone, was likely to think full responsible government inconsistent with colonial status. He would not let the Queen's representative be reduced to a 'mere machine, a passive instrument in the hands of the Executive Council, or any other body'. He did however concede to Roebuck that, when Parliament passed private Acts to incorporate banks, land companies and other institutions in Canada, or the Crown issued charters to similar effect, the rights of the colonial legislature were invaded.

Russell, for the Whigs, was of the same mind as Peel. He supported Metcalfe and blamed only Bagot, who was dead. He could see no future for Canada outside the empire; if the Canadians did follow Peel's grim choice and take themselves out of British protection, they would not remain independent for six months. Howick, though later severely critical of Metcalfe, was silent in the debate, concentrating his energies that day on sugar duties, then also before the Commons.[75]

By September Metcalfe had made up a mixed government, whose dominant member was Draper. To give the ministry a chance, Metcalfe dissolved the assembly on 23 September 'as the least of all evils'[76] and prepared for battle at elections to be held in November. The campaign was as discreditable as Sydenham's had been in 1841. Rioting and bloodshed at the polls followed weeks of scandalous campaigning, marked by angry abuse and malpractices. Metcalfe himself, in pain with cancer, fought as hard as he could, demanding votes for the Queen, loyalty, the British connection, stability and sound government. Ryerson and the Methodists rallied notably to his cause.

In a formal sense Metcalfe won the election, for, with forty-six out of eighty-four seats, he had a small majority; but victory won under such conditions was doubtfully indicative of public opinion and ominous for the future. Fortunately for Metcalfe, the colony had been unusually prosperous in the autumn of 1844: the Canada Corn Act was having its effect and the timber trade was doing well because of the railway boom in Britain. In Canada West Metcalfe benefited from local resentment of the reformers' proposals to remove the capital to Canada East, to suppress the Orangemen and to impose Hincks's 'Algerian' income tax. The governor-general's victory was mainly in the West, where the claims of 'loyalty' split the reformers and gave him nearly thirty seats. In Canada East, where there had been less violence and less hope of victory, the winner was really La Fontaine, who had campaigned for the solidarity and survival of French Canada. His supporters in the new assembly numbered twenty-eight, including some English-speaking members. When attempts were made to establish a new principle requiring concurrent majorities of the representatives of Canada East and Canada West to allow Bills to pass, Draper found himself drawn closer to La Fontaine.

After the elections Metcalfe had another year in Canada before he went home in November 1845, almost blind and scarcely able to eat or speak. Peel and Stanley had him rewarded with a peerage, but in truth he had lost the battle that he sometimes thought he had won. While Draper struggled to maintain his government, every point for which the reformers had argued was quietly conceded. Draper was virtually prime minister and, aided by Metcalfe, played party politics to maintain a majority.[77] The council used patronage to keep itself in office, while Metcalfe, working in darkened rooms, gave them his confidence. In Britain ministers attended to some important concessions that he had recommended in 1843. The amnesty of February 1845 for the rebels of 1837, the substitution by 10 and 11 Vict., c. 71, of a permanent civil list enacted by the colonial legislature for that contained in the Reunion Act, and the lifting of restrictions on the official use of French were agreed to, although not all implemented in Metcalfe's time.[78]

Metcalfe saw how strongly the tide ran against imperial authority in colonial affairs: 'The whole Colony must at times be regarded as a party opposed to Her Majesty's Government. If any question arises . . . in which the interests of the Mother Country and those of the Colony may appear to be different, the great mass of the people . . . will be enlisted against the former.'[79] Even in Canada West men thought that loyalty to Britain earned them slight permanent advantage and that the welfare of the empire at large was not their business, although most of them wished to retain British protection. The critics of union remained more vociferous than its supporters.[80] Should Britain continue to maintain the colonial connection on such terms, by relying on the stream of British investments and immigrants, and a liberal constitutional policy to invigorate the potentially strong ties of kinship and culture?

Gladstone, who had succeeded Stanley at the Colonial Office in December 1845, failed in leadership when he drafted instructions for Metcalfe's successor, Earl Cathcart. The appointment of Cathcart, commander of the forces in Canada, owed something to the Oregon crisis with the United States and to the British hope that a strong soldier would be both a warning to the Americans and an encouragement to the Canadians. Gladstone passed over lightly a plain piece of advice from Stephen: 'Canada appears . . . to have shaken off the colonial relation . . . and . . . become, in everything but name, a distinct state. . . . There are at this moment, in Canada, almost as many Europeans as there were in the United States when they declared their independence – a very pregnant fact in many ways'.[81]

Stephen wished the instructions to be meaningfully meaningless, so that the Canadians might evolve their constitution as they wished. However, the Parliamentary Under-Secretary to Stanley, G. W. Hope, wished for specific instructions on the degree of responsible government to be allowed and a frank statement that threats of separation would produce no concessions.[82] Gladstone compromised. He addressed Cathcart as if Metcalfe had been wholly successful: 'The favour of his Sovereign and the acknowledgement of his country' had rewarded an administration of Canada, 'which . . . may justly be regarded as a model for his successor.' Cathcart was to choose his advisers as far as possible from the moderates, preferring the loyal to the disloyal – that is, honouring if he could Metcalfe's wish never to employ Baldwin or La Fontaine again. He was to leave the responsible government question alone and be assured that threats of separation would never lead to unreasonable demands from the colonists being conceded. Gladstone undermined his own broad assertions of Tory policy by carefully leaving Cathcart so many lines of retreat that, in some respects, the instructions did approach Stephen's proposal of empty 'commonplaces'. Cathcart could have concluded that the new Secretary of State admired Metcalfe's policies, but privately doubted whether they were practicable. It would have been difficult, although not impossible, to have found in the instructions a reflection of the Prime Minister's view, that the Canadians had either to conform to British ideas of self-government or give up their privileged status as a colony.[82]

GREY AND BULLER ON PARTY GOVERNMENT FOR BRITISH NORTH AMERICA

When Grey became Secretary of State for War and the Colonies in July 1846, the Prince Consort told him that the Queen wished Metcalfe's policies to continue.[83] Royalty was on the popular side, for Metcalfe's public triumphs and terrible illness commanded respect and sympathy. Grey, however, had never been an admirer of Metcalfe. He thought his performance in Jamaica greatly overrated; had not Metcalfe 'obtained temporary tranquillity by letting the Assembly have its own way without attempting to effect the reform and reorganization of society so much wanted'.[84] In Canada Metcalfe had imprudently contested the patronage question, which lay at the heart of responsible government by a popular party. 'The truth is', wrote Grey to Lord Elgin some years later, that Metcalfe 'did not comprehend representative government at all, nor from his Indian experience is this wonderful.'[85] In retrospect Grey was sceptical also of Metcalfe's famous victory in 1844, wondering what would happen when some campaigning governor-general lost an election. Sydenham, he knew, had been lucky to avoid a second test. Bagot, on the other hand, had behaved prudently; Grey did not cavil at his decision to admit the French as a party to the executive council.[86]

In constitutional terms Grey's analysis of Canadian problems resembled Peel's. Responsible government by party, which they both understood with the thoroughness of men who had watched it emerge, would necessarily take the selection of ministers and patronage and all other matters of internal policy away from the governor-general and, therefore, the Secretary of State and Parliament. In 1845 Peel, following the view laid down by Russell, still thought that so much independence would be impossible for a colony and that Britain could not in safety and honour allow it. If the Canadians wanted responsible government by party, they would have to become an independent country. Grey, who since 1831 had asked which British interests were served by attempting any greater control over the internal affairs of Canada than the colonists were prepared to accept, and who most earnestly wished the empire to continue, turned the other way. If the sovereign no longer chose her own ministers or controlled policy-making in Britain, why was it necessary for her representative to select his ministers and decide his own policy in respect of purely colonial matters? Were there no parties in Canada to whom control of purely Canadian affairs might be confided? Why was it better to govern Canada through a party in Britain than through a party in the colony?

Grey knew that Canada had virtually obtained party government under Bagot. His own contribution, he later thought, had been to regularise and make perpetual the great change that his predecessors had misunderstood, obstructed and tried to undo. In *Colonial Policy of Lord John Russell's Administration* (1853) he referred to responsible government as having existed in Canada for 'little more than ten years', although not brought into full operation until he was Secretary of State. In a letter of 1851 to Governor Sir Harry Smith on the constitution of the Cape Colony, he implied that the beginnings of responsible government in Canada went back to the Sydenham system, although not firmly established until he himself became Secretary of State.[87] When Grey struck away the restrictions that Russell, Peel, Stanley and Gladstone had placed on responsible government, and allowed full party govenment in all domestic affairs, he was moved by knowledge of the constitutional changes that had occurred in Britain, by strong faith in colonisation and imperial destiny, and by commonsense rejection of futile resistance to changes that could not be prevented for ever or even for long.

Grey came to the Colonial Office as a free trader who was also a powerful advocate of systematic colonisation and a firm believer in imperial destiny. As we have seen, he regarded free trade as a moral imperative: Britain had a duty to see it applied throughout the empire. Free trade did not help him towards responsible government of colonies except in so far as he thought it likely to keep some colonies within the empire and so ensure that they were free traders. On the other hand, systematic colonisation and the grasping of the imperial destiny of large British communities overseas assumed a degree of active, constructive partnership between Britain and Canada that made Peel's logical doubts of whether Canada could lawfully remain a colony seem niggling. The expansive view of empire to which Grey was committed made him impatient of claims that Britain had to safeguard her own honour by restricting the domestic self-government of colonies that might disgrace her, or endeavour to overthrow imperial authority in matters that were necessarily imperial. Grey simply did not believe that those British communities overseas that were judged fit for responsible government would humiliate Britain in the ways that Russell and Peel had feared. So long as Britain remained supreme in commercial policy, defence and other reserved subjects, Grey preferred colonies capable of managing their own affairs to do so, as if the colonists were living in Britain.

Just before he became Secretary of State, Grey warmly praised an *Edinburgh Review* article that he correctly concluded to be the work of

Nassau Senior. It was a review of Cornewall Lewis's *Government of Dependencies*,[88] which already had some influence as a text for anti-imperialists and acquired high standing as an analysis of colonial self-government. Lewis had convinced himself that neither Britain nor any other 'dominant country' derived any real advantages from the possession of colonies other than those that would still be available if the colonies became independent. He also noted that 'no legislative body elected by the people' would willingly confine itself to legislation, for it would inevitably claim the rights to 'superintend the administration of the country, to complain of grievances, and petition for remedies'. 'It soon demands that the principal executive officers should possess its confidence, . . . that they should be taken out of its own body, or rather out of the majority of that body, or at least be removable at the will of the majority.'[89]

Senior commented at length on Lewis's judgements, noting that a legislature that could not require the executive government to have its confidence would develop into a mere opposition. Senior agreed with Lewis that it would be folly to grant a colony 'popular institutions' with the appearance of self-government unless the colony were treated as 'virtually independent'. He based his comment primarily on experience of the parliamentary executive in Britain, in other words on the evidence that no one knew better than Grey did. Over the years Grey had been discussing constitutional questions, most notably House of Lords reform, with Senior and valued his judgement highly.[90] That the *Edinburgh* article interested him is certain; that it helped confirm his judgement in the great steps that he was about to take is probable. Grey relished theoretical demonstrations of the political arguments he was using practically.

The link in Grey's mind between responsible government for Canada, systematic colonisation and imperial destiny may be related with little conjecture to the influence of Charles Buller. Friendship between them had been ripening for seven or eight years. After the Whigs left office in 1841 and Howick's last special privileges in the Colonial Office ended, Buller came to replace Stephen as his principal confidant in colonial matters. Howick had little to do with Stephen between 1840 and 1845, and Stephen, when he met Grey officially again in 1846, found him greatly changed from the young Howick whom he had influenced so much in the 1830s.[91] The vacuum left by the loss of Stephen's counsel was gradually and partly replaced by Buller, who developed so close a relationship with Grey that the new Secretary of State was publicly regarded as the principal link between the official Whigs and the colonial reformers.[92] Unlike Wakefield, Buller had a reputable character, unruffled temper, intellectual integrity and financial probity. In the years when Howick was out of office, the two men discussed colonisation and colonies, Ireland, free trade, British politics and taxation. Buller, whose essay on responsible government[93] was more precise and practical than most of Durham's references to the subject, and whose famous speech in the Commons on 6 April 1843 on systematic colonisation was not tainted with visions of personal advantage,[94] commended himself to Russell as well as Howick. From 1842 on, Howick often had Buller to visit him at his Datchet villa as a family friend. According to Palmerston, Buller in 1845 described Howick as 'the God of his idolatry'.[95] When Grey became Secretary of State, he wanted Buller to be his Parliamentary Under-Secretary. Russell would not agree to concede so much to the colonial reformers and Stephen was shocked. Grey had to take dull, faithful Benjamin Hawes, whom he knew well, to be his coadjutor, but Buller was made Judge Advocate-General with a special duty to assist Grey on colonial matters. It was necessary to keep him away from the Office and he saw Stephen only once.[96]

In 1846 Grey genuinely wished to promote systematic colonisation, but in less than a year he had to admit to Buller that he would never have funds enough to build an empire of settlement: 'It is mortifying to the last degree but ... I can do nothing to promote "systematic colonizatn" — There is not a farthing to be had from the Tsy & without some money ... very little seems possible.' Buller vainly tried to stir him with hopes of lasting fame, but there was nothing to be done. Although Grey continued to work hard to obtain men, money and public works, including railways, for Canada,[97] the original dream of systematic colonisation was shattered, both for Canada and for New Zealand, and Wakefield angrily attacked Grey as a renegade. In October 1847, when Stephen had to be replaced as Permanent Under-Secretary, Russell suggested that Grey should give that post to Hawes and take Buller as Parliamentary Under-Secretary.[98] Partly because he had larger schemes in mind for the reconstruction of the Office, Grey did not take up the offer and Buller became Chief Poor Law Commissioner. His relations with Grey continued cordial until Buller's early death in 1848.

In the vital period from July 1846 to March 1847, while Grey was taking his major decisions on responsible government for British North America, Buller was at his right hand, pressing the case for allowing the reform and for taking a new and larger view of the possibilities of colonisation than either Whigs or Tories had ever held before.

THE RESPONSIBLE GOVERNMENT QUESTION IN NOVA SCOTIA

Nova Scotia, which had the oldest legislature in the empire, was the first to obtain responsible government. Under Glenelg the executive council had been separated from the legislative council, with the understanding that some members of the assembly were, if possible, to become members of the government. Dissatisfied with the implementing of these concessions, the radical Joseph Howe, who had addressed the famous letters on responsible government to Lord John Russell, carried in February 1840, by thirty votes to twelve, a vote of no confidence in the executive council. Sydenham, visting the colony to help solve the problem, concluded that the vote of no confidence in the council had been unconstitutional, for only the governor was 'responsible' and the assembly should have proceeded against him by complaint to London. Most of the colony's discontents, he thought, arose from the failure of governors to follow a vigorous policy of development, which would have given men more urgent interests than abstract theories of government. Hoping for a strong, broadly based council, he persuaded Howe to join it by giving him the impression, as he had done with Baldwin in Canada, that he favoured responsible government by party. But the council had only three reformers — Howe, James B. Uniacke and James McNab; the other six members were all tories. Sydenham thought it a promising coalition of 'all the talents', but it was riven with internal dissensions and sustained in the assembly by unreliable majorities.

The new governor, the tenth Viscount Falkland, had a good start, for he had been a representative Scottish peer and liberal Whip in the Lords. Both reformers and conservatives were disposed to trust him. As the era of good feelings in the colony ended, Falkland found himself in difficulties. The tories hoped to force the reformers off the executive council, making it a one-party body. The ablest moderate, J. W. Johnston, a lawyer and a Baptist, was embroiled with Howe and a large part of the community over aid to sectarian colleges. Johnston and Howe also clashed publicly on whether party government were necessary or practicable in Nova Scotia. The assembly, whose control of the purse was growing as Crown revenues became insufficient to pay civil salaries, was little inclined to heed the governor.

Falkland decided to dissolve the assembly, 'as the only means by which I could hope to escape the necessity of immediately forming a Party Government'.[99] He may have been influenced by Stanley's attitude to Metcalfe's problems. Falkland interpreted the elections that followed the dissolution as a rebuff to the reformers, which they vigorously denied, and before the new assembly met he reconstructed the executive council to rely on Johnston. Following this change and the Metcalfe crisis in Canada, Howe, Uniacke and McNab all resigned, angrily claiming that, because they had a majority in the assembly, Falkland should not have strengthened their opponents on the council.

Johnston maintained dignity, restraint and (on 5 March 1844) a majority of two in the assembly against party government. While Howe exchanged insults with Falkland's supporters and, so he suspected, with Johnston's agents, the government continued painfully on its course. In London Falkland, who was well connected, reaped the benefits of Johnston's good management and was promoted to govern Bombay. The angry Howe emerged with less credit. In February 1846 he attacked

Falkland's comments on colonists in his dispatches to London: 'Some Colonist will, by-and-by, or I am much mistaken', he said, 'hire a black fellow to horsewhip a Lieutenant-Governor.'[100] The assembly censured Howe, who severed his connection with the newspaper *The Novascotian* and retired to his farm in disgust.

In the long run, as Howe perceived, the governor had made the triumph of responsible government certain. By siding with one party he had committed himself to governing through it alone or failing altogether. Sooner or later the other party would win at the elections and then the governor's position would become intolerable. In 1844 Howe claimed that the issue was 'already decided. The Liberals will have party Government . . . and the Tories can form no other.' A year later he wrote, 'Here lies the man who denounced party government that he might form one; and professing justice to all parties, gave every office to his own.'[101]

Falkland was succeeded, on Gladstone's nomination, by Sir John Harvey, a soldier with a reputation for liberality gained in New Brunswick and Newfoundland. Before he reached Nova Scotia, Harvey learned that the colony was divided on the merits of party government and that Falkland had left vacancies on both the legislative and executive councils. Harvey's own preference, which he took to be in accordance with the assembly's resolution of 5 March 1844, was for an executive council made up of men of all parties, a coalition. Howe told him that the problem was too big for such a compromise and neither Howe nor McNab would serve on a coalition council. Uniacke, however, took the opposite view, having concluded that the colony was too small for party government with repeated changes of office and perpetual conflicts of policy. As a true coalition was impossible and party government was undesirable, he believed that Harvey should dissolve the assembly and trust the electorate to solve his problem.

Harvey decided to refer his problems to the new Secretary of State. In so doing he declared against party government in small colonies.[102] His first problem was that the legislative council, with only two vacancies, already had a heavy predominance of conservatives; should he increase its size beyond the normal twenty-one, in order to procure a better balance of parties, more likely to favour a coalition executive council? What should he do about the vacancies on the executive council itself? Should he dissolve the assembly?

A day after the lieutenant-governor unburdened himself to Grey, Howe wrote privately to Buller, whom he had known since 1839, and whose new proximity to power delighted colonial liberals: 'If you have, as I suppose, influence with Earl Grey, request him to dissolve our House, and you will have no more trouble in Nova Scotia for the next four years.'[103] Howe welcomed the Whigs back into office, assured Buller that he looked forward to both responsible government and free trade and rejoiced that he at last had a better line to the Secretary of State than any governor was likely to command. (Buller had already written to Howe praising Grey's colonial policy.)[104]

In deciding on his famous answer to Harvey, Grey seems to have had little help from Stephen, whose minute merely opposed dissolution and regretfully supported an increase of the legislative council. The arguments that Grey put to Russell are not known. A short letter from Russell to Grey agreed that Harvey should let the conservatives govern while they had a majority and turn them out when they lost it. For the architect of the Sydenham system this was a considerable change of policy.[105]

The private, confidential answer that Grey sent to Harvey,[106] after consulting Buller in drafting it, warned him that it would be imprudent to enlarge the legislative council to get round a difficulty that was prospective rather than actual; nor should the assembly be dissolved, as the reformers asked, unless the executive council so advised, or there were some obvious crisis. Grey instructed Harvey to follow a course of action that would lead to party government in Nova Scotia. Harvey was to call on the existing members of the executive council to propose additional members to fill the vacancies on it. If there were no valid objection to their proposals, they must be accepted, and the council, whatever its party composition, should be allowed to govern so long as it had the necessary confidence of the legislature. If the members could not propose satisfactory additions to the council, Harvey, on the analogy of British practice, must apply to the opposition party and, if through their assistance he formed a satisfactory council, there would be 'no impropriety in dissolving the Assembly upon their advice'.

Harvey was instructed never to change his advisers until it had become 'perfectly clear that they are unable with such fair support from yourself as they have a right to expect to carry on the Government of the Province satisfactorily and command the confidence of the Legislature'. He was to identify himself with no party and be wary of refusing the advice of the council, for they would be entitled to resign if he did not accept it, and public opinion might be on their side. If there were a clash between Harvey and the council, he should take care that the grounds of it were clearly recorded 'in written Documents capable of being publicly quoted'. 'Such are the general principles upon which the constitutions granted to the North American Colonies render it necessary that their Government should be conducted.'

Fortunately for the advocates of responsible government, Buller sent Howe well calculated hints of what Grey had written to Harvey.[107] Howe was not to agitate for a dissolution; Harvey had been ordered to adopt responsible government and patience would be rewarded: 'One hostile vote of the House will settle the matter', or Harvey might object to the additional members proposed for the council. Above all, Howe must trust Grey; the case was so good that not even Stanley could thwart them.

Harvey acknowledged Grey's dispatch on 19 November and interpreted it wrongly 'as an instruction, not equivocal, that under certain Constitutional restrictions, clearly enunciated, I may consider it in the light of a "Carte Blanche" to pursue my own responsibility'. Hawes and Stephen both thought that Harvey had genuinely misunderstood the dispatch and Grey set the Governor right. But Harvey had already undermined Grey's policy by asking the executive council without disclosing to them the full purport of Grey's dispatch, to propose new members; in fact he had let the council think that Grey opposed party government and wished the vacancies to be filled from the opposition. Harvey believed that his superior was committing a fundamental mistake. How could Nova Scotia with its small population ever manage responsible government? He sent Grey an able memorandum by Johnston, arguing that in Nova Scotia the principal secretary and the treasurer should be civil servants, clear of the nuisances of politics, the turmoil of elections and the dangers of the spoils system, with another from the opposition arguing the reverse.[108]

Stephen, a tired, sick man, dreaded the pointless disputation that might follow the issue of 'authoritative promulgation of abstract principles of Govt' and wanted no answer sent to the memoranda. Hawes wished Grey to defend responsible government, as every attempt to delay its institution embittered politics in the colonies.[109] Grey consulted Buller and sent two careful answers. On 2 March he told Harvey that he ought not to have involved himself publicly in acrimonious attempts to form a coalition council. Neither in Nova Scotia nor anywhere else would a coalition be acceptable to men of honour: 'The two contesting parties will have to decide their quarrel at present in the Assembly and ultimately at the hustings. And until a decision adverse to your present advisers shall be pronounced in one way or the other, the composition of your Council will require no further interposition on your part.'[110]

A second dispatch, dated 31 March and written after unrecorded consultation with Russell, discussed how responsible government might be introduced into the province. Grey extracted from the memoranda that Harvey had sent more evidence of agreement than the governor had found. Both parties had conceded that the governor must have as advisers those who commanded a majority of the legislature, more particularly the elected house. The liberals conceded further that there were dangers in too many changes of office. From a practical point of view, Nova Scotia could have responsible government if only two or three offices were made political. The colony was small and had a limited revenue; its social state was not suitable to government by rotation of large parties. It would be sufficient to establish the principle of party government if only the provincial secretary, the attorney-general and, perhaps, the solicitor-general held their offices subject to the confidence of the assembly. When conditions in the colony changed, a larger number of offices might be made political. Members of the executive council, other than the two or three named, should be paid civil servants, not sitting in either house. Pensions would have to be paid to existing members of the executive council who were forced to retire, except to those who had specifically been appointed with an obligation to retire on political grounds.

In the elections held on 5 August 1847, according to schedule, the liberals were victorious. Harvey kept out of the campaign but continued to resist party government after the result was known. He did not convene the legislature for five months, the old councillors retaining office meanwhile, and Harvey again told the liberals that party government was unsuitable for the 'minor colonies of North America'. When the assembly met in January it voted out the council by twenty-nine votes to twenty-two. Grey approved Harvey's concluding actions and insisted on pensions for those who had retired on political grounds.[111]

In March, Howe, who in September had warned Buller to prepare Grey for intrigues in London against the liberals, received Buller's congratulations on the 'wisdom and moderation' that the reformers had shown. Buller then admitted that he had seen all Grey's dispatches to Harvey and assured the 'tribune of Nova Scotia' that his thanks would be conveyed to both Grey and Hawes.[112]

Harvey reported the new ministry to Grey on 10 February; it included Howe, McNab and Uniacke, the last as premier. 'I trust', Grey wrote to him on 7 March, 'that the system of responsible government, of which they so justly appreciate and apply the principles, may now be regarded as established in Nova Scotia.' It was, but party feeling had run high, and there were great difficulties over the retirement of Sir Rupert George, who had been provincial secretary and clerk to the council for thirty-five years. Buller was content to let difficulties solve themselves in the colony; responsible government, he wrote to Howe, was coming throughout British North America.[113]

Throughout the difficult correspondence with Harvey, Grey was always clear that he intended to introduce party government. Whether Russell was equally sure is not known. As late as August 1846 he still believed that reunion and Sydenham had 'saved' Canada.[114] There is, however, no hint of disagreement with Grey either in their correspondence or in Grey's book. Buller was sure at the first, and remained sure, that the only real obstacles were conservatives at home and in the colony, who feared popular control, and governors unwilling to give up their powers:

In my eyes the almost sole business of the Colonial Office should be to breed up a supply of Good Colonial Governors: & then leave them &

you to manage your affairs. Our practice is to neglect the one duty, & meddle in every thing else. You are fortunate now in having a Colonial Secretary who has sound views of Colonial Policy: but the good results of Ld Grey's administration cannot be achieved all at once. We must wait some time ere he can find Governors to carry his views into effect.[115]

GREY, ELGIN AND RESPONSIBLE GOVERNMENT IN CANADA

Before they appointed Cathcart as governor-general in 1846, Peel and Gladstone had thought of James Bruce, eighth Earl of Elgin, who had sat in Parliament in 1841—2 as a Tory and gone to govern Jamaica on inheriting the earldom. Elgin had done well in Jamaica, wanted a move, and had been mentioned by the Queen herself.[116] But the Oregon troubles had made the appointment of a soldier desirable and Elgin could not leave Jamaica quickly. When the Whigs took office in July, Elgin's hopes of Canada seemed slight, especially as he had seconded the amendment that had brought down Lord Melbourne's government in 1841. Grey, however, who shared Buller's views on the importance of good governors, decided, after he had met Elgin on 21 July and found him 'a very able man indeed', to send him to Canada. Russell agreed, the Queen cordially approved and Elgin accepted the offer immediately. Perhaps Grey had seen advantages in sending to Canada a Tory approved by the Queen to undo the policy that Stanley and Gladstone had followed.[117]

Grey had not known Elgin when he had him appointed governor-general, except by reputation and through his one brief meeting with him in July.[118] Before Elgin left for Canada in January 1847, however, the two men had come to know one another rather well. Elgin, whose first wife had died in Jamaica, fell in love with Lady Mary Lambton, who was Durham's daughter and Grey's niece. 'I cannot say how glad I shall be if this leads to his marrying her', Grey, normally so reserved, wrote in his Journal. It did. 'The lovers', as Grey privately thought of them, were married on 7 November, in the presence of the Secretary of State. During Elgin's brief courtship Grey saw him often, and they discussed Grey's plans to introduce responsible government into Canada and his hopes to federate all the provinces of British North America for the sake of efficient administration, improved political standards, and free trade among the provinces. Elgin was given a copy of the important dispatch sent to Harvey on 3 November and the understanding between the statesman and the governor seemed complete. The Elgins lunched with the Greys in January, on the eve of the governor-general's departure; Lady Elgin, who was to join him in the spring, stayed a while with the Greys. At the end of January, Elgin wrote cheerfully to his wife that 'I have adopted yr Father's view of Government', a statement that was lovingly connubial rather than politically exact.[119]

Grey's instructions to Elgin, drafted without a word of Durham, were that

> He was to act generally upon the advice of his Executive Council, and to receive as Members of that body those persons, who might be pointed out to him as entitled to be so by their possessing the confidence of the Assembly. But he was carefully to avoid identifying himself with the party from the ranks of which the actual Council was drawn, and to make it generally understood that, if public opinion required it, he was equally ready to accept their opponents as his advisers, uninfluenced by any personal preferences.[120]

So far as the internal affairs of the colony were concerned, the governor-general would normally have to content himself with the influence that office, character and experience might give him. He could not choose his own advisers, or decline to act on advice given him so long as it was limited to the internal affairs of the colony.

Elgin's early dispatches from Canada showed how well he understood his instructions. Elgin gave Grey what he lacked in Nova Scotia, a governor who knew what the Secretary of State was doing and thoroughly agreed with it. 'I am determined', wrote Elgin, 'to do nothing which will put it out of my power to act with the opposite party'; he doubted whether the Draper ministry would last long and was prepared to work with its opponents. He hoped to compensate for the loss of the power of patronage, for which Metcalfe had contended so strongly, by establishing 'a moral influence in the province'. Elgin, who with experience became surer than ever that responsible government in the form of party government was needed in Canada, had already warned Grey that hopes of federation were wholly impracticable, and Grey had temporarily abandoned that part of his plans.[121]

Grey's instructions to Harvey and Elgin were not publicly known in London. The choice that apparently lay before Elgin was summed up in the Tory *Morning Herald* on 23 March 1847:

> The Radical's interpretation of his own war-cry is, that every member of the Executive Administration, except the Governor, should be responsible to the Canadian people, dependent upon the popular voice for his official existence . . . ; while the governor himself, like a mere puppet, should neither by word or deed . . . betray his own individuality, but that every petty appointment should be made by his ministerial advisers, and that he himself should be responsible to the Imperial Government . . . for acts over which he was not allowed to exercise the slightest control.

This radical doctrine of party government was contrasted with the conservative view, that 'the colonial Cabinet ought to enjoy a majority in the Provincial Parliament, or resign their offices to men in whom the assembly confides; but it justly vindicates the independence of the Governor as a representative of the British SOVEREIGN.' The *Morning Herald* thought it unlikely that a man like Elgin would 'barter the prerogatives of the Crown for a short-lived colonial popularity'. Its confidence that a Tory governor-general would do as Stanley and Gladstone would have done was unsupported by any proposal of how Elgin was to resist demands for party government, except for the comment that only 'at home' could they 'meet with effectual counter-action'. Grey was prudent to keep his intentions secret.

Elgin's first major difficulty, touching the principles of responsible government, occurred when Draper thought to strengthen the ministry by adding some French Canadians. Despite some aloofness between Elgin and Draper, the governor-general did agree that 'an alliance [with Draper] would be more natural for the French than the existing alliance with Baldwin'. Elgin assisted cordially, interviewing some of the French leaders himself, and Hincks reported to Baldwin from Montreal that the French were 'panting for office'.[122] The negotiations failed, for Draper had too little to offer. Elgin, however, gained the goodwill of the French by his practical demonstration that he would have welcomed them into office. Draper was forced to look for further strength from Canada West, among the conservatives, and added the young J. A. Macdonald. His actions stirred the tories to hope that they might dominate the government. Draper had hoped to build up a strong, flexible conservative party that would resist the reforming objectives of Baldwin and be a reasonable alternative to both the toryism of Macnab and Sherwood and the everlasting dissidence of the French. To his chagrin, Elgin was less interested in this conservative project than he was in instituting what he called constitutional government. Draper soon decided to retire to high judicial office.

His successor, Henry Sherwood, was a somewhat extreme tory, who clung to office with tenuous majorities while the legislature sat in June and July and survived Baldwin's challenge (in the name of Durham) to introduce full responsible government at once. Elgin told Grey that he was more than ever sure that full responsible government was inevitable in Canada and gave reasons that were somewhat different from those of the Secretary of State in that they emphasised the immediate practicalities:

... when I read Ld Sydenham's despatches I never cease to marvel what study of human nature or of history led him to the conclusion that it would be possible to concede to a pushing enterprising people unencumbered by aristocracy and dwelling in the immediate vicinity of the United States such Constitutional privileges as were conferred ... at the time of the Union, and yet to restrict in practice their powers of self Government as he hoped.[123]

In late autumn Elgin granted a dissolution. Unlike some of his
predecessors, he remained conspicuously neutral throughout the election
of 1847—8, which was more remarkable for violence of weather than of
antagonists. Responsible government was not much a campaign question.
The electors rejected Sherwood's administration because it had failed to
resolve its own internal tensions and provide strong government at a
difficult time. The terrifying crisis of Irish immigration, in the wake of the
Great Famine, and the onset of economic depression, much aggravated by
the change of British commercial policy, would have made it hard for any
government to hold on to office. The electors gave the reformers a large
majority in Canada West and almost total victory in Canada East. *The
Globe* immediately demanded responsible government as in Nova
Scotia.[124]

Sherwood remained in office, as he was entitled to do, until the new
legislature met and the assembly carried a vote of no confidence by
fifty-four votes to nineteen. Elgin then called on Baldwin and La Fontaine,
the 'disloyal democrats' whom Metcalfe would have excluded from office
for ever, to form the new council. Grey had instructed Elgin not to resist
the will of the majority, even if Papineau, who had been elected to the
assembly after returning to Canada, were proposed as a member of the
council. Papineau's republicanism was no less notorious than his conviction that responsible government was a 'delusion and a snare' that
Russell cynically dangled before the French. Elgin was saved such a
humiliation: Baldwin and La Fontaine made reasonable proposals and
allowed him to induce them to include Sullivan in the ministry. Elgin was
delighted with his new advisers, finding them of more talent and of greater
strength in the legislature than their predecessors. All the councillors were
from the same party and their assembly support was party based.[125]

Elgin clearly had a party government, which he intended to influence
with all the power that office, character and experience could command,
but in which he did not intend to be his own prime minister. He would
influence the choice of his advisers and the advice that was given him, but
when influence was expended, he would accept whatever advisers the
assembly gave him and allow them to command the full resources of the
government in all purely colonial matters.[126]

Between them, Grey and Elgin had shown that the British ministry
expected responsible government to work as party government in Canada
and that the French need fear no exclusion from power. Grey, Elgin, and
Russell never imagined that the introduction of party government would
wholly restore the internal tranquillity of the colony or guarantee that it
would not seek incorporation in the United States. Elgin, noting the
strength of the French and the Irish and of American influences,
commented that 'British Institutions have no hold whatsoever on the
affections of certain classes of the inhabitants'.[127] Russell believed that

Britain would need to have an attractive Canadian policy, if the colony were to be saved for the empire, as his imperial vision led him to hope it would be. Particularly, as we shall see, he hestitated over Grey's policy of withdrawing British troops, which were the symbol of British strength and of Canadian defences against the United States.[128] Grey himself pressed ahead with some of the concessions that Metcalfe had sought; the Act 11 and 12 Vict., c. 56, repealed the language restrictions imposed by the Reunion Act. A complete amnesty was granted for the rebellions of 1837. Concessions were timely, for Papineau broke with La Fontaine in March, claiming again that responsible government was an English trick and that justice had not yet been done to the French Canadians. He reiterated his old demands, that French Canada should be separated and ruled by American institutions. His challenge to the union and La Fontaine's attempts to come to terms with it appealed to veteran agitators and to idealistic young radicals, who hated Britain and Canada West. Elgin's answer, approved by Grey, was to trust the French and give up assimilation.[129]

In Montreal and in Canada West there was an almost complementary problem. The conservatives were increasingly dissatisfied with British rule. Had not reunion displaced them from power in favour of a party of radicals and French Canadians, including the 'disloyal and the natural enemies of the British Crown'? The reversal of British commercial policy that had destroyed the preferences of the Canada Corn Act, and the onset of worldwide depression in the late 1840s had undermined British markets for Canadian exports and sorely tried loyal Canadian attitudes to Britain.[130] The inconsistency of British commercial policy seemed unbearable to men whose fortunes were imperilled by the coming of free trade. Prosperity based on wheat and timber and on the building of roads, railways and canals changed to recession and resentment. Men wondered in Canada whether Britain really intended to retain an empire in North America, and knew that in Britain some men questioned whether any case for empire could survive the ending of the old commercial system, while others believed that the colonies would no longer find the burdens of empire, most notably subordination to Britain, endurable when they lost their former economic privileges.

Elgin wrote to Grey of 'the generally uneasy and diseased condition of the public mind' and Grey, in a dark hour, wondered whether Canada were worth keeping. The commercial empire of the St Lawrence seemed to be sinking into ruin, with the extended canals half idle and the colony's credit at such a low ebb that further loans were impossible. The disturbances of 1848 in France and Ireland were alarming and the generally bad outlook turned attention away from responsible government to the more fundamental question of whether the imperial connection could or should survive. In Canada, as in Britain, people asked why Britain should retain

her colonies if she abandoned the old commercial system and allowed full
responsible government.[131]

Some Montreal tories, suffering under the changed conditions, hoped
for American annexation. Many of Papineau's followers looked to a bright
future in the expanding, democratic republic. Free trade and responsible
government were both cold comfort, the former positively damaging to
Canada, the latter temporarily irrelevant. Elgin believed the imperial
connection to be in danger, because so many lines of discontent merged on
the desperate remedy of annexation:

> Whether it be alleged that the French are oppressing the British, or the
> British the French — that Upper Canada Debt presses on Lower Canada,
> or Lower Canada claims on Upper — whether merchants be bankrupt,
> stocks depreciated, roads bad, or seasons unfavourable — annexation is
> invoked as the remedy for all ills imaginary or real. — A great deal of
> this talk is . . . bravado, and a great deal the mere product of
> thoughtlessness — Undoubtedly it is in some quarters the utterance of
> very sincere convictions — And if England will not make the sacrifices
> which are absolutely necessary to put the Colonists here in as good a
> position commercially as the citizens of the States — in order to which
> *free navigation* and *reciprocal trade with the States* are indispensable
> . . . the end may be nearer at hand than we wot of.[132]

Russell was alarmed and thought of tariff reform or federation to ease
North American discontents. Elgin himself believed that only a union of
the colonies of British North America was likely to 'place British interests
in North America on a footing of security', by putting the strains between
English and French Canada into a larger arena. He and Grey had already
noted that the small size of the Canadian legislature gave party government
there special acrimony and limited efficiency and both had thought of a
federal legislature as having at least the political advantages of a larger
electorate.[133]

In October the Annexation Association in Montreal formally called for
a 'friendly and peaceful separation' from Britain and incorporation in the
United States. Most signatories were Montreal businessmen. But the
manifesto overreached itself; few Canadians, English-speaking or French-
speaking, were really sure that they wanted to become additional states of
the American republic. American democracy, overshadowed by conflicts
over slavery and expansion was far from wholly attractive. Prompted by
Elgin, Grey reassured the colonists that Britain would not abandon them,
whatever some of the speeches of his colleagues and other parliamentarians
might seem to imply: 'Her Majesty confidently relies on the loyalty of the
great majority of her Canadian subjects, and she is therefore determined to
exert all the authority which belongs to her, for the purpose of

maintaining the connexion of Canada with this country, being persuaded that the permanence of that connexion is highly advantageous to both.'[134] Grey wanted to supply and encourage the Canadians by every means in his power until, under free trade, the natural advantages of their economic strength began to tell and to hold them fast to Britain. The gradual return of prosperity and Grey's promise of assistance in obtaining a new loan helped convince most colonists that annexation was not in their interest. Farmers with good harvests, French Canadians satisfied with La Fontaine as prime minister, and the solid mass of the people of Canada West indicated, in one way or another by the spring of 1850, that annexation was a lost cause.[135]

The success with which Elgin and Grey overcame 'annexation fever' owed something[136] to their firmness in introducing and defending responsible government, especially when the famous Rebellion Losses Act of 1849 led to a major challenge in Parliament itself to Grey's policy in Canada. The La Fontaine–Baldwin ministry introduced in that year a Bill to compensate inhabitants of old Lower Canada for damage suffered in the rebellions of 1837.[137] Compensation for damage in Upper Canada had been agreed upon in 1838–9 and paid by 1845, when a similar measure for Lower Canada was approved in principle. In 1849 the opposition in the colony protested that the Bill was an indemnity to rebels, which in some ways it was, but the French resolved that it should pass. Baldwin and his supporters knew that, if it did not pass, La Fontaine would reopen the old wounds of racial animosity, to the benefit of Papineau. The annexationists of Montreal saw the Bill as a shameful harbinger of what a French majority would do to Canada; the tories of Canada West were besides themselves with rage that treason should be forgiven. The Bill passed in a house where order was barely preserved and was then approved in the legislative council. Opponents of the Bill put their faith in Elgin, hoping that he would refuse his assent or reserve the Bill for the royal pleasure, or dissolve the assembly and appeal to the country.

Elgin saw his duty clearly. His ministers had passed a fiercely contested measure with clear majorities; there was no ground to refuse his assent, nor to risk the delays and disturbances to imperial relations that would occur if he reserved it. Dissolution would be doubly objectionable: the council had not advised it and an election would produce a conflict from which no one would benefit except the followers of Papineau and Macnab. He explained to Grey:

> If I pass the bill, whatever mischief ensues may probably be repaired if the worst comes to the worst by the sacrifice of me. — Whereas, if the case be referred to England it is not impossible that Her Majesty may only have before Her the alternative of provoking a rebellion in Lower Canada by refusing her assent to a measure deeply affecting the

interests of the Habitans and thus throwing out the whole population into Papineau's hands, or of wounding the susceptibilities of some of the best subjects she has in the Province.[138]

He knew that many loyal colonists would never understand why he felt obliged to assent to the Bill. Grey left the matter to Elgin's discretion and on 25 April he publicly assented. His return to the viceregal residence, made in a carriage at full gallop, was attended by showers of stones, rotten eggs and coarse abuse.

Wild scenes followed in Montreal. The mob burst into the assembly chamber, forced the abandonment of the meeting and set the building on fire. La Fontaine's new house was devastated. When Elgin came to town again, to receive the loyal address of the legislature, his carriage was battered and chased halfway home. 'We were for a time', he wrote to Grey, 'in great danger.... Excesses correct themselves and I have no doubt that the violence of the disaffected will elict a great counter-demonstration.'[139] Elgin thought that the Orange Societies, businessmen seeking annexation and ambitious politicians were to blame for the disturbances, and found them profoundly alarming. Within a week or so, however, the worst of the violence was over and, except in Montreal and a little in Toronto, a majority of the colonists eventually supported the governor-general's stand, that Canada ruled itself.

Grey was in more subtle danger than Elgin. The leading English newspapers attacked Elgin strongly. Only *The Times*,[140] which Grey kept informed, believed that the question was simply one of self-government, not of loyalty and the imperial connection. The Peelite *Morning Chronicle*, which boasted a liberal attitude to colonial reform, blamed Elgin for not having taken firmer steps to shape the Bill.[141] On 14 June Mr Gladstone's conscience would no longer let him be silent. 'I am not prepared', he weightily informed the Commons, 'be the consequences what they may, to be a consenting party to advising the Crown . . . to assent to any Act of a Colonial Legislature, which I believe to be essentially dishonourable to Imperial rights.'[142] No rebel should be compensated. Gladstone did not, however, strike the blow that might have had the gravest consequences for the Anglo-Canadian connection.

That task was reserved to J. C. Herries, a man of over seventy, long a Tory spokesman on finance and trade, who moved that the House disapprove the Act and address the Crown to have it disallowed.[143] Disraeli seconded the motion. In the Lords a powerful attack was mounted against Elgin and the Act by Brougham and Stanley; the latter warned that if the Canadian assembly were not restrained the constitution of a British colony would become 'more absolutely and purely democratic than is even the constitution of the United States'.

In the Commons Russell had little difficulty in defeating Herries' motion, for he had to combat only the obstinacy of the recalcitrant Tories and 'colonial reformers' and the growing distrust of Grey. Peel, whose faith in the empire Grey had doubted only a month before,[144] was on the liberal side. Changing conditions in Britain and Canada, the new idea of self-governing colonies, and the difficult state of Anglo-American relations all helped to emancipate him from the tight-lipped alternative of 1844, that Canada had either to be a colony or be independent. Without discussing the principle of responsible government, the Commons rejected Herries's motion by 291 votes to 150.

In the Lords, however, Grey was in difficulties when Brougham tried to have Elgin's actions disallowed. Brougham opposed the Rebellion Losses Act with angry vehemence and declared that the Canadians wanted such a degree of responsible government as was inconceivable in a colony. He spoke as if party government did not exist in Britain itself and attributed much greater power to the sovereign in choosing her ministers than Victoria really possessed. In general his constitutional position, like that of most lords who supported him, was out of date. Using the words that Russell had spoken a decade before, he concluded that responsible government would always be inconsistent with colonial status 'in matters that touch . . . the honour of the Crown, and the interests of the imperial government'.[145]

Grey was anxious and feared that he spoke 'detestably'. In fact, his speech was well conceived and memorable. The circumstances of each colony, he said, defined the sort of government that Britain could establish there. Generally Britain would try to establish the most liberal form of government that local conditions permitted. Stanley himself had allowed that the executive council in Canada should be composed of men possessing the confidence of the assembly. More was needed, however, because in Canada the executive could properly be controlled by the representatives of the people in all purely colonial matters. Grey referred to Russell's 'tenure of offices' dispatch, to Durham's views on responsible government and to the just expectations of the Canadians, who deserved as much British self-government as could be reconciled with imperial supremacy.

Striking at the heart of the difficulty that had so long prevented full responsible government in Canada, he abandoned all the problems of demarcating imperial and colonial powers and dismissed all doubts on how a governor who was advised by ministers responsible to a colonial assembly could also be accountable to his masters in London. He took a clear commonsense ground for writing these problems out of consideration. It would be imprudent and unsettling, he said, ever to attempt to define the relative powers of the Secretary of State, the governor and the assembly, all of whom were familiar with British political traditions. 'The same . . . is true of our government', he wisely added. 'If Parliament or the Crown should stretch their power to extremes, the whole machinery of government must soon be brought to a standstill.'[146] The Canadians should be credited with political judgement to match that of British ministers in reconciling imperial policy with colonial interests. *Solvitur ambulando*!

The Lords were not sufficiently impressed by Grey's argument that British political wisdom might flourish in British colonies as well as at home. Although he told them that it would be dangerous for Parliament to stretch its powers by disallowing the deliberate act of the representatives of the Canadian people, confirmed by the Queen's representative, the Lords opposed 'subsidies to treason'. Brougham was defeated by only three votes (ninety-nine to ninety-six), a hard-won victory and a strange one in that some Peelite lords voted with the Opposition. Among them was Lincoln, later fifth Duke of Newcastle, then in his most violent 'anti-Grey' phase, who later carried responsible government to lengths that Grey thought mistaken.

Neither Grey nor Russell liked the Rebellion Losses Act, and neither forgot the alarming disturbances that had accompanied its passage in Canada. In 1847 Grey and Elgin had noted how the small size of colonial assemblies changed the nature of party government. As we have seen, Grey had wondered whether federation would help produce a smoother operation of party government, because a larger assembly, chosen from a wider electorate, would be more likely to behave like the House of Commons than ever the assembly of Canada would. In 1849 Grey thought again of how to improve the legislature of Canada without undoing responsible government. He suggested to Russell that the legislative council should be strengthened, perhaps by making it partly elective. If the council were composed of the holders of certain offices and of the elected representatives of various interests, it would have strength and will to check the assembly, so that colonial contests would be contained within the legislature and not embarrass the Queen's representative or the imperial Parliament. 'These are mere speculations', he conceded, when he proposed that Parliament might empower the legislature of Canada to change its own constitution to make the upper house elective, subject to royal approval.[147] Grey's liberal reforms for conservative purposes alarmed Russell, who disliked the departure from British constitutional practice involved in an elected upper house and would not trust the Canadians to amend their own constitution. What would happen if the Crown disapproved a change that the legislature made in pursuance of powers that Parliament had conferred? A few years later Russell successfully faced this problem with the Australian constitution; in 1849 he thought it too alarming to contemplate.

Russell's own plan was to have representatives of the colonists sit in the imperial Parliament. Colonial representation at Westminster was to be proportionate to the contributions of the colonies to defence costs.[148] If colonists sat in the imperial Parliament, the demarcation of imperial and colonial questions would be weighted to the imperial side and imperial influences in colonial legislatures might be strengthened. Elgin saw some merit in Russell's idea, but only for the distant future; though often revived, it was never acted upon.[149]

RESPONSIBLE GOVERNMENT IN CONTEXT

Why did Grey allow responsible government to Nova Scotia and to Canada? The anwers given here are, in the context of British colonial self-government, clear and confirmed by Grey himself. He hoped that responsible government was part of the way to political peace in Nova Scotia and Canada,[150] although neither he nor Elgin was confident that the great concession would be in time to save North America for the empire.[151] Grey thought that the people of both colonies were politically qualified to work the new system. As a believer in the imperial destiny of large colonies of British settlement, and as a systematic coloniser (of sorts), he had faith that liberal reforms might ultimately unite Britain and the colonies in lasting, valued and voluntary union, based on kinship, culture and shared institutions. He thought it possible to limit the grant of responsible government to the domestic affairs of the colonies. Commercial policy, foreign policy, the constitution and the major aspects of strategy and defence were all to be reserved to imperial control. Neither Baldwin, nor Howe, nor any other colonist demanding responsible government at that time seriously contested this reservation of imperial powers, which was made also by Durham, Russell and Buller. Responsible government was granted not because of the coming of free trade, but in accordance with the long tradition of established British policy towards self-government of colonies. Commercial policy had always been reserved to imperial control and the constitutional privileges of colonists had been settled independently of it, according to their ability to operate forms of government that political men in Britain accepted for themselves. From 1831 onwards, with no more inconsistency than any human being normally shows, Grey had asked why the Canadians could not have full liberty to manage their own affairs. He differed from his contemporaries in attributing Canadian discontents to frustrated maturity, not to disaffection or malevolence, and departed from the tradition of British policy only in his readiness to trust French Canadians as much as English Canadians, without relying on futile hopes of assimilation.

In 1853 Grey rejected vigorously the argument that free trade had cleared the way for responsible government by diminishing the need to control the commercial policies of the colonies:

> When Parliament, after a protracted discussion of many years, finally determined upon abandoning the former policy of endeavouring to promote the commerce of the Empire by an artificial system of

restrictions, and upon adopting in its place the policy of Free Trade, it did not abdicate the duty and the power of regulating the commercial policy, not only of the United Kingdom, but of the British Empire. The common interest . . . required that . . . commercial policy should be the same throughout its numerous dependencies.[152]

Free trade was a prescriptive principle of universal validity. Britain had a duty to enforce it and, therefore, had to retain full control of the commercial policy of the whole empire. One of the many reasons for keeping colonies was to make free trade flourish widely. A colony that had responsible government should have its enactments disallowed if tainted by protection, and be subjected to imperial legislation on all matters of external commerce.[153] Grey did not argue, though he could have done, that one reason for granting responsible government was to help keep within the empire those colonies, such as Canada, that suffered under the impact of free trade.

Grey and his contemporaries were wrong about the practicability of the restrictions that they imposed on responsible government. In 1848 Grey criticised the Canadian tariff of 1847 and wanted it revised because of apparently protective tendencies.[154] A year later Canada adopted a tariff that Grey should have disallowed as protective,[155] but in the strained political conditions of that year he chose to regard it as designed merely to raise revenue. In 1850 he could not prevent an agreement among Canada, Nova Scotia and Prince Edward Island establishing differential duties in one another's favour.[156] He strongly opposed the granting of a bounty to hemp production in New Brunswick in 1849–50, but his successors allowed it and it is difficult to see that he could have been any firmer than they were.[157]

By 1854 the Canadians had burst out of Grey's tight free trade system, entering into a short-lived Reciprocity Treaty with the United States; five years later they asserted the right to impose their own customs duties on goods imported from Britain itself. Their motive was less protection than revenue. Unwilling to tax themselves in more painful ways, the Canadians wanted the 'right to impose a tariff on British goods to secure revenue to meet the demands of British capitalists for interest on loans spent on public works to reduce costs of transportation'.[158] Constitutionally, the case for the tariff of 1859 was put by Alexander Galt, the Canadian minister of finace, who drew it up: 'Self-government would be utterly annihilated if the views of the imperial government were to be preferred to those of the people of Canada. Her majesty cannot be advised to disallow such acts, unless her advisers are prepared to assume the administration of the affairs of the colony irrespective of the wishes of the inhabitants.'[159] Responsible government soon existed without Grey's reservation of commercial policy, which could not be maintained against a powerful colony, especially one adjacent to the United States. From the Canadian point of view responsible government and autonomy of commercial policy came to be inseparable, but they were not so in the first place, and autonomy was generally not claimed by the Canadian reformers during their long agitation for responsible government.

As a free trader, Grey continued till his death in 1894 to lament the abandonment of strict imperial control of a uniform commercial policy for the whole empire. His doctrinaire free trade principles withstood even Elgin's quiet observation that the new commercial policy might weaken the empire by building up new alien ties between the colonies and their immediate neighbours or other natural trading partners.[160] Grey had enough faith in the expansive energy of British commerce, and in the ties of British institutions, culture and kinship to overlook the truth in Elgin's remark. Perhaps he thought Elgin overinfluenced by troubles with the Americans on his borders and the Irish and the French in Canada.

Grey and Russell did not expect the liberties granted with full responsible government to be offset by colonies of settlement becoming increasingly dependent on the mother country for money, markets or men. No such latter-day interpretation is fairly to be found in their speeches or writings, or in the works of their contemporaries. The idea has, however, occured to some twentieth-century historians, who have been better attuned to the changing economic interests of empire than to the history of colonial self-government or to the idea of an imperial destiny of British communities overseas. C. A. Wood, Chancellor of the Exchequer under Russell, wrote a letter to Grey (his brother-in-law) that leaves no room for any suggestion that any British minister could have hoped in the late 1840s to control Canada through loans and interest rates: 'We have guaranteed the loan to Canada and we have spent more money than enough upon them in various ways. Their taxation is very light in consequence . . . . They spend our money and their own in their senseless insurrections and then grumble that people are not confident of their being always able to pay the interest.'[161] Elgin, who greatly feared the annexation movement, thought that, if it succeeded, British loans might be repudiated and new capital raised in the United States.[162] Grey himself could not find money for the development of Canada, whether through railways or systematic colonisation, and was alarmed by reports that the British connection was blamed in Canada for retarding the flow of capital into the colony.[163]

Nor was there any ground in the 1840s for believing that Britain could determine the most important aspects of Canadian development by control of immigration. The many Canadian complaints of shiploads of paupers, unskilled Irish labourers and diseased and destitute persons all showed that Britain's need to export people was more urgent than Canada's to receive them. Elgin's argument for sending out British farmers to help settle British North America before the United States could absorb or populate it was imperially, not colonially, oriented.[164] Nor could British control of Canadian markets help sustain British supremacy in North America. Free trade largely destroyed what had formerly been a useful weapon of policy and played its part in producing the annexation movement. The outraged colonists sometimes thought that responsible government was a cunning device to placate them, a sop to palliate the injuries that the new commercial policy inflicted upon them.[165]

The only financial advantage that Grey ever sought to extract from responsible government was, as is well known, that colonies with responsible government might pay the costs of their administration (apart from governors' salaries) and local defence.[166] Molesworth, a strange ally for Grey, commended responsible government for permitting reduction of British military expenditure.[167] Elgin, however, was unenthusiastic, thinking Grey's zeal for economy inexpedient at a time of economic stress, before the merits of responsible government were much appreciated.[168] He saw that 'the adoption of Free Trade ... will doubtless render the English people more than ever jealous of expenditure' on the colonies, but could not concede that responsible government would save Canada for Britain irrespective of what was done about its defences. Russell, as we have seen, had similar doubts. Grey was too doctrinaire to perceive that if the colonies were forced to bear more of their own defence burdens they might have to raise such large revenues from customs duties as would undermine their adherence to free trade.[169]

Grey, Russell, Peel and Elgin all believed that party government was a British institution to which some colonies were fully entitled. They reached this conclusion by different routes and at different times. Grey, Russell and Peel, in that order, were powerfully influenced by faith in the imperial destiny of Britain to build up British communities overseas that would be united to Britain by kinship, culture, the Crown and similarity of institutions. Elgin may have thought so; certainly, as we shall see, he quickly recognised that responsible government was not an institution that ought to be confined to North America.

Under Grey's immediate successors, especially the fifth Duke of Newcastle, the work that Grey did in deciding which colonies were entitled to responsible government was rapidly continued. Newcastle by 1853 saw responsible government not as an unexpected by-product of the Durham Report and free trade, and as something to be introduced in North America only, but as an evolutionary process of constitutional change, in which Britain shared the advanced conventions of her own political life with colonies that became substantial British communities overseas. Newcastle, as we shall see, had to decide several difficult cases of whether to grant or refuse responsible government and, finally, whether to insist that it be prepared for although not requested.

9 The Policy of Responsible Government

This 'responsible Government' will be asked for everywhere, and we must take care to keep at least the Canadian safeguards, especially that no money should be voted except on the proposal of the Crown, and a Civil List.

Russell to Grey, 22 May 1850[1]

Responsible government was established in North America after notably little deliberation in Britain. Grey, who among British statesmen had given the greatest thought to the new policy, was soon uneasy about its consequences and became unwilling to extend it beyond North America.[2] He believed in the empire of settlement and the future of great British communities overseas, but he did not believe in the political fitness of the Cape Colony, or New Zealand or the Australian colonies, to have responsible government. Although he remarked in 1849 that the Australian colonies would eventually qualify to enjoy party government on the British model, he still thought in 1880 that none of them had yet done so, although five of them already possessed it. His disappointment at the breakdown of the fiscal unity of the empire strengthened his distaste for allowing any further relaxations of British control over the self-governing colonies, while his growing conservatism distrusted colonial democracy.[3]

GREY'S CONSTITUTION MAKING IN AUSTRALIA

Grey's constitutional policies in Australia were influenced heavily by recollections of New South Wales in the 1830s, when he had sought a form of government suited to a penal colony with some free settlers. The man who had then compared convict New South Wales with the West Indian slave colonies could not approve responsible government for a colony that, in his view, remained under the most solemn imperial obligation to go on receiving convicts.[4]

When Grey turned his mind to constitution making for Australia, he did not think of responsible government. The earliest problems that he had to solve arose from the dissatisfaction of powerful political groups in New South Wales with imperial land policy and the constitution of 1842, the demand of the Port Phillip District of New South Wales for separation from the rest of the colony, and the desire of South Australia and Tasmania to be granted constitutions as liberal as that established in New South Wales under Stanley. Looking at the Australian colonies, Grey was impressed by the immense distances separating them from one another, the sparse settlement of much of the occupied country, the lack of a class of educated men of independent means, the small populations of all the colonies except New South Wales, and the convict problem in every colony except South Australia. In consultation with Stephen he decided to apply to the Australian colonies a form of government originally intended for the scattered, sparsely populated settlements in New Zealand.[5] This was an elaborate pyramid of institutions, based on elected district councils that would elect the colonial legislatures from among their own members, while these legislatures in turn would elect a federal body from their members. The pyramid plan was little advanced beyond the complicated constitution making with which Grey (Howick) and Macarthur had tried to ensure good government for New South Wales in the 1830s.[6] In the late 1840s, as in the 1830s, Grey was not illiberal, only excessively paternal to colonies regarded as politically incapable of managing their own affairs through British institutions. The federal part of his proposals owed much to his desire to ensure free trade among the Australian colonies and among the colonies in New Zealand, and to his long interest in the federation of British North America.

Grey's proposals were abandoned in New Zealand as unworkable and were strongly condemned in Australia, except in so far as they promised representative institutions to Tasmania, South Australia and the new colony to be made out of the Port Phillip District. Early in 1848 he referred the problems of constitution making in the antipodes to Stephen, despite the latter's retirement from office.[7]

With the ripe wisdom that he commanded when relieved from the daily turmoil of business, Stephen reminded Grey that 'all we have to do for the benefit of a colony, so far as respects its Government, is to create a trustworthy legislature'. A colony should be left to establish its own courts of justice, its own municipal institutions, territorial divisions and fiscal establishment. The only problems in constitution making, so far as the Secretary of State was concerned, were to discover to whom he could honourably transfer power and assess how much power might safely be transferred with proper regard to justice to all the Queen's subjects and the needs of the rest of the empire. In the long run, British colonists would be worthy of strong faith in their political judgement, 'though they will indeed work out a real democracy under monarchial forms'. Stephen would not have hesitated for long over responsible government itself: 'What is called responsible Government, seems to me a panacea for the remediable evils of colonial misrule, wherever it can be safely applied . . . . it can be applied with safety wherever the colonists constitute an intelligent, English, homogenous population; and therefore, . . . it may safely be applied to all the Australian colonies.' In any colonial struggle for liberal institutions, the mother country was 'doomed to defeat'. Half-confidence in British subjects overseas was the 'worst possible policy'. 'A colony really fit for a Representative Legislature, is fit for self-government in the amplest, that is to say, in the Canadian sense of the name.'

Grey was advised to abandon blended legislatures in Australia (only New South Wales then had one, but the other colonies sought the same boon), establish bicameral legislatures and make them the bases of a central congress. 'I would inform each Governor', added Stephen, 'that if the Legislature of the colony desired the introduction of . . . [responsible government], no opposition must be made to them on that subject.'[8]

Grey, though taken aback by Stephen's challenge to his statesmanship and no doubt remembering that Stephen himself had been the original proposer of both blended legislatures and the New Zealand pyramid of institutions, was prepared for a thorough investigation of Australian government. He told Merivale that he disagreed with Stephen's condemnation of the blended legislature in New South Wales, that he thought colonial upper houses did more harm than good, and that strict regard must be had to imperial commercial policy; but he referred the Australian constitutions to the Privy Council Committee of Trade and Plantations — that is, in effect, to himself, Stephen and some others — for prolonged consideration of fundamental questions.[9]

The report of the Privy Council Committee[10] recommended uniform tariffs throughout the Australian colonies, federation, the separation of the Port Phillip District from New South Wales, the establishment in the other colonies of constitutions like that of New South Wales, and liberty to all the colonies to change their blended legislatures into bicameral legislatures. Neither Stephen nor Grey was entirely satisfied with the recommendations; in putting them into the successive draft Bills that led up to the Australian Colonies Government Act of 1850, many changes were made for the sake of expediency. Among the most important was Grey's agreement that the proposed federal legislature could be trusted (as it would be relatively free from provincial selfishness) to amend the Land Sales Act of 1842.[11]

The many Bills that the Colonial Office prepared for the government of the Australian colonies were much delayed because of the weakness of the Russell administration and the fierce controversies surrounding Grey himself, who was being pilloried by the 'colonial reformers'. Grey was blamed for maintaining convict transportation to Australia, for failing to support systematic colonisation, for refusing liberal constitutions to Australia and New Zealand, for weakness towards Canada, for undue tenderness towards the New Zealand Company, for failing to prevent frontier wars at the Cape, for extending the empire and for not extending the empire — blamed, indeed, for any colonial misfortune or mishap that could somehow be attributed to an unpopular minister. The colonial reformers, especially Molesworth and Adderley, with Wakefield in the background, looked to leading Peelites such as Lincoln (later fifth Duke of Newcastle) and Gladstone for help in driving Grey and the Russell government from office.[12] In February 1850 Russell introduced a new Australian Government Bill into the Commons. His able speech on colonial policy[13] owed much to a confidential minute that Grey had prepared for the Cabinet and that he later used in the first chapter of *Colonial Policy of Lord John Russell's Administration*.[14] The essential liberality of the Whig position was made clear in Russell's speech; so were the reasons for not advancing any Australian colony immediately to the political privileges enjoyed in Canada. The Bill was to separate the Port Phillip District from New South Wales, to give the new colony and Tasmania and South Australia blended legislatures, to allow all the colonies to go over to bicameral legislatures when they chose to do so and to authorise the federation of any two or more colonies wishing to enter such a union. Uniform customs duties were not required, but discriminating duties were prohibited.

The Times, which approved Russell's outline of colonial policy, agreed that no Australian colony was ready for a bicameral legislature or responsible government; but the colonial reformers were as unrelenting as bloodhounds in searching to destroy Grey. *The Times* wisely commented that 'The only difference between the Colonial Office and the Colonial Reformers is that the latter are somewhat more arbitrary and dogmatical than the former, for while the former are really leaving the question in the hands of the colonists, the latter are for sending out a cut and dried scheme evidently designed for permanent adoption.'[15] The reformers were trying to make a regular system of colonial self-government. Grey, distrusting their formulas, wanted to proceed pragmatically.

Molesworth[16] prompted *The Times*'s just complaint against the reformers. He bitterly attacked blended legislatures and the failure to distinguish between legislative powers that had to be wholly reserved to Britain and those that could be entirely allowed to the colonies. He asserted that the colonists would not be happy without responsible government and unsuccessfully tried to get the Bill recommitted to ensure that the colonial governments would be in the hands of men responsible to the people's representatives and that the legislatures would consist of two elective houses. Other critics complained that the Australian colonies were being given institutions fundamentally different from those of Britain. Spencer Walpole, the Whig historian, predicted that nominated members in blended legislatures would have a bad influence on legislation in normal times, and be powerless in times of excitement. He was strongly in favour of establishing institutions as nearly as possible the same as those of Britain, so as to stimulate community of outlook between the mother country and the colonies.[17]

The great difficulty with Grey's position was that he could not prove that blended legislatures and a federal system were wanted by the colonists; still less could he show that either was in accordance with British polity or with the understandings implicit in the granting of responsible government in North America. He and other government speakers had to argue that the arrangements proposed were as near to British institutions as existing social and political conditions in the Australian colonies justified. Before the debate was over, the federation clauses, for which the colonists had never asked, had had to be abandoned. The rest of the measure survived in essentials. The Act separated the Port Phillip District, which was erected into the colony of Victoria. It extended the franchise to allow the vote to landholders who had had six months' tenure of a freehold estate of the clear value of £100, or the occupation of a dwelling of the clear annual value of £10, or of a leasehold of the same annual value with at least three years to run, or the tenure of a depasturing licence. The enfranchisement of the squatters was a powerful aid to colonial conservatives, while the £10 franchise soon seemed dangerously democratic in the colony when the gold rushes swelled the numbers of the lower middle classes.

The Act continued many of the provisions of the New South Wales Act of 1842 to which colonists had strongly objected, notably the reservation to imperial control of lands and land revenues and the initiation of money votes by the Crown. Civil lists were established in each colony, with some liberty to the legislatures to alter them. The colonies were allowed to levy customs duties, provided that they were not differential or inconsistent with treaties. Finally, the legislatures were empowered, with the assent of the Queen in council, to alter the electoral laws or to change their blended legislatures into separate legislative houses.

Generally, the Act conferred such boons on Victoria, South Australia and Tasmania that their colonists welcomed it. But in New South Wales the legislative council adopted on Wentworth's motion a declaration and remonstrance, complaining that none of the most desired reforms had been granted, that the detested civil list had been increased, that patronage was still reserved to the Secretary of State and his officials, that land revenue and land policy were still under imperial control, that the Land Sales Act was still in force and that the imperial power of veto over colonial legislation remained as before.

Grey emphasised the large powers of constitutional amendment granted to the colonies and the changes made in customs adminstration, but could not deny that his policy towards the Australian colonies rested on presumptions about their political immaturity and social condition that led him to treat them quite differently from the North American colonies. The colonial reformers misunderstood him and, as *The Times* rightly said, were really more rigid than he. Grey left part of the constitutional future of the colonies, including both bicameralism and (implicitly) responsible government, in their own hands, subject to the royal assent. Molesworth would have inflicted his own notions on the antipodes. Grey, who had followed Stephen's bold counsel on the Canadas in the 1830s, would not follow him in the next decade when he recommended Canadian liberties for Australian colonies.

The Secretary of State who struck away all the doubts and difficulties that had perplexed Grey was the fifth Duke of Newcastle.[18] As Earl of Lincoln, he had voted against Grey (and Elgin) on the Rebellion Losses Act. He had been one of Grey's severest critics among the Peelites and entered office in December 1852 determined to end convict transportation to eastern Australia. He announced in the Lords on 17 February 1853 that transportation to Tasmania would cease at once;[19] the ship that had sailed on 31 December was the last convict transport to go to eastern Australia. Newcastle had another great advantage over Grey: by the time he took office the significance of the Australian gold discoveries was becoming apparent. A vastly accelerated pace of colonial growth, a large increase of the free population, a considerable accession of wealth, and growing recognition in Britain that New South Wales and Victoria had shown remarkable stability in face of upheaval all predisposed Newcastle and his advisers to take a very different view of Australia from Grey's. Newcastle's problem with responsible government was the lack of colonial demand for it rather than doubts of the fitness of the colonies to have it.

Newcastle's clearest statements on the principle of responsible government belong to his second term as Secretary of State, when he had reflected on the differences between himself and his predecessors. In 1861, when he invited the authoritarian Sir George Grey to return to New Zealand as governor, he warned him that 'popular institutions' had been established there. 'For good or evil they exist. I cannot agree with Lord Grey that it would be desirable, even if it were possible, to change them.'[20]

Newcastle had learned the case for responsible government from eminent teachers, among them his old friend Elgin. In February 1853 Elgin told him that responsible government was blocking the growth of republicanism in Canada by its manifest advantages over the 'elected, irresponsible Executives' across the border. Responsible government, Elgin wrote on another occasion, was keeping Canada loyal to the empire and on good terms with the mother country. The political troubles of the colony had become matters of local, rather than of imperial, concern; Elgin had been able to cut down 'the distrust of the intentions and designs of a British governor which previous occurrences had implanted'.[21]

The conclusions that Elgin drew from his experience of applying the policies of Lord Grey coincided well with what Newcastle was learning from another quarter. Newcastle's interests in the Canterbury Association in New Zealand and in the colonial reformers, who migrated there, gave him striking evidence of how free settlers capable of managing their own affairs resented control from home. Before the founding of Canterbury, few of the colonial reformers, perhaps only Durham and Charles Buller, had had any active convictions on responsible government. Wakefield's principles of systematic colonisation required strong imperial control from the centre rather than extensive local devolution. The experience of Canterbury showed some of the reformers how restrictive and irksome central control could be.

John Robert Godley, the driving spirit in the foundation of Canterbury, was a friend of Newcastle. A short stay in the colony taught him the evils of government from a distance. Control by the Canterbury Association in London was as vexatious as control by the Colonial Office. Godley complained to Adderley, a colonial reformer sitting in Parliament, that 'I see . . . fatally exemplified here all the evils of distant government, and I feel . . . strongly the impossibility of our making any decent stand against the Colonial Office till we have purged the beam from our own eye.'[22] Godley soon revolted against Wakefield's tyranny:

> One word about Wakefield's saying this is not [yet] a colony, and should therefore have its affairs managed for it at home. I should like to know how many hundred times I have heard him say, 'Numbers don't signify — the first ship's company is the colony. They should make laws for themselves on board ship . . .'. He cannot bear to have his theories applied to himself. He would make the most intolerable minister that ever lived in Downing-street.[23]

Newcastle knew Adderley well and would have been aware of these complaints. Late in 1852 the Canterbury settlers thanked him for his interest in refoming the government of New Zealand.[24] Godley returned to London in 1853 and wrote to Newcastle, 'Now that I have been a practical colonizer and have seen how these things are managed in fact, I often smile when I think of the ideal Canterbury of which our imagination dreamed.'[25]

When Newcastle decided policy towards the Australian constitutions, he had also the advice of Herman Merivale, Permanent Under-Secretary in the Colonial Office from 1847, who firmly believed in the new system. Before he entered the Colonial Office Merivale had written that:

> It does not follow as a necessary consequence that the attainment of domestic freedom is inconsistent with continued dependence on the imperial sovereignty . . . . Union might be preserved . . . long after the sense of necessary dependence is gone . . . . And the crown may remain, at last, in solitary supremacy, the only common authority recognised by many different legislatures, by many nations politically and socially distinct.[26]

Under Grey he had helped to extend responsible government in British North America. From 1852 onwards, as we shall see, he supported its introduction into the Australian colonies, and in 1854 he favoured it for New Zealand.[27] In 1860 he confidently praised the beneficial effects of responsible government in the great colonies of settlement: 'Old irritations between colony and the mother-country disappear and few traces are left in the public mind. Confidence in and affection for the home country supersede distrust and disloyalty . . . . Social progress, coinciding with . . . political change, may also be a result of it.'[28]

James Stephen also, who had become Regius Professor of Modern History at Cambridge,[29] was sure that New South Wales ought to be allowed 'to take over its own government'. New South Wales, he predicted, would become 'a British dependency in name, and an independent state in reality'. 'My old quarters at the Colonial Office', he whimsically added, 'will soon become useless and may be let out as a toy-shop or as a model lodging house.' New South Wales, endowed with gold and self-government, would forge ahead by attracting emigrants from Britain and manage its affairs with advantage to itself and to British manufacturers.[30]

Sir John Pakington, who succeeded Grey as Secretary of State, tried to settle policy towards the Australian constitutions in 1852. The legislative council of New South Wales had been greatly dissatisfied with the Australian Colonies Government Act of 1850, which had done little to remedy its grievances. The conservatives in the legislative council made it their business to change the constitution, as the Act permitted, so as to win an extensive control, independent of London and of the mass of the colonists, over the colony's domestic affairs.

On 15 January 1852 Governor-General FitzRoy forwarded to Pakington a petition from the legislative council.[31] It complained that only limited powers were entrusted to the local executive, while large powers were retained by the imperial authorities. It offered to assume the whole cost of the government of New South Wales (other than the governor-general's salary) and to grant a fixed civil list to the Crown, if in return Britain would repeal the Waste Lands Act, surrender to the colony 'the entire management of all . . . Revenues' and grant 'a Constitution . . . similar in its outlines to that of Canada'.

FitzRoy reported correctly that the petition was 'supported by the general and deliberate opinion of the most loyal, respectable, influential members of the community' – that is, the elected conservative members of the council and other persons of wealth and standing. The petition did not expressly ask for responsible government and FitzRoy believed that no request for it was implied in the reference to the constitution of Canada. 'Neither the Council or the public', he wrote, 'are anxious for Responsible Government to the extent that it now exists in Canada.' Most people, he thought, understood that New South Wales had neither parties nor sufficient men of independent means to become ministers if obliged to resign on losing the confidence of a fickle, elected legislature.

FitzRoy urged the Secretary of State to grant what the petition appeared to ask: a large transfer of power from London to Sydney and a reform of the constitution of the legislative council to give the colony a bicameral legislature. As in Canada, one house might be nominated and the other elected. Because the existing legislative council already had power, subject to the Queen in council, to establish a bicameral legislature, officials in London wondered whether responsible government might be the real object of the petition.[32] FitzRoy was probably right, however, in thinking the opposite. There had been no considerable demand for responsible government in New South Wales since 1849. He seems either to have ignored or been unimpressed by the incipient divisions of opinion among the colony's political leaders concerning the merits of bicameralism and the composition of the new upper house.

NEW SOUTH WALES VIEWS OF RESPONSIBLE GOVERNMENT, 1844–52

From 1843 or 1844 to 1849 there had been an intermittent demand in New South Wales for the 'Canadian system' of government, meaning, probably, some form of responsible government, not necessarily with a bicameral legislature.[33] Among the advocates of the 'system' was Wentworth, while he was fighting the battle of the elected members of the legislative council against unpopular policies on land, finance and economic development. Some conservatives supported him because they thought the precedent of Canada a proper one for a settled, free colony to follow.

Public support for the 'Canadian system' became strongest in 1849, in circumstances reminiscent of the assembly's attacks on the councils in Upper Canada. The urban middle classes, both liberal and conservative, complained of economic and political subordination to the powerful pastoralists, and, resenting attempts to resume the transportation of convicts, looked for constitutional change to give themselves a majority in the legislature and some control of the executive. The 'illiberal liberal', Robert Lowe, later Chancellor of the Exchequer under Gladstone, was then nearing the end of his New South Wales period and tried to speak for all those who had given up faith in old liberals like Wentworth. The former advocates of change, according to Lowe and his allies, had been interested in reform only 'when a grasping Executive were ruining the pastoral interests of the Colony by tyrannous exactions'.[34] John Lamb, a merchant, who spoke for the traders and businessmen of Sydney, complained that the commercial leaders of the colony were under-represented in a council dominated by pastoralists and officials. Charles Cowper, a devout churchman and adroit politician, interested in railways and development, strenuously attacked convictism as a great moral evil and wanted political power redistributed so that the popular will would prevail.

The liberals of the late 1840s wished for an executive that would be responsible to the legislature, provided, however, that they had a legislature with a reformed electoral franchise to give them power proportionate to their property, education and numbers. They wanted convict transportation ended for ever, because, so long as it continued, the pastoral domination of New South Wales could be maintained. Merchants, professional men, skilled tradesmen (and some small farmers) united in a common cause that had moral conviction and some important, if ill defined, economic objectives. They wanted the economy to be diversified so as to end the limitations of the domestic market and reduce dependence on the unstable export trade. Having watched the advance of responsible government in British North America, they expected that the new system, if adopted in New South Wales, would improve their position just as it appeared to have reduced the power of the entrenched ruling classes in North America. *The Sydney Morning Herald* on three occasions in 1849 outlined the working of responsible government in Canada and referred to its prospects in New South Wales.[35]

At the anti-transportation meeting held in Sydney on 18 June 1849, Lowe merged the two claims, against transportation and for responsible government.[36] Britain, he strangely remarked, would not dare to send convicts to Canada, Nova Scotia or New Brunswick, because those colonies had responsible government. Let New South Wales have responsible government, and transportation would be abandoned immediately; other-wise the colonists should remember the example of the Americans and unite against Britain. The meeting demanded that the colony's government should be in the hands of 'ministers chosen from and responsible to the colonists themselves in accordance with the principles of the British constitution'.

Although the young Henry Parkes, later many times premier of New South Wales, was radical enough to think of the meeting as 'the glorious

18th of June',[37] less excitable observers were perturbed by Lowe's appeal to stand ready to rebel. FitzRoy sent to the Colonial Office a confidential report in which the superintendent of police commented severely on those at the meeting.[38] Among liberals the meeting marked the brief high tide of enthusiasm for responsible government, and before long the tide ran out. Men who combined against transportation were alarmed by talk of rebellion. News of the Rebellion Losses Bill worried advocates of responsible government in New South Wales,[39] the more so because of the emergence in the colony late in 1848 of a small Constitutional Association seeking a liberal electoral franchise and other reforms. Led by Parkes, E. J. Hawksley and J. R. Wilshire, the second mayor of Sydney, it was partly inspired by Chartism and the revolutions of 1848.[40] Against such a background, responsible government suddenly seemed too 'democratic', too liable to place power in the hands of demagogues inciting the Sydney 'mob'. The practical difficulties of introducing responsible government into Nova Scotia suggested that the new system was full of trouble and expense.[41] In the newspapers there was some discussion of modified forms of responsible government that would allow the governor to retain greater powers in determining policy and choosing his advisers than were then exercised by the sovereign in Britain.[42] So great was the change of temper that Lowe (partly also because of Grey's legislative moves in England) did not proceed in the council with resolutions that he had proposed on responsible government.[43] The conservatives were glad, for they had come to fear that responsible government would inevitably produce democracy and republicanism.[44]

Throughout the rest of 1849 and 1850 the liberals were so heavily involved in the sharpened struggle to end convict transportation that the demands for responsible government were almost forgotten. Whatever Lowe might say, a grant of responsible government could not help the anti-transportation cause immediately. Swift political victory was needed and, to be decisive, it had to be won in Britain. Some liberal critics of transportation had become as fearful of democracy, political parties and social conflict as any conservative could be. George Allen, a solicitor and Methodist lay-preacher, thought that the colony was 'too small a community' and too politically immature for responsible government. 'We should very soon have anarchy and confusion'.[45] He wanted the highest offices of government to remain under orders from Downing Street 'for some years to come' and preferred a nominated to an elected upper house.

The conservatives, mostly on good terms with FitzRoy, had nothing to gain from responsible government as it existed in Canada. The memorial addressed to Lord Grey in February 1850 on the subject of the constitution did not ask for responsible government at all but did ask for a nominated upper house, to offset the growth of democracy and complicate political attempts to interfere with the executive government.[46] Wentworth's famous declaration of grievances, which was moved in the council in August 1850, did not ask for responsible government, because it would usher in 'pure democracy'.[47] The liberal *Maitland Mercury*, which supported responsible government, democracy and elected upper houses, explained why the foremost advocate of responsible government in 1844 opposed it in 1850. Six years before, the 'Sydney mob' had supported him and he had hoped to gain by advocating extension of the franchise and responsible government as measures to reduce the power of Britain in the colony. In 1850, when his policy towards transportation and his own economic interests had identified him with the conservatives, the 'mob' turned against him. He thereupon gave up his liberal protestations.[48] Allied as he was to the officials and the great landholders, he had less to gain than before from bringing the executive under the control of the legislature.[49] The *Mercury* did not note that, even in 1850, he may have been willing for some modified form of responsible government, to admit some elected members of a single blended legislative chamber to a share of executive power; he certainly then opposed responsible government in the sense of party government and collective responsibility.[50]

In the council a rising young attorney and journalist, James Martin, who had worked with Lowe on *The Atlas*, gave notice of amendments to Wentworth's motion.[51] He thought it 'the most intolerable grievance' of all, that 'the Executive Government is not responsible to the people's representatives as the Ministers of England are'. The proposed amendments embarrassed Wentworth, who tried to explain his own shift of attitude since 1844 by claiming that conditions had changed. If the amendments were adopted, Sydney (like Paris) would be ruled by the people. The colonial secretary, Deas Thomson, asserted what had become a widely held view in New South Wales, that responsible government had 'not been introduced with any advantage in any of the British possessions' and was incompatible with colonial status.[52]

The council was nearly empty when these statements were made. Martin withdrew his motion because of lack of support. The grievances that interested Wentworth and a majority of the council in 1850 were not the irresponsible executive but the continued imperial control of patronage, of lands and of lands revenue, the reserving of some appropriations from colonial scrutiny and the lack of 'plenary powers in all matters of domestic or municipal government'.

These were claims that most liberals inside and outside the council supported in principle, although unenthusiastically and with no sense of urgency, unless they themselves could control the legislature. Transportation still absorbed their energies. Less than three weeks after Martin withdrew his motion on responsible government, a meeting in the Old

Barrack Square, Sydney, on 16 September condemned the council for supporting transportation and Grey for persisting in a policy rejected by the public conscience of the colony.[53] Even after the council had resolved on 1 October that 'no more convicts ought, under any conditions, to be sent to any part of this colony', the rifts produced by the convict question continued to deepen and persist and turned political opinion away from responsible government.[54]

Responsible government did not find its way back into the council's favour during 1851. In April, when the Australian Colonies Government Act was considered, Wentworth had a select committee appointed to prepare a formal protest.[55] The declaration and remonstrance that the council adopted in May 1851 did not mention responsible government; its principal complaint was that New South Wales lacked full power over its own domestic affairs. Wentworth wanted the colony to have power of legislation free from imperial veto, to have exclusive power to raise and appropriate revenue, and to have an unrestricted power of patronage.[56] The resolutions were carried by eighteen votes to eight, for the conservatives and the liberals joined together against the officials and two of the nominees.

Outside the council, in December 1851, another public meeting in the cause of constitutional reform was convened. This meeting, organised by John Dunmore Lang, Wilshire and others sympathetic with Lowe's position on responsible government (Lowe himself had returned to England in January 1850), supported responsible government, an elected upper house and democratic reform of the electoral system.[57] Generally, in 1851, hostile comment on Wentworth's grievances resolution denounced them as mere showpieces, intended to persuade the public that the conservative leaders were really liberals at heart.[58] The critics misunderstood the conservative dilemma. Conservatives saw that the strength of the liberals was a useful asset in their arguments with Downing Street over the necessity of reform; but they saw also that the asset was dangerous to themselves in the colony, and they wished to keep it under the strictest control.

The conservatives still wanted both a large transfer of authority from London to Sydney and a further increase of their own power in the colony. The Electoral Act of 1851, which may have been the brainchild of James Macarthur,[59] had already distributed representation according to interests rather than population. Landed interests, whether pastoral or agricultural, had received a disproportionate share of political influence, so as to offset the political influence of Sydney, where liberals and radicals were thought to abound and the urban conservatives to be outnumbered. *The Sydney Morning Herald* pointed out that respectable merchants and professional men did not necessarily oppose the pastoralists, but wondered how urban conservatives could be distinguished electorally from liberals and radicals.[60] The legislative council was so safe for the conservatives that responsible government could scarcely have hurt them so long as the electoral franchise and distribution were not changed again. But how long would the Act remain unchanged? Some conservatives thought it too democratic, but it was widely criticised as a clever attempt to circumvent the liberal franchise provisions of the Act of 1850 and, perhaps, to prepare the way for more transportation and an extended monopoly of the land for the pastoralists.[61] Few conservatives, pastoral or urban, were willing to hazard responsible government. Their greatest fear was the growth of democracy, which would bring with it disaster and disorder. The extension of the franchise to the £10-householders in 1851 came to seem full of danger when the gold rushes increased the population and shifted the social foundations of the colony. The imminent rise of lower middle class groups with enough property to have votes alarmed men, even some liberals, who believed in government by an élite of men of property, education and standing. In this respect, the Crown officials, the conservatives and some liberals shared basic concepts of law and authority, which they were prepared to defend together. (FitzRoy significantly noted that Wentworth unnecessarily provoked the 'lower class of voters'.)[62]

One landholding conservative who did favour responsible government for the colony was Edward Hamilton of Liverpool Plains, whom Governor Gipps had thought of as a member of a proposed new imperial order for colonials.[63] As a nominee member of the legislative council from 1843 to 1846 and again in 1848–50, he had boldly supported the resumption of convict transportation for economic reasons and attacked Grey's failure in 1850 to give the colony control of its own civil list and lands revenue.[64] In 1851, exasperated by the 'tyranny' of the Colonial Office in imposing land and immigration policies contrary to the interests of New South Wales, he asked for responsible government as a guarantee that the internal affairs of the colony would be liberated from Downing Street. Britain had denied the colony the use of convict labour and of indentured workers from Asia and the Pacific, and had choked off, as it seemed, the flow of free labour. The Whigs had perverted England with their own nepotism and incompetence, enjoying the fruits of office while the colonies languished in discontent. New South Wales needed complete independence in managing its own internal affairs, and responsible government would be indispensable in order to ensure that the Colonial Office did not limit that independence. Hamilton saw more clearly than most of his contemporaries that, if New South Wales were really to exercise fully the additional powers of self-government that so many leading colonists sought, Downing Street influence would have to be extirpated. Only responsible government could ensure that a governor and the highest officials would not have orders from Downing Street to oppose the interests of the colonists. Hamilton was an exception among his class, a conservative who wanted a nominee, if not a hereditary, upper house, but was willing to try responsible government at once to help rid the colony of Downing Street control.[65]

In 1851 most political men in New South Wales clearly agreed that responsible government was not immediately appropriate to the colony, although it might possibly have to be expected in the long run. The petition on general grievances that the council adopted in December 1851 was founded on Wentworth's declaration and remonstrance and, as we have seen, did not ask for responsible government. The phrase 'a constitution similar in its outlines to that of Canada' did not mean responsible government, but bicameralism and increased powers of self-government, including control of patronage and plenary powers of legislation in all colonial matters. Since 1849 there had been no considered demand for responsible government. Bicameralism itself had had only intermittent attraction for the conservatives. Wentworth, it should be repeated, may not have given up hopes of making the blended council an effective legislature, with elected members exercising some degree of control over the executive, until the financial disputes of late 1851 suggested the desirability of separating nominated and elected members.[66]

The Colonial Office found FitzRoy's report of 1852 difficult to assess. Merivale suggested that the real grievance of the colonists was the imperial control of waste lands and their revenue. 'The rest is thrown in by way of makeweight.' But he supported responsible government for Australia, and inclined to the belief that the colonists were asking for it. Like Stephen, he thought it 'utterly vain to refuse' to the Australians what had been granted to the Canadians. If the colonists asked for responsible government, they should have it.[67]

Pakington, a mild Tory, appears to have accepted FitzRoy's reservations on responsible government. He concluded that the only reforms the colonists sought were those such as control of their revenues and the waste lands, and the establishment of a bicameral legislature as in Canada. He doubted Merivale's opinion that the request for a 'constitution among us similar in its outlines to that of Canada' might convey more than a wish for a bicameral legislature. In September 1852, while at Balmoral with the Queen, he cancelled a draft dispatch sent him by Merivale[68] that promised 'the fullest concessions consistent with the maintenance of the power and authority of the Crown and the interests of the Empire'. Merivale had come close to promising responsible government to New South Wales if the colonists wanted it, and to extending the concession to the other colonies. The dispatch that Pakington sent to FitzRoy on 1 October stated merely that the petition was being studied, and that a considered answer would follow.[69]

After consulting the Cabinet, Pakington himself drafted the well known dispatch of 15 December, which defended Grey's criticisms of most of the colony's complaints, but justified a revision of policy on the ground that the gold rushes had changed conditions in New South Wales and had shown that the colonists were capable of managing their own affairs.[70] The rapid progress of New South Wales made desirable an assimilation of its institutions to those of Britain. New South Wales was promised control of its own lands and territorial revenue and also the reforms of the civil list and the customs service that it had been seeking (some of them already made). In return for these concessions the Secretary of State required constitutional reforms that would distribute political power in the colony according to British ideas of just polity. The council should use its powers to make itself into a bicameral legislature. Pakington suggested, but did not (although colonial conservatives liked to think that he did) firmly require that the new upper house should be nominated by the Crown. He intended only that there should be some normal safeguard against sectional or hasty legislation by an elected assembly; an upper house would be the more necessary because of the increased powers transferred to the colony.[71] The Act of 1850 had not forbidden an elected upper house — the Cape Colony was soon to receive one, and Grey had wished New Zealand to have one also. Pakington did not refer to responsible government and changed Merivale's draft where it came close to mentioning it. He sent copies of the dispatch to the lieutenant-governors of Victoria and South Australia, wishing those colonies to be able to share any concessions made to New South Wales. Tasmania he excluded because of its convict problem, but promised that transportation to the island colony would cease.

Less than a fornight after Pakington's dispatch had been sent, Newcastle, who had become Secretary of State when Aberdeen formed his ministry, received embarrassing news from FitzRoy.[72] The legislative council would refuse supplies for 1854 unless a favourable reply were received to the petition for constitutional reform sent to England eleven months before. FitzRoy again stressed his considered opinion that the council and the colony as a whole strongly desired reform. The council, he wrote, already had a committee at work drafting a new constitution, in which an adequate civil list would be provided.

Newcastle doubted whether substantial reforms of the kind Pakington had had in mind could be necessary so soon after the Act of 1850, and distrusted nominee upper houses, but for the sake of peace decided not to write to Fitzroy on these subjects. He repeated Pakington's promises, assured the colonists that he would honour them, and cautiously described the new constitution that the council was drawing up as 'thought to be similar to that of Canada'. He hinted that the conditions suggested by Pakington might be ignored.[73]

Four days after Newcastle wrote, a confidential dispatch arrived from FitzRoy, to report that a select committee of the legislative council had drafted a new constitution.[74] FitzRoy commented that the committee had been divided on the composition of the upper house of the proposed new legislature. He himself objected to elective upper houses, as steps 'towards Republican Institutions', contrary to imperial precedent and bad in principle, and from experience he disliked blended chambers. For the sake of keeping one house remote from popular pressures, he hoped that the new upper house would be nominated by the Crown. Newcastle, disliking nominee upper houses, found the dispatch unwelcome, but accepted Merivale's advice to send a mere acknowledgement. The legislative council, Merivale wisely thought, would have amended the draft constitution before any advice from London could reach Sydney.[75]

In fact the legislative council was slow to consider the report of its own select committee. In December 1852 it resolved that, 'in consideration of the thinness of the House and the advanced period of the session', the second reading of the Constitution Bill be postponed into the next session.[76] The Council agreed unanimously. Wentworth and Darvall, the leading liberal, both wanted the Bill deferred, Wentworth because the nominees might not vote for the large transfer of power from London to Sydney that he sought, Darvall for fear that the council would support a nominated upper house.

When FitzRoy reported to Newcastle, he at last brought himself to comment on responsible government, which had been referred to quite extensively in the report of the select committee: 'There is no desire among the thinking portion of the community that the system of Self-Government should be carried out to the extent that it is in Canada; . . . I have . . . little doubt that . . . the Council will confirm this opinion.' FitzRoy made this forthright judgement although the committee had formally recommended responsible government: 'The advantages which this colony will derive from the new Constitution are those which must necessarily follow in the train of responsible government, which it is meant to introduce.' The committee had referred approvingly to the dispatch written to Grey on 21 October 1849 by Harvey, the lieutenant-governor of Nova Scotia, extolling some virtues of responsible government.[77] Although the committee did not, either expressly or implicitly, request full responsible government (what FitzRoy called self-government carried to the same lengths as in Canada), it had clearly demanded a limited form of responsible government. The draft constitution provided that some government officials might be elected to the assembly, and established pensions for existing officials who had to retire 'on political grounds'.[78] These provisions made possible, but did not require, individual responsibility of some officials to the assembly. The power of the elected members over official policy would have been increased under this system, because the censure of even one 'minister' would have greatly embarrassed the governor-general. Some heads of departments would have become colonial ministers instead of imperial officials. There would have been little prospect of party government, because the colony had no parties and because the select committee intended some officials to sit in the nominated upper house, secure from the displeasure of the elected members. Responsible government had apparently found its way back into the favour of some of the conservatives on the council, as part of their plan to gain control of all colonial affairs and as an expression of their distrust of the imperial authorities, who had delayed the reforms that the council sought.[79]

When the draft constitution of 1852 (and the new draft prepared in 1853) were discussed in the colony, no politician of standing asked for full responsible government on the Canadian model. The characteristic features of responsible (or party) government as it existed in British North America were that the governor did not choose his advisers (although nominally he appointed them), that they made up a ministry whose advice he normally . took on all colonial matters, and that ministries usually held power only while they were supported collectively by a majority of the elected house of the legislature.

Party government, parties and collective responsibility of ministries were none of them desired by the political leaders of New South Wales in 1852 or 1853. Among the conservatives who were entrenched in power the weightiest judgements still rejected party government as a product of democracy and impracticable in the political circumstances of the colony. James Macarthur told the legislative council during the debates on the 1853 constitution that New South Wales could not have 'two parties of the "ins and the outs" as in England . . . for years'. He predicted a form of responsible government based on individual responsibility without parties:

> The way in which responsible government will be introduced will be this — while the entire government will not be broken up, unless on some extraordinary occasion, no government will be able to stand which does not call into its ranks the active business talent of both houses . . . [to] imagine that the colonial parliament could suddenly, and at once, jump into two great contending parties, is absurd.[80]

Some of the little effective opposition to the conservatives on the council and the two constitutions that they drafted came from an unofficial body of assorted liberals, the New South Wales Constitution Committee, set up late in July 1853.[81] Its leaders included G. K. Holden, a Sydney solicitor, who supported only a modified form of responsible government and gave it a low priority among his constitutional demands, and Parkes, who may have wanted full responsible government. The committee was more interested in the composition of the new upper house than in responsible government and eventually asked for two elected chambers. Responsible government was supported only unenthusiastically.[82] In the legislative council Darvall, rapidly becoming prominent both on the committee and off it, thought that responsible government would have to be limited to something considerably short of Canadian-style party government. *The Sydney Morning Herald* also thought that responsible government as in Canada was not immediately possible.[83]

The little public discussion of the new constitution was polarised by the manoeuvres of the conservatives on the council and concentrated on the tactics of Wentworth and his allies, whose interest in power for themselves was glaringly apparent.[84] The new constitutions were attacked for preferring pastoral to mercantile interests, for giving the squatters a chance to monopolise lands and for obstructing democracy. But constitutional reform could not absorb much popular interest after gold had kindled hopes of quick wealth, and most people cared more for quick returns than for forms of government. Responsible government passed almost without notice — a vague, unknown system that liberals and radicals were prepared to ignore, because it seemed so remote and improbable. In contrast, electoral franchises and electoral distributions carefully devised to favour entrenched conservatives were clear, present dangers that men might oppose actively, even when preoccupied with the distractions of the gold era.

Contemporary comment attributed the 1853 report and Constitution Bill to Wentworth, and posterity has endorsed the verdict although there is no conclusive evidence for it. Wentworth certainly played the foremost role, as chairman of the select committee, and led the debates in the legislative council. Deas Thomson, James Macarthur and the attorney-general, J. H. Plunkett, were, however, also active on the committee and none of them was negligible or bound to Wentworth's leadership. Of the four dominant members of the committee, only Wentworth himself was a spokesman for the squatters; Macarthur was a great pastoralist but his land interests were not those of the squatters and he had regretted Grey's change of policy towards the squatters in 1847; Deas Thomson and Plunkett were both officials. Macarthur had more experience of constitution making than Wentworth had. Relations between Macarthur and Deas Thomson were more intimate than were the relations between either of them and Wentworth.

It is certain that the conservatives dominated the proceedings of the committee. They were the most regular attenders at its thirteen meetings, while the liberals had a poor record:[85]

W. C. Wentworth	13	J. Martin	7
E. Deas Thomson	12	C. Cowper	7
H. G. Douglass	12	G. McLeay	6
J. Macarthur	9	T. A. Murray	3
J. H. Plunkett	9	W. Thurlow	3

Douglass, a surgeon and philanthropist, was a friend of Wentworth. The radical *Empire* remarked that 'the Colonial Secretary, Mr. Wentworth and Dr. Douglass have been permitted by the negligence of the other members to be the chief actors in this despicable performance'. On reflection, a week later, the *Empire* suspected that Macarthur, who disliked public appearances, might have been more influential in the committee's deliberations than appeared.[86]

The only liberals on the committee were Cowper and William Thurlow, a Sydney solicitor. Cowper later described his own role on the committee as thoroughly painful. Before the third reading of the Bill, in December, he declared that he could oppose it no longer, although he had just written to Parkes on the importance of continued resistance. 'He had made suggestions in Committee and in the Council by the adoption of which . . . the Bill might have been rendered more palatable to the people . . . but they had been all made in vain . . . his only course was to wash his hands of any responsibility that might attend the measure.'[87]

NEWCASTLE AND RESPONSIBLE GOVERNMENT

FitzRoy's dispatch of 1 January 1853 requested the Secretary of State to give his own views on the New South Wales constitution. Newcastle decided not to answer immediately, because FitzRoy, when he wrote, had received neither Pakington's dispatch of 15 December nor his own promises of 18 January. While he awaited information from New South Wales, he continued to learn the advantages of responsible government from Elgin, and the Canterbury Association continued to ask for complete self-government in all local matters. Lowe had become a junior colleague of Newcastle in the Aberdeen ministry, and made his opinions known to his friend at the head of the Colonial Office. So did Newcastle's cousin (and FitzRoy's), G. C. Mundy, who had been in New South Wales as deputy adjutant-general, and apparently took a liberal conservative view, agreeable to his colonial friends. John Dunmore Lang, who was in England, wrote to Newcastle warning him against conservative manoeuvres in drafting the constitution.[88]

In the Office, Merivale had come to believe that it would be positively unwise to change the Australian constitutions without introducing full responsible government. He had been persuaded of the fundamental stability of the colony when he saw how successfully it coped with the political and social problems of the gold rushes. Increasingly he handled New South Wales business on the assumption that the colony would soon have a large increase of self-government. The social stratification, which he thought of as a survival of the convict system, probably appeared to him in 1853 as yet another factor ensuring that New South Wales would, if responsible government were granted, be well governed by educated, prosperous landholders and not handed over to the perils of democracy. Merivale was more inclined to wonder that New South Wales was so slow in settling its new constitution than to doubt whether it were ready for responsible government.[89]

In 1853 Newcastle and Merivale had to consider several constitutional problems that set them thinking about the place of responsible government in British imperial policy and the conditions required for its successful introduction into a colony. The affairs of the Cape Colony, Jamaica and Newfoundland may all have helped persuade Newcastle that he ought to intervene, as he ultimately did, to ensure that the new constitutions provided for the introduction of responsible government into the Australian colonies.

The problem of the Cape constitution had been referred by Grey in 1849 to the Privy Council Committee for Trade and Plantations. William Porter, the attorney-general of the colony, had asked whether responsible government would be granted. Grey's answer was given in the committee's report: 'What had been termed "responsible" but what would more correctly be described as "parliamentary or party" government' was not suited to the Cape. The problems of distance and of a strong separatist movement in the Eastern Province, the divisions of Boers, British and indigenous peoples, and the constant threat of frontier wars were all powerful indications against granting a reform for which only a minority of the English liberals at the Cape had ever asked. The most difficult problems of the colony, such as frontiers and relations with the Africans, had all to be settled in London: the colony did not command resources to deal with them. Responsible government that would give power in the colony to a minority incapable of handling imperial problems imperially was inadmissible.[90]

The new Kaffir War, which laid Grey's Cape policy in ruins and made South Africa the 'graveyard of his reputation', delayed his reform of the constitution. When Newcastle became Secretary of State he hastily completed the Cape of Good Hope Ordinance, which gave the Cape, with only a few modifications, the constitution that Grey had designed.[91] The Cape received representative institutions, but not responsible government. Both houses of the new legislature were elective, an important departure in imperial policy, and one that Grey had particularly desired; the innovation reflected British despair at the record of nominated legislative councils in North America and also recognition of the peculiar social conditions at the Cape. The franchise for both houses was colour-blind: property qualifications alone made the houses of parliament closed preserves for the whites. A section of the liberals at the Cape continued until the late 1850s to demand responsible government, but they were defeated by conservatives and by the objections of those living in the frontier provinces, to whom responsible government seemed too cumbersome and too slow for military emergencies.

Newcastle was responsible only at law for the decision, which was really Grey's, not to grant responsible government to the Cape in 1853. In the case of Jamaica, however, he, rather than Grey, formulated policy and took the principal decisions. In 1852 the troubled political situation of Jamaica was deteriorating rapidly, for the era of good feelings under Metcalfe and Elgin had ended.[92] Law and order were at the mercy of an assembly that had become increasingly arrogant, irresponsible and quarrelsome. Clashing with the council, it had seized many executive powers. It had also monopolised control of the colony's finances with disastrous results to Jamaica. The emancipation of the slaves, followed by the coming of free trade, declining prosperity and growing social disorders, produced savage despair and a crisis of labour and finance. In 1848 and 1849 Grey had seriously considered whether a grant of responsible government, as suggested by the governor, Sir Charles Grey, who had been a member of the Gosford Commission to Canada, might improve the methods and temper of the assembly. He had long been worried by the ignorance, selfishness and racial animosities of the colonial politicians. Sir Charles, perplexed by bitter quarrels over salaries, import duties and taxes, hoped that responsible ministries might reduce the force of political collisions. Lord Grey thought that responsible government could not possibly increase the already bloated powers of the assembly, but it might make it more responsibly minded. Nothing came of the idea, which the assembly would not support.[93]

The introduction of responsible government into Jamaica would have been a desperate expedient that could not have been reconciled either with Grey's general principles or with his policy at the Cape. He had already concluded that there was no satisfactory halting place between Crown colony government and responsible government, at least for a colony with such a population as Jamaica's, where politics were poisoned by colour, class, indebtedness and the *damnosa hereditas* of slavery. He had become more disposed to praise the constitutions of the old representative system, in which the legislative and executive councils were the same body, than to transfer the government of Jamaica to a ministry drawn from the assembly, and would not agree with Russell's sweeping propositions that 'those who can lead the majority should hold the chief offices' and that 'responsible government must be established in at least all our larger colonies'.[94]

In 1851, when arrangements to assist the West Indian sugar islands with supplies of coolie labour were being considered, Grey wanted, as a condition of financial assistance to the islands, to limit the powers of the Jamaica assembly by requiring, according to ordinary British practice, that money Bills be proposed only with the consent of the government. The council was to be made a purely legislative body and executive powers were to be transferred to 'an executive committee or cabinet'. The assembly sullenly opposed the plan. Grey himself doubted whether it would work well and events in the colonies soon swept it out of men's minds except as one more indication that the relations of the assembly and the council needed reform.[95]

Soon after taking office, Newcastle found his hand forced by a new financial and constitutional crisis in Jamaica. Barkly, who had succeeded Charles Grey as governor, had done well with similar problems in British Guiana. Newcastle's new policy for Jamaica, based on propositions from Henry Taylor, was to link constitutional reforms with a British guarantee of the whole island's debts, except that owing to Great Britain. Barkly was to set up an executive committee with one or more spokesmen in the assembly and to obtain reform of the civil list, together with a guarantee that the Crown alone could institute money votes. Newcastle would permit only a distant approximation to responsible government in the colony for some time to come, although confident that responsible government would ultimately be granted. Grey and Derby both supported Newcastle's policy, making it a non-party matter.[96]

Barkly, the son of a West India merchant in London, was a good choice for Jamaica. Adroit, tactful and armed with the offer of a loan of £500,000 at low interest, he eventually produced a workable solution. A committee of the assembly reported that responsible government was 'neither required nor practicable in Jamaica'. By its own Reform Act of 1854 (16 and 17 Vict., c. 29) the colony acquired separate executive and legislative councils in addition to the elected assembly. Only the Crown might initiate money votes; the Act included a small civil list. To the privy council, which served as the governor's principal adviser, there was added an executive committee, consisting of the governor, one member of the legislative council and three members of the assembly. The powers and authority of the committee were not those of a ministry under responsible government, for its members owed their duty to the governor alone and he could disregard their advice. In practice, however, a governor might be induced to remove members of the committee who had lost confidence in the assembly, but he was not bound to do so. Taylor advised Newcastle to accept the Reform Act as sufficient compliance with British policy, and a Loan Guarantee Act was passed immediately.[97]

Jamaica neither sought nor received responsible government. Merivale thought that the obstacle to liberal reform was 'the old story of constitutional government without party and without patronage whereby to consolidate a party'.[98] In 1860, when Governor Sir Charles Darling asked the members of the executive committee to declare that the Reform Act had introduced responsible government into Jamaica, they resigned rather than do so. Six years later Jamaica, after the bloody crisis of Morant

Bay, retreated from representative government and became a Crown colony.[99]

If the violent, decaying society of Jamaica was the case in which responsible government could not be granted, Newfoundland was the case in which it could not be refused. From 1848 Newfoundland had an assembly and a legislative council, which was also the executive council. Partly because of the dissatisfaction of the numerous body of Roman Catholics with their treatment by the government and by the legislature, and partly because of the example of the other colonies of British North America, Newfoundland developed its own demand for responsible government.[100] In 1845 the legislature decided that new holders of offices that would be deemed political in the neighbouring colonies should be warned that their tenure was liable to change. Grey approved this decision, but would not yield to an address from the assembly in 1851 asking for responsible government.[101] The address had been carried by a thin house at the end of a fatiguing session and was opposed by the governor, Gaspard Le Marchant, and many professional and business men. Grey and Le Marchant agreed that Newfoundland had shown no clear desire for responsible government and that the colony still lacked the social structure, the political cohesiveness and a large enough assembly (then possessing only fifteen members) for responsible government, in which parties or political groups, not sectarian rivals, would compete for power, control the civil service, govern in the interests of the whole community, and retire from office (without ruin to themselves) when defeated. Pakington thought likewise. So did the Newfoundland merchants and professional men, mainly Protestants, though the Roman Catholics, who comprised the majority of the permanent residents, did not.[102]

Elections in 1852 again returned a majority of liberals, pledged to seek responsible government and also reciprocal free trade with the United States. The new governor, Ker Baillie Hamilton, a soldier of limited political experience, opposed both. The assembly sent two representatives to Newcastle in 1853, pleading for responsible government and other reforms. Philip Francis Little was a Roman Catholic lawyer, with experience in Prince Edward Island, to which responsible government had been granted in 1851. Robert John Parsons was an active politician, especially interested in the commercial and fishing rights of the colony. Hume introduced them to Newcastle, and they tried to persuade him that Grey and Pakington had been misled about political conditions in the island by the clique controlling trade and government: this group had always exaggerated sectarian strife and political instability so as to delay reform. Little and Parsons urged Newcastle to act on the principle, laid down by Grey in 1849, that the government of a North American colony should and could not be carried on contrary to the wishes of its inhabitants.[103]

Newcastle was aware that Hamilton opposed the granting of responsible government to Newfoundland, lest the new system put power into the hands of class-conscious Roman Catholics, who would be at loggerheads with the Protestant élite. At his first interview with the delegates he declared that colonies fit for responsible government ought to have it 'wherever practicable',[104] but questioned whether Newfoundland, due to its lack of people qualified to be ministers, the strength of its internal conflicts, and the inadequate political experience of the colonists there, were qualified for it. By the time that the delegates left England, however, they had the support of many members of Parliament, including Hume and John Bright, and were fairly confident that Newcastle and also Frederick Peel, the Parliamentary Under-Secretary, were swinging to their side.

In late July and early August 1853 Newcastle had the Newfoundland problem as much in mind as larger concerns, especially of foreign policy, permitted. He did not find it easy to decide whether a small colony, with a population of only 120,000 and troubled by sectarian strife, high turnover of population among the propertied classes, and uncertain prosperity, would be able to work responsible government efficiently. No one could have been encouraged by the consequences of Grey's concession of the reform to Prince Edward Island, where the population was only 65,000. Turmoil, maladministration and angry complaints to the Colonial Office would be the penalty of deciding wrongly either way.[105] Late in January 1854 Newcastle decided to separate the executive from the legislative council in Newfoundland and to grant responsible government on conditions suggested by the Protestants and including doubling the size of the assembly (by dividing large electoral districts) and guaranteeing pensions for displaced officials: 'It is perhaps about the severest trial to which "responsible government" can be exposed. But the circumstances which militated against its adoption are not those which have hitherto been assigned by any Secretary of State or could with propriety be brought forward in a despatch — the unhappy antagonism and nearly equal power of two religious Creeds.' Newcastle's conditions were not met for some time, partly because of Hamilton's tactlessness and opposition. Responsible government did not begin in Newfoundland until 1855.[106]

While he had the problem of Newfoundland before him, Newcastle had to remember that the Australian colonies were drawing up new constitutions. All of them had shown some interest in responsible government. If granted to Prince Edward Island and Newfoundland, how could it be refused to New South Wales or Victoria, or, possibly, South Australia and Tasmania? If the Australian colonists were not already asking officially for full responsible government, they assuredly would do so before long.

The wise course was to prevent trouble by making the concession at once. But there was no certainty that even New South Wales, which had shown more interest in responsible government than the other colonies had done, would provide for the system adequately in its new constitution. FitzRoy had reported more than once that the colonists neither sought nor needed more than a limited form of responsible government. Newcastle decided to intervene to ensure that the new constitution provided for responsible government effectively and according to experience in British North America. The decision to shape events in Australia is to be attributed partly to his great difficulties with constitutional problems in other parts of the empire, especially Newfoundland, which reinforced influences already exerted upon him by Elgin, Merivale, Lowe and the Canterbury Association. He was certainly not responding to any Australian agitation for full responsible government for none then existed.

On 4 August 1853 Newcastle sent a private dispatch to FitzRoy, and to the lieutenant-governors of South Australia, Victoria and Tasmania, instructing them that the new constitutions must provide for the coming of responsible government.[107] Merivale explained a year later to a new Secretary of State, Sir George Grey, that Newcastle had 'addressed the Australian Governors confidentially to prepare them for the establishment of responsible government as a probable consequence of the new constitutions'.[108]

Newcastle had perceived some truths that had eluded the shrewd FitzRoy. Whatever 'the most thoughtful' inhabitants of the colony might think, there had, some years before, been many demands for some form of responsible government. The colonial conservatives who wanted power transferred from London to Sydney also wanted responsible government, but only just enough of it to bring the principal officials and finance under colonial control. Sooner or later, in both Britain and the colony, it would be politically inconceivable to introduce a new constitution into a 'British community' that was a 'large colony' overseas (Russell's two tests for responsible government) without providing the accepted form of government in British North America. If most of the Australian colonies were to have new constitutions giving them larger powers of self-government, and to receive full control of the waste lands, revenues and patronage, responsible government was almost a necessary concomitant of other constitutional changes.

Newcastle was sure of his ground and wrote confidently to FitzRoy, in terms of the long tradition of British colonial policy, that political privileges could not be withheld from men to whom 'the maxims now prevalent in British domestic policy afford so strong a right to claim them': 'While public expectation is as yet but little excited on the subject of Responsible Government, . . . we should prepare ourselves to regard its introduction as a change which cannot be long delayed, and for which the way should be smoothed as far as possible by the removal of unnecessary impediments.' The new constitutions should, for example, establish pensions for all officers who would have to retire on political grounds, so that, in future, ministers sitting in the legislature would be the heads of the departments. The report of the 1852 select committee on the constitution had provided pensions for an unstated number of officials who would be 'liable to removal' under the new constitution, but not to their successors. FitzRoy had sent a message to the legislative council on 29 September 1852 stating that he did not know 'what officers it is contemplated should be liable to removal' and that he could not assess whether the provision of £4250 per annum would be adequate.[109] Newcastle required specific and proper provision for officers who would be removed on political grounds from appointments that they had been permitted to regard as theirs for life. He asked the Australians to learn on this point from painful experiences in British North America.

He required also that the new legislatures should be bicameral, because he believed that responsible government would not work with the blended legislatures (in which the heads of departments sat as nominees) that then existed in Australia, nor with any other sort of unicameral legislature. He did not require that the upper houses of the new legislatures be nominated. He was already well aware of the risk, much mentioned in confidential discussions of responsible government in Canada, that ministers controlling the lower elected house would pack the upper nominated house with their own supporters.[110]

FitzRoy received this instructive dispatch on 17 November 1853 by the ship *Vimeirio* and acknowledged it on the same day. Fortunately for him, the new constitution drafted in 1853 by a select committee of the legislative council had again provided for a form of responsible government.[111] He wrote to Newcastle as if responsible government (he did not say what kind) had always been taken for granted as a necessary part of the new constitution, and did not explain why, only ten months before, he had reported that responsible government was not really desired by the 'thinking portion of the community' and that the legislative council was unlikely to approve it.

FitzRoy's comment that the new constitution provided for responsible government was correct, but, as we have seen, short of the whole truth. He intended no deception and enclosed a copy of the draft Bill. He did not point out that the select committee had probably thought of responsible government according to Macarthur's restricted formula of the individual responsibility to the legislature of a few specified officials, who might, in the first instance, be the existing office holders, sitting as elected members in the assembly or as nominees in the council.[112] Collective responsibility had been excluded because it implied party government, which would soon throw out the existing officials and would be halfway to democracy, whose seeds the committee had 'no wish to sow'. Individual responsibility had been included in order to make the colony's leading officials answerable in some degree to the legislature, and so assist a substantial transfer of legislative and executive power from London to Sydney. Probably the difference between the two forms of responsible government eluded FitzRoy. As late as 14 December 1853 he seems to have thought responsible government compatible with election to the assembly of some officials, who would not be liable to removal on political grounds.[113]

THE COLONIAL CONSERVATIVES AND THEIR CONSTITUTION

Whose advice FitzRoy took in answering Newcastle is not known, and no record of how he drafted his dispatch has been found. He did not disclose what Newcastle had written until the council went into committee on the Bill. Newcastle's strong preference for an elected upper house was likely to embarrass the constitution makers in getting their Bill through the council and was personally difficult to FitzRoy because he had only recently sent home his own arguments for a nominee chamber.[114]

When the council did learn of Newcastle's dispatch, the Bill was soon amended to make full responsible government possible. There is no proof, only great probability, that the amendment was made to reconcile him to a measure some of the most vital parts of which he was certain to dislike. Whether prompted by Lowe or not, he would oppose the nominee upper house, distrust the attempts of the landholding conservatives to perpetuate their own power, and resist the provisions aimed at limiting British authority in the colony. To yield what Newcastle asked on responsible government was not a great concession for the conservatives to make: none of them thought party government really possible for some years to come; all of them believed in the efficacy of the elaborate safeguards against constitutional change that had been drafted into the Bill; and no one denied that responsible government was a British institution.

Clause XIX of the draft Constitution Bill listed ten government officials who were to be eligible for election to the legislature and might be regarded as a ministry. Clause LIX provided pensions for only the five most important officials — the colonial secretary, colonial treasurer, auditor-general, attorney-general and solicitor-general — who were all declared liable to retire on political grounds. The five other officials who might be in the legislature had no pensions provided and would have been in a strange situation. Perhaps they would have been mere 'placemen', supporting the government by speaking and voting, possibly against their own convictions, possibly at the risk of losing either their seats by defeat at elections or their posts by dismissal. Probably Clauses XIX and LIX together were intended to embody the plan of merely individual responsibility to the legislature on the part of members of the executive (that was the sense in which the clauses were originally debated in the council). So long as there was no collective responsibility, no member of the executive, pensionable or not, would formally have been compelled to retire unless singled out for a vote of censure; but all would have been under colonial rather than imperial control. Possibly the unpensioned members would have been politically too unimportant to run much risk of earning personal condemnation. Some contemporary comment, including speeches by Wentworth, suggests that the distinction between pensionable officials and non-pensionable officials was based on the unwritten rule of regarding those officials who already sat in both the legislative and executive councils as more answerable for government policy than those who merely sat in the legislature.[115]

It was not until 20 December 1853, when the draft constitution was before the council, that, on the motion of the solicitor-general, Clause XIX was amended, to remove the five unpensioned officials from the legislature altogether.[116] This vital change, which ensured that every official sitting in the assembly depended both on election and on the support of the house, took place in the course of a debate that effectively saw the end of every scheme of individual responsibility as an alternative to collective responsibility. No one could say how long parties might take to emerge[117] and there is evidence that the conservatives expected full responsible government to be slow in coming. The council accepted Wentworth's amendment that not more than one-seventh of the new nominated legislative council should be officials, although both the colonial secretary and the attorney-general saw that a long period of limited responsible government might be implied by the restriction. Wentworth was able to resist liberal attempts to require that the nomination of the new upper house should be deferred until the first assembly had been elected — at which time, presumably, the governor-general would have obtained some advisers from among the new elected members. In effect, the governor-general was left to nominate the new council on five-year terms with such advice as he might get from the existing executive council.[118] The report and papers transmitted to London with the Bill were silent on the change that would be needed in the governor's instructions in order to introduce responsible government, although one of the council's resolutions included a requirement that patronage be exercised in future on the advice of the executive council.[119]

Even with all these reservations, the amendment of Clause XIX was obviously of the highest importance, because, taken in conjunction with the clear change of attitude towards collective responsibility, it did remove, so far as the council could, every obstacle to full responsible government in New South Wales. The remaining steps, to ratify the Bill and issue appropriate instructions to the governor-general, had both to be taken in London.

One reason why so important a change was made in the draft constitution is to be found in the debates themselves. Wentworth, Deas Thomson, Douglass and others all seem to have been impelled — partly by reasoned and historical objections to 'placemen', and by practical and constitutional objections to a large 'ministry' of varying degrees of political responsibility — to give up the notion of individual responsibility.[120] This is not to say that any of the officials or the conservatives experienced a great change of mind on the subject, for they still thought party government unlikely and expected many of the existing officials to continue in office, whether as elected members of the assembly or nominated members of the new council.

There were also, however, other and no less significant reasons why the council changed its mind on responsible government. The conservatives abandoned their objections to party government and collective responsibility partly in the hope that, by so doing, they would be safeguarding those aspects of the constitution that they most prized. The main purpose of their manoeuvres in constitution making had been to transfer large powers from Britain to the colony and to concentrate power there in the hands of men like themselves — educated, propertied and public-spirited. Elaborate clauses distinguished between imperial and colonial matters, so as to withdraw the latter from British supervision and almost merit Frederic Rogers's description 'little less than a legislative Declaration of Independence'.[121] The constitution committee asked for full powers over all the internal affairs of the colony. It also wished the Crown to surrender its power of veto over colonial Bills that were limited to colonial matters and sought to prevent further changes of the colony's boundaries without the consent of its legislature.

No less elaborate were the clauses designed to preserve conservative ascendancy within the colony. At one stage the committee had favoured 'a scheme for creating an hereditary upper House which was much disapproved out of doors'. Public ridicule and the knowledge that Newcastle was firmly against the proposal forced the committee to abandon a project that had been suggested to it by the Canada Act of 1791.[122] But the committee, supported by the governor-general, recommended that the upper house should be nominated by the Crown, the first house for five years, later nominations for life. A nominee upper house was preferred partly because it seemed more British than an elected upper house and was an easy transition from the old blended council. Another, no less important, reason for preferring a nominated to an elected upper house was recollection of what had happened in England in 1832. An upper house that could be 'swamped', just as the House of Lords had nearly been swamped by the creation of more peers, was a safer, more flexible safeguard of conservatism than one that was elected and might be in deadlock with the elected lower house. The electoral system provided for in the constitution avowedly favoured property and interests at the expense of population. Electoral divisions and apportionment of representatives were not to be changed without the approval of two-thirds of the assembly and an absolute majority of the council. Amendments to the constitution required two-thirds majorities in both houses.[123]

Throughout the second half of 1853 angry critics up and down the colony hammered home the charges that the constitution was less liberal than most colonists desired and that it was a conspiracy to entrench conservatives and officials in power for ever.[124] If the legislative council approved the draft constitution, the objectors intended to ask the Colonial Office and Parliament not to give it the force of law.

The conservatives contemplated the colony's predicament (as they thought it) with considerable chagrin. Sir Charles Nicholson, the landowner, physician and scholar, who was speaker of the legislative council, wrote to Macarthur in April 1853 that political and social changes might make the colony a place where no 'man with English feelings will wish to make his permanent home'.[125] How could the colony be saved? No prominent conservative trusted the Colonial Office. As G. W. Rusden (a conservative historian) wrote thirty years later:

> The work of England had been one-sided. She had nurtured only the democratic principle in her colonies. It was nought to English statesmen, excepting Pitt and a few others, that the aristocracy of England was for her sons the priceless heritage which Stephen Langton enshrined in the Great Charter. . . . No class analogous [to the English gentry] was created or encouraged in the colonies except by Pitt in framing a Constitution for Quebec.[126]

British governments, remembering the fate of the Canada Act and the direction of political change at home, had leaned towards democracy and the political power of mere numbers in the colonies, and had not fostered colonial counterparts of the governing classes at home.

Nicholson and Macarthur specially feared the jealous suspicion with which Grey, still active in the Lords, would watch any attempt by the conservatives to make themselves a governing clique. Macarthur and Nicholson wanted an ordered, hierarchical society in New South Wales; Grey and Newcastle both thought that no Secretary of State should protect one section of colonists in dominating the rest (as had occurred in the Canadas). From the standpoint of Nicholson and Macarthur, conscious of their own good intentions, superior education and great local knowledge, the too-evident disposition of the Colonial Office to hold the scales of justice between competing factions was ill informed, dangerously liberal, and subversive of every reasoned attempt to reproduce British society and politics in Australia. Nicholson was sure that Grey in particular had followed policies that would 'republicanise and democratise the country' by abandoning in New South Wales the essential principles of the British constitution.[127]

The second great difficulty facing the conservatives was in New South Wales itself. The clamour for a new constitution was not great, but it was too strong to ignore. The conservatives knew they must draw up their new scheme of government while their own power remained great, and make a lasting settlement that would obviate 'the necessity of constantly manufacturing new Constitutions'. But what settlement could be made? Social conditions were changing rapidly and British precedents were remote from the colonial gold rush period. Wentworth, whom Nicholson and Macarthur still regarded as outside their own social class, was politically the front man for the conservatives, but he was also 'as vacillating ... as any one' in deciding how to shape the new form of government.[128]

Neither Nicholson nor Macarthur wished the proposed new assembly to have full control over the executive; limited responsible government would be enough to make the great officials answerable to them and not to London. Like Wentworth they thought first of how to balance a popular assembly with a sensible, educated, property-owning upper class sitting in the dignity of a new nominated legislative council. Nicholson preferred a nominated upper house, because it was nearer to English precedents than an elected house could ever be, but he admitted the merits of one of Wentworth's suggestions, that only men who had been elected to the assembly (or the old legislative council) might be nominated to the new council. Wentworth's proposal, he thought, would pacify the objectors, while still preserving the colonial house of lords from the follies of youth, the irresponsibility of men without a stake in the land or without satisfactory education, and the dangers of relying on political tyros.

Fortunately, from the conservatives' point of view, the objectors were neither so firm nor so united as Nicholson and Macarthur feared. They were strong in criticism and weak in construction. The colony's leading firebrand, John Dunmore Lang, had been overseas throughout most of the discussions on the new constitution. When he returned to New South Wales late in 1853, Sir John Robertson, a liberal, reforming landowner, who had served on the constitution committee, told him of 'the puny, if not contemptible' agitation against 'Wentworth's New Constitution Bill'.[129] Robertson would have challenged the conservatives on their two basic assumptions. He denied that the constitution of the colony ought necessarily to reproduce the institutions of the mother country; he denied further that the British constitution possessed, even in Britain, the great merits with which it was usually credited. The select committee ought to have looked to any country for institutions that might 'tend to the establishment of civil and religious liberty, equal laws for all sects, and the welfare of the people, giving no man preference or privilege in the state other than his capacity and worth justify, and excluding no just principle on the flimsy pretext of lack of precedent for its adoption'.

Essentially Robertson was not far removed from those Canadian reformers who had insisted on having the right to draw up an autochthonous constitution. Unlike the radicals in Canada, however, he had little support: indifference and faith in British institutions were too strong for him to overcome. There was a general belief in New South Wales that all the constitutions of Europe (save that of Britain) were despotic and that the constitution of the United States, where civil war already threatened, was a disastrous exercise in the selfish republican rule of transitory and tyrannous majorities.[130]

Although Robertson and Lang ignored the brief and casual references to responsible government in the report of the select committee, some liberals in the council protested against the failure to provide adequately for responsible government, as well as to the electoral system and the two-thirds majorities rule. The conservatives were not in a good position to resist. The constitution that they had drawn up had to be enacted and sent to Britain to win parliamentary approval. Its more controversial provisions — the nominated upper house, the gerrymandered electorates and the entrenched provisions against change — had to survive both in the legislative council and in Parliament. Nicholson thought that 'Even if a good measure be adopted ... there is the chance of it being rejected at home — and the chance is ... much augmented by Lowe[131] being in Parliament ... there is nothing he would like better than to knock down any machinery that we might set up.'[132]

Like the liberals, who petitioned Queen and Parliament against the new constitution, its authors had to depend on what the Cabinet and Parliament might decide. As Wentworth, when on his way to London with Deas Thomson to watch over the Bill, wrote to Macarthur:

> I trust I may arrive ... in time to hasten the ratification of our last great measure; ... if it be returned on our hands for amendment, ... it will no longer be possible to frame in the Colony a constitution of a sufficiently conservative character. It would be better to invoke Imperial Legislation, than to encounter so great a risque on this. My first interview with the Duke of Newcastle will show how the cat jumps, and I shall not fail to let my friends in the Colony know, as soon as possible, what they have to expect.[133]

The architects of the constitution counted themselves fortunate to have passed so conservative a measure through the legislature of New South Wales. Because it included elaborate provisions to reduce British authority in the internal affairs of the colony, the powers granted under the Act of 1850 had been exceeded and Parliamentary approval was required.

By allowing at least the possibility of full responsible government, the conservatives made it easier to pass their Bill in the colony and improved their chances in Britain. Newcastle, who would have charge of all proceedings on the Bill, had required provision for full responsible government. If he had eventually to preside over the drafting of a new Bill, as Wentworth feared, his goodwill had to be assured by every safe means at their disposal.

When Wentworth moved the third reading of the Constitution Bill on 21 December 1853, he commended the legislative council for having 'adhered to its compact with the English Government, including that on the Civil List'. Some British statesmen, he said (without mentioning Newcastle by name), had urged an elective upper house; apparently, they had not realised how republican, how utterly inconsistent with monarchy an elected upper house would be. 'The colony had asked for the British constitution', he continued. 'The idea of an American Senate had not been suggested until April 1853.' Among the resolutions that he proposed, there was one on responsible government, which for the first time he justified as part of the British constitution: 'As a necessary consequence [of gaining the British constitution], the Bill established responsible government and placed the appointment to all offices of trust and emolument in the hands of the responsible ministers, thus giving the citizens of New South Wales nearly equal rights with those of England.'[134] Beyond claiming that responsible government would be 'successful and advantageous' and that it was 'the ardent desire of the Council and the country', Wentworth found nothing to say about it. His main claim for the Bill, apart from its British qualities, was that the grievances of 1844, 1848 and 1851 had been redressed; the larger powers of self-government that New South Wales had sought were also included.

In the same debate the liberal Darvall challenged the conservatives with making a calculated attack on the liberties of the people. Had they not hurried through the new constitution, although no fundamental change was urgently needed? The public, he thought, were either actively hostile to the Bill, or silent in astonishment that such a measure had been thought necessary. He did not, however, complain of the inadequate provision made for responsible government. 'There was something wrong with responsible government', he told the council, 'when they had to offer large salaried offices to get support and keep the government together.' He did not take up the acute observation of W. H. Suttor that, 'under responsible government, there could be constant antagonism between the Upper and Lower Houses, and between the aristocratic and democratic parties'. Suttor, a member of the famous pastoral family, feared that the familiar problems of the Canadas might appear in New South Wales after reform, when a democratic assembly collided with a nominated council. He did not, however, foresee how great the democratic triumph in New South

Wales politics would be. Darvall himself foresaw nothing beyond the immediate triumph of the old conservatives in constitution making.[135] The council defeated his efforts to have the Bill postponed.

Darvall, like Cowper, had to put his faith in Newcastle. Pious George Allen, much engaged in prayer for this world and the next, probably summed up the misgivings of the urban middle classes, when he wrote in his journal ten months later, 'It is reported that our new constitution act will probably not be sanctioned by Britain. If not, we shall have to go through the whole matter again. I hope the Governor will hold an election so that the people will consider themselves represented and have no cause for complaint.'[136] In May 1855, Cowper, on learning that responsible government had been conceded to New Zealand, wrote to Parkes that the liberal critics of the constitution ought to have insisted on full responsible government, not as a merely facultative provision, but as a flesh and blood principle, so that the governor's instructions under the new Act would require its immediate introduction.[137]

EQUITY AMONG THE SUBJECTS OF THE QUEEN

Cowper's mild astonishment that responsible government had been established in New Zealand, while in New South Wales liberals and radicals were still not united in demanding it, was equalled by doubts in the Colonial Office of the way in which the concession to New Zealand had been made. Newcastle had not included New Zealand among the colonies to which his dispatch of 4 August 1853 had been sent.[138] The liberal provincial constitution of 1852 had been enacted for New Zealand without a thought of responsible government; indeed, the new general assembly was not expected to meet often for some years to come.[139] Governor George Grey had not called it before going to Europe on leave. The officer administering the government, Colonel R. H. Wynyard, summoned it in January 1854, and events then moved quickly and confusedly, partly owing to the machinations of Wakefield, who had made his home in the colony. Wynyard reported in June that he had virtually conceded responsible government.

His dispatch was unwelcome. Lord Grey might have ruled against Wynyard and revoked the purported concession on the ground that responsible government would not operate fairly to the Maoris, who had no effective share of political power. Merivale, advising Sir George Grey, Bart., who had succeeded Newcastle as Secretary of State, failed to raise this important principle and confined his objections to procedure. He thought responsible government 'very desirable' in New Zealand, but was sorry that Wynyard had not followed precedent in referring the question to Downing Street.[140] The swift pace of events in the colony caught up with this inadequate appraisal and the dispatch drafted on Merivale's advice was never sent. The Cabinet, of which Newcastle was still a member considered New Zealand in November and, in the light of further developments in the colony, decided on no resistance. A dispatch of 8 December ignored all the difficulties of allowing responsible government to the dominant section of a mixed population. Provided that pensions were provided for retiring officials, Wynyard was told, 'Her Majesty's Government have no objection whatever to the establishment of ... responsible government in New Zealand. They have no reason to doubt that it will prove the best method for developing the interests as well as satisfying the wishes of the community.'[141] Later, the problem of New Zealand's policies towards the Maoris made these remarks seem precipitate. At the time, the Colonial Office seems to have regarded the concession as just, inevitable, and unfortunate only in its manner of seeking.

Cowper was right in thinking that if New Zealand had responsible government the Australian colonies would not be allowed to have their new constitutions unless the new system were introduced immediately. And the New South Wales conservatives were right in thinking that no Secretary of State would fail to scrutinise closely their plans for reducing imperial authority in the colony and for entrenching themselves in power. Frederic Rogers, then one of the Law Officers, reported on the former that 'an acquiescence ... in these enactments would appear to be a total abandonment by the Home Government of any right to interfere directly or indirectly with any Colonial Legislation whatever, except within the narrow circle of subjects enumerated' as imperial. New South Wales was asking for power to legislate itself into independence.

This part of Rogers's memorandum is well known. Historians have been less interested in his general reflections on two matters relevant to responsible government as well as to attempted formal restrictions of the prerogative power in colonies. If imperial control were wholly or partly removed, he wondered, would colonies enact measures and perform executive acts discreditable to Britain? Would they pass laws authorising polygamy or the killing of aborigines? Would they repudiate debts or embarrass Britain's foreign relations? Rogers believed that, provided no rigid distinctions were drawn between imperial and colonial areas of authority, Britain had enough formal power and influence to safeguard her own interests. He also recognised that the colonies, however much they differed from Britain in social structure and democratic politics, were British communities overseas and likely to behave according to the standards of the mother country.

Rogers was sure that New South Wales should have responsible government. Emigration was rapidly injecting 'the materials of a healthy public opinion' and habits of conscientious legislation. He expected the necessity of imperial intervention in colonial affairs to diminish, but would not agree that Britain should simply do as asked, and give up all her rights to legislate for the colony. He tried, without success, to think of some methods of arbitrating differences between Britain and the colonies as to which matters were imperial and which colonial. More clear-sighted than the conservatives in the colony, he saw that the granting of responsible government, which was inevitable, would be followed by a great contest between the conservatives, especially pastoralists, and the more liberal parts of the community. He had little faith in and no liking for the entrenched provisions of the constitution, with which the conservatives intended to guard the bastions of their power.[142]

The Secretary of State who made the final decisions on the New South Wales constitution was Lord John Russell. Less liberal among his contemporaries than when he had allowed Grey to concede responsible government in North America, he thought that elected upper houses (such as Victoria desired) were one more means of exposing the authority of the Crown to the 'assaults of democracy'. Responsible government itself, although a necessary reform, would virtually destroy the power of the Crown to play a beneficial role in the colonies to which that reform was granted. He therefore would not agree to reduce any other part of the prerogative power in relation to colonies. If Britain had no authority whatever in New South Wales, the colony would be better independent than nominally linked with a mother country that was powerless in its affairs. He thought it impossible to distinguish formally between imperial and colonial areas of legislation and executive authority. Like Grey he preferred to rely, when imperial and colonial activities touched one another, on commonsense, shared British tradition and, where necessary, the firm use of the prerogative to safeguard the interests of the Queen's subjects, wherever they might be. In justice to all the people of New South Wales and to the empire at large, he would not allow the conservatives of the colony to exclude the imperial authority from their affairs, nor to perpetuate their power by imposing special constitutional barriers to change. Responsible government would not be granted to a colony in which one part of the population was permanently set in authority over the others.[143]

In London prolonged discussions, in which Wentworth sometimes participated,[144] confirmed the official British views that responsible government should be granted, that every prerogative power and the legislative power of Parliament should be preserved unchanged, and that within the colony political privilege and, as far as possible, political power should be distributed equitably.

The Constitution Act, 18 and 19 Vict., c. 54, omitted all the provisions that the conservatives had designed concerning the imperial disallowance of colonial legislation and the powers of the Crown to issue instructions to governors. The Act also omitted the provision to protect the requirements, regarding special majorities, that had been inserted in the original Bill as a safeguard against liberal constitutional change. The conservatives, having triumphed in the colony, were defeated in the end by the insistence of the Secretary of State that responsible government, which they had included in their Bill for such special reasons, required normal relations between Britain and the colony and equity among the Queen's subjects, so as to ensure that power was not transferred to a section or clique. The conservatives were allowed their nominee upper house and had the further satisfaction of seeing the Waste Lands Act repealed by 18 and 19 Vict., c. 56, without reserve except of existing rights. Instructions were issued to the governor for the immediate introduction of responsible government when the new constitution came into force. Victoria, South Australia and Tasmania, which also drafted and received new constitutions at this time, had had their own political conflicts, which in varying degrees had basically resembled the conflict in New South Wales. They also received responsible government. In every colony British responsible government and colonial democracy defeated the conservatives.[145] Merivale later thought that 'The able and wealthy leaders of the old Australian legislatures wanted to transfer power from Downing Street to themselves: they succeeded in transferring it to their inferiors.'[146]

In Britain responsible government emerged as the way in which the power of the Commons and the electorate grew at the expense of the power of the Crown and of the Lords. In the legislative colonies responsible government was the means of increasing both the power of a colony to govern itself, because heads of departments ceased to be imperial officials and became colonial ministers, and also the power of the colonial legislature and electorate to control the colonial executive.

Grey, who made the original great concessions of responsible government, was too limited by doctrinaire free trade opinions, and too burdened by a heavy sense of imperial responsibility for every part of the empire and all the Queen's subjects, to extend responsible government outside North America. His successors, no less confident than he of the great destiny and fundamental good sense of large British communities overseas, were less trammelled by hopes of a uniform commercial policy for the whole empire and, it must be admitted, less scrupulous than he in their concern for indigenous peoples, who might be oppressed if European settlers were left to rule mixed populations without close imperial supervision. Newcastle and Sir George Grey and, more doubtingly, Lord John Russell treated responsible government as a normal institution of British politics, to which colonies with large British populations, political maturity and internal stability were entitled according to the principles of 1791. Although those principles had sometimes been forgotten or thrust aside as inconvenient, they had provided the beginning of an important continuity in British policy towards colonial self-government. British institutions of government were granted, as nearly as local circumstances and colonial status permitted, to all British possessions overseas that were thought capable of working them smoothly according to British notions of political equity. Naturally, what was to be granted varied according to changes in the constitution and political ideas in Britain itself. Most of North America was allowed responsible government, although in some cases doubtfully. Jamaica was not. New Zealand, only questionably meeting the tests, received it in odd circumstances. The Australian colonies had to be ordered to prepare for it and were then allowed to have it only if British authority were preserved, as it was in Canada, and if political powers and privileges were distributed equitably in each colony. British polity had to prevail, allowing for colonial democracy and the stresses of new communities, so that the various British constitutions should be consistent in principle and compatible under the Crown.

References

CHAPTER 1

1 J. S. Mill, *On Liberty*, 308.
2 31 Geo. III, c.31, discussed in Chapter 2.
3 Cruikshank, in Ontario Historical Society, *Papers and Records*, XXVIII, 244f.
4 H. T. Manning, *Revolt of French Canada*, 26f.
5 Grenville to Dorchester, 5 June 1790, in Shortt and Doughty, *Documents*, II, 1024f.
6 J. S. Mill, *On Liberty*, 309.
7 Ibid., 131; *London and Westminster Review* (1838), 241f.

CHAPTER 2

1 Simcoe to Portland, 30 Oct 1795, in Doughty and McArthur, *Documents*, 206f.
2 Report of the Board of Trade, 7 Mar 1768, in Morison, *Sources and Documents*, 72.
3 Shortt and Doughty, *Documents*, I, 163f.
4 Forsyth, *Cases and Opinions on Constitutional Law*, 12f.
5 MacNutt, *The Atlantic Provinces*, 53f.
6 Murray to Lords of Trade, 29 Oct 1764, in Shortt and Doughty, *Documents*, I, 231.
7 F. Masères, 'Considerations on the Expediency of Procuring an Act of Parliament for the Settlement of the Province of Quebec' (London, 1766), in ibid., I, 275f.
8 Murray's commission (28 Nov 1763) and instructions (7 Dec 1763), in ibid., I, 173f., 181f.; *Acts of the Privy Council (Colonial)*, IV, 574f.
9 See *Campbell v. Hall* (1774), discussed below.
10 Board of Trade to Governor Lawrence, 25 Mar 1756, in *Nova Scotia Archives*, I, 711f. (quoted in Labaree, *Royal Government*, 176); MacNutt, *The Atlantic Provinces*, 53f.; Keith, *First British Empire*, 168f.
11 Humphreys and Morley Scott, in *CHR*, XIV (1), 42f.; Burt, 'The Problem of Government, 1760–1774', in *CHBE*, VI, 149f.; Neatby, *Quebec*, 33f. and Chapter 5; Shortt and Doughty, *Documents*, I, 251f., 327f., 370f., 377f.
12 William Petty (1737–1805), second Earl of Shelburne, later first Marquis of Lansdowne.
13 Sir Guy Carleton, first Baron Dorchester (1724–1808).
14 Shelburne to Carleton, 20 June and 17 Dec 1767, in Shortt and Doughty, *Documents*, I, 281f., 287f.; Shelburne to Hillsborough (?), 17 May 1767, Shelburne Papers, 64, 483–91, quoted in Gipson, *The British Empire*, XIII, 150.
15 Carleton to Shelburne, 25 Nov and 24 Dec 1767, 20 Jan 1768, in Shortt and Doughty, *Documents*, I, 281f., 288f., 294.; Carleton to Hillsborough, 20 Nov 1768 (secret), in ibid., I, 325f.
16 Carleton to Shelburne, 20 Jan 1768, in ibid., I, 294f.

17 Donoughue, *British Politics*, 108 and Chapter 5. Commons debates in Cavendish, *Debates on the Canada Bill*; Lords debates in *Journals of the House of Lords*, XXXIV.
18 Wight, *The Legislative Council*, 38.
19 Instructions to Carleton, 3 Jan 1775, in Shortt and Doughty, *Documents*, I, 594f.
20 14 Geo. III, c. 88, in force from 5 Apr 1775.
21 Dorchester to Sydney, 14 June 1787, CO 42/50, quoted in Graham, *British Policy and Canada*, 25; Carleton to Gage, 4 Feb 1775, in Shortt and Doughty, *Documents*, I, 660f.
22 Hinkhouse, *Preliminaries of the American Revolution*, 170f.
23 Donoughue, *British Politics*, 126.
24 Wight, *The Legislative Council*, 37f.
25 Cavendish, *Debates on the Canada Bill*, 61f.
26 Ibid., 246f.
27 Ibid., 72f., 188f., 213, 289.
28 Donoughue, *British Politics*, 121; Taylor and Pringle, *Correspondence of Chatham*, IV, 351f.; B. Williams, in *EHR*, XXII, 756f.
29 Cavendish, *Debates on the Canada Bill*, 27f., 50f., 92, 204, 271f.
30 Keith, *Speeches and Documents*, I, 35f.; Shortt and Doughty, *Documents*, I, 522f.
31 See also *Sammut v. Strickland* (1938), in 3 *All England Law Reports*, 693f.; and per Denning, M. R. in *Sabally v. Attorney-General* (1964), in *All England Law Reports*, 377.
32 In 1769 Mansfield held in *Rex v. Vaughan* (4 *Burrow* Reports, 249f.) that a conquered colony might become a settled colony.
33 Dartmouth to Carleton, 1 and 24 July 1775, CO 43/8.
34 Hey to Thurlow, June 1775, CO 42/35.
35 Instructions to Carleton, 8 Jan 1775, in Shortt and Doughty, *Documents*, II, 594f.; Neatby, *Quebec*, 139.
36 Graham, *British Policy and Canada*, 72; Ritcheson, *Aftermath of Revolution*, 56.
37 North to Haldimand, 12 May 1783, and Connolly to Evan Nepean, 13 June 1783, CO 42/15; additional instructions to Haldimand, 16 July 1783, in Shortt and Doughty, *Documents*, II, 730f.
38 Haldimand to North, 24 Oct 1783, in ibid., II, 735f.
39 Petition of 24 Nov 1784, in ibid., II, 742f.; CO 42/20.
40 Upton, *The Loyal Whig, passim*.
41 Plan of General Directions for Carleton, included in Sydney to Dorchester, 20 Sep 1787 (private), in Shortt and Doughty, *Documents*, II, 863f.
42 Discussion of Petitions, enclosed in Grenville to Dorchester, 20 Oct 1789 (private and secret), in ibid., II, 969f. at 974; Neatby, *Quebec*, 286, note 27; Cruikshank, in Ontario Historical Society, *Papers and Records*, XVIII, 231 and 233; Harlow, 'The New Imperial System, 1783–1815', in *CHBE*, II, 137, note 3.
43 Enclosed in Grenville to Dorchester, 20 Oct 1789 (private and secret), in Shortt and Doughty, *Documents*, II, 975.
44 Grenville to Dorchester, 20 Oct 1789 (public), in ibid., II, 988.
45 Ibid., II, 969f. at 975.
46 Cf. Grenada in Gipson, *The British Empire*, IX, 268f., and XIII, 149; Harlow, *Founding*, II, 773f.; Harlow, 'The New Imperial System, 1783–1815', in *CHBE*, II, 151f.; Keith, *The First British Empire*, 355f.; H. T. Manning, *British Colonial Government*, 64f.
47 Upton, *The Loyal Whig*, 202f.; Neatby, *Quebec*, Chapter 14; Trotter, *Canadian Federation*, 6f.

48 Smith to Dorchester, 5 Feb 1790, in Shortt and Doughty, *Documents*, II, 1018f.
49 Dorchester to Grenville, 5 June 1790, in ibid., II, 1027; Harlow, *Founding*, II, 766f.
50 Ormsby, in *CHR*, XXXIX, 279.
51 Memorandum enclosed in Grenville to Dorchester, 20 Oct 1789 (private and secret), in Shortt and Doughty, *Documents*, II, 970f.
52 Bolton, *The Passing of the Irish Act of Union*, 10f.; Harlow, *Founding*, I, 631f.; P. O'Farrell, *Ireland's English Question*, 63.
53 Cruickshank, in Ontario Historical Society, *Papers and Records*, XXVIII, 155–327.
54 Ibid., XXVIII, 252, 291f.
55 Ibid., XXVIII, 252f.
56 31 Geo. III, c. 31, s. 38.
57 Wight, *The Legislative Council*, 46.
58 Ritcheson, *British Politics and the American Revolution*, 207.
59 Grenville to Dorchester, 20 Oct 1789 (public), in Shortt and Doughty, *Documents*, II, 990; instructions to Dorchester, 16 Sep 1791, in Doughty and McArthur, *Documents*, 13f.
60 Grenville to Dorchester, 20 Oct 1789 (private and secret), in Shortt and Doughty, *Documents*, II, 970f; Harlow, *Founding*, II, 731.
61 22 Geo. III, c. 75, forbade future absentee tenure of colonial posts.
62 Partition by order-in-council, 25 Aug 1791, in Doughty and McArthur, *Documents*, 3.
63 Schuyler, *Fall of the Old Colonial System*, 82f.; Burt, *The United States, Great Britain and British North America*, Chapter 4.
64 D. G. Creighton, *Empire of the St Lawrence*, 193.
65 Liverpool to Craig, 12 Sep 1810, in Kennedy, *Documents*, 276f.
66 Henry, third Earl Bathurst (1762–1834), son of the Lord Chancellor.
67 The term was not used until about 1828 (Craig, *Upper Canada*, 107). See also Saunders, in *Ontario History*, XLIX, 165f.
68 Doughty and Story, *Documents*, 159f., 234f., 272f., 274f., 294f., 305f., 308f., 356f., 362f.; Craig, *Upper Canada*, 118, 121f., 422f., 428f.
69 Maitland to Murray, 18 Sep 1828, CO 42/384.
70 For Mackenzie's writings see Fairley, *Selected Writings of Mackenzie*.
71 Hay to Wilmot-Horton, 18 Nov 1828, Catton Papers; Doughty and Story, *Documents*, 431f.
72 Rolph to W. W. Baldwin, 9 Oct 1828, W. W. Baldwin Papers (Toronto Public Libraries); Dunham, *Political Unrest*, 170.
73 Doughty and Story, *Documents*, 477f.; Clark, *Movements of Political Unrest in Canada*, 350.
74 W. W. Baldwin to Wellington, 3 Jan 1829, CO 42/390; Doughty and Story, *Documents*, 481f.; W. W. Baldwin to R. Baldwin, 25 Jan 1829, R. Baldwin Papers, A. 83 (Toronto Public Libraries).
75 Dunham, *Political Unrest*, 166f.
76 H. T. Manning, *Revolt of French Canada*, 58.
77 Ibid., 70, 207f., 214f.
78 Ibid., Ch. XII *passim*.
79 Craig to Castlereagh, 5 Aug 1808, in Kennedy, *Documents*, 250f.
80 See H. T. Manning, *Revolt of French Canada*, 395, note 18.; L. A. H. Smith, in *CHR*, XXXVIII, 93f.
81 Hamilton, in *Canadian Historical Association Report, 1964*, 89f.
82 Craig to Liverpool, 1 May 1810, in Kennedy, *Documents*, 250f.

83 Castlereagh to Craig, 7 Sep 1809, in Kennedy, *Documents*, 254.
84 Robert Banks Jenkinson, second Earl of Liverpool (1770–1828). See H. T. Manning, *Revolt of French Canada*, 277f.
85 Liverpool to Craig, no date, in Yonge, *Liverpool*, I, 312f.
86 Liverpool to Craig, 12 Sep 1810, in Kennedy, *Documents*, 276f.
87 Ibid.
88 Louis-Joseph Papineau (1786–1871). See Ouellet, *Papineau*, 21.
89 Robinson, *Life of Sir John Beverley Robinson*.
90 Ormsby in *CHR*, XXXIX, 277f.; H. T. Manning, *Revolt of French Canada*, 487, note 12.
91 The triangle of territory in Lower Canada south of the St Lawrence river, bordering the United States of America.
92 Creighton, *Empire of the St Lawrence*, 215; H. T. Manning, *Revolt of French Canada*, 154, 249.
93 Ormsby, in *CHR*, XXXIX, 281; Wade, *French Canadians*, 130; Robinson to Bathurst, April 1822, in Harlow and Madden, *British Colonial Developments*, 224f.
94 Kennedy, *Documents*, 243f.; Doughty and Story, *Documents*, 123f.
95 H. T. Manning, *Revolt of French Canada*, 153.
96 Ormsby, in *CHR*, XXXIX, 277; Thomas Talbot to Wilmot-Horton, 4 Oct 1822, Catton Papers; PAC, *Report 1934*, 128, note 1.
97 Ellice to Wilmot-Horton, 4 [month doubtful] 1822, Catton Papers.
98 2 *PD*, VII, 1199, 1698f., 1729f.
99 2 *PD*, VII, 1731. Castlereagh was then Marquis of Londonderry.
100 Neilson to Papineau, 22 June 1822, quoted in H. T. Manning, *Revolt of French Canada*, 161.
101 Thomas Talbot to Wilmot-Horton, 13 Dec 1822, Catton Papers.
102 Bathurst to Wilmot-Horton, 16 Aug (?) 1826, Bathurst Papers (ML).
103 3 Geo. IV, c. 119; Creighton, *Empire of the St Lawrence*, 223 and 232f.; 6 Geo. IV, c. 59; Doughty and Story, *Documents*, 291f.
104 Creighton, in *CHR*, XII, 120f.
105 Ibid., XII, 126.
106 Dalhousie to Kempt, 22 Nov 1827, quoted in ibid., XII, 134.
107 Doughty and Story, *Documents*, 408f., 416f.; Wilmot-Horton to Bathurst, 4 Oct 1827, and Wellington to Bathurst, 14 Oct 1827, both in Historical Manuscripts Commission, *Report of the Bathurst MSS.*, 645, 647.
108 Kempt to Murray, 27 Sep 1828, quoted by Creighton in *CHR*, XII, 143.
109 Ouellet, *Papineau*, 33.
110 2 *PD*, XIX, 300f.
111 See Chapter 7 below.
112 *PP*, 1828, VII (569), 375–730.
113 *Colonial Advocate*, 25 Sep 1828.
114 Bathurst to Hay, 24 Dec 1828, Bathurst Papers, BM 57/59; Hay to Dalhousie, 28 July 1828, and Hay to Kempt, 29 Sep 1828, CO 324/89.
115 Minutes of Evidence before the Select Committee, *PP*, 1828, VII (569), 240 and 245.
116 Ouellet, *Papineau*, 42.
117 See p. 23f.
118 2 *PD*, XXI, 1326f. (14 May 1829).
119 Jones, *Lord Derby*, 9.
120 H. T. Manning: in *Bulletin of the IHR*, XXX, 41f. at 45; *Revolt of French Canada*, 305.
121 H. T. Manning: in *Bulletin of the IHR*, XXX, 50f.; and in *CHR*, XXXIII, 207f.

122 H. T. Manning, in *CHR*, XXXIII, 203f.
123 Stephen to Murray, 3 Sep 1828, CO 42/218; H. T. Manning, *Revolt of French Canada*, 274f.
124 Howick to Ellice, 10 and 30 May 1834, quoted from the Ellice Papers by H. T. Manning in *Bulletin of the IHR*, XXX, 58, note 2.
125 Burroughs, *The Canadian Crisis*, 50f.
126 *Mirror of Parliament for 1831*, 330f.; 3 *PD*, II, 690 (18 Feb 1831).
127 3 *PD*, II, 693.
128 Kennedy, *Documents*, 262f.
129 Craig, *Upper Canada*, 212.
130 Kennedy, *Documents*, 263f.
131 H. T. Manning, *Revolt of French Canada*, 339f.
132 H. T. Manning, in *Bulletin of the IHR*, XXX, 58.
133 Aylmer to Goderich, 2 Mar 1832, CO 42/236.

CHAPTER 3

1 H. T. Manning, In *CHR*, XXXIII, 203.
2 *Westminster Review*, XLVI (1839), 269.
3 Kriegel, in *EHR*, LXXXVI, 23.
4 Bentham to O'Connell, 31 Aug 1828, quoted in Bowring, *Works of Jeremy Bentham*, X, 598.
5 Hanham, *Reform of the Electoral System*, 8.
6 Fairley, *Selected Writings of Mackenzie*, 318f.; Lindsey *Life and Times of Mackenzie*, 234; H. T. Manning, in *CHR*, XXXIII, 228f.
7 Robert Stephen Rintoul (1787–1858) founded the *Spectator* in 1828 and made it the 'weekly organ of the Wakefield party' (Semmel, *Free Trade Imperialism*, 125).
8 John Black (1783–1855) edited *The Morning Chronicle*, 1817–43.
9 Fairley, *Selected Writings of Mackenzie*, 326f.
10 Ibid., 247; Journal of the third Earl Grey, 20 and 30 June 1833.
11 Fairley, *Selected Writings of Mackenzie*, 323.
12 Memorandum by James Stephen, 30 Mar 1832, CO 537/22.
13 *Fraser's Magazine*, XXXIII (1846), 471f.
14 See Melbourne to Grey, 5 and 7 Jan 1834, Grey to Melbourne, 7 Jan 1834 (copies in Grey of Howick Papers), and Journal of the third Earl Grey, 27 Mar 1833.
15 Saunders, in *Ontario History*, XLIX, 165f. (quotation at 178); Craig, *Upper Canada*, 107f.
16 Craig, in *CHR*, XXIX, 338f.; Colborne to Hay, 8 May 1833, CO 42/244.
17 Craig, in *CHR*, XXIX, 350f.
18 R. R. Palmer, *The Age of the Democratic Revolution: The Challenge* (Princeton, 1959), 215.
19 Fairley, *Selected Writings of Mackenzie*, 259; Craig, in *CHR*, XXIX, 343f.
20 C. W. New, in *CHR* XX, 119f. at 123f.
21 Craig, in *CHR* XXIX, 345f.
22 Creighton, *Empire of the St Lawrence*, 303; Craig, in *CHR* XXIX, 344.
23 'The Massacre of Montreal', in H. T. Manning, *Revolt of French Canada*, 347f.
24 Ellice to Howick, 2 Jan 1832, Grey of Howick Papers.
25 Wade, *The French Canadians*, 141; H. T. Manning, *Revolt of French Canada*, 202, 344.
26 Creighton, *Empire of the St Lawrence*, 276f.; H. T. Manning, *Revolt of French Canada*, 192, 203; Ellice to Howick, 4 Sep 1832, Grey of Howick Papers.
27 Creighton, *Empire of the St Lawrence*, 276f.

28 Aylmer to Goderich, 30 Jan 1833, CO 42/241; Ouellet, *Papineau*, 46f.
29 Petition of the House of Assembly, in Kennedy, *Documents*, 258f.
30 *Correspondent*, 26 Jan 1833.
31 The British constitution was prescriptive. See Chapter 1.
32 Address of the Legislative Council, in Kennedy, *Documents*, 262f.
33 Kennedy, *Documents*, 266f; Ouellet, *Papineau*, 77f., *Montreal Gazette*, 27 May 1834, quoting *Dundas Weekly Post*.
34 Burroughs, *The Canadian Crisis*, 64.
35 3 *PD*, XXII, 767f. (25 April 1834); Burroughs, *The Canadian Crisis*, 64; Leader, *Life and Letters of Roebuck*, 66f; 3 *PD*, XXVI, 669 (9 Mar 1835).
36 3 *PD*, XXII, 790f. (25 Apr 1834).
37 *PP*, 1834, XVIII; Evidence, *PP*, 1837, VII (96); H. T. Manning, in *Bulletin of the IHR*, XXX, 59.
38 3 *PD*, XXV, 920 (4 Aug 1834).
39 Journal of the third Earl Grey, 1 Mar, 5, 9 and 22 May 1834, 3 Nov 1835; 3 *PD*, XXVI, 670 (9 Mar 1835).
40 Spring-Rice to Aylmer, 29 June 1834 (confidential), in PAC, *Report 1931*, 307f. Minutes of the Conference (of Spring-Rice, Roebuck, Viger and Morin) at the Colonial Office, 22 June 1834. Papers of the third Earl Grey, Colonial Papers, Canada, No. 46.
41 Especially, Aylmer to Spring-Rice, 11 Sep and 8 Oct 1834, CO 42/252.
42 Memorandum by Stephen, 19 Aug 1834, minute by Hay, 22 Sep 1834, CO 537/137 (also CO 880/1).
43 Peel to Croker, 14 Apr 1835, in Jennings, *Croker Papers*, II, 273; Peel in the Commons, 3 *PD*, XXVI, 699f. (9 Mar 1835) and XXVIII, 881f. (12 June 1835).
44 Stephen to Howick, 20 Mar 1835, Grey of Howick Papers.
45 3 *PD*, XXVI, 703 (9 Mar 1835); H. T. Manning, in *Bulletin of the IHR*, XXX, 59f.
46 Papineau to Roebuck, 25 Mar 1835, in PAC, *Report 1928*, 22; Creighton, *Empire of the St Lawrence*, 297.
47 Howick's memoranda of 24 Apr and 28 Nov 1835, Papers of the third Earl Grey, Colonial Papers, Canada, nos. 54 and 64; Howick to Glenelg, 11 July 1835, Grey of Howick Papers.
48 Journal of the third Earl Grey, 3 Nov 1835, indicates that some of Howick's ideas may have come from Tocqueville, *Democracy in America.*
49 *The Times*, 23 Dec 1837.
50 Journal of the third Earl Grey, 4 July 1835.
51 Instructions to Gosford Commission, in Kennedy, *Documents* (no. CXVIII), and in CO 537/138. Manning, in *CHR*, XXXIII, 344f.; Stephen to Howick, 25 Oct 1835, Grey of Howick Papers.
52 Manning, in *CHR*, XXXIII, 347f.
53 The King's opinion according to Journal of the third Earl Grey, 3 June and 9 July 1835.
54 Journal of the third Earl Grey, 18, 19 and 27 Nov 1835; Manning and Galbraith, in *CHR*, XLII, 50f.
55 *PP*, 1837, XXIV (50), 14.
56 Journal of the third Earl Grey, 17 Apr 1836.
57 Journal of the third Earl Grey, 18 Nov 1835.
58 Glenelg to Head, 5 Dec 1835, in Kennedy, *Documents*, 412f.; Craig, *Upper Canada*, 233f.
59 Hume to Mackenzie, 5 Dec 1835, in Head, *A Narrative* (London, 1839), 36f.
60 *Correspondent and Advocate*, 18 Feb 1836.
61 Craig, *Upper Canada*, 234f.
62 Head to Glenelg, 5 Feb 1836, CO 42/249; Craig, in *CHR* XXIX, 334.

63 W. W. Baldwin to R. Baldwin, 27 Apr 1836, Baldwin Papers, A. 83.
64 Craig, *Upper Canada*, 236f.
65 *Constitution*, 27 July 1836.
66 Wilson, *Robert Baldwin*, Chapter 3; W. W. Baldwin to R. Baldwin, 17 May 1836, Baldwin Papers, A. 83.
67 W. W. Baldwin to R. Baldwin, 27 Aug 1836, Baldwin Papers, A 83.
68 3 *PD*, CVIII, 550 (8 Feb 1850).
69 R. Baldwin to Glenelg, 13 July 1836, in Kennedy, *Documents*, 335f., and PAC, *Report 1923*, 329f.
70 G. Grey to R. Baldwin, 4 Aug 1836, quoted in Wilson, *Robert Baldwin*, 54.
71 Wilson, *Robert Baldwin*, 57f.
72 *Constitution*, 27 July 1836; W. W. Baldwin to R. Baldwin, 30 July 1836, Baldwin Papers, A. 83.
73 Head to Glenelg, 30 Dec 1836, PAC, Colonial Office Records, Q. 391; H. T. Manning, in *CHR*, XXXIII, 361f.
74 Journal of the third Earl Grey, 14 May, 9 June, 3 July and 12 Aug 1836.
75 Journal of the third Earl Grey, 16—26 Apr, 14 May and 9—15 June 1836.
76 Journal of the third Earl Grey, 21 Apr 1836.
77 CO 537/137; PAC, *Report 1929*, 161f.
78 PAC, *Report 1929*, 161.
79 See Chapter 6 and p. 248f.
80 PAC, *Report 1929*, 170f.
81 Journal of the third Earl Grey, 18, 23, 24 and 29 Aug 1835, and 'Notes from my Journal for 1835', 30 May, 3 and 8 June 1836; Howick to Melbourne, 30 May and 2 June 1836, and Melbourne to Howick, 1 June 1836, Grey of Howick Papers; Papers of the third Earl Grey, Colonial Papers, Nos 63 (dated 30 May 1836) and 64; Broughton, *Recollections of a Long Life*, V, 41f.; 3 *PD*, XXXVIII, 1209f. (14 Apr 1837).
82 Howick to Melbourne, 15 June 1836 (copy), and Melbourne to Howick, 17 June 1836, Grey of Howick Papers.
83 Glenelg to Gosford, 7 June 1836, in Kennedy, *Documents*, 431f.; Journal of the third Earl Grey, 14 June 1836; Howick to Melbourne, 15 June 1836 (copy), Grey of Howick Papers.
84 Elliot to Howick, 18 July 1836, Grey of Howick Papers.
85 Stephen to Howick, 29 Aug 1836, Grey of Howick Papers.
86 Stephen's minute of 15 Nov 1836, CO 537/137; Sir Charles Grey's plan of 17 Nov 1836, *PP*, 1837, XXIV (50), 246f.
87 A. P. Newton, *Federal and Unified Constitutions*, 37; Ward, in *AJPH*, III, 18f.; Higham, in *EHR*, XLI, 190f., 366f.
88 Stephen's minute of 20 Dec 1836, CO 537/137; Burroughs, *The Canadian Crisis*, 85f.
89 Howick to Glenelg, 4 Jan 1837 (copy), Papers of the third Earl Grey, Colonial Papers, No. 69; epitome of proposed Canada Act, 19 Jan 1837, CO 537/137; Journal of the third Earl Grey, 18 and 23 Jan 1837.
90 Journal of the third Earl Grey, 30 Jan and 12 Feb 1837; Stephen to Howick, 2 Jan 1837, Papers of the third Earl Grey, Colonial Papers, No. 67.
91 Memorandum on Canada, Feb 1837, Papers of the third Earl Grey, Colonial Papers, No. 92; 3 *PD*, XXXVI, 1287f. (6 Mar 1837); Kennedy, *Documents*, 434f.; Russell to Howick, 2 Apr 1837, Grey of Howick Papers; Journal of the third Earl Grey, 3 Apr 1837.
92 3 *PD*, XXXVI, 128f., XXXVII, 767f., XXXVIII, 198f. (6 Mar to 24 Apr, 9 May 1837); Journal of the third Earl Grey, 9 May 1837.
93 Memorandum on Canada by Lord John Russell, Apr 1837, Papers of the third Earl Grey, Colonial Papers, No. 93.

94 Howick to Russell, 30 Mar 1837, Russell to Howick, 30 Mar 1837, and Howick to Russell, 7 Apr 1837 (copy), Grey of Howick Papers.
95 Russell carefully said 'removable', implying a discretion (then still existing) in the Crown. See Chapter 6.
96 See comment on Russell's phrase 'independent sovereign' at p. 76f.
97 Memorandum of 2 Nov 1837, Papers of the Third Earl Grey, Colonial Papers, No. 97.
98 Glenelg to Sir A. Campbell, 31 Aug 1836, in PAC, *Report 1931*, 376f.; Howick to Glenelg, 11 July 1835, Grey of Howick Papers.
99 Glenelg to Gosford, 14 July 1837, quoted in PAC, *Report 1931*, 416f.
100 Paper by Howick, 5 Apr 1837, Papers of the third Earl Grey, Colonial Papers, No. 94.
101 Melbourne to Howick, 8 Aug 1837, Grey of Howick Papers.
102 Stephen to J. C. Stephen, 18 Nov 1837, Stephen Papers, Journals, XI, 49f.; Stephen to Arthur, 22 Nov 1837, Arthur Papers (ML); Journal of the third Earl Grey, 20 June, 30 Oct, 1, 7, 10 and 30 Nov, and 1 Dec 1837.
103 Journal of the third Earl Grey, 1 Dec 1837.
104 Journal of the third Earl Grey, 22 Dec 1837.
105 3 *PD*, XXXIX, 1428f. (22 Dec 1837); Journal of the third Earl Grey, 22 Dec 1837.
106 Melbourne to Durham, 22 July 1837, in Reid, *Durham*, II, 137f.; Melbourne to Russell, 31 Dec 1837, in Russell, *Early Correspondence*, II, 213f.; Journal of the third Early Grey, 29 Dec 1837.
107 Stephen to Howick, 28 Dec 1837, Grey of Howick Papers.
108 Papers of the third Earl Grey, Colonial Papers, No. 99.
109 Melbourne to Howick, 2 Jan 1838, Grey of Howick Papers; Journal of the third Earl Grey, 2 Jan 1838.
110 Journal of the third Earl Grey, 29 Dec 1837.
111 Journal of the third Earl Grey, 29 Dec 1837; Papers of the third Earl Grey, Colonial Papers, No. 100.
112 Journal of the third Earl Grey, 2, 3 and 5 Jan 1838.
113 Journal of the third Earl Grey, 23 Dec 1837 and 5 Jan 1838; memorandum on Canada, 3(?) Jan 1838, and Howick to Russell, 2 Jan 1838, both in Russell Papers, PRO 30/22, Box 3.
114 Memorandum read to Cabinet, 30 May 1836, Russell Papers, PRO 30/22, Box 2; Journal of the third Earl Grey, 20 June, and 7 and 30 Nov 1837.
115 Melbourne to Durham, 22 July 1837, in Reid, *Durham*, II, 137f.
116 New, *Durham*, 319, from Lambton Papers, Ellice to Durham, 29 Dec 1837; *The Times*, 7 Apr 1838.
117 Memorandum of January 1838 (?), in Russell, *Early Correspondence*, 215f.; Russell to Melbourne (copy), 25 Oct [1838], Russell Papers, PRO 30/22, Box 3; Ormsby, *Emergence of the Federal Concept*, 15.
118 Journal of the third Earl Grey, 30 Dec 1837; Russell to Melbourne, 25 Oct [1838], Russell Papers, PRO 30/22, Box 3.
119 See Chapter 6. Howick to Ellice, 4 Jan 1838 (Private), Ellice Papers, E. 22 (National Library of Scotland); Martin, *The Durham Report*, 12f.; G. Grey to Howick, 16 Jan 1838, Grey of Howick Papers.
120 Melbourne to Durham, 7 Jan 1838, in Reid, *Durham*, II, 149f.; Durham to Grey, 15 Jan 1838, Grey of Howick Papers (second Earl); New, *Durham*, 531.
121 3 *PD*, XL, 7f. (16 Jan 1838).
122 3 *PD*, XL, 60f. (Grote), 87f. (Buller), 107f. (Warburton), 310f. (Roebuck) (16–29 Jan 1838); also 177, 217 (Melbourne and Brougham) (18 Jan 1838).
123 Gladstone's memorandum on Peel's remarks to Tory leaders, 20 Jan 1838, quoted in Morley, *Gladstone*, I, 641f.

124 The matter went to Cabinet. Journal of the third Earl Grey, 15 and 18—26 Jan 1838; Ormsby, *Emergence of the Federal Concept*, 16.
125 Journal of the third Earl Grey, 19 Jan 1838.
126 Glenelg to Durham, 20 Jan 1838, in PAC, *Report 1923*, 24.
127 Journal of the third Earl Grey, 8 Jan 1838; Papers of the third Earl Grey, Colonial Papers, No. 102.
128 See Chapter 2, p. 16.
129 Roebuck, *Colonies of England*, 190f.; 3 *PD* CX, 1426 (13 May 1850).
130 Durham, *Report*, II, 304; New, *Durham*, 359f., 462.
131 Glenelg to Durham, 20 Jan 1838, in PAC, *Report 1923*, 24.
132 Glenelg to Durham, 21 Apr 1838, in PAC, *Report 1931*, 465.
133 Journal of the third Earl Grey, 8 Feb 1839.
134 Journal of the third Earl Grey, 8, 9 and 15 Jan, 3 Feb, 15 Aug, 20 and 21 Oct, 7 Nov, and 7 Dec 1838, 22, 26 and 31 Jan, 8 Feb, 8 and 17 May 1839. Durham to Glenelg, 13 Sep 1838, CO 42/283; *The Times*, 18 Oct 1838.
135 Journal of the third Earl Grey, 7 Dec 1838; Russell to Melbourne (copy), 9 Dec 1838, Russell Papers, PRO 30/22, Box 3; Melbourne to Russell, 8 and 19 Dec 1838, in Sanders, *Lord Melbourne's Papers*, 440f. 443f.; Durham to G. Grey, 20 Dec 1838, CO 42/284.
136 Ed. C. P. Lucas, 3 vols (Oxford, 1912).
137 Martin, *The Durham Report, passim*.
138 New, *Durham*, 369, 409, 411f.; Craig, *Upper Canada*, 256f.
139 Durham Papers, II, 1—43 (1 Aug 1838), quoted in Wilson, *Life of Robert Baldwin*, 157.
140 R. Baldwin to Durham, 23 July 1858, quoted in PAC, *Report 1923*, 326.
141 Cf. Wrong, *Charles Buller*, 33.
142 3 *PD*, LIV, 741 (29 May 1841).
143 3 *PD*, LIV, 710f. (May 1840).
144 Durham, *Report*, II, 77.
145 Ibid., II, 150f.
146 Ibid., II, 277f.
147 Ibid., II, 279f.
148 Ibid., II, 278.
149 Ibid., II, 279f.
150 Ibid., II, 280.
151 Ibid., II, 279.
152 Ibid., II, 282f.
153 Russell's list of possible disasters in *Mirror of Parliament*, 1840, IV, 342f.
154 Durham, *Report*, II, 283.
155 Ibid., II, 282 and note.
156 Ibid., II, 282.
157 Ibid., II, 70, 292f. ('Hopeless inferiority of the French Canadian race').
158 Ibid., II, 70, 285.
159 Ibid., II, 304, 307f. Durham's exaggerated account of a race war was challenged at once by Russell (3 *PD*, XLVII, 1254f., 3 June 1839) and Nielson (quoted in Hamel, *La Rapport de Durham*, 46).
160 Durham, *Report*, II, 70.
161 Ibid., I, 149f., and II, 113, 324.
162 Labouchere to Barkly, 2 May 1857, in 'Confidential Dispatches from the Secretary of State to the Governor of Victoria', I, Part 1 (Public Library of Victoria).
163 Durham, *Report*, II, 327.
164 J. L. Morison, 'The Mission of the Earl of Durham', in *CHBE*, VI, 306; and *British Supremacy and Canadian Self-Government*, 244.
165 Durham, *Report*, II, 327.

166 See G. Wrong, *Charles Buller*, 101.
167 H. T. Manning: in *CHR*, XXXIII, 203f. and 341f.; and in *Bulletin of the IHR*, XXX, 41f.
168 See Chapters 6 and 8.
169 Journal of the third Earl Grey, 15 and 22 Jan, and 8 May 1839. Howick dutifully supported his wife, Maria Copley of the well known Tory family.
170 Journal of the third Earl Grey, 15 Jan 1839.
171 Howick to Durham, 7 Feb 1839, Grey of Howick Papers; New, *Durham*, 133.
172 Journal of the third Earl Grey, 2 Feb 1839.
173 Durham to Howick, 8 Feb 1839, Grey of Howick Papers; Wakefield to Durham, 9 Feb 1839, Durham Papers, in PAC, *Report 1923*, 200; Journal of the third Earl Grey, 5 Feb 1839.
174 Durham, *Report*, II, 304, and III, 305f.; Glenelg to Durham, 20 Jan 1838; Trotter, in *Canadian Historical Association Report 1925*, 55f.
175 Journal of the third Earl Grey, 9 Jan 1838.
176 3 *PD*, LIV, 746 (29 May 1840).
177 Colonel Charles Grey, later General Grey, Private Secretary to Prince Albert and later to Queen Victoria.
178 Colonel Grey to Grey, 20 July 1838, 25 Feb, 17 Apr, 13 May and 24 June 1839; Ormsby, *Crisis in the Canadas*, 108f.
179 Grey to Colonel Grey, 16 May 1839, Grey of Howick Papers; Colonel Grey to Grey, 24 June 1839; Ormsby, *Crisis in the Canadas*, 110; Colonel Grey to Lady Durham, 12 Apr 1839, quoted in New, *Durham*, 531.
180 See Chapter 6.
181 Howick's proposed minute and minute adopted by Cabinet, both in Journal of the third Earl Grey, 11 May 1839; 3 *PD*, LI, 770 (29 Jan 1839).
182 Journal of the third Earl Grey, 2 Mar and 13 Apr 1839, Papers of the third Earl Grey, Colonial Papers, No. 110 (23 Feb 1839); New, *Durham*, 554, 561.
183 Journal of the third Earl Grey, 30 Mar 1839; Ormsby, *Emergence of the Federal Concept*, 75f.
184 Journal of the third Earl Grey, 26 Mar 1839; Ellice's plan, 21 Dec 1838, CO 880/1.
185 Journal of the third Earl Grey, 30 Mar 1839.
186 Journal of the third Earl Grey, 28 May 1839. See Chapter 6.
187 Arthur to Normanby, 2 July 1839, CO 42/463; New, *Durham*, 542f.; Journal of the third Earl Grey, 2 June 1839; Craig, *Upper Canada*, 265f.
188 3 *PD*, XLVII, 1254f. (3 June 1839).
189 Fifth Resolution, in Kennedy, *Documents*, 435.
190 Ormsby, *Emergence of the Federal Concept*, 48f.; New, *Durham*, 526.
191 3 *PD*, LIII, 1062f. (13 Apr 1840), LIV, 1263f. (29 May 1840); Journal of the third Earl Grey, 27 Apr, 12 June and 7 July 1840.
192 The Union Act, 3 and 4 Vict., c. 35.
193 Liverpool to Craig, 12 Sep 1810, in Kennedy, *Documents*, 276f., discussed in Chapter 2.
194 Russell to Poulett Thomson, 14 Oct 1839, in Kennedy, *Documents*, 522f.
195 In the West Indies and New South Wales as well as in the Canadas. See Chapters 4, 5 and 6.
196 W. Smith, in *Canadian Historical Association Report 1928*, 41f.; Journal of the third Earl Grey, 3 June 1839.
197 Buller to Durham, 4 June 1839, Durham Papers, in PAC, *Report 1923*, 204.
198 Russell to Poulett Thomson and the lieutenant-governors of Upper and Lower Canada, Nova Scotia, New Brunswick, Prince Edward Island, Newfoundland and Bermuda, 16 Oct 1839, CO 42/297; Kennedy, *Documents*, 524f.; Knaplund, in *CHR*, V, 3f.; Kinchen, in *CHR*, XXXVI, 382f.; Butler, in *CHJ*, II, 248f.
199 See p. 253f.

200 CO 13/15.
201 Russell to Poulett Thomson, 7 and 14 Sep 1839; Kennedy, *Documents*, 516f., 522f.
202 Russell to Campbell, 30 Apr 1840, CO 217/174.
203 3 *PD*, LIII, 733f. (13 Apr 1840).
204 Kennedy, *Documents* 480f.; Chisholm, *Speeches and Letters of Howe*.
205 Harvey, in *CHR*, XX, 161f. at 175; Morrell, *British Colonial Policy*, 19; correspondence of Russell and Howe, CO 217/171–4.
206 Reprinted in 1840 as *Responsible Government for Colonies* (later edition, ed. G. M. Wrong; Oxford, 1926); Wakefield to Durham, 26 Dec 1839, Durham Papers, in PAC, *Report 1923*, 206.
207 Wrong, *Charles Buller*, 92f.
208 Ibid., 113, 101.
209 Martin, *The Durham Report*, Chapter 3.
210 See above, p. 75f. 3 *PD*, LIII, 1056f. (13 Apr 1840), LIV, 710f., 724f., 1121f., 1263f. (29 May 1840).
211 Knaplund, in *CHR*, XX, 196.

CHAPTER 4

1 1 *PD*, XXXIX, 496 (18 Feb 1819).
2 Howick to Melbourne, 3 Jan 1839, Grey of Howick Papers.
3 Murray, *The West Indies*, 158, note 75.
4 See Chapter 2.
5 Stokes, *Utilitarians and India, passim.*
6 Ibid., XI.
7 24 Geo. III, c. 25.
8 *PH*, XXV, 1266, 1293 (16 Mar 1786).
9 The law was settled in *Campbell v. Hall* (1774). See Chapter 2.
10 R. Pares, review of Harlow, *Founding* I, in *EHR*, LXVIII (1953), 284; R. Hyam, review of Harlow, *Founding* II, in *Historical Journal* X (1967) 116.
11 1 *PD*, XL, 1077f. (10 June 1819).
12 1 *PD*, XL, 272f. (10 May 1819).
13 1 *PD*, XL 355f. (29 Nov 1819).
14 2 *PD*, VIII, 249f. (25 Feb 1823).
15 Ragatz, *Fall of the Planter Class*, Chapter 1; Penson, in *EHR*, XXXVI, 373f.; Higman, in *HS*, XIII, 1f.
16 H. T. Manning, *British Colonial Government*, 298.
17 Portland to Grey, 5 Sep 1794, and Portland to Williams, 5 Sep 1794, CO 319/12; H. T. Manning, *British Colonial Government*, 341f.
18 E. Williams, *History of Trinidad*, Chapters 5 and 7.
19 Quoted in Murray, *The West Indies*, 68, from G. W. Jordon, *An Examination of the Principles of the Slave Registry Bill* (1816), 41. The statement was made between 1801 and 1804.
20 Picton's instructions, 1 June 1801, CO 296/4.
21 Bolt, *Victorian Attitudes to Race*, 80.
22 Picton to Hobart, 26 June 1801, CO 295/2.
23 Hobart to Picton, 18 Feb 1802, CO 295/2.
24 *PH*, XXXVI, 854f. (27 May 1802); Hobart to Picton, 18 Feb and 26 June 1802, CO 295/2.
25 Hobart to Picton, 9 July 1802, CO 295/2.
26 Instruction, 16 Oct 1802, CO 295/3; dispatches in CO 295/5.
27 Hobart to Picton, 9 Jan and 2 Feb 1804, CO 295/8.
28 Gloster to Hislop, 4 July 1804, in Hislop to Camden, 9 July 1804, CO 295/8.
29 Hobart to Hislop, 3 Nov 1803, CO 296/4.

30 [J. Stephen], *The Crisis of the Sugar Colonies*, 189.
31 Instructions to Smith, undated [1808], CO 380/134; Castlereagh to Hislop, 6 Mar 1809, CO 296/4; Smith to Jenkinson, 14 May 1810, CO, 295/24; Smith to E. Cooke (Under-Secretary), 28 Oct 1809, CO 295/22.
32 Liverpool to Hislop, 15 Mar 1810, CO 296/4; Jenkinson to Smith, 15 Mar 1810 (private), identified in Jenkinson to Hislop, 19 Mar 1810, both CO 296/4.
33 Hislop to Liverpool, 20 May and 19 July 1810, CO 295/23; Smith to Jenkinson, 13 May 1810, CO 295/24; Hislop to Liverpool, 19 July 1810, CO 295/23.
34 Liverpool to Hislop, 27 Nov 1810, CO 296/4; Stephen to Liverpool, 1 Sep 1810, CO 295/25.
35 *PD*, XX, 1341., 610f. (14 May and 13 June 1811).
36 H. T. Manning, *British Colonial Government*, 376f.; Bathurst to Woodford, 27 Sep 1813, CO 296/5.
37 Liverpool to Eldon, 4 Sep 1811, quoted in Murray, *The West Indies*, 81; H. T. Manning, *British Colonial Government*, Chapter 14.
38 Peel to Goulburn, 12–15 Aug 1812, quoted in Gash, *Mr Secretary Peel*, 93f.
39 1 *PD*, XXXI, 772f., 1127f. (13 June–5 July 1815).
40 18 Geo. III, c. 12.
41 Schuyler, in *Political Science Quarterly*, XL, 1f.
42 6 Geo. III, c. 12.
43 *PH*, XXXII, 944f., 991f. (11 Apr 1796); Hobart on Perceval and Law to Hobart, 14 Dec 1801, CO 324/65; H. T. Manning, *British Colonial Government*, 72.
44 CO 29/30; Bathurst to Manchester, 13 Aug 1816, CO 138/47.
45 Ragatz, *Fall of the Planter Class*, 31f.
46 *Edinburgh Review*, XLIII (1825–6), 433f.
47 Stephen to Bathurst, 12 June 1815, Bathurst MSS., BM 57/9.
48 1 *PD* XXXI, 772 (13 June 1815).
49 *Journal of the Jamaica House of Assembly*, XII, 696 (31 Oct 1815); Murray, *The West Indies*, 96f.
50 1 *PD*, XXXIV, 910 (30 May 1816).
51 Manning, *British Colonial Government*, 505.
52 28 June 1816, CO 29/30.
53 Reports on the Acts, CO 323/40; Goulburn to Bathurst, Nov or Dec 1821, Bathurst Papers, BM 57/13.
54 59 Geo. III, c. 120.
55 Schuyler, *Parliament and the British Empire*, Chapter 4.
56 H. T. Manning, *British Colonial Government*, 509.
57 2 *PD*, IX, 257f. (15 May 1823).
58 Bathurst to Murray, 28 May 1823, CO 112/5.
59 Bathurst to Woodford, 28 May 1823, CO 296/6; Bathurst to Officer administering St Lucia, 28 May 1823, CO 254/6.
60 CO 29/30; *PP*, 1824, XXIV, 433.
61 Secret and confidential dispatches of 28 May 1823, CO 29/30.
62 Ragatz, *Fall of the Planter Class*, 413; Burn, *Emancipation and Apprenticeship*, 81.
63 Goulburn to Bathurst, 26 Dec 1820, Bathurst Papers, BM 57/13.
64 *Edinburgh Review*, XL (1824), 226f. and XLIII (1825–6), 419f; Ragatz, *Fall*, 430f.; New, *Brougham*, 289f.; *PP* 1826–7, XVIII (554); Catton Papers, under Sir Benjamin D'Urban.
65 Herbert Taylor to Bathurst, Liverpool to Bathurst, Duke of York to Bathurst, Wellington to Bathurst, Bathurst to George IV, 11, 13 (twice) and 14 Oct, and 6 Dec 1823, all in Bathurst Papers, BM 57/14; Wellington, *Despatches, Correspondence and Memoranda*, II, 151.
66 *Edinburgh Review*, XLI (1824–5), 209f.; New, *Brougham*, 441.
67 CO 29/30; *PP*, 1824, XXIV, 438.

68 Memorandum by Stephen, 30 Mar 1823, CO 111/13.

69 Bathurst to Murray, 9 July 1823, CO 112/5.

70 Orders-in-council of 10 Mar and 14 Aug 1824, CO 111/47. D'Urban to Bathurst, 4 June 1824, CO 111/44; Bathurst to D'Urban, 20 Sep 1824, CO 112/6.

71 Woodford to Bathurst, 26 Aug 1823, CO 295/59; Bathurst in the Lords, 2 *PD*, X, 1046, and Canning in the Commons, ibid., 109 (16 Mar 1824). Bathurst to Governors, 14 July 1824, CO 138/47.

72 Mathieson, *British Slavery*, 136f.

73 Dispatches listed in Ragatz, *Fall of the Planter Class*, 416, note 3; Liverpool to Bathurst, 2 and 12 Jan 1824, and Liverpool to Canning, 9 Jan 1824, in Historical Manuscripts Commission, *Report of the Bathurst MSS.*, 560f.; Canning in Commons, 2 *PD*, XIV, 973 (1 Mar 1826).

74 Wilmot-Horton to Huskisson, 26 Jan 1824, quoted in Murray, *The West Indies*, 131.

75 2 *PD*, X, 1098 (16 Mar 1824).

76 Liverpool to Canning, 9 Jan 1824 (enclosed in Liverpool to Bathurst 12 Jan 1824) and Canning to Bathurst, 14 Feb and 15 Mar 1824, Bathurst MSS., BM 57/15.

77 *Quarterly Review*, XXXII (1825), 516f., and XXXIII (1826), 413f.

78 *Westminster Review*, I (1824), 337f.

79 New, *Brougham*, 442.

80 *Edinburgh Review*, XLIII (1825—6), 432f.

81 New, *Brougham*, 441; *Edinburgh Review*, XLI (1824—5) 209f.

82 Ragatz, *Fall of the Planter Class*, 417.

83 Hibbert to Speaker, House of Assembly, Jamaica, 7 Oct 1825, Bathurst Papers, BM 57/16.

84 Enclosed in Hibbert to Bathurst, 10 Apr 1826, Bathurst Papers, BM 57/16.

85 Memorandum by Stephen, no date [1826—7], CO 320/4.

86 2 *PD*, X, 1046f. (16 Mar 1824).

87 Bathurst to Wilmot-Horton, 16 Aug 1826 and 17 Sep 1828, Bathurst Papers (ML).

88 5 Geo. IV, c. 113.

89 Lushington to Bathurst, 10 June 1824, Bathurst Papers, BM 57/15; letters from acting governor, CO 295/78, other correspondence in CO 295/84; Woodford to Bathurst, 29 Sep 1825, CO 295/67.

90 Bathurst to D'Urban, 6 Oct 1824, CO 324/73.

91 Taylor to Howick, 23 Apr 1832, Grey of Howick Papers; Canning to Bathurst, 20 Oct 1815, Bathurst Papers, BM 57/10.

92 Memorandum by Bathurst, 16 Nov 1825, CO 320/5; Bathurst to D'Urban, 25 Feb 1826, CO 112/6; D'Urban to Wilmot-Horton, 9 Mar 1825, Catton Papers.

93 Murray, *The West Indies*, 131f.; Mathieson, *British Slavery*, 157f.

94 2 *PD*, XIV, 1139f. (7 Mar 1826).

95 2 *PD*, XV, 1308f. (19 May 1826).

96 2 *PD*, XIV, 1140 (17 Mar 1826); Bathurst to governors, 11 May 1826, CO 29/31; *PP* 1826—7, XXV, 61; noe by Stephen, 11 May 1830, CO 323/46.

97 Bathurst to Codrington, 29 May 1826, Bathurst Papers, BM 57/16.

98 Bathurst to Huskisson, 21 Mar 1826, Bathurst Papers, BM 57/16; Minute by Bathurst, 25 Aug 1826, CO 324/15.

99 Murray, *The West Indies*, 158; Murray to governors, 15 Sep 1828, *PP*, 1829, XXV (333), 8.

100 Murray to D'Urban, 4 Feb 1831, CO 112/7.

101 Minute by Howick, 16 June 1832, Papers of the third Earl Grey, Colonial Papers, Colonial Policy, No. 1; Penson, in *Transactions of the RHS*, IX, 126f.

102 Stephen to Goderich, 3 Feb 1831, CO 323/213.

103 *PP*, 1831–2, XLVI, 93f.; Ellice to Howick, no date [1832], Grey of Howick Papers.
104 Ragatz, *Fall of the Planter Class*, 440f.
105 *CHBE*, II, 483f.; *PP*, 1831–2, XX (381) and XXXI 382.
106 *PP*, 1831–2, XLVI (279); Papers of the third Earl Grey, Colonial Papers, Emancipation, No. 56.
107 Goderich to Belmore, 1 Mar 1832, *PP*, 1831–2, XLVII (285), 39.
108 Stephen's report, 21 Nov 1832, CO 323/46.
109 *PP*, 1831–2, II (721); Taylor to Howick, 23 Apr and 15 Aug 1832, and Ellice to Howick, Nov 1832, Grey of Howick Papers; Howick's plan, CO 320/1; Taylor, *Autobiography*, I, 125f.
110 Memoranda by Stephen, Howick and Goderich, Apr 1832, Papers of the third Earl Grey, Colonial Papers, Slavery, Nos. 37, 38, 39; Howick to Goderich, Feb 1832, Goderich to Howick, 4 and 8 Mar 1832, Grey of Howick Papers.
111 Burn, *Emancipation and Apprenticeship*, 94; Goderich to Howick, 26 Apr 1832 (private), Grey of Howick Papers.
112 Goderich to Howick, 4 Mar 1832, Grey of Howick Papers; Francis Baring to Wilmot-Horton, no date [1832], Catton Papers; Higman, in *HS*, XIII, 16.
113 Rough copy of Howick to Grey, 7 Feb 1833, Papers of the third Earl Grey, Colonial Papers, Slavery, No. 30.
114 Draft order of 19 Oct 1833, CO 318/117; order-in-council of 19 Mar 1834, *PP*, 1834, XLIV (152).
115 T. F. Elliot, 'A Few Remarks on the Causes of the Unpopularity of the Colonial Office' (July 1848), CO 325/47.
116 See Chapter 5. Wilmot-Horton to Woodford, 12 Oct 1825, CO 324/98; Woodford to Wilmot-Horton, 31 Dec 1825, CO 295/67; minute by Bathurst, no date [1825], CO 320/1.
117 Wight, *The Legislative Council*, 67, note 1.
118 *PP*, 1826–7, XXIII (883), 37.
119 Wilmot-Horton to Bathurst, 22 Nov 1825, Bathurst Papers, BM 57/16; H. Craig, *Trinidad and Tobago*, 17.
120 Memorandum by Wilmot-Horton, 19 Jan 1827, CO 320/4.
121 P. 93.
122 Bathurst to Wilmot-Horton, 21 Jan 1827, CO 325/35.
123 Memorandum by Stephen, no date [1826–7], CO 320/4.
124 Memorandum by Bathurst, no date [1827], CO 320/4.
125 Bathurst to Bentinck, 26 Apr 1815, Portland Papers, quoted by McLachlan, in *HS*, XIII, 484.
126 Young, *The Colonial Office*, 18.
127 Snelling and Barron, in *Studies in the Growth of Nineteenth Century Government*, 140f.
128 Taylor, *Autobiography*, I, 117.
129 H. T. Manning, *British Colonial Government*, 367f.; Penson, in *Transactions of the RHS*, IX, 113f.; CO 116/137 and 116/165 on the constitutions.
130 Carmichael to Secretary of State, 3 May 1812, CO 111/13; Penson, in *Transactions of the RHS*, 120f.; Carmichael to Liverpool, 28 Apr, 3, 4, 15 and 28 May, and 5 June 1812 (CO 111/12), and 11 and 12 Oct 1812 (CO 111/13); Harlow and Madden, *British Colonial Documents*, 102f.
131 Penson, in *Transactions of the RHS*, IX, 124.
132 Memorandum by Bathurst, no date [1826], CO 111/58.
133 Memoranda of 1 Jan and July 1826, and 30 Sept 1828, CO 111/98.
134 Twiss's memorandum has to be collected from Stephen to Twiss, 25 Aug 1830, CO 111/98.
135 Stephen had considered a 'blended' legislature earlier. See Chapter 5.

136 Draft order-in-council, CO 380/134.
137 Orders-in-council etc., prepared but not sent, CO 380/134 and 380/37; Murray, *The West Indies*, 163, 168.
138 Stephen to Twiss, 25 Aug 1830, CO 111/98; Law Officers to Goderich, 2 Feb 1831, CO 111/118.
139 3 *PD*, VI, 110f. (16 Aug 1831).
140 Goderich to D'Urban, 18 Mar 1831, CO 112/15.
141 D'Urban's commission, 4 Mar 1831, and instructions, 5 Mar 1831, both CO 381/19; Goderich to D'Urban, 18 Mar 1831, CO 112/15, and 6 June 1832, CO 112/16.
142 D'Urban to Goderich, 7, 11 and 12 April 1832, CO 111/121, and 8 Sep 1832, CO 111/122.
143 Goderich to D'Urban, 6 June, 29 Sep, 22 Nov 1832, CO 112/16 (Howick's corrections, CO 111/122); Penson, in *Transactions of the RHS*, IX, 132.
144 Commission and instructions, 21 Mar 1831, CO 381/74.
145 Known as the legislative council from 1863. Wight, *The Legislative Council*, 59, note 5.
146 Note by Adam Gordon, Chief Clerk, Aug 1831, CO 380/134. On New South Wales, see Chapter 5.
147 Howick to Goderich, 11 Oct 1832, Grey of Howick Papers.
148 Goderich to Grant, 25 May 1831, CO 296/10.
149 Goderich to Grant, 30 Jan 1832, CO 296/10.
150 Taylor to Douglas, 4 Oct 1832, Grey of Howick Papers.
151 Taylor's minute to Stephen, no date, CO 295/96, quoted in Murray, *The West Indies*, 170.
152 Burn, *Emancipation and Apprenticeship*, 129; Greville, *Memoirs*, II, 347.
153 Howick and Goderich, 11 Oct 1832, and Taylor to Howick, 4 June and 23 Dec 1831, 1 and 7 Oct 1832, Grey of Howick Papers.
154 Goderich to Howick, 4 Jan 1833, Grey of Howick Papers.
155 Stephen to Howick, 31 Aug 1832, Grey of Howick Papers.
156 For example, 3 *PD* XIV, 648f. (23 July 1832).
157 Goderich to Mulgrave, 5 Feb 1833 (CO 138/54), to McGregor, 11 Feb 1833 (CO 395/5), to L. Smith, 7 Mar 1833 (CO 29/33); Howick to Stephen, 29 Aug 1832, Stephen to Howick, 31 Aug 1832, and Goderich to Howick, 4 Sep 1832, Grey of Howick Papers.
158 Quoted in Parry and Sherlock, *Short History of the West Indies*, 213.
159 Burnley to Stanley, 19 Oct 1833 (CO 295/100), and 28 Jan and 11 Feb 1834 (CO 295/105).
160 Stanley's minute of 12 Mar 1834, CO 295/105; Lefevre to Spring-Rice, 2 Oct 1834, CO 295/105.
161 Spring-Rice to Hill, 17 Oct 1834, CO 296/11.
162 Stanley to Smyth, 22 Feb 1834, CO 112/18; Penson, in *Transactions of the RHS*, IX, 133; Murray, *The West Indies*, 215, 217.
163 3 and 4 William IV, c. 73, s. 23.
164 Stephen to Lefevre, 6 Jan 1834, CO 71/70; Knaplund, *James Stephen*, 107f.
165 Murray, *The West Indies*, Chapter 12.
166 Aberdeen to Smith, 1 Mar 1835, CO 112/18, quoted in Murray, *The West Indies*, 218.
167 Stephen to Glenelg, 22 Feb 1837, CO 323/52, quoted in Knaplund, *James Stephen*, 119f.; Burn, *Emancipation and Apprenticeship*, 192f., 326f.
168 Murray, *The West Indies*, 222–9.
169 Stephen to Howick, 25 Oct 1835, Grey of Howick Papers.

170 Ibid.; draft of Glenelg to Sligo, 15 July 1835, quoted in Burn, *Emancipation and Apprenticeship*, 293.
171 Glenelg to Sligo, 15 Sep 1835, CO 138/57; Glenelg to Sligo, 17 Sep 1835 (confidential), CO 138/57; Burn, *Emancipation and Apprenticeship*, 294f.
172 Ibid., 314, 336; Glenelg to Sligo, 31 Mar 1836, CO 138/59; Sligo to Glenelg, 23, 25 and 27 May 1836, CO 137/211; assembly's protests, CO 140/126.
173 Confidential circular, in Bell and Morrell, *Select Documents*, 401f.; public circular, 2 Apr 1838, CO 318/141.
174 1 and 2 Vict., c. 19; Burn, *Emancipation and Apprenticeship*, 355, note 2; Burns, *History of the British West Indies*, 631f.
175 See Chapter 6.
176 3 *PD*, XLIII, 87f. (28 May 1838); Burn, *Emancipation and Apprenticeship*, 352f.
177 3 *PD*, XLIII, 376f. (3 June 1838).
178 Bell and Morrell, *Select Documents*, 404f.; CO 140/29.
179 Curtin, *Two Jamaicas*, 180.
180 1 and 2 Vict., c. 67.
181 Smith to Glenelg, 3 Dec (private), and 17 Nov 1838, CO 137/230; Murray, *The West Indies*, 186.
182 Smith to Glenelg, 24 Dec (private), and 25 Dec 1838, CO 137/230.
183 [James Spedding], 'The Jamaica Question', in *Edinburgh Review*, LXIX (1839), 527f.
184 Taylor, *Autobiography*, I, 250; Papers of the third Earl Grey, Colonial Papers, Jamaica, No. 5; Taylor to Grey, 5 Apr 1876, Grey of Howick Papers.
185 Taylor, *Autobiography*, I, 244, 250.
186 Taylor to Grey, 5 Apr 1876, Grey of Howick Papers.
187 Journal of the third Earl Grey, 28 and 30 Jan 1839.
188 Grey to Taylor, 30 May 1885, Taylor to Grey, 7 June 1885, and Howick to Melbourne, 30 Jan 1839, all in Grey of Howick Papers.
189 Journal of the third Earl Grey, 28 Jan 1839.
190 28 Jan 1839, Papers of the third Earl Grey, Colonial Papers, West Indies, No. 5; Journal of the third Earl Grey, 30 Jan 1839.
191 See Chapter 6.
192 Minute by Stephen, 22 Feb 1837, CO 323/52, reprinted in Knaplund, *James Stephen*, 119f.
193 Taylor to Howick, 27 Nov 1832, Grey of Howick Papers.
194 3 *PD*, XLVII, 459f., 573f., 765f. (23 and 26 Apr, 3 and 6 May 1839).
195 Gash, *Sir Robert Peel*, 220.
196 Torrens, *Melbourne*, II, 480.
197 Curtin, *Two Jamaicas*, 73; Burge, *Speech*; 3 *PD*, XLVII, 4591 (23 Apr 1839).
198 Schuyler, in *Political Science Quarterly*, XL, 1f.
199 Greville, *Memoirs*, IV, 199.
200 Journal of the third Earl Grey, 7 May 1839; D. Southgate, *The Passing of the Whigs*, 71; Curtin, *Two Jamaicas*, 97.
201 3 *PD*, XLVII, 973f. (7 May 1839).
202 See Chapter 6.
203 3 *PD*, XLVII, 1105f. (30 May 1839).
204 Journal of the third Earl Grey, 15 and 17 May 1839. It became law as 2 and 3 Vict., c. 26.
205 *Sydney Herald*, 28 Aug 1839.
206 Normanby to Smith, 15 Apr 1839, CO 137/238.
207 Gardner, *History of Jamaica*, 395.

208 King, *Sir Richard Bourke*, 245f.
209 Metcalfe to Russell, 29 July 1840, CO 137/256.
210 Morrell, *British Colonial Policy in the Mid-Victorian Age*, Chapter 13.
211 G. Grey to Grey, 15 Apr 1849, Grey of Howick Papers. Cf. Shaw, in *JBS*, IX, 92f; *Edinburgh Review*, XIX (1839), 527f.

CHAPTER 5

1 James Stephen's memorandum on the Colonial Office and colonial policy, no date (1849?), CO 325/47.
2 CO 881/1, No. XX.
3 See Chapter 4.
4 Keith, *The First British Empire*, 231.
5 Order-in-council, 23 Jan 1634, 20 May 1708, in *Acts of the Privy Council (Colonial)* I, 192f., II, 553f.; 10 and 11 William III, c. 25.
6 A. P. Newton, 'Newfoundland to 1783', in *CHBE*, VI, 145.
7 Hamilton to Bathurst, 3 Feb 1821, CO 194/64; Bathurst to Hamilton, 14 Mar 1821, CO 195/17; Currey, *Forbes*, 14f.; Forbes's report, CO 194/69.
8 2 *PD*, VIII, 702f. (25 Mar 1823).
9 2 *PD*, IX, 244f. (14 May 1823).
10 5 Geo. IV, c. 51, 67, 88, the Fisheries, Judicature and Marriage Acts; Bathurst in the Lords, 2 *PD*, XI, 527f. (6 May 1824); McLintock, *Newfoundland*, 158f.
11 Stephen to Wilmot-Horton, 18 Sep 1826, CO 194/73.
12 19 Dec 1831, CO 194/82, reprinted in McLintock, *Newfoundland*, 207f.
13 Goderich to Howick, no date, CO 194/82.
14 Goderich to Cochrane, 27 July 1832, CO 195/18; Stephen to Howick, 23 July 1832, Grey of Howick Papers; Howick to Cochrane, 27 July 1832, CO 195/18.
15 Stephen to Howick, 23 July 1832, Grey of Howick Papers.
16 Address to Cochrane, 9 Jan 1833, CO 197/2.
17 Cochrane to Goderich, 13 Feb 1833, CO 194/85.
18 3 *PD*, XLVII, 552f., LVII, 611f. (26 Apr 1839, 27 Mar 1841); Stephen's minute on Prescott to Russell, 10 Dec 1840, CO 194/109.
19 Harvey to Russell, 6 Oct 1841 (confidential), CO 194/112; Prescott to Stanley, 16 Sep 1840, CO 194/111; Stanley to Harvey, 19 Nov 1841, CO 195/20; Harvey to Stanley, 21 Dec 1841 (separate and confidential), CO 194/112.
20 3 *PD*, LXIII, 875f. (26 May 1842), and LXV, 873f. (30 July 1842).
21 Stephen's minute to Hope, 18 Jan 1842, CO 194/112.
22 Campbell, in *Sydney Law Review*, IV, 343f.; and in *JRAHS*, L, 181f.; Else-Mitchell, in *JRAHS*, XLIX, 1f.; Evatt, in *Australian Law Journal*, XI, 409f.; Windeyer, in *Tasmanian University Law Review*, I, 635f.
23 MacCallum, in *Arts*, VI, 43f.; Fry, in *HS*, XIV, 497f.
24 24 Geo. III, c. 56, and 27 Geo. III, c. 2 (with Letters Patent thereunder, the First Charter of Justice).
25 Field to Goulburn, 13 Nov 1818, Stephen's opinion, and Field to Bigge, 23 Oct 1820, in *HRA*, IV, i, 321, 415, 858.
26 *HRA*, I, i, 1 and 2. (HO 51/146, PC 5/114).
27 *HRA*, IV, i, 77.
28 Bentham's *Plea*, in Bowring, *Works of Jeremy Bentham*, IV, 254f.; W. B. Campbell, 'A Note on Jeremy Bentham's ... "Plea" ...', in *Australian Law Journal*, XXV (1951), 59f.; memorandum by King, 2 Jan 1806, *HRA*, IV, i, 44; Plumer to Macquarie, 4 May 1809, *HRA*, I, vii, 193; Ellis Bent to Bathurst, 1 July 1815, *HRA*, IV, i, 122; J. H. Bent to Macquarie, 2 October 1815 (enclosed

in Macquarie to Bathurst, 30 Feb 1816), *HRA*, I, ix, 3; Field's opinion, Macquarie to Bathurst, 15 May 1818, *HRA*, I, ix, 772.

29 *PP*, 1812, II (306).
30 Bathurst to Macquarie, 23 Nov 1812, *PP*, 1816, XVIII (450).
31 Bathurst to Ellis Bent, 11 Dec 1815, *HRA*, IV, i, 172.
32 Opinion of Law Officers, *HRA*, IV, i, 330 and 412; 59 Geo. III, c. 114, 1 Geo. IV, c. 12, 1 and 2 Geo. IV, c. 8, 3 Geo. IV, c. 96, and 4 Geo. IV, c. 96; Stephen to Wilmot-Horton, 23 July 1823, 20 Mar 1824 and 15 Oct 1825, *HRA*, IV, i, 486, 534, 625.
33 1 *PD*, XXXI, 464f. (18 Feb 1819).
34 Jeremiah O'Flynn, an unauthorised Franciscan priest, was expelled.
35 Castlereagh in the Commons, 1 *PD*, XXXIX, 480 (18 Feb 1819) and 740 (1 Mar 1819); Bathurst to Sidmouth, 23 Apr 1817, and Sidmouth to Bathurst, 25 Apr 1817, CO 201/187; *Quarterly Review*, XII (1815), 43f.
36 1 *PD*, XXXIX, 1124f. (23 Mar 1819) and 1433 (7 Apr 1819), XXXV, 920 (10 Mar 1817), and XXXIX, 464 (18 Feb 1819); H. G. Bennet, *A Letter to Earl Bathurst*, (London, 1820), partly from evidence in *PP*, 1819, VII, (579).
37 Later editions in 1820 and 1824.
38 Wentworth to D'Arcy Wentworth, 10 Apr 1817, 10 Nov 1818, 13 Apr 1819, Wentworth Papers, A. 756; J. Macarthur to Davidson, 3 Sep 1818, Macarthur Papers, XIII.
39 Wentworth, *New South Wales*, 346, 354f., 362f.
40 *PP*, 1819, VII (579); J. Ker, 'Merchants and Merinos', in *JRAHS*, XLVI (1960), 206f.; Currey, *The Brothers Bent*, 109.
41 Wentworth, *New South Wales*, 357f.
42 Macquarie to Bathurst, 1 Sep 1821, *HRA*, I, x, 543.
43 Howick to Melbourne, 19 Feb 1834, Grey of Howick Papers; *Edinburgh Review*, XXXII (1819), 43; *Quarterly Review*, XII (1815), 41f., and XXIV (1820–21), 56f.
44 Ellis, *John Macarthur*, 470f.; Currey, *Forbes*, 40.
45 Appendix to Bigge Report, CO 201/132; McLachlan, in *HS*, X, 435f.
46 Petitions of 1819 and 1821 in Macquarie to Bathurst, 22 Mar 1819 and 22 Oct 1821, *HRA*, I, x, 52 and 549.
47 Eagar to Bathurst, 3 Apr 1823, *HRA*, IV, i, 441.
48 *PP*, 1823, XIV (532); Ritchie, *Punishment and Profit*.
49 *PP*, 1823, X (33).
50 Edward Macarthur to John Macarthur, 12 Aug 1822, Macarthur Papers, XVII.
51 Wentworth Papers, 140; Macarthur Papers, XV.
52 Memorandum by Forbes, 1 Jan 1823, with notes by Wilmot-Horton, CO 201/146; Forbes to Wilmot-Horton, 15 May 1823, *HRA*, IV, i, 480f.
53 McLintock, *Newfoundland*, 154; 2 *PD*, IX, 245f. (14 May 1823).
54 Forbes to Hay, 12 Nov 1827, *HRA*, IV, i, 745.
55 Macarthur to Wilmot-Horton, 11 Oct 1823, Catton Papers.
56 Melbourne, *Constitutional Development*, 96; Forbes to Hay, 12 Nov 1827, *HRA*, IV, i, 745.
57 Stephen to Wilmot-Horton, 27 Sep and 16 Oct 1824 (two letters), CO 48/96; minute by Wilmot-Horton, 12 Nov 1824, CO 324/75; Bathurst to Somerset, 29 Oct 1824 (private and confidential), Bathurst Papers, BM 57/65; additional instructions to Somerset, 9 Feb 1825, CO 49/16. I am indebted to Dr Hazel King for these references.
58 Wilmot-Horton to T. H. Scott, 16 Aug 1823, *HRA*, IV, i, 492.
59 Canning to Wilmot-Horton, 9 July 1823, Catton Papers; 2 *PD*, IX, 1447f. (7 July 1823); *The Times*, 8 July 1823.
60 Melbourne, *Constitutional Development*, 95, 102f.; Currey, *Forbes*, 40f.

61 Melbourne, *Constitutional Development*, 119f.; Macarthur to Wilmot-Horton, 20 Sep 1823, Catton Papers.

62 Macarthur to Wilmot-Horton, 11 and 20 Sep, 11 Oct 1823, Catton Papers; Wilmot-Horton to Scott, 16 Aug 1823, and Scott to Wilmot-Horton, 22 Aug 1823, *HRA*, IV, i, 492 and 496; Bathurst to Brisbane, 19 Jan 1824, *HRA*, I, xi, 195; Melbourne, *Constitutional Development*, 112f.

63 Forbes to Wilmot-Horton, 1 Jan 1827, CO 201/188.

64 Forbes to Wilmot-Horton, 10 Mar 1823, CO 201/146; memorandum by James Stephen, 4 Mar 1828, CO 201/195.

65 At the Cape after 1825 the chief justice sat on the council and examined draft ordinances, but had no power to prevent them from being enacted.

66 Bathurst to Brisbane, 19 Jan 1824, and Brisbane to Bathurst, 21 Nov 1824, *HRA*, I, xi, 195, 406; Currey, *Forbes*, 82; Eddy, *Britain and the Australian Colonies*, 101.

67 Melbourne, *Constitutional Development*, 126f.; *Quarterly Review*, XXXII (1825), 313f.; Field to Marsden, 21 Nov 1824, Marsden Papers.

68 *HRA*, IV, i, 629; *The Australian*, 27 Oct 1825.

69 Address to Bathurst, enclosed in Macarthur to Wilmot-Horton, 11 July 1826, CO 201/179; *HRA*, IV, i, 633. A copy in the Macarthur Papers, XCII, is differently punctuated, with no change of meaning.

70 Darling to Bathurst, 21 Dec 1825, and enclosure, *HRA*, I, xii, 127.

71 Melbourne, *Constitutional Development*, Part II, Chapter 1; *Sydney Gazette*, 5 and 9 Jan 1826; *Monitor*, 19 Apr 1826.

72 Bathurst to Hay, 2 Aug 1826, Bathurst to Hay, 12 July 1826, Bathurst Papers, BM 57/58; Currey, *Forbes*, 126f.; Hay to Darling, 17 July 1826 (private and confidential), CO 324/85.

73 Darling to Bathurst, 1 May 1826, *HRA*, I, xii, 253.

74 Darling to Wilmot-Horton, 15 Dec 1826 (secret and confidential), *HRA*, I, xii, 761.

75 Darling to Bathurst, 1 Feb 1826, and enclosure, *HRA*, I, xii, 144; Darling to Bathurst, 4 Dec 1826, and enclosure, and Darling to Wilmot-Horton, 15 Dec 1826, and enclosure (secret and confidential), *HRA*, I, xii, 716 and 761; Macarthur Jnr to Macarthur Snr, 12 June 1825, Macarthur Papers, XV.

76 Darling to Bathurst, 4 and 15 Dec 1826 (secret), and enclosure *HRA*, I, xii, 716, 749.

77 Darling to Wilmot-Horton, 15 Dec 1826 (secret and confidential), and enclosure, *HRA*, I, xii, 761.

78 Currey, *Forbes*, Chapter 23; *Sydney Gazette*, 30 Jan and 4 Feb 1828; Darling to Hay, 15 Feb 1828, *HRA*, I, xiii, 785.

79 Darling to Bathurst, 31 Jan 1827, and enclosure, and Darling to Hay (secret and confidential), 9 Feb 1827, *HRA*, I, xiii, 50 and 96.

80 Darling to Hay, 17 Dec 1826 (secret and confidential), *HRA*, I, xii, 803; Darling to Hay, 9 Feb 1827 (secret and confidential), *HRA*, I, xiii, 96f.; Melbourne, *Constitutional Development*, 142; Clark, *History of Australia*, II, 57f.; Forbes to Wilmot-Horton, 20 Sep 1827, *HRA*, IV, i, 731f.; James Macarthur to John Macarthur Jnr, 9 June 1827, Macarthur Papers, XXXV.

81 Darling to Stephen, 17 Dec 1827, enclosed in Darling to Hay, 17 Dec 1827, *HRA*, I, xiii, 652f.; Currey, *Forbes*, 197f.; Melbourne, *Constitutional Development*, 140f.

82 Forbes to Wilmot-Horton, 10 Oct 1826, *HRA*, IV, i, 642; Darling to Stephen, 17 Dec 1827, enclosed in Darling to Hay, 17 Dec 1827, *HRA*, I, xiii, 657; Currey, *Forbes*, 271f.

83 Currey, *Forbes*, Chapter 30.

84 Forbes to Hay, 12 Nov 1827, *HRA*, IV, i, 747; Clark, *History of Australia*, II, 83.
85 Macarthur to Wilmot-Horton, 18 July 1825, 11 and 14 July 1826 and 4 June 1827, CO 201/167, 179, 188; Stephen's memorandum, 4 Mar 1828, CO 201/195.
86 Wentworth to Bathurst, 4 Aug 1827, CO 201/189; Stephen's memorandum of 4 Mar 1828, CO 201/193.
87 Quoted by McLachlan in *HSANZ*, X, 445; Dumaresq to Leveson Gower, 29 Apr 1828, CO 201/197.
88 Melbourne, *Constitutional Development*, 145f.
89 4 Mar 1828, CO 201/195.
90 2 *PD*, XVIII, 1430 (1 Apr 1828); Stephen to Arthur, 27 Dec 1828, Arthur Papers (ML), IV.
91 Stephen to Arthur, 24 Mar 1824 and 9 Oct 1826, Arthur Papers (ML), IV; Melbourne, *Constitutional Development*, 147.
92. Currey, *Forbes*, 285.
93 Stephen's opinion in 1834, CO 323/50, f. 401.
94 2 *PD*, XVIII, 1431 (1 Apr 1828).
95 2 *PD*, XVIII, 1559 (19 Apr 1828).
96 McLachlan, in *HSANZ*, X, 444.
97 John Macarthur Jnr to John Macarthur Snr, no date [1828], Macarthur Papers, XV.
98 Murray to Darling, 1 Feb 1829, *HRA*, I, xiv, 623.
99 *The Australian*, 6 Jan 1829.
100 Hall to Murray, 2 May 1829, enclosed in Darling to Murray, 6 July 1829, *HRA*, I, xv, 53f.; *Monitor*, 4 Oct 1828.
101 Darling to Twiss, 7 July 1829, *HRA*, I, xv, 70; Wentworth to Murray, 1 Mar 1829, enclosed in Darling to Murray, 28 May 1829, *HRA*, I, xiv, 793f.
102 Darling to Murray, 8 Nov 1828, *HRA*, I, xiv, 443.
103 2 *PD*, XXIV, 288 (11 June 1830); Edward Macarthur to James Macarthur, 31 May 1831, and to John Macarthur Snr, 29 May 1831, Macarthur Papers, XVII.
104 *The Australian*, 10 Feb 1830; 3 *PD*, XIII, 1089 (28 June 1832).
105 Howick to Melbourne, 19 Feb 1834, Grey of Howick Papers.
106 *Westminster Review*, VIII (1827—8), 219f.; *Edinburgh Review*, XLVII (1828), 87f.; *Quarterly Review*, XXXVII (1828), 1f.
107 Edward Macarthur to John Macarthur, 27 June 1831, Macarthur Papers, XVII; Bourke to Goderich, 6 Feb and 19 Mar 1832, and Bourke to Howick, 28 Feb 1832, *HRA*, I, xvi, 515, 541; Bourke to Stanley, 12 Sep 1833, *HRA*, I, xvii, 213.
108 Bourke to Stanley, 25 Dec 1833 (separate), *HRA*, I, xvii, 302.
109 Forbes's comments on the draft Bill, CO 201/248; Bourke to Glenelg, 26 Dec 1835, *HRA*, I, xviii, 246; Bill in CO 881/1, No. XX.
110 *HRA*, I, xviii, 286.
111 Melbourne, *Constitutional Development*, 207f.; Bland, *Letters to Buller*, 191; *The Australian*, 2 June and 11 Dec 1828.
112 Bourke to Glenelg, 13 Apr 1836, and enclosure, *HRA*, I, xviii, 391; James Macarthur, *New South Wales*, Appendix, 1f., 9f.
113 *The Australian*, 15 Apr 1836.
114 Edward Macarthur to his brothers, 11 May 1834, 9 May 1835, 14 March, 4 Aug and 1 Oct 1836, Macarthur Papers, XVIII; Melbourne, *Constitutional Development*, 213.
115 Bill in CO 881/1, No. XX, and Grey of Howick Papers.
116 Howick to Stephen, 11 Jan 1836, Grey of Howick Papers.

117 Grey (second Earl) to Frederick Grey, 5 Mar 1833, Grey of Howick Papers.
118 Howick to Melbourne, 19 Feb 1834, and Edward Macarthur to Howick, 20 May 1838, Grey of Howick Papers.
119 Howick to Stewart (Treasury), 15 Dec 1830, and 12 Aug 1831, CO 202/26; Journal of the third Earl Grey, 1 Mar and 28 Oct 1834; Howick on 'Secondary Punishment — Transportation', in *Edinburgh Review*, LVIII (1834), 336f.
120 Bourke to Howick, 11 Aug 1833 (private), Grey of Howick Papers; Bourke to Spring-Rice, 23 Mar 1832, Bourke Papers, IX.
121 Howick read *Democracy in America*, in 1835. See Journal of the third Earl Grey, 3 Nov 1835.
122 Journal of the third Earl Grey, 22 Dec 1835, and 8, 12, 18, 27 and 28 Jan 1836.
123 Stephen to Howick, 11 Jan 1836, Grey of Howick Papers.
124 Stephen to Murray, 14 July 1830, CO 323/47.
125 The course of the Bills, CO 881/1, No. XX; Journal of the third Earl Grey, 13 Jan 1836; minute of 1836 for Glenelg, apparently by Stephen, CO 881/1, No. XX.
126 Journal of the third Earl Grey, 27 June 1836; CO 881/1, No. XX, 37f.; 3 *PD*, XXXIV, 1265 (5 July 1836).
127 Forbes to Stephen, 13 Oct 1836, CO 201/257; Melbourne, *Constitutional Development*, 233; Edward Macarthur to Elizabeth Macarthur, 8 Dec 1836, Macarthur Papers, XVIII; Forbes to Stephen, 27 Oct 1836, CO 201/257; Forbes to Bourke, 28 Oct 1836, Bourke Papers, XI.
128 James Macarthur to William Macarthur, 9 Dec 1836, Macarthur Papers, XXXV; minute of 1836 for Glenelg, CO 881/1, No. XX; James Macarthur to William Macarthur, 18 Dec 1836, Macarthur Papers, XXXV, and to George Grey, 2 Jan 1836, CO 201/267.
129 James Macarthur, *New South Wales*, 132f.
130 Forbes to Stephen, 31 Mar 1837, CO 201/266; Forbes to Bourke, 25 Feb 1837, Bourke Papers, XI; James Macarthur to G. Grey, 9 Feb 1837, CO 201/267.
131 Gipps to G. Grey, 23 Aug 1837, Co 881/1, No. XX; G. Grey to Howick, no date [1837], Grey of Howick Papers.
132 Bulwer to the Australian Patriotic Association, 30 May 1837, in *Monitor*, 12 Feb 1838; McLachlan, in *HSANZ*, X, 446; James Macarthur to Glenelg, Oct 1837, CO 881/1, No. XX; Howick's 'Leading Provisions for a N.S.W. Bill', 13 Dec 1837, Papers of third Earl Grey, Colonial Papers, NSW, No. 10.
133 James Macarthur to Glenelg, Oct 1837, CO 881/1, No. XX; Howick to Glenelg, 1 May 1838 (private and confidential), Grey of Howick Papers.
134 James Macarthur to G. Grey, 4 Dec 1837, CO 881/1, No. XX; Memorandum by James Macarthur, 1 Jan 1855, Macarthur Papers, XXXVI; E. Macarthur to Howick, 20 May 1837, Grey of Howick Papers.
135 CO 881/1, No. XX; letter from Eagar, 1 Feb 1838, in *Monitor*, 27 June 1838; Buller to Australian Patriotic Association, 21 Apr 1838, in *The Australian*, 20 Nov 1838; Melbourne, *Constitutional Development*, 224; memorandum by Buller, 11 Feb 1838, CO 881/1, No. XX; Buller to Glenelg, 14 Apr 1838, quoted in Buller to Australian Patriotic Association, *The Australian*, 25 Oct 1838.
136 Melbourne, *Constitutional Development*, 237f.
137 Memorandum by Buller, 11 Feb 1838, CO 881/1, No. XX.
138 3 *PD*, XLII, 479 (9 Apr 1838).
139 James Macarthur to Glenelg, 10 Apr 1838, CO 201/281.
140 Macarthur Papers, XIV, 158.
141 Buller to Glenelg, 14 Apr 1838, quoted in *The Australian*, 20 Oct 1838.
142 Buller to Russell, 15 Apr 1838, Russell Papers, PRO 30/22, Box 3; Buller to Howick, 23 Apr 1838, Grey of Howick Papers.

143 Melbourne, *Constitutional Development*, 240; Clark, *History of Australia*, II, 227; *Monitor*, 12 Mar, 29 June 1838.
144 Melbourne, *Constitutional Development*, 244; Eagar to G. Grey, 18 July 1838, and to Glenelg, 21 July 1838, CO 201/281; Glenelg to Gipps, 24 Aug 1838, enclosed with 1 and 2 Vict., c. 50, *HRA*, I, xix, 559.
145 Forbes to Stephen, 28 Nov 1836, CO 201/257.
146 3 *PD*, XXXVII, 709f. (23 Mar 1837).
147 *Commons Journals*, XCII, 2, 17–18 (8 April 1837); Glenelg to Bourke, 26 May 1837, *HRA*, I, xviii, 763; Shaw, *Convicts and the Colonies*, 268.
148 Bourke to Howick, 17 July 1838, Grey of Howick Papers; Memorandum for Russell, 1838, and Bourke to Buller, 8 Feb 1839, both in Bourke Papers, Uncatalogued MSS. Set 403, Item 6.
149 Journal of the third Earl Grey, throughout Jan 1837; Clark, *History of Australia*, II, 330f.
150 James Macarthur to William Macarthur, 7 June 1837, Macarthur Papers, XXXV; Currey, *Forbes*, 491f., 498; *PP*, 1837, XIX (518), 1837–8, XXII (669).
151 Macarthur's evidence, *PP*, 1837–8, XXII (699), 5 Feb 1838; J. D. Lang, *Historical and Statistical Account of New South Wales* (London, 1837, 1st ed.: 1834), I, 331f., 320f.; Lang, *Transportation and Colonization*, 228n.; Mudie, *Felony of New South Wales*, 12f., 235f.; *PP*, 1837, XIX (518), 170f.
152 3 *PD*, XLI, 484 (6 Mar 1838). See Chapter 6.
153 3 *PD*, XLIX, 1239 (5 Aug 1839).
154 Edward Macarthur to his brothers, 13 Mar 1839, Macarthur Papers, XVIII; *Sydney Herald*, 9 Dec 1839; Journal of third Earl Grey, 26 Aug 1839.
155 Russell to Howick, 15 Oct 1839, Grey of Howick Papers.
156 *V & P* (LC, NSW), 26 June, 3 and 17 July 1838.
157 *Sydney Herald*, 4, 7, 14 Jan, 26 Apr and 3 May 1839; *The Australian*, Jan 1839 (*passim*) and 5 Feb 1839; Gipps to Normanby, 23 Nov 1839, *HRA*, I, xx, 400.
158 Bland, *Letters to Buller*, 2f.; Buller to Australian Patriotic Association, 2 Sep 1839, in *The Australian*, 3 Apr 1840; Edward Macarthur to his brothers, 13 Mar 1839 and 10 Apr 1840, Macarthur Papers, XVIII; Bland, *Letters to Buller*, 28f., 140f.
159 Journal of the third Earl Grey, 29 Aug 1839, 21 Feb 1841; Howick to G. Grey, 23 Jan 1839 (private), Grey of Howick Papers; *The Australian*, 24 Jan 1839; *Sydney Herald*, 6 May and 21 Sep 1840.
160 After Madgwick, *Immigration into Eastern Australia*, 223.
161 D. Beer, in *JRAHS*, LIV (1968), 205f.
162 *The Sydney Herald*, became *The Sydney Morning Herald* in Aug 1842, having become a daily on 1 Oct 1840.
163 *Sydney Herald*, 11 Jan, 17 June, 11 July and 28 Aug 1839, and 6 Mar 1840; *The Australian*, 9 and 11 July 1839. See p. 299.
164 Gipps to Glenelg, 1 Jan 1839, *HRA*, I, xix, 719.
165 Burroughs, *Britain and Australia*, 231f.
166 *PP*, 1840, III (45), 207; 3 *PD*, LV, 360 (30 June 1840), 451, 1073 (6 and 29 July 1840); Melbourne, *Constitutional Development*, 255f.; Edward Macarthur to Russell, 9 Aug 1840, Macarthur Papers, XVIII.
167 Bland, *Letters to Buller*, 156f., 166; *The Australian*, 10 and 12 Nov 1840 and 21 Jan 1841; Edward Macarthur to Colonial Land and Emigration Commissioners, 18 Mar 1840, Macarthur Papers, XCII; *Sydney Herald*, 5, 6 Jan and 5, 6 Feb 1841; *V & P* (LC, NSW), 10 Dec 1840.
168 Tapp, *Early New Zealand*, Chapter 7.
169 Edward Macarthur to Peel, no date, Macarthur Papers, XIX; Edward Macarthur to Stanley and Russell, Sep 1841 (draft), Macarthur Papers, XCII; Melbourne, *Constitutional Development*, 257, 341; Edward Macarthur, *Colonial Policy of 1840 and 1841* (London, 1841).

352   *Colonial Self-Government*

170 *Sydney Herald*, 10 Feb, 6 and 30 Mar, 25 May, 15 June 1840, and 24 June 1851.
171 *Sydney Herald*, 8 Jan, 6 Feb 1841; *The Australian*, 9 Jan, 6 Feb 1841.
172 Roe, *Quest for Authority*, 82f.; Bland, *Letters to Buller*, 158f.; *The Australian*, 5 Nov 1840; Russell, quoted by Melbourne in *CHBE*, VII(1), 163.
173 For example, Bland, *Letters to Buller*, 158f.
174 *Sydney Herald*, 24 July and 25 Dec 1841; *The Australian*, 4, 8, 18, 21 and 29 Jan 1842; *V & P* (LC, NSW), 20 June 1841; Melbourne, *Constitutional Development*, 261f.; Buller to the Australian Patriotic Association, 31 May 1840, in *The Australian*, 12 Nov 1840.
175 Edward Macarthur to Russell, Mar 1841, CO 201/215; 3 *PD*, LVII, 598, 974 (25 Mar, 22 Apr 1841); Russell to Gipps, 21 July 1841, *HRA*, I, xxi, 440.
176 *Sydney Herald*, 2 Sep and 9 Oct 1841, 17 Feb 1842.
177 Buller to Stanley, Nov 1841 (private and confidential), CO 206/62; *Sydney Herald*, 21 Mar 1842.
178 Compare *Sydney Herald*, 11 Jan 1842.
179 Gipps to Russell, 14 Sep 1841, *HRA*, I, xxi, 510; *Sydney Herald*, 5 Jan 1842.
180 Edward Macarthur to his brothers, 2 Mar 1842, Macarthur Papers, XIX; Stanley to Gipps, 5 Sept 1842, CO 202/45; Bourke to Lord Monteagle (Spring-Rice), 7 July 1842, Bourke Papers, IX.
181 Stanley to Gipps, 5 Sep 1842 (private), CO 202/45.
182 Memorandum of December 1841, CO 281/331; Ward, *Earl Grey*, 28, 46; Melbourne, *Constitutional Development*, Part IV, Chapter 6.
183 See Chapter 8.
184 Stanley to Gipps, 5 Sep 1842 (private), CO 202/45.
185 *SMH*, 1 July 1842, 24 Apr 1867.
186 *SMH*, 18 Aug 1842.
187 Stephen's minute on draft circular to governors, CO 537/91.
188 Memorandum by Stephen (no date, 1848), CO 881/1, No. I.
189 Ward, in *JMH*, XXXI, 189f.
190 CO 881/1, No. XX; Stephen's memorandum on the Colonial Office, CO 325/47; Morrell, *British Colonial Policy*, 43f. See Chapter 7 below.
191 Bourke to Lord Monteagle (Spring-Rice), 7 July 1842, Bourke Papers, IX; Melbourne, *Constitutional Development*, Part IV.

CHAPTER 6

1 Pares, in *EHJ*, VII, 120.
2 Grey, *Parliamentary Government*, 4.
3 See pp. 23 and 44; Craig, *Upper Canada*, 203; New, in *CHR*, XX, 119–35.
4 See Chapter 8.
5 Kemp, *King and Commons*, 78, 87f.
6 24 *PH*, 364f., 432f., 483, 690, 709f.; Foord, *His Majesty's Opposition*, 394f.; Emden, *The People and the Constitution*, 154f.; Christie, *The End of North's Ministry*, and Cannon, *The Fox—North Coalition* (both *passim*).
7 Kemp, *King and Commons*, 131.
8 Quoted from Barrington to Mitchell, 13 Dec 1762 (British Museum Add. MSS. 6834, 52), in Namier, *England in the Age of the American Revolution*, I, 58.
9 Lewis, *Essays on the Administration of Great Britain*, ed. E. Head, 88f.
10 Kemp, *King and Commons*, 80f., 134.
11 Foord, in *EHR*, LXII, 506.
12 Foord, *His Majesty's Opposition*, 470. 'His Majesty's Opposition' was probably first so called by John Cam Hobhouse in 1826; 2 *PD*, XV, 137 and 149.

13 Bathurst to Hay, 23 Oct 1828, Bathurst Papers, BM 57/59; cf. H. Gally Knight to Wilmot-Horton, 15 Feb [1828], Catton Papers; Mitchell, *The Whigs in Opposition*, Chapters 9 and 10.
14 S. R. Lushington to W. Kingston, 26 Mar 1827; Aspinall, *Letters of George IV*, III, 207f.
15 3 *PD*, XI, 757 (22 Mar 1832).
16 Greville, *Memoirs*, II, 367 (22 Feb 1833).
17 Greville, *Memoirs*, III, 28f. (3 Sep 1833).
18 See Chapters 2 and 3.
19 3 *PD*, LIV, 730f. (29 May 1840).
20 *The Times*, 10 May 1839 (leading article).
21 Hardcastle, *Life of Lord Campbell*, I, 467.
22 Journal of the third Earl Grey, 6 Aug 1833, 14 July 1834; Prest, *Russell*, 69, 72f.; Melbourne to William IV, 10 July 1834; Peel to William IV, 13 July 1834, in Peel, *Memoirs*, II, 3f., 9f.; Kitson Clark, *Peel and the Conservative Party*, 175f., 191f.
23 William IV to Melbourne, 14 Nov 1834, in Peel, *Memoirs*, II, 22; Gash, *Reaction and Reconstruction*, 6f.
24 Journal of the third Earl Grey, 16 Nov 1834.
25 W. I. Jennings, *Cabinet Government*, 299; Evatt, *The King and his Dominion Governors*, 105; Melbourne to Grey, 14 November 1834, in Sanders, *Lord Melbourne's Papers*, 225; Greville, *Memoirs*, 16 Nov 1834, III, 147; William IV to Peel, 22 Feb 1835, in Parker, *Peel*, II, 287f.; Kitson Clark, *Peel*, 194f.
26 Trevelyan, *Lord Grey of the Reform Bill*, 341.
27 Peel, *Memoirs*, II, 31f.
28 3 *PD*, XXVI, 215f. (24 Feb 1835); Todd, *Parliamentary Government in England*, I, 112; Emden, *The People and the Constitution*, 150.
29 Greville, *Memoirs*, III, 223 (23 Feb 1835); Hamilton, in *Canadian Historical Association Report 1964*, 89–104; Hardcastle, *Campbell*, II, 58; Peel *Memoirs*, II, 43f., 51; Gash, *Politics, 232.*
30 *Weekly Political Register*, 13 Dec 1834.
31 Melbourne to Grey, 23 Jan 1835, in Sanders, *Lord Melbourne's Papers*, 238.
32 Greville, *Memoirs*, III, 166 (27 Nov 1834).
33 *Westminster Review*, I (1824), 2, and XXII (1835), 259f.; *Spectator*, VII (1834), 1102, 1182. Regarding Upper Canada, cf. *Correspondent and Advocate*, 22 Jan 1835.
34 Gash, *Politics*, 335.
35 Dudley Ryder, Viscount Sandon, member for Liverpool, later second Earl of Harrowby. 3 *PD*, XXVI, 151f. (24 Feb 1835).
36 G. W. F. Howard, Viscount Morpeth, later seventh Earl of Carlisle, member for the West Riding. 3 *PD*, XXVI, 167f. (24 Feb 1835).
37 Kemp, *King and Commons*, 79.
38 3 *PD*, XXVI, 464 (27 Feb 1835); Erskine May, *Constitutional History of England*, II, 151; Greville, *Memoirs*, III, 223 (23 Feb 1835); L. J. Jennings, *Croker Papers*, II, 266; Greville, *Memoirs*, III, 242, (28 Mar 1835).
39 Hardcastle, *Campbell*, II, 62; Greville, *Memoirs*, III, 208f.
40 3 *PD*, XXVI, 471 (27 Feb 1835).
41 *Fraser's Magazine*, XI (1835), 361f.
42 Creevey to Countess Grey, 2 Feb 1835, Hickleton Papers, A/1/4/26.
43 Gash, *Reaction and Reconstruction*, 165.
44 Journal of the third Earl Grey, 18 and 20 Feb, 8, 10 and 11 Apr 1835; Prest, *Russell*, 72f, 85f.
45 Journal of the third Earl Grey, 27 Feb 1835.

46 Ellice to Durham, 19 Mar 1835, Lambton Papers, quoted in Aspinall, *Lord Brougham and the Whig Party* (Manchester, 1927), 293.

47 3 *PD*, XXVI, 474 (27 Feb 1835); Kitson Clark, *Peel*, 211f. and 238f.; Namier *Personalities and Powers*, 17; Gash, *Sir Robert Peel*, 106f.

48 Parker, *Peel*, II, 293; Peel, *Memoirs*, II, 89; Gash, *Peel*, 114.

49 Parker, *Peel*, II, 294f.

50 Davis, *Age of Grey and Peel*, 255; 3 *PD*, XXVI, 374 (30 Mar 1835); Parker, *Peel*, II, 301f.; Journal of the third Earl Grey, 4 Apr 1835; Prest, *Russell*, 90f.

51 Parker, *Peel*, II, 302; Journal of the third Earl Grey, 11 Apr 1835; Malmesbury, *Memoirs*, I, 62.

52 Parker, *Peel*, 299f.

53 Peel to William IV, 29 Mar 1835; Peel, *Memoirs*, II, 91f.; Peel to Croker, 5 July 1837, in L. J. Jennings, *Croker Papers*, II, 316f.

54 Journal of the third Earl Grey, 8, 10 and 11 Apr 1835; Gash, *Peel*, 127f.

55 *Edinburgh Review*, LXI (1835), 10, LXII (1835), 185f.

56 *Quarterly Review*, LVII (1836), 231f., and LIX (1837), 244f.

57 *Fraser's Magazine*, XII (1835), 301f., 674f.

58 Gash, *Peel*, 125.

59 *Westminster Review*, XXV (1837), 279f., and XXVIII (1838), 1f.; *Fraser's Magazine*, XVI (1837), 267f.; Journal of the third Earl Grey, throughout this period; Grey to C. A. Wood, 3 Feb and 10 Nov 1837, Hickleton Papers, A/2/73.

60 3 *PD*, XXXIX, 1428f. (22 Dec 1837); Journal of the third Earl Grey, 22 Dec 1837; Morley, *Gladstone*, I, 614f.

61 C. Buller, *Sketch of Lord Durham's Mission*, in Durham, *Report*, III, 338f.; 3 *PD*, XLIV, 1127f. (10 Aug 1838); Journal of the third Earl Grey, 15 Aug 1838.

62 Journal of the third Earl Grey, 21 and 24 Oct 1838; Russell to Melbourne, 2 and 12 Dec 1838, in Russell, *Early Correspondence*, 236f.

63 *Fraser's Magazine*, XIX (1839), 180f.

64 Greville, *Memoirs*, IV, 133 (23 Aug 1838).

65 3 *PD*, XLI, 476f. (6 Mar 1838); Gash, *Peel*, 203f.; Greville, *Memoirs*, IV, 78 (9 Mar 1838); Grey to Howick, 7 and 20 Jan 1839, and Howick to Grey, 22 Jan 1839, Grey of Howick Papers; Grey to Wood, 8 Nov 1838, Hickleton Papers, A/2/73; Prest, *Russell*, 139; Gash, *Reaction and Reconstruction*, 153; Sanders, *Lord Melbourne's Papers*, 380; C. E. Stephen, *The First Sir James Stephen* (Gloucester, 1906), 51.

66 Chapter 4, p. 118.

67 Journal of the third Earl Grey, 31 Jan 1839; Russell to Melbourne, 2 Feb 1839, Russell Papers (PRO 30/22, Box 3).

68 Howick to Melbourne, 30 Jan 1839, Russell to Howick, 31 Jan 1839 (two letters), and Howick to Russell, 31 Jan 1839 (two letters), Grey of Howick Papers; Journal of the third Earl Grey, 1 Feb 1839.

69 Howick to Grey, 20 Aug 1839, Grey of Howick Papers.

70 Journal of the third Earl Grey, 4 and 5 Feb 1839; Grey to Howick, 16 Feb 1839, and Howick to Grey, 14 Aug 1839, Grey of Howick Papers.

71 Grey to Howick, 2 Feb 1839, Howick to Grey, 14 and 18 Feb 1839, Grey of Howick Papers.

72 Journal of the third Earl Grey, 9 Feb 1839. Correspondence of Howick and Melbourne, Feb 1839, Grey of Howick Papers; Melbourne to Victoria, 10 Feb 1839, in Benson and Esher, *Letters of Queen Victoria*, I, 184.

73 Melbourne to Victoria, 22 Mar 1839, in ibid., I, 188.

74 Melbourne to Victoria, 26 Apr 1839, in ibid., I, 193.

75 3 *PD*, XLVII, 459, 573, 765, 970f. (23 and 26 Apr, 3 and 6 May 1839); Greville, *Memoirs*, 6 May 1839, IV, 199; Journal of the third Earl Grey, 6 May 1839; Gash, *Peel*, 220; Prest, *Russell*, 146.

76 Melbourne to Victoria, 7 May 1839, in Benson and Esher, *Letters of Queen Victoria*, I, 194; *The Times*, 8 May 1839; Journal of the third Earl Grey, 7 May 1839; 3 *PD*, XLVII, 976f.

77 Russell later claimed as much. See 3 *PD*, LVIII, 1213 (4 June 1841).

78 *The Times*, 8 May 1839.

79 Melbourne to Victoria, 7 May 1839 (second letter), in Benson and Esher, *Letters of Queen Victoria*, I, 195f.; Gash, *Peel*, 220f.; Peel to Victoria, 10 May 1839, in Parker, *Peel*, 396f.; Gash, *Reaction and Reconstruction*, 24f.; Kitson Clark, *Peel*, 417; Melbourne to Victoria, 9 May 1839, in Benson and Esher, *Letters of Queen Victoria*, I, 204; Extracts from the Queen's Journal, 9 and 10 May 1839, in ibid., I, 207f.; Greville, *Memoirs*, IV, 216 (12 May 1839).

80 Greville, *Memoirs*, IV, 214 (12 May 1839).

81 Journal of the third Earl Grey, 9 and 11 May 1839. Cabinet minute (May 1839), in Benson and Esher, *Letters of Queen Victoria*, I, 315f.

82 3 *PD*, LI, 770 (29 Jan 1839).

83 Journal of the third Earl Grey, 9 and 14 May 1839.

84 Greville, *Memoirs*, IV, 219.

85 Greville, *Memoirs*, IV, 214, 216f.; Graham to Croker, 22 May 1839, in L. J. Jennings, *Croker Papers*, II, 356; Gash, *Peel*, 225; memorandum by Anson, 4 May 1841, in Benson and Esher, *Letters of Queen Victoria*, I, 337.

86 Journal of the third Earl Grey, 15 and 17 May, 20—30 Aug, 25 Sep and 19 Oct 1839; Howick to Grey, 5, 14, 20, 27, 28 and 29 Aug 1839, and Grey to Howick, 22, 28, 29 and 31 Aug 1839, Grey of Howick Papers.

87 Howick to Grey, 20 and 27 Aug 1839, Grey of Howick Papers; Torrens, *Melbourne*, II, 313; Prest, *Russell*, 139.

88 Howick to Grey, 20, 27 and 28 Aug 1839, Grey of Howick Papers.

89 Journal of the third Earl Grey, 20 Aug 1839; J. W. Croker, 'Conduct of Ministers', in *Quarterly Review*, LXV (1839), 283f.; Normanby to Russell, 4 June 1839, Russell Papers (PRO 30/22, Box 3); Journal of the third Earl Grey, 10 Oct 1839.

90 The defeat by 104 votes over Prince Albert's allowance was particularly significant. See *The Times*, 5 Feb 1840.

91 Grey to Wood, 30 Oct 1839, Hickleton Papers, A/2/73.

92 Journal of the third Earl Grey, 16 Jan 1840; Gash, *Peel*, 238f.; Grey to Howick, 21 Jan 1840, Grey of Howick Papers.

93 3 *PD*, LI, 650f., 737f., 835f., 936, 1073f. (28—31 Jan 1840); Journal of the third Earl Grey, 21 and 28 Jan 1840.

94 Journal of the third Earl Grey, 21 Jan 1840.

95 Grey to Howick, 4 Feb 1840, Grey of Howick Papers.

96 *The Times* (5 Feb 1840) denied this because Peel's administration was 'in all respects *an experiment*'.

97 Grey to Howick, 2 and 4 Feb 1840, and Howick to Grey, 1 and 4 Feb 1840, Grey of Howick Papers.

98 Grey to Howick, 21 Jan and 2 Feb 1840, and Howick to Grey, 4 Feb 1840, Grey of Howick Papers.

99 Howick to Grey, 14 and 24 Feb 1840, Grey of Howick Papers; *Fraser's Magazine*, XXII (1840), 373f.; Grey to Howick, 1 and 5 Mar 1841, Grey of Howick Papers.

100 *The Times*, 28 Apr 1841; Kitson Clark, *Peel*, 473; Gash, *Peel*, 251.

101 Journal of the third Earl Grey, 26—29 April 1841.

102 Journal of the third Earl Grey, 14, 15, 19 and 20 May 1841; *Quarterly Review*, LXVIII (1841), 238f.

103 Memoranda by Anson, 4, 5, 9 and 10 May 1841, in Benson and Esher, *Letters of Queen Victoria*, I, 337, 339, 341, 344; Melbourne to Victoria, 7 May 1841, in ibid., I, 340; Gash, *Peel*, 258f.; memorandum by Peel, 11 May 1841, in Parker, *Peel*, II, 455f.

104 Journal of the third Earl Grey, 19 May 1841; Greville, *Memoirs*, V, 1f.

105 Extract from the Queen's Journal, 15 May 1841, in Benson and Esher, *Letters of Queen Victoria*, I, 347; Melbourne to Russell, 13 and 14 May 1841, in Sanders, *Lord Melbourne's Papers*, 417, 418.

106 Palmerston to Melbourne, 14 May 1841, in ibid., 419.

107 Journal of the third Earl Grey, 3, 19 and 22 May 1841.

108 Kitson Clark, *Peel*, 478f.

109 Extracts from the Queen's Journal, 17 and 18 May 1841, in Benson and Esher, *Letters of Queen Victoria*, I, 350f.

110 Melbourne to Russell, 13 and 14 May 1841, in Sanders, *Lord Melbourne's Papers*, 417 and 418; Journal of the third Earl Grey, 18 May 1841.

111 'Present State and Conduct of the Parties', in *Edinburgh Review*, LXXI (1840), 285f.; Gash, *Peel*, 255f.

112 Journal of the third Earl Grey, 24 May 1841.

113 Journal of the third Earl Grey, 24 May 1841; Palmerston to Melbourne, 14 May 1841, in Sanders, *Lord Melbourne's Papers*, 419.

114 3 PD, LVIII, 803f. (4 June 1841).

115 Emden, *The People and the Constitution*, 157.

116 Ibid., 156; Greville, *Memoirs*, II, 65; Foord, *His Majesty's Opposition*, 464; Kemp, *King and Commons*, 79.

117 Melbourne to Russell, 14 May 1841, in Sanders, *Lord Melbourne's Papers*, 418.

118 Journal of the third Earl Grey, 4 and 8 June 1841; Prest, *Russell*, 181f.; 3 PD, LVIII, 1274 (7 June 1841); Maxwell, *Creevey Papers*, II, 10f.

119 Grey to Howick, 1 Mar 1841, Grey of Howick Papers; Journal of third Earl Grey, 22 and 26 May 1841.

120 J. W. Croker, 'The Old and New Ministries', in *Quarterly Review*, LXVIII (1841), 494f.; *Edinburgh Review*, LXXV (1842), 189f.

121 Greville, *Memoirs*, V, 21f (11 July 1841); Gash, *Reaction and Reconstruction*, 28, note 3.; Gash, *Peel*, 264f.

122 Hamilton, in *Canadian Historical Association Report 1964*, 100.

123 *The Times*, 31 July 1841.

124 *The Times*, 5 Aug 1841.

125 3 PD, LIX, 71 (24 Aug 1841).

126 Gash, *Peel*, 265.

127 *The Times*, 28, 30 and 31 Aug, 20 Sep 1841.

128 3 PD, LIX, 175f. (24 Aug 1841); Emden, *The People and the Constitution*, 163.

129 Ibid., 165.

130 Broughton, *Recollections of a Long Life*, VI, 40.

131 Melbourne to Victoria, no date [c. 11 Sep 1841], in Benson and Esher, *Letters of Queen Victoria*, I, 385; Keith, *The British Cabinet System*, 23; Victoria to Russell, 16 July 1846, in Benson and Esher, *Letters of Queen Victoria*, II, 108.

132 Emden, *The People and the Constitution*, 159; Kemp, *King and Commons*, 76f.

133 Russell, in *Memorials of Life and Times of Charles James Fox*, 3 vols (London, 1859–66), II, 245; Emden, *The People and the Constitution*, 206f.

134 Hanham, *Nineteenth Century Constitution*, 172, 174f.

135 Holdsworth, *A History of English Law*, XIII, 257; Kemp, *King and Commons*, 145; Emden, *The People and the Constitution*, 162f.

136 3 PD, LIV, 728 (29 May 1841).

137 Journal of the third Earl Grey, 21 and 22 May, and 4 June 1841.

138 Journal of the third Earl Grey, 26 May, 1, 4 and 10 July, 2 and 7 Oct 1841, 22 and 30 May, 2 and 10 June 1842; correspondence between Howick and Russell (several letters), July—Sep 1842, Grey of Howick Papers.

139 Sandon to Peel, 15 June 1844, and Peel to Sandon, 17 June 1844, in Parker, *Peel*, III, 150f., 152.

140 Tufnell to Russell, no date, Russell Papers (PRO 30/22, Box 4).

141 Graham to Lord Heytesbury, 12 Apr 1845, Graham Papers, Netherby, quoted in Gash, *Reaction and Reconstruction*, 152.

142 Journal of the third Earl Grey, 15—19 Dec 1845; Grey to Russell, 16 Dec 1845, and Russell to Grey, 17, 18 and 19 Dec 1845, Grey of Howick Papers.

143 Parker, *Peel*, II, 249, 251; Peel, *Memoirs*, II, 234f. 238f.; Greville, *Memoirs*, V, 339 (21 Dec 1845); Journal of the third Earl Grey, 15—31 Dec 1845, 5 and 20 Jan 1846.

144 1st Baron Stanmore, *Sidney Herbert*, 2 vols (London, 1906), I, 56; Greville, *Memoirs*, V, 339f. (21—24 Dec 1845); Peel to Prince Albert, 18 Dec 1845, in Parker, *Peel*, III, 252f.; Conacher, in *EHR*, LXXIII, 432f.

145 Heytesbury, from Parker, *Peel*, III, 290.

146 Journal of the third Earl Grey, 6 Feb 1845.

147 *Quarterly Review*, LXXVIII (1846), 538f., 566f.

148 3 *PD*, LXXXIII, 90 (22 Jan 1846).

149 Peel, *Memoirs*, II, 231; Wellington to Croker, 6 Jan 1846, in L. J. Jennings, *Croker Papers*, III, 519.

150 R. Blake, *Disraeli* (London, 1956), 162f., 178, 183, 239f.; 3 *PD*, LXXXIII, 123 (22 Jan 1846); Blake, *Disraeli*, 226f.; Gash, *Peel*, 596.

151 3 *PD*, LXXXVII, 959 (25 June 1846).

152 Ellenborough to Peel, 29 May 1846, quoted in Gash, *Reaction and Reconstruction*, 15; Gash, *Peel*, 599.

153 Peel to Ellenborough, 30 May 1846, Ellenborough Papers (PRO 30/12/21).

154 Journal of the third Earl Grey, 2 and 3 June 1846.

155 Parker, *Peel*, III, 365.

156 Peel's memorandum of 21 June 1846, enclosed in Peel to Queen Victoria, 26 June 1846 (secret), Peel Papers, Royal Archives, Windsor (microfilm).

157 Wellington to Peel, 21 June 1846, Parker, *Peel*, II, 365f.

158 292 to 219 votes. Journal of the third Earl Grey, 26 June 1846.

159 *The Times*, 30 June 1846.

160 Grey, *Parliamentary Government*, 4.

161 Butt, *The Power of Parliament*, 77f.; Gash, *Politics*, 395. Grey (*Parliamentary Government*, 198) preferred 'parliamentary government' or 'party government' to 'responsible government'.

162 Senior, *Historical and Philosophical Essays*, 2 vols, (London, 1865), II, 219f.

CHAPTER 7

1 Beaglehole, in *Bulletin of IHR*, VII, 184f.

2 Merivale, *Lectures*, I, 134.

3 Pares, in *EHJ*, VII, 130.

4 Morrell, *British Colonial Policy*, 505.

5 Shaw, *Great Britain and the Colonies*, 24f.

6 Schuyler, *Fall of the Old Colonial System, passim*.

7 Gallagher and Robinson, in *EHJ*, 2nd series, VI, 1f.

8 Galbraith, in *AHR*, LXVII, 34f.

9 Shaw, *Great Britain and the Colonies*, 25.

10 MacDonagh, in *EHJ*, XIV, 500.

11 See Chapters 8 and 9. Crook, *American Democracy in English Politics, passim.*
12 Ricardo, *Works,* IX, 269 and note.
13 2 *PD,* XVII, 805 (15 May 1827); Jones, '*Prosperity Robinson*', 35, 99, 101, 234f.
14 For example, 2 *PD,* VII, 1121.
15 3 *PD,* XLVI, 777 (15 Mar 1839).
16 Gash, *Peel,* 639.
17 L. Brown, *The Board of Trade and the Free Trade Movement* (Oxford, 1958), 6.
18 Prest, *Russell,* 191; Semmel, *Free Trade Imperialism,* 196.
19 Journal of the third Earl Grey, 2 and 12 Feb, 13 Aug 1829, 2 and 26 Jan, 12 and 14 Mar, 6 and 31 May 1830.
20 Ward, in *HSANZ,* IX, 244–62.
21 Wakefield, *Art of Colonization,* in *Collected Works,* 771.
22 A. Smith, *Wealth of Nations,* 590.
23 Ibid., 353f., 384f., 415f., 574f., 690.
24 Benians, in *CHJ,* I, 249f.
25 Malthus: *Essay on Population,* 2nd ed., 437f.; *Additions,* 109, 117f.
26 K. Smith, *The Malthusian Controversy,* 326f.
27 Poynter, *Society and Pauperism,* 149, note 117.
28 *Quarterly Review,* XXV (1824), 297f.
29 Malthus, *Additions,* 111f., 119, 199; Semmel, *Free Trade Imperialism,* 74f.
30 Wagner, in *Political Science Quarterly,* XLVI, 257f.
31 *Quarterly Review,* XXIX (1828), 214f.
32 Ricardo, *Works,* V, 16, note.
33 Bowring, *Works of Jeremy Bentham,* IV, 408, 411, 418; Stark, *Economic Writings of Bentham,* III, 68, 299.
34 J. Mill, *Elements of Political Economy,* 3rd ed., 211f.; *Westminster Review,* II (1824), 290f.
35 *Westminster Review,* XIII (1830), 47f., XIV (1831), 101, and XXIV (1836), 29; Kittrell, in *Southern Economic Journal,* XXXI, reprinted in Shaw, *Great Britain and the Colonies,* 46f.
36 2 *PD,* VII, 250 (25 Feb 1823); 3 *PD,* XLV, 648 (23 Feb 1832).
37 Wakefield, *England and America,* in *Collected Works,* 582f.
38 J. Mill, 'Colony', Supplement to *Encyclopaedia Britannica,* supplement to 4th, 5th and 6th eds, III, 275f.
39 *Westminster Review,* III (1825), 449f., and VIII (1827), 25; Nesbitt, *Benthamite Reviewing,* 63.
40 2 *PD,* VIII, 250 (25 Feb 1823).
41 Brougham, Inquiry, I, 159f., 168f., 194f., 214f., 266f.
42 R. Torrens, *Economists Refuted* (London, 1808), 33f.; Torrens, *External Corn Trade* (London, 1815), 148f., 288f., 321f.; Torrens, *The Poor's Rate* (London, 1817), 524, quoted in Knorr, *British Colonial Theories,* 279; Semmel, *Free Trade Imperialism,* 60f.
43 *Quarterly Review,* V (1811), 416f., VI (1811), 496f., and VIII (1812), 355.
44 Ibid., XXXIII (1824–5), 410f.
45 Ibid., XXXIX (1829), 340.
46 Ibid., XXXIII (1825–6), 428.
47 Cf. Thrall, *Rebellious Fraser's,* 123f. and Chapter 6, *passim.*
48 Huskisson, *Speeches,* II, 287; also III, 110, 286f., 313.
49 Morrell, *British Colonial Policy,* 4.
50 Ritchie, *Punishment and Profit,* 91f.; MacMillan, *Scotland and Australia,* Chapter 3.

51 Jenks, *Migration of British Capital*, 52f.; Roberts, *The Squatting Age in Australia*, 138.
52 *PP*, 1826–7, V, 225.
53 *Edinburgh Review*, XLVII (1828), 97; *Quarterly Review*, XXXII (1825), 333.
54 H. T. Manning, in *JBS*, V, 92f.
55 Imlah, *Economic Elements*, 181; Porter, *Progress of the Nation*, 143.
56 Sidmouth to Liverpool, 5 Apr 1817, Sidmouth Papers (Exeter), quoted in Ritchie, *Punishment and Profit*, 90.
57 *PP*, 1819, II, 529, quoted in Madgwick, *Immigration into Eastern Australia*, 73.
58 Burroughs, *Britain and Australia*, 384.
59 Corry, *Money, Saving and Investment*, 37; Wagner, in *Political Science Quarterly*, XLVI, 267.
60 Crook, *American Democracy in English Politics*, 38 and Chapter 2, *passim*.
61 See note 38 above.
62 Himes, in *Economic History*, III, 267f.
63 'Manual of Political Economy', in Bowring, *Works of Jeremy Bentham*, III, 76; 'Population and Colonization', Bentham Papers, CLI, 108.
64 Knorr, *British Colonial Theories*, 267, note 77; Halévy, *Growth of Philosophic Radicalism*, 510; Bowring, *Works of Jeremy Bentham*, IV, 418.
65 Quoted in Semmel, *Free Trade Imperialism*, 80f.
66 T. Chalmers, *Christian and Economic Polity* (London, 1821), viii, quoted in Knorr, *British Colonial Theories*, 272, note 13.
67 R. J. Wilmot-Horton, *Causes and Remedies of Pauperism*, Part I, 22f., 36f., 49f.; 2 *PD*, XVI, 480 (15 Feb 1827).
68 Wilmot-Horton, *Causes and Remedies of Pauperism*, 22.
69 Torrens, *The Poor's Rate*, quoted in Knorr, *British Colonial Theories*, 271, note 8; correspondence between Torrens and Wilmot-Horton, Catton Papers.
70 2 *PD* XVI, 482 (15 Feb 1827), XIX, 1503, 1508 (24 June 1828), XXI, 1724 (4 June 1829).
71 Kittrell, in *Southern Economic Journal*, XXXI, reprinted in Shaw, *Great Britain and the Colonies*, 64f.; N. W. Senior, *Industrial Efficiency and Social Economy*, 2 vols (New York and London, 1928), I, 342, 351f.
72 *Westminster Review*, VI (1826), 343, 370f.
73 2 *PD*, XIV, 1364 (14 Mar 1826), and XVI, 509 (15 Feb 1827); Ghosh, in *Economica*, XXXI, 385f., reprinted in Shaw, *Great Britain and the Colonies*, 45f.
74 3 *PD*, II, 875f. (22 Feb 1831); *Edinburgh Review*, LIII, 547; *Quarterly Review*, XLV (1831), 139f.; Burroughs, *Britain and Australia*, 69f.; H. Ellis to Wilmot-Horton, 5 June 1832, Catton Papers; Papers of the third Earl Grey, Colonial, Emigration, No. 5; Goderich to Emigration Commissioners, 4 Aug 1832, CO 384/27.
75 Wilmot-Horton to Howick, 17 Feb 1831, Grey of Howick Papers; Ghosh, in *Economica*, XXXI, 385f.
76 H. T. Manning, in *JBS*, V, 92.
77 Gouger to Wilmot-Horton, 3 Feb 1830, quoted by Pike in *HSANZ*, VII, 205.
78 Wilmot-Horton to Tennant, 23 Apr 1831, quoted in Pike, *HSANZ*, VII, 210; *The Times*, 17 June 1830.
79 Philipp, *A Great View of Things*, 2, and Bibliography; Wakefield on opponents: *England and America*, in *Collected Works*, 514, 542, 567f.; *Art of Colonization*, in ibid., 769f., 785f., 882f. (from Buller), 903f.
80 Shaw, in *JBS*, IX, 91 and note.
81 *PP*, 1847, VI [Cmd 737], quoted on 4383.

82 Buller to J. S. Mill, 13 Oct 1838, reprinted in PAC, *Report 1928,* Appendix F., 76; H. T. Manning, in *JBS,* V. 92.
83 Philipp, *A Great View of Things,* Chapter 3; Mills, *Colonization of Australia,* Chapter 5; Burroughs, *Britain and Australia,* 12f.; Pike, *Paradise of Dissent,* Chapters 3 and 5; Winch, *Classical Political Economy,* Chapters 5 and 6; Semmel, *Free Trade Imperialism,* Chapters 4 and 5.
84 Wakefield, *England and America,* in *Collected Works,* 353, 373.
85 Ibid., 410f.
86 Torrens, *The Poor's Rate,* 524; Senior, *Remarks on Emigration* (London, 1831), 4f.
87 *Edinburgh Review,* LXXV (1842), 540.
88 Grampp, *The Manchester School of Economics,* 7f.; Schuyler, *Fall of the Old Colonial System,* Chapter 7.
89 3 *PD,* LXVIII, 501 (6 June 1843).
90 See Chapter 3, pp. 68–9, on Durham; Russell, 3 *PD,* LXXXI, 667 (17 June 1845), and Russell to Grey, 19 Aug 1848, Grey of Howick Papers; Grey, *Colonial Policy,* I, 281f., and 3 *PD,* LXXXVIII, 907 (20 Aug 1846).
91 Tucker, *Progress and Profits,* 185f.; Semmel, *Free Trade Imperialism,* 192f.; Torrens, *Colonization of South Australia,* 231f.
92 Winch, in *Economica,* XXX (1963), reprinted in Shaw, *Great Britain and the Colonies,* 93f.; Blaug, *Ricardian Economics,* 90f.; Tucker, Progress and Profits, 183f.
93 *The Times,* 2 July 1834.
94 J. S. Mill, *Principles of Political Economy,* 1909 ed., 728, 731, 971.
95 *Edinburgh Review,* LXXI (1840), 443; Merivale, *Lectures,* 1928 ed., 170f.
96 Sidney, *Three Colonies of Australia,* 2nd ed., 95.
97 Morrell, *British Colonial Policy,* 8.
98 *Edinburgh Review,* LXXI (1841), 519.
99 Semmel, *Free Trade Imperialism,* 108f., 119f.; Philipp, *A Great View of Things,* 4f., 18f., 58f., 72 note 1, 77f., 83f.
100 3 *PD,* CL, 38f. (10 Aug 1848), also Howick to Russell, 18 Jan 1845, Russell Papers (Duke University).
101 Grey, *Colonial Policy,* I, 328f.; Grey to F. Baring, 6 Oct 1849, Grey of Howick Papers.
102 *Economist,* 22 June 1848, quoted in Schuyler, *Fall of the Old Colonial System,* 234.
103 Lewis, *Government of Dependencies,* 226f.
104 Mundy, *Our Antipodes,* III, 83.; Knorr, *British Colonial Theories,* 310f., 356f.
105 *Quarterly Review,* LXVIII (1841), 88.
106 *Westminster Review,* XXXV (1840), 132, 141; R. Walsh (ed.), *Select Speeches of William Windham and William Huskisson* (Philadelphia, 1845), 543; *Quarterly Review,* XXXIX (1829), 340.
107 3 *PD,* LXX, 205 (22 June 1843).
108 Torrens, *The Budget* (London, 1844), 300, 318.
109 3 *PD,* XLIV, 730 (29 May 1840).
110 Merivale, *Lectures,* I, 134.
111 Cf. Stokes, *The English Utilitarians and India,* xiii.
112 Quoted in Knorr, *British Colonial Theories,* 315.
113 Grey, *Colonial Policy,* I, 13.
114 Curtin, *Image of Africa,* 374f.; Knorr, *British Colonial Theories,* 382–8.
115 Grey, *Colonial Policy,* I, 15f. Cf. Fowell Buxton, 3 *PD,* XXIX, 549.
116 Cf. O. Macdonagh, in *EHJ,* XIV, 489f., reprinted in Shaw, *Great Britain and the Colonies,* 167f.
117 Ward, in *AJPH,* III, 18f.

118 3 *PD*, LXXXVI, 1307.
119 3 *PD*, LXXXI, 665f. (17—19 June 1845). Also New South Wales debate of 22 Apr 1841, 3 *PD*, LVII, 974f.
120 Semmel, *Free Trade Imperialism*, 126f.
121 Ward, *British Policy in the South Pacific*, Chapters 9 and 10.
122 Koebner, *Imperialism*, 67.
123 Stanley to Grey, 27 June 1845, *PP*, 1845, XXXIII (HC 517—I), 8; Stanley to Grey, 28 June 1845 (private), CO 406/4.
124 Shaw, *Great Britain and the Colonies*, 6.
125 Koebner, *Imperialism*, 60.
126 3 *PD*, LXIII, 533f. (13 May 1842).
127 3 *PD*, LXXXIII, 262 (27 Jan 1846).
128 3 *PD*, LXXXIII, 850f., 867f., 1165f.
129 3 *PD*, LXXXVI, 1307f.
130 Gladstone to Cathcart, 3 June 1846, *PP*, 1846, XXVII (extract in Bell and Morrell, *Select Documents*, 345).
131 Russell to Grey, 19 Aug 1849, Grey of Howick Papers.
132 The phrase is Russell's in Russell to Grey, 19 Aug 1849, Grey of Howick Papers.
133 Wakefield, *Collected Works*, 875.
134 Ibid., 879.
135 Ibid., 882f., 769f.
136 Ibid., 859f.
137 Ibid., 719f.
138 Wakefield did foresee trouble. See *PP*, 1836, XI, 823.
139 J. S. Mayer, *Alexis de Tocqueville* (New York, 1960), 11f.
140 3 *PD*, CLXII, 965 (21 May 1852).
141 Crook, *American Democracy in English Politics*, 47f., 177f.
142 *Edinburgh Review*, LXXV (1842), 11.
143 Crook, *American Democracy in English Politics*, 91.
144 *Edinburgh Review*, LXXVI (1847), 391.
145 *Quarterly Review*, LIII (1835), 183f.; Crook, *American Democracy in English Politics*, 121f.
146 Durham, *Report*, I, 282f., and II, 264f., 297, 151, 267, 170f., 212f., 262.
147 3 *PD*, CV, 937 (26 May 1849).
148 Roebuck, *The Colonies of England*, 16f.
149 Ward, in *HS*, XIV, 594.
150 3 *PD*, CX, 1182 (6 May 1850).
151 Crook, *American Democracy in English Politics*, 23f., 78 note 3.
152 *Edinburgh Review*, LXXII (1846), 141.
153 Crook, *American Democracy in English Politics*, 27.
154 Journal of the third Earl Grey, 24 Oct 1853 and 31 Aug 1856.

CHAPTER 8

 1 Kennedy, *Statutes, Treaties and Documents*, 495.
 2 3 *PD*, LIV, 746 (29 May 1840).
 3 J. S. Mill, *On Liberty*, 308f.
 4 See Chapter 3. Also Martin, *The Durham Report*, Chapters 3 and 4.
 5 Russell's phrase, in Russell to Grey, 19 Aug 1849, Grey of Howick Papers.
 6 See Chapter 7.
 7 Buller in the Commons, 3 *PD*, LXXXV, 36 (30 May 1844).
 8 Stacey, *Canada and the British Army*, 25.
 9 Grey, *Colonial Policy*, I, 5.
10 Swinfen, *Imperial Control of Colonial Legislation*, 106f.

11 Schuyler, *Fall of the Old Colonial System*, Chapters 4 and 5; Bodelsen, *Mid-Victorian Imperialism*, 32f.
12 Morrell, *British Colonial Policy*, Chapter 19.
13 Grey, *Colonial Policy*, I, 22f., 26f.
14 For example, Morrell, *British Colonial Policy*, Chapter 18; Careless, *Union of the Canadas*, Chapters 1—7; and Ormsby, *The Emergence of the Federal Concept, passim.*
15 Careless, *Union of the Canadas*, xii.
16 Wade, *The French Canadians*, 225.
17 Quoted in Scrope, *Sydenham*, 172.
18 See pp. 77 and 285.
19 Sydenham to Russell, 18 July 1841, CO 42/280; Ormsby, *The Emergence of the Federal Concept*, 86f.
20 Baldwin to Sydenham, 18 Feb 1841, and Draper to Baldwin, 22 Feb 1841, both in Baldwin Papers.
21 Baldwin to Glenelg, 13 July 1836, in Kennedy, *Documents*, 339.
22 Sydenham to Baldwin, 1 Mar 1841, Baldwin to Sydenham, 5 Mar 1841, and Sydenham to Arthur, 27 Feb and 18 Mar 1841, all in Sanderson, *Arthur Papers*, III, 371f.
23 Poulett Thomson to the assembly of Upper Canada, 14 Jan 1840, in Kennedy, *Documents*, 432.
24 Journal of the third Earl Grey, 16 Apr, 2 and 7 Sep 1841.
25 Baldwin to Sydenham, 12 June 1841, Baldwin Papers. Sydenham to Russell: 12 June 1841, in Knaplund, *Letters*, 143; 23 June 1841, CO 42/479.
26 Kennedy, *Documents*, 455f.; Sydenham to Russell, 27 June 1841, in Knaplund, *Letters*, 145f.
27 Hincks to William Baldwin, 7 July 1841, Baldwin Papers.
28 Sydenham to Russell, 4 Aug 1841, in Knaplund, *Letters*, 157.
29 Kennedy, *Documents*, 457f.
30 Morrell, *British Colonial Policy*, 50; Metcalf, in *CHR*, XLII, 303.
31 Ormsby, *The Emergence of the Federal Concept*, 102.
32 Journal of the third Earl Grey, 8 June 1841; Peel to Stanley, 31 Aug 1843, quoted in Careless, *Union of the Canadas*, 230, note 88; Peel to Stanley, 5 Oct 1841, Ormsby, *The Emergence of the Federal Concept*, 102.
33 Sydenham to Russell, 27 May 1841, in Scrope, *Sydenham*, 244.
34 Buller to Peel, 9 Sep 1841, quoted by Knaplund in *CHR*, VIII, 43.
35 Stanley to Peel, 19 July 1841, in ibid., VIII, 41.
36 Stanley to Bagot, 8 Oct 1841, in Kennedy, *Documents*, 458.
37 Bagot to Stanley, 23 Feb 1842 (confidential), in Kennedy, *Documents*, 461.
38 Draper to Bagot, 16 July 1842, and Harrison to Bagot, 11 July 1842, in Kennedy, *Documents*, 468f., 464f.; Stanley to Bagot, 16 Oct 1842, Bagot Papers.
39 Bagot to Stanley, 12 June 1842, in Kennedy, *Documents*, 463f.
40 Bagot to Stanley, 10 July 1842, Bagot Papers, quoted in Careless, *Union of the Canadas*, 65f.
41 Bagot to Stanley, 28 July 1842, in Kennedy, *Documents*, 469f.
42 Bagot to Stanley, 13 Sep 1842 (private), in CO 537/140.
43 Stanley to Peel, 27 Aug 1842, Bagot Papers.
44 Bagot to Stanley, 6 Sep 1842 (private and confidential), CO 537/140.
45 Bagot to Stanley, 26 Sep 1842 (three dispatches with enclosures), in Kennedy, *Documents*, 475f.
46 CO 537/140.
47 Leacock, *Baldwin, La Fontaine, Hincks*, 140.
48 Careless, *Union of the Canadas*, 70.

49 Stanley to Bagot, 1 Sep 1842, in Kennedy, *Documents*, 472f.
50 *The Times*, 18 Oct 1842.
51 Arbuthnot to Peel, 18 Oct 1842, in Parker, *Peel*, III, 382.
52 Greville, *Memoirs*, II, 117.
53 Bagot to Stanley, 28 Oct 1842, Bagot Papers.
54 Stanley to Bagot, 2 and 3 Nov 1842, in Kennedy, *Documents*, 483f., 486f.
55 Stanley to Bagot, 3 Dec 1842, quoted in Morrell, *British Colonial Policy*, 58.
56 Bagot to Stanley, 11 Dec 1842, Bagot Papers.
57 Stanley to Metcalfe, 29 May 1843, CO 537/141.
58 Stanley to Metcalfe, 18 Aug 1843, CO 537/142.
59 Metcalfe to Stanley, 24 Apr 1843 (confidential), and 12 May 1843, CO 537/142.
60 Stanley to Metcalfe: 29 May 1843, CO 537/141; 1 Nov 1843, in Morrell, *British Colonial Policy*, 60.
61 Metcalfe to Stanley, 5 Aug 1843, CO 537/142.
62 Ibid.
63 Metcalfe to Stanley, 9 Oct 1843, CO 537/142.
64 Baldwin to Glenelg, 13 July 1836, in Kennedy, *Documents*, 340. Metcalfe to Stanley: 26 Nov 1843, CO 537/142; 26 Nov 1843 (private), Derby Papers, quoted in Careless, *Union of the Canadas*, 83; 11 Dec 1843, CO 42/509.
65 Quoted in Careless, *Union of the Canadas*, 83.
66 Wade, *The French Canadians*, 228.
67 Kaye, *Papers of Lord Metcalfe*, 533f.
68 Metcalfe to Stanley, 25 Feb 1844, Derby Papers, quoted in Careless, *Union of the Canadas*, 87.
69 3 *PD*, LXIX, 640 (19 May 1843).
70 Gash, *Peel*, 374f., 500.
71 Peel to Stanley, 2 Feb 1844, Peel Papers, quoted in Morrell, *British Colonial Policy*, 64.
72 H. T. Manning, in *CHR*, XLVIII, 1f.; [Wakefield], *Metcalfe's Government of Canada*.
73 *Spectator*, 6 Jan 1844.
74 3 *PD*, LXXXV, 31f. (30 May 1844).
75 Journal of the third Earl Grey, 30 May 1844.
76 Metcalfe to Stanley, 17 Sep 1844, CO 537/143.
77 Metcalf, in *CHR*, XLII, 312f.
78 Ormsby, in *Canadian Historical Association Report 1961*, 35f.; Bell, *Colonial Administration*, 307f.
79 Metcalfe to Stanley, 13 May 1845, in Kaye, *Papers of Lord Metcalfe*, 475f.
80 Elgin to Grey, 7 May 1847, in Doughty, *Elgin—Grey Papers*, I, 34.
81 Minute by Stephen on Cathcart's draft instructions, CO 380/5.
82 Minute by Hope, CO 42/351; Gladstone to Cathcart, 3 Feb 1846, CO 43/146.
83 Albert to Grey, 3 Aug 1846, in Jagow, *Letters of the Prince Consort*, 105.
84 Journal of the third Earl Grey, 11 July 1842.
85 Grey to Elgin, 5 Apr 1849, in Doughty, *Elgin—Grey Papers*, I, 316f.
86 Grey, *Colonial Policy*, I, 204.
87 Memorandum on colonial policy, 8 Feb 1849, Papers of the third Earl Grey, Colonial Papers, No. 3; Ward, in *HSANZ*, IX, 244f.; Grey, *Colonial Policy*, I, 34.
88 *Edinburgh Review*, LXXXIII (1846), 512f.; Journal of the third Earl Grey, 27 Apr 1846.
89 Lewis, *Government of Dependencies*, 324, 293.
90 See Chapter 3.
91 Stephen to Howick, [day unknown] Feb 1845, Grey of Howick Papers; Stephen's Diary, 12 July 1846.

92 J. R. M. Butler, 'Colonial Self-Government, 1838—1852', in *CHBE*, II, 369.
93 See Chapter 3.
94 3 *PD*, LXVIII, 484, (6 Apr 1843).
95 Journal of the third Earl Grey, 9 June 1843 to 29 June 1846; Buller to Howick, 27 Mar 1843, 1 Dec 1845, 14 Jan and 25 Apr 1846, Grey of Howick Papers; Palmerston to Russell, 20 Dec 1844, Russell Papers (PRO 30/22, Box 4).
96 Journal of the third Earl Grey, 3, 4 and 7 July 1846; Stephen's Diary, 12 July 1846.
97 Grey to Buller, 23 Feb 1847, Grey of Howick Papers; Semmel, *Free Trade Imperialism*, 122f.; Buller to Grey, 15 Mar 1847, Grey of Howick Papers; Morrell, *British Colonial Policy*, Chapter 17.
98 Russell to Grey, 17 Oct 1847, Grey of Howick Papers.
99 Falkland to Stanley, 28 Nov 1843, CO 217/184.
100 Chisholm, *Joseph Howe*, I, 594.
101 Chisholm, *Joseph Howe*, I, 494, 541.
102 Harvey to Grey, 15 Sep 1846 (private and confidential), CO 217/193.
103 Howe to Buller, 16 Sep 1846, quoted by Martin in *CHR*, VI, 318.
104 Buller to Howe, 10 Sep 1846, in ibid., VI, 316; Stephen's minute of 30 Sep 1846, CO 217/193.
105 Russell to Grey, 30 Oct and 4 Aug 1846, Grey of Howick Papers.
106 Grey to Harvey, 3 Nov 1846 (private and confidential), CO 217/193; *PP*, 1847—8, XLII (621), 7—9.
107 Buller to Howe, 16 Nov 1846, quoted by Martin in *CHR*, VI, 320f.
108 Harvey to Grey, 19 Nov and 2 Dec 1846 (private and confidential), CO 217/193; Grey to Harvey, 22 Dec 1846, CO 217/193; Grey to Harvey, 23 Dec 1846 (private and confidential), CO 218/34; memoranda of 28 and 30 Jan 1847, enclosed in Harvey to Grey, 2 Feb 1847 (No. 222), CO 217/193.
109 Minutes by Stephen and Hawes, 17 Feb, and by Grey, 18 Feb 1847, on Harvey to Grey, 2 Feb 1847 (No. 222), CO 217/193.
110 Grey to Harvey, 2 Mar 1847, CO 218/34; Buller to Grey, 1 Mar [1847], Grey of Howick Papers.
111 Harvey to Grey, 10 Aug, 2 Sep and 16 Dec 1847, CO 217/196; Harvey to Grey, 29 Jan 1848, and Grey to Harvey, 21 Feb 1848, CO 217/197.
112 Howe to Buller, 2 Sep 1847, and Buller to Howe, 23 Mar 1848, quoted by Martin in *CHR*, VI, 322f., 323f.
113 Grey to Harvey, 7 Mar 1848, CO 218/34; Buller to Howe, 24 Mar 1848, quoted by Martin in *CHR*, VI, 328.
114 Russell to Grey, 4 Aug 1846, Grey of Howick Papers.
115 Buller to Howe, 10 Sep 1846, quoted by Martin in *CHR*, VI, 316.
116 Elgin to Grey, 16 and 18 July 1846, and Grey to Elgin, 4 Aug 1846, in Doughty, *Elgin—Grey Papers*, I, 1f.
117 Journal of the third Earl Grey, 21 July, 1—6 Aug 1846; Russell to Grey, 31 July 1846, and Gladstone to Grey, 13 Aug 1846, Grey of Howick Papers.
118 Elgin to Grey, 29 Oct 1847, in Doughty, *Elgin—Grey Papers*, I, 75.
119 Journal of the third Earl Grey, 6 and 8 Oct, 7 Nov 1846, 4 and 5 Jan 1847; Elgin to Grey, 8 Dec 1846, in Doughty, *Elgin—Grey Papers*, I, 51; Grey, *Colonial Policy*, I, 208f.; Martin, *The Durham Report*, 67f.; Morrell, *British Colonial Policy*, 448.
120 Grey, *Colonial Policy*, I, 213f.
121 Elgin to Grey, 27 Mar (secret), 7 May (private) and 13 July 1847 (private and confidential), in Doughty, *Elgin—Grey Papers*, I, 21, 34f., 58.
122 Metcalf, in *CHR*, XLII, 316; Hincks to Baldwin, 25 and 27 Mar 1847, Baldwin Papers.
123 Elgin to Grey, 26 Apr 1847, in Doughty, *Elgin—Grey Papers*, I, 29.

124 Elgin to Grey, 9 and 24 Dec 1847, 7 and 22 Jan 1848, in ibid., I, 101, 102, 117, 118f.; *Globe*, 16 and 23 Feb 1848.
125 Grey to Elgin, 22 Feb 1848 (private), and Elgin to Grey, 22 Jan and 17 Mar 1848, in Doughty, *Elgin—Grey Papers*, I, 120, 119, 134f.
126 Elgin to Grey, 13 July 1847 and 27 Mar 1848, in ibid., I, 58, 139.
127 Elgin to Grey, 5 Feb 1848, in ibid., I, 123.
128 Russell to Grey, 12 and 16 Mar 1848, Grey to Russell, 14 Mar 1848, Grey of Howick Papers.
129 Elgin to Grey, 4 May 1848, in Doughty, *Elgin—Grey Papers*, I, 148.
130 Elgin to Grey, 16 Nov 1848, in ibid., I, 256.
131 Elgin to Grey, 22 Nov 1848 and 4 Jan 1849, and Grey to Elgin, 22 Mar and 15 Nov 1848, in ibid., I, 260, 278, 125, 262.
132 Elgin to Grey, 14 Mar 1849, in ibid., I, 307.
133 Russell to Grey, 1 Jan, 3 and 6 Aug 1849, Grey of Howick Papers; Elgin to Grey, 27 May and 1 Mar 1849, and Grey to Elgin, 16 June 1847, in Doughty, *Elgin—Grey Papers*, I, 45, 300, 47f.
134 Grey to Elgin, 9 Jan 1850, *PP*, 1850, XXXVIII [Cmd 1181] 24.
135 Grey to Elgin, 18 May 1849, in Doughty, *Elgin—Grey Papers*, I, 351.
136 Elgin to Grey, 30 Nov 1848, and Grey to Elgin, 26 Dec 1848, in ibid., I, 262f. 266.
137 Elgin to Grey, 1 Mar 1849, in ibid., I, 299f.
138 Elgin to Grey, 14 Mar and 12 Apr 1849, in ibid., I, 309, 338f.
139 Elgin to Grey, 30 Apr 1849, in ibid., I, 350.
140 *The Times*, 16 and 17 May 1849; Grey to Elgin, 18 May 1849, in Doughty, *Elgin—Grey Papers*, I, 351.
141 *Morning Chronicle*, 16 June 1849.
142 3 *PD*, CVI, 191 (14 June 1849); Grey to Elgin, 14 June 1849, in Doughty, *Elgin—Grey Papers*, I, 360.
143 3 *PD*, CVI, 243 (Commons, 14 June 1849) and 450 (Lords, 19 June 1849).
144 See Chapter 9; Grey to Elgin, 18 May 1849, in Doughty, *Elgin—Grey Papers*, I, 351.
145 3 *PD*, CVI, 461f.
146 Grey to Elgin, 22 June 1849, in Doughty, *Elgin—Grey Papers*, I, 372; 3 *PD*, CVI, 492.
147 Grey to Elgin, 16 June 1847, 13 and 22 June 1849, in Doughty, *Elgin—Grey Papers*, I, 47f., 372f., and IV, 1475; Grey to Russell, 31 July 1849, Grey of Howick Papers.
148 Russell to Grey, 19 Aug and 13 Oct 1849, Grey of Howick Papers.
149 Elgin to Grey, 23 May 1848, in Doughty, *Elgin—Grey Papers*, I, 179.
150 Elgin to Grey, 30 Nov 1848, and Grey to Elgin, 26 Dec 1848, in ibid., I, 263f., 266.
151 Elgin to Grey, 26 Apr and 18 May 1848, and Grey to Elgin, 18 May 1848, in ibid., I, 144, 186, 146.
152 Grey, *Colonial Policy*, I, 281f.
153 Ibid., I, 274f.; Bell, *Colonial Administration*, 324f.
154 Grey to Elgin, 31 Mar 1848, CO 43/139; Swinfen, *Imperial Control of Colonial Legislation*, 109.
155 Grey to Elgin, 11 Oct 1849 (draft with notes), CO 42/558; Grey, *Colonial Policy*, I, 235.
156 Masters, *Reciprocity Treaty of 1854*, xxi f.
157 Grey, *Colonial Policy*, I, 279f.; Grey to Head, 19 Aug 1850, Grey of Howick Papers.
158 Innis, *Essays in Canadian Economics*, 206; Swinfen, *Imperial Control of Colonial Legislation*, 109f.

159 Enclosed in Head to Newcastle, 11 Nov 1859, CO 42/618.
160 Elgin to Grey, 6 June 1848, in Doughty, *Elgin—Grey Papers*, I, 182.
161 Wood to Grey, 13 Nov 1850, Grey of Howick Papers.
162 Elgin to Grey, 23 Apr 1849, in Doughty, *Elgin—Grey Papers*, I, 329.
163 Morrell, *British Colonial Policy*, Chapter 17; Grey to Russell, 18 Nov 1850, Grey of Howick Papers.
164 Elgin to Grey, 7 May, 13 July, 13 Aug and 30 Sep 1847, 2 Mar and 24 Aug 1848, etc., in Doughty, *Elgin—Grey Papers*, I, 34, 58, 63, 72, 127, 226.
165 Masters, *Short History of Canada*, 28.
166 Schuyler, *Fall of the Old Imperial System*, 217f.; Grey, *Colonial Policy*, I, 117f., 257; Grey to Elgin, 22 Mar 1848, in Doughty, *Elgin—Grey Papers*, I, 125f.
167 3 *PD*, CIII, 1010, and CXV, 1838.
168 Elgin to Grey, 2 Mar and 26 Apr 1848, in Doughty, *Elgin—Grey Papers*, I, 128, 144.
169 Knorr, *British Colonial Theories*, 355.

CHAPTER 9

1 Russell to Grey, 22 May 1850, Grey of Howick Papers.
2 See Chapter 8 and below.
3 Minute of 22 Feb 1850 on FitzRoy to Grey, 13 Oct 1849, CO 201/416; 'Earl Grey on Victorian Politics', in *Victorian Review*, I (1880), 857f.; Grey, 'Past and Present Policy in South Africa' and 'How shall we retain the Colonies?', in *Nineteenth Century*, V (1879), 583f. and 985f.
4 Ward, *Grey and the Australian Colonies*, Chapters 2—4.
5 Stephen's minute of 10 July 1806 on G. Grey to Gladstone, CO 209/42; Ward, *Grey and the Australian Colonies*, 35f.
6 See Chapter 5. Also Ward, *Grey and the Australian Colonies*, Chapter 2; Morrell, *British Colonial Policy*, Chapters 13 and 15.
7 Minute of 17 Mar 1848, CO 881/1, No. I.
8 Minute, no date, by Stephen, on the above, CO 881/1, No. I.
9 Ward, *Grey and the Australian Colonies*, Chapter 4; Ward, in *JMH*, XXXI, 189f.; Grey to Merivale, 9 May 1848, CO 881/1, No. I.
10 CO 881/1, Nos. II and III; also *PP*, 1849, XXXV [Cmd 1074], 33f.
11 3 *PD*, CVII, 464f. (18 July 1849).
12 Ward: in *JRAHS*, L, 321f., and in *HSANZ*, IX, 244f.
13 3 *PD*, CVIII, 535f. (8 Feb 1850).
14 Minute of 7 Mar 1850, Grey of Howick Papers, Colonial Papers; Ward, *Grey and the Australian Colonies*, 115, note 20.
15 *The Times*, 9 Feb and 30 Apr 1850.
16 3 *PD*, CIX, 1319f. (22 Mar 1850).
17 3 *PD*, CIX, 1272f. (22 Mar 1859).
18 Ward, in *JRAHS*, L, 323f,; Morrell, *British Colonial Policy in the Mid-Victorian Age*, 16f.
19 3 *PD*, CXXIV, 165f. (17 Feb 1853).
20 Newcastle to G. Grey, 5 June 1861, NeC 10,885.
21 Elgin to Newcastle, 4 Feb, 23 Apr and 21 May 1853, NeC 9552.
22 Godley to Adderley, 18 June 1851, in Adderley, *Letters of Godley to Adderley*, 177.
23 Godley to Adderley, 17 Mar 1852, in ibid., 184.
24 A. Matthias to Newcastle, 20 Dec 1852, NeC 9650; F. A. Weld to Newcastle, 26 Dec 1852, NeC 9601.

25 Godley to Newcastle, 9 July 1853, NeC 9605a.
26 Merivale, *Lectures*, 2nd ed. (1861), 532f.
27 Merivale to Hawes, 15 Sep 1848 (CO 217/199); Merivale's minutes on Head to Grey, 28 Feb 1852, and on Wynyard to Newcastle, 9 June 1854, both CO 209/123.
28 Merivale, *Lectures*, 641.
29 Ward, in *JMH*, XXXI, 189f.
30 J. Stephen to A. Stephen, [day and month doubtful] 1852, Papers of A. Stephen (ML).
31 FitzRoy to Grey, 15 Jan 1852, CO 201/450.
32 Merivale to G. Grey, 21 May 1854, CO 201/467.
33 Irving, in *HSANZ*, XI, 192f.
34 *Atlas*, 29 Apr 1848; Knight, *Illiberal Liberal*, 108f.
35 *SMH*, 13, 17 and 20 Jan 1849; also *Maitland Mercury*, 18 and 21 Apr 1849; *PA*, 27 Jan, 10 Feb and 14 Apr 1849.
36 *SMH*, 19 June 1849; FitzRoy to Grey, 30 June 1849, and E. S. Hall to Grey, 14 Nov 1849, CO 201/414; Knight, *Illiberal Liberal*, 224.
37 *PA*, 23 June 1849.
38 Enclosed in FitzRoy to Grey, 30 June 1849, CO 201/414.
39 *SMH*, 31 July and 27 Aug 1849; *Maitland Mercury*, 5 Sep 1849; *PA*, 25 Aug 1849.
40 *PA*, 9 and 30 Dec 1848; *Daily News*, 22 Nov 1848; *Atlas*, 23 Dec 1848; *SMH*, 23 Dec 1848; *Objects, Laws and Regulations of the Constitutional Association*, (Sydney, 1848), ML.
41 Fairbanks case reported, *SMH*, 30 July and 17 Aug 1849.
42 Irving, in *HSANZ*, XI, 199; *Maitland Mercury*, 15 Sep 1849; letter from 'An Australian', *SMH*, 20 Sep 1849.
43 *SMH*, 12 June, 6 and 10 Aug 1849; *V & P* (LC, NSW), 1849, I, 234; Knight, *Illiberal Liberal*, 231.
44 *SMH*, 10 Aug and 12 Sep 1849; *PA*, 15 Sep 1849.
45 George Allen Journal (ML), 7 May and 22 June 1850.
46 *SMH*, 21 Feb 1850, interpreted in light of Denison to Deas Thomson, 7 May 1851, Deas Thomson Papers (ML), II.
47 *SMH* 27 and 28 Aug 1850.
48 *Maitland Mercury*, 27 Feb, 24 Aug and 7 Sep 1850; *SMH*, 13 Sep 1850.
49 Melbourne, *Early Constitutional Development*, 2nd ed., 363.
50 Irving, 'The Development of Liberal Politics in New South Wales' (Ph. D. thesis), 396.
51 *SMH*, 21 and 28 Aug 1850.
52 *SMH*, 28 Aug 1850; *V & P* (LC, NSW), 1850, I, 26 and 27 Aug 1850; *Freeman's Journal*, 29 Aug 1850.
53 *SMH*, 18 Sep 1850; *PA*, 21 Sep 1850; FitzRoy to Grey, 8 Oct 1850, *PP*, 1851, XLV [Cmd 1361], 187.
54 Ward, *Grey and the Australian Colonies*, 60f. and Chapter 8, *passim*; Roe, *Quest for Authority*, 53, 72, 198f.; Parkes, *Australian History*, I, 10.
55 *V & P* (LC, NSW), 8 Apr 1851.
56 *V & P* (LC, NSW), 1 May 1851; FitzRoy to Grey, 18 June 1851, CO 201/441; Melbourne, *Constitutional Development*, 379f.; *SMH*, 9 Apr, 2 and 7 May 1851.
57 *SMH*, 22, 29 Dec 1851; *PA*, 27 Dec 1851.
58 *Empire*, 10 and 14 Apr 1851.
59 Diaries, etc., of Emily Macarthur, March 1851, Macarthur Papers (restricted), A. 4351.
60 *SMH*, 26 Mar 1851; also Denison to Deas Thomson, 26 Mar 1851, Deas Thomson Papers, II, 568.

61 *Empire*, 10 Apr 1851; C. Nicholson to A. Cunninghame, 12 Feb 1851, Cunninghame Papers (ML), A. 3180.
62 FitzRoy to Grey, 21 Feb 1852, CO 201/451.
63 *HRA*, I, xxxiv, 127.
64 Hamilton to Macarthur, 27 Oct 1846, Macarthur Papers A. 2922; Hamilton to Clive, 11 Sep 1850, Collaroy Papers, A. 2407.
65 Hamilton to G. Clive, 21 June 1852, Collaroy Papers, A. 2401; Hamilton to Wentworth, 7 Sep 1853, Autograph Letters of Henry Parkes, A. 63.
66 *V & P* (LC, NSW), 29 Sep and 19 Oct 1851; *Empire*, 31 Aug 1851.
67 Minute of 19 June on FitzRoy to Grey, 15 Jan 1852, CO 201/450; Merivale to G. Grey, 21 June 1854, CO 201/467.
68 Pakington to Merivale, 30 Sep 1852, CO 201/450.
69 Pakington to FitzRoy, 1 Oct 1852, CO 201/450.
70 Pakington to FitzRoy, 15 Dec 1852, CO 201/450, referring to Grey to FitzRoy, 23 Jan 1852, *PP*, 1852, XXXIV [Cmd 1534], 10f.; minutes by Elliot, Merivale and Desart on FitzRoy to Grey, 21 Feb 1852, CO 201/451.
71 Denison to Deas Thomson, 3 June 1853 (Deas Thomson Papers, II, 715), interpreted the dispatch correctly.
72 FitzRoy to Pakington, 31 Aug 1852 (received 27 Dec), CO 201/453.
73 Newcastle to FitzRoy, 18 Jan 1853, CO 201/453.
74 FitzRoy to Pakington, 1 Nov 1852, CO 201/455.
75 Newcastle to FitzRoy, 1 Feb 1853, CO 201/455.
76 *SMH*, 13 Dec 1852, *V & P* (LC, NSW), 16 Dec 1852; FitzRoy to Pakington, 1 Jan 1853 (confidential), CO 201/463.
77 Harvey to Grey, 31 Oct 1849, *PP*, 1849, XXXIV, [Cmd 1126], 51.
78 *SMH*, 22 Sep 1852.
79 Irving, in *HSANZ*, XI, 200; *SMH*, 22 Sep and 10 Dec 1852.
80 Silvester, *Speeches in the Legislative Council*, 133.
81 Loveday, in *JRAHS*, XLII, 187f.
82 *SMH*, 23 Nov 1853; *Empire*, 1 Oct and 26 Nov 1853.
83 *SMH*, 30 Nov 1853.
84 *SMH*, 29 Jan, 19 and 25 Feb, 2 Apr, 6, 7 and 17 Sep and 9 Nov 1853; *Empire*, 7 Mar, 2 Apr and 1 Oct 1853; *PA*, 19 Mar 1853.
85 *V & P* (LC, NSW), 1853, II, 123f.
86 *Empire*, 14 June, 6 and 15 Aug 1853.
87 *Empire*, 1 Oct 1853; *SMH*, 9 Dec 1853; Cowper to Parkes, 25 Nov 1853, Parkes Papers (ML), VI.
88 FitzRoy to Pakington (confidential), 1 Jan 1853, and minutes thereon, CO 201/463; Mundy to Deas Thomson, 4 Mar 1853, Deas Thomson Papers, III; Lang to Kerr, 30 Apr 1853, William Kerr Papers, II.
89 Minutes by Merivale on FitzRoy to Grey, 2 Jan, 26 May and 29 June 1852 (CO 201/452), 26 Aug 1852 (CO 201/453), and FitzRoy to Pakington, 20 Oct 1852 (CO 201/454); Merivale, *Lectures*, 642f.
90 Morrell, *British Colonial Policy*, 276f.; W. Porter to H. Smith, 17 Mar 1848, H. Smith to Grey, 29 July 1848, and Grey to Smith, 20 Jan 1851, all CO 48/289; Grey to Smith (cancelled draft), 20 Jan 1851, CO 48/308; PC Committee Report, *PP*, 1850, XXXVIII [Cmd 1137], 100f.; Ward, in *AJPH*, III, 18f.
91 *PP*, 1852–3, LXVI, 244 [Cmd 1635], 24f. [Cmd 1636]; Newcastle in the Lords, 3 *PD*, CXXVIII, 248f. (16 June 1853).
92 See Chapter 4; Grey, *Colonial Policy*, I, 294f.; Morrell, *British Colonial Policy in the Mid-Victorian Age*, Chapters 12 and 13, and *British Colonial Policy*, Chapter 11.
93 Correspondence of Grey and C. E. Grey in CO 137/302 and CO 138/68.

94 Russell to Grey, 19 Oct 1851, Grey of Howick Papers.

95 Correspondence in *PP*, 1852—3, LXVII (HC 76); minute, 7 June 1852, CO 137/315.

96 3 *PD*, CXXVII, 947f. (30 June 1853).

97 Barkly to Newcastle: 10 Dec 1853, NeC 9553; 10 Apr 1854, *PP*, 1854, XLII [Cmd 1906], 89f. Minute by Taylor on Barkly to Newcastle, 10 Apr 1854, CO 137/323, 17 and 18 Vict., c. 54.

98 Sires, in *Journal of Comparative Legislation*, XXII, 188f.; minute by Merivale on Darling to Stanley, 10 June 1858, CO 137/337.

99 Morrell, *British Colonial Policy in the Mid-Victorian Age*, Chapter 13.

100 Gunn, *Political History of Newfoundland*, Chapter 9; *PP*, 1854—5, XXXVI (HC 273).

101 Le Marchant to Grey, 10 Apr 1849, CO 194/31; Grey to Le Marchant, 13 Dec 1851, CO 195/21.

102 Le Marchant to Grey, 26 Feb 1852, CO 194/36.

103 Hume to Newcastle, 25 July 1853, Little and Parsons to Newcastle, 25, 28 July 1853, CO 194/140.

104 *PP*, 1854, XXXVI (HC 273), 19, 26.

105 See Head to Grey, 6 Nov 1850, CO 188/113; Elgin to Grey, 14 Sep 1847, in Doughty, *Elgin—Grey Papers*, I, 68f.; Grey to Bannerman, 31 Jan 1851, CO 227/10; Grey, *Colonial Policy*, I, 274.

106 Newcastle to Hamilton, 21 Feb 1854, CO 195/21; Gunn, *Political History of Newfoundland*, 134f.

107 Newcastle to FitzRoy, 4 Aug 1853, *PP*, 1854, XLIV, 62f.

108 Merivale to G. Grey, CO 201/467, f. 460.

109 Enclosed in FitzRoy to Pakington, 1 Nov 1852, CO 201/455.

110 For example, Ellice to Grey, 12 Mar 1853, Grey of Howick Papers.

111 FitzRoy to Newcastle (confidential), 17 Nov 1853, CO 201/467; *V & P* (LC, NSW), 1853, II, 119f.; Melbourne, *Constitutional Development*, 401f.

112 Silvester, *Speeches in the Legislative Council*, 74, 133.

113 *SMH*, 15 Dec 1853; Irving, in *HSANZ*, XI, 205.

114 Ward, in *JRAHS*, L, 326f. FitzRoy to Newcastle, 4 Oct 1853 (CO 201/466) had argued for a nominee upper house.

115 Douglass and Wentworth in *SMH*, 15 Dec 1853; Wentworth, *SMH*, 21 Dec 1853; Irving, in *HSANZ*, XI, 202.

116 *SMH*, 21 Dec 1853.

117 Deas Thomson's views, *SMH*, 9 and 21 Dec 1853; Irving, in *HSANZ*, XI, 212f.

118 *SMH*, 9 Dec 1853.

119 The Bill was silent on the powers of the new upper house on money Bills. Main, in *HSANZ*, VII, 377.

120 Irving, in *HSANZ*, XI, 202f. and references therein.

121 F. Rogers to R. W. Church, 23 Sep 1854, in Blachford, *Letters*, 157.

122 FitzRoy to Newcastle, 17 Nov 1853, CO 201/467; *SMH*, 6 Dec 1853; Cowper to Parkes, 25 Nov 1853, Parkes Correspondence (ML), VI.

123 Clauses XVII and XLII.

124 Petitions in FitzRoy to Newcastle, 10, 11 and 18 Nov 1853, CO 201/467; *Empire*, 14 June, 6 Aug and 1 Oct 1853; Loveday, in *JRAHS*, XLII, 187f.

125 Nicholson to J. Macarthur, 21 Apr 1853, Macarthur Papers, A. 2923.

126 Rusden, *Australia*, III, 72f.

127 Nicholson to Cunninghame, Cunninghame Papers, III, A. 3180.

128 Nicholson to Macarthur, 21 Apr 1853, Macarthur Papers, A. 2923.

129 Robertson to Lang, 26 Nov 1853, Lang Papers, VI, A. 2226; also P. P. King to P. G. King, 18 Aug 1853, King Papers, A. 1977.

130 *SMH*, 23 Aug 1853.
131 For Lowe's attitude, see Melbourne, *Constitutional Development*, 420f.; Ward, *Grey and the Australian Colonies*, 367f.
132 Nicholson to Macarthur, 21 Apr 1853, Macarthur Papers, A. 2923.
133 Wentworth to Macarthur, 3 Apr 1853, Macarthur Papers, A. 2923.
134 *SMH*, 22 Dec 1853.
135 *SMH*, 8 and 21 Dec 1853.
136 George Allen Journal (ML), 25 Oct 1854.
137 Cowper to Parkes, [day and month doubtful] May 1855, Parkes Papers, XVI.
138 Cf. Morrell, *British Colonial Policy in the Mid-Victorian Age*, 17.
139 On responsible government in New Zealand, see ibid., 202f.
140 Minute by Merivale, 11 Nov 1854, on Wynyard to Newcastle, 9 June 1854, CO 209/123.
141 Grey to officer administering the government, 8 Dec 1854, and minutes by Merivale and Grey, 6 and 7 Dec 1854, CO 209/124.
142 Rogers's report on the Constitution Acts, 6 Sep 1854, CO 881/1, No. VII.
143 Paper by Russell, no date, CO 881/1, No. IX.
144 Wentworth to Macarthur, 15 July 1854, Macarthur Papers, XXVII, A. 2923; Sir George Grey on Deas Thomson to Colonial Office, 26 Feb 1855, CO 201/492; W. C. Wentworth, *A Reply to Lowe's Speech in the House of Commons*.
145 Russell to Denison, 20 July 1855, CO 202/66; *SMH*, 1 Nov 1855; *Freeman's Journal*, 6 Oct, 3 and 10 Nov 1855.
146 Merivale, *Lectures*, 644.

Bibliography

The Bibliography is arranged as follows.

I. Official sources: British and colonial.
II. Other sources: (A) manuscripts;
                 (B) contemporary newspapers, periodicals and reviews;
                 (C) printed books (both primary and secondary, and including printed collections of primary sources);
                 (D) articles and chapters;
                 (E) unpublished works.

I. OFFICIAL SOURCES

(A) *Colonial Office papers at the Public Record Office, London*

'Original correspondence', 'entry books' and in some cases executive council minutes, newspapers, Blue Books and statutes of Canada, Nova Scotia, New Brunswick, Newfoundland, Prince Edward Island, Jamaica, Trinidad, British Guiana, West Indies (General), Cape of Good Hope, New South Wales, Victoria, Van Diemen's Land (Tasmania), South Australia, New Zealand. Also the series, CO 323, CO 324, CO 380, CO 381, CO 386, CO 537, CO 881, and colonial papers in PC 1 and PC 2. All these papers are listed and described in *Guide to the Contents of the Public Record Office*, 2 vols (London: HMSO, 1963).

(B) *British Parliamentary papers, debates and statutes*

Parliamentary Papers (PP): Bills; reports of select committees; reports of commissioners; accounts and papers.
Debates: Cobbett's *Parliamentary History of England*; Hansard's *Parliamentary Debates*; *Mirror of Parliament*.
Journals of the House of Lords.
Journals of the House of Commons.
The Statutes at Large.

(C) *Legislative papers, debates and statutes of the colonies*

Journals of the Legislative Assembly of the Province of Canada (and appendices), to 1852.
Votes and Proceedings of the Legislative Council of New South Wales, 1843–55.
Votes and Proceedings of the Legislative Council of Tasmania (with papers), 1846–55.
Acts and Ordinances of New South Wales, 1824–56.

Acts of Council (Tasmania), 1826—55.
The Laws of Jamaica, 7 vols, Jamaica, 1802—24.
Votes and Proceedings of the House of Representatives (of New Zealand), 1854.

(D) *Unpublished official sources of the colonies*

Public Archives of New South Wales:
    Executive Council Minutes, 1824—55, and appendices, record group NEC;
    Colonial Secretary's Papers, record group NCS;
    Papers of the Governor, record group NG.
    (On all the above see *Guides to the State Archives of NSW*, issued by the Archives
      Authority of NSW.)
Public Archives of Canada:
    see under Manuscripts (Bagot, Derby, Elgin).

II. OTHER SOURCES

(A) *Manuscripts*

Allen, George: Papers, ML.
Arnold, W. M.: Correspondence, ML.
Autograph Letters of Notable Australians, ML.
Arthur Papers, ML.
Bagot Papers, PAC.
Baldwin Papers, Provincial Archives, Toronto.
Bathurst Papers, British Museum, Add MSS. Loan 57/9—17, 22, 57—59, 65—66.
Bathurst Papers, Letters of the third Earl Bathurst to Wilmot-Horton, 1825—7,
    ML.
Blaxland Family Papers, ML.
Bourke Papers, ML.
Bentham Papers, University College, London.
Brisbane Papers, ML.
Catton Papers, Derby Central Library (papers of R. Wilmot-Horton).
Collaroy Station Papers, ML.
Cowper, Charles: Papers and Correspondence, ML.
Cunninghame Family Papers, ML.
Darvall, Sir John Bayley: Papers, 1823—69, ML.
Deas Thomson Papers, ML.
Deniehy, Daniel Henry: Letters to Sir H. Parkes, 1854—7, ML.
Derby (Stanley), Papers (microfilm), PAC.
Durham Papers, PAC.
Elgin Papers, (microfilm), PAC.
Ellice Papers, E. 22, National Library of Scotland.
Elyard Family Papers, ML.
Fairfax Family Papers, ML.
Forbes Papers, ML.
Grey of Howick Papers, University of Durham.
Hickleton Papers, York City Library, by permission (papers of the first Viscount
    Halifax).
Kemp, Charles: Diary, ML.
Kerr Papers, ML.
Lang, Rev. John Dunmore: Papers and Correspondence, ML.

Lang, John Dunmore: Papers, NLA.
Macarthur Family Papers, ML (restricted and unrestricted). See *Catalogue of MSS. . . . in the ML* (Sydney, 1967), Item 1—45A.
Manning, Sir William: Papers, ML.
Marsden Papers, ML.
Murray, T. A.: Papers, NLA.
Newcastle Papers, Fifth Duke of Newcastle, Nottingham University Archives.
Norton Cole MSS. (Adderley Papers), Birmingham University Library (by kindness of Professor C. E. Carrington).
Parkes, Sir H.: Papers, Correspondence, Autographed Letters from Notable Australians, Autographed Letters from Prominent Men in Great Britain and Australia, ML.
Peel Papers, Royal Archives, Windsor (microfilm).
Peel Papers, British Museum, Add. MSS. 40329—33, 40391—401.
Russell Papers (Lord John Russell), PRO 30/22.
Russell Papers, Duke University, Durham, NC.
Spark, Alexander Brodie: Diary 1836—56, ML.
Stephen, Sir Alfred: Papers, ML.
Stephen, James: Diary and Papers, Cambridge University Library, Add. MSS. 7511(F), 7349(C).
Wentworth Papers, ML.
Windeyer Papers, ML.

(B) *Contemporary newspapers, periodicals and reviews*

Britain:
   The Annual Register, The Colonial Gazette, The Economist, The Edinburgh Review, Fraser's Magazine, The London and Westminster Review, The Morning Chronicle, The Quarterly Review, Spectator, The Times, The Westminster Review.

Australia:
   New South Wales: *The Australian, The Atlas, Daily News, Empire, Freeman's Journal, Maitland Mercury, The Monitor, People's Advocate and NSW Vindicator, The Sydney Herald, The Sydney Gazette, The Sydney Morning Herald.*
   Victoria: *Age, Argus.*
   South Australia: *Adelaide Observer, Adelaide Times.*
   Tasmania: *Hobart Town Advertiser, Hobart Town Courier, Launceston Examiner.*

Canada:
   Available through the Canadian Library Association Newspaper Microfilming Project: *The Globe* (1844—9), *Canadian Correspondent* (1833—4), *The Correspondent and Advocate* (1834—6), *The Constitution* (1836—7), *The Montreal Gazette* (1832).

(C) *Printed Books, including both primary and secondary sources*

*Collections of documents.

1. *Britain*

Aspinall, A. (ed.), *Letters of King George IV, 1812—1830*, 3 vols (Cambridge, 1938).
Aspinall, A., *Politics and the Press, c. 1780—1850* (London, 1949).

Aspinall, A. (ed.), *Three Early Nineteenth Century Diaries* (London, 1952).

*Aspinall, A. and Smith, E. A. (eds), *English Historical Documents*, XI, 1783—1832 (London, 1959).

Austin, John, *A Plea for the Constitution* (London, 1859).

Bagehot, Walter, *The English Constitution* (London, 1867). (Ed. R. H. S. Crossman: London, 1963.)

*Benson, C., and Viscount Esher, *The Letters of Queen Victoria: Selection from Her Majesty's Correspondence*, 1st series, 1837—61, 3 vols (London, 1907).

Black, R. Collison, *Economic Thought and the Irish Question, 1817—1870* (Cambridge, 1964).

Blackstone, W., *Commentaries on the Laws of England*, 4 vols (London, 1765—9).

Blaug, M., *Ricardian Economics* (New Haven, 1958).

Bolton, G. C., *The Passing of the Irish Act of Union* (Oxford, 1966).

Bowring, J. (ed.), *The Works of Jeremy Bentham*, 11 vols (London, 1838—43).

Brock, W. R., *Lord Liverpool and Liberal Toryism 1820—1827* (London, 1941).

Broughton, Lord (J. C. Hobhouse), *Recollections of a Long Life*, ed. Lady Dorchester, 6 vols (London, 1909).

Bryce, J., *The American Commonwealth*, 3 vols (London, 1888).

Brown, F. K., *Fathers of the Victorians* (Cambridge, 1961).

Burn, W. L., *The Age of Equipoise* (London, 1964).

Butt, R., *The Power of Parliament* (London, 1967).

Butterfield, H., *George III and the Historians* (London, 1957).

Cannon, J., *Parliamentary Reform, 1640—1832* (Cambridge, 1973).

Cannon, J., *The Fox—North Coalition. Crisis of the Constitution, 1782—4* (Cambridge, 1970).

Christie, I. R., *The End of North's Ministry, 1780—1782* (London, 1958).

*Cobden, R., *Speeches on Questions of Public Policy, etc.*, ed. J. Bright and J. E. Thorold Rogers (London, 1870).

Conacher, J. B., *The Aberdeen Coalition 1852—1855* (Cambridge, 1968).

Conacher, J. B., *The Emergence of British Parliamentary Democracy in the Nineteenth Century* (New York, 1971).

Corry, B. A., *Money, Saving and Investment in English Economics, 1800—1850* (London, 1962).

Cowherd, R. G., *The Politics of English Dissent* (New York, 1956; London, 1959).

Crook, D. P., *American Democracy in English Politics, 1815—1850* (London, 1969).

Davis, H. W. C., *Age of Grey and Peel* (Oxford, 1929).

De Lolme, J. L., *The Constitution of England* (London, 1775).

Dictionary of National Biography.

Dunn, J., *The Political Thought of John Locke* (Cambridge, 1969).

Emden, C. S., *The People and the Constitution*, 2nd ed. (Oxford, 1956). (1st ed.: 1933).

*Emden, C. S. (ed.), *Selected Speeches on the Constitution*, 2 vols (Oxford, 1939).

Erskine, May T., *Constitutional History of England, 1760—1860*, 2 vols (London, 1861—3), 3rd ed. (London, 1871).

Fitzroy, A. M., *History of the Privy Council* (London, 1928).

Foord, A. S., *His Majesty's Opposition 1714—1830*, (Oxford, 1964).

Forsyth, W., *Cases and Opinions on Constitutional Law and Various Points of English Jurisprudence* (London, 1869).

*Fortescue, J. (ed.), *The Correspondence of King George III*, V (London, 1928). (*Additions and Corrections* by L. B. Namier: London, 1937).

Gash, N., *Mr Secretary Peel* (London, 1961).

Gash, N., *Politics in the Age of Peel* (London, 1953).

Gash, N., *Reaction and Reconstruction in English Politics, 1832–1852* (Oxford, 1965).

Gash, N., *Sir Robert Peel. The Life of Sir Robert Peel after 1830* (London, 1972).

*Gooch, G. P. (ed.), *The Later Correspondence of Lord John Russell. 1840–1878*, 2 vols (London, 1925).

*Grant, W. L., and Munro, J. (eds), *Acts of the Privy Council of England*, Colonial Series, 1766–83, 6 vols (London, 1908–12).

Grampp, W. D., *The Manchester School of Economics* (Stanford, 1964).

Greville, C. C. F., *The Greville Memoirs. A Journal of the Reign of King George IV, William IV and Queen Victoria*, revised ed., 8 vols (London, 1896).

Grey, Henry George (third Earl), *Parliamentary Government Considered with Reference to a Reform of Parliament: An Essay* (London, 1858 and 1864).

Griffith, G. T., *Population Problems of the Age of Malthus* (Cambridge, 1926).

Halévy, E., *The Growth of Philosophic Radicalism* (London, 1928; Boston, 1935).

Hanham, H. J., *The Reform of the Electoral System in Great Britain, 1832–1914* (London, 1968).

Hanham, H. J. (ed.), *The Nineteenth-Century Constitution 1815–1914* (Cambridge, 1969).

Hardcastle, M. S. (ed.), *Life of . . . Lord Campbell*, 2 vols (London, 1881).

Holdsworth, W., *A History of English Law*, 16 vols (London, 1903–66).

Hood Phillips, O., *Leading Cases in Constitutional Law* (London, 1952).

Howse, E. M., *Saints in Politics* (London, 1952).

Huskisson, W., *Speeches . . . with a Biographical Memoir*, 3 vols (London, 1831).

*Jagow, K. (ed.), *Letters of the Prince Consort, 1831–1861* (London, 1931).

Jenks, L. H., *The Migration of British Capital to 1875*, (New York, 1927; London, 1963).

Jennings, W. I., *Cabinet Government* (Cambridge, 1936).

*Jennings, L. J. (ed.), *The Croker Papers*, 3 vols (London, 1884).

Jones, W. D., *'Prosperity Robinson' . . . Viscount Goderich* (New York, 1967).

Judd, G. P., *Members of Parliament, 1734–1832* (New Haven, 1955).

Keith, A. B., *The British Cabinet System, 1830–1938* (London, 1939). (2nd ed., London, 1952).

Kemp, B., *King and Commons, 1660–1832* (London, 1957).

Kitson Clark, G., *Peel and the Conservative Party*, 2nd ed. (London, 1964). (1st ed.: 1929.)

Maccoby, S., *English Radicalism, 1832–1852* (London, 1935).

Malmesbury, Lord, *Memoirs of an Ex-Minister*, 2 vols (London, 1886).

Malthus, T. R., *An Essay on Population*, 1st, 2nd and 3rd eds (London, 1798, 1803, 1806).

Malthus, T. R., *Additions to the Fourth and Former Editions of an Essay on the Principle of Population* (London, 1817).

Malthus, T. R., *Principles of Political Economy* (London, 1820).

Manning, D. J., *The Mind of Jeremy Bentham* (London, 1968).

Martineau, J., *The Life of Henry Pelham, Fifth Duke of Newcastle* (London, 1908).

*Maxwell, H. E. (ed.), *The Creevey Papers*, 2 vols (London, 1903).

*Melville, L. (ed.), *The Huskisson Papers* (London, 1931).

Mitchell, A., *The Whigs in Opposition, 1815–1830* (Oxford, 1967).

Morley, J., *Life of William Ewart Gladstone*, 3 vols (London, 1903).

Morley, J., *Life of Richard Cobden*, 2 vols (London, 1908).

Namier, L. B., *England in the Age of the American Revolution*, 2nd ed. (London, 1961). (1st ed.: 1930.)

Namier, L. B., *Personalities and Powers* (London, 1955).

Namier, L. B., *The Structure of Politics at the Accession of George III*, 2nd ed. (London, 1957). (1st ed., 2 vols.: 1929.)

Namier, L. B., and Brooke, J., *The History of Parliament: The House of Commons, 1754—1790*, 3 vols (London, 1964).

Nesbitt, G. L., *Benthamite Reviewing* (New York, 1934).

Pares, R., *King George III and the Politicians* (Oxford, 1953 and 1967).

Parker, C. S., *Life and Letters of Sir James Graham, 1792—1861* (London, 1907).

*Parker, C. S. (ed.), *Sir Robert Peel, from his Private Papers*, 3 vols (London 1891—9).

*Peel, G. (ed.), *The Private Letters of Sir Robert Peel* (London, 1920).

Peel, Sir Robert, *Memoirs*, ed. Lord Stanhope and E. Cardwell, 2 vols (London, 1856—7).

Peel, Sir Robert, *The Speeches of . . . delivered in the House of Commons*, 4 vols (London, 1853).

Pocock, J. G. A., *Politics, Language and Time* (New York, 1971).

Porter, G. R., *The Progress of the Nation*, 3 vols (London, 1836—43).

Poynter, J. R., *Society and Pauperism . . . 1795—1834* (Melbourne, 1969).

Prest, J., *Lord John Russell* (London, 1972).

*Reid, S., *Life and Letters of . . . Durham*, 2 vols (London, 1926).

Ricardo, D., *Works*, ed. R. Sraffa, 10 vols (Cambridge, 1951—2).

Robbins, L., *The Theory of Economic Policy in English Classical Political Economy* (London, 1961).

Robbins, L., *Robert Torrens and the Evolution of Classical Economics* (London, 1958).

Rudé, G., *Wilkes and Liberty* (Oxford, 1962).

*Russell, Lord John, *Early Correspondence of Lord John Russell, 1805—1840*, ed. R. Russell, 2 vols (London, 1913).

*Russell, Lord John, *The Later Correspondence of Lord John Russell, 1840—1878*, ed. G. P. Gooch, 2 vols (London, 1925).

*Sanders, L. C. (ed.), *Lord Melbourne's Papers* (London, 1889).

Schuyler, R. L. (ed.), *Josiah Tucker: A Selection from His Economic and Political Writings* (New York, 1931).

Senior, Nassau W., *Historical and Philosophical Essays*, 2 vols (London, 1865).

Smith, Adam, *An Inquiry into the Nature and Causes of the Wealth of Nations* (1776). (Ed. E. Cannon, 2 vols.: London, 1904 and 1930.)

Smith, K., *The Malthusian Controversy* (London, 1951).

Southgate, D., *The Passing of the Whigs, 1832—1886* (London, 1962).

Stark, W. (ed.), *Economic Writings of Jeremy Bentham*, 3 vols (London, 1952).

*Taylor, W. S., and Pringle, J. H. (eds), *Correspondence of William Pitt, Earl of Chatham*, 4 vols (London, 1838—40).

The Times, History of The Times, II: 'The Tradition Established, 1841—1884' (London, 1939).

Thrall, M. M. H., *Rebellious Fraser's* (New York, 1934).

Torrens, W. M., *Memoirs of Viscount Melbourne*, 2 vols (London, 1878).

Trevelyan, G. M., *Lord Grey of the Reform Bill* (London, 1920).

Tucker, G. S. L., *Progress and Profits in British Economic Thought, 1650—1850* (Cambridge, 1960).

Turberville, A. S., *The House of Lords in the Age of Reform, 1784—1837* (London, 1958).

Turberville, A. S., *The House of Lords in the Eighteenth Century* (London, 1927).

*Wellington, Duke of, *Despatches, Correspondence and Memoranda*, ed. his son, 8 vols (London, 1867—80).

Williams, E. N., *The Eighteenth Century Constitution*, (Cambridge, 1960).

Wilmot-Horton, R., *The Causes and Remedies of Pauperism in the United Kingdom . . .* (London, 1830).

Yonge, C. D., *Life and Administration of 2nd Earl of Liverpool*, 3 vols (London, 1868).

*Young, G. M., and Handcock, W. D. (eds), *English Historical Documents*, XII (1), 1833—74 (London, 1956).

Young, G. M., *Victorian England. Portrait of an Age* (London, 1936). (Reprinted 1949.)

2. Britain in relation to the empire

Adderley, C. B. (Lord Norton), *The Australian Colonies Government Bill Discussed* (London, [1850]).

Adderley, C. B., *Review of 'The Colonial Policy of Lord John Russell's Administration'. . . and of Subsequent Colonial History* (London, 1869).

Adderley, C. B. (ed.), *Extracts from Letters of John Robert Godley to C. B. Adderley* (London, 1863).

Bearce, G. D., *British Attitudes towards India, 1784—1858* (London, 1961).

Beer, G. L., *The Old Colonial System, 1660—1754*, 2 vols (New York, 1912). (Reprinted 1933.)

*Bell, K. N., and Morrell, W. P. (eds), *Select Documents on British Colonial Policy, 1830—1860* (Oxford, 1928).

Bell, S. S., *Colonial Administration of Great Britain* (London, 1859). (Reprinted 1968.)

Blachford, Lord, *Letters of Frederic [Rogers], Lord Blachford*, ed. G. S. Marindin (London, 1896).

Benians, E. A., *et. al.* (eds), *Cambridge History of the British Empire*, 8 vols (Cambridge, 1929—59).

Bodelsen, C. A., *Studies in Mid-Victorian Imperialism* (Copenhagen, 1924). (Reprinted: London, 1960.)

Bolt, C., *Victorian Attitudes to Race* (London, 1971).

Brougham, Henry (first Baron), *An Inquiry into the Colonial Policy of the European Powers*, 2 vols (Edinburgh, 1803).

Buller, C., *Responsible Government for Colonies* (London, 1840). (Ed. E. M. Wrong, in *Charles Buller and Responsible Government*: Oxford, 1926.)

Cairns, H. A. C., *Prelude to Imperialism: British Reactions to Central African Society, 1840—1850* (London, 1965).

Carlyle, T., *Latter-Day Pamphlets* (London, 1850).

Carrothers, W. A., *Emigration from the British Isles* (London, 1929 and 1965).

Cavendish, Sir Henry, *Debates of the House of Commons in the Year 1774, on the Bill for the Government of the Province of Quebec*, ed. J. Wright (London, 1839). (Reprinted 1966.)

Cell, J. W., *British Colonial Administration in the Mid-Nineteenth Century: The Policy-Making Process* (New Haven, 1970).

Chalmers, G., *Opinions of Eminent Lawyers on Various Points of English Jurisprudence*, 2 vols (London, 1914).

Clark, C., *A Summary of Colonial Law* (London, 1834).

Curtin, P. D., *The Image of Africa* (Madison, 1964).

Drescher, S., *Tocqueville and England* (Cambridge, Mass., 1964).

Egerton, H. E., *Origin and Growth of the English Colonies and of their System of Government* (London, 1904).

Evatt, H. V., *The King and his Dominion Governors*, 2nd ed. (London, 1936).

Gipson, L. H., *The British Empire before the American Revolution*, 13 vols (Caldwell, Idaho, and New York, 1936—68).

Godley, J. R., *Extracts from letters to C. B. Adderley* (London, 1863).

Grey, Henry George (third Earl), *The Colonial Policy of Lord John Russell: Administration*, 2nd ed., 2 vols (London, 1853).

Harlow, V. T., *The Founding of the Second British Empire, 1763—1793*, 2 vols (London, 1952 and 1964).

*Harlow, V. T., and Madden, F. (eds), *British Colonial Developments, 1774—1834. Select Documents* (Oxford, 1953).

Hitchins, F. H., *The Colonial Land and Emigration Commission* (Philadelphia, 1931).

Imlah, A. H., *Economic Elements in the Pax Britannica* (Cambridge, Mass., 1958).

Johnston, H. J. M., *British Emigration Policy, 1815—1830* (Oxford, 1972).

Keith, A. B., *Constitutional History of the First British Empire* (Oxford, 1930).

Keith, A. B., *Responsible Government in the Dominions*, 3 vols (Oxford, 1912). (2nd ed, 2 vols: 1928.)

*Keith, A. B. (ed.), *Selected Speeches and Documents on British Colonial Policy. 1763—1917* (Oxford, 1961).

Klingberg, F. J., *The Anti-Slavery Movement in England* (New Haven, 1926).

Knaplund, P., *Gladstone and Britain's Imperial Policy* (London, 1927).

Knaplund, P., *James Stephen and the British Colonial System, 1813—1847* (Madison, 1953).

Knorr, K. E., *British Colonial Theories, 1570—1850* (Toronto, 1944). (Reprinted: London, 1963.)

Koebner, R., *Empire* (Cambridge, 1961).

Koebner, R., and Schmidt, H. D., *Imperialism* (Cambridge, 1965).

Leader, R. E. (ed.), *Life and Letters of John Arthur Roebuck* (London, 1898).

Lewis, G. Cornewall, *An Essay on the Government of Dependencies* (London, 1841). (Ed. C. P. Lucas: Oxford, 1891.)

Lewis, G. C., *Essays on the Administration of Great Britain from 1783 to 1820, contributed to the 'Edinburgh Review'*, ed. E. Head (London, 1864).

Lillibridge, G. D., *Beacon of Freedom* (Philadelphia, 1954; London, 1955).

Lively, J., *The Social and Political Thought of Alexis de Tocqueville* (Oxford, 1962).

*Madden, F., *Imperial Constitutional Documents. 1765—1965. A Supplement* (Oxford, 1953).

Mander-Jones, P. (ed.), *Manuscripts in the British Isles relating to Australia, New Zealand and the Pacific* (Canberra, 1972).

Manning, H. T., *British Colonial Government after the American Revolution, 1783—1820* (New Haven, 1933). (Reprinted: Hamden, 1966.)

Mansergh, N., *The Commonwealth Experience* (London, 1969).

Mathieson, W. L., *British Slavery and its Abolition, 1823—1838* (London, 1926).

Mellor, G. R., *British Imperial Trusteeship, 1783—1850* (London, 1951).

Merivale, H., *Lectures on Colonization and Colonies*, 2 vols (London, 1841—2). (2nd ed.: 1861.)

Mill, J., *Elements of Political Economy*, 3rd ed. (London, 1826). (1st ed.: 1821.)

Mill, J. S., *On Liberty and Considerations on Representative Government*, ed. R. B. McCallum (Oxford, 1946).

Mill, J. S., *Principles of Political Economy* (London, 1909), 1st ed. (London, 1848).

Mills, A., *Colonial Constitutions* (London, 1856).

Molesworth, W., *Selected Speeches of William Molesworth on Questions relating to Colonial Policy*, ed. H. E. Egerton (London, 1903).

Morrell, W. P., *British Colonial Policy in the Age of Peel and Russell* (Oxford, 1930). (Note: within the present work, references to Morrell, *British Colonial Policy* should be understood as referring to this title.)

Morrell, W. P., *British Colonial Policy in the Mid-Victorian Age* (Oxford, 1969).

New, C. W., *Lord Durham* (Oxford, 1929).

Newton, A. P., *Federal and Unified Constitutions . . . Constitutional Documents* (London, 1923).

O'Farrell, P., *Ireland's English Question* (London, 1971).

Platt, D. C. M., *Finance, Trade and Politics in British Foreign Policy, 1815–1914* (Oxford, 1968).

Philipp, J., *A Great View of Things: ... Wakefield* (Melbourne, 1971).

Roebuck, J. A., *The Colonies of England* (London, 1849). (Reprinted London, 1968.)

Robinson, K., and Madden, F., *Essays in Imperial Government Presented to Margery Perham* (Oxford, 1963).

Robinson, R., Gallagher, J., and Denny, Alice, *Africa and the Victorians: The Official Mind of Imperialism* (London, 1961).

Schuyler, R. L., *The Fall of the Old Colonial System* (New York, 1945). (Reprinted: Hamden, 1966.)

Schuyler, R. L., *Parliament and the British Empire* (New York, 1929).

Semmel, B., *The Rise of Free Trade Imperialism* (Cambridge, 1970).

Shaw, A. G. L., *Great Britain and the Colonies, 1815–1865* (London, 1970).

Stokes, A., *A View of the Constitutions of the British Colonies* (London, 1783).

Stokes, E., *The English Utilitarians and India* (Oxford, 1959).

Swinfen, D. B., *Imperial Control of Colonial Legislation 1813–1865* (Oxford, 1970).

Taylor, (Sir) Henry, *Autobiography*, 2 vols (London, 1885).

Thomas, Brinley, *Migration and Economic Growth: A Study of Great Britain and the Atlantic Economy* (Cambridge, 1954).

Tocqueville, Alexis de, *Democracy in America*, translated by H. Reeve, 4 vols (London, 1835–43). (Revised by P. Bradley, 2 vols: New York, 1953.)

Todd, A., *Parliamentary Government in the British Colonies*, 2nd ed., edited by his son (London 1894).

*Wakefield, E. G., *The Collected Works of Edward Gibbon Wakefield*, ed. M. F. Lloyd Prichard (London, 1968).

Wight, M., *The Development of the Legislative Council, 1606–1945* (London, 1946).

Winch, D. N., *Classical Political Economy and the Colonies* (London, 1965).

Winks, R. W. (ed.), *Historiography of the British Empire–Commonwealth* (Durham, NC, 1966).

Wrong, E. M., *Charles Buller and Responsible Government* (Oxford, 1926).

Young, D. M., *The Colonial Office in the Early Nineteenth Century* (London, 1961).

3. The American colonies

Andrews, C. M., *Colonial Self-Government, 1652–1689* (New York, 1904).

Andrews, C. M., *The Colonial Background of the American Revolution* (New Haven, 1924 and 1961).

Andrews, C. M., *The Colonial Period of American History*, 4 vols (New Haven, 1934–8).

Bailyn, B., with the assistance of Jean N. Garrett, *Pamphlets of the American Revolution, 1750–1796*, I, 1750–65 (Cambridge, Mass., 1965).

Bailyn, B., *The Ideological Origins of the American Revolution* (Cambridge, Mass., 1967). (Reprinted 1968.)

*Beloff, M. (ed.), *The Debate on the American Revolution* (London, 1949).

Boorstin, D. J., *The Americans. The Colonial Experience* (New York, 1968).

Clark, D. M., *British Opinion and the American Revolution* (New Haven, 1930). (Reprinted: New York, 1966.)

Dickerson, O. M., *American Colonial Government, 1696–1765* (Cleveland, 1912).

Donoughue, B., *British Politics and the American Revolution* (London, 1964).

Gipson, L. H., *The Coming of the Revolution, 1763–1775* (New York, 1954).

Greene, E. B., *The Provincial Government in the English Colonies of North America* (Cambridge, Mass., 1898).

Greene, J. P., *The Quest for Power: The Lower Houses of Assembly in the Southern Royal Colonies, 1689–1776* (Chapel Hill, NC, 1963).

Greene, J. P. (ed.), *Great Britain and the American Colonies, 1606–1763* (Columbia, SC, 1970).

Hinkhouse, F. J., *The Preliminaries of the American Revolution as seen in the English Press, 1763–1775* (New York, 1926).

*Jensen, M. (ed.), 'American Colonial Documents to 1776', vol. IX of *English Historical Documents*, ed. D. C. Douglas (London, 1955).

Knollenberg, B., *Origin of the American Revolution, 1759–1766*, revised ed. (New York, 1961).

Labaree, L. W., *Royal Government in America* (New Haven, 1930).

McIlwain, C. H., *The American Revolution: A Constitutional Interpretation* (New York, 1923).

Miller, J. C., *Origins of the American Revolution* (Stanford, 1959).

Morgan, E. S., *The Birth of the Republic, 1763–89* (Chicago, 1956).

Morgan, E. S. and H. M., *The Stamp Act Crisis: Prologue to Revolution* (Chapel Hill, NC, 1953). (Revised ed.: New York, 1963.)

*Morison, S. E., *Sources and Documents illustrating the American Revolution, 1764–1788*, 2nd ed. (Oxford, 1951). (1st ed.: 1923.)

Mullett, C. F., *Fundamental Law and the American Revolution, 1760–1776* (New York, 1933).

Pole, J. R., *Political Representation in England and the Origins of the American Republic* (London, 1966).

Pownall, T., *The Administration of the Colonies* 4th ed. (London, 1768).

Ritcheson, C. R., *British Politics and the American Revolution* (Norman, Okla., 1954).

Robbins, C., *The Eighteenth Century Commonwealthman* (Cambridge, Mass., 1959).

Russell, E. B., *The Review of American Colonial Legislation* (New York, 1935).

Smith, J. H., *Appeals to the Privy Council from the American Plantations* (New York, 1950).

Sosin, J. M., *Agents and Merchants. British Colonial Policy and the Origins of the American Revolution, 1762–1775* (Lincoln, Nebr., 1965).

4. British North America

Beck, J. M., *The Government of Nova Scotia* (Toronto, 1959).

Beck, J. (ed.), *Joseph Howe: Voice of Nova Scotia* (Toronto, 1964).

Brebner, J. B., *North Atlantic Triangle* (New Haven, 1945).

Burroughs, P., *The Colonial Reformers and Canada, 1830–1849* (Toronto, 1969).

*Burroughs, P., *British Attitudes Towards Canada, 1822–1849* (Scarborough, Ont., 1971).

Burroughs, P., *The Canadian Crisis and British Colonial Policy, 1828–1841* (London, 1972).

Burt, A. L., *The Old Province of Quebec* (Minneapolis, 1933).

Burt, A. L., *The United States, Great Britain and British North America* (New Haven, 1940).

*Canada, Dominion of, *Reports of the Public Archives* for the years 1923 (Durham Papers), 1928 (Roebuck Papers and letter from Buller to J. S. Mill), 1929 (Glenelg minute of 30 Apr 1836), 1930–2 (Calendar of Series 'G' of Public Archives; see CHBE, VI, 825).

Careless, J. M. S., *Brown of the Globe*, 2 vols (Toronto, 1959—63).
Careless, J. M. S., *The Union of the Canadas* (Toronto, 1967).
Chisholm, J. A. (ed.), *Speeches and Public Lectures of Joseph Howe* (London, 1909).
Clark, S. D., *Movements of Political Protest in Canada 1640—1840* (Toronto, 1959).
Coupland, R., *The Quebec Act* (Oxford, 1925).
Craig, G. M., *Upper Canada . . . 1784—1841* (Toronto, 1963).
Creighton, D. G., *The Empire of the St Lawrence* (Toronto, 1956).
Cruikshank, E. A. (ed.), *Correspondence of . . . Simcoe*, 5 vols (Toronto, 1923—31).
*Doughty, A. G. (ed.), *The Elgin—Grey Papers, 1846—52*, 4 vols (Ottawa, 1937).
*Doughty, A. G., and McArthur, D. A. (eds), *Documents relating to the Constitutional History of Canada, 1791—1818* (Ottawa, 1914).
*Doughty, A. G., and Story, N. (eds), *Documents relating to the Constitutional History of Canada, 1819—1828* (Ottawa, 1935).
Dunham, A., *Political Unrest in Upper Canada, 1815—1836* (London, 1927; Toronto, 1963).
*Durham, John George Lambton, first Earl of, *Lord Durham's Report on the Affairs of British North America*, ed. C. P. Lucas, 3 vols (Oxford, 1912).
*Egerton, H. E., and Grant, W. L. (eds), *Canadian Constitutional Development . . . Selected Speeches and Dispatches* (London, 1907).
*Fairley, M. (ed.), *Selected Writings of William Lyon Mackenzie* (Toronto, 1960).
Glazebrook, G. P. de T., *Sir Charles Bagot in Canada* (Oxford, 1929).
*Godley, J. R., *Letters from America*, 2 vols (London, 1844).
Graham, G. S., *British Policy and Canada, 1774—1791* (London, 1930).
Gunn, G. E., *The Political History of Newfoundland, 1832—1864* (Toronto, 1966).
Hamel, M. T., *La Rapport de Durham* (Quebec, 1948).
Horton, R. Wilmot-, *Exposition and Defence of Earl Bathurst's Administration of the Affairs of Canada . . . 1822 to 1827* (London, 1828).
Innis, H. A., *Essays in Canadian Economic History*, ed. Mary Q. Innis (Toronto, 1956).
Innis, H. A., *The Fur Trade in Canada* (New Haven, 1930 and 1965; Toronto, 1956).
Kaye, J. W., *Life and Correspondence of Charles, Lord Metcalfe*, 2 vols (London, 1854).
Kaye, J. W. (ed.), *Selections from the Papers of Lord Metcalfe* (London, 1855).
*Kennedy, W. P. M. (ed.), *Statutes, Treaties and Documents of the Canadian Constitution, 1713—1929* 2nd ed. (Oxford, 1930).
Kennedy, W. P. M., *The Constitution of Canada, 1834—1937*, 2nd ed. (Oxford, 1938). (1st ed.: 1922.)
Kerr, D. G. G., *Sir Edmund Head* (Toronto, 1954).
Kilbourn, W., *The Firebrand, William Lyon MacKenzie and the Rebellion in Upper Canada* (Toronto, 1956). (Revised ed.: 1964.)
Kinchen, O. A., *Lord Russell's Canadian Policy* (Lubbock, Texas, 1945).
Knaplund, P. (ed.), *Letters from Lord Sydenham to Lord John Russell* (London, 1931).
Landon, F., *Western Ontario and the American Frontier* (Toronto, 1941 and 1967).
Leacock, S. B., *Baldwin, LaFontaine, Hincks* (Oxford and Toronto, 1926), 1st ed. (Toronto, 1907).
Lower, A. R. M., *Canadians in the Making* (Toronto, 1958).
McKinnon, F., *The Government of Prince Edward Island* (Toronto, 1951).

McLintock, A. H., *The Establishment of Constitutional Government in Newfoundland, 1783–1832* (London, 1941).
MacNutt, W. S., *The Atlantic Provinces . . . 1712–1857* (Toronto, 1965).
MacNutt, W. S., *New Brunswick, A History, 1784–1867* (Toronto, 1963).
Manning, H. T., *The Revolt of French Canada, 1800–1835* (London, 1962).
Martin, C., *Empire and Commonwealth* (Oxford, 1929).
Martin, G., *The Durham Report and British Policy* (Cambridge, 1972).
Masters, D. C., *The Reciprocity Treaty of 1854* (Toronto, 1963).
Masters, D. C., *Short History of Canada* (New York, 1958).
Monet, J., *The Last Cannon Shot: A Study of French Canadian Nationalism* (Toronto, 1970).
Morison, J. L., *British Supremacy and Canadian Self-Government 1839–1854* (Glasgow, 1919).
Morison, J. L., *The Eighth Earl of Elgin* (London, 1928).
Neatby, H., *Quebec. The Revolutionary Age, 1760–1791* (Toronto, 1966).
Ormsby, W., *The Emergence of the Federal Concept in Canada, 1839–1845* (Toronto, 1969).
Ormsby, W. (ed.), *Crisis in the Canadas: 1838–39. The Grey Journal and Letters* (London, 1965).
Ouellet, F., *Histoire économique et sociale du Quebec, 1760–1850* (Montreal, 1966).
Ouellet, F., *Louis-Joseph Papineau: A Divided Soul* (Ottawa, 1960).
Parker, D. W., *Guide to the Documents in the Manuscript Room at the Public Archives of Canada*, I (Ottawa, 1914).
Robinson, J. B., *Canada and the Canada Bill* (London, 1840).
Robinson, C. W., *Life of Sir John Beverley Robinson* (Edinburgh, 1904).
Roy, J. A., *Joseph Howe* (Toronto, 1935).
Sanderson, C. R. (ed.), *The Arthur Papers*, 3 vols (Toronto, 1917–9).
Scrope, G. Poulett, *Memoir of . . . Lord Sydenham* (London, 1844).
*Shortt, A., and Doughty, A. G. (eds), *Documents relating to the Constitutional History of Canada, 1759–1791*, 2nd ed. (Ottawa, 1928). 2 vols.
Stacey, C. P., *Canada and the British Army, 1846–1871: A Study in . . . Responsible Government*, revised ed. (Toronto, 1963). (1st ed.: London, 1936.)
Trotter, R. G., *Canadian Federation* (Toronto and London, 1924).
Tucker, G. N., *The Canadian Commercial Revolution, 1845–51* (New Haven, 1936).
Upton, L. F. S., *The Loyal Whig. William Smith of New York and Quebec* (Toronto, 1969).
Wade, M., *The French Canadians. 1760–1945* (Toronto, 1955).
[Wakefield, E. G.], *A View of Sir Charles Metcalfe's Government of Canada,* (London, 1844).
Wilson, G. E., *The Life of Robert Baldwin* (Toronto, 1933).
Walrond, T. (ed.), *Letters and Journals of James, Eighth Earl of Elgin* (London, 1872).
Wrong, G. M., *The Eighth Earl of Elgin* (London, 1905).

5. *Australia*

Bland, W. (ed.), *Letters to Charles Buller Jnr. from the Australian Patriotic Association* (London, 1849).
Burroughs, P., *Britain and Australia, 1831–1855* (Oxford, 1967).
Chapman, H. S., *Parliamentary Government; or Responsible Ministries for the Australian Colonies* (Hobart, 1854).
Clark, C. M. H., *History of Australia*, I, II, III (Melbourne, 1962, 1968, 1973).

Clark, C. M. H. (ed.), *Select Documents in Australian History, 1788—1850* and ..., *1851—1900* (Sydney, 1950 and 1955).

Currey, C. H., *The Brothers Bent* (Sydney, 1968).

Currey, C. H., *Sir Francis Forbes* (Sydney, 1968).

Eddy, J. J., *Britain and the Australian Colonies, 1818—1831* (Oxford, 1969).

Ellis, M. H., *John Macarthur* (Sydney, 1955).

*Gilchrist, A. (ed.), *John Dunmore Lang*, 2 vols (Melbourne, 1951).

Gollan, R. A., *Radical and Working Class Politics ... Eastern Australia, 1850—1910* (Melbourne, 1960).

Historical Records of Australia, ed. F. Watson (for Library Committee of the Parliament of the Commonwealth), Series I (26 vols), III (6 vols), IV (1 vol.).

Kiddle, M. L., *Men of Yesterday* (Melbourne, 1961).

King, H., *Richard Bourke* (Melbourne, 1971).

Knight, R., *Illiberal Liberal. Robert Lowe ..., 1842—1850* (Melbourne, 1966).

Lansbury, C., *Arcady in Australia ... Australia in Nineteenth-Century English Literature* (Melbourne, 1970).

Lumb, R. D., *The Constitutions of the Australian States* (St. Lucia, 1963). (2nd ed.: 1965.)

Macarthur, Edward, *Colonial Policy of 1840 and 1841* (London, 1841).

Macarthur, James, *New South Wales, its Present State and Future Prospects* (London, 1837).

Macarthur-Onslow, S., *Some Early Records of the Macarthurs of Camden* (Sydney, 1914).

Macmillan, D. S., *Scotland and Australia, 1788—1850* (London, 1967).

Madgwick, R. B., *Immigration into Eastern Australia, 1788—1851* (London, 1937). (Reprinted: Sydney, 1969.)

Melbourne, A. C. V., *Early Constitutional Development in Australia: New South Wales, 1788—1856* (Oxford, 1934). (2nd ed., edited by R. B. Joyce: St. Lucia, 1963.)

Melbourne, A. C. V., *William Charles Wentworth* (Brisbane, 1934).

Mills, R. C., *The Colonization of Australia, 1829—1842* (London, 1915).

Nadel, G., *Australia's Colonial Culture* (Melbourne, 1957).

Parkes, H., *Fifty Years in the Making of Australian History*, 2 vols (London, 1892).

Pike, D. (ed.), *Australian Dictionary of Biography*, I—IV (Melbourne, 1966—72).

Pike, D., *Paradise of Dissent, South Australia, 1829—1857* (London, 1957).

Ritchie, J., *Punishment and Profit: The Reports of Commissioner John Bigge* (Melbourne, 1970).

Roberts, S. H., *History of Australian Land Settlement, 1788—1920* (Melbourne, 1924).

Roberts, S. H., *The Squatting Age in Australia, 1835—1847* (Melbourne, 1935 and 1965).

Roe, M., *Quest for Authority in Eastern Australia, 1835—1851* (Melbourne, 1965).

Rusden, G. W., *History of Australia*, 3 vols (London, 1883).

Serle, G., *The Golden Age ... Victoria, 1851—1861* (Melbourne, 1963).

Shaw, A. G. L., *Convicts and the Colonies* (London, 1966).

Sidney, S., *The Three Colonies of Australia* (London, 1852). (2nd ed.: 1853.)

*Silvester, E. K. (ed.), *The Speeches in the Legislative Council of New South Wales, on the Second Reading of the Bill for framing a new Constitution for a Colony* (Sydney, 1853).

Ward, J. M., *Earl Grey and the Australian Colonies, 1846—1857* (Melbourne, 1958).

Ward, J. M., *Empire in the Antipodes. The British in Australasia: 1840—1860* (London, 1966).

Webb, G. H. F. (ed.), *Debate in the Legislative Council of Victoria on the New Constitution Bill* (Melbourne, 1854).
Wentworth, W. C., *Statistical Account of the British Settlement in Australasia* (London, 1820, and later editions).

6. *New Zealand*

Carrington, C. E., *John Robert Godley of Canterbury* (Christchurch, 1950).
* McIntyre, W. D., and Gardner, W. J., *Speeches and Documents on New Zealand History* (Oxford, 1971).
McLintock, A. H., *Crown Colony Government in New Zealand* (Wellington, 1958).
Marais, J. S., *The Colonization of New Zealand* (Oxford, 1927).
Miller, H. G., *Race Conflict in New Zealand, 1814—1865* (Auckland, 1966).
Morrell, W. P., *The Provincial System in New Zealand, 1852—1876* (London, 1932; Christchurch, 1964).
Rutherford, J., *Sir George Grey* (London, 1961).
Scott, K. J., *The New Zealand Constitution* (Oxford, 1962).
Sinclair, K., *Origins of the Maori Wars* (Wellington, 1957).
Tapp, E. J., *Early New Zealand. A Dependency of New South Wales, 1788—1841* (Melbourne, 1958).
Ward, J. M., *British Policy in the South Pacific, 1786—1893* (Sydney, 1948 and 1950).
Wood, G. A., *A Guide for Students of New Zealand History* (Dunedin, 1973).

7. *The West Indies*

Burge, W., *Speech of W. Burge at the Bar of the House of Commons against the Bill . . . for the Government of Jamaica* (London, 1839).
Burn, W. L., *Emancipation and Apprenticeship in the British West Indies* (London, 1937).
Burns, A., *History of the British West Indies* (London, 1954).
Clementi, C., *Constitutional History of British Guiana* (London, 1927).
Craig, H., *The Legislative Council of Trinidad and Tobago* (London, 1952).
Curtin, P. D., *Two Jamaicas: the Role of Ideas in a Tropical Colony, 1830—1865* (Cambridge, Mass., 1955).
Eisner, G., *Jamaica, 1830—1930* (Manchester, 1961).
Gardner, W. J., *A History of Jamaica, from its Discovery by Christopher Columbus to 1872*, 2nd ed. (London, 1909). (1st ed.: 1873.)
Millette, J., *Genesis of Crown Colony Government: Trinidad, 1783—1810* (Curepa, Trinidad, 1970).
Murray, D. J., *The West Indies and the Development of Colonial Government, 1801—1834* (Oxford, 1965).
Pares, R., *War and Trade in the West Indies, 1739—1763* (Oxford, 1936).
Parry, J. H., and P. M. Sherlock, *Short History of the West Indies* (London, 1963), 1st ed. (London, 1956).
Penson, L. M., *Colonial Agents in the British West Indies* (London, 1924).
Ragatz, L. J., *Absentee Landlords in the British Caribbean, 1750—1833* (London, 1931).
Ragatz, L. J., *A Guide to the Study of British Caribbean History, 1763—1834* (Washington, DC, 1932).
Ragatz, L. J., *The Fall of the Planter Class in the British Caribbean, 1763—1833* (Washington, DC, 1928).
[Stephen, J.], *The Crisis of the Sugar Colonies* (London, 1802).

Williams, E. E., *Capitalism and Slavery* (Chapel Hill, NC, 1944). (2nd ed.: London, 1964.)
Woodcock, H. I., *Laws and Constitution of the British Colonies in the West Indies*, 2nd ed. (London, 1938).
Wrong, H. H., *The Government of the West Indies* (Oxford, 1923).

8. *Africa*

Cory, G. E., *The Rise of South Africa*, 5 vols (London, 1910—30).
*Eybers, G. W., *Select Constitutional Documents Illustrating South African History, 1795—1910* (London, 1918).
Galbraith, J. S., *Reluctant Empire: British Policy on the South African Frontier, 1834—1854* (Berkeley and Los Angeles, 1963).
Marais, J. S., *The Cape Coloured People, 1652—1937* (London, 1939).
Martin, E. C., *The British West African Settlements, 1750—1821* (London, 1927).
Muller, C. F. J., van Jaarsveld, F. A., and van Wink, T., *Select Bibliography of South African History* (Pretoria, 1966).
Walker, E. A., *A History of Southern Africa*, 3rd ed. (London, 1957).

D *Articles and chapters*

Aspinall, A., 'The Cabinet Council, 1783—1835', in *Proceedings of the British Academy*, XXVIII (1952), 145f.
Beaglehole, J. C., 'The Colonial Office, 1782—1854', in *HSANZ*, I (1941), 170f.
Beaglehole, J. C., 'The Royal Instructions to Colonial Governors, 1783—1854', in *Bulletin of the IHR*, VII (1930), 184f.
Beer, D., 'A Note on Lord Durham's Report and the NSW Press, 1839', in *JRAHS*, LIV (1968), 205f.
Beer, S. H., 'The Representation of Interests in British Government', in *American Political Science Review*, LI (1957), 613f.
Benians, E. A., 'Adam Smith's Project of Empire', in *CHJ*, I (1925), 249f.
Bolton, G. C., 'The Founding of the Second British Empire', in *EHR*, XIX (1966), 1957.
Brown, G. W., 'The Durham Report and the Upper Canada Scene', in *CHR*, XX (1939), 136f.
Butler, J. R. M., 'Notes on the Origins of Lord John Russell's Dispatch of October 16, 1839, on the Tenure of Crown Offices in the Colonies', in *CHJ*, II (1928), 248f.
Campbell, E., 'Prerogative Rule in New South Wales, 1788—1823', in *JRAHS*, L (1964), 181f.
Campbell, E., 'The Royal Prerogative to Create Colonial Courts', in *Sydney Law Review*, IV (1964), 343f.
Cell, J. W., 'The Colonial Office in the 1850's', in *HSANZ*, XII (1965), 43f.
Conacher, J. B., 'Peel and the Peelites, 1846—1850', in *EHR*, LXXIII (1958), 431f.
Craig, G. M., 'The American Impact on the Upper Canadian Reform Movement before 1837', in *CHR*, XXIX (1948), 333f.
Creighton, D. G., 'The Struggle for Financial Control in Lower Canada, 1818—1831', in *CHR*, XII (1931), 120f.
Cruikshank, E. A., 'Genesis of the Canada Act', in Ontario Historical Society, *Papers and Records*, XXVIII (1932), 155f.
Currey, C. H., 'William Charles Wentworth and the Making of the Constitution of New South Wales', in *JRAHS*, XLII (1956), 144f.
Dobie, E., 'The Dismissal of Lord Glenelg from the Office of Colonial Secretary', in *CHR*, XXIII (1942), 280f.

Dyster, B., 'Support for the Squatters, 1844', in *JRAHS*, LI (1965), 41f.

Else-Mitchell, R., 'The Foundation of New South Wales and the Inheritance of the Common Law', in *JRAHS*, XLIX (1963), 1f.

Evatt, H. V., 'The Legal Foundations of New South Wales', in *Australian Law Journal*, XI (1938), 409f.

Fetter, F. W., 'The Authorship of Economic Articles in the *Edinburgh Review*, 1802—47', in *JPE*, LXI (1953), 232f.

Fetter, F. W., 'The Economic Articles in the *Quarterly Review* and their Authors, 1809—1852', in *JPE*, LXVI (1958), 47f. and 154f.

Fetter, F. W., 'The Economic Articles in the *Westminster Review* and their Authors, 1824—1851', in *JPE*, LXX (1962), 570f.

Fetter, F. W., 'Robert Torrens: Colonel of Marines and Political Economist', in *Economica*, XXIX (1962), 152f.

Fieldhouse, D., 'Imperialism. An Historiographical Revision', in *EHJ*, XIV (1964), 187f.

Foord, A. S., 'The Waning of the Influence of the Crown', in *EHR*, LXII (1947), 484f.

Fox, G., 'The Reception of Lord Durham's Report in the English Press', in *CHR*, XVI (1935), 276f.

Fry, H. T., ' "Cathay and the Way thither": the Background to Botany Bay', in *HS*, XIV (1971), 477f.

Galbraith, J. S., 'Myths of the Little England Era', in *AHR*, LXVII (1961), 34f.

Gallagher, J., and Robinson, R., 'The Imperialism of Free Trade', in *EHJ*, 2nd series, VI (1953), 1f.

Ghosh, R. N., 'The Colonization Controversy: R. J. Wilmot-Horton and the Classical Economists', in *Economica*, XXXI (1964), 385f.

Ghosh, R. N., 'Malthus on Emigration and Colonization: Letters to Wilmot-Horton', in *Economica*, XXX (1963), 44f.

Hamilton, W. B., 'Constitutional and Political Reflections on the Dismissal of Lord Grenville's Ministry', in *Canadian Historical Association Report* 1964, 89f.

Harvey, D. C., 'Nova Scotia and the Durham Mission', in *CHR*, II (1939), 161f.

Harvey, D. C., 'The Civil List and Responsible Government in Nova Scotia', in *CHR*, XXVIII (1947).

Herron, D. G., 'Sir G. Grey and the Summoning of the First General Assembly', in *HSANZ*, VIII (1959), 364f.

Higham, C. S. S., 'Sir Henry Taylor and the Establishment of Crown Colony Government in the West Indies', in *Scottish Historical Review*, XXIII (1925—6), 92f.

Higham, C. S. S., 'The General Assembly of the Leeward Islands', in *EHR*, XLI (1926), 190f., 366f.

Higman, D. W., 'The West India Interest, 1807—1833', in *HS*, XIII (1967), 1f.

Himes, N. E., 'Jeremy Bentham and the Genesis of Neo-Malthusianism', in *Economic History*, III (1936), 267f.

Humphreys, R. A., 'Lord Shelburne and the Proclamation of 1763', in *EHR*, XLIX (1934), 241f.

Humphreys, R. A., 'Lord Shelburne and British Colonial Policy, 1766—1768', in *EHR*, (1935), 257f.

Humphreys, R. A., and Morley Scott, S., 'Lord Northington and the Laws of Canada', in *CHR*, XIV (1933), 42—61.

Hutchison, T. W., 'Bentham as an Economist', in *Economic Journal*, LXVI (1956), 288f.

Irving, T. H., 'The Idea of Responsible Government in New South Wales before 1856', in *HSANZ*, XI (1964), 190f.

Kinchen, O. A., 'The Stephen–Russell Reforms in Official Tenure', in *CHR*, XXVI (1945), 382f.

Kittrell, E. R., 'Development of the Theory of Colonization', in *Southern Economic Journal*, XXXI (1965).

Knaplund, P., 'Extracts from Gladstone's Private Political Diary touching Canadian Questions in 1840', in *CHR*, XX (1939), 195f.

Knaplund, P., 'Gladstone's Views on British Colonial Policy', in *CHR*, IV (1923), 304f.

Knaplund, P., 'Sir James Stephen and British North American Problems, 1840–1847', in *CHR*, V (1924), 3f.

Knaplund, P., 'The Buller–Peel Correspondence regarding Canada, 1841', in *CHR*, VIII (1927), 41f.

Kriegel, A. D., 'The Irish Policy of Lord Grey's Government', in *EHR*, LXXXVI (1971), 22f.

Loveday, P., ' "Democracy" in New South Wales: the Constitution Committee of 1853', in *JRAHS*, XLII (1956), 187f.

Loveday, P., 'The Legislative Council in New South Wales, 1856–1870', in *HSANZ*, XI (1965), 481f.

Lower, A. R. M., 'Lawrence H. Gipson and the First British Empire: an Evaluation', in *JBS*, III (1963), 57f.

MacCallum, D. M., 'Empty Historical Boxes of the Early Days: Laying Clio's Ghosts on the Shores of New Holland', in *Arts*, VI (1969), 44f.

MacDonagh, O., 'The Anti-Imperialism of Free Trade', in *EHJ*, XIV (1962), 489f.

McLachlan, N. D., 'Bathurst at the Colonial Office, 1812–27: a Reconnaissance', in *HS*, XIII (1969), 477f.

McLachlan, N. D., 'Edward Eagar (1787–1866): a Colonial Spokesman in Sydney and London', in *HSANZ*, X (1963), 431f.

MacNutt, W. S., 'The Coming of Responsible Government to New Brunswick', in *CHR*, XXXIII (1952), 111f.

MacNutt, W. S., 'New Brunswick's Age of Harmony', in *CHR*, XXXII (1951), 105f.

McRae, K. D., 'An Upper Canadian Letter of 1829 on Responsible Government', in *CHR*, XXXI (1950), 288f.

Madden, F., 'Some Origins and Purposes in the formation of British Colonial Government', in K. Robinson and F. Madden, *Essays in Imperial Government Presented to M. Perham* (Oxford, 1963), 1–22.

Main, J. M., 'Making Constitutions in New South Wales and Victoria, 1853–1854', in *HSANZ*, VII (1956), 369f.

Manning, H. T., 'Colonial Crises before the Cabinet, 1828–1835', in *Bulletin of the IHR*, XXX (1957), 41f.

Manning, H. T., 'The Civil List of Lower Canada', in *CHR*, XXIV (1943), 124f.

Manning, H. T., 'The Colonial Policy of the Whig Ministers, 1800–1837', in *CHR*, XXXIII (1952), 203f. and 341f.

Manning, H. T., 'Edward Wakefield and the Beauharnois Canal', in *CHR*, XLVIII (1967), 1f.

Manning, H. T., 'Who Ran the British Empire 1830–1850?', in *JBS*, V (1965), 88f.

Manning, H. T., and Galbraith, J. S., 'The Appointment of Francis Bond Head: a New Insight', in *CHR*, XLII (1961), 50f.

Marshall, P., 'The First and Second British Empire: a Question of Demarcation', in *History*, XLIX (1964), 13f.

Martin, C., 'The Correspondence between Joseph Howe and Charles Buller, 1845–1848', in *CHR*, VI (1927), 310f.

Masters, D. C., 'A. T. Galt and Canadian Fiscal Autonomy', in *CHR*, XV (1934).

Metcalf, G., 'Draper Conservatism and Responsible Government in the Canadas, 1836–1847', in *CHR*, XLII (1961), 300f.

Morton, W. L., 'The Local Executive in the British Empire', in *EHR*, LXXVIII (1963), 463f.

Neale, R. S., 'John Stuart Mill on Australia: a Note', in *HS*, XIII (1968), 239f.

Neale, R. S., 'Roebuck's Constitution and the Durham Proposals', in *HS*, XIV (1971), 579f.

New, C. W., 'Lord Durham and the British Background of his Report', in *CHR*, XX (1939), 49f.

Ormsby, W. G., 'Sir Charles Metcalf and the Canadian Union', in *Canadian Historical Association Report 1961*, 1135f.

Ormsby, W. G., 'The Civil List Question in the Provinces of Canada', in *CHR*, XXXV, 93f.

Ormsby, W. G., 'The Problem of Canadian Union, 1822–28', in *CHR*, XXXIX (1958), 277f.

Pares, R., 'The Economic Factors in the History of Empire', in *EHJ*, VII (1937), 119f.

Penson, L. M., 'The London West India Interest in the Eighteenth Century', in *EHR*, XXXVI (1921), 373f.

Penson, L. M., 'The Making of a Crown Colony: British Guiana, 1803–33', in *Transactions of the RHS*, IX (1926), 107f.

Pike, D., 'Wilmot-Horton and the National Colonization Society', in *HSANZ*, VII (1956), 205f.

Rich, E. E., 'Canadian History, Review Article', in *HJ*, XIV (1971), 827f.

Roe, M., 'Colonial Society in Embryo', in *HSANZ*, VII (1956), 149f.

Saunders, R. A., 'What was the Family Compact?', in *Ontario History*, XLIX (1957), 165f.

Schuyler, R. L., 'The Constitutional Claims of the West Indies', in *Political Science Quarterly*, XL (1925), 1f.

Shaw, A. G. L., 'British Attitudes to the Colonies', in *JBS*, IX (1969), 73f.

Simons, B. R., 'T. R. Malthus on British Society', in *Journal of the History of Ideas*, XVI (1955).

Sires, R. V., 'Constitutional Change in Jamaica', in *Journal of Comparative Legislation*, XXII (1940), 188f.

Smith, L. A. H., '*Le Canadien* and the British Constitution', in *CHR*, XXXVIII (1957), 93f.

Smith, W., 'The Reception of the Durham Report in Canada, in *Canadian Historical Association Report 1928*, 41f.

Snelling, R. C., and Barron, T. J., 'The Colonial Office and its Permanent Officials, 1801–1914', Chapter 6 in *Studies in the Growth of Nineteenth Century Government*, ed. G. Sutherland (London, 1972).

Thomas, W., 'James Mill's Politics: the "Essay on Government" and the Movement for Reform', in *HJ*, XII (1969), 249f.

Trapido, S., 'Origins of the Cape Franchise Qualifications of 1853', in *Journal of African History*, V (1964), 37f.

Trotter, R. G., 'Durham and the Idea of Federal Union of Dutch North America', in *Canadian Historical Association Report 1925*, 55f.

Wagner, D. O., 'British Economists and the Empire', in *Political Science Quarterly*, XLVI (1931), 257f.

Ward, J. M., 'The Colonial Policy of Lord John Russell's Administration', in *HSANZ*, IX (1960), 244f.

Ward, J. M., 'Australian Policy of the Earl of Newcastle', in *JRAHS*, L (1964), 321f.

Ward, J. M., 'The New Empire', in *HS*, XIV (1971), 591f.

Ward, J. M., 'Retirement of a Titan: James Stephen, 1847—50', in *JMH*, XXXI (1959), 189f.
Ward, J. M., 'The Third Earl Grey and Federalism', in *AJPH*, III (1957), 18f.
Williams, B., 'Chatham and the Representation of the Colonies in Imperial Parliament', in *EHR*, XXII (1907), 756f.
Williams, E. T., 'The Cabinet in the Eighteenth Century', in *History*, XXII (1937), 240f.
Williams, E. T., 'The Colonial Office in the Thirties', in *HSANZ*, II (1943), 141f.
Wilson, C., ' "Mercantilism": Some Vicissitudes of an Idea', in *EHJ*, X (1957), 181f.
Winch, D. N., 'Classical Economics and the Case for Colonization', in *Economica*, XXX (1963), 387f.
Windeyer, W. J. V., 'A Birthright and Inheritance — the Establishment of the Rule of Law in Australia', in *Tasmanian University Law Review*, I (1962), 635f.
Windeyer, W. J. V., 'Responsible Government. Highlights, Sidelights and Reflections', in *JRAHS*, XLII (1956), 257f.

(E) *Unpublished work*

Irving, T. H., 'The Development of Liberal Politics in New South Wales, 1843—1855', Ph.D. thesis (Sydney, 1967).
Herron, D. G., 'The Structure and Course of New Zealand Politics, 1853—1858', Ph.D. thesis (New Zealand, 1959).

Index